THE RAGHUVAṂŚA

OF KĀLIDĀSA

With the Commentary Sañjīvanī of Mallinātha

CANTOS I-V

Edited with a Literal English Translation, and Copious Notes by

M. R. KALE

MOTILAL BANARSIDASS PUBLISHERS
PRIVATE LIMITED • DELHI

Reprint: Delhi, 1972, 1991, 1997, 2005, 2008

ISBN: 978-81-208-0861-4

MOTILAL BANARSIDASS
41 U.A. Bungalow Road, Jawahar Nagar, Delhi 110 007
8 Mahalaxmi Chamber, 22 Bhulabhai Desai Road, Mumbai 400 026
236, 9th Main III Block, Jayanagar, Bangalore 560 011
203 Royapettah High Road, Mylapore, Chennai 600 004
Sanas Plaza, 1302 Baji Rao Road, Pune 411 002
8 Camac Street, Kolkata 700 017
Ashok Rajpath, Patna 800 004
Chowk, Varanasi 221 001

Printed in India

BY JAINENDRA PRAKASH JAIN AT SHRI JAINENDRA PRESS,
A-45 NARAINA, PHASE-I, NEW DELHI 110 028
AND PUBLISHED BY NARENDRA PRAKASH JAIN FOR
MOTILAL BANARSIDASS PUBLISHERS PRIVATE LIMITED,
BUNGALOW ROAD, DELHI 110 007

CONTENTS

INTRODUCTION.

I. THE SANSKRIT KÂVYA.

Before the student enters upon a critical and detailed study of the Raghuvaṃśa it is necessary that he should be acquainted with the salient features of what is called Kâvya in Sanskrit.[1] Sanskrit rhetoricians have divided all kinds of literary compositions into two main divisions, दृश्य (what is capable of being seen) and श्रव्य (what can only be heard or chanted). All the varieties of dramatic pieces come under the दृश्य class, while everything else can be broadly described as श्रव्य. The श्रव्य Kávya[2] again, has been further sub-divided, on considerations of its form, according as it is written in verse, or in prose, or in mixed verse and prose.[3] (1) Compositions in verse or metrical form are the commonest specimens of श्रव्य Kâvya. They generally fall into two classes, the distinction being based chiefly on their length:[4]—(a) महाकाव्यs or 'Great Poems', such as the Raghuvaṃśa, the Śiśupâlavadha &c., (b) and खण्डकाव्यs or 'Small Poetical Pieces', a class which includes all minor lyrical poetry and such works as the Meghadùta, the Shâminîvilâsa, the Amaruśataka &c. (2) Prose works are comparatively rare in Sanskrit; their main kinds are two[5]—Kathâ (*e. g.* the Kâdambarî of Báṇabhaṭṭa) and Âkhyâyiká (*e. g.* the Harshacharita of the same author). (3) Works in which prose and

---

1 The information given here has been briefly summarized from the Kav.-D. and the Sáh.-D. For a *historical* outline of Kâvya literature the student is recommended to consult eny standard History (*e. g.* Macdonell's) of Sanskrit Literature.

2 The student should be on his guard against the common conception that Kâvya, 'Poetry', is *metrical* composition. Kâvya originally signifies any literary piece, whether in prose or in verse; in popular usage it has been chiefly applied to verse.

3 पद्यं गद्यं च मिश्रं च तत्त्रिधैव व्यवस्थितम् । Daṇḍin.

4 This is clear from the words of Viśvanâtha who says खण्डकाव्यं भवेत्काव्यस्यैकदेशानुसारि च; 'a Khaṇḍa kâvya treats of some *portion* of (the subjects that fill a whole) Mahákâvya.'

5 अपादः पदसंतानो गद्यमाख्यायिकाकथे । इति तस्य प्रभेदौ द्वौ ॥ Daṇḍin. The Agnipurâṇa mentions five kinds, *viz.* आख्यायिका कथा खण्डकथा परिकथा तथा । कथानिकेति मन्यन्ते गद्यकाव्यं च पञ्चधा ॥

verse are mixed are classed as Champùs (*e. g.* the Bhâratachampû, the Viśvagunâdarśa-champú, &c.).[6]

The student will thus notice that, along with dramas, the महाकाव्यs and खण्डकाव्यs have been the most popular forms of literary composition, and have attracted the best geniuses to try their hand at them. It is true that the Khaṇḍa Kàvya attracted more attention, chiefly because it is short and requires less expenditure of time and energy; and that the number of extant Mahâkâvyas, therefore, is not very large. But what is here lacking in quantity has been amply made up in quality. For in dignity of style, depth of thought and majesty of movement, the Mahâkâvya is far and away the best expression which the Sanskrit literary artist has found for his genius. The Raghuvaṃśa is a Mahákàvya, which the Sâh.–D.[7] defines as follows:—

सर्गबन्धो महाकाव्यं तत्रैको नायकः सुरः ।
सद्वंशः क्षत्रियो वापि धीरोदात्तगुणान्वितः ॥
एकवंशभवा भूपाः कुलजा बहवोऽपि वा ।
शृङ्गारवीरशान्तानामेकोऽङ्गी रस इष्यते ॥
अङ्गानि सर्वेऽपि रसाः सर्वे नाटकसंधयः ।
इतिहासोद्भवं वृत्तमन्यद्वा सज्जनाश्रयम् ॥
चत्वारस्तस्य वर्गाः स्युस्तेष्वेकं च फलं भवेत् ।
आदौ नमस्क्रियाशीर्वा वस्तुनिर्देश एव वा ॥

---

6 गद्यपद्यमयं काव्यं चम्पूरित्यभिधीयते । Sàh.—D. If we set aside the distinction between श्रव्य aud दृश्य, and consider *form* alone, it is also possible to class dramas as 'mixed Kâvya,' as indeed has been done by Daṇḍin who says मिश्राणि नाटकादीनि (K.—D. I. 31).

7 We give above the definition of the Sáh.—D. which is more detailed, since its author, who lived in the fifteenth century, had all the famous Mahákávyas before him, including even the later specimens. The definition of Daṇḍin (of the sixth century) is earlier and concise, and we give it below for comparison with that of Viśvanátha:-
सर्गबन्धो महाकाव्यमुच्यते तस्य लक्षणम् । आशीर्नमस्क्रियावस्तुनिर्देशो वापि तन्मुखम् ॥
इतिहासकथोद्भूतमितरद्वा सदाश्रयम् । चतुर्वर्गफलायत्तं चतुरोदात्तनायकम् ॥
नगरार्णवशैलर्तुचन्द्रार्कोदयवर्णनैः । उद्यानसलिलक्रीडामधुपानरतोत्सवैः ॥
विप्रलम्भैर्विवाहैश्च कुमारोदयवर्णनैः । मन्त्रदूतप्रयाणाजिनायकाभ्युदयैरपि ॥
अलंकृतमसंक्षिप्तं रसभावनिरन्तरम् । सर्गैरनतिविस्तीर्णैः श्रव्यवृत्तैः सुसंधिभिः ॥
सर्वत्र भिन्नवृत्तान्तैरुपेतं लोकरञ्जनम् । काव्यं कल्पान्तरस्थायि जायते सदलंकृति ॥
Other definitions, more or less similar, will be found in Agnipuraṇa (337), Kávyálaṃkára (I), Sarasvati-Kaṇṭhâbharaṇa (V.), &c.

क्वचिन्निंदा खलादीनां सतां च गुणकीर्तनम् ।
एकवृत्तमयैः पद्यैरवसानेऽन्यवृत्तकैः ॥
नातिस्वल्पा नातिदीर्घा सर्गा अष्टाधिका इह ।
नानावृत्तमयः क्वापि सर्गः कश्चन दृश्यते ॥
सर्गान्ते भाविसर्गस्य कथायाः सूचनं भवेत् ।
संध्यासूर्येन्दुरजनीप्रदोषध्वान्तवासराः ॥
प्रातर्मध्याह्नमृगयाशैलर्तुवनसागराः ।
संभोगविप्रलम्भौ च मुनिस्वर्गपुराध्वराः ॥
रणप्रयाणोपयममन्त्रपुत्रोदयादयः ।
वर्णनीया यथायोगं साङ्गोपाङ्गा अमी इह ॥
कवेर्वृत्तस्य वा नाम्ना नायकस्येतरस्य वा ।
नामास्य सर्गोपादेयकथया सर्गनाम तु ॥

(*Parichchheda VI.*)

Thus, a Mahákâvya should be divided into chapters, called सर्ग**s** or Cantos. The hero should be either a divine personage, or a Kshatriya of noble descent and possessed of the qualities of a Dhîrodâtta[8] Hero. This is when the poem is concerned with the description of the life of a single hero (as in the Śiśupálavadha or the Vikramâṅkadevacharita); if like the Raghuvaṃśa it has for its theme a number of Heroes, then they should all be Kshatriya princes sprung from the same race, and of pure descent. The prominent sentiment (रस) should be either शृङ्गार, वीर or शान्त, others being introduced as accessories. The subject-matter should be arranged as in a náṭaka with the necessary changes. The plot may be historical, or may have for its subject-matter the glorious deeds of the good and the virtuous. The object of such compositions should be the attainment of the four aims of human pursuit—*i. e.* they should be written in such a way that their study would point out the means of attaining them. It should open with a verse or verses expressive of a salutation to a deity, or a blessing conferred on the readers, or a hinting of the subject-matter; these may sometimes be followed by censure of villains and praise of the good (as in the Vikramâṅkadevacharita). A Mahákávya should be divided into सर्गs not less than eight[9] which should be neither too

---

8. A 'Dhîrodâtta' ('self-controlled and exalted') Hero is one who is magnanimous, exceedingly grave, forbearing, not boastful, resolute one whose high spirit is concealed, and who is faithful to his promise (महासत्त्वोऽतिगम्भीरः क्षमावानविकत्थनः । स्थिरो निगूढाहंकारो धीरोदात्तो दृढव्रतः ॥ D.—R. III.)

9. Some restrict the number to thirty; *cf.* अष्टसर्गान्न तु न्यूनं त्रिंशत्सर्गाच्च नाधिकम् । Iśânasamhitâ; but the *Haravijaya* possesses as many as fifty cantos. So the rule is not absolute.

long nor too short[10] They should be composed in the same metre, which should change only at the end; sometimes (as a variety) a सर्ग may be written in a nnmber of metres. The contents of the next Canto should be indicated at the end of the preceding one. It should describe, at more or less length, such incidents and topics as twilight, the rise of the sun and the moon, the night, the evening, darkness, the day, morning, noon, hunting, mountains, seasons, forests, oceans, the union and separation of lovers, sages, heaven, cities, sacrifices, battles, invasions, marriage ceremonies, advice, the birth of a son, &c. &c. It should be named after the poet, or the plot, or the Hero, or some other person; while each Sarga should be named in accordance with its own contents (*e. g.* the 6th canto of the Ragh. is named स्वयंवरवर्णन).

It should be borne in mind that these elaborate rules were evolved after a minute examination of all available specimens. The works of early poets like Kálidasa will not therefore be found to conform strictly to the definition given above, nor is it necessary that they should do so, provided they follow the broad lines laid down. For Daṇḍin himself says, न्यूनमप्यत्र यैः कैश्चिदङ्गैः काव्यं न दुष्यति। यद्युपात्तेषु संपत्तिराराधयति तद्विदः॥ (I. 20). Thus the Raghuvaṃśa, though it does not describe everyone of all those incidents and topics, still conforms mostly the definition given, as the student can verify for himself. Thus, it has for its theme a number of noble kings born of the same family. The predominent sentiment is शृङ्गार, though वीर and करुण are often introduced as accessories (*e. g.* in Canto III. and VIII.). It is named after Raghu, the most eminent among its many heroes. The subject of the next Canto is indicated towards the close of the previous one; *e. g.* it is evident from what is said at the end of Canto V. that the *Svayamvara* of Indumatî would be described in Canto VI. The metre changes at the end of each Canto, and the ninth Canto is written in a number of different metres. प्रातःकाल is described in Canto V., मृगया in IX., ऋतु in XVI. and XIX., संभोग in XIX., रण in VII., उपयम in VII., पुत्रोदय in III. Each Canto is named after the most important event described in it. Other particulars the student can find out for himself. Technically, the Raghuvaṃsa is quite a representative specimen of its class; as regards

10. The Iśâna-Saṃhitá explains that the number of stanzas in a single canto should not exceed 200, and should not be less than 30.

its other merits and distinguishing features, we shall have a few remarks to make, but these more properly belong to a subsequent Section.

II. KA'LIDA'SA.

(A) HIS LIFE, WORKS AND POETRY.

His Life. To turn now to the poet it must be admitted that we have absolutely no trustworthy information regarding the personal history of Kálidâsa, by universal consent the greatest of Indian poets. The curiosity of the querist who would ask.–'Where and when was he born?' 'Who were his parents?' 'When did he die?' &c.—must ever remain unsatisfied. The poet has studiously observed complete silence about himself in his works. Read them howsoever we may, we find no allusion, no incident mentioned, that may directly shed any light either on his personal history or on any remarkable event of his life. Under these circumstances we have to content ourselves with gathering what little information we can about a poet of world-wide repute from external sources, and a few incidents found here and there in his works, which may be supposed to have a distant bearing upon the history of his life. Reserving for another Section the question of the date of the poet, we proceed here to state the few facts that can thus be known about him. A time-honoured tradition, supported by internal and external evidence, associates the name of Kâlidâsa with that of the epoch-making king Vikramâditya of Ujjayinî. The keen interest and admiration with which the poet describes the Mahâkâla, the Śiprâ, and other beauties of Ujjayinî, unmistakably point to the conclusion that he must have been a native of that city. And the various covert references[11] to the name of Vikrama in fully eulogistic terms, which are doubtless meant to immortalize king Vikramâditya, are inexplicable if that monarch be not regarded as the poet's patron. Kâlidâsa also betrays considerable acquaintance with court-life in his works. This circumstance, coupled with the fact that there is no allusion in his writings to the goddess of wealth having ever frowned upon him, shows that he was in affluent

---

11. *E. g.*, अनुत्सेकः खलु विक्रमालंकारः (Vikr.), विक्रममहिम्ना वर्धते भवान् (*Ibid.*)&c.

circumstances, and had not the misfortune ever to drink the bitter cup of poverty. He was a Brâhmaṇa by caste and was a devout worshipper of Śiva, though by no means a sectarian. Ae seems to have travelled a good deal, at least in Northern India. For, as Dr. Bhau Dâjî remarks, he is the only poet who describes a living saffron flower, the plant of which grows in Kashmir. His graphic description of the Himâlayan scenes looks very much like that of one who was an eye-witness. Unlike Bhavabûti and many other brother-poets, he appears to have enjoyed great popularity during his lifetime. He was 'an admirer of field-sports,' and 'describes their beneficial effcets with the exactness of a true sportsman.' Though fond of pleasures he was not the unscrupulous voluptuary he is supposed to be by some critics, as is clear from the many noble sentiments expressed in the Śákuntala.[12] It also appears from the same play that he was against love-marriages, though always actuated with the most generous sentiments towards the fair sex. His works bear further testimony to his considerable acquaintance with the Vedas, the philosophy taught by the Upanishads, the Epics and the Purâṇas, the Bhagavadgîtá, the systems of Sâṃkhya, Yoga, and Vedânta as propounded by Bâdarâyaṇa, Medicine, and the rudiments of Astronomy. Beyond these few facts nothing is known for certain about our poet at present. It is inevitable that, during the course of time, a number of fanciful stories and legends should have clustered round the popular hero of literary India. Thus there is a story which relates how the poet was born a blockhead and a dunce, but had wisdom bestowed upon him in consequence of his subsequent propitiation of the goddess Kálî, whence his name *Kâlidâsa*. Another story makes him a friend of King Kumâradâsa of Ceylon, in whose city Kâlidâsa was murdered by a courtesan. No reliance need be placed on such accounts. Many such stories will be found in the Sanskrit Bhojaprabandha, and in a collection which, under the title of *Tales of King Bhoja and Poet Kálidása*, is a popular book in many Indian vernaculars. A few conjectures have been advanced as to some other particulars, but to test their veracity falls strictly within the province of the antiquary.

His Works. The poet's silence about himself in his works gave an opportunity to many unscrupulous inferior poets to father their own works upon him. The following is

12. *Cf.* अनिर्वर्णनीयं परकलत्रं &c. Śâk. V. and our note *ad loc.*

a list of the works generally attributed to him:—(1) शाकुन्तल (2) विक्रमोर्वशीय (3) मालविकाग्निमित्र (4) रघुवंश (5) कुमारसंभव (6) मेघदूत (7) कुन्तेश्वरदौत्य (8) ऋतुसंहार (9) अम्बास्तव (10) कल्याणस्तव (11) कालीस्तोत्र (12) काव्यनाटकालंकाराः (?) (13) and (14) two गङ्गाष्टकs (15) घटकर्पर (16)) चण्डिकादण्डकस्तोत्र (17) चर्चास्तव (18) ज्योतिर्विदाभरण (19) दुर्घटकाव्य (20) नलोदय (21) नवरत्नमाला (22) पुष्पबाणविलास (23) मकरन्दस्तव (24) and (25) two मङ्गलाष्टकs (?) (26) महापद्मषट्क (27) रत्नकोश (28) राक्षसकाव्य (29) लक्ष्मीस्तव (30) लघुस्तव (31) विद्वद्विनोदकाव्य (32) वृन्दावनकाव्य (33) वैद्यमनोरमा (34) श्रुतिचन्द्रिका (35) शृङ्गारतिलक (36) शृङ्गाररसाष्टक (37) शृङ्गारसारकाव्य (38) श्यामलादण्डक (39) श्रुतबोध (40) सप्तश्लोकीरामायण and (41) सेतुबन्ध. Of these the first six are acknowledged by all critics to be undoubtedly his. (7) is not yet discovered, but is known only in a quotation by the Kashmirian scholar Kshemendra, in his Auchityavichâracharchá. The authorship of (8) is somewhat doubtful; while the remaining ones are certainly to be dismissed as the productions of other poets. There is another fact also which should be borne in mind in this connexion. In Sanskrit literary history there have been *many poets who bore the name Kâlidâs*, and at least three were known to Râjaśekhara who wrote एकोऽपि जीयते हन्त कालिदासो न केनचित्। शृङ्गारे ललितोद्गारे कालिदासत्रयी किमु ॥ It is possible, therefore, that other Kálidâsas than the author of the Raghuvaṃsa are responsible for the trifling pieces mentioned above. Here, then, we are concerned with the first six only. The most convenient and reliable method of studying the development of a poet's mind and its relation to his productions would be to read his works in their chronological order. But we have no external evidence, whatsoever, to ascertain the chronology of Kâlidâsa's works. It must, therefore, be based wholly on internal evidence. Judged as such the works would stand in this order—Poems—कुमार०, मेघदूत and रघुवंश; Plays-मालविका०, विक्रमो० and शाकुन्तल or, both indiscriminately as—कुमार०, मालविका०, विक्रमो०, मेघदूत, शाकुन्तल; and रघुवंश. Space will not permit us even to refer to these briefly. We will only remark in passing that the last three are the outcome of the poet's matured poetic faculties and riper years.

His Poetry.

Kálidása is indisputably the greatest master-mind in Sanskrit poetry. His genius has been recognized in India from very early times. He has been and will ever be enshrined in the hearts of his countrymen as the Prince of Indian poets. Most Indian successors of Kálidása have expressed in suitable words their admiration of the poet who stood far ahead of them in the perfection of his art. Thus Báṇabhaṭṭa, the famous author of the Kádambarî, speaks of him in the following words:—

निर्गतासु न वा कस्य कालिदासस्य सूक्तिषु ।
प्रीतिर्मधुरसार्द्रासु मञ्जरीष्विव जायते ॥

"When Kâlidâsa's sweet sayings, charming with sweet sentiment, went forth, who did not feel delight in them as in honey-laden flowers?" Kumârila, who flourished about the first half of the eighth century, has quoted with approval the passage from the Śâkuntala सतां हि संदेहपदेषु वस्तुषु प्रमाणमन्तःकरणप्रवृत्तयः. There is a Subhâshita which says:—

पुरा कवीनां गणनाप्रसङ्गे कनिष्ठिकाऽधिष्ठितकालिदासा ।
अद्यापि तत्तुल्यकवेरभावादनामिका सार्थवती बभूव ॥

"While once the poets were being counted, 'Kâlidása' (as being the first) occupied the last finger. But the ring-finger remained true to its name (अनामिका=nameless), since his second has not yet been found (by whom it can be occupied)". Pandit Govardhanâchârya thus speaks of our poet:—

साकूतमधुरकोमलविलासिनीकण्ठकूजितप्राये ।
शिक्षासमयेऽपि मुदे रतलीलाकालिदासोक्ती ॥

"Two things only *viz.* love-sport and Kâlidása's peotry, delight the heart even at the time of instruction, as they mostly consist of the sweet, tender and touching words of a sportful girl." Almost every Pandit has in his mouth the following memorable verse—

काव्येषु नाटकं रम्यं तत्र रम्या शकुन्तला ।
तत्रापि च चतुर्थोऽङ्कस्तत्र श्लोकचतुष्टयम् ॥

"Among Kávyas the drama is the most charming. Among dramas Śâkuntala is specially charming. Even there the fourth Act is the best, and lastly, four ślokas[13] therein are especially most beautiful". The highest place is assigned to Kálidasa among poets for the construction of happy similes, when it is said—

उपमा कालिदासस्य भारवेरर्थगौरवम् ।
दण्डिनः पदलालित्यं माघे सन्ति त्रयो गुणाः ॥

Among later writers, Jayadeva has called our poet कविकुलगुरु 'the lord of poets' and the विलास or 'Graceful Play' of the Muse of Poetry.[14]

That his countrymen should place him at the head of all Sanskrit poets, unparalleled and unsurpassed by those who have

13 They are—यास्यत्यद्य शकुन्तलेति &c.; शुश्रूषस्व गुरून् &c.; अभिजनवतो भर्तुः श्लाघ्ये &c.; and भूत्वा चिराय चतुरन्तमहीसपत्नी &c.

14 भासो हासः कविकुलगुरुः कालिदासो विलासः ।

preceded or followed him, is natural enough; but he has evoked spontaneous outpourings of praise and manifestations of admiration even from foreign scholars and poets who had access to his works either directly or through translations. Goethe has voluntarily bestowed the highest meed of praise on him—so much was he enraptured by the charms of Kâlidâsa's Muse and struck with his poetic genius. This is what he says about the Śâkuntala--

"Wouldst thou the young year's blossoms and the fruits of its decline,
And all by which the soul is charmed, enraptured, feasted, fed ?
Wouldst thou the earth and heaven itself in one sole name combine ?
I name thee, O Śakuntalâ, and all at once is said." [15]

When we remember that Goethe himself was the greatest poet of Germany and one of the greatest of the world, we realize the importance of his estimate of our poet. The well-known philosopher and traveller, Humboldt, pronounces the following judgment-- 'Kâlidása is a masterly describer of the influence which Nature exercises upon the minds of lovers. Tenderness in the expression of feelings and richness of creative fancy have assigned to him his lofty place among the poets of all nations." The celebrated critic, Schlegel, has assigned him a very high position amongst the glorious company of the 'Sons of Song'. Several eminent modern orientalists have also offered their tribute of praise to our Indian Shakespeare, as Sir William Jones was the first to call him--the very comparison of Kâlidâsa to Shakespeare is the highest form of eulogy that could be bestowed upon him by foreign critics. Sir Monier-Williams, while writing about the Śâkuntala, thus expresses himself:—"No composition of Kâlidâsa displays more the richness of his poetical genius, the exuberance of his imagination, the warmth and play of his fancy, his profound knowledge of the human heart, his delicate appreciation of its most refined and tender emotions, his familiarity with the workings and counter-workings of its conflicting feelings--in short more entitles him to rank as the Shakespeare of India." Prof. Lassen calls him "the brightest star in the firmament of Indian poetry."

Wh thus find that Kâlidâsa has established sovereignty in the hearts of all alike. Now it may be asked, 'What is that in

15. As translated from the German by Mr. E. B. Eastwick.

Kâlidâsa which establishes his undisputed claim to the highest honour which is thus bestowed upon him ?' Unless this question is satisfactorily answered Kâlidâsa's merits as a poet cannot be said to be determined.[16] His poetic genius has brought Sanskrit poetry to the highest elegance and refinement. His style is peculiarly pure and chaste. It has 'neither the laxity of the Purâṇas nor the extravagant colouring of later poems.' It is unartificial and characterized by brevity consistent with perspicuity. An unaffected simplicity of expression and an easy-flowing language mark his writings which are embellished with similes unparalleled for their beauty and appropriateness, and with pithy general sayings. His diction is marked by the absence of long compounds, involved constructions, over-wrought rhetoric, and artificial puns. Kâlidâsa excels other poets in his description of the sublime and the beautiful. It is a principle recognized by all modern critics that 'Nature must be the life and essence of poetry'; and in respect of this, Kâlidâsa may be said to be essentially a poet of Nature (of course in the limited sense of the term which it is possible to attach to it in those times of gay luxury and general prosperity). He describes with most effective touches the gorgeous scenery of the mountain Himâlaya—its snow-clad and mineral-covered summits, the peaks where sunshine ever reigns, the fragrant and cool breezes blowing there, the wilds with the hunters, the musk-deer, the potent herbs shedding lustre at night, the *chamara* deer, the Mânasa lake &c.; and his description of the Ganges and the peaceful hermitage-life is very striking and life-like. His descriptive powers are great, and some of the scenes in the Śák., the Megh., and the Ragh. are so enchanting as to hold his readers spell-bound. And as regards ध्वनिकाव्य, the kind of poetry which suggests more than what it expresses, he is a master of acknowledged skill.

(B) HIS DATE.

The problem of the date of Kâlidâsa is a vexed one and it has yet to be finally settled. The earliest mention of Kâlidâsa by name is in the Aihole Inscription dated 634 A. D., and it furnishes the 7th Century A. D. as the downward limit of the poet's date. Tradition mentions Kálidâsa as a contemporary and a court-poet of king Vikramâditya. One king of that name founded the era known after him, which is accepted as commencing with 57 B. C. Some antiquarians once did not accept this date as the correct one, but

16. For this the student is referred to pp. 27-29 of our introduction to the Śâkuntala, 5th ed.

brought Vikramâditya down to A. D. 544, propounding what was known as the **Korur Theory.** The battle of Korur marked a turning-point in Indian history, Vikramâditya having defeated the Mlechchhas in it. Curiously enough, Mr. Fergusson held that to commemorate the battle an era was invented, and that its beginning was placed back 600 years. So he put the true date of Vikramâditya at 544 A. D., and this theory for a time held sway, since no inscription was discovered bearing a date prior to 600 of the Vikrama era. But the discovery of the Mandasor Inscription, which is dated Saṃvat 529, made this theory untenable, and the traditionary date ramained unshaken. Then there is the theory of the *Nine Gems* Nine eminent men called the 'Nine Gems' adorned the court of ·king Vikramâditya—

धन्वन्तरिक्षपणकामरसिंहशङ्कुवेतालभट्टघटकर्परकालिदासाः ।
ख्यातो वराहमिहिरो नृपतेः सभायां रत्नानि वै वररुचिर्नव विक्रमस्य ॥

Of these अमरसिंह is said to have lived between 414 A. D. and 642 A. D. Varâhamihira is believed to have died in 587 A.. D. On the strength of these dates of Kâlidâsa's supposed contemporaries, Dr. Kern placed him in the latter half of the sixth century. But in this there are many *a priori* conclusions and speculations as to probabilities. If the tradition proves anything definitely, it proves the connexion of Kâlidâsa with King Vikramâditya; but as regards the contemporaneity of the nine authors, the tradition cannot be true. Next there is the theory of Renaissance propounded by Prof. Max Müller. He divided the whole Sanskrit literary period into two parts. The first began with the Vedas and ended which the first century A. D. Then came an *interregnum*, a period during which foreigners invaded India and so literary activity was dormant. The professor placed the RENAISSANCE of Sanskrit learning in the sixth century A. D. with the reign of Vikramâditya. But, as has been shown by Drs. Peterson and Bühler, the period called *interregnum* was really not destitute of literary productivity, and, therefore, if Kâlidâsa is to be considered as the first poet of the new school, he must be placed considerably earlier than Prof. Max Müller did.

There are some minor things which have been pushed into the controversy. These are—(1) the alleged covert references to Dinnâga and Nichula in the Meghadûta, the former a foe and the latter a friend of Kâlidâsa; (2) the identity of Mâtṛigupta, a king of Kashmir, and Kâlidâsa (for, names in Sanskrit are often titles, and Mátṛigupta, *lit.* 'protected by the mother,' may also be taken as Kâligupta or Kâlidâsa); (3) and the supposed astronomical references in the works of Kâlidâsa to the astronomical theories of A'ryabhaṭa, who lived in 476 A. D. Prof. R. N. Apte has examined all these at some length, and on the first point he comes to the conclusion that Diṅnâga and Nichula were not contemporaries of the great Kâlidâsa, but must have been contemporaries of *some other Kâlidâsa.* On the second point he observes that Mátṛigupta and Kálidàsa were two different persons, since they are differently quoted by Kshemendra and other writers and commentators. The supposed astronomical references have really no astronomical significance at all, and it cannot be said that Ka'lidása was acquainted with the astronomical works of Áryabhaṭa. Mr. K. B. Pathak, the latest exponent of the 6th century theory, repeats the arguments given above, but principally bases his conclusion on his theory about the Hùṇa kings, allusion to whom is made by the poet in the Raghuvaṃśa. He argues that since there is no mention made of the Hùṇas in the Rámâyaṇa, the conclusion follows that Kálidása unconsciously refers to the Hûṇa kings of his own time who held sway over the Punjab and Kashmir, in the second quarter of the sixth century. But this rests merely on assumption; for there are references to the Hùṇas even in the Mahábhárata. Prof. Apte has also shown that just beyond Bactria or the threshold of ancient India, the Hùṇas had constituted a powerful empire from the middle of the 3rd century B. C. to the end of the 1st or the 2nd century A. D.

Modern European scholars are generally inclined to hold that Kâlidâsa must have flourished under one or more of the Gupta kings. The Gupta period (about 300–650 A. D.) was noted in ancient Indian history for a revival of Sanskrit learning and arts. The late Mr. Vincent A. Smith (see his *Early History of India.* p. 304, 3rd ed. 1914) believed that Kâlidâsa must have lived in the reigns of the first two, or even in that of the third, of the Gupta Kings:—

Chandragupta II. (c. 357–413)
Kumâragupta I. (413–455)
Skandagupta (455—480)

Both Chandragupta II. and Skandagupta had adopted the title of *Vikramâditya.* To quote the words of Mr. Smith, "It is not unlikely that the earliest works of Kâlidâsa...........may have been composed before A. D. 413, that is to say, while Chandragupta II. was on the throne; but I am inclined to regard the reign of Kumâragupta I. (413–455) as the time during which the poet's later works were composed, and it seems possible, that the whole of his literary career fell within the limits of that reign. It is also possible that he may have continued writing after the accession of Skandagupta". Mr. Smith thus makes Kâlidâsa's literary career extend over a period of not less than thirty years. Note that, even according to Mr. Smith, there is nothing wrong in the tradition about a Vikramáditya having been our poet's patron; only we must arrive at an understanding as to *which* Vikramâditya is meant, because various kings in the history of ancient India called themselves by that title. We ourselves hold, for reasons given below, that we must accept as our poet's patron that king Vikramáditya whose traditional era commences at 56 B. C. The attempt to place Kâlidâsa in the court of the Gupta kings rests merely on the fact that Chandragupta II. was named Vikramáditya. But the existence of prior kings of that title is now a certainty.[17]

Vatsabhûti, the author of the Mandasor inscription, copies several ideas from Kâlidâsa; the latter must, therefore, have lived prior to 472 A. D. Again, Aśvaghosha, the author of a life of the great Buddha in Sanskrit, has numerous passages similar to those occurring in the works of Kâlidâsa. Now, Kâlidâsa was an original poet borrowing his subjects from Válmîki and other ancient authors; Aśvaghosha was more a philosopher than a poet, and may, with greater probability, be supposed to have borrowed his ideas from Kâlidâsa. The date of Aśvaghosha is given as 78 A. D.; and if we suppose him to have borrowed from Kâlidâsa, the latter will have to be placed earlier than 78 A. D. And in this view Dr. Peterson also concurs when he says '*Kálidâsa stands near the beginning of the Christian era, if, indeed, he does not overtop it.*'

There is also internal evidence pointing to the same conclusion. We have first the evidence obtained from the state of the law of inheritance and the penalty for theft as they are indicated in passages in the Śâkuntala. The passage in the sixth Act of the drama, announcing the death of the merchant Dhanamitra who died

17. The Râjataraṃgiṇî mentions an earlier Vikramâditya, a contemporary of Pratâpâditya of Kashmir.

heirless, seems to Prof. Apte to refer to a period when the widow of a deceased person could not inherit his estate. Such a period is to be found only before the Christian era, when Manu, Âpastamba and Vasishṭha held sway, and Bṛihaspati, Śankha, Likhita and Yájñavalkya had not yet written their Codes. The penalty for theft, as indicated in the prologue to the sixth Act, seems to have been the extreme one, and there is also a passage of similar import in the Vikramorvaśíya (आत्मनो वधमाहर्ता &c. V, I.). The penalty for theft has been from time to time mitigated with the progress of civilization. Manu and Âpastamba lay down the extreme penalty, the option of fine being introduced later on, as we find it in the Smṛiti of Bṛihaspati. These two circumstances tend to show that Kálidâsa flourished at a period which is anterior to Bṛihaspati, the latter being generally placed in the first century A. D.

Prof. Apte further calls attention to the fact that there is no reference to the Nyâya philosophy in the works of Kâlidâsa [except perhaps in Ragh. XIII. 1, in which the word शब्दगुणं (आकाशं) occurs, but which the poet might have borrowed from the Sámkhyas], and concludes that he must have lived *before* the development of that philosophy. Then again we have the evidence of style. The artificiality of diction and the fondness for long compounds and double-meaning words which mark the writings of Daṇdin (who in his Kâvyâdarśa says that an abundance of compounds constitutes the quality of *ojas* in poetry), Bâṇa, Bhavabhúti (7th century A. D.) and other mediæval writers, are entirely absent in Kâlidâsa's writings—a fact which shows that he must be placed some six or seven centuries before them, a period necessary to cause such a revolution in the art of literary composition, considering the scanty means of the propagation of learning in those times. It thus becomes clear that Kâlidâsa lived in the first century B. C. at the latest.[18]

18. Prof. S. Ray refers to the discovery in 1909–10 of the Bhita medallion, which pictures a scene which looks exactly like the opening scene of the Śâkuntala. The medallion is assigned to the Sunga period (184 B. C.-72 B. C.), and Prof. Ray assumes that Kâlidâsa is anterior to the date of the medallion, though the Archæological Survey authorities, holding to the Vincent Smith date, are inclined to dispute the identification of the scene with the one in the Play.

III. THE POEM.

(1) Summary of the Story.

Before the student proceeds to a detailed study of his actual text, it is advisable that he should make himself familiar with the contents of the poem as a connected whole. We, therefore, give below briefly the story of the *Raghuvaṃsa* as presented in its nineteen Cantos :—

Canto I. After saluting Śiva and Párvatî, the poet eulogizes the virtues of the kings of the race of Raghu, whose history he proposes to describe. The royal line of the Raghus originally sprang from the Sun, whose son, Manu, was the first king in this race. In direct descent from Manu came the supremely eminent King Dilîpa, with whose history the poem properly begins. Dilîpa is an ideal king, being a most efficient, benign and virtuous ruler. He has a queen called Sudakshiṇâ, the very type of courtesy and kindliness, and the only thing that mars their happiness is that they have no issue. In course of time Dilîpa decides to consult his family-priest, Vasishṭha, as to what holy rites &c. he might perform that would bless him with a son and heir. Leaving the government of his kingdom to his ministers, Dilîpa starts for Vasishṭha's hermitage in the company of his wife. In the evening they reach their destination and make known their wishes to the preceptor. Vasishṭha explains that a curse, formerly pronounced upon the King by the divine cow Surabhi, but unknown to him, was the bar in the way, and for that purpose he should have to propitiate Surabhi's daughter, Nandinî, who was his (Vasishṭha's) own cow. If she were pleased, she could grant that wish of his. Vasishṭha then explains to the royal pair how to serve the cow; after which they retire for the night.

Canto II. The next morning Dilîpa begins the daily routine of disciplined service of the cow, Nandinî. He regularly accompanies her every morning, after she was worshipped, to the forest and back again to the hermitage in the evening when she returned from the pasturage. Twenty-one days thus pass away. On the 22nd day, the cow, wishing to test the devotion of her follower, enters a cave of the Himâlayas, overgrown with grass, for grazing. As the King's eyes are riveted on the mountain scenery, she creates an illusory lion pouncing upon her. The King's attention is suddenly called back by Nandinî's cry; and what does he see? The cow in the grip of a formidable lion, imploringly looking at him. Instantly the King's hand passes to the arrow-case, but just as he seizes an arrow his hand remains fixed there. To add to the wonder of the already bewildered King, the lion speaks in human voice telling him that he was a servant of Śiva, posted there to guard the trees, with orders not to leave the place, but to live on whatever came within his reach, and claims the cow as his rightful prey. The King finds himself in a fix; it was his primary duty to save the cow at any cost. What was he to do? He could not shoot an arrow; but he could offer himself up in lieu of the cow, as they had both entered the cave together; for Śiva's order to the lion was that he should eat whatever came within his grasp. This the magnanimous King does. After a long conversation with the lion he succeeds in prevailing upon the latter to eat him up and let go the cow. The King thus stands the test; the illusion vanishes and instead of the terribe leap of the lion there falls on the King a shower of flowers from heaven. The well-pleased cow confers on the King the wished-for blessing, and they return home. The king informs the sage and his queen of the cow's favour. Their object being gained Vasishṭha sends back the royal couple, and they enter their capital amidst the rejoicings of the citizens. In a short time Sudakshiṇà shows signs of pregnancy.

Canto III. A son is then born to Dilîpa. He is named Raghu, as one destined to be the most illustrious of the kings of the solar race, the family being named after him. He is brought up and educated with due care. He is then married and installed as heir-apparent (*Yuvaràja*). After this, Dilîpa, who had already performed 99 horse-sacrifices, wishes to perform the hundredth to complete the list. Indra, Lord of the gods, in jealousy secretly steals the sacrificial horse to prevent the completion of the rite. To Raghu was entrusted the duty of guarding the horse; and ordinarily he would have been unable to trace the horse. But Nandinî, whose protege he was in a way, appears on the scene and bestows upon him superhuman sight. Raghu then sees Indra carrying away the horse, and fights with him most gallantly. Indra of course triumphs over Raghu in the end; but he is so highly pleased with Raghu's bravery that, although he could not restore the horse, he promises, to bestow upon his father, Dilîpa, the whole merit obtainable from the sacrifice, had it been duly completed, as a mark of his appreciation of Raghu's valour. Indra also acquaints Dilîpa, at Raghu's request, with what had occurred; highly gratified at the account, Dilîpa accords his son a hearty welcome when he goes back to his court. A short while after he installs Raghu on the throne as King, and himself retires, with his queen, to the forest, as was the wont of the kings of Ikshvâku's race.

Canto IV. King Raghu now begins to rule, and all are made to feel his equal justice and cautious vigilance. When autumn comes, Raghu decides to start upon an expedition of conquest (*Dig-vijaya*). Proceeding first to the east, he marches right up to the eastern ocean, where he vanquishes the Suhmas and the Vaṅgas. Crossing the river Kapiśâ he goes through Utkala to the Kaliṅga country. He conquers its ruler and then marches to the south. After subduing the Páṇḍya kings there, he crosses the Sahya mountain, and subjugates the *Aparânta* districts along the western coast. Then by land he proceeds northwards, where he conquers the Pârasîkas. Thence he traverses as far as the Sindhu river, where he defeats the Hûṇas and the Kâmbojas. Thence he proceeds across the Himálayas, where he brings the Utsavasaṅketas under his sway. Descending to the plains he finally conquers Prâgjyotisha and Kâmarûpa, and returns to his capital laden with glory and wealth. He then performs the *Vis'vajit* sacrifice (indicative of universal conquest), in which he gives away to Brâhmaṇas (by way of Dakshiṇá) everything that he possessed.

Canto V. While Raghu had thus practically beggared himself in the Viśvajit sacrifice, an ascetic called Kautsa came to him. He wanted money, as much as fourteen crores, to enable him to pay his *guru*, his tuition fees. Raghu had nothing with him, but he did not like to have it said of him that a supplicant, not gaining his object from Raghu, had to seek it from some other person. In order, therefore, to satisfy Kautsa's demand he planned an expedition against Kubera, the God of wealth, to obtain the money from him. Divining his intention Kubera filled Raghu's treasury with a shower of gold during the night, and Raghu gave all that to Kautsa. The latter, departing, blessed his benefactor that he would soon obtain a valiant son. This son is then born, and is named Aja. When Aja, who is properly educated, reaches the marriageable age, a messenger comes to Raghu from King Bhoja of the Vidarbha country to invite the prince to be present at the Svayaṃvara ceremony of his sister, Indumati, which was shortly to take place. The invitation is accepted and Aja goes accordingly. On his way he happens to kill a wild elephant, who turns out to be a Gandharva born in that form owing to a curse. The Gandharva gives to Aja a certain miraculous weapon (*astra*) called Saṃmohana. On reaching Bhoja's city, Aja rests for the night, and in the next morning goes to the hall where the Svayaṃvara ceremony was to be held.

Canto VI. There he takes his seat in the assembly of numerous other kings who had come from far and near for the Svayaṃvara ceremony. The Princess Indumatî enters, accompanied by her clever maid Sunandá, who takes her in turn to each one of the royal suitors and describes him and his qualifications in a few well-chosen words. The Princess passes by them all, including among them the rulers of Magadha, Aṅga, Avantî, Anûpa, Śûrasena, Kaliṅga and Pâṇḍya. Finally she comes to Aja, whom she chooses as her husband, to the deep chagrin of the other kings who feel envious and humiliated.

Canto VII. The actual wedding-ceremony of Aja and Indumatî then takes place in the royal palace, after which all depart for their respective countries. The slighted kings, however, bear a grudge against Aja, and they, therefore, waylay his party on his way back to Ayodhyá. A very fierce fight ensues. Aja entrusts his bride to the care of his minister, and personally takes an active part in the slaughter of his foes, whom he completely vanquishes by means of the miraculous 'Saṃmohana' *astra* which the Gandharva had given him before. He then returns to the capital; and his father entrusts the kingdom to his care, wishing to live in retirement.

Canto VIII. Aja begins to reign and Raghu continues to live near by, in secluded retirement, when after a few years he departs this life. Aja gives him a suitable funeral. In course of time Indumatî gives birth to a son who is named Daśaratha. Aja pleases all by his excellent rule. A change comes over his happy life when once, while he and his royal consort were sporting in a pleasure-garden, a wreath of flowers falls from the sky below upon Indumatî who instantly drops down dead. The grief of the King at this unexpected stroke of misfortune knows no bounds. After the funeral was over, as Aja still remained plunged in sorrow and took no interest in life, his preceptor Vasishṭha sent to him a disciple with a message to cheer him. It was explained to Aja how his wife had formerly been a celestial nymph (*apsaras*) who had to come down upon the earth owing to a curse, and who left as soon as the curse ceased to operate when the garland fell upon her from heaven. Life being an accident and death the rule, a firm-minded, wise ruler like Aja, should cease to brood over his grief. Thus ran the message, and the King received it dutifully as coming from his *guru*, though it had little visible effect upon him. He spent some eight years more after this, all the while mourning for his lost wife, whom he finally went to join in the next world.

Canto IX. After his father, Daśaratha rules over Ayodhyâ as nobly as his predecessors. His greatness was such that even Indra himself on occasions asked his assistance in his own wars. Once, having enjoyed all the pleasures of the spring season with its attendant festivities, he plans a long hunting trip. He spends several days in that engrossing and delightful sport. One morning he starts after a deer, alone and without followers. In his pursuit he comes to the river Tamasá, where he hears the noise of a pot being filled with water. He mistakes it for the trumpet of a wild elephant, and discharges an arrow in that direction, aiming at the sound only, as he could not see the mark. As a matter of fact a young ascetic-boy was filling his jar there; and the arrow hit him fatally. His parents, who were blind, were at hand. The King, who was horrified at what he had unwillingly done, related to them what had happened. As the boy died, his sorrow-stricken father cursed the King as the author of his bereavement, with the words: "You, too, like me, shall die, in your old age, grieving for your son." The King had no son then; so he received the curse as a sort of qualified blessing, since it meant that at any rate a son was bound to be born to him before he died. The aged couple burned themselves on the funeral pyre of their son, and Daśaratha returned to his city, full of grief not unmixed with a little anticipatory joy at the prospect of a son.

Canto X. Some ten thousand years pass, but still Daśaratha remains without the expected son. At last, holy sages proceed to perform on his behalf a special kind of sacrifice intended to bring about the birth of a son. Now at about this time it so happens that the gods, who were continually harassed and persecuted by the dreaded and powerful demon Râvaṇa, carry their tale of grievances to their lord Vishṇu, who tells them how, by virtue of a boon given by Brahmá, Râvaṇa was immune from death at the hands of all except human beings, whom he despised and hence had left out of the boon. Vishṇu, therefore, promises that he would be born as a *man*, as a son of King Daśaratha of Ayodhya, and that at his hands Râvaṇa would meet death.—Now, out of the fire of that sacrifice which was being performed for Daśaratha, there arises a being who gives consecrated food (*charu*) to the King, who gives it to his three wives. Into this food Vishṇu had entered spiritually, and thus Daśaratha's wives, who conceive afterwards, all bear sons who are partial incarnations (*avataras*) of Vishṇu. Râma was the eldest of them, born of Kausalya. Of Kaikeyî was born Bharata, and of Sumitrá were born the twins, Lakshmaṇa and Śatrughna.

CANTO XI. The sage Viśvâmitra, who wanted protection from demons in his sacrificial work, now comes to Daśaratha with a request that the King should send Ráma with him for that purpose. Accordingly Ráma, and also Lakshmaṇa, accompany Viśvâmitra to his hermitage; on their way Râma kills the demoness Tâḍakâ. In the hermitage of Viśvâmitra, Râma routs the demons after having killed their leaders Subáhu and Mārîcha. On the completion of his sacrifice, Viśvâmitra goes to Mithilâ at the invitation of king Janaka of that city, taking with him the two princes. On their way Râma restores to her original form Ahalyâ, the wife of Gautama, who had been cursed by him to be reduced to the form of a stone. On reaching Mithilá, Viśvâmitra tells Janaka that Ráma was anxious to see the famous bow in his possession. It had been announced that whoever should succeed in bending that bow, would be given Janaka's daughter, Sîtâ, in marriage. No king had yet succeeded in bending the bow, and Janaka wondered how a mere boy should dare to make the attempt. Râma, however, bends the bow, and with such force that it cracks; he thus wins the princess Sîtá for his bride. Daśaratha is then invited to Mithilá, when Râma is married to Sîtâ; her sister is given to Lakshmaṇa, and Bharata and Śatrughna were married to the two nieces of Janaka. On their way back to Ayodhyá, they are stopped by the Brâhmaṇa Paraśurāma, who had vowed vengeance on all Kshatriyas, and whose anger was stirred into action on hearing of that bow-breaking exploit of Râma, a Kshatriya. He, therefore, challenges Râma to bend his (Paraśurāma's) bow, which was stronger than that of Janaka. Râma bends that too, and humbles the pride of Paraśurāma, who recognizes in his adversary the supreme lord Vishṇu, and makes peace with him. The party then safely arrive in Ayodhyâ.

Canto XII. King Daśaratha, who had grown old and was nearing his end, declares his intention to set Râma on the throne, when Kaikeyî contrives, by means of two boons which her husband had promised her, to have Ráma exiled for fourteen years and to have her son Bharata installed King. Râma quite willingly undertakes to go to the forest, and the old King, grieving at being separated from his beloved son, dies heart-broken, thus fulfilling the old man's curse (Canto IX). Bharata declines to accept the sovereignty earned by intrigue, and after vainly trying to persuade Râma to come back, himself remains a sort of exile at Nandigráma, and from that place he rules the kingdom as Ráma's representative. In his journey to the forest Râma is accompanied by Sîtâ and Lakshmaṇa. He there kills Virādha, Dûshaṇa, Khara, and other demons, the news of whose death is carried to Rāvaṇa in Lankâ by his sister Śûrpaṇakhâ, whom Lakshmaṇa had disfigured. Râvaṇa comes and carries off Sîtá in Râma's absence. Râma makes friends with Sugrîva, the monkey-Chief, and through his retainer Maruti discovers the whereabouts of Sîtá. Building a bridge over the sea, Ráma with Sugrîva's army crosses into Lankâ, and is engaged in a series of battles with the hosts of Râvaṇa, whose death he finally accomplishes. Ráma recovers Sîtá, gives Ravaṇa's kingdom to his brother Vibhîshaṇa, and starts back for Ayodhyā in the well-known aerial car, Pushpaka, along with Sugrîva and Vibhîshaṇa and their armies.

Canto XIII. The journey of Râma from Lankâ to Ayodhyā by air is here described. Râma points out to Sîtâ the various objects and places of interest on the way, including, in order, Janasthána, the mountain Mālyavat, the lake Pampâ, the Godâvarî, Pañchavaṭî, the dwelling-places of the sages Agastya Śâtakarṇi and Śarabhanga, the mountain Chitrakûṭa, the stream Mandâkinî, the rivers Gangâ and Yamunâ, and lastly the Sarayû. After they had seen the Sarayû they observe Bharata advancing with an army to welcome the home-coming king. Râma gets down from the Pushpaka, and the meeting of the brothers is touchingly described. Then Râma again gets into the car and arrives at last in a garden outside Ayodhyâ, his capital.

Canto XIV. There in the garden Ráma and Lakshmaṇa see their mothers who greet them with joy. Ráma is then formally crowned King of Ayodhyâ with due pomp and ceremony. He then gives the armies of Sugrîva and Vibhîshaṇa leave to depart, and restores Pushpaka to its original rightful owner, Kubera. In course of time Sîtā shows signs of pregnancy. She expresses a desire again to visit the once-familiar regions along the banks of the Ganges. While Ráma promises her that, a scandal reaches his ear about his unquestioning acceptance of Sîtâ after her residence in a stranger's house for a long time. A strong sense of duty towards his subjects both as the dispenser of law and justice and the up-holder of social order compels him to abandon Sîtâ as a concession to this scandal, although he knew her to be pure and innocent. He, therefore, orders Lakshmaṇa to take Sîtâ away and leave her on the banks of the Ganges near the hermitage of Vālmîki who, he thinks, would find her and take due care of her. Lakshmaṇa very reluctantly performs this task; and when Sîtâ knows why she is abandoned, she cries loud and long, though she would not blame Râma so much as she blamed herself. Vâlmîki takes her to his hermitage where afterwards in due time she gives birth to twins. Râma continues to discharge his kingly duties as usual, but without marrying again.

Canto XV. Now, certain sages who were harassed by the demon Lavaṇa apply to Râma for protection, who sends off Śatrughna on that mission. Śatrughna happens to halt at Vālmîki's hermitage on his way, and it so chances that that very night Sîta gives birth to twins. Śatrughna proceeds against Lavaṇa, whom he kills in battle, and builds for himself a city called Madhurá on the banks of the Yamunâ. Sîta's sons were named Kuśa and Lava; they were duly brought up and educated by the venerable Vālmîki, who also teaches them to sing his own poem 'Rāmāyaṇa', celebrating the exploits of their father. After some time Śatrughna returns to Ayodhyā, but says nothing to Râma about Kuśa and Lava, at the express bidding of Vālmîki, who bided his own time. Rama's killing of Śambûka is then related. Śambûka was a Śûdra practising penance; this was against the rule, and this transgression caused other distresses in the state; it was therefore imperative that Śambûka should be killed. This done, Râma performs a horse-sacrifice, to which holy men are invited from everywhere. Among them is Vālmîki, who brings with him his two pupils, the princes Kuśa and Lava

They sing the Râmayâṇa in the presence of Ráma, and charm all by their sweet singing as also by the majesty of their demeanour. Râma is then told that they are his sons, and Vâlmîki then asks him to take back Sîtá. Râma agrees to do it if she would satisfy the public about her purity. Sîtá, therefore, calls upon the Earth to receive her in her bosom, if she (Sîtâ) was really and truly pure. The Earth then appears in corporeal form and takes off Sîtâ, whom Ráma thus loses for ever, although he gets his two sons. After a time Râma begins to feel his end approaching. He puts his brothers, nephews and sons in charge of separate, small principalities. Lakshmaṇa dies, and soon Ráma also leaves this world of mortals and ascends to heaven, after having completed his special work here.

Canto XVI. After the death of Râma, his son Kuśa, who ruled in the city of Kus'âvatî, is visited in a dream by the guardian deity (*Adhidevatâ*) of the city of Ayodhyā, which being kingless lay now a deserted ruin. She invites him to come back to his father's capital and to re-people it and restore it to its former glory. He consents, and coming back to Ayodhyâ re-endows it with its former splendour, and rules there in future. Once, while he is sporting in the river Sarayû, his bracelet drops in its waters and sinks to the bottom. He orders the river to be searched, but the ornament could not be recovered; at the suggestion that it was probably taken by the Nága Kumuda, who resided in a part of the river, Kus'a takes up a missile (*astra*) to destroy the Nâga, who hurriedly comes up, leading by the hand his sister Kumudvatî. It was she who had taken the bracelet in curiosity. Kumuda requests Kuśa to accept his sister as his wife; Kus a agrees and the two are then married.

Canto XVII. Kuśa gets from Kumudvati a son, called Atithi, who ascends the throne on the death of his father, who was killed in a fight with the demon Durjaya. Atithi is possessed of great political wisdom, and the Canto describes at some length some of the main principles of the science of Polity (Râja Nîti) which Atithi sedulously acted upon.

Canto XVIII. This Canto barely enumerates, without any illuminating details, the various kings, twenty-one in all, that succeeded Atithi. They were Nishadha, Nala, Nabhas, Puṇḍarîka, Kshemadhanvan, Devánîka, Ahînagu, Páriyátra, Sila, Unnâbha,

Vajranâbha, Śankhaṇa, Vyushitâśva, Viśvasaha, Hiraṇyanâbha, Kausalya, Brahmishṭha, Putra, Pushya, Dhruvasandhi, and Sudarśana. The last of these (Sudarśana) ascends the throne when a young boy of six, his father having been killed by a lion. After he attains youth he is married.

CANTO XIX. Sudarśana gets a son, Agnivarṇa by name, whom he instals king and himself retires into the forest. Agnivarṇa turns out to be a voluptuous, pleasure-seeking sensualist. The Canto describes at length his amorous sports and pastime. Agnivarṇa pays the penalty of having drunk too deep at the fountain of dissipation, and he falls a victim to consumption. At his death his wife was pregnant; she ascended the throne as the Queen-regent, and looked after the affairs of state on behalf of her unborn child. And here the story somewhat abruptly ends.

(2) THE SOURCES OF THE RAGHUVAṂŚA.

In ancient Sanskrit literature history in the modern sense of the term is not to be found. It either merges in mythology or becomes for the most part indistinguishable from it; hence, although the Raghuvaṃśa is based on historical material, the latter is so slender that it can be disposed of in a few lines. Briefly summarized it amounts to this, that in the solar dynasty that ruled at Ayodhyâ, there were four great kings, Dilîpa, Raghu, Aja and Daśaratha; after these came Râma, the greatest of all and the incarnation of divine Vishṇu; after him came 24 kings, the last being Agnivarṇa, who died without issue, leaving his queen *enceinte*. The account of the solar race must have been a matter of common knowledge in the times of Kâlidâsa; but, with certain embellishments, it had been already presented in narrative form by the authors of the various Purâṇas, and in particular by Vâlmîki, the author of the celebrated epic, Râmâyaṇa. It is obvious that Kâlidâsa was acquainted with this literature, and derived his details from the same, choosing and discarding matter as suited his purpose. Indeed he prominently mentions with deep reverence the Râmâyaṇa and its author (*cf.* वृत्तं रामस्य वाल्मीकेः कृतिस्तौ किन्नरस्वनौ। किं तद्येन मनो हर्तुमलं स्यातां न शृण्वताम् ॥ XV. 64), and he has utilized it for the Râma-portion of his work. But the Râmâyaṇa does not cover the whole ground of the Ragh.; and Kâlidâsa has referred to certain other accounts of the solar race, rather vaguely, when he speaks of it as having been described before by "former writers" (पूर्वसूरिभिः I. 4). Here the use of the plural is significant, and it obviously includes others besides Válmîki. By the others we can only understand the compilers of the Purâṇas. The Purâṇas are not all modern works, and many of them have been shown to date from times much anterior to the Christrian era. Of these Purâṇas he seems to have used the Vishṇu-, the Vâyu-, and the Padma- in particular. A word of caution, however, is here necessary. The Purâṇas *in their present form* bear evidences of having been re-modelled and re-written at various periods, and their current recensions may not be those with which our poet was familiar. Indeed, in some of them (*e. g.* in the Padma-P.) it appears as though the stories had been revised in the light of the works of Kâlidása. Hence, any remarks which one would be inclined to pass on the so-called "changes" made by the poet in his sources must be made with due reservations, since we may not have before us the actual version which was accessible to Kâlidása, but some later redaction of it. [19]

With these preliminary remarks, we shall proceed to examine the poem itself. In the first place, the list of kings as given by the poet does not exactly agree with any that are available to us, [20] but agrees nearest with the one in the Vishṇu-Purâṇa, with a slight difference. The Purâṇa mentions a number of Kings before Dilîpa, but these are omitted by Kâlidâsa. The Vishṇu-Purâṇa (as also the Vâyu-P.) represents Raghu as the son of one Dîrghabâhu, grandson of Dilîpa; while Kâlidâsa mentions him as the son of Dilîpa himself. Kâlidâsa's account stops with Agnivarṇa, while the Vishṇu-P. enumerates a number of kings after him; but there is no incongruency here, since our poem is probably incomplete, a point which we have discussed elsewhere.

Thus the line of succession in the Ragh. practically agrees with that of the Vishṇu-P. and may be accepted as being historically true. But what about the various incidents specially described in

---

19. This might be said to some extent of the Râmâyaṇa also. There are at present three different recensions of the Râmâyaṇa extant, and "about one-third of the ślokas in each recension occurs in neither of the other two." (Macdonell's *History of Sanskrit Literature*, p. 303).

20. Thus the Râm. (Bala. Sarga 70) gives the genealogy quite differently.

the Ragh. in the life of each king? Are they all historical facts? The poet has not portrayed for us the whole life of each king, but only such episodes as suited his poetic purpose or the requirements of a Mahâkávya. Thus the bare facts he mentions about king Dilîpa are his childless state, his service of a cow, the birth of his son Raghu, and his horse-sacrifice. He devotes the first three Cantos to these, and the parallel account will be found in the Uttarakhaṇḍa of the Padma-Purâṇa. We forbear from quoting it here, which the curious student may consult in the original. As regards the incidents in the lives of Raghu and Aja, no references can be found in the accounts that have been published till now. For example, the *dig-vijaya* of Raghu, the Kautsa episode, the battle in Canto VII, or the tragic end of Aja's queen in Canto VIII, have not yet been traced to their sources. Kâlidása could hardly have invented these, and they must be lying embedded in accounts that have not yet been brought to light.

From Canto IX onwards the poet closely follows the Rámâyaṇa. Kálidâsa was an admirer and a diligent student of the great epic. Indeed, as has been pointed out by Pandit R. Krishnamachariar,[21] the name "Raghuvaṃśa" of the poem itself seems to have been directly suggested by, and borrowed from, the Râmāyaṇa, where it occurs twice (रघुवंशस्य चरितं चकार भगवान्मुनिः I. 3. 9; अहं च रघुवंशश्च लक्ष्मणश्च महाबलः VI. 1. 11.). It is no wonder, therefore, that Vâlmîki should have been the model of Kálidása. What changes he makes in the Ṛámáyaṇa account are such as are necessary for poetic and dramatic effect. Thus in the Râm. Daśaratha shoots the young ascetic-boy, who dies first, and then the parents are taken to him by the King; while in the Ragh. the poet makes the boy die in the presence of his parents, which enhances the tragic effect of Daśaratha's deed. In Canto X Kâlidása makes the gods approach Vishṇu directly; while in the Râmâyaṇa they approach Brahmâ first, and then comes Vishṇu to whom they repeat their grievances. In Canto XII the poet goes over the account very hurriedly, disposing of important events in single verses and phrases even,[22] as if anxious not to narrate at length what had been so well narrated by Vâlmíki. Even here, some of the accounts differ from those of the

---

21. In his *Raghuvaṃs'avimars'a*, Srirangam 1908, p. 130.

22. *E. g.* The whole story of the purification of Sitâ in fire he gives in one single word जातवेदोविशुद्धां (verse 104).

Rámáyaṇa. For example, the crow-story (vv. 21–23) is given differently by Vâlmîki; the reason of the burial of Virâdha (verse 30), again, is not the same as that found in the Râmáyaṇa. But these are trifling variations. The thirteenth Canto is based on sarga 123 of the Yuddha-Káṇḍa of the Rám. It provides an excellent contrast between the methods of the two poets. While the narrative of Válmîki is crude and simple, that of Kálidása is brilliant with high-wrought imagery. Thus, to take a single instance where Válmîki merely wrote असौ सुतनु शैलेन्द्रश्चित्रकूटः प्रकाशते, Kálidása expanded the same into (XIII. 47)—

धारास्वनोद्गारिदरीमुखोऽसौ शृङ्गाग्रलग्नाम्बुदवप्रपङ्कः ।
बध्नाति मे बन्धुरगात्रि चक्षुर्दृप्तः ककुद्मानिव चित्रकूटः ॥

Cantos XIV and XV strictly follow the Rámáyaṇa. From Canto XVI onwards, the poet goes beyond the story of the epic, and has recourse to Puráṇas. Here, too, the exact references have not yet been brought to light, and it cannot be said, for instance, whether the episode of Kumudvatî's espousal had any basis or was invented by the poet. The description of राजनीति in Canto XVII is evidently based on that given in ancient treatises like Kauṭilyás Arthaśástra,[23] a work which Kâlidâsa appears to have closely studied. The remaining portion of the poem only enumerates the kings in succession, and calls for no special comment.

THE SOLAR DYNASTY

[We give below in parallel columns, for ready reference, the kings of the solar race as enumerated in the Vishṇu-Purâṇa (IV.), in the Râmâyaṇa (1. 70 and II. 110), and in the Raghuvaṃśa. The student will observe how closely Kâlidâsa has followed the Vishṇu-P. list. Before Raghu, Ikshvâku was the most celebrated king of Ayodhyâ and the family was named after him (see I. 72; VI. 71; XV. 44; XIV. 55 &c.). Nimi, a son of Ikshvāku, was the founder of the Nimi dynasty that reigned at Mithilâ.]

23. This standard ancient treatise on the science of Politics has been only recently discovered and published at Mysore. It is frequently quoted by Mallinâtha and is the original on which the well-knoun Kâmandakîya Nîtisâra is based.

Vishṇu-Purâṇa.	Râmâyaṇa.	Raghuvaṃśa
ब्रह्मन्	ब्रह्मन्	विवस्वत्
दक्षप्रजापति	मरीचि	मनु
अदिति	कश्यप	... ...
विवस्वत्	विवस्वत्	दिलीप
मनु	मनु	रघु
इक्ष्वाकु	इक्ष्वाकु	अज
विकुक्षि (or शशाद)	कुक्षि	दशरथ
परंजय (or ककुत्स्थ)	विकुक्षि	राम
अनेनस्	बाण	कुश
पृथु	अनरण्य	अतिथि
विष्वगश्व	पृथु	निषध
आर्द्र	त्रिशङ्कु	नल
युवनाश्व	धुंधुमार	नभस्
श्रावस्त	युवनाश्व	पुण्डरीक
बृहदश्व	मांधातृ	क्षेमधन्वन्
कुवलयाश्व (or धुंधुमार)	सुसंधि	देवानीक
दृढाश्व	ध्रुवसंधि	अहीनगु
हर्यश्व	भरत	पारियात्र
निकुम्भ	असित	शिल
संहताश्व	सगर	उन्नाभ
कृशाश्व	असमञ्ज	वज्रणाभ
प्रसेनजित्	अंशुमत्	शङ्खण
युवनाश्व	दिलीप	व्युषिताश्व
मांधातृ	भगीरथ	विश्वसह
पुरुकुत्स	ककुत्स्थ	हिरण्यनाभ
त्रसदस्यु	रघु	कौसल्य
संभूत	कल्माषपाद	ब्रह्मिष्ठ
अनरण्य	शङ्खण	पुत्र
पृषदश्व	सुदर्शन	पुष्य
हर्यश्व	अग्निवर्ण	ध्रुवसंधि
वसुमनस्	शीघ्रग	सुदर्शन
त्रिधन्वन्	मरु	अग्निवर्ण
त्रैय्यारुण	प्रशुश्रुक	
सत्यव्रत (or त्रिशङ्कु)	अम्बरीष	
हरिश्चन्द्र	नहुष	
रोहिताश्व	ययाति	
हरित	नाभाग	
चञ्चु	अज	
	दशरथ	
	राम	

Vishnu-Purâṇa.	Vishṇu-Puráṇa.	Vishṇu-Puráṇa.
विजय	देवानीक	दल (or शिल)
रुरुक	दशरथ	उक्थ
वृक	इलविल	वज्रणाभ
बाहु	विश्वसह	शङ्खनाभ
सगर	दिलीप	व्युषिताश्व
असमञ्जस	खट्वाङ्ग	विश्वसह
अंशुमत्	दीर्घबाहु	हिरण्यनाभ
दिलीप	रघु	......
भगीरथ	अज	......
श्रुत	दशरथ	......
नाभाग	राम	पुष्प
अम्बरीष	कुश	ध्रुवसंधि
सिन्धुद्वीप	अतिथि	सुदर्शन
अयुताश्व	निषध	अग्निवर्ण
ऋतुपर्ण	नल	शीघ्र
सर्वकाम	नभस्	मरु
सुदास	पुण्डरीक	प्रसुश्रुत
मित्रसह (or कल्माषपाद)	क्षेमधन्वन्	सुगवि
अश्मक	अहीनगु (or रुरु)	अमर्ष
मूलक	पारियात्र	महस्वत्
		विश्रुतवत्
		बृहद्बल

(3) GENERAL AND CRITICAL REMARKS.

The student who has closely followed the preceding summary could not have failed to be immediately struck with the abrupt ending of the poem; this, and the absence of a suitable benedictory stanza which generally marks the close of Sanskrit compositions, have given rise to an important question, *viz.* whether the present nineteen Cantos are the whole poem, and whether the poet might not have written more Cantos than have descended to us. No decisive answer can be given to this question. The student might compare how the Kumárasambhava, too, similarly ends in an abrupt manner at the end of its 8th Canto ; here some later poet has filled the deficiency by composing nine more Cantos. But no such thing has been done in the case of the Raghuvaṃśa. All the MSS. of the poem yet discovered agree in ending the poem where it ends at present. All the commentators, again, who belong to different provinces of the land and different periods of time, seem to have believed the poem to be complete, and they all conclude their commentaries formally at the end of the nineteenth Canto; and one of them, Hemádri, incidentally remarks at the beginning of the 16th Canto that the Rámáyaṇa, the poet's source for the history up to that portion, being exhausted, he now gives *four* more Cantos from other sources. There is a persistent tradition, however, which says that the complete poem originally contained as many as 25 Cantos; and there is nothing that goes against this tradition. On the contrary many things tend to confirm it. As a general rule Sanskrit poets studiously avoid a tragic result; and even when they cannot avoid it, they are anxious to give it an agreeable finish. And we cannot reasonably suppose Kálidása to have gone against a practice of such long standing as led the later writers on poetics to lay down a rule that the death of the hero should never be actually represented (नाधिकारिवधं क्वापि D.-R. III. 40). "Further" remarks Mr. S. P. Pandit, "he (Kâlidâsa), who is on all hands praised for the happy choice of his subjects and the thorough execution of his plans, cannot be supposed to have brought down the history of the most celebrated ancient Indian kings to such a sorry end. It is natural to imagine that his object must have been some such as to connect some one of the dynasties of kings existing in his time with the race anciently descended from the sun. The Vishṇu-Puráṇa enumerates no less than 37 princes after Agnivarṇa, of whom it represents 8 as having reigned up to the war of the Mahábhárata and the rest after that event * * * * * The line of Kings, therefore, mentioned by our poet, not being complete, the conclusion is inevitable either that the poet did not finish his work, or if he did, it has not descended to us in its entirety." The absence of any trace of additional Cantos having ever existed lends weight to the former conclusion. We think it highly likely that Kálidása, though he might have intended to write more Cantos, was somehow prevented from carrying out his intention.

Another feature, that calls for notice on a review of the contents of the poem as a whole, is the evident lack of unity of plot. This, however, is part of the very design of the poem, and can hardly be accounted as a blemish. The poet did not choose a single episode, nor even the life of a single hero; but the lives of a number of famous kings; it is unfair to expect unity of plot in a work of such character. On the contrary, it amounts to a triumph of skill on the poet's part to have welded together his detached episodes without incongruity in presentation. Moreover, a unity of plot of a certain kind does exist, if we remember that the incidents mentioned in the poem are all to be interpreted as part of the central idea running through the poem, *viz.* the portraying of the leading characteristics of an ideal king according to the Aryan standard. Viewed in this light, even the slight charge of "a formless plot" vanishes into background, and we see the Raghuvaṃśa for what it is, being a word-painting, in the most polished phraseology of an accomplished poet, of the ideal of kingship; *that* is the theme of the Raghuvṃśa, and not so much the complete life-history of each King. It is, therefore, inevitable that, as remarked by Dr. Ryder, we must regard the Raghuvaṃśa as a poem "in which single episodes take a stronger hold upon the reader than does the unfolding of an ingenious plot."

It is in the Raghuvaṃśa, as in the Śâkuntala, that Kâlidása is seen at his best. The poem has been most popular in India from very early times and has evoked an unending chorus of praise from the learned and beginners alike. Stray lines, detached stanzas, and even whole Cantos of the poem are on the lips of many a cultured Indian to whom Kálidâsa's muse embodies the very essence of the pleasure derivable from poetry: क इह रघुकारे न रमते, says a well-known subháshita. Almost every Canto of the poem makes a special appeal to the reader by reason of some peculiar grace, whether of mellifluous style, or of life-like description, or of dramatic dialogue. Let the student examine the various Cantos for himself. In the very opening stanzas (5–9) of the first Canto the poet strikes the key-note of the whole poem in a rèsumè of the accomplishments of the kings of the Raghu line. Then follows the description of Dilîpa's good rule as well as that of his journey to Vasishṭha's hermitage, which is of a kind that leaves its impress on the mind long after it is read, bringing usually before us the benign ruler and his simple subjects by such stanzas as हैयंगवीनमादाय घोषवृद्धानुपस्थितान् । नामधेयानि पृच्छन्तौ वन्यानां मार्गशाखिनाम् ॥ Then in Canto II the meeting of Dilîpa with the lion, and in Canto III Raghu's encounter with Indra are classic examples, known to almost every Indian Sanskrit-reading school-boy, of spirited and balanced dialogue and bright narration, apart from the noble ideals of self-sacrifice and personal valour which they vividly place before him. In the fourth Canto we have a striking description of the main parts of the country; it is impossible to forget the word-pictures which the poet draws in such stanzas as बलैरध्युषितास्तस्य विजिगीषोर्गताध्वनः । मारीचोद्भ्रान्तहारीता मलयाद्रेरुपत्यकाः ॥ or विनीताध्वश्रमास्तस्य सिन्धुतीरविचेष्टनैः । दुधुवुर्वाजिनः स्कन्धाँल्लग्नकुङ्कुमकेसरान् ॥ Canto V describes the magnanimity of Raghu, who gave to the sage Kautsa wealth in excess of his demands; it is, as we have said elsewhere, probably the most characteristic kingly trait. This Canto contains also the famous address of the bards (*Vaitâlikas*) to prince Aja at dawn. The passage from तस्याधिकारपुरुषैः (V. 63) to the end of the Canto is one of the best known in the works of Kālidāsa, where the poet has expressed beautiful thoughts in language which is most rhythmical and charming. The expression here is so sweet and so pleasing, the harmony between sound and sense is carried here to such exquisite perfection, that it is not without reason that a tradition has grown up around this passage as to its having been written by the Muse of Poetry, the goddess Sarasvatî herself. The sixth Canto contains rapid pen-portraits of the various kings in the Svayamvara ; here Kálidása reveals himself as a master of the art of sketching a character with a few telling strokes. The seventh Canto contains a description of a typical Âryan wedding, similar to the one in the seventh Canto of the Kum., and the student can see that the marriage-customs have not much altered materially during twenty centuries. The description of the fight (VII. 35-63), it must be allowed, is rather tame and conventional. The eighth Canto contains the famous अजविलाप or lament of King Aja at the death of his wife Indumatî. It is fine poetry, but it suffers by comparison with the corresponding रतिविलाप in Kum. IV. It is more natural in a woman, as being of the weaker sex, to indulge in lamentation ; while when a man grieves it is a sign of weakness which does not enlist our sympathy so much: the poet has therefore better succeeded in portraying a lamenting Rati. At the end of this Canto is the beautiful message sent to Aja by his *guru* Vasishtha, concerning the evanescence of this world and the futility of human sorrow for departed relatives. The ninth Canto attracts many owing to the charming यमकs introduced. This is the only place in all the works of Kâlidása where he tries his hand at चित्रकाव्य ; he has succeeded well without putting an undue strain on the construction of the Sloka, as other inferior poets do when they try to employ यमकs. The Canto also cantains fine descriptions of spring and deer-hunt.

In the tenth Canto we have the passage where the gods praise Vishṇu, which has its counterpart in Kum. II.; it does not possess any particular interest. In the eleventh we have a life-like description of the journey of the two boy-princes to Viśvâmitra's hermitage; its chief feature is the encounter of Râma with Paraśurâma, and the graceful way in which the poet brings the former out of it. The twelfth Canto has become one of the weakest in the whole poem, as the entire story of the Rámáyaṇa from the death of Daśaratha in Ayodhyâ to the killing of Râvaṇa in Lankâ has been very hurriedly gone over. The poet felt the necessity of abridging it in this manner; for otherwise his poem would have grown interminably long. Dr. Ryder observes (pp. 150–151)—"It may well be doubted whether the cantos dealing with Ráma are the most successful. They are too compressed, too briefly allusive. Kálidása attempts to tell the story in about one-thirtieth of the space given to it by his great predecessor, Vâlmîki. The result is much loss by omission and much loss by compression. Many of the best episodes of the Râmâyaṇa are quite omitted by Kâlidása: for example, the story of the jealous humpback who eggs on Queen Kaikeyî to demand her two boons; the beautiful scene in which Sîtá insists on following Râma into the forest; the account of the somnolent giant Pot-ear...Other fine episodes are so briefly alluded to as to lose all their charm: for example, the story of the golden deer that attracts the attention of Ràma while Râvaṇa is stealing his wife; the journey of the monkey Hanumat to Rávaṇa's fortress and his interview with Sîtá. The Ráma-story, as told by Válmîki, is one of the great epic stories of the world. It has been for two thousand years and more the story *par excellence* of the Hindus...There is, therefore, real matter for regret in the fact that so great a poet as Kâlidâsa should have treated it in a way not quite worthy of it and of himself."

While we recognize the force of this criticism, we cannot quite agree with the learned scholar in his explanation. Dr. Ryder says that Kálidása did not care to put himself "into direct competition with Vâlmîki," and thus to challenge comparison with him. While Kâlidâsa doubtless felt great admiration for Vâlmîki and his work, the real explanation of the weakness of the twelfth and the fifteenth cantos is, in our opinion, to be sought elsewhere. It is that the poet felt the need of abridging somewhere, and these are the parts of the story where he has chosen to do it; whenever our poet has had to relate incidents in a catalogue fashion, as for instance in Cantos XII., XV. and XVIII., he is never at his best. But whenever he gives full play to his fancy, his poetry is as good as, even better than, Vâlmîki's. For example, the famous journey back to Ayodhyá from Lanká (Canto XIII.) is to be found in the original Rámáyaṇa also; if we compare the two we see that our poet has excelled his predecessor in acuteness of observation, in the elegance of style and in the vividness of expression (vide *supra* p. xxvii). The fourteenth Canto is rather colourless, but the sixteenth makes up the deficiency, containing as it does Kuśa's interview with the guardian-deity of Ayodhyá, and further on, the charming description of summer beginning with अगस्त्यचिह्नादयनात्समीपं &c. (śl. 44). The next Canto (XVII.) gives a detailed description of administrative policy, which would probably read dry to those not interested in the subject. The ending Canto describes amorous sports, much in the manner of the eighth Canto of the Kumárasambhava. We thus see that, barring a few exceptions, every canto of this poem has some attractive feature or other which endears it to the reader on that account; there is no wonder, therefore, if the whole poem has found admirers by the million, and has become, in the words of Sanskrit rhetoricians, मूर्धाभिषिक्त of all the Kávyas in popularity.

If we were to compare the Ragh. with the two other poems of Kálidâsa, it would be found inferior to them in unity of plot; but, as we have remarked above, this happens because it treats of a number of Kings and not of one definite episode. It might also be said that the Meghadûta excels the Ragh. in perfection of polish, though here too the comparison would be slightly unjust since the Meghadûta is a small piece, while the Ragh. is twelve times larger; in a large work one cannot expect equal finish in every part.

One chief reason of Kálidâsa's superiority over other poets is his brilliantly polished style; there is no other Sanskrit poet who possesses an equal command over language so simple and withal so graceful. In fact, all the works of Kálidása are written in what the later rhetoricians have called the *Vaidarbhi* style, the ten chief excellences belonging to which are thus given by Daṇḍin:—
श्लेषः प्रसाद समता माधुर्यं सुकुमारता । अर्थव्यक्तिरुदारत्वमोजःकान्तिसमाधयः ॥
(K.—D. I. 41). Kálidása abhors the looseness and laxity of the epics

the superfluous piling of epithets found in lesser poets, and the artificiality of diction which is observable even in writers like Báṇa and Mágha. He studiously avoids all meretricious ornament and the cheap tinsel of verbal tricks. His strength lies in the music of his words and in the swift conveying of precise and beautiful ideas. He employs no figures of speech except the commonest ones, and in particular he delights in *Upamá*, of which he is a recognised master. He is a great lover of nature, and all his similes and illustrations are drawn from his close observation of natural phenomena. We note down a few here, chosen at random:

नक्षत्रताराग्रहसंकुलापि ज्योतिष्मती चन्द्रमसैव रात्रिः । (VI. 22)
द्रुमसानुमतां किमन्तरं यदि वायौ द्वितयेऽपि ते चलाः । (VIII. 90)
दिवसं शारदमिव प्रारम्भसुखदर्शनम् । (X. 9)
अंशैरनुययुर्विष्णुं पुष्पैर्वायुमिव द्रुमाः । (X. 49)
मनो बहुर्निदाघान्ते श्यामाभ्रा दिवसा इव । (X. 83)
बालार्कप्रतिमेवाप्सु वीचिभिन्ना पतिष्यतः ।
रराज रक्षःकायस्य कण्ठच्छेदपरंपरा ॥ XII. 100)

The student can select many more; the whole work richly abounds with them. Over the Raghuvaṃśa, as Dr. Ryder observes, "is shed the magic charm of Kálidása's style;" and it is this magic charm of style, coupled with the discriminating choice of episodes and topics, that constitutes the main element in the universal admiration which the Raghuvaṃśa has continued to elicit from an appreciating and critical public.

(4) THE PRINCIPAL CHARACTERS.

The poet has devoted the major part of his poem (Cantos I.—XV.) to describing the five chief princes of the Raghu race, whose collective virtues he has briefly summarized for us at the very beginning in these memorable lines:—

… आजन्मशुद्धानामाफलोदयकर्मणाम् ।
आसमुद्रक्षितीशानामानाकरथवर्त्मनाम् ॥
यथाविधिहुताग्नीनां यथाकामार्चितार्थिनाम् ।
यथापराधदण्डानां यथाकालप्रबोधिनाम् ॥
त्यागाय संभृतार्थानां सत्याय मितभाषिणाम् ।
यशसे विजिगीषूणां प्रजायै गृहमेधिनाम् ॥
शैशवेऽभ्यस्तविद्यानां यौवने विषयैषिणाम् ।
वार्द्धके मुनिवृत्तीनां योगेनान्ते तनुत्यजाम् ॥
रघूणां … … … … (I. 5–9)

This, in brief, is the ancient Hindu ideal of Kingship; and it is here illustrated by a series of brilliant portraits which aim at showing the culture and civilization of ancient India at their best. It is true that a poet's powers of depicting a character are best seen in a play, which is a दृश्य काव्य, while in a long poem dealing with a series of kings characters will occupy—comparatively—a secondary place, it being the poet's object to make each canto an attractive piece of poetry by exhibiting his powers of narration and description in melodious and poetical language.[24] Nevertheless, there will be sufficient scope for character-painting if the poet takes care to choose just suitable episodes for detailed narration, relegating minor incidents to the back-ground, or even omitting them altogether. Kálidása has done this, and he has skilfully selected those incidents in the careers of his heroes which possess an absorbing *dramatic* interest; thus the reader, when he comes to Dilîpa's contest with the lion, or to Raghu's with Indra, feels the whole scene being acted before his eyes as though on a real stage. It is such scenes that leave a permanent impression on the reader, without being simply bald statements of facts in metrical language.

The poet begins with King **Dilîpa**. His general virtues are described in ślokas **13-29** of canto I.; it is a description which, it may be remarked in passing, applies in a great or less degree to all good and noble kings. We can hardly understand him that way; if we are to know him better, we must have something more definite than a conventional description. Dilîpa had no issue and he decides to consult Vasishṭha on that account, which shows his great reverence for his spiritual *guru* and his faith in the efficacy of religious rites in attaining the desired end. Vasishṭha enjoins upon him service of the holy cow in his possesion; the readiness with which the King accepts the task, and the rigorous exactitude with which he performs it, show how simple and duty-loving his nature was. With him kingly grace was not incompatible with simplicity. But the trait of character which raises him far above the level of ordinary kings is his interview with the lion wherein he offers his own body in exchange for that of the cow, recalling the famous instance of Śibi saving the pigeon in a similar manner. The moral may be given in the

---

24. If this were not so, where was the necessity of describing in detail a model Government under the obscure King Atithi (Canto XVII), when it could, with better propriety, have been done under Raghu?

poet's own words—क्षतात्किल त्रायत इत्युदग्रः क्षत्रस्य शब्दो भुवनेषु रूढः। राज्येन किं तद्विपरीतवृत्तेः प्राणैरुपक्रोशमलीमसैर्वा॥. "The highest duty of the ruler is to look after the weak and to save them from the aggressive strong." In due time, when his son Raghu is born, he abdicates his throne in his favour, and retires to the forest.

Raghu is the next king. He was the most illustrious of his line, since not only is the poem named "Raghu-vaṃs'a" after him, but even his equally illustrious successor, Râma, is more often known by such titles as राघव, रघुपति, रघुनाथ and the like. While yet a young man, Raghu was entrusted with the task of guarding his father's sacrificial horse; we know how he had to fight with the redoubtable Indra, the chief of the immortals. His intrepid bravery won him Indra's admiration and his father's blessing. In the poet's own words, the incident brings out Raghu's वीर्यातिशय (III. 62). Raghu's merits as a ruler will be found in s'lokas 8-13 of canto IV., which also describes how Raghu brought the whole of India under his sway. It would appear that he was the first prince of his race who undertook, and brought to a successful termination, this wide, arduous and glorious campaign of universal conquest; and that is perhaps one reason why he came to be regarded as the greatest of his race, since doubtless a king who first brought a whole country under one *chhatra* could not have failed to win universal applause and approbation. It is, however, in a subsequent incident that his crowning achievement lies, which brought him undying[25] fame. Having given away all his wealth as gift to Bráhmaṇas in a sacrifice, Raghu had practically become a beggar, so much so that even the vessels in his household were earthen and not of gold. But when the sage Kautsa comes to him for money he cannot turn him away; he wishes to satisfy his want; and the God of Wealth showers down gold, all of which he makes over to Kautsa. It is more than Kautsa wants, but the king insists on his taking all, as it was obtained for him; as the poet beautifully expresses it—जनस्य साकेतनिवासिनस्तौ द्वावप्यभूतामभिनन्द्यसत्त्वौ। गुरुप्रदेयाधिकनिःस्पृहोऽर्थी नृपोऽर्थिकामादधिकप्रदश्च॥ (V. 31) The incident reveals the highest type of selfless nobility in a king, illustrating the complete harmony between भोग (enjoyment) and त्याग (renun-

25. That this was also the popular conception is shown by a later reference to Raghu, when in canto VI. he is described as महाक्रतोर्विश्वजितः प्रयोक्ता। चतुर्दिगावर्जितसंभृतां यो मृत्पात्रशेषामकरोद्विभूतिम्॥ आरूढमद्रीनुदधीन्वितीर्णं भुजंगमानां वसतिं प्रविष्टम्। ऊर्ध्वं गतं यस्य न चानुबन्धि यशः परिच्छेत्तुमियत्तयाऽलम्॥ (76–77).

ciation) and the **यथाकामार्चितार्थित्व** and **त्यागाय संभृतार्थत्व** of Raghu ; we should not hesitate to name it as probably the most striking episode in the whole book. After seeing his son married, Raghu departed this worldly existence by means of *yoga* (VIII. 24; *cf.* **योगेनान्ते तनुत्यजाम्**).

The next King is **Aja**. He is presented in the three-fold character of the best warrior (VII. 57 ff.), the best ruler, a second copy as it were of Raghu (VIII. 4 ff.), and the most loving husband (VIII. 38 ff.). Thus he is shown to have proved himself a conquering hero, when he routed the hosts of his rival kings on his way back from the Svayaṃvara. The poet describes in the beginning of canto VIII, how Aja ruled wisely and justly; but what he has elected to describe at length is the death of Aja's queen, Indumatî, and his consequent grief. It appears that Kálidása had an object in giving prominence to this; probably here he wanted to present a contrast with the character of Ráma, showing that if a King of Raghu's race could cast off his wife under pressure of circumstances (as Râma will be described in the sequel to have done), there was here one, the intensity of whose love was so great that when he lost his wife he could not survive her but died pining for her. And the poet has done it very skilfully.

The next ruler is **Das'aratha**, whose general merits are described in the beginning of the 9th Canto. He is as great a warrior and as wise a ruler as his two immediate predecessors and also a great performer of sacrifices. (See IX. 5, 10, 20, 21 &c.) He was neither much given to chase nor addicted to any of the principal vices of men (s'l. 7). But in fulfilment of a decree of fate he once went a-hunting and there inadvertently killed an ascetic youth; and the father of the young ascetic cursed the King that he would die of grief for his son. This son is Râma, at separation from whom Das'aratha died as foretold. The poet explains away this one instance of breach of duty on the part of Das'aratha with the remark **अपथे पदमर्पयन्ति हि श्रुतवन्तोऽपि रजोनिमीलिताः** (IX. 74).

Finally we come to **Râma**. Here Kâlidâsa instinctively felt overshadowed by the genius of his great predecessor Vâlmîki, and the vastness of the material before him; and he has, therefore, hurriedly gone over the chief incidents in Râma's career—how out of filial love and obedience he went out into the forest and killed the demon-king Râvaṇa in Laṅkâ. Râma's abandonment of Sîtâ, some think, is a sort of blot on his otherwise immaculate character; the poet, therefore, explains why Sîtâ was abandoned,

It was not because Râma thought her guilty, but because he wanted not even a breath of criticism against him among his subjects. As a King he felt it was his duty to lay down an example of rigid moral purity, and to show that all his acts were above suspicion. Râma's killing of Śambûka is then related, which too was an act done with the intention of regulating the conduct of his subjects as a whole, and not of punishing Śambûka individually; for after all Śambûka *did* go to heaven as he wished (XV. 53). We thus realize how Râma has been portrayed particularly as a sovereign who is most anxious to rule his people with scrupulous punctiliousness, following in his own person whatever he wanted his people to follow, even when it entailed suffering on himself. No kingly ideal of later times can enjoin a better precept or point to a worthier model; and it is but fitting in the nature of things that *Râma-Râjya* should become in popular parlance a common expression for the ideal Government, where the interests of the people are placed first, even before those of the sovereign.

(5) THE GEOGRAPHY OF THE POEM.

Besides the Meghadûta the Raghuvaṃśa is the only work of Kâlidâsa which contains a number of references to the geography of India as it was known to him in those days. These are to be found in the 4th, 6th and 13th cantos, but more particularly in the 4th, which describes the *dig-vijaya* of Raghu. The student can easily identify these places on the map[26] which is reproduced elsewhere, and the detailed explanations would be found in our Notes. He should especially trace the course of Raghu's tour of conquest. Starting from Ayodhyá, Raghu first marches towards the *East*, where he conquers the Suhmas and the Vaṅgas. He then crosses the river Kapiśâ, which takes him to the *South*. Here he conquers, in order, the Utkalas, the Kaliṅgas, the Pâṇdyas, the Keralas, and the Aparântas on the western coast. In the *West* and in the north-west he subdues the Pârasikas, the Hûnas and the Kâmbojas; and in the *North* and the north-east, the Utsavasaṅketas, the Prâgjyotishas, and the Kâmarûpas, returning thence to his capital. Most of the principal rivers and mountains have been mentioned here; *e.g.* the Sahya and Himâlaya ranges,

26. We are greatly indebted to the Map given in Pandit R. Krishnamachariar's *Raghuvaṃs'avimars'a* (1908), from which we have borrowed some of these identifications.

and the Ganges, the Kâverî and the Indus rivers. In the 6th Canto, on the occasion of describing the various kings assembled in Kuṇḍina, the capital of the Vidarbhas in Central India, the principal provinces of India have naturally been mentioned; these are Magadha, Aṅga, Avanti, Anûpa, Śúrasena, Kaliṅga, Pâṇḍya and Uttara-Kosala. As all the chief princes were expected to have come there, it is almost certain, as observed by Mark Collins,[27] that "we may see in this list a reflex of the principal kingdoms of India in the times of Kâlidâsa." The 13th Canto supplies some additional names of places lying in a straight line between Ceylon and Ayodhyâ; *e. g.* the mountain Málvavat, the lake Pampâ, the river Godávarî, the mountain Chitrakûṭa and the rivers Yamunâ and Sarayû. The description of many of these places is far from being conventional or traditional; it very often reads like such as would be given by an eye-witness, and it is pretty certain that our poet must have travelled widely with an observant eye. No other poet in classical Sanskrit literature has described the country in such a familiar and vivid manner.

---

(6) MALLINÂTHA.

There exist a large number of commentaries on this poem, but none of them is so well-known or so often studied as that of Mallinâtha, who enjoys a supreme position as the standard authority in the interpretation of Kâlidâsa's poems. While writing about Kálidása we had to remark above that he says absolutely nothing about himself in his writings, and the same is true of his great scholiast, Mallinâtha. Pandit Vámanácharya Zalktîkar, the editor of the Kâvyaprakáśa, wrote that Mallinátha was a Bráhmaṇa of the Kâśyapa gotra, and that his descendants were still living at Gajendragad in the Satara District. But the learned Pandit was hasty in his identification; for Mr. M. S. Śâstrî (in his "Second Report on the Search of Sanskrit MSS.") has shown that Mallinátha was a native of Tailangaṇa (Ândhra), which fact is now accepted as established. He had a son named Kumárasvámin, who was also an erudite scholar, and wrote a commentary on the Pratáparudrîya. In addition to his three commentaries on the three poems of Kâlidâsa, Mallinátha is credited to have written (*a*) commentaries on अमरकोश, एकावली, काव्यादर्श, किरातार्जुनीय, तन्त्रवार्तिक, तार्किकरक्षा, नलोदय, नैषधीयचारित, प्रशस्तपादभाष्य, भट्टिकाव्य

27. *The Geographical Data of the Raghuvaṃs'a and Das'akumâra-charita* (1907), p. 17.

लघुशब्देन्दुशेखर, शिशुपालवध, and सारमञ्जरी ; and (*b*) independently, these works—भट्टारकाव्य, रघुवीरचरितकाव्य, वैद्यकल्पतरु, and वैद्यरत्नमाला. It is possible that some of these productions belong to some other Mallinátha than our commentator; for there have been many Mallinâthas, just as there have been many Kálidâsas.

The date of Mallinâtha can be fixed with tolerable certainty. He has written a com. on the Ekâvalî, a work on alaṃkâra which frequently refers to King Vîra--Narasiṃha, whose reign extended up to 1314 A. D. Mallinâth also often quotes the Pratâparudrîya, another work on alaṃkára, which mentions King Pratâparudra who reigned from 1295 to 1323 A.D. Sir Dr. Bhandárkar has shown (p. xxi of his Preface to his 2nd ed. of the Mâl.–Mādh.) that Mallinâtha must be placed before the lexicographer Medinikâra, the latest limit for whose date is 1431 A.D. Hence it is clear that the date of Mallinâtha approximately falls somewhere between 1325 and 1425 A.D. Most probably he belongs to the latter half of the 14th century.

Mallinâtha is a commentator of great merit and literary acumen. He was a profound grammarian, well versed in the Nyâya and Vaiśeshika philosophies, and thoroughly acquainted with Pauraṇic as well as secular literature, as he himself tells us in his introductory ślokas to the commentary on the Ragh.; and the extreme popularity of his commentaries shows that this is not an idle boast. His commentaries are pre-eminently adapted to the needs of the advanced general reader. They are sufficiently expressive without being prolix. He never makes an unnecessary display of his knowledge, but strictly follows the principle he himself lays down, *viz.*, नामूलं लिख्यते किंचिन्नानपेक्षितमुच्यते. He is perhaps the only commentator on the poems of Kálidâsa who shows a critical appreciation of poetry and endeavours to preserve, as far as possible, the genuine readings of the poet, studiously rejecting the spurious substitutions of single words and phrases, and the occasional interpolations of whole s'lokas. To his commentaries on the three poems of Kálidása he has given the title संजीवनी, meaning thereby that his commentaries *re-inspire with life* the words of Kâlidâsa "that lay in a swoon under the effect of the poison of bad commentaries." Every student of Kâlidâsa now recognizes that this was no vain presumption ; Malli.'s commentaries have eclipsed all others, and he stands unrivalled as *the* commentator of Kâlidâsa's poetical works.

Important Abbreviations.

:o:

A. G.—Apte's Guide to Sanskrit Composition.

Ak., Amar.—Amarakośa.

Ath.-V.—Atharva-Veda.

Ba'l.-Ra'm.—Bála-Râmâyan (play).

Bg.—Bhagavadgîtâ

Bhar.—Bhartṛihari's Śatakas (N. and V.).*

Bhatti.—Bhaṭṭi-Kâvya.*

Bh.-P.—Bhâgavata-Purâṇa.

Brih.-Sam.—Bṛihatsaṃhitâ.

Brih.-Up.—Bṛihadâraṇyakopanishad.

Chh.-Up.—Chhândogyopanishad.

D.-K.—Daśakumâracharita.*

D.-R.—Daśarupaka

Gi't.—Gîtagovinda.

H.-Ch.—Harshacharita.

Hem.—Hemâdri.

Hitop.—Hitopadeśa.*

H. S. Gr.—Higher Sanskrit Grammar (by M. R. Kâle).

Hv.—Harivaṃśa.

Ka'd.—Kâdambarî *

Ka'm. N.—Kâmandaka's Nîtisâra

Ka's'.—Kâs'ikâ of Vâmana.

Ka's'.—Kh.—Káśîkhaṇḍa.

Katha's.—Kathásaritságara.

K'av., K. D.—Kâvyâdarśa of Daṇḍin.

Kir.—Kirâtârjunîya.*

K.-P.—Kāvya-Prakâśa.

Kum.—Kumârasaṃbhava.*

Mah.-Bh.—Mahá-Bhárata.

Ma'lav.—Mâlavikâgnimitra.*

Malli.—Mallinâth.

Ma'l.-Ma'dh.—Mâlatî Mâdhava*

Ma'rk.-P.—Mârkaṇḍeya-Purâṇa.

Megh.—Meghadûta.*

Mrich.—Mṛichchhakaṭika.

Mud.—Mudrârâkshasa.

Mv.—Mahâvîracharita.

M-W.—Monier-Williams.

Nag.—Nagananda*

N.-Ch.—Naishadhîya-Charita.

Pan.—Pâṇini's Ashṭâdhyâyî.

Pt.—Pañchatantra.*

Ragh.—Raghuvaṃs'a.*

Ra'm.—Râmâyaṇa of Vâlmîki.

Ratn.—Ratnâvalî.*

Rig.-V.—Ṛig-Veda.

Ritus.—Ritusaṃhâra.*

Śa'k.—Śâkuntala.*

Sa'm.-K—Sâṃkhya-Kârikâ.

S.-D.—Sâhitya-Darpaṇa.

S.-D.-S.—Sarvadarśana-saṃgraha.

Sid.-K.—Siddhântakaumudî.

Śiś.—Śiśupâlavadha.

Tark.—Tarkasaṃgraha.

Up.—Upanishad.

Uttar.—Uttararâmacharita.*

Vall.—Vallabhadeva.

Va'rt.—Vârttika.

Venî.—Veṇîsaṃhâra.*

Vikr.—Vikramorvaśîya.

Vish.-P.—Vishṇu Puráṇa.

Yog.-S.—Yogasûtras.

&c. &c. &c.

* Annoted by the Editor.

॥ श्रीः ॥

रघुवंशः ।

संजीवन्या समेतः ।

प्रथमः सर्गः ।

मातापितृभ्यां जगतो नमो वामार्धजानये[1] ।
सद्यो दक्षिणदृक्पातसंकुचद्वामदृष्टये ॥

अन्तरायतिमिरोपशान्तये शान्तपावनमचिन्त्यवैभवम् ।
तन्नरं वपुषि कुञ्जरं मुखे मन्महे किमपि तुन्दिलं महः[2] ॥

शरणं करवाणि शर्मदं ते चरणं वाणि चराचरोपजीव्यम् ।
करुणामसृणैः कटाक्षपातैः कुरु मामम्ब कृतार्थसार्थवाहम्[3] ॥

[4]वाणीं काणभुजीमजीगणदवाशासीच्च वैयासकी-
मन्तस्तन्त्रमरंस्त पन्नगगवीगुम्फेषु चाजागरीत् ।
वाचामाकलयद्रहस्यमखिलं यश्चाक्षपादस्फुरां
लोकेऽभूद्यदुपज्ञमेव विदुषां सौजन्यजन्यं यशः ॥

मल्लिनाथकविः सोऽयं मन्दात्मानुजिघृक्षया ।
व्याचष्टे कालिदासीयं काव्यत्रयमनाकुलम् ॥

कालिदासगिरां सारं कालिदासः सरस्वती ।
चतुर्मुखोऽथ वा साक्षाद्विदुर्नान्ये तु मादृशाः ॥

तथाऽपि दक्षिणावर्तनाथाद्यैः क्षुण्णवर्त्मसु ।
वयं च कालिदासोक्तिष्ववकाशं लभेमहि ॥

भारती कालिदासस्य दुर्व्याख्याविषमूर्छिता ।
एषा संजीवनी टीका तामद्योज्जीवयिष्यति ॥

इहान्वयमुखेनैव सर्वं व्याख्यायते मया ।
नामूलं लिख्यते किंचिन्नानपेक्षितमुच्यते ॥

इह खलु सकलकविशिरोमणिः कालिदासः 'काव्यं यशसेऽर्थकृते व्यवहारविदे शिवेतरक्षतये

---

१ कथंभूताय मातापितृस्वरूपाय । वामार्धजानये वामार्धं जाया यस्य तस्मै । पुनः कीदृशाय। दक्षिणदृक्पातेन शिवस्य दृष्टिपातेनेत्यर्थः संकुचन्ती वामा पार्वत्या इत्यर्थः दृष्टिः यस्य। २ गजाननाख्यं तेजः मन्महे इ० । ३ कृतार्थसार्थवाहम्-साधुनिर्व्यूढटीकाकरणभारमिति श्लिष्टोऽर्थः । ४ वाणीं काणभुजीं-कणभुक्प्रणीतं वैशेषिकदर्शनम् । वैयासकीं-व्यासकृतानि अष्टादश पुराणानि । अन्तस्तन्त्रं तन्त्रशास्त्रे । पन्नगगवीगुम्फेषु पातञ्जलमहाभाष्ये इत्यर्थः । अक्षपादस्फुरां वाचां गौतमप्रणीतन्यायदर्शनस्य इ० । यदुपज्ञं-उपज्ञा आद्यज्ञानं यस्य उपज्ञा यदुपज्ञम् । 'उपज्ञोपक्रमं तदाद्याचिख्यासायाम्' (२।४।२१) इति सूत्रेण तत्पुरुषस्य नपुंसकत्वम् । यस्माद्उपज्ञा यस्य इति वा ।

सद्यः परनिर्वृतये कान्तासंमिततयोपदेशयुजे ॥ ' इत्याद्यालंकारिकवचनप्रामाण्यात्काव्यस्यानेकश्रेयःसाधनताम्, ' काव्यालापांश्च वर्जयेत् ' इत्यस्य निषेधशास्त्रस्यासत्काव्यविषयतां च पश्यन् रघुवंशाख्यं महाकाव्यं चिकीर्षुः चिकीर्षितार्थाविघ्नपरिसमाप्तिसंप्रदायाविच्छेदलक्षणफलसाधनभूतविशिष्टदेवतानमस्कारस्य शिष्टाचारपरिप्राप्तत्वात् 'आशीर्नमस्क्रिया वस्तुनिर्देशो वाऽपि तन्मुखम् । ' इत्याशीर्न्नोदाद्यन्यतमस्य प्रबन्धमुखलक्षणत्वात्काव्यनिर्माणस्य विशिष्टशब्दार्थप्रतिपत्तिमूलकत्वेन विशिष्टशब्दार्थयोश्च ' शब्दजातमशेषं तु धत्ते शर्वस्य वल्लभा । अर्थरूपं यदखिलं धत्ते मुग्धेन्दुशेखरः ॥ ' इति वायुपुराणसंहितावचनबलेन पार्वतीपरमेश्वरायत्तत्वदर्शनात्तत्प्रतिपित्सया तावेवाभिवादयते—

वागर्थाविव संपृक्तौ वागर्थप्रतिपत्तये ।
जगतः पितरौ वन्दे पार्वतीपरमेश्वरौ ॥ १ ॥

वागर्थाविवेत्येकं पदम् । इवेन सह समासो विभक्त्यलोपश्च पूर्वपदप्रकृतिस्वरत्वं चेति वक्तव्यम् । एवमन्यत्रापि द्रष्टव्यम् । **वागर्थाविव** शब्दार्थाविव **संपृक्तौ** नित्यसंबद्धावित्यर्थः । नित्यसंबद्धयोरुपमानत्वेनोपादानात् । ' नित्यः शब्दार्थसंबन्धः ' इति मीमांसकाः । **जगतः** लोकस्य **पितरौ** । माता च पिता च पितरौ । 'पिता मात्रा' इति द्वन्द्वैकशेषः । ' मातापितरौ पितरौ मातरपितरौ प्रसूजनयितारौ । ' इत्यमरः । एतेन शर्वशिवयोः सर्वजगज्जनकतया वैशिष्ट्यमिष्टार्थप्रदानशक्तिः परमकारुणिकत्वं च सूच्यते । पर्वतस्यापत्यं स्त्री पार्वती । ' तस्यापत्यम् ' इत्यण् । ' टिड्ढाणञ्– ' इत्यादिना ङीप् । पार्वती च परमेश्वरश्च **पार्वतीपरमेश्वरौ** । परमशब्दः सर्वोत्तमत्वद्योतनार्थः । मातुरभ्यर्हितत्वादल्पाक्षरत्वाच्च पार्वतीशब्दस्य पूर्वनिपातः । **वागर्थप्रतिपत्तये** शब्दार्थयोः सम्यग्ज्ञानार्थम् । **वन्दे** अभिवादये । अत्रोपमालंकारः स्फुट एव । तथोक्तम्–' स्वतःसिद्धेन भिन्नेन संपन्नेन च धर्मतः । साम्यमन्येन वर्ण्यस्य वाच्यं चेदेकगोपमा ॥ ' इति । प्रायिकश्चोपमालंकारः कालिदासोक्तकाव्यादौ । भूदेवताकस्य सर्वगुरोर्मगणस्य प्रयोगाच्छुभलाभः सूच्यते । तदुक्तम्–' शुभदो मो भूमिमयः ' इति । वकारस्यामृतबीजत्वात्प्रचयगमनादिसिद्धिः ॥

संप्रति कविः स्वाहंकारं परिहरति ' क्व सूर्य– ' इत्यादिश्लोकद्वयेन—

क्व सूर्यप्रभवो वंशः क्व चाल्पविषया मतिः ।
तितीर्षुर्दुस्तरं मोहादुडुपेनास्मि सागरम् ॥ २ ॥

प्रभवत्यस्मादिति प्रभवः कारणम् । ' ऋदोरप् । ' ' अकर्तरि च कारके संज्ञायाम् । ' इति साधुः । सूर्यः प्रभवो यस्य स **सूर्यप्रभवः वंशः क्व** । अल्पो विषयो ज्ञेयोऽर्थो यस्याः सा [**अल्पविषया**] मे **मतिः** प्रज्ञा **च क्व** । द्वौ क्वशब्दौ महदन्तरं सूचयतः । सूर्यवंश-

---

१ का० प्र० १, २. २ का० द० १, १४. आशीर्वस्तुनमस्कारनिर्देशात्प्रथमं कविः । काव्यं कुर्वन्नविघ्नेन कीर्तिं प्रीतिं च विन्दति ॥ इति सरस्वतीकण्ठाभरणम् । ३ अत्र नित्यसमास इति पाठो दृश्यते किं तु स प्रामादिक इव भाति महाभाष्ये नित्यशब्दरहितस्यैव पाठस्योपलम्भात् । अन्यथा ' उद्बाहुरिव वामनः ' इत्यादिप्रयोगाणामसाधुत्वापत्तेः । ४ अभ्यर्हितत्वात् पूज्यत्वात् । " अल्पाच्तरम् । " पा० २. २. ३४. अभ्यर्हितं च । वार्ति० । मातुरभ्यर्हितत्वे याज्ञवल्क्यः । * एते मान्या यथापूर्वमेभ्यो माता गरीयसी ॥ इति उक्तं च–पितृतोऽपि गुरुर्माता नास्ति मातृसमो गुरुः । पतिना गुरवस्त्याज्या नैव माता कदाचन । गर्भधारणपोषाभ्यां तेन माता गरीयसी ॥ तथा च–उपाध्यायान् दशाचार्य आचार्याणां शतं पिता । सहस्रं तु पितॄन्माता गौरवेणातिरिच्यते ॥ इति । पार्वत्या जगन्मातृत्वात् श्रेष्ठत्वं ज्ञेयम् ।

नावलम्बयितुं न शक्नोमीत्यर्थः । तथा च तद्विषयप्रबन्धनिरूपणं तु दूरापास्तमिति भावः तथा हि । **दुस्तरं** तरितुमशक्यम् । 'ईषद्दुःसुषु–' इत्यादिना खल्प्रत्ययः । **सागरं मोहाद्** अज्ञानाद् **उडुपेन** प्लवेन । 'उडुपं तु प्लवः कोलः' इत्यमरः । अथ वा चर्मावनद्धेन पानपात्रेण । 'चर्मावनद्धमुडुपं प्लवः काष्ठं करण्डवत् ।' इति सज्जनः । **तितीर्षुः** तरीतुमिच्छुः **अस्मि** भवामि । तरतेः सन्नन्तादुप्रत्ययः । अल्पसाधनैरधिकारम्भो न सुकर इति भावः । इदं च वंशोत्कर्षकथनं स्वप्रबन्धमहत्त्वार्थमेव । तदुक्तम् 'प्रतिपाद्यमहिम्ना च प्रबन्धो हि महत्तरः ।' इति ॥

मन्दः कवियशःप्रार्थी गमिष्याम्युपहास्यताम् ।
प्रांशुलभ्ये फले लोभादुद्बाहुरिव वामनः ॥ ३ ॥

किं च । **मन्दः** मूढः । 'मूढाल्पापटुनिर्भाग्या मन्दाः स्युः ।' इत्यमरः । तथाऽपि **कवियशःप्रार्थी** । कवीनां यशः काव्यनिर्माणेन जातं तत्प्रार्थनाशीलोऽहं प्रांशुना उन्नतपुरुषेण लभ्ये प्राप्ये [**प्रांशुलभ्ये**] **फले** फलविषये **लोभाद् उद्बाहुः** फलग्रहणायोच्छ्रितहस्तः **वामनः** खर्वः इव । 'खर्वो ह्रस्वश्च वामनः' इत्यमरः । **उपहास्यताम्** उपहासविषयताम् । 'ऋहलोर्ण्यत्' इति ण्यत्प्रत्ययः । **गमिष्यामि** प्राप्स्यामि ॥

मन्दश्चेत्तर्हि त्यज्यतामयमुद्योग इत्यत आह—

अथ वा कृतवाग्द्वारे वंशेऽस्मिन्पूर्वसूरिभिः ।
मणौ वज्रसमुत्कीर्णे सूत्रस्येवास्ति मे गतिः ॥ ४ ॥

अथ वा पक्षान्तरे पूर्वैः सूरिभिः [**पूर्वसूरिभिः**] कविभिर्वाल्मीकादिभिः **कृतवाग्द्वारे** कृतं रामायणादिप्रबन्धरूपा या वाक् सैव द्वारं प्रवेशो यस्य तस्मिन् । **अस्मिन्** सूर्यप्रभवे **वंशे** कुले । जन्मनैकलक्षणः संतानो वंशः । वज्रेण मणिवेधकसूचीविशेषेण । 'वज्रं त्वस्त्री कुलिशशस्त्रयोः । मणिवेधे रत्नभेदे' इति केशवः । समुत्कीर्णे विद्धे [**वज्रसमुत्कीर्णे**] **मणौ** रत्ने **सूत्रस्य इव मे** मम **गतिः** संचारः **अस्ति** । वर्णनीये रघुवंशे मम वाक्प्रसरोऽस्तीत्यर्थः ॥

एवं रघुवंशे लब्धप्रवेशस्तत्कीर्तनं प्रतिजानानः 'सोऽहम्' इत्यादिभिः पञ्चभिः श्लोकैः कुलकेनाह—

सोऽहमाजन्मशुद्धानामाफलोदयकर्मणाम् ।
आसमुद्रक्षितीशानामानाकरथवर्त्मनाम् ॥ ५ ॥

सः अहम् । 'रघूणामन्वयं वक्ष्ये' (१ । ९) इत्युत्तरेण संबन्धः । किंविधानां रघूणा-

---

१ अत्र उडुपेन सागरतरणवन्मन्मत्या सूर्यवंशवर्णनमसंभावितमित्युपमायां पर्यवसानान्निदर्शनालंकारः । उद्धृतश्चायं श्लोकः काव्यप्रकाशकृता वाक्यार्थनिदर्शनोदाहरणत्वेन ।

२ यथा मन्दः शनैश्चरः कवेः शुक्रस्य यशःप्रार्थी उपहास्यतां याति—इति केचित् छायार्थं प्रदर्शयन्ति । केचित् फले कार्यसिद्धौ उपहास्यतां गमिष्यामीति योजयन्ति । केचित्तु मन्दः काकः कस्य ब्रह्मणः वेः पक्षिणः हंसस्य इति व्याख्यान्ति । एतत्त्रयं च सहृदयानामहृदयंगमत्वादुपेक्ष्यम् ।

३ अत्र भिन्नलिङ्गत्वेन औपम्यं न दुष्टम् । तथा च वामनः "इष्टः (लिङ्गभेदः) पुंनपुंसकयोः प्रायेण ।" का० सू० ४. २. १३. इह मणिशब्दोपादानेन वंशस्य अनर्घ्यत्वं निर्मलत्वं च दर्शितं इति केचित् । केचित्तु सूत्रोपमानेन आत्मनः सूक्ष्मबुद्धित्वं कविना सूचितमित्याहुः ।

४ एकान्वयी पञ्चान्यूनश्लोकसंघातः कुलकम् । तदुक्तं—द्वाभ्यां युग्ममिति प्रोक्तं त्रिभिः श्लोकैर्विशेषकम् । कलापकं चतुर्भिः स्यात्तदूर्ध्वं कुलकं स्मृतम् ॥ इति ।

मित्यत्रोत्तराणि विशेषणानि योज्यानि । आ जन्मनः । जन्मारभ्येत्यर्थः । 'आङ्मर्यादाभिविध्योः' इत्यव्ययीभावः । शुद्धानाम् **आजन्मशुद्धानाम्** । सुप्सुपेति समासः । एवमुत्तरत्रापि द्रष्टव्यम् । निषेकादिसर्वसंस्काराणामित्यर्थः । [**आफलोदयकर्मणाम्**] आफलोदयमा फलसिद्धेः कर्म येषां ते तथोक्तास्तेषाम् । प्रारब्धान्तगामिनामित्यर्थः । [**आसमुद्रक्षितीशानाम्**] आसमुद्रं क्षितेरीशानाम् । सार्वभौमाणामित्यर्थः । [**आनाकरथवर्त्मनाम्**] आनाकं रथवर्त्म येषां तेषाम् । इन्द्रसहचारिणामित्यर्थः । अत्र सर्वत्राङोऽभिविध्यर्थत्वं द्रष्टव्यम् । अन्यथा मर्यादार्थत्वे जन्मादिषु शुद्ध्यभावप्रसङ्गात् ॥

यथाविधिहुताग्नीनां यथाकामार्चितार्थिनाम् ।
यथापराधदण्डानां यथाकालप्रबोधिनाम् ॥ ६ ॥

विधिमनतिक्रम्य यथाविधि । 'यथाऽसादृश्ये' इत्यव्ययीभावः । तथा हुतशब्देन सुप्सुपेति समासः । एवं 'यथाकामार्चित–' इत्यादीनामपि द्रष्टव्यम् । यथाविधि हुताः अग्नयो यैस्तेषां [**यथाविधिहुताग्नीनाम्**] । यथाकाममभिलाषमनतिक्रम्यार्चितार्थिनाम् [**यथाकामार्चितार्थिनाम्**] । यथापराधमपराधमनतिक्रम्य दण्डो येषां तेषाम् [**यथापराधदण्डानाम्**] । यथाकालं कालमनतिक्रम्य प्रबोधिनां प्रबोधनशीलानाम् [**यथाकालप्रबोधिनाम्**] । चतुर्भिर्विशेषणैर्देवतायजनार्थिसत्कारदण्डधरत्वप्रजापालनसमयजागरूकत्वादीनि विवक्षितानि ॥

त्यागाय संभृतार्थानां सत्याय मितभाषिणाम् ।
यशसे विजिगीषूणां प्रजायै गृहमेधिनाम् ॥ ७ ॥

त्यागाय सत्पात्रे विनियोगस्त्यागस्तस्मै । 'त्यागो विहापितं दानम्' इत्यमरः । **संभृतार्थानां** संचितधनानाम् । न तु दुर्व्यापाराय । **सत्याय मितभाषिणां** मितभाषणशीलानाम् । न तु पराभवाय । **यशसे** कीर्तये । 'यशः कीर्तिः समज्ञा च' इत्यमरः । **विजिगीषूणाम्** विजेतुमिच्छूनाम् । न त्वर्थसंग्रहाय । **प्रजायै** संतानाय **गृहमेधिनाम्** दारसंग्रहाणाम् । न तु कामोपभोगाय । अत्र 'त्यागाय' इत्यादिषु 'चतुर्थी तदर्थ––' इत्यादिना तादर्थ्ये चतुर्थीसमासविधानज्ञापकाच्चतुर्थी । गृहैर्दारैर्मेधन्ते संगच्छन्त इति गृहमेधिनः । 'दारेष्वपि गृहाः' इत्यमरः । 'जाया च गृहिणी गृहम्' इति हलायुधः । 'मेधृ संगमे' इति धातोर्णिनिः । एभिर्विशेषणैः परोपकारित्वं सत्यवचनत्वं यशःपरत्वं पितॄणां शुद्धत्वं च विवक्षितानि ॥

---

१ एतेन तेषामाग्निहोत्रित्वं सूचितम् । यथाह मनुः–"वैवाहिकेऽग्नौ कुर्वीत गृह्यं कर्म यथाविधि । पञ्चयज्ञविधानं च पक्तिं चान्वाहिकीं गृही ॥" इ०. २ "अपराधानुरूपं च दण्डं दण्ड्येषु दापयेत्" इति विष्णुस्मृतेः । अत्र कामन्दकः–"उद्वेजयति तीक्ष्णेन मृदुना परिभूयते । दण्डेन नृपतिस्तस्माद्युक्तदण्डः प्रशस्यते ॥ त्रिवर्गं वर्धयत्याशु राज्ञो दण्डो यथाविधि । प्रणीतो वाऽसमञ्जस्याद्वनस्थानपि कोपयेत् ॥" इ०. ३ यथाकालं शास्त्रोक्तकाले । ब्राह्मे मुहूर्ते इत्यर्थः । प्रबोधः शयनादुत्थानं येषामिति वा । तथा च मनुः–'उत्थाय पश्चिमे यामे कृतशौचः समाहितः । हुताग्निर्ब्राह्मणांश्चार्च्य प्रविशेत्स शुभां सभाम् ॥' इ०. ४ बहुभाषणे असत्यमपि स्यादिति हेतोः इत्य० । उक्तं च मनुना–"सत्यं ब्रूयात्प्रियं ब्रूयान्न ब्रूयात्सत्यमप्रियम् । प्रियं च नानृतं ब्रूयादेष धर्मः सनातनः ॥ ॥" इ०. ५ "पुत्रार्थं क्रियते भार्या पुत्रः पिण्डप्रयोजनः ।" इति स्मरणात् । केचित् गृहमेधः विवाहः अस्त्येषामिति व्याचक्षते । गृहे गृहस्थधर्मे मेधा येषामिति वा ।

शैशवेऽभ्यस्तविद्यानां यौवने विषयैषिणाम् ।
वार्द्धके मुनिवृत्तीनां योगेनान्ते तनुत्यजाम् ॥ ८ ॥

[**शैशवे**] शिशोर्भावः शैशवं बाल्यम् । 'प्राणभृज्जातिवयोवचनोद्गात्रादिभ्योऽञ्—' इत्यञ्प्रत्ययः । 'शिशुत्वं शैशवं बाल्यम्' इत्यमरः । तस्मिन्वयसि **अभ्यस्तविद्यानाम्** । एतेन ब्रह्मचर्याश्रमो विवक्षितः । [**यौवने**] यूनो भावो यौवनं तारुण्यम् । युवादित्वादण्प्रत्ययः । 'तारुण्यं यौवनं समम्' इत्यमरः । तस्मिन्वयसि **विषयैषिणां** भोगाभिलाषिणाम् । एतेन गृहस्थाश्रमो विवक्षितः । वृद्धस्य भावो वार्द्धकं वृद्धत्वम् । 'द्वन्द्वमनोज्ञादिभ्यश्च' इति वुञ्प्रत्ययः । 'वार्द्धकं वृद्धसंघाते वृद्धत्वे वृद्धकर्मणि ।' इति विश्वः । संघातार्थेऽत्र 'वृद्धाच्च' इति वक्तव्यात्सामूहिको वुञ् । तस्मिन् **वार्द्धके** वयसि मुनीनां वृत्तिरिव वृत्तिर्येषां तेषाम् [**मुनिवृत्तीनाम्**] । एतेन वानप्रस्थाश्रमो विवक्षितः । **अन्ते** शरीरत्यागकाले **योगेन** परमात्मध्यानेन । 'योगः संनहनोपायध्यानसंगतियुक्तिषु ।' इत्यमरः । तनुं देहं त्यजन्तीति तेषां **तनुत्यजां** देहत्यागिनाम् । 'कायो देहः क्लीबपुंसोः स्त्रियां मूर्तिस्तनुस्तनूः ।' इत्यमरः । 'अन्येभ्योऽपि दृश्यते' इति क्विप् । एतेन भिक्षुकाश्रमो विवक्षितः ॥

रघूणामन्वयं वक्ष्ये तनुवाग्विभवोऽपि सन् ।
तद्गुणैः कर्णमागत्य चापलाय प्रचोदितः ॥ ९ ॥

सोऽहं लब्धप्रवेशः **तनुवाग्विभवोऽपि** स्वल्पवाणीप्रसारोऽपि **सन्** । तेषां रघूणां गुणैः **तद्गुणैः** आजन्मशुद्ध्यादिभिः कर्तृभिः । **कर्णं** मम श्रोत्रं **आगत्य चापलाय** चापलं चपलकर्माविमृश्यकरणरूपं कर्तुम् । युवादित्वात्कर्मण्यण् । 'क्रियार्थोपपदस्य—' इत्यादिना चतुर्थी । **प्रचोदितः** प्रेरितः सन् । **रघूणामन्वयं** तद्विषयप्रबन्धं **वक्ष्ये** । कुलकम् ॥

संप्रति स्वप्रबन्धपरीक्षार्थं सतः प्रार्थयते—

तं सन्तः श्रोतुमर्हन्ति सदसद्व्यक्तिहेतवः ।
हेम्नः संलक्ष्यते ह्यग्नौ विशुद्धिः श्यामिकाऽपि वा ॥ १० ॥

तं रघुवंशाख्यं प्रबन्धं सदसतोर्गुणदोषयोर्व्यक्तेर्हेतवः [**सदसद्व्यक्तिहेतवः**] कर्तारः **सन्तः श्रोतुमर्हन्ति** । तथा **हि** । **हेम्नः विशुद्धिः** निर्दोषस्वरूपं **श्यामिकाऽपि**

---

१ यथाह मनुः—गृहस्थस्तु यदा पश्येद्वलीपलितमात्मनः । अपत्यस्यैव चापत्यं तदारण्यं समाश्रयेत् ॥ संत्यज्य ग्राम्यमाहारं सर्वं चैव परिच्छदम् । पुत्रेषु भार्यां निक्षिप्य वनं गच्छेत्सहैव वा ॥ २ अत्र मनुः—इन्द्रियाणां निरोधेन रागद्वेषक्षयेण च । अहिंसया च भूतानाममृतत्वाय कल्पते ॥...प्रियेषु स्वेषु सुकृतमप्रियेषु च दुष्कृतम् । विसृज्य ध्यानयोगेन ब्रह्माभ्येति सनातनम् ॥ इ०.

रघूणां आजन्मशुद्ध्यादयो गुणाः अस्मिन्नेव ग्रन्थे कविना वर्णिताः तेषां क्रमेण दिग्दर्शनम्—(१) आजन्म०–तृ० स० १०, १८ श्लो० (२) आफलोदय०–अ० स० २२ श्लो० (३) आसमुद्र०–प्र० स० ३० श्लो० (४) आनाक०–पं० स० २७ श्लो० (५) यथाविधि०–पं० स० २५, अ० स० २५, पं० स० १८ श्लो० (६) यथाकामा०–पं० सर्गे कौत्सोपाख्यानं, ए० स० २ श्लो० (७) यथापराध०–च० स० ८ श्लो० (८) यथाकाल०–प्र० स० १५ श्लो० (९) त्यागाय–च० स० ८६ श्लो० (१०) सत्याय–प्र० स० २९ श्लो०, द्वा० सर्गे दशरथस्य प्रतिज्ञापालनवर्णनं च । (११) यशसे–च० स० ४३ श्लो० (१२) प्रजायै–प्र० स० २५ श्लो० (१३) शैशवे– तृ० स० २८, २९ श्लो०, अष्टा० ४६ श्लो० (१४) यौवने–प्र० स० २१ श्लो०, अ० स० अजविलासवर्णनं च । (१५) वार्द्धके–तृ० स० ७० श्लो०, अ० स० ११ श्लो० (१६) योगेन–अ० स० १० श्लो०

श्यामिकारूपो हेमान्तरसंसर्गात्मको दोषोऽपि **या अग्नौ संलक्ष्यते** । नान्यत्र । तद्वदत्रापि सन्त एव गुणदोषविवेकाधिकारिणः । नान्य इति भावः ॥

वर्ण्यं वस्तूपक्षिपति--

वैवस्वतो मनुर्नाम माननीयो मनीषिणाम् ।
आसीन्महीक्षितामाद्यः प्रणवश्छन्दसामिव ॥ ११ ॥

मनस ईषिणो मनीषिणो धीराः । विद्वांस इति यावत् । पृषोदरादित्वात्साधुः । तेषां [**मनीषिणां**] **माननीयः** पूज्यः । **छन्दसां** वेदानाम् । 'छन्दः पद्ये च वेदे च' इति विश्वः । **प्रणवः** ओंकारः **इव** । महीं क्षियन्तीशत इति महीक्षितः क्षितीश्वराः । क्षिधातोरैश्वर्यार्थात्क्विप् तुगागमश्च । तेषां [**महीक्षिताम्** ।] **आद्यः** आदिभूतः । विवस्वतः सूर्यस्यापत्यं पुमान् **वैवस्वतो नाम** वैवस्वत इति प्रसिद्धो **मनुः आसीत** ॥

तदन्वये शुद्धिमति प्रसूतः शुद्धिमत्तरः ।
दिलीप इति राजेन्दुरिन्दुः क्षीरनिधाविव ॥ १२ ॥

शुद्धिरस्यास्तीति शुद्धिमान् । तस्मिन् **शुद्धिमति तदन्वये** तस्य मनोरन्वये वंशे । 'अन्ववायोऽन्वयो वंशो गोत्रं चाभिजनं कुलम् ।' इति हलायुधः । अतिशयेन शुद्धिमान् **शुद्धिमत्तरः** । 'द्विवचनविभज्योप–' इत्यादिना तरप् । **दिलीपः इति** प्रसिद्धो राजा इन्दुरिव **राजेन्दुः** राजश्रेष्ठः । उपमितं व्याघ्रादिना समासः । **क्षीरनिधौ इन्दुः इव प्रसूतः** जातः ॥

'व्यूढ–' इत्यादित्रिभिः श्लोकैर्दिलीपं विशिनष्टि–

व्यूढोरस्को वृषस्कन्धः शालप्रांशुर्महाभुजः ।
आत्मकर्मक्षमं देहं क्षात्रो धर्म इवाश्रितः ॥ १३ ॥

व्यूढं विपुलमुरो यस्य स **व्यूढोरस्कः** । 'उरःप्रभृतिभ्यः कप्' । 'व्यूढं विपुलं भद्रं स्फारं समं वरिष्ठं च ।' इति यादवः । वृषस्य स्कन्ध इव स्कन्धो यस्य स [**वृषस्कन्धः**] । 'सप्तम्युपमान–' इत्यादिनोत्तरपदलोपी बहुव्रीहिः । शालो वृक्ष इव प्रांशुरुन्नतः **शालप्रांशुः** । 'प्राकारवृक्षयोः शालः शालः सर्जतरुः स्मृतः ।' इति यादवः । 'उच्चप्रांशून्नतोदग्रोच्छ्रितास्तुङ्गे' इत्यमरः । **महाभुजः** महाबाहुः । **आत्मकर्मक्षमं** स्वव्यापा-

---

१ उपदेशं विदुः शुद्धं सन्तस्तमुपदेशिनः । श्यामायते न युष्मासु यः काञ्चनमिवाग्निषु ॥ इति मालविकाग्निमित्रे द्वितीयाङ्के समानार्थः श्लोकांशः । २ दीक्षितादीनां मते 'शकन्ध्वादिषु पररूपं वाच्यं' इति वार्तिकेन साधुः । ३ प्रकर्षेण यथा तथा नूयते स्तूयते अनेन इति प्रणवः । अत्र मनुः–ब्रह्मणः प्रणवं कुर्यादादावन्ते च सर्वदा । स्रवत्यनोंकृतं पूर्वं परस्ताच्च विशीर्यते ॥ इ० प्रणवः सर्ववेदेषु...इ० भगवद्गीता । ४ (१) स्वायंभुवः (२) स्वारोचिषः (३) उत्तमः (४) तामसः (५) रैवतः (६) चाक्षुषः (७) वैवस्वतः (८) सावर्णिः (९) दक्षसावर्णिः (१०) ब्रह्मसावर्णिः (११) धर्मसावर्णिः (१२) रुद्रसावर्णिः (१३) देव (रौच्य) सावर्णिः (१४) इन्द्रसावर्णिः–इत्येते चतुर्दश मनवः । तेषां वैवस्वतः सप्तमः । ५ ततः शतसहस्रांशुर्मथ्यमानात्तु सागरात् । प्रसन्नात्मा समुत्पन्नः सोमः शीतांशुरुज्ज्वलः ॥ इति महाभारतम् । ६ यद्वा—"यः पद्मलोचनश्छत्रध्वजवज्राङ्किताङ्घ्रिकः । चतुर्हस्तः स्वहस्तेन शालप्रांशुः स उच्यते ॥" इत्युक्तलक्षणोपेतः । ७ शौर्यं तेजो धृतिर्दाक्ष्यं युद्धे चाप्यपलायनम् । दानमीश्वरभावश्च क्षात्रं कर्म स्वभावजम् ॥ भ. गीता १८–४३.

रानुरूपं **देहम् आश्रितः** प्राप्तः **क्षात्रः** क्षत्रसंबन्धी **धर्मः इव** स्थितः । मूर्तिमान्क्षात्र इव स्थित इत्युत्प्रेक्षा ॥

सर्वातिरिक्तसारेण सर्वतेजोभिभाविना ।
स्थितः सर्वोन्नतेनोर्वीं क्रान्त्वा मेरुरिवात्मना ॥ १४ ॥

सर्वातिरिक्तसारेण सर्वेभ्यो भूतेभ्योऽधिकबलेन । 'सारो बले स्थिरांशे च' इत्यमरः । सर्वाणि भूतानि तेजसाभिभवतीति सर्वतेजोभिभावी तेन [**सर्वतेजोभिभाविना**] । सर्वेभ्यः उन्नतेन [**सर्वोन्नतेन**] **आत्मना** शरीरेण । 'आत्मा देहे धृतौ जीवे स्वभावे परमात्मनि ।' इति विश्वः । **मेरुरिव उर्वीम् क्रान्त्वा** आक्रम्य **स्थितः** । मेरावपि विशेषणानि तुल्यानि । 'अष्टाभिश्च सुरेन्द्राणां मात्राभिर्निर्मितो नृपः । तस्मादभिभवत्येष सर्वभूतानि तेजसा ॥' इति मनुवचनाद्राज्ञः सर्वतेजोभिभावित्वं ज्ञेयम् ॥

आकारसदृशप्रज्ञः प्रज्ञया सदृशागमः ।
आगमैः सदृशारम्भ आरम्भसदृशोदयः ॥ १५ ॥

आकारेण मूर्त्या सदृशी प्रज्ञा यस्य सः [**आकारसदृशप्रज्ञः**] । **प्रज्ञया सदृशागमः** प्रज्ञानुरूपशास्त्रपरिश्रमः । **आगमैः** सदृश आरम्भः कर्म यस्य स [**सदृशारम्भः**] तथोक्तः । आरभ्यत इत्यारम्भः कर्म । तत्सदृश उदयः फलसिद्धिर्यस्य स[**आरम्भसदृशोदयः**]तथोक्तः॥

भीमकान्तैर्नृपगुणैः स बभूवोपजीविनाम् ।
अधृष्यश्चाभिगम्यश्च यादोरत्नैरिवार्णवः ॥ १६ ॥

भीमैश्च कान्तैश्च [**भीमकान्तैः**] **नृपगुणैः** राजगुणैस्तेजःप्रतापादिभिः कुलशीलदाक्षिण्यादिभिश्च **स** दिलीपः **उपजीविनाम्** आश्रितानाम् । यादोभिर्जलजन्तुभिः । 'यादांसि जलजन्तवः' इत्यमरः । रत्नैश्च [**यादोरत्नैः**] **अर्णवः इव अधृष्यः** अनभिभवनीयः **च अभिगम्यः** आश्रयणीयः **च बभूव** ॥

रेखामात्रमपि क्षुण्णादा मनोर्वर्त्मनः परम् ।
न व्यतीयुः प्रजास्तस्य नियन्तुर्नेमिवृत्तयः ॥ १७ ॥

नियन्तुः शिक्षकस्य सारथेश्च **तस्य** दिलीपस्य संबन्धिन्यो नेमीनां चक्रधाराणां

---

१ अत्र उपमेयस्य दिलीपस्य उपमानेन क्षात्रधर्मेण सह एकरूपतया संभावनाद् उत्प्रेक्षालंकारः । इयं च इवशब्दप्रयोगात् वाच्या । तदुक्तं साहित्यदर्पणे–भवेत्संभावनोत्प्रेक्षा प्रकृतस्य परात्मना । वाच्या प्रतीयमाना सा प्रथमा द्विविधा मता । वाच्येवादिप्रयोगे स्यादप्रयोगे परा पुनः ॥ इ०.२ मेरोरपि सौवर्णत्वात्सर्वतेजोभिभावित्वम् । मिनोति क्षिपति उन्नतत्वाज्ज्योतींषि इति मेरुः । ३ आगमलक्षणं यथा–सर्ववेदः क्रियामूलमृषिभिर्यद्दृष्टदर्शिभिः । कालो देशः क्रिया कर्ता कारणं कार्यमागमः ॥ सिद्धं सिद्धैः प्रमाणैस्तु हितं चात्र परत्र च । आगमः शास्त्रमाप्तानामाप्तास्तत्त्वार्थवेदिनः ॥ शृण्वतां जायते भक्तिस्ततो गुरुमुपासते । स च विद्यागमान्वीक्षिविद्यायुक्तस्त्वभितो नृपः ॥ इ० ४ अर्णांसि भूमान्यत्र सन्ति इति अर्णवः । अर्णसो लोपश्च । पा० ५. २. १०९ (वा०) इति वः सलोपश्च । ५ तेजो बलं सत्त्ववत्ता प्रभावः पालकाद्भुता । अधृष्यस्य गुणानेतान्नृपस्य मुनयो विदुः ॥ इति बृहस्पतिः । 'कुलं सत्त्वं वयः शीलं दाक्षिण्यं क्षिप्रकारिता । असंविसंवादिता सत्यं वृद्धसेवा कृतज्ञता ॥ दैवसंपन्नता बुद्धिरक्षुद्रपरिवारिता । शक्यसामन्तता चैव तथा च दृढभक्तिता ॥ दीर्घदर्शित्वमुत्साहः शुचिता स्थूललक्ष्यता । विनीतता धार्मिकता गुणाः साध्याभिगामिकाः ॥' इति कामन्दकः.

वृत्तिरिव वृत्तिर्व्यापारो यासां ताः [**नेमिवृत्तयः**]। 'चक्रधारा प्रधिर्नेमिः' इति यादवः। 'चक्रं रथाङ्गं तस्यान्ते नेमिः स्त्री स्यात्प्रधिः पुमान्।' इत्यमरः। **प्रजाः** । **आ मनोः** मनुमारभ्येत्यभिविधिः । पदद्वयं चैतत्। समासस्य विभाषितत्वात्। **क्षुण्णाद्** अभ्यस्तात्प्रहताच्च **वर्त्मनः** आचारपद्धतेरध्वनश्च **परं** अधिकम्। इतस्ततः इत्यर्थः। रेखा प्रमाणमस्येति **रेखामात्रं** रेखाप्रमाणम्। ईषदपीत्यर्थः। 'प्रमाणे द्वयसज्–' इत्यादिना मात्रच्प्रत्ययः। परशब्दविशेषणं चैतत्। [**अपि**] **न व्यतीयुः** नातिक्रान्तवत्यः । कुशलसारथिप्रेषिता रथनेमय इव तस्य प्रजाः पूर्वक्षुण्णमार्गं न जहुरिति भावः॥

प्रजानामेव भूत्यर्थं स ताभ्यो बलिमग्रहीत्।
सहस्रगुणमुत्स्रष्टुमादत्ते हि रसं रविः॥ १८॥

स राजा **प्रजानां** भूत्या अर्थाय **भूत्यर्थं** वृद्ध्यर्थं **एव**। 'अर्थेन सह नित्यसमासः सर्वलिङ्गता **च** वक्तव्या।' ग्रहणक्रियाविशेषणं चैतत्। **ताभ्यः** प्रजाभ्यो **बलिं** षष्ठांशरूपं करं **अग्रहीत्**। 'भागधेयः करो बलिः' इत्यमरः। तथा **हि**। **रविः** सहस्रं गुणा यस्मिन्कर्मणि तद्यथा तथा **सहस्रगुणं** सहस्रधा **उत्स्रष्टुं** दातुम् । उत्सर्जनक्रियाविशेषणं चैतत्। **रसं** अम्बु **आदत्ते** गृह्णाति[3]। 'रसो गन्धे रसे स्वादे तिक्तादौ विषरागयोः। शृङ्गारादौ द्रवे वीर्ये देहधात्वम्बुपारदे॥' इति विश्वः॥

संप्रति बुद्धिशौर्यसंपन्नस्य तस्यार्थसाधनेषु परानपेक्षत्वमाह—

सेना परिच्छदस्तस्य द्वयमेवार्थसाधनम्।
शास्त्रेष्वकुण्ठिता बुद्धिर्मौर्वी धनुषि चातता॥ १९॥

तस्य राज्ञः **सेना** चतुरङ्गबलम्। परिच्छाद्यतेऽनेनेति **परिच्छदः** उपकरणं बभूव। छत्रचामरादितुल्यमभूदित्यर्थः। 'पुंसि संज्ञायां घः प्रायेण' इति घप्रत्ययः। 'छादेर्घेऽद्व्युपसर्गस्य' इत्युपधाह्रस्वः। अर्थस्य प्रयोजनस्य तु साधनं [**अर्थसाधनं**] **द्वयमेव**। **शास्त्रेषु अकुण्ठिता** अव्याहता **बुद्धिः**। 'व्यापृता' इत्यपि पाठः। **धनुषि आतता** आरोपिता **मौर्वी** ज्या **च**। 'मौर्वी ज्या शिञ्जिनी गुणः' इत्यमरः। नीतिपुरःसरमेव तस्य शौर्यमभूदित्यर्थः॥

राज्यमूलं मन्त्रसंरक्षणं तस्यासीदित्याह—

तस्य संवृतमन्त्रस्य गूढाकारेङ्गितस्य च।
फलानुमेयाः प्रारम्भाः संस्काराः प्राक्तना इव॥ २०॥

संवृतमन्त्रस्य गुप्तविचारस्य । 'वेदभेदे गुप्तवादे मन्त्रः' इत्यमरः। शोकहर्षादिसूचको भ्रुकुटीमुखरागादिराकारः । [**गूढाकारेङ्गितस्य**] इङ्गितं चेष्टितं हृदयगतविकारो वा। 'इङ्गितं हृद्गतो भावो बहिराकार आकृतिः ।' इति सज्जनः । गूढे

---

१ राज्ञः विपथगामिनां नियन्तृत्वे याज्ञवल्क्यः—कुलानि जातीः श्रेणीश्च गणाञ्जनपदानपि । स्वधर्माच्चलितान् राजा विनीय स्थापयेत्पथि ॥ इति। २ म. स्मृ. स. अ. १२८–१३२. ३ दशमसर्गे ५८ श्लो० द्रष्टव्यः । स राजा प्रजाभ्यः गृहीतेन करेण यज्ञादिकं ततान। तेन तुष्टैर्देवैर्वृष्टिस्तयान्नं तेन प्रजापुष्टिरिति परंपरया बलेर्भूत्यर्थता । इति चारित्रवर्धनः। ४ सेनापरिच्छदः इति वा एकं समस्तं षष्ठयन्तं पदम्। सेना परिच्छद् उपकरणं यस्य तस्य। ५ शास्त्रेषु–दण्डनीत्यादिषु। ६ यतः–आकारैरिङ्गितैर्गत्या चेष्टया भाषितेन च । नेत्रवक्त्रविकारैश्च लक्ष्यतेऽन्तर्गतं मनः॥ म० स्मृ० ७. २६; एतेन तस्य गाम्भीर्यं सूचितम्।

आकारेङ्गिते यस्य । स्वभावचापलाद् भ्रमपरंपरया मुखरागादिलिङ्गैर्वाऽतृतीयगामिमन्त्रस्य **च तस्य** । प्रारभ्यन्त इति **प्रारम्भाः** सामाद्युपायप्रयोगाः । प्रागित्यव्ययेन पूर्वजन्मोच्यते तत्र भवाः **प्राक्तनाः** । 'सायंचिर-' इत्यादिना ट्युल्प्रत्ययः* ॥ **संस्काराः** पूर्वकर्मवासना **इव** । फलेन कार्येणानुमेया अनुमातुं योग्या [**फलानुमेयाः**] आसन् । अत्र याज्ञवल्क्यः-'मन्त्रमूलं यतो राज्यमतो मन्त्रं सुरक्षितम् । कुर्याद्यथा तन्न विदुः कर्मणामा फलोदयात् ॥' इति ॥

संप्रति सामाद्युपायान्वितैवात्मरक्षादिकं कृतवानित्याह—

जुगोपात्मानमत्रस्तो भेजे धर्ममनातुरः ।
अगृध्नुराददे सोऽर्थमसक्तः सुखमन्वभूत् ॥ २१ ॥

[**सः**] **अत्रस्तः** अभीतः सन् । 'त्रस्तो भीरुभीरुकभीलुकाः' इत्यमरः । त्रासोपाधिमन्तरेणैव त्रिवर्गसिद्धेः प्रथमसाधनत्वादेव **आत्मानं** शरीरं **जुगोप** रक्षितवान्[१] । **अनातुरः** अरुग्ण एव **धर्मं** सुकृतं **भेजे** । अर्जितवानित्यर्थः । **अगृध्नुः** अगर्धनशील एव **अर्थमाददे** स्वीकृतवान् । 'गृध्नुस्तु गर्धनः । लुब्धोऽभिलाषुकस्तृष्णक्समौ लोलुपलोलुभौ ॥' इत्यमरः । 'त्रसिगृधिधृषिक्षिपेः क्नुः' इति क्नुप्रत्ययः । **असक्तः** आसक्तिरहित एव **सुखम् अन्वभूत्** ॥

परस्परविरुद्धानामपि गुणानां तत्र साहचर्यमासीदित्याह—

ज्ञाने मौनं क्षमा शक्तौ त्यागे श्लाघाविपर्ययः ।
गुणा गुणानुबन्धित्वात्तस्य सप्रसवा इव ॥ २२ ॥

ज्ञाने परवृत्तान्तज्ञाने सत्यपि **मौनं** वाङ्नियमनम् । यथाह कामन्दकः-'नान्योपतापि वचनं मौनं व्रतचरिष्णुता ।' इति । **शक्तौ** प्रतीकारसामर्थ्येऽपि **क्षमा** अपकारसहनम् । अत्र चाणक्यः-'शक्तानां भूषणं क्षमा' इति । **त्यागे** वितरणे सत्यपि [**श्लाघाविपर्ययः**] श्लाघाया विकत्थनस्य विपर्ययोऽभावः । अत्राह मनुः-'न दत्त्वा परिकीर्तयेत्' इति । इत्थं **तस्य गुणा** ज्ञानादयो [**गुणानुबन्धित्वात्**] गुणैर्विरुद्धैर्मौनादिभिरनुबन्धित्वात्सहचारित्वात् । सह प्रसवो जन्म येषां ते **सप्रसवाः** सोदराः **इव** अभूवन् । विरुद्धा अपि गुणास्तस्मिन्नविरोधेनैव स्थिता इत्यर्थः ॥

द्विविधं वृद्धत्वम्, ज्ञानेन वयसा च । तत्र तस्य ज्ञानेन वृद्धत्वमाह—

अनाकृष्टस्य विषयैर्विद्यानां पारदृश्वनः ।
तस्य धर्मरतेरासीद्वृद्धत्वं जरसा विना ॥ २३ ॥

विषयैः शब्दादिभिः । 'रूपं शब्दो गन्धरसस्पर्शाश्च विषया अमी ।' इत्यमरः । **अनाकृष्टस्य** अवशीकृतस्य । **विद्यानां** वेदवेदाङ्गादीनां **पारदृश्वनः** परमन्तं दृष्टवतः ।

---

*तुडागमश्च । १ म. स्मृ. ७. १४७–१४८ श्लो. द्रष्टव्यौ । २ 'सततं आत्मानं गोपायीत' इति श्रुते । 'आत्मानं सततं रक्षेद्दारैरपि धनैरपि' इति मनुस्मरणाच्च । ३ उक्तं च-'ज्ञानेनाशुनमर्थस्य रक्षणं वर्धनं तथा । सत्पात्रे प्रतिपत्तिश्च राजवृत्तं चतुर्विधम् ॥' इति । अनुरूपभावः किरातार्जुनीये 'वसूनि वाञ्छन्न वशी' इत्यादौ । अनासक्ततया विषयोपभोगे कामन्दकः-'सेवेत विषयान्काले त्यक्त्वा तत्परतां वशी । सुखं हि फलमर्थस्य तन्निरोधे वृथा श्रियः ॥' इति । ४ आन्वीक्षिकी त्रयी वार्ता दण्डनीतिश्च शाश्वती । विद्याश्चतस्र एवैता लोकसंस्थितिहेतवः ॥ इति कामन्दकोक्ताश्चतस्रो विद्या वा । यदुक्तं कविनैव तृतीयसर्गे-'धियः समग्रैः' इत्यादि (३०) श्लोके.

दृशेः क्वनिप् । [**धर्मरतेः**] धर्मे रतिर्यस्य **तस्य** राज्ञः **जरसा** जरया **विना** । 'विस्रसा जरा ' इत्यमरः । ' षिद्भिदादिभ्योऽङ् ' इत्यङ्प्रत्ययः । ' **जराया जरसन्यतरस्याम्** ' इति जरसादेशः । **वृद्धत्वं** वार्द्धकं **आसीत्** । तस्य यूनोऽपि विषयवैराग्यादिज्ञानगुणसंपत्त्या ज्ञानतो वृद्धत्वमासीदित्यर्थः । नाथस्तु चतुर्विधं वृद्धत्वमिति कृत्वा ' अनाकृष्टस्य ' इत्यादिना विशेषणत्रयेण वैराग्यज्ञानशीलवृद्धत्वान्युक्तानीत्यवोचत् ॥

प्रजानां विनयाधानाद्रक्षणाद्भरणादपि ।
स पिता पितरस्तासां केवलं जन्महेतवः ॥ २४ ॥

[**प्रजानां**] प्रजायन्त इति प्रजा जनाः । ' उपसर्गे च संज्ञायाम् ' इति डप्रत्ययः । 'प्रजा स्यात्संततौ जने' इत्यमरः । तासां [**विनयाधानात्**] विनयस्य शिक्षाया आधानात् करणात् । सन्मार्गप्रवर्तनादिति यावत् । **रक्षणात्** भयहेतुभ्यस्त्राणात् । आपन्निवारणादिति यावत् । **भरणात्** अन्नपानादिभिः पोषणात् **अपि** । अपिः समुच्चये । **स** राजा **पिता** अभूत् । **तासां पितरः** तु **जन्महेतवः** जन्ममात्रकर्तारः **केवलं** उत्पादका एवाभूवन् । जननमात्र एव पितॄणां व्यापारः । सदा शिक्षारक्षारक्षणादिकं तु स एव करोतीति तस्मिन्पितृव्यपदेशः । आहुश्च–' स पिता यस्तु पोषकः ' इति ॥

स्थित्यै दण्डयतो दण्ड्यान्परिणेतुः प्रसूतये ।
अप्यर्थकामौ तस्यास्तां धर्म एव मनीषिणः ॥ २५ ॥

दण्डमर्हन्तीति दण्ड्याः । ' दण्डादिभ्यो यः ' इति यप्रत्ययः । ' अदण्ड्यान्दण्डयन्राजा दण्ड्यांश्चैवाप्यदण्डयन् । अयशो महदाप्नोति नरकं चैव गच्छति ॥ ' इति शास्त्रवचनात् । तान् **दण्ड्यान्** एव **स्थित्यै** लोकप्रतिष्ठायै **दण्डयतः** शिक्षयतः । **प्रसूतये** संतानार्थैव **परिणेतुः** दारान्परिगृह्णतः । **मनीषिणः** विदुषः । दोषज्ञस्येति यावत् । ' विद्वान्विपश्चिद्दोषज्ञः सन्सुधीः कोविदो बुधः । धीरो मनीषी ' इत्यमरः । **तस्य** दिलीपस्य **अर्थकामौ अपि धर्म एवास्तां** जातौ । अस्तेर्लङ् । अर्थकामसाधनयोर्दण्डविवाहयोर्लोकस्थापनप्रजोत्पादनरूपधर्मार्थत्वेनानुष्ठानादर्थकामावपि धर्मशेषतामापादयन्स राजा धर्मोत्तरोऽभूदित्यर्थः । आह च गौतमः–'न पूर्वाह्णमध्यंदिनापराह्णानफलान्कुर्यात् । यथाशक्ति धर्मार्थकामेभ्यस्तेषु धर्मोत्तरः स्यात् । ' इति ॥

दुदोह गां स यज्ञाय सस्याय मघवा दिवम् ।
संपद्विनिमयेनोभौ दधतुर्भुवनद्वयम् ॥ २६ ॥

स राजा **यज्ञाय** यज्ञं कर्तुं **गां** भुवं **दुदोह** । करग्रहणेन रिक्तां चकारेत्यर्थः । **मघवा**

---

१ यदाह मनुः—' न तेन वृद्धो भवति येनास्य पलितं शिरः । यो वै युवाऽप्यधीयानस्तं देवाः स्थविरं विदुः ॥ ' इति । २ अत्र मनुः–स्याच्चाम्नायपरो लोके वर्तेत पितृवन्नृषु । (अ. ७,८०). शरीरकृत्प्राणदाता यस्य चान्नानि भुञ्जते । क्रमेणैते त्रयोऽप्युक्ताः पितरो धर्मशासने ॥ इति भारते । कन्यादाताऽन्नदाता च ज्ञानदाताऽभयप्रदः । जन्मदो मन्त्रदो ज्येष्ठभ्राता च पितरः स्मृताः ॥ इत्यन्यत्रापि. ३ " पुत्रार्थं क्रियते भार्या पुत्रः पिण्डप्रयोजनः । " इति स्मरणात् । ' पुत्रप्रयोजना दाराः पुत्रः पिण्डप्रयोजनः । हितप्रयोजनं मित्रं धनं सर्वप्रयोजनम् ॥ ' इति चाणक्यनीतौ । ४ यतः त्रिवर्गो धर्ममूलः । " त्रिवर्गोऽयं धर्ममूलो नरेन्द्र राज्यं चेदं धर्ममूलं वदन्ति । धर्मे राजन् वर्तमानः स्वशक्त्या पुत्रान् सर्वान् पाहि पाण्डोः सुतांश्च ॥ " इति महाभारते धृतराष्ट्रं प्रति विदुरोक्तिरेतदेव दर्शयति । ५ गौः स्वर्गे च बलीवर्दे रश्मौ च कुलिशे पुमान् । स्त्री सौरभेयीदृग्बाणदिग्वाग्भूष्वप्सु भूम्नि च ॥ इ० मेदिनी ।

देवेन्द्रः **सस्याय** सस्यं वर्धयितुं **दिवं** स्वर्गं दुदोह । द्युलोकान्महीलोके वृष्टिमुत्पादयामासेत्यर्थः । ' क्रियार्थोपपदस्य—' इत्यादिना यज्ञसस्याभ्यां चतुर्थी । एवं **उभौ** [**संपद्विनिमयेन**] संपदो विनिमयेन परस्परमादानप्रतिदानाभ्यां **भुवनद्वयं दधतुः** पुपुषतुः । राजा यज्ञैरिन्द्रलोकमिन्द्रश्चोदकेन भूलोकं पुपोषेत्यर्थः । उक्तं च दण्डनीतौ—' राजा त्वर्थान्समाहृत्य कुर्यादिन्द्रमहोत्सवम् । प्रीणितो मेघवाहस्तु महतीं वृष्टिमावहेत् ॥ ' इति ।

न किलानुययुस्तस्य राजानो रक्षितुर्यशः ।
व्यावृत्ता यत्परस्वेभ्यः श्रुतौ तस्करता स्थिता ॥ २७ ॥

राजानः अन्ये नृपाः **रक्षितुः** भयेभ्यस्त्रातुः **तस्य** राज्ञः **यशः न अनुययुः किल** नानुचक्रुः खलु । कुतः **यद्** यस्मात्कारणात् **तस्करता** चौर्यं **परस्वेभ्यः** परधनेभ्यः स्वविषयभूतेभ्यः **व्यावृत्ता** सती **श्रुतौ** वाचकशब्दे **स्थिता** प्रवृत्ता । अपहार्याभावात्तस्करशब्द एवापहृत इत्यर्थः । अथ वा । ' अत्यन्तासत्यपि ह्यर्थे ज्ञानं शब्दः करोति हि ' इति न्यायेन शब्दे स्थिता स्फुरिता न तु स्वरूपतोऽस्तीत्यर्थः ॥

द्वेष्योऽपि संमतः शिष्टस्तस्यार्तस्य यथौषधम् ।
त्याज्यो दुष्टः प्रियोऽप्यासीदङ्गुलीवोरगक्षता ॥ २८ ॥

शिष्टः जनो **द्वेष्यः** शत्रुः **अपि । आर्तस्य** रोगिणः **औषधं यथा** औषधमिव **तस्य संमतः** अनुमत आसीत् । **दुष्टः** जनः **प्रियः अपि** प्रेमास्पदीभूतोऽपि **उरगक्षता** सर्पदष्टा **अङ्गुली इव** । ' छिन्द्याद्बाहुमपि दुष्टात्मनः ' इति न्यायात् । **त्याज्यः आसीत्** । तस्य शिष्ट एव बन्धुर्दुष्ट एव शत्रुरित्यर्थः ।

तस्य परोपकारित्वमाह—

तं वेधा विदधे नूनं महाभूतसमाधिना ।
तथा हि सर्वे तस्यासन्परार्थैकफला गुणाः ॥ २९ ॥

वेधाः स्रष्टा । ' स्रष्टा प्रजापतिर्वेधाः ' इत्यमरः । **तं** दिलीपम् । समाधीयतेऽनेनेति समाधिः कारणसामग्री । महाभूतानां यः समाधिस्तेन **महाभूतसमाधिना विदधे** ससर्ज **नूनं** ध्रुवम् । इत्युत्प्रेक्षा । **तथा हि । तस्य** राज्ञः **सर्वे गुणाः** रूपरसादिमहाभूतगुणवदेव परार्थः परप्रयोजनमेवैकं मुख्यं फलं येषां ते तथोक्ताः [**परार्थैकफलाः**] **आसन्** । महाभूतगुणोपमानेन कारणगुणाः कार्यं संक्रामन्तीति न्यायः सूचितः ॥

---

१ अत्र भगवद्गीता—सहयज्ञाः....॥ देवान्भावयतानेन ते देवा भावयन्तु वः । परस्परं भावयन्तः श्रेयः परमवाप्स्यथ ॥ इष्टान् भोगान्हि वो देवा दास्यन्ते यज्ञभाविताः ॥ अ० ३ श्लो० १०-१२. अस्य तुल्यार्थः श्लोकः शाकुन्तले—तव भवतु बिडौजाः प्राज्यवृष्टिः प्रजासु त्वमपि विततयज्ञः स्वर्गिणः प्रीणयस्व । युगशतपरिवर्तानेवमन्योन्यकृत्यैः नयतमुभयलोकानुग्रहश्लाघनीयैः ॥ २ श्रूयते इति श्रुतिः ध्वनिः तस्मिन् स्वमात्रं स्थिता ॥ इति नाथः । ३ धर्मणाधिगतो यैस्तु वेदः सपरिबृंहणः । ते शिष्टा ब्राह्मणा ज्ञेयाः श्रुतिप्रत्यक्षहेतवः ॥ इति मनु (अ० १२ श्लोक १०९). ४ अत्रोपमानोपमेययोः भिन्नलिङ्गत्वं न दोषः सहृदयानामनुद्वेगकरत्वात् । तदुक्तं दण्डिना— न लिङ्गवचने भिन्ने न हीनाधिकतापि वा । उपमादूषणायालं यत्रोद्वेगो न धीमताम् ॥ इति । का० द० २. ५१. ५ मन्ये शङ्के ध्रुवं प्रायो नूनमित्येवमादिभिः । उत्प्रेक्षा व्यज्यते शब्दैरिवशब्दोऽपि तादृशः ॥ का० द० २. २३४.

स वेलावप्रवलयां परिखीकृतसागराम् ।
अनन्यशासनामुर्वीं शशासैकपुरीमिव ॥ ३० ॥

स दिलीपः । [**वेलावप्रवलयां**] वेलाः समुद्रकूलानि । 'वेला कूलेऽपि वारिधेः' इति विश्वः । ता एव वप्रवलयाः प्राकारवेष्टनानि यस्यास्ताम् । 'स्याच्चयो वप्रमस्त्रियाम् । प्राकारो वरणः शालः प्राचीनं प्रान्ततो वृतिः ॥' इत्यमरः । [**परिखीकृतसागरां**] परितः खातं परिखा दुर्गवेष्टनम् । 'खातं खेयं तु परिखा' इत्यमरः । 'अन्येष्वपि दृश्यते' इत्यत्र पिशब्दात्खनेर्डप्रत्ययः । अपरिखाः परिखाः संपद्यमानाः कृताः परिखीकृताः सागरा यस्यास्ताम् । अभूततद्भावे च्विः । अविद्यमानमन्यस्य राज्ञः शासनं यस्यास्तां **अनन्यशासनाम् उर्वीम् एकपुरीम् इव शशास** । अनायासेन शासितवानित्यर्थः ॥

तस्य दाक्षिण्यरूढेन नाम्ना मगधवंशजा ।
पत्नी सुदक्षिणेत्यासीदध्वरस्येव दक्षिणा ॥ ३१ ॥

तस्य राज्ञो मगधवंशे जाता **मगधवंशजा** । 'सप्तम्यां जनेर्डः' इति डप्रत्ययः एतेनाभिजात्यमुक्तम् । [**दाक्षिण्यरूढेन**] दाक्षिण्यं परच्छन्दानुवर्तनम्[१] । 'दक्षिणः सरलादारपरच्छन्दानुवर्तिषु ।' इति शाश्वतः । तेन रूढं प्रसिद्धम् । तेन **नाम्ना अध्वरस्य**[२] यज्ञस्य **दक्षिणा** दक्षिणाख्या पत्नी **इव** । **सुदक्षिणा इति** प्रसिद्धा **पत्नी आसीत्**[३] । अत्र श्रुतिः—'यज्ञो गन्धर्वस्तस्य दक्षिणाप्सरसः' इति । 'दक्षिणाया दाक्षिण्यं नामर्त्विजो दक्षिणत्वप्रापकत्वम् । ते दक्षन्ते दक्षिणां प्रतिगृह्य' इति च ॥

कलत्रवन्तमात्मानमवरोधे महत्यपि ।
तया मेने मनस्विन्या लक्ष्म्या च वसुधाधिपः ॥ ३२ ॥

वसुधाधिपः अवरोधे अन्तःपुरवर्गे **महति** सति **अपि** । **मनस्विन्या** दृढचित्तया । पतिचित्तानुवृत्त्यादिनिर्बन्धक्षमयेत्यर्थः । **तया** सुदक्षिणया **लक्ष्म्या चात्मानं कलत्रवन्तं** भार्यावन्तं **मेने** । 'कलत्रं श्रोणिभार्ययोः' इत्यमरः । वसुधाधिप इत्यनेन वसुधया चेति गम्यते ॥

तस्यामात्मानुरूपायामात्मजन्मसमुत्सुकः ।
विलम्बितफलैः कालं स निनाय मनोरथैः ॥ ३३ ॥

स राजा । **आत्मानुरूपायां तस्याम्** [**आत्मजन्मसमुत्सुकः**] आत्मनो जन्म यस्यासावात्मजन्मा पुत्रः । तस्मिन्समुत्सुकः । यद्वा आत्मनो जन्मनि पुत्ररूपेणोत्पत्तौ समुत्सुकः सन् । 'आत्मा वै पुत्रनामासि' इति श्रुतेः[४] । विलम्बितं फलं पुत्रप्राप्तिरूपं येषां तैः [**विलम्बितफलैः**] **मनोरथैः** कदा मे पुत्रो भवेदित्याशाभिः **कालं निनाय** यापयामास ॥

---

१ औदार्यं वा । २ अध्वरस्य—न ध्वरतीति अध्वरः हिंसारहितः । न हि अग्निना सर्वतः पालितं यज्ञं राक्षसा हिंसितुं प्रभवन्ति इति ऋग्वेदभाष्ये सायनः (ऋ० १. १. ४) । ध्वरतिः हिंसाकर्मा तत्प्रतिषेधो निपातः अहिंस्रः । इति निरुक्ते यास्कः । अध्वानं स्वर्गमार्गं राति ददातीति वा । न ध्वरः अध्वरः अकुटिलः शास्त्रोक्त इति वा । ३ दक्षिणा यज्ञपत्नी च दीक्षा सर्वस्य पूजिता । यया विना हि विश्वेषु सर्वं कर्म हि निष्फलम् ॥ इति स्मरणात् । ४ आत्मा वै जायते पुत्रः । इति श्रुत्यन्तरम् ।

संतानार्थाय विधये स्वभुजादवतारिता ।
तेन धूर्जगतो गुर्वी सचिवेषु निचिक्षिपे ॥ ३४ ॥

तेन दिलीपेन । संतानोऽर्थः प्रयोजनं यस्य तस्मै **संतानार्थाय विधये** अनुष्ठानाय **स्वभुजात् अवतारिता** अवरोपिता **जगतः** लोकस्य **गुर्वी धूः** भारः **सचिवेषु निचिक्षिपे** निहिता ॥

अथाभ्यर्च्य विधातारं प्रयतौ पुत्रकाम्यया ।
तौ दंपती वसिष्ठस्य गुरोर्जग्मतुराश्रमम् ॥ ३५ ॥

अथ धुरोऽवतारानन्तरं **पुत्रकाम्यया** आत्मनः पुत्रेच्छया । 'काम्यच्च' इति पुत्रशब्दात्काम्यच्प्रत्ययः । 'अ प्रत्ययात्' इति पुत्रकाम्यधातोरकारप्रत्ययः । ततष्टाप् । तया **तौ दंपती** जायापती । राजदन्तादिषु जायाशब्दस्य दमिति निपातनात्साधुः । **प्रयतौ** पूतौ **विधातारं** ब्रह्माणं **अभ्यर्च्य** । 'स खलु पुत्रार्थिभिरुपास्यते' इति मान्त्रिकाः **गुरोः** कुलगुरोः **वसिष्ठस्य आश्रमं जग्मतुः** । पुत्रप्राप्त्युपायापेक्षयेति शेषः ॥

स्निग्धगम्भीरनिर्घोषमेकं स्यन्दनमास्थितौ ।
प्रावृषेण्यं पयोवाहं विद्युदैरावताविव ॥ ३६ ॥

स्निग्धो मधुरो गम्भीरो निर्घोषो यस्य तं [**स्निग्धगम्भीरनिर्घोषं**] **एकं स्यन्दनं** रथम् । प्रावृषि भवः प्रावृषेण्यः । 'प्रावृष एण्यः' इत्येण्यप्रत्ययः । तं **प्रावृषेण्यं पयोवाहं** मेघं **विद्युदैरावतौ इव** । **आस्थितौ** आरूढौ । जग्मतुरिति पूर्वेण संबन्धः । इरा आपः । 'इरा भूवाक्सुराप्सु स्यात्' इत्यमरः । 'इरावान्समुद्रः । तत्र भव ऐरावतोऽभ्रमातङ्गः । 'ऐरावतोऽभ्रमातङ्गैरावणाभ्रमुवल्लभाः ।' इत्यमरः । 'अभ्रमातङ्गत्वं चाभ्रस्थत्वादभ्ररूपत्वाद्वा' इति क्षीरस्वामी । अत एव मेघारोहणं विद्युत्साहचर्यं च घटते । किं च विद्युत ऐरावतसाहचर्यादैरावतीसंज्ञा । ऐरावतस्य स्त्री ऐरावतीति क्षीरस्वामी । तस्मात्सुष्ठूक्तं विद्युदैरावताविवेति । एकरथारोहणोक्त्या कार्यसिद्धिबीजं दंपत्योरत्यन्तसौमनस्यं सूचयति ॥

मा भूदाश्रमपीडेति परिमेयपुरःसरौ ।
अनुभावविशेषात्तु सेनापरिवृताविव ॥ ३७ ॥

पुनः किंभूतौ दंपती । **आश्रमपीडा मा भूत्** मास्तु **इति** हेतोः । 'माङि लुङ्' इत्याशीरर्थे लुङ् । 'न माङ्योगे' इत्यडागमनिषेधः । **परिमेयपुरःसरौ** परिमितपरिचरौ । **अनुभावविशेषात् तु** तेजोविशेषात् **सेनापरिवृतौ इव** स्थितौ ॥

सेव्यमानौ सुखस्पर्शैः शालनिर्यासगन्धिभिः ।
पुष्परेणूत्किरैर्वातैराधूतवनराजिभिः ॥ ३८ ॥

पुनः कथंभूतौ । सुखः शीतलत्वात्प्रियः स्पर्शो येषां तैः [**सुखस्पर्शैः**] **शाल-**

---

१ मेघस्योपरि मेघो यः स ऐरावत उच्यते । इ० दक्षिणावर्तः. २ विद्युत्साम्यात्सुदक्षिणाया अलौकिकी देहकान्तिः, ऐरावतसाम्याद्दिलीपस्य लोकोत्तरः वपुःप्रकर्षः, मेघसाम्याद्रथस्य विशालत्वादिकं च सूचितानि । 'विद्युदैरावते इव' इति पाठे तु ऐरावतं इन्द्रधनुः इत्यत्र पुंनपुंसकयोः भिन्नलिङ्गस्यानिष्टत्वात् उपमादूषणं चिन्तनीयम् । इति चारित्रवर्धनः ।

निर्यासगन्धिभिः सर्जतरुनिस्यन्दगन्धवद्भिः । 'शालः सर्जतरुः स्मृतः' इति शाश्वतः । उत्किरन्ति विक्षिपन्तीत्युत्किराः । 'इगुपध-' इत्यादिना किरतेः कप्रत्ययः । पुष्परेणूनामुत्किरास्तैः [**पुष्परेणूत्किरैः**] आधूता मान्द्यादीषत्कम्पिता वनराजयो यैस्तैः [**आधूतवनराजिभिः**] **वातैः सेव्यमानौ** ॥

मनोभिरामाः शृण्वन्तौ रथनेमिस्वनोन्मुखैः ।
षड्जसंवादिनीः केका द्विधा भिन्नाः शिखण्डिभिः ॥ ३९ ॥

रथनेमिस्वनोन्मुखैः । मेघध्वनिशङ्कयोन्नमितमुखैरित्यर्थः । **शिखण्डिभिः** मयूरैः **द्विधा भिन्नाः** । शुद्धविकृतभेदेनाविकृतावस्थायां च्युताच्युतभेदेन वा षड्जो द्विविधः । तस्मात्तद्रूपात्केका अपि द्विधा भिन्ना इत्युच्यते । अत एवाह-**षड्जसंवादिनीः** इति । षड्भ्यः स्थानेभ्यो जातः षड्जः । तदुक्तम्—'नासां कण्ठमुरस्तालु जिह्वां दन्तांश्च संस्पृशन् । षड्भ्यः संजायते यस्मात्तस्मात्षड्ज इति स्मृतः ॥' इति । स च तन्त्रीकण्ठजन्मा स्वरविशेषः । 'निषादर्षभगान्धारषड्जमध्यमधैवताः । पञ्चमश्चेत्यमी सप्त तन्त्रीकण्ठोत्थिताः स्वराः ॥' इत्यमरः । षड्जेन संवादिनीः सदृशीः । तदुक्तं मातङ्गेन—'षड्जं मयूरो वदति' इति । **मनोभिरामाः** मनसः प्रियाः । के मूर्ध्नि कायन्ति ध्वनन्तीति केका मयूरवाण्यः । 'केका वाणी मयूरस्य' इत्यमरः । ताः **केकाः शृण्वन्तौ** । इति श्लोकार्थः ॥

परस्पराक्षिसादृश्यमदूरोज्झितवर्त्मसु ।
मृगद्वन्द्वेषु पश्यन्तौ स्यन्दनाबद्धदृष्टिषु ॥ ४० ॥

विश्रम्भाददूरं समीपं यथा भवति तथोज्झितं वर्त्म यैस्तेषु [**अदूरोज्झितवर्त्मसु**] **स्यन्दनाबद्धदृष्टिषु** स्यन्दने रथ आबद्धासञ्जिता दृष्टिर्नेत्रं यैस्तेषु । 'दृग्दृष्टिर्नेत्रलोचनचक्षुर्नयनाम्बुजेक्षणाक्षीणि ।' इति हलायुधः । कौतुकवशाद्रथासक्तदृष्टिष्वित्यर्थः । मृग्यश्च मृगाश्च मृगाः । 'पुमान्स्त्रिया' इत्येकशेषः । तेषां द्वन्द्वेषु मिथुनेषु [**मृगद्वन्द्वेषु**] 'स्त्रीपुंसौ मिथुनं द्वन्द्वम्' इत्यमरः । परस्पराक्ष्णां सादृश्यं [**परस्पराक्षिसादृश्यम्**] **पश्यन्तौ** । द्वन्द्वशब्दसामर्थ्यान्मृगीषु सुदक्षिणाक्षिसादृश्यं दिलीपो दिलीपाक्षिसादृश्यं च मृगेषु सुदक्षिणेत्येवं विवेक्तव्यम् ॥

श्रेणीबन्धाद्वितन्वद्भिरस्तम्भां तोरणस्रजम् ।
सारसैः कलनिर्ह्रादैः क्वचिदुन्नमिताननौ ॥ ४१ ॥

श्रेणीबन्धात् पङ्क्तिबन्धनाद्धेतोः **अस्तम्भाम्** आधारस्तम्भरहिताम् । तोरणं बहिर्द्वारम् । 'तोरणोऽस्त्री बहिर्द्वारम्' इत्यमरः । तत्र या स्रग्विरच्यते तां **तोरणस्रजं वितन्वद्भिः** । कुर्वद्भिरिवेत्यर्थः । उत्प्रेक्षाव्यञ्जकेवशब्दप्रयोगाभावेऽपि गम्योत्प्रेक्षेयम् । **कलनिर्ह्रादैः** अव्यक्तमधुरध्वनिभिः **सारसैः** पक्षिविशेषैः करणैः । **क्वचित् उन्नमिताननौ** । 'सारसो मैथुनी कामी गोनर्दः पुष्कराह्वयः ।' इति यादवः ॥

पवनस्यानुकूलत्वात्प्रार्थनासिद्धिशंसिनः ।
रजोभिस्तुरगोत्कीर्णैरस्पृष्टालकवेष्टनौ ॥ ४२ ॥

प्रार्थनासिद्धिशंसिनः अनुकूलत्वादेव मनोरथसिद्धिसूचकस्य **पवनस्यानुकूल-**

१ प्रार्थनायाः सिद्धिः तां शंसितुं शीलमस्य । "शुभगन्धे च शब्दे च सानुकूले च मारुते । प्रस्थाने सर्वकार्याणां सर्वसिद्धिर्ध्रुवं भवेत् ॥" इति पालकाप्ये ।

त्वात् गन्तव्यदिगभिमुखत्वात् । **तुरगोत्कीर्णैः रजोभिः** अस्पृष्टा अलका देव्या वेष्टनमुष्णीषं च राज्ञो ययोस्तौ तथोक्तौ [**अस्पृष्टालकवेष्टनौ**]। 'शिरसा वेष्टनशोभिना सुतः' (८ स० १२ श्लो०) इति वक्ष्यति ॥

सरसीष्वरविन्दानां वीचिविक्षोभशीतलम् ।
आमोदमुपजिघ्रन्तौ स्वनिःश्वासानुकारिणम् ॥ ४३ ॥

सरसीषु वीचिविक्षोभशीतलम् ऊर्मिसंघट्टनेन शीतलं स्वनिःश्वासमनुकर्तुं शीलमस्येति **स्वनिःश्वासानुकारिणम्** । एतेन तयोरुत्कृष्टस्त्रीपुंसजातीयत्वमुक्तम् । [1]**अरविन्दानाम् आमोदम् उपजिघ्रन्तौ** घ्राणेन गृह्णन्तौ ॥

ग्रामेष्वात्मविसृष्टेषु यूपचिह्नेषु यज्वनाम् ।
अमोघाः प्रतिगृह्णन्तावर्घ्यानुपदमाशिषः ॥ ४४ ॥

आत्मविसृष्टेषु स्वदत्तेषु । यूपो नाम संस्कृतः पशुबन्धाय दारुविशेषः । यूपा एव चिह्नानि येषां तेषु [**यूपचिह्नेषु**] **ग्रामेषु अमोघाः** सफलाः **यज्वनां** विधिनेष्टवताम् । 'यज्वा तु विधिनेष्टवान्' इत्यमरः । 'सुयजोर्ङ्वनिप्' इति ङ्वनिप्प्रत्ययः । **आशिषः** आशीर्वादान् । अर्घः पूजाविधिः । तदर्थं द्रव्यमर्घ्यम् । 'पादार्घाभ्यां च' इति यत्प्रत्ययः । 'षट् तु त्रिष्वर्घ्यमर्घार्थे पाद्यं पादाय वारिणि' इत्यमरः । अर्घ्यस्यानुपदमन्वक् [**अर्घ्यानुपदम्**] अर्घ्यस्वीकारानन्तरमित्यर्थः । **प्रतिगृह्णन्तौ** स्वीकुर्वन्तौ । पदस्य पश्चादनुपदम् । पश्चादर्थेऽव्ययीभावः । 'अन्वगन्वक्षमनुगेऽनुपदं क्लीबमव्ययम् ।' इत्यमरः ॥

हैयंगवीनमादाय घोषवृद्धानुपस्थितान् ।
नामधेयानि पृच्छन्तौ वन्यानां मार्गशाखिनाम् ॥ ४५ ॥

ह्यस्तनगोदोहोद्भवं घृतं **हैयंगवीनम्** । ह्यः पूर्वेद्युर्भवम् । 'तत्तु हैयंगवीनं यद्ध्योगोदोहोद्भवं घृतम् ।' इत्यमरः । 'हैयंगवीनं संज्ञायाम्' इति निपातः । तत्सद्योघृतं **आदाय उपस्थितान्घोषवृद्धान्** । 'घोष आभीरपल्ली स्यात्' इत्यमरः । **वन्यानां मार्गशाखिनां नामधेयानि पृच्छन्तौ** । 'दुह्याच्–' इत्यादिना पृच्छतेर्द्विकर्मकत्वम् । कुलकम् ॥

काऽप्यभिख्या तयोरासीद्व्रजतोः शुद्धवेषयोः ।
हिमनिर्मुक्तयोर्योगे चित्राचन्द्रमसोरिव ॥ ४६ ॥

व्रजतोः गच्छतोः **शुद्धवेषयोः** उज्ज्वलनेपथ्ययोः **तयोः** सुदक्षिणादिलीपयोः । **हिमनिर्मुक्तयोः चित्राचन्द्रमसोः इव योगे** सति **काऽपि** अनिर्वाच्या **अभिख्या** शोभा **आसीत्** । 'अभिख्या नामशोभयोः' इत्यमरः । 'आतश्चोपसर्गे' इत्यङ्प्रत्ययः । चित्रा नक्षत्रविशेषः । शिशिरापगमे चैत्र्यां चित्रापूर्णचन्द्रमसोरिवेत्यर्थः ॥

---

१ अरविन्दं–अरं शीघ्रं लिप्सां विन्दतीति । अरकाराणि दलानि तत्सादृश्याद् अराः तानि विन्दतीति वा । पा० ३. १. १३८. अस्य च अतिमनोहारिगन्धयात् मदनबाणता । तदुक्तं–अरविन्दमशोकं च चूतं च नवमल्लिका । नीलोत्पलं च पञ्चैते पञ्चबाणस्य सायकाः ॥ इति । २ हीनाधिकत्वं वचनलिङ्गभेदो विपर्ययः । असादृश्यासंभवौ च दोषाः सप्तोपमागताः ॥ इति प्राचीनसंमता उपमादोषाः । किं तु यत्र धीमतां नोद्वेगस्तत्रैते उपमां दूषयितुं नालं (का॰ द॰ २. ५१). नव्यास्तु कालपुरुषविध्यादिभेदस्यापि उपमादूषकतामाहुः । तेनात्र चित्राचन्द्रमसोरभिख्या न खलु आसीत् अपि तु सर्वदा भवत्येव, सुदक्षिणादिलीपयोस्तु तादृशी शोभा आसीदिति उपमानोपमेययोः कालभेदात् भग्नप्रक्रमत्वं नाम दोषः । कवयस्तावत्कालादीनां दूषकत्वं स्फुटं प्रतीयमानमपि प्रायः न गणयन्ति ।

तत्तद्भूमिपतिः पत्न्यै दर्शयन्प्रियदर्शनः ।
अपि लङ्घितमध्वानं बुबुधे न बुधोपमः ॥ ४७ ॥

प्रियं दर्शनं स्वकर्मकं यस्यासौ **प्रियदर्शनः** योग्यदर्शनीय इत्यर्थः । **भूमिपतिः पत्न्यै तत्तद्** अद्भुतं वस्तु **दर्शयन् लङ्घितं** अतिवाहितं **अपि अध्वानं न बुबुधे** न ज्ञातवान् । [**बुधोपमः**] सन् बुधः सौम्य उपमोपमानं यस्येति विग्रहः । इदं विशेषणं तत्तद्दर्शयन्नित्युपयोगितयैवास्य ज्ञातृत्वसूचनार्थम् ॥

स दुष्प्रापयशाः प्रापदाश्रमं श्रान्तवाहनः ।
सायं संयमिनस्तस्य महर्षेर्महिषीसखः ॥ ४८ ॥

दुष्प्रापयशाः दुष्प्रापमन्यदुर्लभं यशो यस्य स तथोक्तः । **श्रान्तवाहनो** दूरोपगमनात्क्लान्तयुग्यः । महिष्याः सखा **महिषीसखः** । 'राजाहःसखिभ्यष्टच्' इति टच्प्रत्ययः । सहायान्तरानिरपेक्ष इति भावः । **स** राजा । **सायं** सायंकाले **संयमिनः** नियमवतः **तस्य महर्षेः** वसिष्ठस्य **आश्रमं प्रापत्** प्राप । पुषादित्वादङ् ॥

तमाश्रमं विशिनष्टि—

वनान्तरादुपावृत्तैः समित्कुशफलाहरैः ।
पूर्यमाणमदृश्याग्निप्रत्युद्यातैस्तपस्विभिः ॥ ४९ ॥

वनान्तरात् अन्यस्माद्वनात् **उपावृत्तैः** प्रत्यावृत्तैः । समिधश्च कुशांश्च फलानि चाहर्तुं शीलं येषामिति समित्कुशफलाहराः तैः [**समित्कुशफलाहरैः**] । 'आङि ताच्छील्ये' इति हरतेराङ्पूर्वादच्प्रत्ययः । अदृश्यैर्दर्शनायोग्यैरग्निभिर्वैतानिकैः प्रत्युद्याताः प्रत्युद्गताः तैः [**अदृश्याग्निप्रत्युद्यातैः**] **तपस्विभिः पूर्यमाणम्** । 'प्रोष्यागच्छतामाहिताग्नीनामग्नयः प्रत्युद्यान्ति' इति श्रुतेः । यथाह—'कामं पितरं प्रोषितवन्तं पुत्राः प्रत्याधावन्ति । एवमेत(एवं ह वैत-) मग्नयः प्रत्याधावन्ति सशकलान्दारूनिवाहरन् ।' इति ॥

आकीर्णमृषिपत्नीनामुटजद्वाररोधिभिः ।
अपत्यैरिव नीवारभागधेयोचितैर्मृगैः ॥ ५० ॥

नीवाराणां भाग एव भागधेयोंऽशः । 'रूपनामभागेभ्यो धेयः' इति वक्तव्यसूत्रात्स्वाभिधेये धेयप्रत्ययः । तस्योचितैः । [**नीवारभागधेयोचितैः**] । अत एवोटजानां पर्णशालानां द्वाररोधिभिः [**उटजद्वाररोधिभिः**] द्वाररोधकैः **मृगैः** । **ऋषिपत्नीनाम् अपत्यैः इव** । **आकीर्णं** व्याप्तम् ॥

---

१ प्रियं दर्शनं दर्शनीयचक्षुर्जातं यस्य इति । वस्तूनां दर्शनं स्वकर्तृकं यस्य इति वा । 'प्रियदर्शनः अपूर्ववस्तुद्रष्टा बुधश्चन्द्रपुत्रो ग्रहस्तेन तुल्योऽपि न बुबुधे इति विरोधाभासोऽलंकारः' इ० चारित्रवर्धनः । २ संयमः अस्यास्तीति संयमी तस्य । ध्यानधारणासमाधित्रयं संयमपदवाच्यम् इति सर्वदर्शनसं० । ३ अत्र अनुप्रासालंकारः । ४ 'स्कन्धासक्तसमित्कुशैः' इ० पा. ५ अस्मात् श्लोकात्परं " **आकीर्यमाणमासन्नविधिभिः समिदाहरैः । वैखानसैरदृश्याग्निप्रत्युद्गमनवृत्तिभिः ॥** " इत्यतिरिक्तं श्लोकं केचित्पठन्ति । ६ उटेभ्यः तृणपर्णादिभ्यः जायते इति उटजः । ७ अपत्यैः—न पतन्ति पितरोऽनेन इति अपत्यम् । तथा च यास्कः-अपत्यं कस्मात्, अपततं भवति पितुः सकाशादित्य पृथक्ततं भवति, अनेन जातेन सता पिता नरकं न पततीति वा ।

सेकान्ते मुनिकन्याभिस्तत्क्षणोज्झितवृक्षकम् ।
विश्वासाय विहङ्गानामालवालाम्बुपायिनाम् ॥ ५१ ॥

सेकान्ते वृक्षमूलसेचनावसाने **मुनिकन्याभिः** । सेक्त्रीभिः । आलवालेषु जलावापप्रदेशेषु यदम्बु तत्पायिनाम् [**आलवालाम्बुपायिनाम्**] । 'स्यादालवालमावालमावापः' इत्यमरः । **विहङ्गानां** पक्षिणां **विश्वासाय** विश्रम्भाय । 'समौ विश्वासविश्रम्भौ' इत्यमरः । तत्क्षणं सेकक्षण उज्झिता वृक्षका ह्रस्ववृक्षा यस्मिंस्तम् [**तत्क्षणोज्झितवृक्षकम्**] । ह्रस्वार्थे कप्रत्ययः ॥

आतपात्ययसंक्षिप्तनीवारासु निषादिभिः ।
मृगैर्वर्तितरोमन्थमुटजाङ्गनभूमिषु ॥ ५२ ॥

आतपस्यात्ययेऽपगमे सति संक्षिप्ता राशीकृता नीवारास्तृणधान्यानि यासु तासु [**आतपात्ययसंक्षिप्तनीवारासु**] । 'नीवारास्तृणधान्यानि' इत्यमरः । उटजानां पर्णशालानामङ्गनभूमिषु चत्वरभागेषु [**उटजाङ्गनभूमिषु**] । 'पर्णशालोटजोऽस्त्रियाम्' इति, 'अङ्गनं चत्वराजिरे' इति चामरः । **निषादिभिः** उपविष्टैः **मृगैः** वर्तितो निष्पादितो रोमन्थश्चर्वितचर्वणं यस्मिन्नाश्रमे तम् [**वर्तितरोमन्थम्**] ॥

अभ्युत्थिताग्निपिशुनैरतिथीनाश्रमोन्मुखान् ।
पुनानं पवनोद्धूतैर्धूमैराहुतिगन्धिभिः ॥ ५३ ॥

अभ्युत्थिताः प्रज्वलिताः । होमयोग्या इत्यर्थः । 'समिद्धेऽग्नावाहुतीर्जुहोति' इति वचनात् । तेषामग्नीनां पिशुनैः सूचकैः [**अभ्युत्थिताग्निपिशुनैः** ।] **पवनोद्धूतैः** । आहुतिगन्धो येषामस्तीत्याहुतिगन्धिनः तैः [**आहुतिगन्धिभिः**] **धूमैः आश्रमोन्मुखान् अतिथीन्** **पुनानं** पवित्रीकुर्वाणम् । कुलकम् ॥

अथ यन्तारमादिश्य धुर्यान्विश्रामयेति सः ।
तामवारोहयत्पत्नीं रथादवततार च ॥ ५४ ॥

अथ आश्रमप्राप्त्यनन्तरं **स** राजा **यन्तारं** सारथिम् । धुरं वहन्तीति धुर्या युग्याः । 'धुरो यड्ढकौ' इति यत्प्रत्ययः । 'धूर्वहे धुर्यधौरेयधुरीणाः सधुरंधराः' इत्यमरः । **धुर्यान्** रथाश्वान् **विश्रामय** विनीतश्रमान्कुरु **इति आदिश्य** आज्ञाप्य **तां पत्नीं रथाद् अवारोहयद्** अवतारितवान्स्वयं **च अवततार** । 'विश्रमय' इति ह्रस्वपाठे 'जनीजॄष्-' इति मित्त्वे 'मितां ह्रस्वः' इति ह्रस्वः । दीर्घपाठे 'मितां ह्रस्वः' इति सूत्रे 'वा चित्तविरागे' इत्यतो 'वा' इत्यनुवर्त्य व्यवस्थितविभाषाश्रयणत्वाद्ध्रस्वाभाव इति वृत्तिकारः ॥

तस्मै सभ्याः सभार्याय गोप्त्रे गुप्ततमेन्द्रियाः ।
अर्हणामर्हते चक्रुर्मुनयो नयचक्षुषे ॥ ५५ ॥

सभायां साधवः **सभ्याः** । 'सभाया यः' इति यप्रत्ययः । **गुप्ततमेन्द्रियाः**

---

१ आ समन्तात् लवं जललवं आलाति गृह्णातीति आलवालम् । २ अतति गच्छतीति अतिथिः । 'ऋतन्यञ्जि-' (उ० ४. २) इति इथिन् । यद्वा न विद्यते द्वितीया तिथिः यस्य एकत्र एकरात्रमेवावस्थानात् इति अतिथिः । तथा च मनुः—एकरात्रं तु निवसन्नतिथिर्ब्राह्मणः स्मृतः । अनित्यं हि स्थितो यस्मात्तस्मादतिथिरुच्यते ॥ अ० ३. १०२.

अत्यन्तनियमितेन्द्रियाः **मुनयः सभार्याय गोप्त्रे** रक्षकाय। नयः शास्त्रमेव चक्षुस्तत्त्वावेदकं प्रमाणं यस्य तस्मै **नयचक्षुषे**। अत एव **अर्हते** प्रशस्ताय। पूज्यायेत्यर्थः। 'अर्हः प्रशंसायाम्' इति शतृप्रत्ययः। **तस्मै** राज्ञे **अर्हणां** पूजां **चक्रुः**। 'पूजा नमस्यापचितिः सपर्यार्चार्हणाः समाः।' इत्यमरः॥

विधेः सायंतनस्यान्ते स ददर्श तपोनिधिम्।
अन्वासितमरुन्धत्या स्वाहयेव हविर्भुजम्॥ ५६॥

स राजा **सायंतनस्य** सायंभवस्य। 'सायंचिरम्–' इत्यादिना ट्युल्प्रत्ययः। **विधेः** जपहोमाद्यनुष्ठानस्य **अन्ते** अवसाने **अरुन्धत्या अन्वासितं** पश्चादुपवेशनेनोपसेवितम्। कर्मणि क्तः। उपसर्गवशात्सकर्मकत्वम्। 'अन्वास्यैनाम्' इत्यादिवदुपपद्यते। **तपोनिधिं** वसिष्ठम्। **स्वाहया** स्वाहादेव्या। 'अथाग्नायी स्वाहा च हुतभुक्प्रिया' इत्यमरः। अन्वासितं **हविर्भुजमिव ददर्श**। 'समित्पुष्पकुशाग्न्यम्बुमृदन्नाक्षतपाणिकः। जपं होमं च कुर्वाणो नाभिवाद्यो द्विजो भवेत्॥' इत्यनुष्ठानस्य मध्येऽभिवादननिषेधाद्विधेरन्ते ददर्शेत्युक्तम्। अन्वासनं चात्र पतिव्रताधर्मत्वेनोक्तम्; न तु कर्माङ्गत्वेन। विधेरन्त इति कर्मणः समाप्त्यभिधानात्॥

तयोर्जगृहतुः पादान्राजा राज्ञी च मागधी।
तौ गुरुर्गुरुपत्नी च प्रीत्या प्रतिननन्दतुः॥ ५७॥

मागधी मगधराजपुत्री **राज्ञी** सुदक्षिणा **राजा च तयोः** अरुन्धतीवसिष्ठयोः **पादान् जगृहतुः**। 'पादः पदाङ्घ्रिश्चरणोऽस्त्रियाम्' इत्यमरः। पादग्रहणमभिवादनम्। **गुरुपत्नी गुरुश्च** कर्तारौ। सा च स च **तौ** सुदक्षिणादिलीपौ कर्मभूतौ। **प्रीत्या** हर्षेण **प्रतिननन्दतुः**। आशीर्वादादिभिः संभावयांचक्रतुरित्यर्थः॥

तमातिथ्यक्रियाशान्तरथक्षोभपरिश्रमम्।
पप्रच्छ कुशलं राज्ये राज्याश्रममुनिं मुनिः॥ ५८॥

मुनिः। अतिथ्यर्थमातिथ्यम्। 'अतिथेर्ञ्यः' इति ञ्यप्रत्ययः। आतिथ्यस्य क्रिया। तया शान्तो रथक्षोभेण यः परिश्रमः स यस्य स तं तथोक्तम् [**आतिथ्यक्रियाशान्तरथक्षोभपरिश्रमम्**]। राज्यमेवाश्रमस्तत्र मुनिम् [**राज्याश्रममुनिम्**]। मुनितुल्यमित्यर्थः। **तं** दिलीपं **राज्ये कुशलं पप्रच्छ**। पृच्छतस्तु द्विकर्मकत्वमुक्तम्। यद्यपि राज्यशब्दः पुरोहितादिष्वन्तर्गतत्वाद्राजकर्मवचनः तथाप्यत्र सप्ताङ्गवचनः। 'उपपन्नं ननु शिवं सप्तस्वङ्गेषु' (१।६०) इत्युत्तरविरोधात्। तथाह मनुः–'स्वाम्यमात्यपुरं राष्ट्रं कोशदण्डौ तथा सुहृत्। सप्तैतानि समस्तानि लोकेऽस्मिन्राज्यमुच्यते॥' इति। तत्र 'ब्राह्मणं कुशलं पृच्छेत्क्षत्रबन्धुमनामयम्। वैश्यं क्षेमं

---

१ पादानित्यत्र 'पादौ' इति चारित्रवर्धनः पठति व्याचष्टे च–ननु पादानिति वक्तव्ये पादाविति कथं द्विवचनप्रयोगः। पादजातेर्द्वित्वविवक्षितत्वात्। स्त्रीणां चक्षुरित्यादिवन्न दोषः। उक्तं च वामनेन "स्तनादीनां द्वित्वविशिष्टा जातिः प्रायेण।" इति। यथा माघे 'स्तनौ दधानास्तरुण्यः' इति। मागधीपदेन विशिष्टवंशत्वं लभ्यते। तेन च गुरुजनचरणप्रणामौचित्यं द्योत्यते। ननु कथं राजा राज्ञीत्यादीनामेकवचनानां जगृहतुः प्रतिननन्दतुः इति द्विवचनक्रियाभिः संबन्धः। 'द्वयोर्नाम्नोर्बहूनां वा यदि वाक्यं समुच्चये। अङ्गवच्चाश्रिता संख्या पदादौ वा विशेषतः॥' इति विकल्पविधानान्न दोषः इति।

समागम्य शूद्रमारोग्यमेव च ॥' इति मनुवचने सत्यपि तस्य राज्ञो महानुभावत्वाद्ब्राह्मणोचितः कुशलप्रश्न एव कृत इत्यनुसंधेयम् । अत एवोक्तम् 'राज्याश्रममुनिम्' इति ॥

अथाथर्वनिधेस्तस्य विजितारिपुरः पुरः ।
अर्थ्यामर्थपतिर्वाचमाददे वदतां वरः ॥ ५९ ॥

अथ प्रश्नानन्तरं **विजितारिपुरः** विजितशत्रुनगरः **वदतां** वक्तॄणां **वरः** श्रेष्ठः । 'यतश्च निर्धारणम्' इति षष्ठी । **अर्थपतिः** राजाथर्वणोऽथर्ववेदस्य निधिः [**अथर्वनिधेः**] **तस्य** मुनेः **पुरः** अग्रे **अर्थ्याम्** अर्थादनपेताम् । 'धर्मपथ्यर्थन्यायादनपेते' इति यत्प्रत्ययः । **वाचमाददे** । वक्तुमुपक्रान्तवानित्यर्थः । अथर्वनिधेरित्यनेन पुरोहितकृत्याभिज्ञत्वात्तत्कर्मनिर्वाहकत्वं मुनेरस्तीति सूच्यते । यथाह कामन्दकः—'त्रय्यां च दण्डनीत्यां च कुशलः स्यात्पुरोहितः । अथर्वविहितं कुर्यान्नित्यं शान्तिकपौष्टिकम् ॥' इति[1] ॥

उपपन्नं ननु शिवं सप्तस्वङ्गेषु यस्य मे ।
दैवीनां मानुषीणां च प्रतिहर्ता त्वमापदाम् ॥ ६० ॥

हे गुरो । **सप्तसु अङ्गेषु** स्वाम्यमात्यादिषु । 'स्वाम्यमात्यसुहृत्कोशराष्ट्रदुर्गबलानि च । सप्ताङ्गानि' इत्यमरः । **शिवं** कुशलं **उपपन्नं ननु** युक्तमेव । नन्ववधारणे । 'प्रश्नावधारणानुज्ञानुनयामन्त्रणे ननु ।' इत्यमरः । कथमित्यत्राह । **यस्य मे दैवीनां** देवेभ्य आगतानां दुर्भिक्षादीनाम् **मानुषीणां** मनुष्येभ्य आगतानां चौरभयादीनाम् [**च**] । उभयत्रापि 'तत आगतः' इत्यण् । 'टिड्ढाणञ्–' इत्यादिना ङीप् । **आपदां** व्यसनानां **त्वं प्रतिहर्ता** वारयितासि । अत्राह कामन्दकः—'हुताशनो जलं व्याधिर्दुर्भिक्षं मरणं तथा । इति पञ्चविधं दैवं मानुषं व्यसनं ततः ॥ आयुक्तकेभ्यश्चौरेभ्यः परेभ्यो राजवल्लभात् । पृथिवीपतिलोभाच्च नराणां पञ्चधा मतम् ॥' इति ॥

तव मन्त्रकृतो मन्त्रैर्दूरात्प्रशमितारिभिः ।
प्रत्यादिश्यन्त इव मे दृष्टलक्ष्यभिदः शराः ॥ ६१ ॥

दूरात् परोक्ष एव **प्रशमितारिभिः** । मन्त्रान्कृतवान्मन्त्रकृत् । 'सुकर्मपापमन्त्रपुण्येषु कृञः' इति क्विप् । तस्य **मन्त्रकृतो** मन्त्राणां स्रष्टुः प्रयोक्तुर्वा **तव मन्त्रैः** कर्तृभिः दृष्टं प्रत्यक्षं यल्लक्ष्यं तन्मात्रं भिन्दन्तीति **दृष्टलक्ष्यभिदः मे शराः प्रत्यादिश्यन्त इव** । वयमेव समर्थाः किमेभिः पिष्टपेषकैरिति निराक्रियन्त इवेत्युत्प्रेक्षा । 'प्रत्यादेशो निराकृतिः' इत्यमरः । त्वन्मन्त्रसामर्थ्यादेव नः पौरुषं फलतीति भावः ॥

संप्रति दैविकापत्प्रतीकारमाह—

हविरावर्जितं होतस्त्वया विधिवदग्निषु ।
वृष्टिर्भवति सस्यानामवग्रहविशोषिणाम् ॥ ६२ ॥

हे होतः त्वया विधिवत् अग्निषु आवर्जितं प्रक्षिप्तं **हविः** आज्यादिकं कर्तृ । अवग्रहो वर्षप्रतिबन्धः । 'अवे ग्रहो वर्षप्रतिबन्धे' इत्यप्प्रत्ययः । 'वृष्टिर्वर्षं तद्विघातेऽवग्राहावग्रहौ समौ ।' इत्यमरः । तेन विशोषिणां **विशुष्यतां** [**अवग्रहविशो-**

---

१ पुरोहितं च कुर्वीत दैवज्ञमुदितोदितम् । दण्डनीत्यां च कुशलमथर्वाङ्गिरसे तथा ॥ इति मिताक्षरायाम् । आचा. १३. ५.

षिणाम्] **सस्यानां वृष्टिर्भवति** । वृष्टिरूपेण सस्यानुपजीवयतीति भावः । अत्र मनुः—' अग्नौ दत्ताहुतिः सम्यगादित्यमुपतिष्ठते । आदित्याज्जायते वृष्टिर्वृष्टेरन्नं ततः प्रजाः ' इति ॥

पुरुषायुषजीविन्यो निरातङ्का निरीतयः ।
यन्मदीयाः प्रजास्तस्य हेतुस्त्वद्ब्रह्मवर्चसम् ॥ ६३ ॥

आयुर्जीवितकालः । पुरुषस्यायुः पुरुषायुषम् । वर्षशतमित्यर्थः । ' शतायुर्वै पुरुषः ' इति श्रुतेः । ' अचतुर– ' आदिसूत्रेणाच्प्रत्ययान्तो निपातः । **मदीयाः प्रजाः** । पुरुषायुषं जीवन्तीति **पुरुषायुषजीविन्यः** । **निरातङ्काः** निर्भयाः । ' आतङ्को भयमाशङ्का ' इति हलायुधः । **निरीतयः** अतिवृष्ट्यादिरहिता इति **यत् तस्य** सर्वस्य **त्वद्ब्रह्मवर्चसं** तव व्रताध्ययनसंपत्तिरेव **हेतुः** । ' व्रताध्ययनसंपत्तिरित्येतद्ब्रह्मवर्चसम् । ' इति हलायुधः । ब्रह्मणो वर्चो ब्रह्मवर्चसम् । ' ब्रह्महस्तिभ्यां वर्चसः ' इत्यच्प्रत्ययः । ' अतिवृष्टिरनावृष्टिर्मूषिकाः शलभाः शुकाः । अत्यासन्नाश्च राजानः षडेता ईतयः स्मृताः ॥ ' इति कामन्दकः ॥

त्वयैवं चिन्त्यमानस्य गुरुणा ब्रह्मयोनिना ।
सानुबन्धाः कथं न स्युः संपदो मे निरापदः ॥ ६४ ॥

ब्रह्मा योनिः कारणं यस्य तेन [**ब्रह्मयोनिना**] ब्रह्मपुत्रेण[1] **गुरुणा त्वया एवम्** उक्तप्रकारेण **चिन्त्यमानस्य** अनुध्यायमानस्य । अत एव **निरापदः**[2] व्यसनहीनस्य **मे संपदः सानुबन्धाः** सानुस्यूतयः । अविच्छिन्ना इति यावत् । **कथं न स्युः** । स्युरेवेत्यर्थः ॥

संप्रत्यागमनप्रयोजनमाह—

किं तु वध्वां तवैतस्यामदृष्टसदृशप्रजम् ।
न मामवति सद्वीपा रत्नसूरपि मेदिनी ॥ ६५ ॥

किं तु तव एतस्यां वध्वां स्नुषायाम् । ' वधूर्जाया स्नुषा चैव ' इत्यमरः । अदृष्टा सदृश्यनुरूपा प्रजा येन तं [**अदृष्टसदृशप्रजम्**] **मां सद्वीपा** अपि । रत्नानि सूयत इति **रत्नसूः अपि** । ' सत्सूद्विष– ' इत्यादिना क्विप् । **मेदिनी न अवति** न प्रीणाति । अवधातू रक्षणगतिप्रीत्याद्यर्थेषूपदेशादत्र प्रीणने । रत्नसूरपीत्यनेन सर्वरत्नेभ्यः पुत्ररत्नमेव श्लाघ्यमिति सूचितम् ॥

तदेव प्रतिपादयति—

नूनं मत्तः परं वंश्याः पिण्डविच्छेददर्शिनः ।
न प्रकामभुजः श्राद्धे स्वधासंग्रहतत्पराः ॥ ६६ ॥

मत्तः परं मदनन्तरम् । ' पञ्चम्यास्तसिल् ' । **पिण्डविच्छेददर्शिनः** पिण्डदानविच्छेदमुत्प्रेक्षमाणाः वंशोद्भवा **वंश्याः** पितरः । स्वधेत्यव्ययं पितृभोज्ये वर्तते ।

---

१ ब्रह्मणः मानसपुत्रेण इत्यर्थः । तथा च मत्स्यपुराणे—मरीचिरभवत्पूर्वं ततोऽत्रिर्भगवानृषिः । अङ्गिराश्चाभवत्पश्चात्पुलस्त्यस्तदनन्तरम् ॥ ततः पुलहनामा वै ततः क्रतुरजायत । प्रचेताश्च ततः पुत्रो वसिष्ठश्चाभवत्पुनः ॥ पुत्रो भृगुरभूत्तत्र नारदोऽपि चिरादभूत् । दशेमान्मानसान्ब्रह्मा जपन्पुत्रानजीजनत् ॥ इति । २ निर्गता आपदः याभ्यः इति ' संपदः ' इत्यस्य विशेषणं वा ।

तस्याः संग्रहे तत्पराः आसक्ताः [**स्वधासंग्रहतत्पराः**] सन्तः **श्राद्धं** पितृकर्माणि । 'पितृदानं निवापः स्याच्छ्राद्धं तत्कर्म शास्त्रतः ।' इत्यमरः । **प्रकामभुजः**[१] पर्याप्तभोजिनः **न** भवन्ति **नूनं** सत्यम् । 'कामं प्रकामं पर्याप्तम्' इत्यमरः । निर्धना ह्यापद्धनं कियदपि संगृह्णन्तीति भावः ॥

मत्परं दुर्लभं मत्वा नूनमावर्जितं मया ।
पयः पूर्वैः स्वनिःश्वासैः कवोष्णमुपभुज्यते ॥ ६७ ॥

मत्परं मदनन्तरम् । 'अन्यारात्—' इत्यादिना पञ्चमी । **दुर्लभं** दुर्लभ्यं **मत्वा मया आवर्जितं** दत्तं **पयः पूर्वैः** पितृभिः **स्वनिःश्वासैः** दुःखजैः **कवोष्णम्** ईषदुष्णं यथा तथा **उपभुज्यते**[२] । **नूनम्** इति तर्के । कवोष्णमिति कुशब्दस्य कवादेशः । 'कोष्णं कवोष्णं मन्दोष्णं कदुष्णं त्रिषु तद्वति ।' इत्यमरः ॥

सोऽहमिज्याविशुद्धात्मा प्रजालोपनिमीलितः ।
प्रकाशश्चाप्रकाशश्च लोकालोक इवाचलः ॥ ६८ ॥

इज्या यागः । 'व्रजयजोर्भावे क्यप्' इति क्यप्प्रत्ययः । तया विशुद्धात्मा विशुद्धचेतनः [**इज्याविशुद्धात्मा**] प्रजालोपेन संतत्यभावेन निमीलितः कृतनिमीलनः । [**प्रजालोपनिमीलितः**] **सोऽहम्** । लोक्यत इति लोकः न लोक्यत इत्यलोकः । लोकश्चालोकश्चात्र स्त इति लोकश्चासावलोकश्चेति वा **लोकालोकः** चक्रवालः **अचलः इव** । 'लोकालोकश्चक्रवालः' इत्यमरः । प्रकाशत इति **प्रकाशश्च** देवर्णविमोचनात्[३] । न प्रकाशत इति **अप्रकाशश्च** पितृणामविमोचनात् । पचाद्यच् । अस्मीति शेषः । लोकालोको[४]ऽप्यन्तः सूर्यसंपर्काद्बहिस्तमोव्याप्त्या च प्रकाशश्चाप्रकाशश्चेति मन्तव्यम् ॥

ननु तपोदानादिसंपन्नस्य किमपत्यैरित्यत्राह—

लोकान्तरसुखं पुण्यं तपोदानसमुद्भवम् ।
संततिः शुद्धवंश्या हि परत्रेह च शर्मणे ॥ ६९ ॥

समुद्भवत्यस्मादिति समुद्भवः कारणम् । तपोदाने समुद्भवो यस्य तत् **तपोदानसमुद्भवं** यत् **पुण्यं** तल्लोकान्तरे परलोके सुखं सुखकरम् [**लोकान्तरसुखम्**] । शुद्धवंशे भवा **शुद्धवंश्या संततिः हि परत्र** परलोके **इह च** लोके **शर्मणे** सुखाय । 'शर्मशातसुखानि च' इत्यमरः । भवतीति शेषः ॥

तया हीनं विधातर्मां कथं पश्यन्न दूयसे ।
सिक्तं स्वयमिव स्नेहाद्वन्ध्यमाश्रमवृक्षकम् ॥ ७० ॥

विधातः स्रष्टः । **तया** संतत्या **हीनम्** अनपत्यं **माम्** । **स्नेहात्** प्रेम्णा

१ प्रकामभुजः—प्रकामं यथा तथा भुञ्जते इति । २ दिलीपानन्तरं पयो न प्राप्स्याम इति शोकावेशात् निर्गच्छद्भिः निःश्वासैः ईषदुष्णं पितरः स्वीकुर्वते इति तात्पर्यार्थः इति चारित्रवर्धनः । अस्य समानार्थः श्लोकः शाकुन्तले–अस्मात्परं बत यथाश्रुति संभृतानि को नः कुले निवपनानि नियच्छतीति । नूनं प्रसूतिविकलेन मया प्रसिक्तं धौताश्रुसेकमुदकं पितरः पिबन्ति ॥ ३ देवानां ऋणविमोचनात् यागादिक्रियया इत्य० । ४ स्वादूदकस्य परतो लोकालोकाचलो महान् । लोकस्य चाप्यलोकस्य मध्ये गिरिरवस्थितः ॥ प्राकार इव संवेष्ट्य लोकान्सर्वान् महामते । लोकालोकाचलो नाम तेनासौ परिकीर्तितः ॥ इति पद्मपुराणे ।

स्वयम् एव सिक्तं जलसेकेन वर्धितं **वन्ध्यम्** अफलम् । 'वन्ध्योऽफलोऽवकेशी च' इत्यमरः । आश्रमस्य वृक्षकं [**आश्रमवृक्षकम्**] वृक्षपोतम् **इव । पश्यन् कथं न दूयसे** न परितप्यसे । विधातरित्यनेन समर्थोऽप्युपेक्षस इति गम्यते ॥

असह्यपीडं भगवन्नृणमन्त्यमवेहि मे ।
अरुंतुदमिवालानमनिर्वाणस्य दन्तिनः ॥ ७१ ॥

हे भगवन् । मे मम **अन्त्यमृणं** पैतृकमृणम् । **अनिर्वाणस्य** मज्जनरहितस्य । 'निर्वाणं निर्वृतौ मोक्षे विनाशे गजमज्जने ।' इति यादवः । **दन्तिनः** गजस्य । अरुर्मर्म तुदतीति **अरुंतुदं** मर्मस्पृक् । 'व्रणोऽस्त्रियामीर्ममरुः' इति, 'अरुंतुदस्तु मर्मस्पृक्' इति चामरः । 'विध्वरुषोस्तुदः' इति खश्प्रत्ययः । 'अरुर्द्विषत्–' इत्यादिना मुमागमः । **आलानं** बन्धनस्तम्भः **इव** । 'आलानं बन्धनस्तम्भे' इत्यमरः । असह्या सोढुमशक्या पीडा दुःखं यस्मिंस्तत् [**असह्यपीडम्**] **अवेहि** । दुःसहदुःखजनकं विद्धीत्यर्थः । 'निर्वाणोत्थानशयनानि त्रीणि गजकर्माणि' इति पालकाप्ये । 'ऋणं देवस्य यागेन ऋषीणां दान [पाठ] कर्मणा । संतत्या पितृलोकानां शोधयित्वा परिव्रजेत्' ॥

तस्मान्मुच्ये यथा तात संविधातुं तथाऽर्हसि ।
इक्ष्वाकूणां दुरापेऽर्थे त्वदधीना हि सिद्धयः ॥ ७२ ॥

हे **तात तस्मात्** पैतृकादृणाद् **यथा मुच्ये** मुक्तो भवामि । कर्मणि लट् । **तथा संविधातुं** कर्तुम् **अर्हसि । हि** यस्मात्कारणाद् **इक्ष्वाकूणाम्** इक्ष्वाकुवंश्यानाम् । तद्राजत्वाद्बहुष्वणो लुक् । **दुरापे** दुष्प्राप्ये **अर्थे सिद्धयः त्वदधीनाः** त्वदायत्ताः । इक्ष्वाकूणामिति शेषे षष्ठी[2] । 'न लोक–' इत्यादिना कृद्योगे षष्ठीनिषेधात् ॥

इति विज्ञापितो राज्ञा ध्यानस्तिमितलोचनः ।
क्षणमात्रमृषिस्तस्थौ सुप्तमीन इव ह्रदः ॥ ७३ ॥

इति राज्ञा विज्ञापितः ऋषिः ध्यानेन स्तिमिते लोचने यस्य **ध्यानस्तिमितलोचनः** निश्चलाक्षः सन् **क्षणमात्रम् । सुप्तमीनः**[3] **ह्रदः इव तस्थौ** ॥

सोऽपश्यत्प्रणिधानेन संततेः स्तम्भकारणम् ।
भावितात्मा भुवो भर्तुरथैनं प्रत्यबोधयत् ॥ ७४ ॥

स मुनिः **प्रणिधानेन** चित्तैकाग्र्येण **भावितात्मा** शुद्धान्तःकरणो **भुवो भर्तुः** नृपस्य **संततेः स्तम्भकारणं** संतानप्रतिबन्धकारणं **अपश्यत् । अथ** अनन्तरम् **एनं** नृपं **प्रत्यबोधयत्** । स्वदृष्टं ज्ञापितवानित्यर्थः । एनमिति 'गतिबुद्धि–' इत्यादिनाणि कर्तुः कर्मत्वम् ॥

---

१ एष वा अनृणो यः पुत्री यज्वा ब्रह्मचारी वा । इति श्रुतेः । २ अत्र षष्ठीविषये चारित्रवर्धनः– कथं कर्तरि षष्ठी । 'आक्षिपन्त्यरविन्दानि मुग्धे तव मुखश्रियम् । कोषदण्डसमग्राणां किमेषामस्ति दुष्करम् ॥' इत्यादावालंकारिकैरादृतत्वान्न दोषः । यदाह भोजः–इदं हि शास्त्रमाहात्म्यदर्शनालसचेतसाम् । अपशब्दवदाभाति न च सौभाग्यमुज्झति ॥ इति. ३ सुप्ताः निष्पन्दत्वेनावस्थिता इत्यर्थः मत्स्याः मीनाः जलजन्तव इति यावत् यस्मिन् सः । अत्र "सुप्तमीनः" इति शब्देन सर्वेषामेव जलजन्तूनां निश्चेष्टत्वं, "स्तिमितलोचनः" इत्यनेन सर्वेषामेव बहिरिन्द्रियाणां वृत्तिनिरोधः गम्यते ।

पुरा शक्रमुपस्थाय तवोर्वीं प्रतियास्यतः ।
आसीत्कल्पतरुच्छायामाश्रिता सुरभिः पथि ॥ ७५ ॥

पुरा पूर्वं **शक्रम्** इन्द्रं **उपस्थाय** संसेव्य **उर्वीं प्रति** भुवमुद्दिश्य **यास्यतः** गमिष्यतः **तव पथि कल्पतरुच्छायां आश्रिता सुरभिः** कामधेनुः **आसीत्** । तत्र स्थितेत्यर्थः ॥

ततः किमित्याह—

धर्मलोपभयाद्राज्ञीमृतुस्नातामिमां स्मरन् ।
प्रदक्षिणक्रियार्हायां तस्यां त्वं साधु नाचरः ॥ ७६ ॥

ऋतुः पुष्पम् । रज इति यावत् । ' ऋतुः स्त्रीकुसुमेऽपि च ' इत्यमरः । ऋतुना निमित्तेन स्नातां [**ऋतुस्नातां**] **इमां राज्ञीं** सुदक्षिणां धर्मस्यात्वभिगमनलक्षणस्य लोपाद् भ्रंशाद्भयं तस्मात् [**धर्मलोपभयात्**] **स्मरन्** ध्यायन् । ' मृदङ्गं दैवतं विप्रं घृतं मधु चतुष्पथम् । प्रदक्षिणानि कुर्वीत विज्ञातांश्च वनस्पतीन् ॥ ' इति शास्त्रात् **प्रदक्षिणक्रियार्हायां** प्रदक्षिणकरणयोग्यायां **तस्यां** धेन्वां **त्वं साधु** प्रदक्षिणादिसत्कारं **न आचरः** नाचरितवानसि । व्यासक्ता हि विस्मरन्तीति भावः । ऋतुकालाभिगमने मनुः—' ऋतुकालाभिगामी स्यात्स्वदारनिरतः सदा । ' इति । अकरणे दोषमाह पराशरः—' ऋतुस्नातां तु यो भार्यां स्वस्थः सन्नोपगच्छति । बालगोघ्नापराधेन विध्यते नात्र संशयः ॥ ' इति ॥

अवजानासि मां यस्मादतस्ते न भविष्यति ।
मत्प्रसूतिमनाराध्य प्रजेति त्वां शशाप सा ॥ ७७ ॥

यस्मात् कारणात् **माम् अवजानासि** तिरस्करोषि । **अतः** कारणात् **मत्प्रसूतिं** मम संततिं **अनाराध्य** असेवयित्वा **ते** तव **प्रजा न भविष्यति इति सा** सुरभिः **त्वां शशाप** । ' शप आक्रोशे ' ॥

कथं तदस्माभिर्न श्रुतमित्याह—

स शापो न त्वया राजन्न च सारथिना श्रुतः ।
नदत्याकाशगङ्गायाः स्रोतस्युद्दामदिग्गजे ॥ ७८ ॥

हे **राजन् स शापः त्वया न श्रुतः । सारथिना च न** श्रुतः । अश्रवणे हेतुमाह—क्रीडार्थमागता उद्दामानो दाम्न उद्गता दिग्गजा यस्मिंस्तथोक्ते [**उद्दामदिग्गजे**] **आकाशगङ्गायाः** मन्दाकिन्याः **स्रोतसि** प्रवाहे **नदति** ध्वनति ॥

अस्तु प्रस्तुते किमायातमित्यत्राह—

ईप्सितं[3] **तदवज्ञानाद्विद्धि सार्गलमात्मनः ।**
प्रतिबध्नाति हि श्रेयः पूज्यपूजाव्यतिक्रमः ॥ ७९ ॥

तदवज्ञानात् तस्या धेनोः अवज्ञानाद् अपमानाद् **आत्मनः** स्वस्याप्तुमिष्टं **ईप्सितं** मनोरथम् । आप्नोतेः सन्नन्तात् क्तः ईकारश्च । **सार्गलं** सप्रतिबन्धं **विद्धि** जानीहि । तथा **हि** । पूज्यपूजाया व्यतिक्रमोऽतिक्रमणं [**पूज्यपूजाव्यतिक्रमः**] **श्रेयः प्रतिबध्नाति** ॥

---

१ ऋतौ भार्यामुपेयात् इति श्रुतेः । २ ऐरावतः पुण्डरीको वामनः कुमुदोऽञ्जनः । पुष्पदन्तः सार्वभौमः सुप्रतीकश्च दिग्गजाः ॥ इत्यमरः । ३ अवेहि तदवज्ञानात्–अवैमि तदपध्यानाद्–यत्नापेक्षं मनोरथम् । इ० पाठा०.

तर्हि गत्वा तामाराधयानि । सा वा कथंचिदागमिष्यतीत्याशा न कर्तव्येत्याह—

हविषे दीर्घसत्रस्य सा चेदानीं प्रचेतसः ।
भुजंगपिहितद्वारं पातालमधितिष्ठति ॥ ८० ॥

सा च सुरभिः **इदानीं** दीर्घं सत्रं चिरकालसाध्यो यागविशेषो यस्य तस्य [**दीर्घसत्रस्य**] **प्रचेतसः हविषे** दध्याज्यादिहविरर्थं **भुजंगपिहितद्वारं** भुजंगावरुद्धद्वारं ततो दुष्प्रवेशं **पातालम् अधितिष्ठति** । पाताले तिष्ठतीत्यर्थः । 'अधिशीङ्स्थासां कर्म' इति कर्मत्वम् ॥

तर्हि का गतिरित्यत आह—

सुतां तदीयां सुरभेः कृत्वा प्रतिनिधिं शुचिः ।[1]
आराधय सपत्नीकः प्रीता कामदुघा हि सा ॥ ८१ ॥

तस्याः सुरभेः इयं तदीया तां [**तदीयां**] **सुतां सुरभेः प्रतिनिधिं कृत्वा शुचिः** शुद्धः । सह पत्न्या वर्तत इति **सपत्नीकः** सन् । 'नद्यृतश्च' इति कप्प्रत्ययः । **आराधय । हि** यस्मात्कारणात् **सा प्रीता** तुष्टा सती । कामान्दोग्धीति **कामदुघा** भवति । 'दुहः कब्घश्च' इति कप्प्रत्ययः घादेशश्च ॥

इति वादिन एवास्य होतुराहुतिसाधनम् ।
अनिन्द्या नन्दिनी नाम धेनुराववृते वनात् ॥ ८२ ॥[2]

इति वादिनः वदत **एव होतुः** हवनशीलस्य । 'तृन्' इति तृन्प्रत्ययः । **अस्य** मुनेराहुतीनां साधनं कारणम् [**आहुतिसाधनम्**] । नन्दयतीति व्युत्पत्त्या **नन्दिनी नाम अनिन्द्या** अगर्ह्या प्रशस्ता **धेनुः वनात् आववृते** प्रत्यागता । 'अव्याक्षेपो भविष्यन्त्याः कार्यसिद्धेर्हि लक्षणम् ।' इति भावः ॥

सप्रति धेनुं विशिनष्टि—

ललाटोदयमाभुग्नं पल्लवस्निग्धपाटला ।
बिभ्रती श्वेतरोमाङ्कं संध्येव शशिनं नवम् ॥ ८३ ॥

पल्लवस्निग्धा चासौ पाटला च [**पल्लवस्निग्धपाटला**] । संध्यायामप्येतद्विशेषणं योज्यम् । ललाटे उदयो यस्य स ललाटोदयः तं [**ललाटोदयम्**] । **आभुग्नं** ईषद्वक्रम् । 'आविद्धं कुटिलं भुग्नं वेल्लितं वक्रमित्यपि ।' इत्यमरः । 'ओदितश्च' इति निष्ठातस्य नत्वम् । श्वेतरोमाण्येवाङ्कस्तं [**श्वेतरोमाङ्कं**] **बिभ्रती । नवं शशिनं** बिभ्रती **संध्येव** । स्थिता ॥

भुवं कोष्णेन कुण्डोध्नी मेध्येनावभृथादपि ।
प्रस्नवेनाभिवर्षन्ती वत्सालोकप्रवर्तिना ॥ ८४ ॥[3]

कोष्णेन किंचिदुष्णेन । 'कवं चोष्णे' इति चकारात्कादेशः । **अवभृथादपि** अवभृथस्नानादपि **मेध्येन** पवित्रेण । 'पूतं पवित्रं मेध्यं च' इत्यमरः । वत्सस्यालोकेन प्रदर्शनेन प्रवर्तिना प्रवहता [**वत्सालोकप्रवर्तिना**] **प्रस्नवेन** क्षीराभिस्यन्दनेन

---

१ स त्वमेकान्तरां तस्या मदीयां वत्समातरम् ।……सा वां कामान् प्रदास्यति ॥ इ. पा.
२ अस्मात्परमयमधिकः श्लोक उपलभ्यते क्वचित्—**ताम्रां ललाटजां रेखां बिभ्रती सा सितेतराम् । संध्या प्रातिपदेनेव प्रति-श्रुति-भिन्ना हिमांशुना ॥** ३ प्रकृष्टं स्नौति इ० **प्रस्नवः** ।

भुवम् अभिवर्षन्ती सिञ्चन्ती । कुण्डमिवोध आपीनं यस्याः सा **कुण्डोध्नी** । 'ऊधस्तु क्लीबमापीनम्' इत्यमरः । 'ऊधसोऽनङ्' इत्यनङादेशः । 'बहुव्रीहेरूधसो ङीष्' इति ङीष् ॥

रजःकणैः खुरोद्धूतैः स्पृशद्भिर्गात्रमन्तिकात् ।
तीर्थाभिषेकजां शुद्धिमादधाना महीक्षितः ॥ ८५ ॥

खुरोद्धूतैः अन्तिकात् समीपे **गात्रं स्पृशद्भिः** । 'दूरान्तिकार्थेभ्यो द्वितीया च' इति चकारात्पञ्चमी । रजसां कणैः [**रजःकणैः**] । मही क्षियत ईष्टे इति महीक्षित्तस्य [**महीक्षितः**] । तीर्थाभिषेकेण जातां **तीर्थाभिषेकजाम्** । **शुद्धिं आदधाना** कुर्वाणा । एतेन वायव्यं स्नानमुक्तम् । उक्तं च मनुना—'आग्नेयं भस्मना स्नानमवगाह्यं तु वारुणम् । आपोहिष्ठेति च ब्राह्मं वायव्यं गोरजः स्मृतम् ॥' इति ॥

तां पुण्यदर्शनां दृष्ट्वा निमित्तज्ञस्तपोनिधिः ।
याज्यमाशंसितावन्ध्यप्रार्थनं पुनरब्रवीत् ॥ ८६ ॥

निमित्तज्ञः शकुनज्ञः **तपोनिधिः** वसिष्ठः । पुण्यं दर्शनं यस्यास्तां [**पुण्यदर्शनां**] **तां** धेनुं **दृष्ट्वा** । आशंसितं मनोरथः । 'नपुंसके भावे क्तः' । तत्रावन्ध्यं सफलं प्रार्थनं यस्य स तम् [**आशंसितावन्ध्यप्रार्थनम्**] । अवन्ध्यमनोरथमित्यर्थः । याजयितुं योग्यं **याज्यं** पार्थिवं **पुनः अब्रवीत्** ॥

अदूरवर्तिनीं सिद्धिं राजन्विगणयात्मनः ।
उपस्थितेयं कल्याणी नाम्नि कीर्तित एव यत् ॥ ८७ ॥

हे **राजन् आत्मनः** कार्यस्य **सिद्धिं** [2]**अदूरवर्तिनीं** शीघ्रभाविनीं **विगणय** विद्धि । **यद्** यस्मात्कारणात् **कल्याणी** मङ्गलमूर्तिः । 'बह्वादिभ्यश्च' इति ङीष् । **इयं** धेनुः **नाम्नि कीर्तिते** कथिते सति **एव उपस्थिता** ॥

वन्यवृत्तिरिमां शश्वदात्मानुगमनेन[3] गाम् ।
विद्यामभ्यसनेनेव प्रसादयितुमर्हसि ॥ ८८ ॥

वने भवं वन्यं कन्दमूलादिकं वृत्तिराहारो यस्य तथाभूतः [**वन्यवृत्तिः**] सन् । **इमां गां शश्वत्** सदा । आ प्रसादादविच्छेदेनेत्यर्थः । आत्मनस्तव कर्तुः अनुगमनेनानुसरणेन [**आत्मानुगमनेन**] । **अभ्यसनेन** अनुष्ठातुरभ्यासेन **विद्याम् इव** । **प्रसादयितुं** प्रसन्नां कर्तुं **अर्हसि** ॥

गवानुसरणप्रकारमाह—

प्रस्थितायां प्रतिष्ठेथाः स्थितायां स्थितिमाचरेः ।
निषण्णायां निषीदास्यां पीताम्भसि पिबेरपः ॥ ८९ ॥

अस्यां नन्दिन्यां **प्रस्थितायां प्रतिष्ठेथाः** प्रयाहि । 'समवप्रविभ्यः स्थः' इत्यात्मनेपदम् । **स्थितायां** निवृत्तगतिकायां **स्थितिम् आचरेः** स्थितिं कुरु । तिष्ठेत्यर्थः । **निषण्णायां** उपविष्टायां **निषीद** उपविश । विध्यर्थे लोट् । पीतमम्भो यया तस्यां **पीताम्भसि** सत्यां **अपः पिबेः** पिब ॥

---

१ कुड्यन्ति जलं होमाग्निं वेति कुण्डं जलाधारः होमाधारो वा पात्रविशेषः । २ अत्र विरोधो नञर्थः । तदुक्तं—तत्सादृश्यमभावश्च तदन्यत्वं तदल्पता । अप्राशस्त्यं विरोधश्च नञर्थाः षट् प्रकीर्तिताः ॥ ३ सम्यगाराधनेन इ. पा.

वधूर्भक्तिमती चैनामर्चितामा तपोवनात् ।
प्रयता[1] प्रातरन्वेतु सायं प्रत्युद्व्रजेदपि ॥ ९० ॥

वधूः जाया च **भक्तिमती प्रयता** सती गन्धादिभिः **अर्चिताम् एनां** गां **प्रातः आ तपोवनात्** । आङ् मर्यादायाम् । पदद्वयं चैतत् । **अन्वेतु** अनुगच्छतु । **सायं अपि प्रत्युद्व्रजेत्** प्रत्युद्गच्छेत् । विध्यर्थे लिङ् ॥

इत्याप्रसादादस्यास्त्वं परिचर्यापरो भव ।
अविघ्नमस्तु ते स्थेयाः पितेव धुरि पुत्रिणाम् ॥ ९१ ॥

इति अनेन प्रकारेण **त्वम् आ प्रसादात्** प्रसादपर्यन्तम् । 'आङ् मर्यादाभिविध्योः' इत्यस्य वैभाषिकत्वादसमासत्वम् । **अस्याः** धेनोः **परिचर्यापरः** शुश्रूषापरः **भव** । **ते** तव **अविघ्नं** विघ्नस्याभावः **अस्तु** । 'अव्ययं विभक्ति–' इत्यादिनार्थाभावेऽव्ययीभावः । **पितेव पुत्रिणां** सत्पुत्रवताम् । प्रशंसायामिनिप्रत्ययः । **धुरि** अग्रे **स्थेयाः** तिष्ठेः । आशीरर्थे लिङ् । 'एर्लिङि' इत्याकारस्यैकारादेशः । त्वत्सदृशो भवत्पुत्रोऽस्त्विति भावः ॥

तथेति प्रतिजग्राह प्रीतिमान्सपरिग्रहः ।
आदेशं देशकालज्ञः[2] शिष्यः शासितुरानतः ॥ ९२ ॥

देशकालज्ञः । देशोऽग्निसंनिधिः कालोऽग्निहोत्रावसानसमयः । विशिष्टदेशकालोत्पन्नमपि ज्ञानमव्याहतमिति जानन् । अत एव **प्रीतिमान् शिष्यः** अन्तेवासी राजा **सपरिग्रहः** सपत्नीकः । 'पत्नीपरिजनादानमूलशापाः परिग्रहाः ।' इत्यमरः । **आनतः** विनयनम्रः सन् । **शासितुः** गुरोः **आदेशं** आज्ञां **तथेति प्रतिजग्राह** स्वीचकार ॥

अथ प्रदोषे[4] दोषज्ञः संवेशाय विशांपतिम् ।
सूनुः सूनृतवाक्स्रष्टुर्विससर्जोदितश्रियम्[3] ॥ ९३ ॥

अथ प्रदोषे रात्रौ **दोषज्ञः** विद्वान् । 'विद्वान्विपश्चिद्दोषज्ञः' इत्यमरः । **सूनृतवाक्** सत्यप्रियवाक् । 'प्रियं सत्यं च सूनृतम्' इति हलायुधः । **स्रष्टुः सूनुः** ब्रह्मपुत्रो मुनिः । अनेन प्रकृतकार्यनिर्वाहकत्वं सूचयति । **उदितश्रियं विशांपतिं** मनुजेश्वरम् । 'द्वौ विशौ वैश्यमनुजौ' इत्यमरः । **संवेशाय** निद्रायै । 'स्यान्निद्रा शयनं स्वापः स्वप्नः संवेश इत्यपि' इत्यमरः । **विससर्ज** आज्ञापयामास ॥

सत्यामपि तपःसिद्धौ नियमापेक्षया मुनिः ।
कल्पवित्कल्पयामास वन्यामेवास्य संविधाम् ॥ ९४ ॥

कल्पवित् व्रतप्रयोगाभिज्ञो **मुनिः** । **तपःसिद्धौ सत्यामपि** । तपसैव राजयोग्याहारसंपादनसामर्थ्ये सत्यपीत्यर्थः । **नियमापेक्षया** तदाप्रभृत्येव व्रतचर्यापेक्षया । **अस्य** राज्ञः **वन्यामेव** । संविधीयतेऽनयेति **संविधाम्** । कुशादिशयनसामग्रीम् । 'आतश्चोपसर्गे' इति कप्रत्ययः । 'अकर्तरि च कारके संज्ञायाम्' इति कर्माद्यर्थत्वम् । **कल्पयामास** संपादयामास ॥

---

१ प्रयातां, प्रयतां इ. पा. २ देशकालज्ञत्वेन गोरक्षणप्रवृत्तिकारणत्वं सूच्यते इति चारित्रवर्धनः । ३ ऊर्जितश्रि० इ. पा. ४ प्रारब्धाः प्रकृष्टा वा दोषाः चौर्यादिभयानि यस्मिन् ।

निर्दिष्टां कुलपतिना स पर्णशाला-
मध्यास्य प्रयतपरिग्रहद्वितीयः ।
तच्छिष्याध्ययननिवेदितावसानां
संविष्टः कुशशयने निशां निनाय ॥ ९५ ॥

स राजा **कुलपतिना** मुनिकुलेश्वरेण वसिष्ठेन **निर्दिष्टां पर्णशालामध्यास्य** अधिष्ठाय । तस्यामधिष्ठानं कृत्वेत्यर्थः । 'अधिशीङ्-' इत्यादिनाधारस्य कर्मत्वम् । कर्मणि द्वितीया । प्रयतो नियतः परिग्रहः पत्नी द्वितीयो यस्येति [**प्रयतपरिग्रहद्वितीयः**] स तथोक्तः । कुशानां शयने [**कुशशयने**] **संविष्टः** सुप्तः सन् । तस्य वसिष्ठस्य शिष्याणामध्ययनेनापररात्रे वेदपाठेन निवेदितमवसानं यस्यास्तां [**तच्छिष्याध्ययननिवेदितावसानां**] **निशां निनाय** गमयामास । अपररात्रेऽध्ययने मनुः—'निशान्ते न परिश्रान्तो ब्रह्माधीत्य पुनः स्वपेत् ।' इति । 'न चापररात्रमधीत्य पुनः स्वपेत्' इति गौतमश्च । प्रहर्षिणीवृत्तमेतत् । तदुक्तम्—'म्नौ ज्रौ गस्त्रिदशयतिः प्रहर्षिणीयम्' ॥

इति महामहोपाध्यायकोलाचलमल्लिनाथसूरिविरचितया संजीवनीसमाख्यया
व्याख्यया समेतो महाकविश्रीकालिदासकृतौ रघुवंशे महाकाव्ये
वसिष्ठाश्रमाभिगमनो नाम प्रथमः सर्गः ।

द्वितीयः सर्गः ।

आशासु राशीभवदङ्गवल्लीभासैव दासीकृतदुग्धसिन्धुम् ।
मन्दस्मितैर्निन्दितशारदेन्दुं वन्देऽरविन्दासनसुन्दरि त्वाम् ॥

अथ प्रजानामधिपः प्रभाते जायाप्रतिग्राहितगन्धमाल्याम् ।
वनाय पीतप्रतिबद्धवत्सां यशोधनो धेनुमृषेर्मुमोच ॥ १ ॥

अथ निशानयनानन्तरं **यशोधनः प्रजानामधिपः** प्रजेश्वरः **प्रभाते** प्रातःकाले जायया सुदक्षिणया । प्रतिग्राहयित्र्या । प्रतिग्राहिते स्वीकारिते गन्धमाल्ये यया सा जायाप्रतिग्राहितगन्धमाल्या तां तथोक्ताम् [**जायाप्रतिग्राहितगन्धमाल्याम्**] । पीतं पानमस्यास्तीति पीतः । पीतवानित्यर्थः । 'अर्शआदिभ्योऽच्' इत्यच्प्रत्ययः । 'पीता गावो भुक्ता ब्राह्मणाः' इति महाभाष्ये दर्शनात् । पीतः प्रतिबद्धो वत्सो यस्यास्तां [**पीतप्रतिबद्धवत्सां**] **ऋषेः धेनुं वनाय** वनं गन्तुम् । 'क्रियार्थोपपद-' इत्यादिना चतुर्थी । **मुमोच** मुक्तवान् । जायापदसामर्थ्यात्सुदक्षिणायाः पुत्रजननयोग्यत्वमनुसंधेयम् । तथा हि श्रुतिः—'पतिर्जायां प्रविशति गर्भो भूत्वेह मातरम् । तस्यां पुनर्नवो

---

१ अन्वैषीत् इ. पा. २ कुलस्य मुनिसमूहस्य पतिः । कुलपतिलक्षणं यथा—मुनीनां दशसाहस्रं योऽन्नदानादिपोषणात् । अध्यापयति विप्रर्षिरसौ कुलपतिः स्मृतः ॥ इति । ३ हे अरविन्दासनसुन्दरि लक्ष्मि दिक्षु राशीभवन्ती अनवरतं समन्ततः प्रसरणात् संघीभवन्ती या अङ्गवल्ल्याः भाः कान्तिः तया एव धावल्यातिशयात् निर्जितः दुग्धसिन्धुः यया ताम् । मन्दस्मितैः ईषद्धासैः निन्दितः तिरस्कृतः शारदेन्दुः यया एतादृशीं त्वां वंदे ।

भूत्वा दशमे मासि जायते । तज्जाया जाया भवति यदस्यां जायते पुनः । ' इति । यशोधन इत्यनेन पुत्रवत्ताकीर्तिलाभाद्राजार्हे गोरक्षणे प्रवृत्त इति गम्यते । अस्मिन्सर्गे वृत्तमुपजातिः—' अनन्तरोदीरितलक्ष्मभाजौ पादौ यदीयावुपजातयस्ताः । ' इति ॥

तस्याः खुरन्यासपवित्रपांसुमपांसुलानां धुरि कीर्तनीया ।
मार्गं मनुष्येश्वरधर्मपत्नी श्रुतेरिवार्थं स्मृतिरन्वगच्छत् ॥ २ ॥

पांसवो दोषा आसां सन्तीति पांसुलाः स्वैरिण्यः । ' स्वैरिणी पांसुला ' इत्यमरः । ' सिध्मादिभ्यश्च ' इति लच्प्रत्ययः । **अपांसुलानां** पतिव्रतानां **धुरि** अग्रे **कीर्तनीया** परिगणनीया **मनुष्येश्वरधर्मपत्नी** । खुरन्यासैः पवित्राः पांसवो यस्य तं [**खुरन्यासपवित्रपांसुम्**] । ' रेणुर्द्वयोः स्त्रियां धूलिः पांसुर्ना न द्वयो रजः । ' इत्यमरः । **तस्याः** धेनोः **मार्गम्** । **स्मृतिः** मन्वादिवाक्यं **श्रुतेः** वेदवाक्यस्य **अर्थं** अभिधेयं **इव** । **अन्वगच्छत्** अनुसृतवती च । यथा स्मृतिः श्रुतिक्षुण्णमेवार्थमनुसरति तथा सापि गोखुरक्षुण्णमेव मार्गमनुससारेत्यर्थः । धर्मपत्नीत्यत्राश्वघासादिवत्तादर्थ्ये षष्ठीसमासः प्रकृतिविकाराभावात् । पांसुलपथप्रवृत्तावप्यपांसुलानामिति विरोधालंकारो ध्वन्यते ॥

निवर्त्य राजा दयितां दयालुस्तां सौरभेयीं सुरभिर्यशोभिः ।
पयोधरीभूतचतुःसमुद्रां जुगोप गोरूपधरामिवोर्वीम् ॥ ३ ॥

दयालुः कारुणिकः । ' स्याद्दयालुः कारुणिकः ' इत्यमरः । ' स्पृहिगृहि–' इत्यादिनालुच्प्रत्ययः । **यशोभिः सुरभिः** मनोज्ञः । ' सुरभिः स्यान्मनोज्ञेऽपि ' इति विश्वः । **राजा तां दयितां निवर्त्य सौरभेयीं** कामधेनुसुतां नन्दिनीम् । धरन्तीति धराः । पचाद्यच् । पयसां धराः पयोधराः स्तनाः । ' स्त्रीस्तनाब्दौ पयोधरौ ' इत्यमरः । अपयोधराः पयोधराः संपद्यमानाः पयोधरीभूताः । अभूततद्भावे च्विः । ' कुगतिप्रादयः ' इति समासः । पयोधरीभूताश्चत्वारः समुद्रा यस्यास्तां [**पयोधरीभूतचतुःसमुद्रां**] ' अनेकमन्यपदार्थे ' इत्यनेकपदार्थग्रहणसामर्थ्यात्त्रिपदो बहुव्रीहिः । **गोरूपधराम् उर्वीम् इव जुगोप** ररक्ष । भूरक्षणप्रयत्नेनेव ररक्षेति भावः । धेनुपक्षे पयसा दुग्धेनाधरीभूताश्चत्वारः समुद्रा यस्याः सा तथोक्ताम् । दुग्धतिरस्कृतसागरामित्यर्थः ॥

व्रताय तेनानुचरेण धेनोर्न्यषेधि शेषोऽप्यनुयायिवर्गः ।
न चान्यतस्तस्य शरीररक्षा स्ववीर्यगुप्ता हि मनोः प्रसूतिः ॥ ४ ॥

व्रताय धेनोः अनुचरेण । न तु जीवनायेति भावः । **तेन** दिलीपेन **शेषः** अवशिष्टः **अपि अनुयायिवर्गः** अनुचरवर्गः । **न्यषेधि** निवर्तितः । शेषत्वं सुदक्षिणापेक्षया । कथं तर्ह्यात्मरक्षणमत आह—न चेति । **तस्य** दिलीपस्य **शरीररक्षा च अन्यतः** पुरुषान्तरात् **न** । कुतः । **हि** यस्मात्कारणात् **मनोः** । प्रसूयत इति **प्रसूतिः** संततिः **स्ववीर्यगुप्ता** स्ववीर्येणैव रक्षिता । न हि स्वनिर्वाहकस्य परापेक्षेति भावः ॥

---

१ पतिं धर्मरतं पत्नी साध्वी शुश्रूषते तु या । नित्यं त्वनन्यहृदया धर्मपत्नीं तु तां विदुः ॥ २ धर्माय पत्नी इति वक्तव्येपि धर्मस्य पत्नी इति तादर्थ्ये षष्ठीसमासः अश्वस्य घास इतिवत् । ३ पांसुलमार्गमनुसरन्ती अपि कथं पांसुस्पर्शरहितानां धुरि कीर्तनीया इति आपाततः [न तु अर्थावबोधानन्तरं] विरोधः । तेनात्र विरोधाभासः अलंकारः ।

आस्वादवद्भिः कवलैस्तृणानां कण्डूयनैर्दंशनिवारणैश्च ।
[1]अव्याहतैः स्वैरगतैः स तस्याः सम्राट् समाराधनतत्परोऽभूत् ॥ ५ ॥

सम्राट् मण्डलेश्वरः । 'येनेष्टं राजसूयेन मण्डलस्येश्वरश्च यः । शास्ति यश्चाज्ञया राज्ञः स सम्राट्' इत्यमरः । **स** राजा । **आस्वादवद्भिः** रसवद्भिः । स्वादयुक्तैरित्यर्थः । **तृणानां कवलैः** ग्रासैः । 'ग्रासस्तु कवलार्थकः' इत्यमरः । **कण्डूयनैः** खर्जनैः । दंशानां वनमक्षिकाणां निवारणैः [**दंशनिवारणैः**] । 'दंशस्तु वनमक्षिका' इत्यमरः । **अव्याहतैः** अप्रतिहतैः **स्वैरगतैः** स्वच्छन्दगमनैः **च** । **तस्याः** धेन्वाः **समाराधनतत्परः** शुश्रूषासक्तः **अभूत्** । तदेव परं प्रधानं यस्येति तत्परः । 'तत्परे प्रसितासक्तौ' इत्यमरः ॥

स्थितः स्थितामुच्चलितः प्रयातां निषेदुषीमासनबन्धधीरः ।
जलाभिलाषी जलमाददानां छायेव तां भूपतिरन्वगच्छत् ॥ ६ ॥

भूपतिः तां गां **स्थितां** सतीं **स्थितः** सन् । स्थितिरूर्ध्वावस्थानम् । **प्रयातां** प्रस्थितां **उच्चलितः** प्रस्थितः । **निषेदुषीं** निषण्णाम् । उपविष्टामित्यर्थः । 'भाषायां सदवसश्रुवः' इति क्वसुप्रत्ययः । 'उगितश्च' इति ङीप् । आसनबन्ध उपवेशने धीरः स्थितः [**आसनबन्धधीरः**] । उपविष्टः सन्नित्यर्थः । **जलम् आददानां** पिबन्तीं **जलाभिलाषी** । पिबन्नित्यर्थः । इत्थं **छाया इव अन्वगच्छत्** अनुसृतवान् ॥

स न्यस्तचिह्नामपि राजलक्ष्मीं तेजोविशेषानुमितां दधानः ।
आसीदनाविष्कृतदानराजिरन्तर्मदावस्थ इव द्विपेन्द्रः ॥ ७ ॥

न्यस्तानि परिहृतानि चिह्नानि छत्रचामरादीनि यस्यास्तां तथाभूतां [**न्यस्तचिह्नाम्**] **अपि** तेजोविशेषेण प्रभावातिशयेनानुमितां [**तेजोविशेषानुमितां**] सर्वथा राजैवायं भवेदित्यूहितां **राजलक्ष्मीं दधानः स** राजा । **अनाविष्कृतदानराजिः** बहिरप्रकटितमदरेखः । अन्तर्गता मदावस्था यस्य सः **अन्तर्मदावस्थः** । तथाभूतः **द्विपेन्द्रः इव आसीत्** ॥

लताप्रतानोद्ग्रथितैः स केशैरधिज्यधन्वा विचचार दावम् ।
रक्षापदेशान्मुनिहोमधेनोर्वन्यान्विनेष्यन्निव दुष्टसत्त्वान् ॥ ८ ॥

लतानां वल्लीनां प्रतानैः कुटिलतन्तुभिरुद्ग्रथिता उन्नमय्य ग्रथिता ये केशास्तैः [**लताप्रतानोद्ग्रथितैः केशैः**] उपलक्षितः । 'इत्थंभूतलक्षणे' इति तृतीया । **स** राजा अधिज्यमारोपितमौर्वीकं धनुर्यस्य सः **अधिज्यधन्वा** सन् । 'धनुषश्च' इत्यनङादेशः । **मुनिहोमधेनोः रक्षापदेशात्** रक्षणव्याजात् । **वन्यान्** वने भवान् **दुष्टसत्त्वान्** दुष्टजन्तून् । 'द्रव्यासुव्यवसायेषु सत्त्वमस्त्री तु जन्तुषु ।' इत्यमरः । **विनेष्यन्** शिक्षयिष्यन् **इव** । **दावं** वनम् । 'वने च वनवह्नौ च दवो दाव इहेष्यते ।' इति यादवः । **विचचार** । वने चचारेत्यर्थः । 'देशकालाध्वगन्तव्याः कर्मसंज्ञा ह्यकर्मणाम्' इति दावस्य कर्मत्वम् ॥

---

१ अव्याहतस्वैरगतैः इति वल्लभचारित्रवर्धनौ पठतः । २ छाया इति लुप्तोपमानं न भिन्नलिङ्गत्वदोषदुष्टम् । 'न लिङ्गवचने भिन्ने न हीनाधिकतापि वा ।' इति दण्डिवचनात् । ३ अत्रान्तर्मदत्वाद्भद्रजातीयो गज इष्टः । तदाह वल्लभः—'भद्रो मन्दो मृगश्चेति संकीर्णश्चेति जातयः । चतस्रः करिणां तासां भद्रोऽन्तर्मद एव यः ॥' इति । ४ अत्र क्रियोत्प्रेक्षा ।

'विसृष्ट—' इत्यादिभिः षड्भिः श्लोकैस्तस्य महामहिमतया द्रुमादयोऽपि राजोपचारं चक्रुरित्याह—

विसृष्टपार्श्वानुचरस्य तस्य पार्श्वद्रुमाः पाशभृता समस्य ।
उदीरयामासुरिवोन्मदानामालोकशब्दं वयसां विरावैः ॥ ९ ॥

विसृष्टाः पार्श्वानुचराः पार्श्ववर्तिनो जना येन तस्य [**विसृष्टपार्श्वानुचरस्य**] **पाशभृता** वरुणेन **समस्य** तुल्यस्य । 'प्रचेता वरुणः पाशी' इत्यमरः । अनुभावोऽनेन सूचितः । **तस्य** राज्ञः पार्श्वयोर्द्रुमाः [**पार्श्वद्रुमाः**] । **उन्मदानां** उत्कटमदानां **वयसां** खगानाम् । 'खगबाल्यादिनोर्वयः' इत्यमरः । **विरावैः** शब्दैः । आलोकस्य शब्दं वाचकमालोकयेति शब्दम् [**आलोकशब्दम्**] । जयशब्दमित्यर्थः । 'आलोको जयशब्दः स्यात्' इति विश्वः । **उदीरयामासुरिव** अवदन्निव । इत्युत्प्रेक्षा ॥

मरुत्प्रयुक्ताश्च मरुत्सखाभं तमर्च्यमारादभिवर्तमानम् ।
अवाकिरन्बाललताः प्रसूनैराचारलाजैरिव पौरकन्याः ॥ १० ॥

मरुत्प्रयुक्ताः वायुना प्रेरिताः **बाललताः** [**च**] **आरात्** समीपे **अभिवर्तमानम्** । 'आराद् दूरसमीपयोः' इत्यमरः । मरुतो वायोः सखा मरुत्सखोऽग्निः । स इवाभातीति तं **मरुत्सखाभम्** । 'आतश्चोपसर्गे' इति कप्रत्ययः । **अर्च्यं** पूज्यं **तं** दिलीपं **प्रसूनैः** पुष्पैः । **पौरकन्याः** पौराश्च ताः कन्या आचारार्थैर्लाजैः **आचारलाजैः इव** । **अवाकिरन्** । तस्योपरि निक्षिप्तवत्य इत्यर्थः । सखा हि सखायमागतमुपचरतीति भावः ॥

धनुर्भृतोऽप्यस्य दयार्द्रभावमाख्यातमन्तःकरणैर्विशङ्कैः ।
विलोकयन्त्यो वपुरापुरक्ष्णां प्रकामविस्तारफलं हरिण्यः ॥ ११ ॥

धनुर्भृतः अपि अस्य राज्ञः । एतेन भयसंभावना दर्शिता । तथापि **विशङ्कैः** निर्भीकैः **अन्तःकरणैः** । कर्तृभिः । दयया कृपारसेनार्द्रो भावोऽभिप्रायो यस्य तत् **दयार्द्रभावं** तत् **आख्यातम्** । दयार्द्रभावमेतदित्याख्यातमित्यर्थः । 'भावः सत्तास्वभावाभिप्रायचेष्टात्मजन्मसु ।' इत्यमरः । तथाविधं **वपुः विलोकयन्त्यः हरिण्यः अक्ष्णां** प्रकामविस्तारस्य अत्यन्तविशालतायाः फलं [**प्रकामविस्तारफलम्**] **आपुः** । 'विमलं कलुषीभवच्च चेतः कथयत्येव हितैषिणं रिपुं च ।' इति न्यायेन स्वान्तःकरणवृत्तिप्रामाण्यादेव विश्रब्धं ददृशुरित्यर्थः ॥

स कीचकैर्मारुतपूर्णरन्ध्रैः कूजद्भिरापादितवंशकृत्यम् ।
शुश्राव कुञ्जेषु यशः स्वमुच्चैरुद्गीयमानं वनदेवताभिः ॥ १२ ॥

स दिलीपः **मारुतपूर्णरन्ध्रैः** अत एव **कूजद्भिः** स्वनद्भिः । **कीचकैः** वेणुविशेषैः । 'वेणवः कीचकास्ते स्युर्ये स्वनन्त्यनिलाद्धताः ।' इत्यमरः । वंशः सुषिरवाद्यविशेषः । 'वंशादिकं तु सुषिरम्' इत्यमरः । आपादितं संपादितं वंशस्य कृत्यं कार्यं

---

१ 'आलोकस्य दर्शनस्य शब्दः आलोकशब्दस्तम् । जय जीवेत्याद्यालोकशब्दः । जय जय महाराज प्रभो स्वामिन् पादमवधार्यतामित्यालोकशब्दः' । इति वल्लभः । २ बाललतानां प्रफुल्लत्वादल्पावयवत्वाच्च प्रफुल्लवदनश्रीभिः स्वल्पवयस्काभिः पौरकन्याभिः साम्यम् । पुष्पाणां लाजानां च शुभ्रत्वान्माङ्गलिकत्वाच्चान्योन्यसादृश्यम् । लाजवर्षा वयोवृद्धाभिरपि क्रियते । चतुर्थसर्गे २७ श्लोको द्रष्टव्यः ।

यस्मिन्कर्मणि तत्तथा **[आपादितवंशकृत्यम्]**। **कुञ्जेषु** लतागृहेषु । 'निकुञ्जकुञ्जौ वा क्लीबे लतादिपिहितोदरे ।' इत्यमरः। **वनदेवताभिः उच्चैः उद्गीयमानं** उच्चैर्गीयमानं **स्वं यशः शुश्राव** श्रुतवान् ॥

पृक्तस्तुषारैर्गिरिनिर्झराणामनोकहाकम्पितपुष्पगन्धी ।
तमातपक्लान्तमनातपत्रमाचारपूतं पवनः सिषेवे ॥ १३ ॥

गिरिषु निर्झराणां **[गिरिनिर्झराणां]** वारिप्रवाहाणाम् । 'वारिप्रवाहो निर्झरो झरः' इत्यमरः। **तुषारैः** सीकरैः । 'तुषारौ हिमसीकरौ' इति शाश्वतः। **पृक्तः** संपृक्तः। **[अनोकहाकम्पितपुष्पगन्धी]** अनोकहानां वृक्षाणामाकम्पितानीषत्कम्पितानि पुष्पाणि तेषां यो गन्धः सोऽस्यास्तीत्याकम्पितपुष्पगन्धी । ईषत्कम्पितपुष्पगन्धवान् । एवं शीतो मन्दः सुरभिः **पवनः** वायुः **अनातपत्रं** व्रतार्थं परिहृतच्छत्रम् । अत एव **आतपक्लान्तं** आचारेण पूतं **[आचारपूतं]** शुद्धं **तं** नृपं **सिषेवे** । आचारपूतत्वात्स राजा जगत्पावनस्यापि सेव्य आसीदिति भावः ॥

शशाम वृष्ट्याऽपि विना दवाग्निरासीद्विशेषा फलपुष्पवृद्धिः ।
ऊनं न सत्त्वेष्वधिको बबाधे तस्मिन्वनं गोप्तरि गाहमाने ॥ १४ ॥

गोप्तरि तस्मिन् राज्ञि **वनं गाहमाने** प्रविशति सति **वृष्ट्या विना अपि**। **दवाग्निः** वनाग्निः। 'दवदावौ वनानले' इति हैमः। **शशाम**। फलानां पुष्पाणां च वृद्धिः **[फलपुष्पवृद्धिः]** विशेष्यत इति **विशेषा** अतिशयिता **आसीत्**। कर्मार्थे घञ्प्रत्ययः। **सत्त्वेषु** जन्तुषु मध्ये। 'यतश्च निर्धारणम्' इति सप्तमी। **अधिकः** प्रबलो व्याघ्रादिः **ऊनं** दुर्बलं हरिणादिकं **न बबाधे** ॥

संचारपूतानि दिगन्तराणि कृत्वा दिनान्ते निलयाय गन्तुम् ।
प्रचक्रमे पल्लवरागताम्रा प्रभा पतङ्गस्य मुनेश्च धेनुः ॥ १५ ॥

पल्लवस्य रागो वर्णः पल्लवरागः। 'रागोऽनुरक्तौ मात्सर्ये क्लेशादौ लोहितादिषु ।' इति शाश्वतः। स इव ताम्रा **पल्लवरागताम्रा पतङ्गस्य** सूर्यस्य **प्रभा** कान्तिः। 'पतङ्गः पक्षिसूर्ययोः' इति शाश्वतः। **मुनेर्धेनुश्च**। **दिगन्तराणि** दिशामवकाशान् । 'अन्तरमवकाशावधिपरिधानान्तर्धिभेदतादर्थ्ये।' इत्यमरः । संचारेण पूतानि शुद्धानि **[संचारपूतानि] कृत्वा दिनान्ते** सायंकाले **निलयाय** अस्तमयाय । धेनुपक्षे आलयाय च **गन्तुं प्रचक्रमे** ॥

---

१ गान्धारग्रामेण गीयमानमित्यर्थः । तदुक्तं नारदेन—षड्जमध्यमनामानौ ग्रामौ गायन्ति मानवाः । न तु गान्धारनामानं स लभ्यो देवयोनिभिः ॥ इति । अनुरञ्जकवाद्यं विना गीतं न मनोरममित्युक्तमापादितवंशकृत्यमिति । अत्र भरतः—गाता यं यं स्वरं गच्छेत्तं तं वंशेन तानयेत् । इति । अनुरूपश्लोकः कुमारसंभवे—यः पूरयन्कीचकरन्ध्रभागान्दरीमुखोत्थेन समीरणेन । उद्गास्यतामिच्छति किंनराणां तानप्रदायित्वमिवोपगन्तुम् ॥ इति । २ अनसः शकटस्य गतिं हन्ति इति अनोकहः । 'वृक्षा दुमोऽपि राज्ञोपचारं चक्रुः' इति चारित्रवर्धनः। वायोरनुरूपं वर्णनं कुमारसंभवे—भागीरथीनिर्झरशीकराणां वोढा मुहुः कम्पितदेवदारुः । यद्वायुरन्विष्टमृगैः किरातैरासेव्यते भिन्नशिखण्डिबर्हः ॥ इति । ३ 'गत्यर्थकर्मणि द्वितीयाचतुर्थ्यौ चेष्टायामनध्वनि' इति चतुर्थी ।

तां देवतापित्रतिथिक्रियार्थामन्वग्ययौ मध्यमलोकपालः ।
बभौ च सा तेन सतां मतेन श्रद्धेव साक्षाद्विधिनोपपन्ना ॥ १६ ॥

मध्यमलोकपालः भूपालः । देवतापित्रतिथीनां क्रिया यागश्राद्धदानानि ता एवार्थः प्रयोजनं यस्याः तां [**देवतापित्रतिथिक्रियार्थाम्**] **तां** धेनुं **अन्वग्** अनुपदं **ययौ** । 'अन्वगन्वक्षमनुगेऽनुपदं क्लीबमव्ययम् ।' इत्यमरः । **सतां मतेन** सद्भिर्मान्येन । 'गतिबुद्धि–' इत्यादिना वर्तमाने क्तः । 'क्तस्य च वर्तमाने' इति षष्ठी । **तेन** राज्ञा **उपपन्ना** युक्ता **सा** धेनुः । सतां मतेन **विधिना** अनुष्ठानेनोपपन्ना **साक्षात्** प्रत्यक्षा **श्रद्धा** आस्तिक्यबुद्धिः **इव बभौ च** ॥

स पल्वलोत्तीर्णवराहयूथान्यावासवृक्षोन्मुखबर्हिणानि ।
ययौ मृगाध्यासितशाद्वलानि श्यामायमानानि वनानि पश्यन् ॥ १७ ॥

स राजा । पल्वलेभ्योऽल्पजलाशयेभ्य उत्तीर्णानि निर्गतानि वराहाणां यूथानि कुलानि येषु तानि [**पल्वलोत्तीर्णवराहयूथानि**] । बर्हाण्येषां सन्तीति बर्हिणः मयूराः । 'मयूरो बर्हिणो बर्ही' इत्यमरः । 'फलबर्हाभ्यामिनच्प्रत्ययो' वक्तव्यः । आवासवृक्षाणामुन्मुखा बर्हिणा येषु तानि [**आवासवृक्षोन्मुखबर्हिणानि**] । श्यामायमानानि वराहबर्हिणादिमालिनिम्ना[२] अश्यामानि श्यामानि भवन्तीति **श्यामायमानानि** । 'लोहितादिडाज्भ्यः क्यष्' इति क्यष्प्रत्ययः । 'वा क्यषः' इत्यात्मनेपदे शानच् । मृगैरध्यासिता अधिष्ठिताः शाद्वला येषु तानि [**मृगाध्यासितशाद्वलानि**] । शादाः शष्पाण्येषु देशेषु सन्तीति शाद्वलाः शष्पश्यामदेशाः । 'शाद्वलः शादहरिते' इत्यमरः । 'शादः कर्दमशष्पयोः' इति विश्वः । 'नडशादाड्ड्वलच्' इति ड्वलच्प्रत्ययः । **वनानि पश्यन्ययौ** ॥

आपीनभारोद्वहनप्रयत्नाद्गृष्टिर्गुरुत्वाद्वपुषो नरेन्द्रः ।
उभावलंचक्रतुरञ्चिताभ्यां तपोवनावृत्तिपथं गताभ्याम् ॥ १८ ॥

गृष्टिः सकृत्प्रसूता गौः । 'गृष्टिः सकृत्प्रसूता गौः' इति हलायुधः । **नरेन्द्रः** च **उभौ** यथाक्रमम् । आपीनमूधः । 'ऊधस्तु क्लीबमापीनम्' इत्यमरः । आपीनस्य भारोद्वहने प्रयत्नात्प्रयासात् [**आपीनभारोद्वहनप्रयत्नात्**[३]] । **वपुषः गुरुत्वाद्** आधिक्याच्च । **अञ्चिताभ्यां** चारुभ्यां **गताभ्यां** गमनाभ्यां तपोवनादावृत्तेः पन्थास्तं **तपोवनावृत्तिपथम्** । 'ऋक्पूः–' इत्यादिना समासान्तोऽप्रत्ययः । **अलंचक्रतुः** भूषितवन्तौ ॥

वसिष्ठधेनोरनुयायिनं तमावर्तमानं वनिता वनान्तात् ।
पपौ निमेषालसपक्ष्मपङ्क्तिरुपोषिताभ्यामिव लोचनाभ्याम् ॥ १९ ॥

---

१ तदुक्तं याज्ञवल्क्येन–श्रद्धाविधिसमायुक्तं कर्म यत्क्रियते नृभिः । सुविशुद्धेन भावेन तदानन्त्याय कल्पते । विधिहीनं भवेद्दुष्टं कृतमश्रद्धया च यत् । तद्धरन्त्यसुरास्तस्य मूढस्य दुष्कृतात्मनः ॥ इति । २ संध्यागमस्य पाटलिम्ना किंचिद्धूसराणीकानि वनानि वराहादीनां नीलिम्ना श्यामीभूतानीति सुष्ठूक्तमेव टीकाकृता । अत्र नैशतमसावृतत्वादधुनानां श्यामत्वमिति केचिन्मन्यन्ते तन्न साधु । धेनोः संध्यावसानात्प्रागेवारण्यान्निवृत्तेः । कविवर्णनात्तथा चमत्कृतेरभावाच्च । ३ आपीनस्य विशालत्वमुक्तमेव प्राक् 'पयोधरीभूतचतुःसमुद्राम्' 'भुवं कोष्णेन कुण्डोध्नी' इत्यादिना । राज्ञो वपुषो गुरुत्वं चोक्तं 'व्यूढोरस्को वृषस्कन्धः' इत्यत्र ।

वसिष्ठधेनोः अनुयायिनं अनुचरं **वनान्ताद् आवर्तमानं** प्रत्यागतं **तं** दिलीपं **वनिता** सुदक्षिणा निमेषेष्वलसा मन्दा पक्ष्मणां पङ्क्तिर्यस्याः सा [**निमेषालसपक्ष्मपङ्क्तिः**] । निर्निमेषा सतीत्यर्थः । **लोचनाभ्याम्** । करणाभ्याम् । **उपोषिताभ्याम् इव** । उपवासो भोजननिवृत्तिः । तद्वद्भ्यामिव । वसतेः कर्तरि क्तः । **पपौ** । यथोपोषितोऽतितृष्णया जलमधिकं पिबति तद्वदतितृष्णयाऽधिकं व्यलोकयदित्यर्थः ॥

पुरस्कृता वर्त्मनि पार्थिवेन प्रत्युद्गता पार्थिवधर्मपत्न्या ।
तदन्तरे सा विरराज धेनुर्दिनक्षपामध्यगतेव संध्या ॥ २० ॥

वर्त्मनि पार्थिवेन पृथिव्या ईश्वरेण । 'तस्येश्वरः' इत्यञ्प्रत्ययः । **पुरस्कृता** अग्रतःकृता । धर्मस्य पत्नी । धर्मार्थपत्नीत्यर्थः । अश्वघासादिवत्तादर्थ्ये षष्ठीसमासः । पार्थिवस्य धर्मपत्न्या [**पार्थिवधर्मपत्न्या**] **प्रत्युद्गता सा धेनुः तदन्तरे** तयोर्दंपत्योर्मध्ये । दिनक्षपयोर्दिनरात्र्योर्मध्यगता [**दिनक्षपामध्यगता**] **संध्या इव विरराज** ॥

प्रदक्षिणीकृत्य पयस्विनीं तां सुदक्षिणा साक्षतपात्रहस्ता ।
प्रणम्य चानर्च विशालमस्याः शृङ्गान्तरं द्वारमिवार्थसिद्धेः ॥ २१ ॥

अक्षतानां पात्रेण सह वर्तेते इति साक्षतपात्रौ हस्तौ यस्याः सा [**साक्षतपात्रहस्ता**] **सुदक्षिणा पयस्विनीं** प्रशस्तक्षीरां **तां** धेनुं **प्रदक्षिणीकृत्य प्रणम्य च अस्याः** धेन्वाः **विशालं शृङ्गान्तरं** शृङ्गमध्यम् । **अर्थसिद्धेः** कार्यसिद्धेः **द्वारं** प्रवेशमार्गम् **इव** । **आनर्च** अर्चयामास । अर्चतेर्भौवादिकाल्लिट् ॥

वत्सोत्सुकाऽपि स्तिमिता सपर्यां प्रत्यग्रहीत्सेति ननन्दतुस्तौ ।
भक्त्योपपन्नेषु हि तद्विधानां प्रसादचिह्नानि पुरःफलानि ॥ २२ ॥

सा धेनुः **वत्सोत्सुका अपि** वत्से उत्कण्ठितापि **स्तिमिता** निश्चला सती **सपर्यां** पूजां **प्रत्यग्रहीत् इति** हेतोः **तौ** दंपती **ननन्दतुः** । पूजास्वीकारस्यानन्दहेतुत्वमाह—भक्त्येति । पूज्येष्वनुरागो भक्तिः । तया [**भक्त्या**] **उपपन्नेषु** युक्तेषु विषये **तद्विधानाम्** । तस्या धेन्वा विधेव विधा प्रकारो येषां तेषाम् । महतामित्यर्थः । प्रसादस्य चिह्नानि लिङ्गानि [**प्रसादचिह्नानि**] पूजास्वीकारादीनि **पुरःफलानि** पुरोगतानि प्रत्यासन्नानि फलानि येषां तानि **हि** । अविलम्बितफलसूचकलिङ्गदर्शनादानन्दो युज्यत इत्यर्थः ॥

गुरोः सदारस्य निपीड्य पादौ समाप्य सांध्यं च विधिं दिलीपः ।
दोहावसाने पुनरेव दोग्ध्रीं भेजे भुजोच्छिन्नरिपुर्निषण्णाम् ॥ २३ ॥

भुजोच्छिन्नरिपुः दिलीपः सदारस्य दारैररुन्धत्या सह वर्तमानस्य **गुरोः** उभयोरपीत्यर्थः । 'भार्या जायाथ पुंभूम्नि दाराः' इत्यमरः । **पादौ निपीड्य** अभिवन्द्य

---

१ अतितृष्णया सादरं ददर्श । सतृष्णमालोकनं पानमुच्यते । उत्प्रेक्षालंकारः । २ लोहितत्वाद्धेनोः संध्यासाम्यम् । क्षपाऽत्र चन्द्रालोकरमणीया ग्राह्या । दिनक्षपासाम्याद्राज्ञःप्रभावजतेजसोज्ज्वलत्वं राज्या अतिस्निग्धमधुरत्वं ध्वनितम् । 'समासे लिङ्गभेदाप्रतीतेर्दिनशब्दस्य नोपमादोषः । यदाह—इष्टः पुन्नपुंसकयोः प्रायेण । इति चा०. ३ आत्मसिद्धेः इ. दिनकरः पठति । ४ 'प्रसितोत्सुकाभ्यां तृतीया' च इति सप्तमी तृतीया च स्यात् ।

सांध्यं संध्यायां विहितं **विधिं** अनुष्ठानं **च समाप्य । दोहावसाननिषण्णां** आसीनां **दोग्ध्रीं** दोहनशीलाम् । 'तृन्' इति तृन्प्रत्ययः । धेनुं **एव भेजे पुनः** सेवितवान् । दोग्ध्रीमिति निरुपपदप्रयोगात्कामधेनुत्वं गम्यते ॥

तामन्तिकन्यस्तबलिप्रदीपामन्वास्य गोप्ता गृहिणीसहायः ।
क्रमेण सुप्तामनु संविवेश सुप्तोत्थितां प्रातरनूदतिष्ठत् ॥ २४ ॥

गोप्ता रक्षकः **गृहिणीसहायः** पत्नीद्वितीयः सन् । उभावपीत्यर्थः । [**अन्तिकन्यस्तबलिप्रदीपाम्**] अन्तिके न्यस्ता बलयः प्रदीपाश्च यस्यास्तां तथोक्तां **तां** पूर्वोक्तां निषण्णां धेनुम् **अन्वास्य** अनूपविश्य **क्रमेण सुप्तामनु** अनन्तरं **संविवेश** सुष्वाप । **प्रातः सुप्तोत्थिताम् अनूदतिष्ठद्** उत्थितवान् । अत्रानुशब्देन धेनुराजव्यापारयोः पौर्वापर्यमुच्यते । क्रमशब्देन धेनुव्यापाराणामेव । इत्यपौनरुक्त्यम् । 'कर्मप्रवचनीययुक्ते—' इति द्वितीया ॥

इत्थं व्रतं धारयतः प्रजार्थं समं महिष्या महनीयकीर्तेः ।
सप्त व्यतीयुस्त्रिगुणानि तस्य दिनानि दीनोद्धरणोचितस्य ॥ २५ ॥

इत्थम् अनेन प्रकारेण **प्रजार्थं** संतानाय **महिष्या समम्** अभिषिक्तपत्न्या सह । 'कृताभिषेका महिषी' इत्यमरः । **व्रतं धारयतः** । महनीया पूज्या कीर्तिर्यस्य तस्य । [**महनीयकीर्तेः**] दीनानामुद्धरणं दैन्यविमोचनम् । तत्रोचितस्य परिचितस्य [**दीनोद्धरणोचितस्य**] **तस्य** नृपस्य । त्रयो गुणा आवृत्तयो येषां तानि **त्रिगुणानि** त्रिरावृत्तानि **सप्त दिनानि** एकविंशतिर्दिनानि **व्यतीयुः** ॥

अन्येद्युरात्मानुचरस्य भावं जिज्ञासमाना मुनिहोमधेनुः ।
गङ्गाप्रपातान्तविरूढशष्पं गौरीगुरोर्गह्वरमाविवेश ॥ २६ ॥

अन्येद्युः अन्यस्मिन्दिने द्वाविंशे दिने । 'सद्यः परुत्परारि—' इत्यादिना निपातनादव्ययम् । 'अथात्राह्नाय पूर्वेऽह्नीत्यादौ पूर्वोत्तरापरात् । तथाधरान्यान्यतरेतरात्पूर्वेद्युरादयः' इत्यमरः । **मुनिहोमधेनुः आत्मानुचरस्य भावम्** अभिप्रायं दृढभक्तिभावम् 'भावोऽभिप्राय आशयः' इति यादवः । **जिज्ञासमाना** ज्ञातुमिच्छन्ती । 'ज्ञाश्रुस्मृदृशां सनः' इत्यात्मने[1]पदे शानच् । प्रपतत्यस्मिन्निति प्रपातः पतनप्रदेशः । गङ्गायाः प्रपातस्तस्यान्ते समीपे विरूढानि जातानि शष्पाणि बालतृणानि यस्मिंस्तत् [**गङ्गाप्रपातान्तविरूढशष्पम्**] । 'शष्पं बालतृणं घासः' इत्यमरः । **गौरीगुरोः** पार्वतीपितुः **गह्वरं** गुहाम् **आविवेश** ॥

सा दुष्प्रधर्षा मनसाऽपि हिंस्रैरित्यद्रिशोभाप्रहितेक्षणेन ।
अलक्षिताभ्युत्पतनो नृपेण प्रसह्य सिंहः किल तां चकर्ष ॥ २७ ॥

सा धेनुः **हिंस्रैः** व्याघ्रादिभिः **मनसापि दुष्प्रधर्षा** दुर्धर्षा **इति** हेतोरद्रिशोभायां प्रहितेक्षणेन दत्तदृष्टिना [**अद्रिशोभाप्रहितेक्षणेन**] **नृपेण** अलक्षितम-

---

१ सन्नन्तस्य ज्ञाधातोरात्मनेपदित्वात् शानच् । गौरीगुरोर्हिमाचलस्य । २ दुःखेन प्रधार्यते इति दुष्प्रधर्षा । कर्मणि खल् । सिंहः—हिनस्ति मारयतीति पृषोदरादित्वात्सिद्धम् । हिंसेर्वर्णविपर्ययः । तदुक्तम्–'सिंहो वर्णविपर्ययात्' । किल–अलीकार्थेन किलशब्देन सिंहाक्रमणं मायामात्रमिति सूचितम् ।

भ्युत्पतनमभिमुख्येनोत्पतनं यस्य स [**अलक्षिताभ्युत्पतनः**] **सिंहः तां धेनुं प्रसह्य** हठात् । ' प्रसह्य तु हठार्थकम् ' इत्यमरः । **चकर्ष** । **किल** इत्यलीके ॥

तदीयमाक्रन्दितमार्तसाधोर्गुहानिबद्धप्रतिशब्ददीर्घम् ।
रश्मिष्विवादाय नगेन्द्रसक्तां निवर्तयामास नृपस्य दृष्टिम् ॥ २८ ॥

गुहानिबद्धेन प्रतिशब्देन प्रतिध्वनिना दीर्घम् [**गुहानिबद्धप्रतिशब्ददीर्घम्**] तस्या इदं **तदीयम्** । **आक्रन्दितम्** आर्तघोषणम् । आर्तेष्वापन्नेषु साधोर्हितकारिणः [**आर्तसाधोः**] **नृपस्य नगेन्द्रसक्तां दृष्टिम्** । **रश्मिषु** प्रग्रहेषु । ' किरणप्रग्रहौ रश्मी ' इत्यमरः । **आदाय इव** गृहीत्वेव । **निवर्तयामास** ॥

स पाटलायां गवि तस्थिवांसं धनुर्धरः केसरिणं ददर्श ।
अधित्यकायामिव धातुमय्यां लोध्रद्रुमं सानुमतः प्रफुल्लम् ॥ २९ ॥

धनुर्धरः स नृपः **पाटलायां** रक्तवर्णायां **गवि तस्थिवांसं** स्थितम् । ' क्वसुश्च ' इति क्वसुप्रत्ययः । **केसरिणं** सिंहम् । **सानुमतः** अद्रेः धातोर्गैरिकस्य विकारो धातुमयी तस्याम् [**धातुमय्यां**] **अधित्यकायां** ऊर्ध्वभूमौ । ' उपत्यकाद्रेरासन्ना भूमिरूर्ध्वमधित्यका ' इत्यमरः । ' उपाधिभ्यां त्यकन्नासन्नारूढयोः ' इति त्यकन्प्रत्ययः । प्रफुल्लो विकसितस्तम् [**प्रफुल्लम्**] । ' फुल्ल विकसने ' इति धातोः पचाद्यच् । ' प्रफुल्तम् ' इति तकारपाठे ' ञिफला विशरणे ' इति धातोः कर्तरि क्तः । ' उत्परस्यातः ' इत्युकारादेशः । लोध्राख्यं द्रुमम् [**लोध्रद्रुमम्**] **इव ददर्श** ॥

ततो मृगेन्द्रस्य मृगेन्द्रगामी वधाय वध्यस्य शरं शरण्यः ।
जाताभिषङ्गो नृपतिर्निषङ्गादुद्धर्तुमैच्छत्प्रसभोद्धृतारिः ॥ ३० ॥

ततः सिंहदर्शनानन्तरं **मृगेन्द्रगामी** सिंहगामी । शरणं रक्षणम् । ' शरणं गृहरक्षित्रोः ' इत्यमरः । ' शरणं रक्षणे गृहे ' इति यादवः । शरणे साधु **शरण्यः** । ' तत्र साधुः ' इति यत्प्रत्ययः । प्रसभेन बलात्कारेणोद्धृता अरयो येन सः [**प्रसभोद्धृतारिः**] **नृपतिः** राजा **जाताभिषङ्गः** जातपराभवः सन् । ' अभिषङ्गः पराभवः ' इत्यमरः । **वध्यस्य** वधार्हस्य । ' दण्डादिभ्यो यः ' इति यप्रत्ययः । **मृगेन्द्रस्य वधाय निषङ्गात्** तूणीरात् । ' तूणोपासङ्गतूणीरनिषङ्गा इषुधिर्द्वयोः । ' इत्यमरः । **शरम् उद्धर्तुम् ऐच्छत्** ॥

वामेतरस्तस्य करः प्रहर्तुर्नखप्रभाभूषितकङ्कपत्रे ।
सक्ताङ्गुलिः सायकपुङ्ख एव चित्रार्पितारम्भ इवावतस्थे ॥ ३१ ॥

प्रहर्तुः तस्य वामेतरः दक्षिणः **करः** । नखप्रभाभिर्भूषितानि विच्छुरितानि कङ्कस्य पक्षिविशेषस्य पत्राणि यस्य तस्मिन् [**नखप्रभाभूषितकङ्कपत्रे**] । ' कङ्कः

---

१ अत्र करणस्यैवाधिकरणविवक्षायां सप्तमी । यथोक्तम्—' व्याददाने चतुर्थी स्याद्दर्शने कथनेऽपि च । आदाय करणे योगे सप्तमी कैश्चिदुच्यते ॥' इति सु० ।

२ धातुमय्याम्—इत्यत्र प्राचुर्यार्थे मयट् । हिमाद्रिशिखराणां धातुमयत्वं वर्णितं कुमारसंभवे—यश्चाप्सरोविभ्रममण्डनानां संपादयित्रीं शिखरैर्बिभर्ति । बलाहकच्छेदविभक्तरागामकालसंध्यामिव धातुमत्ताम् ॥ इति केसरिपदेन प्रफुल्लत्वात्साम्यामिति चा० वि० । ३ मृगेन्द्रवद्गन्तुं शीलमस्य ।

पक्षिविशेषे स्याद्बकाकारे युधिष्ठिरे । ' इति विश्वः । ' कङ्कस्तु कर्कटः ' इति यादवः । सायकस्य पुङ्खे [**सायकपुङ्खे**] कर्तर्याख्ये मूलप्रदेशे **एव** । ' कर्तरी पुङ्खे ' इति यादवः । **सक्ताङ्गुलिः** सन् । **चित्रार्पितारम्भः** चित्रलिखितशरोद्धरणोद्योगः **इव** । **अवतस्थे** ॥

बाहुप्रतिष्टम्भविवृद्धमन्युरभ्यर्णमागस्कृतमस्पृशद्भिः ।
राजा स्वतेजोभिरदह्यतान्तर्भोगीव मन्त्रौषधिरुद्धवीर्यः ॥ ३२ ॥

[**बाहुप्रतिष्टम्भविवृद्धमन्युः**] बाहोः प्रतिष्टम्भेन प्रतिबन्धेन । ' प्रतिबन्धः प्रतिष्टम्भः ' इत्यमरः । विवृद्धमन्युः प्रवृद्धरोषः **राजा** [**मन्त्रौषधिरुद्धवीर्यः**] मन्त्रौषधिभ्यां रुद्धवीर्यः प्रतिबद्धशक्तिः **भोगी** सर्पः **इव** । ' भोगी राजभुजंगयोः ' इति शाश्वतः । **अभ्यर्णम्** अन्तिकम् । ' उपकण्ठान्तिकाभ्यर्णाभ्यग्रा अप्यभितोऽव्ययम् । ' इत्यमरः । **आगस्कृतम्** अपराधकारिणम् **अस्पृशद्भिः स्वतेजोभिः अन्तः अदह्यत** । ' अधिक्षेपाद्यसहनं तेजः प्राणात्ययेष्वपि । ' इति यादवः ॥

तमार्यगृह्यं निगृहीतधेनुर्मनुष्यवाचा मनुवंशकेतुम् ।
विस्माययन्विस्मितमात्मवृत्तौ सिंहोरुसत्त्वं निजगाद सिंहः ॥ ३३ ॥

निगृहीता पीडिता धेनुर्येन स [**निगृहीतधेनुः**] **सिंहः** । [**आर्यगृह्यं**] आर्याणां सतां गृह्यं पक्ष्यम् । ' पदास्वैरिबाह्यापक्ष्येषु च ' इति क्यप् । मनुवंशस्य केतुं चिह्नं केतुवद्व्यावर्तकम् [**मनुवंशकेतुम्**] । सिंह इवोरुसत्त्वो महाबलस्तम् [**सिंहोरुसत्त्वम्**] । [**आत्मवृत्तौ**] आत्मनो वृत्तौ बाहुस्तम्भरूपे व्यापारेऽभूतपूर्वत्वाद **विस्मितम्** । कर्तरि क्तः । **तं** दिलीपं **मनुष्यवाचा** करणेन पुनः **विस्माययन्** विस्मयमाश्चर्यं प्रापयन् **निजगाद** । ' स्मिङ् ईषद्धसने ' इति धातोर्णिचि वृद्धावायादेशे शतृप्रत्यये च सति विस्माययन्निति रूपं सिद्धम् । ' विस्मापयन् ' इति पाठे पुगागममात्रं वक्तव्यम् । तच्च ' नित्यं स्मयतेः ' इति हेतुभयविवक्षायामेवेति ' भीस्म्योर्हेतुभये ' इत्यात्मनेपदे विस्मापयमान इति स्यात् । तस्मान्मनुष्यवाचा विस्माययन्निति रूपं सिद्धम् । करणविवक्षायां न कश्चिद्दोषः ॥

अलं महीपाल तव श्रमेण प्रयुक्तमप्यस्त्रमितो वृथा स्यात् ।
न पादपोन्मूलनशक्ति रंहः शिलोच्चये मूर्छति मारुतस्य ॥ ३४ ॥

हे **महीपाल तव श्रमेण अलम्** । साध्याभावाच्छ्रमो न कर्तव्य इत्यर्थः । अत्र गम्यमानसाधनक्रियापेक्षया श्रमस्य करणत्वात्तृतीया । उक्तं च न्यासोद्द्योते--' न केवलं श्रूयमाणैव क्रिया निमित्तं करणभावस्य । अपि तर्हि गम्यमानापि ' इति । ' अलं भूषणपर्याप्ति-

---

१ अधिक्षेपापमानादेः प्रयुक्तस्य परेण यत् । प्राणत्यागेऽप्यसहनं तत्तेजः समुदाहृतम् ॥ इति भरतश्च । २ आर्यगृह्यम्–आर्यैर्गृह्यते स्वाश्रयत्वेन सेव्यते इत्यार्यगृह्यस्तम् । साधुपक्षाश्रितमित्यर्थः । आर्यलक्षणं यथा–कर्तव्यमाचरन्कार्यमकर्तव्यमनाचरन् । तिष्ठति प्रकृताचारे स तु आर्य इति स्मृतः ॥ इति । विस्माययन्—इत्यत्र ' विस्मापयन् ' इति दिनकरादयः पठन्ति । किं त्वयं पाठो व्याकरणदोषदुष्टत्वाद्धेयः । तथा हि । यत्र हेतुत एव (न तु कर्तृतः) भयस्य विस्मयस्य चोत्पत्तिस्तत्र णिजन्तयोः भीस्मिधात्वोः परस्मैपदमेव स्यात्स्मिधातोः पुगागमश्च न स्यात् । अत्र तु हेतुत एव विस्मयस्य विवक्षितत्वात्पुगागमाप्राप्तेर्विस्माययन्नित्येव साधु ।

शक्तिवारणवाचकम् ।' इत्यमरः । **इतः** अस्मिन्मयि । सार्वविभक्तिकस्तसिः । **प्रयुक्तम् अपि अस्त्रं वृथा स्यात्** । तथा हि । [**पादपोन्मूलनशक्ति**] पादपोन्मूलने शक्तिर्यस्य तत्तथोक्तं **मारुतस्य रंहः** वेगः **शिलोच्चये** पर्वते **न मूर्च्छति** न प्रसरति ॥

कैलासगौरं वृषमारुरुक्षोः पादार्पणानुग्रहपूतपृष्ठम् ।
अवेहि मां किंकरमष्टमूर्तेः कुम्भोदरं नाम निकुम्भमित्रम् ॥ ३५ ॥

[**कैलासगौरं**] कैलास इव गौरः शुभ्रस्तम् । 'चामीकरे च शुभ्रे च गौरमाहुर्मनीषिणः ।' इति शाश्वतः । **वृषं** वृषभम् **आरुरुक्षोः** आरोढुमिच्छोः । स्वस्योपरि पदं निक्षिप्य वृषमारोहत इत्यर्थः । अष्टौ मूर्तयो यस्य स तस्य **अष्टमूर्तेः** शिवस्य [**पादार्पणानुग्रहपूतपृष्ठम्**] पादार्पणं पादन्यासस्तदेवानुग्रहः प्रसादस्तेन पूतं पृष्ठं यस्य तं तथोक्तं **निकुम्भमित्रं कुम्भोदरं नाम किंकरं माम् अवेहि** विद्धि । 'पृथिवी सलिलं तेजो वायुराकाशमेव च । सूर्याचन्द्रमसौ सोमयाजी चेत्यष्टमूर्तयः' इति यादवः ॥

अमुं पुरः पश्यसि देवदारुं पुत्रीकृतोऽसौ वृषभध्वजेन ।
यो हेमकुम्भस्तननिःसृतानां स्कन्दस्य मातुः पयसां रसज्ञः ॥ ३६ ॥

पुरः अग्रतः **अमुं देवदारुं पश्यसि** । इति काकुः । **असौ** देवदारुः वृषभो ध्वजे यस्य स तेन [**वृषभध्वजेन**] शिवेन **पुत्रीकृतः** पुत्रत्वेन स्वीकृतः । अभूततद्भावे च्विः । **यः** देवदारुः **स्कन्दस्य मातुः** गौर्या हेम्नः कुम्भ एव स्तनः । तस्मान्निःसृतानां [**हेमकुम्भस्तननिःसृतानां**] **पयसाम्** अम्बूनां **रसज्ञः** स्वादज्ञः । स्कन्दपक्षे हेमकुम्भ इव स्तन इति विग्रहः । पयसां क्षीराणाम् । 'पयः क्षीरं पयोऽम्बु च' इत्यमरः । स्कन्दसमानप्रेमास्पदमिति भावः ॥

कण्डूयमानेन कटं कदाचिद्वन्यद्विपेनोन्मथिता त्वगस्य ।
अथैनमद्रेस्तनया शुशोच सेनान्यमालीढमिवासुरास्त्रैः ॥ ३७ ॥

कदाचित्कटं कपोलं **कण्डूयमानेन** कर्षता । 'कण्ड्वादिभ्यो यक्' इति यक् । ततः शानच् । **वन्यद्विपेनास्य** देवदारोः । **त्वक् उन्मथिता** । **अथ अद्रेः तनया** गौरी । **असुरास्त्रैः आलीढं** क्षतम् । सेनां नयतीति सेनानीः स्कन्दः । 'पार्वतीनन्दनः स्कन्दः सेनानीः' इत्यमरः । 'सत्सूद्विष–' इत्यादिना क्विप् । तम् [**सेनान्यम्**] **इव** । **एनं** देवदारुं **शुशोच** ॥

---

१ अयमेव भावोऽष्टमसर्गे–'द्रुमसानुमतां किमन्तरं यदि वायौ द्वितयेऽपि ते चलाः ।'' भवानिनरानभिभवितुं शक्तोऽपि मादृशान्विनाशयितुं न शक्नोतीति भावः । २ निकुम्भो गणभेदः कुम्भकर्णपुत्रो वेति चा० । पार्वतीवाहनः सिंहः इति वल्लभः । निकुम्भतुल्यमिति वल्लभः पठति । ३ भिन्नकण्ठध्वनिर्धीरैः काकुरित्यभिधीयते । इ. साहित्यदर्पणम् । अत्र कण्ठस्वरभङ्गीविशेषेण 'पश्यसि' इत्यनेन पश्यस्येव इत्यर्थः प्रतीयते ।

तदाप्रभृत्येव वनद्विपानां त्रासार्थमस्मिन्नहमद्रिकुक्षौ ।
व्यापारितः शूलभृता विधाय सिंहत्वमङ्कागतसत्त्ववृत्ति ॥ ३८ ॥

तदा तत्कालः प्रभृतिरादिर्यस्मिन्कर्मणि तत्तथा **तदाप्रभृति एव वनद्विपानां त्रासार्थं** भयार्थं **शूलभृता** शिवेन । अङ्कं समीपमागताः प्राप्ताः सत्त्वाः प्राणिनो वृत्तिर्यस्मिंस्तद[1] [**अङ्कागतसत्त्ववृत्ति**] । 'अङ्कः समीप उत्सङ्गे चिह्ने स्थानापराधयोः ।' इति केशवः । **सिंहत्वं विधाय** । **अस्मिन् अद्रिकुक्षौ** गुहायाम् **अहं व्यापारितः** नियुक्तः ॥

तस्यालमेषा क्षुधितस्य तृप्त्यै प्रदिष्टकाला परमेश्वरेण ।
उपस्थिता शोणितपारणा मे सुरद्विषश्चान्द्रमसी सुधेव ॥ ३९ ॥

परमेश्वरेण प्रदिष्टो निर्दिष्टः कालो भोजनवेला यस्याः सा [**प्रदिष्टकाला**] **उपस्थिता** प्राप्ता **एषा** गोरूपा **शोणितपारणा** रुधिरस्य व्रतान्तभोजनम् । **सुरद्विषः** राहोः चन्द्रमस इयं **चान्द्रमसी सुधा इव** । **क्षुधितस्य** बुभुक्षितस्य **तस्य** अङ्कागतसत्त्ववृत्तेः **मे** मम सिंहस्य **तृप्त्यै अलं** पर्याप्ता[2] । 'नमःस्वस्ति–' इत्यादिना चतुर्थी ॥

स त्वं निवर्तस्व विहाय लज्जां गुरोर्भवान्दर्शितशिष्यभक्तिः ।
शस्त्रेण रक्ष्यं यदशक्यरक्षं न तद्यशः शस्त्रभृतां क्षिणोति ॥ ४० ॥

स एवमुपायशून्यः **त्वं लज्जां विहाय निर्वतस्व** । **भवान्** त्वं **गुरोः** [**दर्शितशिष्यभक्तिः**] दर्शिता प्रकाशिता शिष्यस्य कर्तव्या भक्तिर्येन स तथोक्तोऽस्ति । ननु गुरुधनं विनाश्य कथं तत्समीपं गच्छेयमत आह–शस्त्रेणेति । **यत् रक्ष्यं** धनं **शस्त्रेण** आयुधेन । 'शस्त्रमायुधलोहयोः' इत्यमरः । अशक्या रक्षा यस्य तद् **अशक्यरक्षम्** । रक्षितुमशक्यमित्यर्थः । **तद्** रक्ष्यं नष्टमपि **शस्त्रभृतां यशः न क्षिणोति** न हिनस्ति । अशक्यार्थेष्वप्रतिविधानं न दोषायेति भावः ॥

इति प्रगल्भं पुरुषाधिराजो मृगाधिराजस्य वचो निशम्य ।
प्रत्याहतास्त्रो गिरिशप्रभावादात्मन्यवज्ञां शिथिलीचकार ॥ ४१ ॥

पुरुषाणामधिराजो[3] [**पुरुषाधिराजः**] नृपः **इति प्रगल्भं मृगाधिराजस्य वचः निशम्य** श्रुत्वा [**गिरिशप्रभावात्**] गिरिशस्येश्वरस्य प्रभावात् **प्रत्याहतास्त्रः** कुण्ठितास्त्रः सन् **आत्मनि** विषये **अवज्ञाम्** अपमानं **शिथिलीचकार** । तत्याजेत्यर्थः । अवज्ञातोऽहमिति निर्वेदं न प्रापेत्यर्थः । समानेषु हि क्षत्रियाणामभिमानः । न सर्वेश्वरं प्रतीति भावः ॥

प्रत्यब्रवीच्चैनमिषुप्रयोगे तत्पूर्वभङ्गे वितथप्रयत्नः ।
जडीकृतस्त्र्यम्बकवीक्षणेन वज्रं मुमुक्षन्निव वज्रपाणिः ॥ ४२ ॥

---

१ मम समीपे ये जीवा आगच्छन्ति तान्भक्षित्वा जीवामीत्यर्थः । इ. सु० । २ अलमत्यर्थं क्षुधितस्य मे तृप्त्यै इयं शोणितपारणोपस्थितेति वल्लभसंमतोऽन्वयः । ३ अधिको राजाधिराजः । राजाहःसखिभ्यष्टच् ।

स एव पूर्वः प्रथमो भङ्गः प्रतिबन्धो यस्य तस्मिन् **तत्पूर्वभङ्गे इषुप्रयोगे वितथप्रयत्नः** विफलप्रयासः। अत एव **वज्रं** कुलिशं **मुमुक्षन्** मोक्तुमिच्छन्। अम्बकं लोचनम्। 'दृग्दृष्टिनेत्रलोचनचक्षुर्नयनाम्बकेक्षणाक्षीणि।' इति हलायुधः। त्रीण्यम्बकानि यस्य स त्र्यम्बको हरः। तस्य वीक्षणेन [**त्र्यम्बक[1]वीक्षणेन**] **जडीकृतः** निष्पन्दीकृतः। वज्रं पाणौ यस्य स **वज्रपाणिः** इन्द्रः। 'प्रहरणार्थेभ्यः परे निष्ठासप्तम्यौ भवत इति वक्तव्यम्।' इति पाणेः सप्तम्यन्तस्योत्तरनिपातः। स इव स्थितो नृपः **एनं सिंहं प्रत्यब्रवीत् च**। 'बाहुं[2] सवज्रं शक्रस्य क्रुद्धस्यास्तम्भयत्प्रभुः' इति महाभारते॥

संरुद्धचेष्टस्य मृगेन्द्र कामं हास्यं वचस्तद्यदहं विवक्षुः।
अन्तर्गतं प्राणभृतां हि वेद सर्वं भवान्भावमतोऽभिधास्ये॥ ४३॥

हे **मृगेन्द्र संरुद्धचेष्टस्य** प्रतिबद्धव्यापारस्य मम **तत्** वचो वाक्यं **कामं हास्यं** परिहसनीयम्। **यद्** वचः 'स त्वं मदीयेन' (२-४५) इत्यादिकं **अहम् विवक्षुः** वक्तुमिच्छुरस्मि। तर्हि तूष्णीं स्थीयतामित्याशङ्क्येश्वरकिंकरत्वात्सर्वज्ञं त्वां प्रति न हास्यमित्याह—अन्तरिति। **हि** यतः **भवान्प्राणभृतां अन्तर्गतं** हृद्गतं वाग्वृत्त्या बहिरप्रकाशितमेव **सर्वं भावं वेद** वेत्ति। 'विदो लटो वा' इति णलादेशः। **अतः अहम् अभिधास्ये** वक्ष्यामि। वच इति प्रकृतं कर्म संबध्यते। अन्ये त्वीदृग्वचनमाकर्ण्यासंभावितार्थमेतदित्युपहसन्ति। अतस्तु मौनमेव भूषणम्। त्वं तु वाङ्मनसयोरेकविध एवायमिति जानासि। अतोऽभिधास्ये यद्वचोऽहं विवक्षुरित्यर्थः॥

मान्यः स मे स्थावरजङ्गमानां सर्गस्थितिप्रत्यवहारहेतुः।
गुरोरपीदं धनमाहिताग्नेर्नश्यत्पुरस्तादनुपेक्षणीयम्॥ ४४॥

प्रत्यवहारः प्रलयः। [**स्थावर[3]जङ्गमानां**] स्थावराणां तरुशैलादीनां जङ्गमानां मनुष्यादीनां [**सर्गस्थितिप्रत्यवहारहेतुः**] सर्गस्थितिप्रत्यवहारेषु हेतुः **स** ईश्वरो **मे** मम **मान्यः** पूज्यः। अलङ्घ्यशासन इत्यर्थः। शासनं च 'सिंहत्वमङ्कागतसत्त्ववृत्ति' (२।३८) इत्युक्तरूपम्। तर्हि विसृज्य गम्यताम्। नेत्याह—गुरोरपीति। **पुरस्ताद्** अग्रे **नश्यद् इदम् आहिताग्नेः[4] गुरोः धनम् अपि** गोरूपम् **अनुपेक्षणीयम्**। आहिताग्नेरिति विशेषणेनानुपेक्षाकारणं हविःसाधनत्वं सूचयति॥

---

१ अस्य व्युत्पत्तिर्महाभारते द्रोणपर्वणि यथा—तिस्रो देव्यो यदा चैनं भजन्ते भुवनेश्वरम्। द्यौरापः पृथिवी चैव त्र्यम्बकस्तु ततः स्मृतः॥ २ अयं संपूर्णश्लोको द्रोणपर्वणि यथा—'असूयतश्च शक्रस्य वज्रेण प्रहरिष्यतः। बाहुं सवज्रं तं तस्य क्रुद्धस्यास्तम्भयद्विभुः'॥ पुरा किल देवैरभ्यर्थितेन शिवेन दह्यमानानि त्रिपुरपुराणि द्रष्टुमद्भुतं शिशुमङ्के धारयन्ती देवी पार्वत्युपस्थिता। सा च सुरान्दृष्ट्वाऽपृच्छत्—'ब्रूत कोऽयं बालः' इति। तदा बालस्याप्रतिमं तेजो दृष्ट्वेन्द्रोऽसूयया वज्रमुद्यम्य तं हन्तुं प्रचक्रमे। बालरूपधारी शंकरश्च तस्य तं हस्तं स्तम्भयांचकार। पश्चाद्देवैः प्रसादिते शंकरे शक्रस्य बाहुः प्रकृतिं प्राप्तः। इत्येषा भारती कथात्रानुसंधेया। भा. द्रो. प. अ. २००, अनुशासनप. अ. ६०. ३ स्थानशीलाः स्थावराः। 'स्थेशभासपिसकसो वरच्' इति वरच्। जङ्गम्यन्ते वक्रं गच्छन्तीति जङ्गमाः। गत्यर्थानां 'नित्यं कौटिल्ये—' इति यङ्। स्वाम्यादिमते भृशार्थे यङ्। ४ आहितोऽग्निर्येन। 'अग्न्याहितः' इत्यपि रूपम्।

स त्वं मदीयेन शरीरवृत्तिं देहेन निर्वर्तयितुं प्रसीद ।
दिनावसानोत्सुकबालवत्सा विसृज्यतां धेनुरियं महर्षेः ॥ ४५ ॥

सः अङ्कागतसत्त्ववृत्तिः **त्वं मदीयेन देहेन [शरीरवृत्तिं]** शरीरस्य वृत्तिं जीवनं **निर्वर्तयितुं** संपादयितुं **प्रसीद । [दिनावसानोत्सुकबालवत्सा]** दिनावसान उत्सुको माता समागमिष्यतीत्युत्कण्ठितो बालवत्सो यस्याः सा **महर्षेः इयं धेनुः विसृज्यताम्** ॥

अथान्धकारं गिरिगह्वराणां दंष्ट्रामयूखैः शकलानि कुर्वन् ।
भूयः स भूतेश्वरपार्श्ववर्ती किंचिद्विहस्यार्थपतिं बभाषे ॥ ४६ ॥

अथ [भूतेश्वरपार्श्ववर्ती] भूतेश्वरस्य पार्श्ववर्त्यनुचरः **स** सिंहः **[गिरिगह्वराणां]** गिरेर्गह्वराणां गुहानाम् । 'देवखातबिले गुहा । गह्वरम्' इत्यमरः । **अन्धकारं** ध्वान्तं **दंष्ट्रामयूखैः शकलानि** खण्डानि **कुर्वन्** । निरस्यन्नित्यर्थः । **किंचिद् विहस्य अर्थपतिं** नृपं **भूयः बभाषे** । हासकारणम् 'अल्पस्य हेतोर्बहु हातुमिच्छन्' (२।४७) इति वक्ष्यमाणं द्रष्टव्यम् ॥

एकातपत्रं जगतः प्रभुत्वं नवं वयः कान्तमिदं वपुश्च ।
अल्पस्य हेतोर्बहु हातुमिच्छन्विचारमूढः प्रतिभासि मे त्वम् ॥ ४७ ॥

एकातपत्रम् एकच्छत्रं **जगतः प्रभुत्वं** स्वामित्वम् **नवं वयः** यौवनम् **इदं कान्तं** रम्यं **वपुश्च** । इत्येवं **बहु अल्पस्य हेतोः** अल्पेन कारणेन । अल्पफलायेत्यर्थः । 'षष्ठी हेतुप्रयोगे' इति षष्ठी । **हातुं** त्यक्तुम् **इच्छन् त्वं** विचारे कार्याकार्यविमर्शे मूढो मूर्खः **[विचारमूढः] मे** मम **प्रतिभासि** ॥

भूतानुकम्पा तव चेदियं गौरेका भवेत्स्वस्तिमती त्वदन्ते ।
जीवन्पुनः शश्वदुपप्लवेभ्यः प्रजाः प्रजानाथ पितेव पासि ॥ ४८ ॥

तव भूतेष्वनुकम्पा कृपा **[भूतानुकम्पा] चेत्** । 'कृपा दयाऽनुकम्पा स्यात्' इत्यमरः । कृपैव वर्तते चेदित्यर्थः । तर्हि **त्वदन्ते** तव नाशे सति **इयम् एका गौः** । स्वस्ति क्षेममस्या अस्तीति **स्वस्तिमती । भवेत्** । जीवेदित्यर्थः । 'स्वस्त्याशीः-क्षेमपुण्यादौ' इत्यमरः । हे **प्रजानाथ जीवन्पुनः पिता इव प्रजा उपप्लवेभ्यः**

---

१ 'उत्सुकबालवत्सत्वेन द्वयोरपि (नन्दिन्यास्तद्वत्सस्यापि) नाशः सूचितः ।' इति चा. 'प्रसीद' इत्यत्र 'यतस्व' 'विसृज्यताम्' इत्यत्र 'विमुच्यताम्' इति व० चा० सु० पठन्ति । २ 'शकलानि' इति 'अन्धकारम्' इत्यस्य विधेयविशेषणम् । मध्ये मध्ये दन्तकिरणानां प्रवेशात्तत्रान्धकारो व्यवच्छिन्न इत्यर्थः । 'गिरिगह्वराणाम्' इत्यत्र 'गिरिकन्दराणाम्' इति पाठः । ३ एकातपत्रम्—प्रतिद्वंद्विनृपान्तराभावादद्वितीयमातपत्रं यस्मिन् तत् । आतपात्त्रायत इति आतपत्रमत्र राजच्छत्रम् । ४ 'एका गौः स्वस्तिमती भवेत्' अनेन त्वयि मृते सकलं जगद्विपद्ग्रस्तं भवेदतस्तवातिनृशंसतैव प्रसज्येतेति सूचितम् । तदुक्तं कामन्दकीये—'यदि न स्यान्नरपतिः सम्यङ्नेता ततः प्रजा । अकर्णधारा जलधौ विप्लवेतेह नौरिव ॥' इति ।

विघ्नेभ्यः **शश्वत्** सदा । ‘ पुनःसदार्थयोः शश्वत् ’ इत्यमरः । **पासि** रक्षसि । स्वप्राणव्यये-नैकधेनुरक्षणाद्वरं जीवितेनैव शश्वदखिलजगत्त्राणमित्यर्थः ॥

न धर्मलोपादियं प्रवृत्तिः किं तु गुरुभयादित्यत आह—

अथैकधेनोरपराधचण्डाद्गुरोः कृशानुप्रतिमाद्बिभेषि ।
शक्योऽस्य मन्युर्भवता विनेतुं गाः कोटिशः स्पर्शयता घटोध्नीः ॥४९॥

अथ इति पक्षान्तरे । अथ वा [**एकधेनोः**] एकैव धेनुर्यस्य तस्मात् । अयं कोप-कारणोपन्यास इति ज्ञेयम् । अत एवापराधे गवोपेक्षालक्षणे सति चण्डादतिकोपनात् [**अपराधचण्डात्**] । ‘ चण्डस्त्वत्यन्तकोपनः ’ इत्यमरः । अत एव [**कृशानुप्रति-मात्**] कृशानुः प्रतिमोपमा यस्य तस्मादग्निकल्पाद् । **गुरोः बिभेषि** इति काकुः । ‘ भीत्रार्थानां भयहेतुः ’ इत्यपादानात्पञ्चमी । अल्पवित्तस्य धनहानिरतिदुःसहेति भावः । **अस्य** गुरोः **मन्युः** क्रोधः । ‘ मन्युर्दैन्ये क्रतौ क्रुधि ’ इत्यमरः । घटा इवोधांसि यासां ता **घटोध्नीः** । ‘ ऊधसोऽनङ् ’ इत्यनङादेशः । ‘ बहुव्रीहेरूधसो ङीष् ’ इति ङीष् । **कोटिशः गाः स्पर्शयता** प्रतिपादयता । ‘ विश्राणनं वितरणं स्पर्शनं प्रतिपादनम् । ’ इत्यमरः । **भवता विनेतुम्** अपनेतुं **शक्यः** ॥

तद्रक्ष कल्याणपरंपराणां भोक्तारमूर्जस्वलमात्मदेहम् ।
महीतलस्पर्शनमात्रभिन्नमृद्धं हि राज्यं पदमैन्द्रमाहुः ॥ ५० ॥

तत् तस्मात्कारणात् **कल्याणपरंपराणां भोक्तारम्** । कर्मणि षष्ठी । ऊर्जो बल-मस्यास्तीति **ऊर्जस्वलम्** । ‘ ज्योत्स्नातमिस्रा—’ इत्यादिना वलच्प्रत्ययान्तो निपातः । **आत्मदेहं रक्ष** । ननु गामुपेक्ष्यात्मदेहरक्षणे स्वर्गहानिः स्यात् । नेत्याह—महीतलेति । **हि ऋद्धं** समृद्धं **राज्यं** महीतलस्पर्शनमात्रेण भूतलसंबन्धमात्रेण भिन्नम् [**महीतल-स्पर्शनमात्रभिन्नम्**] **ऐन्द्रं** इन्द्रसंबन्धि **पदं** स्थानं **आहुः** । स्वर्गान्न भिद्यत इत्यर्थः ॥

एतावदुक्त्वा विरते मृगेन्द्रे प्रतिस्वनेनास्य गुहागतेन ।
शिलोच्चयोऽपि क्षितिपालमुच्चैः प्रीत्या तमेवार्थमभाषतेव ॥ ५१ ॥

मृगेन्द्रे एतावद् उक्त्वा विरते सति **गुहागतेन अस्य** सिंहस्य **प्रतिस्वनेन शिलोच्चयः** शैलः **अपि प्रीत्या तम् एव अर्थं क्षितिपालम् उच्चैः अभाषत इव** । इत्युत्प्रेक्षा । भाषिरयं ब्रुविसमानार्थत्वाद्द्विकर्मकः । ब्रुविस्तु द्विकर्मकेषु पठितः । तदुक्तम्— ‘ दुहियाचिरुधिप्रच्छिभिक्षिचिञामुपयोगनिमित्तमपूर्वविधौ । ब्रुविशासिगुणेन च यत्सचते तदकीर्तितमाचरितं कविना ॥ ’ इति ॥

निशम्य देवानुचरस्य वाचं मनुष्यदेवः पुनरप्युवाच ।
धेन्वा तदध्यासितकातराक्ष्या निरीक्ष्यमाणः सुतरां दयालुः ॥ ५२ ॥

---

१ अत्र कण्ठध्वनिविशेषेण ‘ त्वं बिभेषि ’ किं तु न ते भयं युक्तमित्यर्थसूचनात्काकुः । २ सति देहे धर्मार्थकाममोक्षाः पुरुषार्थाः साध्यन्ते । ते च कल्याणपरंपरासाधकाः । अयमत्रार्थ उक्तः कुमारसंभवेऽपि ‘ शरीरमाद्यं खलु धर्मसाधनम् ’ इति । ऊर्जस्वलमित्यनेन भोगसामर्थ्यमुक्तम् । उक्तं च ‘ भोज्यं भोजनशक्तिश्च......। विभवो दानशक्तिश्च नाल्पस्य तपसः फलम् ॥ ’ इति ।

देवानुचरस्य ईश्वरकिंकरस्य सिंहस्य **वाचं निशम्य मनुष्यदेवः**[1] राजा **पुनः अपि उवाच** । किंभूतः सन् । तेन सिंहेन तदध्यासितं व्याक्रमणम् । 'नपुंसके भावे क्तः ।' ते कातरे अक्षिणी यस्य तादृशया [**तदध्यासितकातराक्ष्या**[2]] । 'बहुव्रीहौ सक्थ्यक्ष्णोः स्वाङ्गात्षच् ' इति षच् । ' षिद्गौरादिभ्यश्च ' इति ङीष् । किं वा वक्ष्यतीति भीत्यैवं स्थित-येत्यर्थः । **धेन्वा निरीक्ष्यमाणः** अत एव **सुतरां दयालुः** सन् । सुतरामित्यत्र ' द्विवचनविभज्य–' इत्यादिना सुशब्दात्तरप् । ' किमेत्तिङव्यय–' इत्यादिनाम्प्रत्ययः । ' तद्धितश्चासर्वविभक्तिः ' इत्यव्ययसंज्ञा ॥

किमुवाचेत्याह—

क्षतात्किल त्रायत इत्युदग्रः क्षत्रस्य शब्दो भुवनेषु रूढः ।
राज्येन किं तद्विपरीतवृत्तेः प्राणैरुपक्रोशमलीमसैर्वा ॥ ५३ ॥

' क्षणु हिंसायाम् ' इति धातोः संपदादित्वात्क्विप् । ' गमादीनाम् ' इति वक्तव्यादनु-नासिकलोपे तुगागमे च क्षदिति रूपं सिद्धम् । क्षतो नाशात्त्रायत इति क्षत्रः । सुपीति योगविभागात्कः । तामेतां व्युत्पत्तिं कविरर्थतोऽनुक्रामति—क्षतादित्यादिना । **उदग्रः** उन्नतः **क्षत्त्रस्य** क्षत्त्रवर्णस्य **शब्दः** वाचकः । क्षत्त्रशब्दः इत्यर्थः । **क्षतात्त्रायते इति** व्युत्पत्त्या **भुवनेषु रूढः**[3] **किल** प्रसिद्धः खलु । नाश्वकर्णादिवत्केवलरूढः । किं तु पङ्कजादिवद्योगरूढ इत्यर्थः । ततः किमित्यत आह—[**तद्विपरीतवृत्तेः**] तस्य क्षत्त्र-शब्दस्य विपरीतवृत्तेर्विरुद्धव्यापारस्य क्षतत्त्राणमकुर्वतः पुंसः **राज्येन किम् उपक्रोश-मलीमसैः** निन्दामलिनैः । ' उपक्रोशो जुगुप्सा च कुत्सा निन्दा च गर्हणे । ' इत्यमरः । ' ज्योत्स्नातमिस्रा–' इत्यादिना मलीमसशब्दो निपातितः । ' मलीमसं तु मलिनं कच्चरं मल-दूषितम् । ' इत्यमरः । तैः **प्राणैर्वा**[4] किम् । निन्दितस्य सर्वं व्यर्थमित्यर्थः । एतेन ' एकातपत्रम् ' (२ । ४७) इत्यादिना श्लोकद्वयेनोक्तं प्रत्युक्तमिति वेदितव्यम् ॥

' अथैकधेनोः ' (२ । ४९) इत्यत्रोत्तरमाह—

कथं नु शक्योऽनुनयो महर्षेर्विश्राणनाच्चान्यपयस्विनीनाम् ।
इमामनूनां सुरभेरवेहि रुद्रौजसा तु प्रहृतं त्वयाऽस्याम् ॥ ५४ ॥

अनुनयः क्रोधापनयः । चकारो वाकारार्थः । **महर्षेः अनुनयः च** वान्यासां पयस्वि-नीनां दोग्ध्रीणां गवां [**अन्यपयस्विनीनाम्**] **विश्राणनाद्** दानात् । 'त्यागो वितरणं

---

१ मनुष्यदेवः–मनुष्येषु देव इव स्थितत्वात् । तदुक्तं मनुना–' महती देवता ह्येषा नररूपेण तिष्ठति । ' इति । २ ' तदध्यासनकातराक्ष्या ' इति वल्लभचारित्रवर्धनौ पठतः । ३ अस्य व्युत्प-त्तिर्महाभारते शान्तिपर्वणि यथा–ब्राह्मणानां क्षतत्त्राणात्ततः क्षत्त्रिय उच्यते इति । मनुरप्याह–ब्राह्मं प्राप्तेन संस्कारं क्षत्त्रियेण यथाविधि । सर्वस्यास्य यथान्यायं कर्तव्यं परिरक्षणम् ॥ इति । एवं किरातार्जुनीयेऽपि–स क्षत्त्रियस्त्राणसहः सतां यः इत्यादि । ४ अनुरूपभावः किरातार्जु-नीये–अभिमानधनस्य गत्वरैरसुभिः स्थास्नु यशश्चिचीषतः । अचिरांशुविलासचञ्चला ननु लक्ष्मीः फलमानुषङ्गिकम् ॥ इति ।

दानमुत्सर्जनविसर्जने । विश्राणनं वितरणम् ' इत्यमरः । **कथं नु शक्यः** । न शक्य इत्यर्थः । अत्र हेतुमाह-**इमां** गां **सुरभेः** कामधेनोः । ' पञ्चमी विभक्ते ' इति पञ्चमी । **अनूनाम्** अन्यूनाम् **अवेहि** जानीहि । तर्हि कथमस्याः परिभवोऽभूदित्याह—रुद्रौजसेति । **अस्यां** गवि **त्वया** कर्त्रा **प्रहृतं तु** प्रहारस्तु । 'नपुंसके भावे क्तः' । **रुद्रौजसा** ईश्वरसामर्थ्येन । न तु स्वयमित्यर्थः । ' सप्तम्यधिकरणे च ' इति सप्तमी ॥

तर्हि किं चिकीर्षितमित्यत्राह—

सेयं स्वदेहार्पणनिष्क्रयेण न्याय्या मया मोचयितुं भवत्तः ।
न पारणा स्याद्विहता तवैवं भवेदलुप्तश्च मुनेः क्रियार्थः ॥ ५५ ॥

सा इयं गौः **मया** निष्क्रीयते प्रत्याह्रियतेऽनेन परगृहीतमिति निष्क्रयः प्रतिशीर्षकम् । ' एरच् ' इत्यच्प्रत्ययः । स्वदेहार्पणमेव निष्क्रयस्तेन [**स्वदेहार्पणनिष्क्रयेण**] **भवत्तः** त्वत्तः । 'पञ्चम्यास्तसिल्' । **मोचयितुं न्याय्या** न्यायादनपेता । युक्तेत्यर्थः । ' धर्मपथ्यर्थ-' इत्यादिना यत्प्रत्ययः । **एवं** सति **तव पारणा** भोजनं **विहता न स्यात्** । **मुनेः** क्रिया होमादिः । स एवार्थः प्रयोजनम् । स [**क्रियार्थः**] **च अलुप्तः भवेत्** । स्वप्राणव्ययेनापि स्वामिगुरुधनं संरक्ष्यमिति भावः ॥

अत्र भवानेव प्रमाणमित्याह—

भवानपीदं परवानवैति महान्हि यत्नस्तव देवदारौ ।
स्थातुं नियोक्तुर्न हि शक्यमग्रे विनाश्य रक्ष्यं स्वयमक्षतेन ॥ ५६ ॥

परवान् स्वामिपरतन्त्रो **भवानपि** । ' परतन्त्रः पराधीनः परवान्नाथवानपि ' इत्यमरः । **इदं** वक्ष्यमाणम् **अवैति** । भवताऽनुभूयत एवेत्यर्थः । ' शेषे प्रथमः ' इति प्रथमपुरुषः । किमित्यत आह–**हि** यस्माद्धेतोः । ' हि हेतावधारणे ' इत्यमरः । **तव देवदारौ** विषये **महान् यत्नः** । महता यत्नेन रक्ष्यत इत्यर्थः । इदं शब्दोक्तमर्थं दर्शयति–स्थातुमिति । **रक्ष्यं** वस्तु **विनाश्य** विनाशं गमयित्वा **स्वयमक्षतेन** अव्रणेन । नियुक्तेनेति शेषः । **नियोक्तुः** स्वामिनः **अग्रे स्थातुं शक्यं न हि** ॥

सर्वथा चैतदप्रतिहार्यमित्याह—

किमप्यहिंस्यस्तव चेन्मतोऽहं यशःशरीरे भव मे दयालुः ।
एकान्तविध्वंसिषु मद्विधानां पिण्डेष्वनास्था खलु भौतिकेषु ॥ ५७ ॥

किमपि किं वा **अहं तव अहिंस्यः मतश्चेत्** तर्हि **मे** [**यशःशरीरे**] यश एव शरीरं तस्मिन् । **दयालुः** कारुणिको **भव** । ' स्याद्दयालुः कारुणिकः ' इत्यमरः । ननु मुख्यमुपेक्ष्यामुख्यशरीरे कोऽभिनिवेशः । अत आह–एकान्तेति । **मद्विधानां** मादृशानां विवेकिनाम् **एकान्तविध्वंसिषु** अवश्यविनाशिषु **भौतिकेषु** पृथिव्या-

---

१ ' सेयम् ' इत्यत्र कर्मपदं तुमन्तक्रियया यद्यप्यनुक्तमेव तथापि ' न्यायादनपेता ' एतदर्थकस्य ' न्याय्या ' इति पदस्यान्तर्गततद्धितप्रत्ययेन विशेषणोक्तत्वात्कर्मणि द्वितीया न भवति । अनुक्ते कर्मणि द्वितीयाविधानात् । उक्ते कर्मणि तु प्रातिपदिकमात्रे प्रथमा । अभिधानं तु प्रायेण तिङ्कृत्तद्धितसमासैः । क्वचिन्निपातेनापि । अत्र तु तद्धितप्रत्ययेन ।

दिभूतविकारेषु **पिण्डेषु** शरीरेषु **अनास्था खलु** अनपेक्षैव । 'आस्था त्वालम्बना-स्थानयत्नापेक्षासु कथ्यते ।' इति विश्वः ।

सौहार्दादहमनुसरणीयोऽस्मीत्याह—

संबन्धमाभाषणपूर्वमाहुर्वृत्तः स नौ संगतयोर्वनान्ते ।
तद्भूतनाथानुग नार्हसि त्वं संबन्धिनो मे प्रणयं विहन्तुम् ॥ ५८ ॥

संबन्धं सख्यम् । [**आभाषणपूर्वम्**] आभाषणमालापः पूर्वं कारणं यस्य तम् **आहुः** । 'स्यादाभाषणमालापः' इत्यमरः । **स** तादृक्संबन्धः **वनान्ते संगतयोः नौ** आवयोः **वृत्तः** जातः । **तत्** ततो हेतोर्हे **भूतनाथानुग** शिवानुचर । एतेन तस्य महत्त्वं सूचयति । अत एव **संबन्धिनो** मित्रस्य **मे प्रणयं** याच्ञाम् । 'प्रणयास्त्वमी । विश्रम्भयाच्ञाप्रेमाणः' इत्यमरः । **विहन्तुं त्वं नार्हसि** ॥

तथेति गामुक्तवते दिलीपः सद्यः प्रतिष्टम्भविमुक्तबाहुः ।
स न्यस्तशस्त्रो हरये स्वदेहमुपानयत्पिण्डमिवामिषस्य ॥ ५९ ॥

तथेति गाम् उक्तवते हरये सिंहाय । 'कपौ सिंहे सुवर्णे च वर्णे विष्णौ हरिं विदुः ।' इति शाश्वतः । **सद्यः** तत्क्षणे **स** प्रतिष्टम्भात्प्रतिबन्धाद्विमुक्तो बाहुर्यस्य [**प्रतिष्टम्भ-विमुक्तबाहुः**] **दिलीपः न्यस्तशस्त्रः** त्यक्तायुधः सन् । **स्वदेहम्** । **आमिषस्य** मांसस्य । 'पललं क्रव्यमामिषम्' इत्यमरः । **पिण्डम्** कवलम् **इव उपानयत** समर्पित-वान् । एतेन निर्ममत्वमुक्तम् ॥

तस्मिन्क्षणे पालयितुः प्रजानामुत्पश्यतः सिंहनिपातमुग्रम् ।
अवाङ्मुखस्योपरि पुष्पवृष्टिः पपात विद्याधरहस्तमुक्ता ॥ ६० ॥

तस्मिन्क्षणे उग्रं सिंहनिपातमुत्पश्यतः उत्प्रेक्षमाणस्य तर्कयतः **अवाङ्-मुखस्य** अधोमुखस्य । 'स्यादवाङप्यधोमुखः' इत्यमरः । **प्रजानां पालयितुः** राज्ञः **उपरि** उपरिष्टात् । 'उपर्युपरिष्टात्' इति निपातः । [**विद्याधरहस्तमुक्ता**] विद्या-धराणां देवयोनिविशेषाणां हस्तैर्मुक्ता **पुष्पवृष्टिः पपात** ॥

उत्तिष्ठ वत्सेत्यमृतायमानं वचो निशम्योत्थितमुत्थितः सन् ।
ददर्श राजा जननीमिव स्वां गामग्रतः प्रस्रविणीं न सिंहम् ॥ ६१ ॥

राजा । अमृतमिवाचरतीति **अमृतायमानं** तत् । 'उपमानादाचारे' इति क्यङ् । ततः शानच् । **उत्थितम्** उत्पन्नम् । 'हे **वत्स उत्तिष्ठ**' इति **वचः**

---

१ एवं कुमारसंभवे—'यतः सतां संनतगात्रि संगतं मनीषिभिः साप्तपदीनमुच्यते ।' इति । 'संगतं दर्शनात्सताम्' इति हितोपदेशेऽपि ।

२ 'उग्रे सिंहनिपाते शङ्कितस्योपरि कोमला पुष्पवृष्टिः पपातेति वैचित्र्यम्' इति पा० ।

३ 'कर्तुः क्यङ् सलोपश्च' इति सूत्रेणेत्यर्थः । यत्तु कस्मिंश्चिन्मुद्रितपुस्तकेषु 'क्यच्' इति पाठ उपलभ्यते स प्रामादिक इति भाति ।

निशम्य श्रुत्वा । **उत्थितः सन्** । अस्तेः शतृप्रत्ययः । **अग्रतः** अग्रे प्रस्रवः क्षीरस्रावोऽस्ति यस्याः सा तां **प्रस्रविर्णी गां स्वां जननीमिव ददर्श** । **सिंहं न** ददर्श ॥

तं विस्मित धेनुरुवाच साधो मायां मयोद्भाव्य परीक्षितोऽसि ।

ऋषिप्रभावान्मयि नान्तकोऽपि प्रभुः प्रहर्तुं किमुतान्यहिंस्राः ॥ ६२ ॥

विस्मितम् आश्चर्यं गतम् । कर्तरि क्तः । **तं** दिलीपं **धेनुः उवाच** । किमित्यत्राह–हे **साधो मया मायामुद्भाव्य** कल्पयित्वा **परीक्षितोऽसि** । **ऋषिप्रभावान्मयि अन्तकः** यमः **अपि प्रहर्तुं न प्रभुः** न समर्थः । अन्ये हिंस्राः घातुकाः [**अन्यहिंस्राः**] । 'शरारुर्घातुको हिंस्रः' इत्यमरः । 'नमिकम्पि–' इत्यादिना रप्रत्ययः । **किमुत** सुष्ठु । न प्रभव इति योज्यम् । 'बलवत्सुष्ठु किमुत स्वस्त्यतीव च निर्भरे ।' इत्यमरः ॥

भक्त्या गुरौ मय्यनुकम्पया च प्रीताऽस्मि ते पुत्र वरं वृणीष्व ।

न केवलानां पयसां प्रसूतिमवेहि मां कामदुघां प्रसन्नाम् ॥ ६३ ॥

हे **पुत्र गुरौ भक्त्या** । **मय्यनुकम्पया च** । ते तुभ्यं **प्रीताऽस्मि** । 'क्रियाग्रहणमपि कर्तव्यम्' इति चतुर्थी । **वरं** देवेभ्यो वरणीयमर्थम् । 'देवाद्वृते वरः श्रेष्ठे त्रिषु क्लीबं मनाक्प्रिये ।' इत्यमरः । **वृणीष्व** स्वीकुरु । तथा हि । **मां केवलानां पयसां प्रसूतिं** कारणं **न अवेहि** न विद्धि । किं तु **प्रसन्नां** माम् [**कामदुघाम्**] कामान्दोग्धीति कामदुघा तामवेहि । 'दुहः कब्घश्च' इति कप्रत्ययः ॥

ततः समानीय स मानितार्थी हस्तौ स्वहस्तार्जितवीरशब्दः ।

वंशस्य कर्तारमनन्तकीर्तिं सुदक्षिणायां तनयं ययाचे ॥ ६४ ॥

ततः मानितार्थी । स्वहस्तार्जितो वीर इति शब्दो येन स [**स्वहस्तार्जितवीरशब्दः**] । एतेनास्य दातृत्वं दैन्यराहित्यं चोक्तम् । **स** राजा **हस्तौ समानीय** संधाय । अञ्जलिं बद्ध्वेत्यर्थः । **वंशस्य कर्तारं** प्रवर्तयितारम् । अत एव रघुकुलमिति प्रसिद्धिः । **अनन्तकीर्तिं** स्थिरयशसं **तनयं सुदक्षिणायां ययाचे** ॥

संतानकामाय तथेति कामं राज्ञे प्रतिश्रुत्य पयस्विनी सा ।

दुग्ध्वा पयः पत्रपुटे मदीयं पुत्रोपभुङ्क्ष्वेति तमादिदेश ॥ ६५ ॥

सा पयस्विनी गौः । [**संतानकामाय**] संतानं कामयत इति संतानकामः । 'कर्मण्यण्' । तस्मै **राज्ञे तथेति** । काम्यत इति कामो वरः । कर्मार्थे घञ्प्रत्ययः । तं [**कामं**] **प्रतिश्रुत्य** प्रतिज्ञाय 'हे **पुत्र मदीयं पयः पत्रपुटे** पत्रनिर्मिते पात्रे **दुग्ध्वा उपभुङ्क्ष्व** पिब' **इति तमादिदेश** आज्ञापितवती । 'उपयुङ्क्ष्व' इति वा पाठः ॥

---

१ राज्ञः सत्त्वोत्कर्षं दृष्ट्वा तस्मिन्धेनोरपत्यस्नेहस्तथा प्रकटीबभूव यथा तस्याः स्तनमण्डलात्क्षीरधाराः सहसा प्रावर्तन्त इति भावः । 'प्रस्रवस्तु स्नेहवशाज्जनन्या अपि स्यात्' इति चा० ।

२ 'विस्मयस्तु केसरिणोऽदर्शनात्' इति चा० ।

३ 'गोः पयोदाने सामर्थ्यं न वरदाने इत्याह––न केवलानामिति ।' इति चा० ।

वत्सस्य होमार्थविधेश्च शेषमृषेरनुज्ञामधिगम्य मातः ।
ऊधस्यमिच्छामि तवोपभोक्तुं षष्ठांशमुर्व्या इव रक्षितायाः ॥ ६६ ॥

हे **मातः वत्सस्य** वत्सपीतस्य शेषम् । वत्सपीतावशिष्टमित्यर्थः । होम एवार्थः तस्य विधिरनुष्ठानम् तस्य [**होमार्थविधेः**] **च शेषम्** । होमावशिष्टमित्यर्थः । **तव** । ऊधसि भवम् **ऊधस्यं** क्षीरम् । 'शरीरावयवाच्च' इति यत्प्रत्ययः । **रक्षिताया उर्व्याः षष्ठांशं** षष्ठभागम् **इव** । **ऋषेः अनुज्ञामधिगम्य उपभोक्तुमिच्छामि** ॥

इत्थं क्षितीशेन वसिष्ठधेनुर्विज्ञापिता प्रीततरा बभूव ।
तदन्विता हैमवताच्च कुक्षेः प्रत्याययावाश्रममश्रमेण ॥ ६७ ॥

इत्थं क्षितीशेन विज्ञापिता वसिष्ठस्य धेनुः [**वसिष्ठधेनुः**] **प्रीततरा** । पूर्वं शुश्रूषया प्रीता । संप्रत्यनया विज्ञापनया प्रीततरा अतिसंतुष्टा **बभूव** । **तदन्विता** तेन दिलीपेनान्विता **हैमवतात्** हिमवत्संबन्धिनः **कुक्षेः** गुहायाः सकाशाद् **अश्रमेण** अनायासेन **आश्रमं प्रत्याययौ** आगता **च** ॥

तस्याः प्रसन्नेन्दुमुखः प्रसादं गुरुर्नृपाणां गुरवे निवेद्य ।
प्रहर्षचिह्नानुमितं प्रियायै शशंस वाचा पुनरुक्तयेव ॥ ६८ ॥

प्रसन्नेन्दुरिव मुखं यस्य **स** [**प्रसन्नेन्दुमुखः**] **नृपाणां गुरुः** दिलीपः [**प्रहर्षचिह्नानुमितं**] प्रहर्षचिह्नैर्मुखरागादिभिरनुमितमूहितं **तस्याः** धेनोः **प्रसादम्** अनुग्रहं प्रहर्षचिह्नैरेव ज्ञातत्वात् **पुनरुक्तया इव वाचा गुरवे निवेद्य** विज्ञाप्य पश्चात् **प्रियायै शशंस** । कथितस्यैव कथनं पुनरुक्तिः । न चेह तदस्ति किं तु चिह्नैः कथितप्रायत्वात्पुनरुक्तयेव स्थितयेत्युत्प्रेक्षा ॥

स नन्दिनीस्तन्यमनिन्दितात्मा सद्वत्सलो वत्सहुतावशेषम् ।
पपौ वसिष्ठेन कृताभ्यनुज्ञः शुभ्रं यशो मूर्तमिवातितृष्णः ॥ ६९ ॥

अनिन्दितात्मा अगर्हितस्वभावः । सत्सु वत्सलः प्रेमवान् **सद्वत्सलः** । 'वत्सांसाभ्यां कामबले' इति लच्प्रत्ययः । **वसिष्ठेन कृताभ्यनुज्ञः** कृतानुमतिः **स** राजा [**वत्सहुतावशेषम्**] वत्सस्य हुतस्य चावशेषं पीतहुतावशिष्टं [**नन्दिनी-**

---

१ औधस्यमिति पा०. २ अत्र मनुः—आददीताथ षड्भागं द्रुमांसमधुसर्पिषाम् । गन्धौषधिरसानां च पुष्पमूलफलस्य च ॥ पत्रशाकतृणानां च चर्मणां वैदलस्य च । मृन्मयानां च भाण्डानां सर्वस्याश्ममयस्य च ॥ इति स. अ. । राजापि फलमाप्नोति रक्षितायाः क्षितेरपि इति च । ३ अत्र 'प्रकृत्यादिभ्य उपसंख्यानम्' इति तृतीया । ४ उक्तं च मनुना—आकारैरिङ्गितैर्गत्या चेष्टया भाषितेन च । नेत्रवक्त्रविकारैश्च गृह्यतेऽन्तर्गतं मनः ॥ **अष्ट० २९.** ५ वत्सो वत्सकृतं पानमिति यावत् । हुतं होमादिविधिश्च ते **वत्सहुते** तयोरवशिष्टम् । अत्रानुप्रासः स्फुट एव । होमविधेश्च । वत्सानिपीत० इ० पा०

स्तन्यम्] नन्दिन्याः स्तन्यं क्षीरम् । **शुभ्रं मूर्तं** परिच्छिन्नं **यश इव** । **आततृष्णः** सन् **पपौ** ॥

प्रातर्यथोक्तव्रतपारणान्ते प्रास्थानिकं स्वस्त्ययनं प्रयुज्य ।
तौ दंपती स्वां प्रति राजधानीं प्रस्थापयामास वशी वसिष्ठः ॥ ७० ॥

वशी वसिष्ठः प्रातः । [**यथोक्तव्रतपारणान्ते**] यथोक्तस्य पूर्वोक्तस्य व्रतस्य गोसेवारूपस्याङ्गभूता या पारणा तस्या अन्ते **प्रास्थानिकं** प्रस्थानकाले भवम् । तत्कालोचितमित्यर्थः । 'कालाट्ठञ्' इति ठञ्प्रत्ययः । 'यथाकथंचिद्गुणवृत्त्यापि काले वर्तमानात्प्रत्यय इष्यते ।' इति वृत्तिकारः । ईयते प्राप्यतेऽनेनेत्ययनं **स्वस्त्ययनं** शुभावहमाशीर्वादं **प्रयुज्य** । **तौ दंपती स्वां राजधानीं** पुरीं **प्रति प्रस्थापयामास** ॥

प्रदक्षिणीकृत्य हुतं हुताशमनन्तरं भर्तुररुन्धतीं च ।
धेनुं सवत्सां च नृपः प्रतस्थे सन्मङ्गलोदग्रतरप्रभावः ॥ ७१ ॥

नृपः हुतं तर्पितम् । [**हुताशम**] हुतमश्नातीति हुताशोऽग्निः । 'कर्मण्यण्' । तं **भर्तुः** मुनेः **अनन्तरम्** । प्रदक्षिणानन्तरमित्यर्थः । **अरुन्धतीं च सवत्सां धेनुं च प्रदक्षिणीकृत्य** । प्रगतो दक्षिणं प्रदक्षिणम् । 'तिष्ठद्गुप्रभृतीनि च' इत्यव्ययीभावः । ततश्च्विः । अप्रदक्षिणं प्रदक्षिणं संपद्यमानं कृत्वा प्रदक्षिणीकृत्य । [**सन्मङ्गलोदग्रतरप्रभावः**] सद्भिर्मङ्गलैः प्रदक्षिणाभिर्मङ्गलाचारैरुदग्रतरप्रभावः सन् । **प्रतस्थे** ॥

श्रोत्राभिरामध्वनिना रथेन स धर्मपत्नीसहितः सहिष्णुः ।
ययावनुद्धातसुखेन मार्गं स्वेनेव पूर्णेन मनोरथेन ॥ ७२ ॥

धर्मपत्नीसहितः सहिष्णुः व्रतादिदुःखसहनशीलः **स** नृपः **श्रोत्राभिरामध्वनिना** कर्णाह्लादकरस्वनेन अनुद्धातः पाषाणादिप्रतिघातरहितः । अत एव सुखयतीति सुखः । तेन [**अनुद्धातसुखेन**] **रथेन स्वेन पूर्णेन** सफलेन **मनोरथेनेव मार्गं** अध्वानं **ययौ** । मनोरथपक्षे ध्वनिः श्रुतिः । अनुद्धातः प्रतिबन्धनिवृत्तिः ॥

तमाहितौत्सुक्यमदर्शनेन प्रजाः प्रजार्थव्रतकर्शिताङ्गम् ।
नेत्रैः पपुस्तृप्तिमनाप्नुवद्भिर्नवोदयं नाथमिवौषधीनाम् ॥ ७३ ॥

अदर्शनेन प्रवासनिमित्तेन **आहितौत्सुक्यं** जनितदर्शनोत्कण्ठम् । प्रजार्थेन संतानार्थेन व्रतेन नियमेन कर्शितं कृशीकृतमङ्गं यस्य तम् [**प्रजार्थव्रतकर्शिता-**

---

१ 'यशसि धवलता वर्ण्यते हासकीर्त्योः' इति कविसमयः । तेन हासस्य धवलत्वेन वर्णनम् ।
२ 'प्रतिबध्नाति हि श्रेयः पूज्यपूजाव्यतिक्रमः' इति हेतोः सर्वान्प्रदक्षिणीचकारेति भावः । 'सतां मङ्गलैः प्रीतवह्निगोब्राह्मणप्रदक्षिणीकरणैः' इति सु० । 'मङ्गलद्रव्यैर्वा' इति चा० । 'उदग्रतरो महीयान्प्रभावः पौरुषं यस्य' इति च चा० । 'अनन्तरं भर्तुः' इत्यत्र 'ततश्च होतारम्' इति, 'सन्मङ्गलोदग्रतरप्रभावः' इत्यत्र 'सन्मङ्गलोदग्रतरानुभावः' इति व. सु. पठतः । ३ उत्प्रेक्षालंकारः । ४ तोत्कण्ठं इ. पा. ५ प्रजार्थं व्रत० इ. पा.

न्नम्] **नवोदयं** नवाभ्युदयं **प्रजाः तृप्तिम् अनाप्नुवद्भिः** अतिगृध्नुभिः **नेत्रैः** । **ओषधीनां नाथं** सोमम् इव । **तं** राजानं **पपुः** । अत्यास्थया ददृशुरित्यर्थः । चन्द्रपक्षे अदर्शनं कलाक्षयनिमित्तम् । प्रजार्थे लोकहितार्थं व्रतं देवताभ्यः कलादाननियमः । 'तं च सोमं पपुर्देवाः पर्यायेणानुपूर्वशः ।' इति व्यासः । उदय आविर्भावः । अन्यत्समानम् ॥

पुरंदरश्रीः पुरमुत्पताकं प्रविश्य पौरैरभिनन्द्यमानः ।
भुजे भुजङ्गेन्द्रसमानसारे भूयः स भूमेर्धुरमाससञ्ज ॥ ७४ ॥

पुरः पुरीरसुराणां दारयतीति पुरंदरः शक्रः । 'पूःसर्वयोर्दारिसहोः' इति खच्प्रत्ययः । 'वाचंयमपुरंदरौ च' इति मुमागमो निपातितः । तस्य श्रीरिव श्रीर्यस्य स [**पुरंदरश्रीः**] । **स** नृपः **पौरैः अभिनन्द्यमानः** । **उत्पताकम्** उच्छ्रितध्वजम् । 'पताका वैजयन्ती स्यात्केतनं ध्वजमस्त्रियाम् ।' इत्यमरः । **पुरं प्रविश्य** भुजङ्गेन्द्रेण समानसारे तुल्यबले [**भुजङ्गेन्द्रसमानसारे**] । 'सारो बले स्थिरांशे च न्याय्ये क्लीबं वरे त्रिषु ।' इत्यमरः । **भुजे भूयः भूमेः धुरमाससञ्ज** स्थापितवान् ॥

अथ नयनसमुत्थं ज्योतिरत्रेरिव द्यौः
सुरसरिदिव तेजो वह्निनिष्ठ्यूतमैशम् ।
नरपतिकुलभूत्यै गर्भमाधत्त राज्ञी
गुरुभिरभिनिविष्टं लोकपालानुभावैः ॥ ७५ ॥

अथ द्यौः सुरवर्त्म । 'द्यौः स्वर्गसुरवर्त्मनोः' इति विश्वः । **अत्रेः** महर्षेर्नयनयोः समुत्थमुत्पन्नं **नयनसमुत्थम्** । 'आतश्चोपसर्गे' इति कप्रत्ययः । **ज्योतिः इव** । चन्द्रमिवेत्यर्थः । 'ऋक्षेशः स्यादत्रिनेत्रप्रसूतः' इति हलायुधः । चन्द्रस्यात्रिनेत्रोद्भूतत्वमुक्तं हरिवंशे—'नेत्राभ्यां वारि सुस्राव दशधा द्योतयद्दिशः । तद्गर्भविधिना हृष्टा दिशो देव्यो दधुस्तदा ॥ समेत्य धारयामासुर्न च ताः समशक्नुवन् । स ताभ्यः सहसैवाथ दिग्भ्यो गर्भः प्रभान्वितः ॥ पपात भासयँल्लोकाञ्छीतांशुः सर्वभावनः ॥' इति । **सुरसरिद्** गङ्गा [**वह्निनिष्ठ्यूतम्**] वह्निना निष्ठ्यूतं विक्षिप्तम् । 'च्छ्वोः शूडनुनासिके च' इत्यनेन निपूर्वात्ष्ठीवतेर्वकारस्य ऊठ् । 'नुन्ननुत्तास्तनिष्ठ्यूतविद्धाक्षिप्तेरिताः समाः ।' इत्यमरः । **ऐशं तेजः** स्कन्दम् **इव** । अत्र रामायणम्—'ते गत्वा पर्वतं राम कैलासं धातुमण्डितम् । अग्निं नियोजयामासुः पुत्रार्थं सर्वदेवताः ॥ देवकार्यमिदं देव समाधत्स्व हुताशन । शैलपुत्र्यां महातेजो गङ्गायां तेज उत्सृज ॥ देवतानां प्रतिज्ञाय गङ्गामभ्येत्य पावकः । गर्भं धारय वै देवि देवतानामिदं प्रियम् ॥ इत्येतद्वचनं श्रुत्वा दिव्यं रूपमधारयत् । स तस्या महिमां दृष्ट्वा समन्तादवकीर्य च ॥ समन्ततस्तु तां देवीमभ्यषिञ्चत पावकः । सर्वस्रोतांसि पूर्णानि गङ्गाया रघुनन्दन ॥' इति । **राज्ञी**

---

१ उक्तं च देवीपुराणे-कलाः षोडश सोमस्य शुक्ले वर्धयते रविः । अमृतेनामृतं कृष्णे पीयते देवतैः क्रमात् ॥ इति । विशेषस्तूक्तः पञ्चमसर्गे १६ श्लो॰ टिप्पणीषु । चन्द्रो हि उदितः सन्नोषधीः स्वकिरणैः संवर्धयति । अतः स ओषधीनाथ इत्युच्यते ।

सुदक्षिणा नरपतेर्दिलीपस्य कुलभूत्यै [**नरपतिकुलभूत्यै**] संततिलक्षणायै **गुरुभिः** महद्भिः लोकपालानामनुभावैः [**लोकपालानुभावैः**] तेजोभिः **अभिनिविष्टम्** अनुप्रविष्टं **गर्भमाधत्त**। दधावित्यर्थः। अत्र मनुः[१]—'अष्टानां लोकपालानां वपुर्धारयते नृपः।' इति। अत्र 'आधत्त' इत्यनेन स्त्रीकर्तृकधारणामात्रमुच्यते। तथा मन्त्रे च दृश्यते—'यथेयं पृथिवी मह्युत्ताना गर्भमादधे। एवं त्वं गर्भमाधेहि दशमे मासि सूतवे॥' इत्याश्वलायनानां सीमन्तमन्त्रे स्त्रीव्यापारधारण आधानशब्दप्रयोगदर्शनादिति। मालिनीवृत्तमेतत्। तदुक्तम्—'ननमयययुतेयं मालिनी भोगिलोकैः।' इति लक्षणात्॥

इति महामहोपाध्यायकोलाचलमल्लिनाथसूरिविरचितया संजीवनीसमाख्यया व्याख्यया समेतो महाकविश्रीकालिदासकृतौ रघुवंशे महाकाव्ये नन्दिनीवरप्रदानो नाम द्वितीयः सर्गः॥

तृतीयः सर्गः।

उपाधिगम्योऽप्यनुपाधिगम्यः[२] समावलोक्योऽप्यसमावलोक्यः।
भवोऽपि योऽभूदभवः शिवोऽयं जगत्यपायादपि नः स पायात्॥

'राज्ञी गर्भमाधत्त' (२।७५) इत्युक्तम्। संप्रति गर्भलक्षणानि वर्णयितुं प्रस्तौति—

अथेप्सितं[३] भर्तुरुपस्थितोदयं[४] सखीजनोद्वीक्षणकौमुदीमुखम्।
निदानमिक्ष्वाकुकुलस्य संततेः सुदक्षिणा दौहृदलक्षणं दधौ॥ १॥

अथ गर्भधारणानन्तरं **सुदक्षिणा उपस्थितोदयं** प्राप्तकालं **भर्तुः** दिलीपस्य **ईप्सितं** मनोरथम्। भावे क्तः। पुनः [**सखीजनोद्वीक्षणकौमुदीमुखम्**] सखी-

---

१ इन्द्रानिलयमार्काणामग्नेश्च वरुणस्य च। चन्द्रवित्तेशयोश्चैव मात्रा निर्हृत्य शाश्वतीः॥ यस्मादेषां सुरेन्द्राणां मात्राभ्यो निर्मितो नृपः। तस्मादभिभवत्येष सर्वभूतानि तेजसा॥ इति च सप्तमाध्याये मनुः॥ २ उपाधिना देहादिना गम्यो दृग्गोचरः अनुपाधेरतीन्द्रियत्वात्। एवंभूतोऽप्यनुपाधिगम्य इति विरोधः। अनुपाधिभिर्निरस्ताविद्याद्युपाधिभिरेव गम्यो निर्गुणत्वेन ज्ञातुं शक्य इति परिहारः। समैः समाहितमतिभिरवलोकयितुं समाधौ प्रत्यक्षीकर्तुं शक्यः। तादृशोऽप्यसमावलोक्य इति विरोधः। परिहारपक्षे असमानि विषमाणि त्रीणीनि यावदवलोक्यानि नेत्राणि यस्य। भावे ण्यत्। यद्वा असममपर्याप्तमवलोक्यं दृग्विषयीभूतं यस्य स तथा इति परिहारः। भवति सर्वमिति भवो विश्वात्मकः। तथाभूतोऽप्यभव इति विरोधः। परिहारस्तु नास्ति भवो यस्य सोऽभवोऽजोऽसंगो वा। नास्ति भवो यस्मात्स तथा संसारस्य विच्छेदक इति वा इत्यर्थात्। स तादृशः शिवो जगति नः अपायात् पायात्।

३ **ततो विशांपत्युरनन्यसंततेर्मनोरथं किंचिदिवोदयोन्मुखम्।**
अनन्यसौहार्दरसस्य दोहदं प्रिया प्रपेदे प्रकृतिप्रियंवदा॥

इति दिनकरः संपूर्णश्लोकमन्यथा पठति।

४ उपस्थितः प्राप्त उदयः पुत्रोत्पत्तिलक्षणो यस्य यस्माद्वा। इति चा०।

जनस्योद्वीक्षणानां दृष्टीनां कौमुदीमुखं चन्द्रिकाप्रादुर्भावम् । यद्वा कौमुदी नाम दीपोत्सवतिथिः । तदुक्तं भविष्योत्तरे—' कौ मोदन्ते जना यस्यां तेनासौ कौमुदी मता । ' इति । तस्या मुखं प्रारम्भम् । अत एव ' सखीजनोद्वीक्षणकौमुदीमहम् ' इति पाठं केचित्पठन्ति । **इक्ष्वाकुकुलस्य संततेः** अविच्छेदस्य **निदानं** मूलकारणम् । ' निदानं त्वादिकारणम् ' इत्यमरः । एवंविधं **दौर्हृदलक्षणं** गर्भचिह्नं वक्ष्यमाणं **दधौ** । स्वहृदयेन गर्भहृदयेन च द्विहृदया गर्भिणी । यथाह वाग्भटः—' मातृजन्यस्य हृदयं मातुश्च हृदयं च तत् । संबद्धं तेन गर्भिण्याः श्रेष्ठं श्रद्धाभिमाननम् ॥ ' इति । तत्संबन्धित्वाद्गर्भो दौर्हृदमित्युच्यते । सा च तद्योगाद्दौर्हृदिनीति । तदुक्तं संग्रहे—' द्विहृदयां नारी दौर्हृदिनीमाचक्षते ' इति । अत्र दौर्हृदलक्षणस्येप्सितत्वेन कौमुदीमुखत्वेन च निरूपणाद्रूपकालंकारः । अस्मिन्सर्गे वंशस्थं वृत्तम्—' जतौ तु वंशस्थमुदीरितं जरौ । ' इति लक्षणात् ॥

संप्रति क्षामताख्यं गर्भलक्षणं वर्णयति—

[2]शरीरसादादसमग्रभूषणा मुखेन साऽलक्ष्यत लोध्रपाण्डुना ।
तनुप्रकाशेन विचेयतारका प्रभातकल्पा शशिनेव शर्वरी ॥ २ ॥

शरीरस्य सादात्कार्श्यात् [**शरीरसादात्**] **असमग्रभूषणा** परिमिताभरणा लोध्रपुष्पेणेव पाण्डुना [**लोध्रपाण्डुना**] **मुखेन** उपलक्षिता **सा** सुदक्षिणा । [**विचेयतारका**] विचेया मृग्यास्तारका यस्यां सा तथोक्ता । विरलनक्षत्रेत्यर्थः । **तनुप्रकाशेन** अल्पकान्तिना **शशिना** उपलक्षितेषदसमाप्तप्रभाता **प्रभातकल्पा** । प्रभातादीषदूनेत्यर्थः । 'तसिलादिष्वाकृत्वसुचः' इति प्रभातशब्दस्य पुंवद्भावः । **शर्वरी** रात्रिः **इव** । **अलक्ष्यत** । शरीरसादादिगर्भलक्षणमाह वाग्भटः—' क्षामता गरिमा कुक्षेर्मूर्च्छा छर्दिररोचकम् । जृम्भा प्रसेकः सदनं रोमराज्याः प्रकाशनम् ॥ ' इति ॥

तदाननं मृत्सुरभि क्षितीश्वरो रहस्युपाघ्राय न तृप्तिमाययौ ।
करीव सिक्तं पृषतैः पयोमुचां शुचिव्यपाये वनराजिपल्वलम् ॥ ३ ॥

क्षितीश्वरो रहसि मृत्सुरभि मृदा सुगन्धि तस्या आननं **तदाननं** सुदक्षिणामुखम् । **उपाघ्राय तृप्तिं नाययौ** । कः कमिव । **शुचिव्यपाये** ग्रीष्मावसाने । ' शुचिः शुद्धेऽनुपहते शृङ्गाराषाढयोः सिते । ग्रीष्मे हुतवहेऽपि स्यादुपधाशुद्धमन्त्रिणि ॥ ' इति विश्वः । **पयोमुचां** मेघानां **पृषतैः** बिन्दुभिः । ' पृषन्ति बिन्दुपृषताः ' इत्यमरः । **सिक्तम्** उक्षितं [**वनराजिपल्वलम्**] वनराज्याः पल्वलम् उपाघ्राय **करी** गज

---

१ इक्ष्वाकुर्नाम वैवस्वतमनोः पुत्रः । तदुत्पत्तिर्भागवते—' क्षवतस्तु मनोर्जज्ञ इक्ष्वाकुर्घ्राणतः सुतः । ' इति ।

२ **मुखेन सा केतकपत्रपाण्डुना कृशाङ्गयष्टिः परिमेयभूषणा ।**
स्थिताल्पतारां करुणेन्दुमण्डलां विभातकल्पां रजनीं व्यडम्बयत् ॥

इति वल्लभसुमत्यादयः पठन्ति । ३ अर्हे कृत्यतृचश्चेति योग्यतायामचो यत् । ४ ' रहः समाघ्राय ' इति व० चा० पठतः । ५ ' सरसि जलपाते सौरभ्यामिति पल्वलोक्तिः ' इति चा० ।

इव । अत्र करिवनराजिपल्वलानां कान्तकामिनीवदनसमाधिरनुसंधेयः । गर्भिणीनां मृद्भक्षणं लोकप्रसिद्धमेव । एतेन दोहदाख्यं गर्भलक्षणमुच्यते ॥

दोहदलक्षणे हेत्वन्तरमुत्प्रेक्षते—

दिवं मरुत्वानिव भोक्ष्यते भुवं दिगन्तविश्रान्तरथो हि तत्सुतः ।
अतोऽभिलाषे प्रथमं तथाविधे मनो बबन्धान्यरसान्विलङ्घ्य सा ४

हि यस्माद् **दिगन्तविश्रान्तरथः** चक्रवर्ती तस्याः सुतः **तत्सुतः मरुत्वान्** इन्द्रः । 'इन्द्रो मरुत्वान्मघवा' इत्यमरः । **दिवं** स्वर्गम् **इव** । **भुवं भोक्ष्यते** । 'भुजोऽनवने' इत्यात्मनेपदम् । **अतः प्रथमं सा** सुदक्षिणा **तथाविधे** भूविकारे मृद्रूपे । अभिलष्यत इत्यभिलाषो भोग्यवस्तु तस्मिन् [**अभिलाषे**] । कर्मणि घञ्प्रत्ययः । रस्यन्ते स्वाद्यन्त इति रसा भोग्यार्थाः । अन्ये च ते रसाश्च तान् [**अन्यरसान्**] **विलङ्घ्य** विहाय **मनः बबन्ध** । विदधावित्यर्थः । दोहदहेतुकस्य मृद्भक्षणस्य पुत्रभूभोगसूचकार्थत्वमुत्प्रेक्षते ॥

न मे ह्रिया शंसति किंचिदीप्सितं स्पृहावती वस्तुषु केषु मागधी ।
इति स्म पृच्छत्यनुवेलमादृतः प्रियासखीरुत्तरकोसलेश्वरः ॥ ५ ॥

मगधस्य राज्ञोऽपत्यं स्त्री **मागधी** सुदक्षिणा । 'द्व्यञ्मगधकलिङ्गसूरमसादण्' इत्यण्प्रत्ययः । **ह्रिया किंचित्** किमपि **ईप्सितम्** इष्टं **मे** मह्यं **न शंसति** नाचष्टे । **केषु वस्तुषु स्पृहावती इत्यनुवेलम्** अनुक्षणम् **आदृतः** आदरवान् । कर्तरि क्तः । 'आदृतौ सादरार्चितौ' इत्यमरः । [**प्रियासखीः**] प्रियायाः सखीः सहचरीः **उत्तरकोसलेश्वरः** दिलीपः **पृच्छति स्म** पप्रच्छ । 'लट् स्मे' इत्यनेन भूतार्थे लट् । सखीनां विश्रम्भभाजित्वादिति भावः ॥

उपेत्य सा दोहददुःखशीलतां यदेव वव्रे तदपश्यदाहृतम् ।
न[2] हीष्टमस्य त्रिदिवेऽपि भूपतेरभूदनासाद्यमधिज्यधन्वनः ॥ ६ ॥

दोहदं गर्भिणीमनोरथः । 'दोहदं दौर्हृदं श्रद्धा लालसं च समं स्मृतम् ।' इति हलायुधः । **सा** सुदक्षिणा । [**दोहददुःखशीलतां**] दोहदेन गर्भिणीमनोरथेन दुःखशीलतां दुःखस्वभावताम् **उपेत्य** प्राप्य **यद्** वस्तु **वव्रे** आचकाङ्क्ष **तद् आहृतम्** आनीतम् । भर्त्रेति शेषः । **अपश्यदेव** । अलभतेत्यर्थः । कुतः । **हि** यस्माद् **अस्य भूपतेः त्रिदिवेऽपि** स्वर्गेऽपि **इष्टं** वस्तु **अनासाद्यम्** अनवाप्यं **नाभूत्** । किं याच्ञया ।

---

१ 'भुवम्' इत्यत्र 'महान्' इति, 'तत्सुतः' इत्यत्र 'मत्सुतः' इति केचित्पठन्ति । २ 'अस्य' इत्यत्र 'अस्याः' इति, 'अभूदनासाद्यम्' इत्यत्र 'बभूव दुष्प्राप्यम्' इति चा० आदर्शः पठन्ति । ३ त्रिदिवे-त्रयो ब्रह्मविष्णुरुद्रा दीव्यन्त्यत्रेति त्रिदिवः । हलश्चेति घञ् । संज्ञापूर्वकत्वान्न गुणः । यद्वा सात्त्विकराजसतामसभेदेन त्रिविधा दीव्यन्ति व्यवहरन्ति प्रकाशन्ते वा । घञर्थे कविधानम् । वृत्तिविषये संख्याशब्दस्य पूरणार्थत्वम् । अपिशब्दबलेन का कथा मर्त्यलोके इति गम्यते ।

नेत्याह-**अधिज्यधन्वनः** इति । न हि वीरपत्नीनामलभ्यं नाम किंचिदस्तीति भावः । अत्र वाग्भटः-' पादशोफो विदाहोऽन्ते श्रद्धा च विविधात्मिका ' इति । एतच्च पत्नीमनोरथ-पूरणाकरणे दृष्टदोषसंभवात् । न तु राज्ञः प्रीतिलौल्यात् । तदुक्तम्--' देयमप्यहितं तस्यै हिताय हितमल्पकम् । श्रद्धाविघाते गर्भस्य विकृतिश्च्युतिरेव वा ॥ ' अन्यत्र च--' दोहद-स्याप्रदानेन गर्भो दोषमवाप्नुयात् । ' इति ॥

क्रमेण निस्तीर्य च दोहदव्यथां प्रचीयमानावयवा रराज सा ।
पुराणपत्रापगमादनन्तरं लतेव संनद्धमनोज्ञपल्लवा ॥ ७ ॥

सा सुदक्षिणा **क्रमेण दोहदव्यथां च निस्तीर्य प्रचीयमानावयवा** पुष्य-माणावयवा सती । पुराणपत्राणामपगमान्नाशात् [**पुराणपत्रापगमात्**] **अनन्तरं** संनद्धाः संजाताः प्रत्यग्रत्वान्मनोज्ञाः पल्लवा यस्याः सा [**संनद्धमनोज्ञपल्लवा**] **लतेव रराज** ॥

लक्षणान्तरं वर्णयति---

दिनेषु गच्छत्सु नितान्तपीवरं तदीयमानीलमुखं स्तनद्वयम् ।
तिरश्चकार भ्रमराभिलीनयोः सुजातयोः पङ्कजकोशयोः श्रियम् ॥८॥

दिनेषु दोहददिवसेषु **गच्छत्सु** सत्सु **नितान्तपीवरम्** अतिस्थूलम् । **आनील-मुखम्**] आ समन्तान्नीले मुखे चूचुके यस्य तत् । **तदीयं स्तनद्वयम्** [**भ्रमराभि-लीनयोः**] भ्रमरैरभिलीनयोरभिव्याप्तयोः **सुजातयोः** सुन्दरयोः **पङ्कजकोशयोः** मुकुलयोः **श्रियं तिरश्चकार** । अत्र वाग्भटः--' अम्लेष्टता स्तनौ पीनौ श्वेतान्तौ कृष्णचूचुकौ ' इति ॥

निधानगर्भामिव सागराम्बरां शमीमिवाभ्यन्तरलीनपावकाम् ।
नदीमिवान्तःसलिलां सरस्वतीं नृपः ससत्त्वां महिषीममन्यत ॥ ९ ॥

नृपः ससत्त्वाम् आपन्नसत्त्वाम् । गर्भिणीमित्यर्थः । ' आपन्नसत्त्वा स्याद्गुर्विण्यन्तर्वत्नी च गर्भिणी । ' इत्यमरः । **महिषीम्** । निधानं निधिर्गर्भे यस्यास्तां [**निधान-गर्भाम्**] **सागराम्बरां** समुद्रवसनाम् [**इव**] भूमिमित्यर्थः । ' भूतधात्री रत्नगर्भा विपुला सागराम्बरा । ' इति कोशः । अभ्यन्तरे लीनः पावको यस्यास्तां [**अभ्यन्तर-**

---

१ गर्भिण्यास्तत्तदिच्छायां विशेषेण प्रयुज्यते । दोहदस्या० इ. म्पूर्ण. दोहदः । २ उपोढगात्रा-वचया इति, संनद्धत्वम संपद्धेति च पा०. ३ ' तामङ्कमारोप्य कृशाङ्गयष्टिं वर्णान्तराक्रान्तपयो-धराग्राम् । ' इति १४ सर्ग । सुजातयोः-' सुजातं सुन्दरं प्रोक्तं सम्यग्जातं च वर्तुलम् । ' इति विक्रमः । तिरश्चकार-अत्रोपमानादुपमेयस्य शोभाधिक्यवर्णनात् व्यतिरेकालंकारः । ' उपमाना-द्यदन्यस्य व्यतिरेकः स एव सः । ' इति तल्लक्षणम् । नितान्तपीवरमित्यत्र ' मधूकपाण्डुरम् ' ' आनील- ' इत्यत्र च ' आश्याम- ' ' भ्रमराभिलीनयोः ' इत्यत्र च ' भ्रमरावलीढयोः ' इति पाठान्तराणि । ' दिनेषु गच्छत्सु मधूकपाण्डुरं तदीयमाश्याममुखं स्तनद्वयम् । समुद्गयोर्वारणदन्त-कोशयोर्बभार कान्तिं गवलापिधानयोः ॥ ' इत्यपि केचित्पठन्ति ।

लीनपावकाम्] **शमीमिव** । शमीतरौ वह्निरस्तीत्यत्र लिङ्गं शमीगर्भादग्निं जनयतीति । **अन्तःसलिलाम्** अन्तर्गतजलां **सरस्वतीं नदीमिव** । **अमन्यत** । एतेन गर्भस्य भाग्यवत्त्वतेजस्वित्वपावनत्वानि विवक्षितानि ॥

प्रियानुरागस्य मनःसमुन्नतेर्भुजार्जितानां च दिगन्तसंपदाम् ।
यथाक्रमं पुंसवनादिकाः क्रिया धृतेश्च धीरः सदृशीर्व्यधत्त सः ॥ १० ॥

धीरः स राजा प्रियायामनुरागस्य स्नेहस्य [**प्रियानुरागस्य**] मनसः समुन्नतेरौदार्यस्य [**मनःसमुन्नतेः**] [**च**] । भुजेन भुजबलेन करेण वार्जितानाम् [**भुजार्जितानाम्**] । न तु वाणिज्यादिना । दिगन्तेषु संपदाम् [**दिगन्तसंपदाम्**] । **धृतेः** पुत्रो मे भविष्यतीति संतोषस्य **च** । 'धृतिर्योगान्तरे धैर्ये धारणाध्वरतुष्टिषु ।' इति विश्वः । **सदृशीः** अनुरूपाः । पुमान्सूयतेऽनेनेति पुंसवनम् । तदादिर्यासां ताः [**पुंसवनादिकाः**] **क्रियाः यथाक्रमं** क्रममनतिक्रम्य **व्यधत्त** कृतवान् । आदिशब्देनानवलोभनसीमन्तोन्नयने गृह्येते । अत्र मासि द्वितीये तृतीये वा पुंसवनम् । यदाह—'पुंसा नक्षत्रेण चन्द्रमा युक्तः स्यात् ।' इति पारस्करः । 'चतुर्थेऽनवलोभनम्' इत्याश्वलायनः । 'षष्ठेऽष्टमे वा सीमन्तोन्नयनम' इति याज्ञवल्क्यः ॥

सुरेन्द्रमात्राश्रितगर्भगौरवात्प्रयत्नमुक्तासनया गृहागतः ।
तयोपचाराञ्जलिखिन्नहस्तया ननन्द पारिप्लवनेत्रया नृपः ॥ ११ ॥

गृहागतः नृपः सुरेन्द्राणां लोकपालानां मात्राभिरंशैराश्रितस्यानुप्रविष्टस्य गर्भस्य गौरवाद्भारात् [**सुरेन्द्रमात्राश्रितगर्भगौरवात्**] प्रयत्नेन मुक्तासनया [**प्रयत्नमुक्ता-**

---

१ पुरा किल तारकावधार्थं सेनान्यं स्रष्टुकामा देवा ब्रह्मोपदेशादिरमन्ततोऽग्निमन्विष्यन्तस्तं शमीगर्भे ददृशुः देवकार्ये च नियोजयामासुः । ततः प्रभृति शमीगर्भ एवाग्नेरिवासस्थानमभूत् । इत्युक्त्वा निःसृतो ऽश्वत्थादग्निर्वारणसूचितः । प्रविवेश शमीगर्भमथ वह्निः सुषुप्सया ॥... इत्युक्त्वा तं शमीगर्भं वह्निमालक्ष्य देवताः । तदायतनं चक्रुः पुण्यं सर्वक्रियास्वपि ॥ इत्यादिः भारतकथात्रानुसंधेया । विशेषस्त्वनुशासनपर्वणि पञ्चाशीतितमेऽध्याये द्रष्टव्यः । शमीगर्भस्थोऽग्निर्मन्थनादेव व्यज्यते इति सुप्रसिद्धमेतत् । अनुरूपमाह शाकुन्तले—'दुष्यन्तेनाहितं तेजो दधानां भूतये भुवः । अवेहि तनयां ब्रह्मन्नग्निगर्भां शमीमिव ॥' इति । नदीति—'म्लेच्छदेशेषु सा ह्यन्तर्धाय भूयः पुण्यप्रदेशेषूद्भवति' इति वल्लभः । 'सरस्वत्या ऊर्ध्वं वालुकाः पातालान्तर्गतं जलमिति वार्तामात्रम् ।' इति चा० । अत्रोपमेयसुनायाः ससत्त्वाया माहिष्या एकस्या एव बहूपमानत्वान्मालोपमालंकारः । 'मालोपमा यदेकस्योपमानं बहु दृश्यते ।' इति साहित्यदर्पणोक्तेः ।

२ पुंसवनं नाम सुपुत्रजननार्थं गर्भिण्याः संस्कारविशेषः । स च तृतीयमासोपक्रमे शुद्धदिने दंपतीभ्यां करणीयः । यदाह शौनकः—'व्यक्ते गर्भे तृतीये तु मासे पुंसवनं भवेत् । गर्भेऽव्यक्ते तृतीये चेच्चतुर्थे मासि वा भवेत् ॥' इति । वसिष्ठश्च—'कुर्यात्पुंसवनं प्रसिद्धविषये गर्भे तृतीयेऽथ वा । मासि स्फीततनौ तुषारकिरणे पुष्येऽथ वा वैष्णवे' ॥ इति । अस्मिन्विधौ पतिः पत्न्याः पृष्ठदेशे स्थितोऽव्यवहितं तस्या नाभिदेशं स्पृशन् इमं मन्त्रं पठति—'पुमांसौ मित्रावरुणौ पुमांसावश्विनावुभौ । पुमानग्निश्च वायुश्च पुमान्गर्भस्तवोदरे ॥' अन्यं च—'पुमानग्निः पुमानिन्द्रः पुमान्देवो बृहस्पतिः । पुमांसं पुत्रं विन्दस्व तं पुमाननुजायताम् ॥' इति । 'धृतेः' इत्यत्र 'श्रुतेः' इति दिनकरस्य पाठः । तत्र श्रुतेः पुत्रज्ञानस्येत्यर्थः ।

सनया]। आसनादुत्थितयेत्यर्थः। उपचारस्य। अञ्जलौ अञ्जलिकरणे खिन्नहस्तया [**उपचारा-ञ्जलिखिन्नहस्तया**] **पारिप्लवनेत्रया** तरलाक्ष्या । ' चञ्चलं तरलं चैव पारिप्लवपरिप्लवे ' इत्यमरः । **तया** सुदक्षिणया **ननन्द** । ' सुरेन्द्रमात्राश्रित-' इत्यत्र मनुः—' अष्टाभिश्च सुरेन्द्राणां मात्राभिर्निर्मितो नृपः । ' इति ॥

कुमारभृत्याकुशलैरनुष्ठिते भिषग्भिराप्तैरथ गर्भभर्मणि ।
पतिः प्रतीतः प्रसवोन्मुखीं प्रियां ददर्श काले दिवमभ्रितामिव ॥१२॥

अथ । कुमारभृत्या बालचिकित्सा । ' संज्ञायां समजनिषद-' इत्यादिना क्यप् । तस्यां कुशलैः कृतिभिः [**कुमारभृत्याकुशलैः**]। ' कृती कुशलः ' इत्यमरः । **आप्तैः** हितैः **भिषग्भिः** वैद्यैः । ' भिषग्वैद्यौ चिकित्सके ' इत्यमरः। गर्भस्य भर्मणि भरणे [**गर्भ-भर्मणि**] । ' भरणे पोषणे भर्म ' इति हैमः । ' भृतिर्भर्म ' इति शाश्वतः । भृञो मनि-न्प्रत्ययः । ' गर्भकर्मणि ' इति पाठे गर्भाधानप्रतीतावौचित्यभङ्गः । **अनुष्ठिते** कृते सति । **काले** दशमे मासि । अन्यत्र ग्रीष्मावसाने । प्रसवस्य गर्भमोचनस्योन्मुखीं [**प्रसवोन्मुखीम्**] । आसन्नप्रसवामित्यर्थः । ' स्यादुत्पादे फले पुष्पे प्रसवो गर्भमोचने ' इत्यमरः । **प्रियां** भार्याम् । अभ्राण्यस्याः संजातान्यभ्रिता ताम् [**अभ्रिताम्**] । ' तदस्य संजातं तारकादिभ्य इतच् । ' इतीतच्प्रत्ययः । **दिवमिव** । **पतिः** भर्ता **प्रतीतः** हृष्टः सन् । ' ख्याते हृष्टे प्रतीतः ' इत्यमरः । **ददर्श** दृष्टवान् ॥

ग्रहैस्ततः पञ्चभिरुच्चसंश्रयैरसूर्यगैः सूचितभाग्यसंपदम् ।
असूत पुत्रं समये शचीसमा त्रिसाधना शक्तिरिवार्थमक्षयम् ॥ १३ ॥

ततः शच्येन्द्राण्या समा [**शचीसमा**] । ' पुलोमजा शचीन्द्राणी ' इत्यमरः । सा सुदक्षिणा **समये** प्रसूतिकाले सति । दशमे मासीत्यर्थः । ' दशमे मासि जायते ' इति श्रुतेः । **उच्चसंश्रयैः** उच्चसंश्रयैस्तुङ्गस्थानगैः **असूर्यगैः** अनस्तमितैः । कैश्चिद्यथासंभवं

---

१ तदुक्तं भावप्रकाशे–अक्षिपक्ष्माणि चाप्यस्याः संमील्यन्ते विशेषतः । इति । २ कुमार-भृत्या नामाष्टाङ्गस्यायुर्वेदस्याङ्गविशेषः । तदुक्तं सुश्रुते-' शल्यं शालाक्यं कायचिकित्सा भूतविद्या कौमारभृत्यं अगदतन्त्रं रसायनतन्त्रं वाजीकरणतन्त्रमिति । कौमारभरणं नाम कुमारभरणधात्रीशोधनार्थं दुष्टस्तन्यग्रहसमुत्थानां च व्याधीनामुपशमनार्थम् ' । इति । ' अजा-तेपि कुमारे कुमारभृत्याप्रयोगो न दोषाय, कुमारभृत्या गर्भभर्मणि प्रजने च क्रियेत इति कौटिल्य-वचनात् । ' इति चारि०. ३ ' गर्भभर्मणि ' इत्यत्र ' गर्भकर्मणि ' ' गर्भवेश्मनि ' ' गर्भरक्षणे ' इति पाठान्तराणि । ' पतिः प्रतीतः प्रसवोन्मुखीम् ' इत्यत्र ' निरत्ययाय प्रसवाय तस्थुषीम् ' इति पाठान्तरं चारित्रवर्धनः समुद्धरति । ४ अत्र चारित्रवर्धनव्याख्या यथा–ग्रहाणां द्विविधमुच्चत्वं राशिकृतं भागकृतं च । तत्र प्रथमराशौ सूर्यस्योच्चता दशभागेषु । वृषे शीतगोस्त्रिषु भागेषु हरौ कुजस्याष्टाविंशेषु । कन्यायां बुधस्य पञ्चदशसु भागेषु । कर्के गुरोः पञ्चसु भागेषु । मीने शुक्रस्य सप्तविंशतिभागेषु । तुलायां शनेर्विंशतिभागेषु ॥ असूर्यगैः–सर्वे ग्रहाः सूर्यराशिगता अस्त-मिता उच्यन्ते । उक्तं च-' क्रूराक्रान्तः क्रूरगतः क्रूरदृष्टस्तु यो ग्रहः । विरश्मितां प्रपन्नश्च स विनष्टो बुधैः स्मृतः ॥ ' इति । पञ्चभिः सूचितभाग्यसंपदम्–' एकेन ग्रहेण सुखी द्वाभ्यां श्रेष्ठः त्रिभिर्नृपतुल्यश्चतुर्भिर्नृपः पञ्चभिर्देवतुल्यः ' इति भाग्यसंपत् ।

पञ्चभिः ग्रहैः सूचिता भाग्यसंपद्यस्य तं [**सूचितभाग्यसंपदम्**] **पुत्रम्** । त्रीणि प्रभावमन्त्रोत्साहात्मकानि साधनान्युत्पादकानि यस्याः सा **त्रिसाधना शक्तिः** । 'शक्तय-स्तिस्रः प्रभावोत्साहमन्त्रजाः । ' इत्यमरः । **अक्षयमर्थमिव । असूत** । ' षूङ् प्राणिगर्भ-विमोचने ' इत्यात्मनेपदिषु पठ्यते । तस्माद्धातोः कर्तरि लङ् । अत्रेदमनुसंधेयम्---'अज-वृषभमृगाङ्गनाकुलीरा झषवणिजौ च दिवाकरादितुङ्गाः । दशशिखिमनुयुक्तिथीन्द्रियांशैस्त्रिनवक-विंशतिभिश्च तेऽस्तनीचाः ॥ ' इति । सूर्यादीनां सप्तानां ग्रहाणां मेषवृषभादयो राशयः श्लोकोक्तक्रमाविशिष्टा उच्चस्थानानि । स्वस्वतुङ्गापेक्षया सप्तमस्थानानि च नीचानि । तत्रोच्चेष्वपि दशमादयो राशित्रिंशांशा यथाक्रममुच्चेषु परमोच्चा नीचेषु परमनीचा इति जातकश्लोकार्थः । अत्रांशस्त्रिंशो भागः । यथाह नारदः---'त्रिंशद्भागात्मकं लग्नम्' इति । सूर्यप्रत्यासत्तिर्ग्रहा-णामस्तमयो नाम । तदुक्तं लघुजातके---'रविणास्तमयो योगो वियोगस्तूदयो भवेत्' इति । ते च स्वोच्चस्थाः फलन्ति नास्तगा नापि नीचगाः । तदुक्तं राजमृगाङ्के--'स्वोच्चे पूर्णं स्वर्क्षकेऽर्धं सुहृद्भे पादं द्विड्भेऽल्पं शुभं खेचरेन्द्रः । नीचस्थायी नास्तगो वा न किंचित्पादं नूनं स्वत्रिकोणे ददाति ॥ ' इति । तदिदमाह कविरुच्चसंस्थैरसूर्यगैरिति च । एवं सति यस्य जन्मकाले पञ्चप्रभृतयो ग्रहाः स्वोच्चस्थाः स एव तुङ्गो भवति । तदुक्तं कूटस्थीये--' सुखिनः प्रकृष्टकार्या राजप्रतिरूपकाश्च राजानः । एकाद्वित्रिचतुर्भिर्जायन्तेऽतः परं दिव्याः ॥ ' इति । तदिदमाह पञ्चभिरिति ॥

दिशः प्रसेदुर्मरुतो ववुः सुखाः प्रदक्षिणार्चिर्हविरग्निराददे ।
बभूव सर्वं शुभशंसि तत्क्षणं भवो हि लोकाभ्युदयाय तादृशाम् १४

तत्क्षणं तस्मिन्क्षणे । कालाध्वनोरत्यन्तसंयोगे द्वितीया । **दिशः प्रसेदुः** प्रसन्ना बभूवुः । **मरुतः** वाताः **सुखाः** मनोहराः **ववुः** । **अग्निः प्रदक्षिणार्चिः** सन् **हविराददे** स्वीचकार । इत्थं **सर्वं शुभशंसि** शुभसूचकं **बभूव** । तथा **हि । तादृशां** रघुप्रकाराणां **भवः** जन्म **लोकाभ्युदयाय** । भवतीति शेषः । ततो देवा अपि संतुष्टा इत्यर्थः ॥

अरिष्टशय्यां परितो विसारिणा सुजन्मनस्तस्य निजेन तेजसा ।
निशीथदीपाः सहसा हतत्विषो बभूवुरालेख्यसमर्पिता इव ॥ १५ ॥

---

१ अजेति मल्लिनाथोद्धृतश्लोकस्यायमर्थः-रवेरुच्चस्थानं मेषराशिः, सोमस्य वृषराशिः, मङ्गलस्य मकरराशिः, बुधस्य कन्याराशिः, बृहस्पतेः कर्कटकराशिः, शुक्रस्य मीनराशिः, शनेश्च तुलाराशिः (वणिक्) । दश-दशांशाः । शिख-त्र्यंशाः । मनुयुक्-द्विगुणिताश्चतुर्दश (अष्टाविंशतिः) अंशाः । तिथि-पञ्चदशांशाः । इंद्रिय-पञ्चांशाः, त्रिनवक-सप्तविंशतिरंशाः, विंशतिरंशाश्च । एतेषु भागेषु तुङ्गाः । ते पूर्वोक्ताः सूर्योदयोऽस्ते स्वस्थानापेक्षया सप्तमस्थाने स्थिता नीचाः । असूर्यगैरित्येनन कुमारस्य यशःसौभाग्यं न कदाप्यस्मिञ्जगत्यस्तमेष्यतीति सूचितम् । २ अनुरूपवर्णनं कुमारसंभवे-'प्रसन्नदिक्पांशुविविक्तवातं शङ्खस्वनानन्तरपुष्पवृष्टि । शरीरिणां स्थावरजङ्गमानां सुखाय तज्जन्मदिनं बभूव' इति । अग्रे दशमसर्गेपि 'निर्दोषमभवत्सर्वमाविष्कृतगुणं जगत्' इति ।

'अरिष्टं सूतिकागृहम्' इत्यमरः। अरिष्टे सूतिकागृहे शय्यां तल्पं [**अरिष्टशय्यां**] **परितः** अभितः। 'अभितःपरितःसमयानिकषाहाप्रतियोगेपु दृश्यते' इति द्वितीया। **विसारिणा। सुजन्मनः** शोभनोत्पत्तेः। 'जनुर्जननजन्मानि जनिरुत्पत्तिरुद्भवः।' इत्यमरः। **तस्य** शिशोः **निजेन** नैसर्गिकेण **तेजसा सहसा हतत्विषः** क्षीणकान्तयो **निशीथदीपाः**। 'अर्धरात्रनिशीथौ द्वौ' इत्यमरः। **आलेख्यसमर्पिताः** चित्रार्पिताः **इव बभूवुः**। निशीथशब्दो दीपानां प्रभाधिक्यसंभावनार्थः॥

जनाय शुद्धान्तचराय शंसते कुमारजन्मामृतसंमिताक्षरम्।
अदेयमासीत्त्रयमेव भूपतेः शशिप्रभं छत्रमुभे च चामरे॥ १६॥

भूपतेः दिलीपस्य **अमृतसंमिताक्षरम्** अमृतसमानाक्षरम्। 'सरूपसमसंमिताः' इत्यादि दण्डी। **कुमारजन्म** पुत्रोत्पत्तिं **शंसते** कथयते **शुद्धान्तचराय** अन्तःपुरचारिणे **जनाय त्रयमेवादेयमासीत्**। किं तत्। **शशिप्रभम्** उज्ज्वलं **छत्रम् उभे चामरे च**। छत्रादीनां राज्ञः प्रधानाङ्गत्वादिति भावः॥

निवातपद्मास्तिमितेन चक्षुषा नृपस्य कान्तं पिबतः सुताननम्।
महोदधेः पूर इवेन्दुदर्शनाद्गुरुः प्रहर्षः प्रबभूव नात्मनि॥ १७॥

निवातो निर्वातप्रदेशः। 'निवातावाश्रयावातौ' इत्यमरः। तत्र यत्पद्मं तद्वत्स्तिमितेन निष्पन्देन [**निवातपद्मास्तिमितेन**] **चक्षुषा** नेत्रेण **कान्तं** सुन्दरं **सुताननं** पुत्रमुखं **पिबतः** तृष्णया पश्यतः **नृपस्य गुरुः** उत्कटः **प्रहर्षः** कर्ता **इन्दुदर्शनाद्** गुरुः **महोदधेः पूरः** जलौघः **इव आत्मनि** शरीरे **न प्रबभूव** स्थातुं न शशाक। अन्तर्न माति स्मेति यावत्। न ह्यल्पाधारेऽधिकं मीयत इति भावः। यद्वा हर्ष आत्मनि स्वास्मिन्विषय न प्रबभूव। आत्मानं नियन्तुं न शशाक। किं तु बहिर्निर्जगामेत्यर्थः॥

स जातकर्मण्यखिले तपस्विना तपोवनादेत्य पुरोधसा कृते।
दिलीपसूनुर्मणिराकरोद्भवः प्रयुक्तसंस्कार इवाधिकं बभौ॥ १८॥

स दिलीपसूनुः। तपस्विना पुरोधसा पुरोहितेन। 'पुरोधास्तु पुरोहितः' इत्यमरः। वसिष्ठेन। तपस्वित्वात्तदनुष्ठितं कर्म सवीर्यं स्यादिति भावः। **तपोवनादेत्य** आगत्य। **अखिले** समग्रे **जातकर्मणि** जातस्य कर्तव्यसंस्कारविशेषे **कृते**

---

१ अनुरूपः श्लोकोग्रे दशमे-रघुवंशप्रदीपेन—इत्यादिः। २ अस्मात्परं चा. ष. सु. प्रभृतयः श्लोकमेकमधिकं योजयन्ति—

समीक्ष्य पुत्रस्य चिरान्मुखं पिता निधानकुम्भस्य युवेव दुर्गतः।
मुदा शरीरे प्रबभूव नात्मनः पयोधिरिन्दूदयमूर्छितो यथा॥

३ 'शुद्धान्तः स्यादन्तःपुरम्' इत्याभिधानचिन्तामणिः। ४ 'वातस्याभावो निवातम्' इति चा०। अनुरूपः श्लोकः कुमारसंभवे-'भवत्संभावनोत्थाय परितोषाय मूर्च्छते। अपि व्याप्तदिगन्तानि नाङ्गानि प्रभवन्ति मे॥' इति।

सति । प्रयुक्तः संस्कारः शाणोल्लेखनादिर्यस्य स तथोक्तः [**प्रयुक्तसंस्कारः**] । **आकरोद्भवः** खनिप्रभवः । 'खनिः स्त्रियामाकरः स्यात्' इत्यमरः । **मणिरिव** । **अधिकं बभौ** । वसिष्ठमन्त्रप्रभावात्तेजिष्ठोऽभूदित्यर्थः । अत्र मनुः—'प्राङ्नाभिवर्धनात्पुंसो जातकर्म विधीयते' इति ॥

सुखश्रवा मङ्गलतूर्यनिस्वनाः प्रमोदनृत्यैः सह वारयोषिताम् ।
न केवलं सद्मनि मागधीपतेः पथि व्यजृम्भन्त दिवौकसामपि ॥ १९ ॥

सुखः सुखकरः श्रवः श्रवणं येषां ते **सुखश्रवाः** । श्रुतिसुखा इत्यर्थः । **मङ्गलतूर्यनिस्वनाः** मङ्गलवाद्यध्वनयो **वारयोषितां** वेश्यानाम् । 'वारस्त्री गणिका वेश्या रूपाजीवा' इत्यमरः । **प्रमोदनृत्यैः** हर्षनर्तनैः **सह मागधीपतेः** दिलीपस्य **सद्मनि केवलं** गृह एव **न व्यजृम्भन्त** । किं तु । द्यौरोको येषां ते दिवौकसो देवाः । पृषोदरादित्वात्साधुः । तेषां [**दिवौकसाम्**] **पथि** आकाशे **अपि** व्यजृम्भन्त । तस्य देवांशत्वाद्देवोपकारित्वाच्च देवदुन्दुभयोऽपि नेदुरिति भावः ॥

न संयतस्तस्य बभूव रक्षितुर्विसर्जयेद्यं सुतजन्महर्षितः ।
ऋणाभिधानात्स्वयमेव केवलं तदा पितॄणां मुमुचे स बन्धनात् ॥ २० ॥

रक्षितुः सम्यक्पालनशीलस्य **तस्य** दिलीपस्य । अत एव चौराद्यभावात् । **संयतः** बद्धो **न बभूव** नाभूत् । किं तेनात आह—विसर्जयेदिति । सुतजन्मना हर्षितस्तोषितः [**सुतजन्महर्षितः**] सन् । **यं** बद्धं **विसर्जयेत्** विमोचयेत् । किं तु **स** राजा **तदा पितॄणाम् ऋणाभिधानात् बन्धनात् केवलम्** एकं यथा तथा । **स्वयमेव** । एक एवेत्यर्थः । 'केवलः कृत्स्न एकश्च केवलश्चावधारितः ।' इति शाश्वतः । **मुमुचे** । कर्मकर्तरि लिट् । स्वयमेव मुक्त इत्यर्थः । अस्मिन्नर्थे—'एष वा अनृणो यः पुत्री' इति श्रुतिः प्रमाणम् ॥

श्रुतस्य यायादयमन्तमर्भकस्तथा परेषां युधि चेति पार्थिवः ।
अवेक्ष्य धातोर्गमनार्थमर्थविच्चकार नाम्ना रघुमात्मसंभवम् ॥ २१ ॥

अर्थवित् शब्दार्थज्ञः **पार्थिवः** पृथिवीश्वरो दिलीपः । **अयम् अर्भकः** बालकः **श्रुतस्य** शास्त्रस्य **अन्तं** पारं **यायात्** । **तथा युधि परेषां** शत्रूणामन्तं पारं **च** यायात् । यातुं शक्नुयादित्यर्थः । 'शकि लिङ् च' इति शक्यार्थे लिङ् । **इति** हेतोः **धातोः** 'अघिवघिलघि गत्यर्थाः' इति लघिधातोर्गमनाख्यमर्थं [**गमनार्थम्**] अर्थवित्त्वाद्

---

१ स्वर्गपक्षे स्वर्गवासिनीनामुर्वशीमेनकारम्भाद्यानाम् । समानभावो दशमे-पुत्रजन्मप्रवेश्यानां तूर्याणां तस्य पुत्रिणः । आरम्भं प्रथमं चक्रुर्देवदुन्दुभयो दिवि ॥ २ उत्सवविशेषे राज्ञामपराधिविमोचनं प्रसिद्धम्-'युवराजाभिषेके च परचक्रावमर्दने । पुत्रजन्मनि वा मोक्षो बद्धस्य हि विधीयते ॥' इ. हेमा. ३ तल्लक्षणं यथा-क्रियमाणं तु यत्कर्म स्वयमेव प्रसिध्यति । सुकरैः स्वैर्गुणैः कर्तुः कर्मकर्तेति तद्विदुः ॥ अत्र पुत्रवत्तारूपेण गुणेनैव मुक्तत्वात्कर्मकर्तरिप्रयोगः । 'विसर्जयेत्' इत्यत्र 'विमोचयेत्' इति दि. चा. पठतः ।

अवेक्ष्य आलोच्य । आत्मसंभवं पुत्रं नाम्ना रघुं चकार । 'लङ्घिवंह्योर्नलोपश्च' इत्यत्र सूत्रे 'बालमूललघ्वलमङ्गुलीनां वा लो रत्वमापद्यते' इति वैकल्पिके रेफादेशे रघुरिति रूपं सिद्धम् । अत्र शङ्खः—'अशौचे तु व्यतिक्रान्ते नामकर्म विधीयते ।' इति ॥

पितुः प्रयत्नात्स समग्रसंपदः शुभैः शरीरावयवैर्दिने दिने ।
पुपोष वृद्धिं हरिदश्वदीधितेरनुप्रवेशादिव बालचन्द्रमाः ॥ २२ ॥

स रघुः **समग्रसंपदः** पूर्णलक्ष्मीकस्य **पितुः** दिलीपस्य **प्रयत्नात् शुभैः** मनोहरैः **शरीरावयवैः हरिदश्वदीधितेः** सूर्यस्य रश्मेः । 'भास्वद्विवस्वत्सप्ताश्वहरिदश्वोष्णरश्मयः' इत्यमरः । **अनुप्रवेशाद्बालचन्द्रमा इव । दिने दिने** प्रतिदिनम् । 'नित्यवीप्सयोः' इति द्विर्वचनम् । **वृद्धिं पुपोष ।** अत्र वराहसंहितावचनम्—'सलिलमये शशिनि रवेर्दीधितयो मूर्छितास्तमो नैशम् । क्षपयन्ति दर्पणोदरनिहिता इव मन्दिरस्यान्तः ॥' इति ॥

उमावृषाङ्कौ शरजन्मना यथा यथा जयन्तेन शचीपुरंदरौ ।
तथा नृपः सा च सुतेन मागधी ननन्दतुस्तत्सदृशेन तत्समौ ॥२३॥

उमावृषाङ्कौ पार्वतीवृषभध्वजौ **शरजन्मना** कार्तिकेयेन । 'कार्तिकेयो महासेनः शरजन्मा षडाननः ।' इत्यमरः । **यथा** ननन्दतुः । **शचीपुरंदरौ जयन्तेन** जयन्ताख्येन सुतेन । 'जयन्तः पाकशासनिः' इत्यमरः । **यथा** ननन्दतुः । **तथा तत्समौ** ताभ्यामुमावृषाङ्काभ्यां शचीपुरंदराभ्यां च समौ समानौ **सा मागधी नृपश्च तत्सदृशेन** ताभ्यां कुमारजयन्ताभ्यां सदृशेन **सुतेन ननन्दतुः** । मागधी प्रागुक्ताख्याता ॥

रथाङ्गनाम्नोरिव भावबन्धनं बभूव यत्प्रेम परस्पराश्रयम् ।
विभक्तमप्येकसुतेन तत्तयाः परस्परस्योपरि पर्यचीयत ॥ २४ ॥

रथाङ्गनाम्नी च रथाङ्गनामा च रथाङ्गनामानौ चक्रवाकौ । 'पुमान्स्त्रिया' इत्येकशेषः । तयोः

---

१ आत्म०—संभवत्यस्मादिति संभवः । आत्मा संभवो यस्य तत् । 'आत्मा वै पुत्रनामासि' इति श्रुतेः । २ 'श्रीमूर्यस्य सुषुम्ना (अमा) नाम कला तस्याः प्रवेशाद्वृद्धिं पुष्णाति । चन्द्रमाः किल सूर्यस्य सुषुम्नां नाम नाडिकामनुप्रविश्य वर्धते' इति वल्ल. । अमावास्यायां चन्द्रो रवौ गच्छति प्रतिपदि निःसरति, तत उदयं प्राप्य यथा दिने दिने वर्धते तथा अयमपि ववृधे । इ. चा० । अनुरूपवर्णनं कुमारसंभवे-दिने दिने सा परिवर्धमाना लब्धोदया चान्द्रमसीव लेखा । पुपोष लावण्यमयान्विशेषान् ज्योत्स्नान्तराणीव कलान्तराणि ॥ इति ३ । शरेषु जन्मास्य । तस्य शरवणे उत्पन्नत्वात् । इयं कथा कुमारसंभवे दशमसर्गे द्रष्टव्या । अत्र वामनपुराणम्—एतस्मिन्नन्तरे देव्यः कृत्तिकाः षट् सुतेजसः । ददृशुः स्वेच्छया यान्त्यो बालं शरवणे स्थितम् ॥ इत्यादि । ४ 'विभक्तमप्येकसुतेन तत्तयोः परस्परस्योपरि पर्यहीयत' इति वल्लभः पठति । 'न व्यहीयत' इति चारित्रवर्धनदिनकरादयः ।

[**रथाङ्गनाम्नोः**] **इव तयोः** दंपत्योः **भावबन्धनं**[1] हृदयाकर्षकं **परस्पराश्रयम्** अन्योन्यविषयं **यत्प्रेम बभूव** । **तद्** एकेन केवलेन ताभ्यामन्येन वा । 'एके मुख्यान्यकेवलाः' इत्यमरः । सुतेन [**एकसुतेन**] **विभक्तमपि** कृतविभागमपि **परस्परस्योपरि पर्यच्चीयत** ववृधे । कर्मकर्तरि लङ् । अकृत्रिमत्वात्स्वयमेवोपचितमित्यर्थः । यदेकाधारं वस्तु तदाधारद्वये विभज्यमानं हीयते । अत्र तु तयोः प्रागेकैककर्तृकमेकैकविषयं प्रेम संप्रति द्वितीयविषयलाभेऽपि नाहीयत । प्रत्युतोपचितमेवाभूदिति भावः ॥

उवाच[2] धात्र्या प्रथमोदितं वचो ययौ तदीयामवलम्ब्य चाङ्गुलिम् ।
अभूच्च नम्रः प्रणिपातशिक्षया पितुर्मुदं तेन ततान सोऽर्भकः ॥२५॥

सोऽर्भकः शिशुः । 'पोतः पाकोऽर्भको डिम्भः पृथुकः शावकः शिशुः ।' इत्यमरः । **धात्र्या** उपमात्रा । 'धात्री जनन्यामलकीवसुमत्युपमातृषु ।' इति विश्वः । प्रथममुदितमुपदिष्टं [**प्रथमोदितं**] **वचः उवाच** । **तदीयाम् अङ्गुलिम् अवलम्ब्य ययौ च** । [**प्रणिपातशिक्षया**] प्रणिपातस्य शिक्षयोपदेशेन **नम्रः अभूच्च** । इति यत् **तेन पितुः मुदं ततान** ॥

तमङ्कमारोप्य शरीरयोगजैः सुखैर्निषिञ्चन्तमिवामृतं त्वचि ।
उपान्तसंमीलितलोचनो नृपश्चिरात्सुतस्पर्शरसज्ञतां ययौ ॥ २६ ॥

शरीरयोगजैः सुखैः त्वचि त्वगिन्द्रिये **अमृतं निषिञ्चन्तं** वर्षन्तम् **इव तं** पुत्रम् **अङ्कमारोप्य** मुदातिभावादुपान्तयोः प्रान्तयोः संमीलितलोचनः [**उपान्तसंमीलितलोचनः**] सन् । **नृपः चिरात् सुतस्पर्शरसज्ञतां**[3] **ययौ** । रसः स्वादः ॥

अमंस्त चानेन परार्ध्यजन्मना स्थितेरभेत्ता स्थितिमन्तमन्वयम् ।
स्वमूर्तिभेदेन गुणाग्र्यवर्तिना पतिः प्रजानामिव सर्गमात्मनः ॥२७॥

स्थितेः अभेत्ता मर्यादापालकः स नृपः **परार्ध्यजन्मना**[4] उत्कृष्टजन्मना **अनेन**

---

[1] भावस्यान्योन्यचित्तवृत्तेर्बन्धनं संश्लेषणम् । 'चेतोवृत्तिगुम्फनम्' इति व० । 'चित्तवृत्तिबन्धनस्थानं मैत्रीकरणम्' इति चा० । अनुरूपभाव उत्तरचरिते—'आनन्दग्रन्थिरेकोयमपत्यमिति बध्यते' इति । [2] अयं श्लोकः वत्सलरसस्योदाहरणत्वेनोदाहृतः साहित्यदर्पणकृता । वत्सलरसस्य लक्षणं च तेनोक्तम्—'स्फुटं चमत्कारितया वत्सलं च रसं विदुः ।' इति तस्य स्थाय्यादिभावविचारस्तत्रैवालोच्यः । 'उवाच' इत्यत्र 'यदाह' इति, 'ततान सोऽर्भकः' इत्यत्र 'शिशुस्ततान सः' इति पा०. [3] सुतस्पर्शो हि निरतिशयसुखकारित्वेन प्रसिद्धः । उक्तं च भारते—'न वाससां न रामाणां नापां स्पर्शस्तथाविधः । शिशोरालिङ्ग्यमानस्य स्पर्शः सूनोर्यथा सुखः ॥' 'पुत्रस्पर्शात्सुखतरः स्पर्शो लोके न विद्यते' इति च । अनुरूपभावो हर्षचरिते—ससंभ्रममुपसृतं चैनं (पुत्रम्) ...उरसि निवेश्य विशन्निव प्रेम्णा सुधाकरमण्डलमध्ये मज्जन्निवामृतमये महासरसि इ० । 'सर्वाङ्गीणः स्पर्शः सुतस्य किल—' इ. विक्रमोर्वशीये (५।११) च । [4] परस्मिन्नर्धे भवं परार्ध्यं श्रेष्ठम् । रघुपक्षे लोकपालांशत्वादिना विष्णुपक्षे विश्वपालनादिना च श्रेष्ठत्वं ज्ञेयम् ।

रघुणा **अन्वयं** वंशम् । **प्रजानां पतिः** ब्रह्मा । गुणाः सत्त्वादयः । तेष्वन्यतमेन मुख्येन सत्त्वेन वर्तते व्याप्रियत इति गुणाध्यवर्ती तेन [**गुणाध्यवर्तिना**] स्वस्य मूर्तिभेदेन [**स्वमूर्तिभेदेन**[1]] अवतारविशेषेण विष्णुना **आत्मनः सर्ग** सृष्टिम् **इव** । **स्थितिमन्तं** प्रतिष्ठावन्तम् **अमंस्त** मन्यते स्म च । मन्यतेरनुदात्तत्वादिट्प्रतिषेधः । अत्रोपमानोपमेययोरितरेतरविशेषणानीतरेतरत्र योज्यानि । तत्र रघुपक्षे गुणा विद्याविनयादयः । 'गुणोऽप्रधाने रूपादौ मौर्व्यां सूदे वृकोदरे । सत्त्वे सत्त्वादिसंध्यादिविद्यादिहरितादिषु ' इति विश्वः । शेषं सुगमम् ॥

स वृत्तचूलश्चलकाकपक्षकैरमात्यपुत्रैः सवयोभिरन्वितः ।
लिपेर्यथावद्ग्रहणेन वाङ्मयं नदीमुखेनेव समुद्रमाविशत् ॥ २८ ॥

'चूडा कार्या द्विजातीनां सर्वेषामेव धर्मतः । प्रथमेऽब्दे तृतीये वा कर्तव्या श्रुतिचोदनात् ॥' इति मनुस्मरणात्तृतीये वर्षे **वृत्तचूलः**[2] निष्पन्नचूडाकर्मा सन् । डलयोरभेदः । **स** रघुः । 'प्राप्ते तु पञ्चमे वर्षे विद्यारम्भं च कारयेत् ।' इति वचनात्पञ्चमे वर्षे **चलकाकपक्षकैः** चञ्चलशिखण्डकैः । 'बालानां तु शिखा प्रोक्ता काकपक्षः शिखण्डकः ' इति हलायुधः । **सवयोभिः** स्निग्धैः । 'स्निग्धो वयस्यः सवयाः' इत्यमरः । **अमात्यपुत्रैः अन्वितः** सन् **लिपेः** पञ्चाशद्वर्णात्मिकाया मातृकायाः **यथावद्ग्रहणेन** सम्यग्बोधेनोपायभूतेन **वाङ्मयं**[3] शब्दजातम् । नद्या मुखं द्वारम् । 'मुखं तु वदने मुख्यारम्भे द्वाराभ्युपाययोः ।' इति यादवः । तेन [**नदीमुखेन**] कश्चिन्मकरादिः **समुद्रमिव** । **आविशत्** प्रविष्टः । ज्ञातवानित्यर्थः ॥

अथोपनीतं विधिवद्विपश्चितो विनिन्युरेनं गुरवो गुरुप्रियम् ।
अवन्ध्ययत्नाश्च बभूवुरत्र ते क्रिया हि वस्तूपहिता प्रसीदति ॥२९॥

'गर्भाष्टमेऽब्दे कुर्वीत ब्राह्मणस्योपनायनम् । गर्भादेकादशे राज्ञो गर्भाच्च द्वादशे विशः ॥' इति मनुस्मरणाद् **अथ** गर्भैकादशेऽब्दे **विधिवदुपनीतं गुरुप्रियम्**

---

1 स्वमूर्तिभेदेन–पुत्रपक्षे स्वस्य आत्मन एव मूर्तिभेदो रूपान्तरेण प्रादुर्भावः तेन । 'आत्मा वै जायते पुत्रः ' इति स्मरणात् । विष्णुपक्षे मूर्तिभेदः स्वरूपान्तरम् । तदुक्तं कुमारसंभवे–' एकैव मूर्तिर्बिभिदे त्रिधा सा–' इत्यादि । कौर्मे च–' रजोगुणमयं चान्यद्रूपं तस्यैव धीमतः । चतुर्मुखः स भगवान् जगत्स्रष्टा प्रवर्तते ॥ सत्त्वं गुणमुपाश्रित्य विष्णुर्विश्वेश्वरः स्वयम् ।' इति । 'ब्रह्मत्वे सृजते लोकान्विष्णुत्वे पालयत्यपि । रुद्रत्वे संहरत्येव तिस्रोऽवस्थाः स्वयंभुवः ॥' इत्युक्तत्वान्मूर्तिभेदत्वम् । इ. चा. दिनकरश्च । २ 'वृत्तचूडः' 'वृत्तचौलः' इ. पा. ३ वेदचतुष्टयं वर्जयित्वान्यत्सर्वं शास्त्रजातमित्यर्थः । लिपेर्ग्रहणेन–तया तदध्यापनात् । तदुक्तं–अकारादिक्षकारान्ता वर्णमाला यया पुनः । समस्तं वाङ्मयं व्याप्तं त्रैलोक्यमिव विष्णुना ॥ गुरवः प्रियाः यस्य स तम् । गुरुभक्तमित्यर्थः । न हि विद्या गुरुभक्तिं विना फलति । तदुक्तं श्वेताश्वतरोपनिषदि–यस्य देवे परा भक्तिर्यथा देवे तथा गुरौ । तस्यैते कथिता ह्यर्थाः प्रकाशन्ते महात्मनः ॥ इति । यद्वा प्रीणातीति प्रियः । इगुपधेत्यादिना प्रीधातोः कः । गुरूणां प्रियस्तम् । गुरोः शिष्यवात्सल्यं विना शिष्यस्य विद्यालाभासंभवात् ।

एनं रघुं **विपश्चितः** विद्वांसः **गुरवो विनिन्युः** शिक्षितवन्तः । ते गुरवः अत्र अस्मिन्रघौ **अवन्ध्ययत्नाश्च बभूवुः** । तथा हि । **क्रिया** शिक्षा । 'क्रिया तु निष्कृतौ शिक्षाचिकित्सोपायकर्मसु ।' इति यादवः । वस्तुनि पात्रभूते उपहिता प्रयुक्ता [**वस्तूपहिता**] **प्रसीदति**[1] फलति । 'क्रिया हि द्रव्यं विनयति नाद्रव्यम्' इति कौटिल्यः ॥

धियः समग्रैः स गुणैरुदारधीः क्रमाच्चतस्रश्चतुरर्णवोपमाः ।
ततार विद्याः पवनातिपातिभिर्दिशो हरिद्भिर्हरितामिवेश्वरः ॥ ३० ॥

अत्र कामन्दकः—'शुश्रूषा श्रवणं चैव ग्रहणं धारणं तथा । ऊहापोहोऽर्थविज्ञानं तत्त्वज्ञानं च धीगुणाः ॥' इति । 'आन्वीक्षिकी त्रयी वार्ता दण्डनीतिश्च शाश्वती । एता विद्याश्चतस्रस्तु लोकसंस्थितिहेतवः ॥' इति च । **उदारधीः** उत्कृष्टबुद्धिः **स** रघुः **समग्रैर्धियः गुणैः** । चत्वारोऽर्णवा उपमा यासां ताः **चतुरर्णवोपमाः** । 'तद्धितार्थोत्तरपदसमाहारे च' इत्युत्तरपदसमासः । **चतस्रः विद्याः**[2] । **हरितां** दिशाम् **ईश्वरः** सूर्यः **पवनातिपातिभिः**[3] **हरिद्भिः** निजाश्वैः । 'हरित्ककुभि वर्णे च तृणवाजिविशेषयोः ।' इति विश्वः । चतस्रो **दिशः इव** । **क्रमात्ततार** । चतुरर्णवोपमत्वं दिशामपि द्रष्टव्यम् ॥

त्वचं स मेध्यां परिधाय रौरवीमशिक्षतास्त्रं पितुरेव मन्त्रवत् ।
न केवलं तद्गुरुरेकपार्थिवः क्षितावभूदेकधनुर्धरोऽपि सः ॥ ३१ ॥

स रघुः । 'कार्ष्णरौरवबास्तानि चर्माणि ब्रह्मचारिणः । वसीरन्नानुपूर्व्येण शाणक्षौमादिकानि च ॥' इति मनुस्मरणात् **मेध्यां** शुद्धां **रौरवीं** रुरुसंबन्धिनीम् । 'रुरुर्महा-

---

१ अत्र समानार्थाः श्लोकांशाः—'पात्रविशेषन्यस्तं गुणान्तरं व्रजति शिल्पमाधातुः ।' इति मालविकाग्निमित्रे । 'नाद्रव्ये निहिता काचित्क्रिया फलवती भवेत्' इति हितोपदेशे । 'चीयते बालिशस्यापि सत्क्षेत्रपतिता कृषिः ।' इति मुद्राराक्षसे । 'प्रभवति शुचिर्बिम्बोद्ग्राहे मणिर्न मृदां चयः' इति उत्तररामचरिते । 'धीगेषु सत्कविवचो लभते विकासम्' इत्यन्यत्र च । २ 'विद्याश्चतस्र एवैता योगक्षेमाय देहिनाम्' इति पाठो वङ्गदेशमुद्रितपुस्तकेषु । आन्वीक्षिक्यात्मविज्ञानं धर्माधर्मौ त्रयीस्थितौ । अर्थानर्थौ तु वार्तायां दण्डनीतौ नयानयौ ॥ इति च काम० । (१) आन्वीक्षिकी—अनु प्रत्यक्षपरोक्षाभ्यामीक्षितस्यार्थस्य श्रवणोत्तरमीक्षणं परीक्षणमन्वीक्षा, सा प्रयोजनं यस्याः सा आत्मविद्या । 'प्रयोजनम्' इति ठक् । यया च ज्ञातया परमार्थतत्त्वमीक्षमाणो मुमुक्षुर्हर्षशोकौ जहाति । तदुक्तं कामन्दकेन—'आन्वीक्षिक्यात्मविद्या स्यादीक्षणात्सुखदुःखयोः । ईक्षमाणस्तया तत्त्वं हर्षशोकौ व्युदस्यति ॥' इति । मत्वा धीरो हर्षशोकौ जहाति' इति काठकश्रुतेश्च । 'आन्वीक्षिकी तर्कविद्या तत्त्वज्ञानोपयोगिनी । 'आन्वीक्षिकीं चात्मविद्याम्' इति मनुना पार्थक्येन निर्देशात् । न्याय आन्वीक्षिकी पञ्चाध्यायी गौतमेन प्रणीता' इति मधुसूदनः । (२) त्रयी—त्रयीशब्दो वेदवाचक इति सम्यगवस्थापितं भानुजीदीक्षितैरमरटीकायाम् । तेनात्र साङ्गो वेदो ग्राह्यः । उक्तं च कामन्दकेन—'अङ्गानि वेदाश्चत्वारो मीमांसा न्यायविस्तरः । धर्मशास्त्रं पुराणं च त्रयीदं सर्वमुच्यते' इति । (३) वार्ता—वृत्तिरस्त्यस्याम् । 'पाशुपाल्यं कृषिः पुण्यं वार्ता वार्तानुजीविनाम्' इति कामन्दकः । (४) दण्डनीतिः—अखिलं राज्यशासनतन्त्रम् । काम० २, १५. ३ 'पवनातिवर्तिभिः' इति व० चा० पठतः ।

कृष्णसारः ' इति यादवः । **त्वचं** चर्म **परिधाय** वसित्वा **मन्त्रवत्** समन्त्रकम् **अस्त्रम्** आग्नेयादिकं **पितुरेव** उपाध्यायाद् **अशिक्षत** अभ्यस्तवान् । ' आख्यातोपयोगे ' इत्यपादानसंज्ञा । पितुरेवेत्यवधारणमुपपादयति—नेति । **तद्गुरुः** एकः अद्वितीयः पार्थिवः [**एकपार्थिवः**] **केवलं** पृथिवीश्वर एव **नाभूत्** । किं तु **क्षितौ स** दिलीप एको धनुर्धरः **एकधनुर्धरः**] **अपि** अभूत् ॥

महोक्षतां वत्सतरः स्पृशन्निव द्विपेन्द्रभावं कलभः श्रयन्निव ।
रघुः क्रमाद्यौवनभिन्नशैशवः पुपोष गाम्भीर्यमनोहरं वपुः ॥ ३२ ॥

रघुः क्रमाद् यौवनेन भिन्नशैशवो निरस्तशिशुभावः [**यौवनभिन्नशैशवः**] सन् । [**महोक्षतां**] महानुक्षा महोक्षो महर्षभः । ' अचतुर–' आदिसूत्रेण निपातनादकारान्तत्वम् । तस्य भावस्तत्ता तां **स्पृशन्** गच्छन् **वत्सतरः** दम्य **इव** । ' दम्यवत्सतरौ समौ ' इत्यमरः । **द्विपेन्द्रभावं** महागजत्वं **श्रयन्** व्रजन् **कलभः** करिपोतः **इव** । गाम्भीर्येणाचापलेन मनोहरं [**गाम्भीर्यमनोहरम्**] **वपुः पुपोष** ॥

अथास्य गोदानविधेरनन्तरं विवाहदीक्षां निरवर्तयद्गुरुः ।
नरेन्द्रकन्यास्तमवाप्य सत्पतिं तमोनुदं दक्षसुता इवाबभुः ॥ ३३ ॥

' गौर्नादित्ये बलीवर्दे क्रतुभेदर्षिभेदयोः । स्त्री तु स्याद्दिशि भारत्यां भूमौ च सुरभावपि ॥ पुंस्त्रियोः स्वर्गवज्राम्बुरश्मिदृग्बाणलोमसु ॥' इति केशवः । गावो लोमानि केशा दीयन्ते खण्ड्यन्तेऽस्मिन्निति व्युत्पत्त्या गोदानं नाम ब्राह्मणादीनां षोडशादिषु वर्षेषु कर्तव्यं केशान्ताख्यं कर्मोच्यते । तदुक्तं मनुना—' केशान्तः षोडशे वर्षे ब्राह्मणस्य विधीयते । राजन्यबन्धोर्द्वाविंशे वैश्यस्य द्व्यधिके ततः ॥' इति । **अथ गुरुः** पिता । ' गुरुर्गीष्पतिपित्रादौ ' इत्यमरः । **अस्य गोदानविधेरनन्तरं विवाहदीक्षां निरवर्तयत्** । कृतवानित्यर्थः । अथ **नरेन्द्रकन्याः तं** रघुम् [**दक्षसुताः**] दक्षस्य सुता रोहिण्यादयः **तमोनुदं** चन्द्रम् **इव** । ' तमोनुदोऽग्निचन्द्रार्काः ' इति विश्वः । **सत्पतिम् अवाप्य आबभुः** । रघुरपि तमोनुत् । अत्र मनुः—' वेदानधीत्य वेदौ वा वेदं वापि यथाक्रमम् । अविप्लुतब्रह्मचर्यो गृहस्थाश्रममाविशेत् ॥ ' इति ॥

संप्रति यौवराज्ययोग्यतामाह—

युवा युगव्यायतबाहुरंसलः कपाटवक्षाः परिणद्धकंधरः ।
वपुःप्रकर्षादजयद्गुरुं रघुस्तथाऽपि नीचैर्विनयाददृश्यत ॥ ३४ ॥

---

१ कलभः—' पञ्चवर्षदेशीयः करिशावकः ' इति सुभूतिः । ' त्रिंशद्वर्षस्तु कलभः ' इति वैजयन्ती । २ गम्भीरम० इ० पा. गाम्भीर्यम्—भयशोकादिभिर्मनसोऽविकृतत्वम् । ' भीशोकक्रोधहर्षाद्यैर्गाम्भीर्यं निर्विकारता ' इति साहित्यदर्पणे । ३ ' गोप्रशंसारूपस्तद्दानप्रकारः ' इ. हे. । मङ्गलार्थो गोवितरणरूप आचारविशेषः इ. केचित् । ब्रह्मचर्यमाषोडशाब्दं ततो गोदानानन्तरं दारकर्म इ. चाणक्यः । ४ अश्विन्याद्याः सप्तविंशतिः । तदुक्तं पाद्मे—' अश्विन्याद्यास्तु दक्षस्य ह्युपयेमे सुता विधुः । ' इति । तमोनुदम्–रघुपक्षे तमः पापमोहादिकं नुदति निवारयतीति स तम् । ' तमोपहम् ' इति दि. व. पठतः ।

युगा। युगो नाम धुर्यस्कन्धगः सच्छिद्रप्रान्तो यानाङ्गभूतो दारुविशेषः। 'यानाद्यङ्गे युगः पुंसि युगं युग्मे कृतादिषु।' इत्यमरः। युगवद्व्यायतौ दीर्घौ बाहू यस्य सः [**युगव्यायतबाहुः**]। अंसावस्य स्त इति **अंसलः** बलवान्। मांसलश्चेति वृत्तिकारः। 'बलवान्मांसलोंऽसलः' इत्यमरः। 'वत्सांसाभ्यां कामबले' इति लच्प्रत्ययः। **कपाटवक्षाः परिणद्धकंधरः** विशालग्रीवः। 'परिणाहो विशालता' इत्यमरः। **रघुः** [**वपुःप्रकर्षात्**] वपुषः प्रकर्षाद् आधिक्याद्यौवनकृतात् **गुरुं** पितरम् **अजयत्**। **तथापि विनयात्** नम्रत्वेन **नीचैः** अल्पकः **अदृश्यत**। अनौद्धत्यं च विवक्षितम्॥

संप्रति तस्य यौवराज्यमाह—

ततः प्रजानां चिरमात्मना धृतां नितान्तगुर्वीं लघयिष्यता धुरम्।
निसर्गसंस्कारविनीत इत्यसौ नृपेण चक्रे युवराजशब्दभाक्॥ ३५॥

ततः आत्मना चिरं धृतां नितान्तगुर्वीम्। 'वोतो गुणवचनात्' इति ङीप्। **प्रजानां धुरं** पालनप्रयासं **लघयिष्यता** लघु करिष्यता। 'तत्करोति तदाचष्टे' इति लघुशब्दाण्णिच्। ततो 'लृटः सद्वा' इति शतृप्रत्ययः। **नृपेण** दिलीपेन **असौ** रघुर्निसर्गेण स्वभावेन संस्कारेण शास्त्राभ्यासजनितवासनया च विनीतो नम्रः [**निसर्गसंस्कारविनीतः**] **इति** हेतोः। [**युवराजशब्दभाक्**] युवराज इति शब्दं भजतीति तथोक्तः। 'भजो ण्विः' इति ण्विप्रत्ययः। **चक्रे** कृतः। 'द्विविधो विनयः स्वाभाविकः कृत्रिमश्च' इति कौटिल्यः। तदुभयसंपन्नत्वात्पुत्रं युवराजं चकारेत्यर्थः। अत्र कामन्दकः—'विनयोपग्रहान्भूत्यै कुर्वीत नृपतिः सुतान्। अविनीतकुमारं हि कुलमाशु विशीर्यते। विनीतमौरसं पुत्रं यौवराज्येऽभिषेचयेत्॥' इति॥

नरेन्द्रमूलायतनादनन्तरं तदास्पदं श्रीर्युवराजसंज्ञितम्।
अगच्छदंशेन गुणाभिलाषिणी नवावतारं कमलादिवोत्पलम्॥३६॥

गुणान्विनयादीन्सौरभ्यादींश्चाभिलषतीति **गुणाभिलाषिणी श्रीः** राज्यलक्ष्मीः पद्माश्रया च नरेन्द्रो दिलीप एव मूलायतनं प्रधानस्थानं तस्मात् [**नरेन्द्रमूलायतनाद्**] अपादानात् **अनन्तरं** संनिहितम्। युवराज इति संज्ञास्य संजाता तं **युवराजसंज्ञितम्**। तारकादित्वादितच्प्रत्ययः। आत्मनः पदं स्थानमास्पदम्। 'आस्पदं प्रतिष्ठायाम्' इति निपातः। स रघुरित्यास्पदं **तदास्पदम्**। **कमलात्** चिरं स्थानात् **नवावतारम्** आचिरोत्पन्नम् **उत्पलमिव**। **अंशेन अगच्छत्**। स्त्रियो हि यूनि रज्यन्ते इति भावः॥

विभावसुः सारथिनेव वायुना घनव्यपायेन गभस्तिमानिव।
बभूव तेनातितरां सुदुःसहः कटप्रभेदेन करीव पार्थिवः॥ ३७॥

---

१ 'मनोज्ञस्कन्धः' इति सु०। २ युवा चासौ राजा च युवराजः। 'राजाहःसखिभ्यष्टच्'।
३ 'प्रभावः शुचिना मैत्री त्यागः सत्यं क्षमाऽऽर्जवम्। कुलं शीलं दमश्चेति गुणाः संपत्तिहेतवः॥' इति कामन्दकः।

सारथिना सहायभूतेन । एतद्विशेषणमुत्तरवाक्येष्वप्यनुषञ्जनीयम् । **वायुना विभावसुः** वह्निः **इव** । ‘सूर्यवह्नी विभावसू’ इत्यमरः । **घनव्यपायेन**[1] शरत्समयेन सारथिना **गभस्तिमान्** सूर्यः **इव** । [**कटप्रभेदेन**] कटो गण्डः । ‘गण्डः कटो मदो दानम्’ इत्यमरः । तस्य प्रभेदः स्फुटनम् । मदोदय इत्यर्थः । तेन **करीव** । **पार्थिवः** दिलीपः **तेन** रघुणा **अतितरां** अत्यन्तं **सुदुःसहः** सुदुःसहो **बभूव** ॥

नियुज्य तं होमतुरङ्गरक्षणे धनुर्धरं राजसुतैरनुद्रुतम्[2] ।
अपूर्णमेकेन शतक्रतूपमः शतं क्रतूनामपविघ्नमाप सः ॥ ३८ ॥

शतक्रतुरिन्द्र उपमा यस्य स **शतक्रतूपमः स** दिलीपः । ‘शतं वै तल्या राजपुत्रा देवा आशापालाः’ इत्यादिश्रुत्या **राजसुतैः अनुद्रुतम्** अनुगतं **धनुर्धरं तं** रघुं [**होमतुरङ्गरक्षणे**] होमतुरङ्गाणां रक्षणे **नियुज्य** । **एकेन** क्रतुना **अपूर्णम्** एकोनं **क्रतूनाम्** अश्वमेधानां **शतम् अपविघ्नं** अपगतविघ्नं यथा तथा **आप** ॥

ततः परं तेन मखाय यज्वना तुरङ्गमुत्सृष्टमनर्गलं पुनः ।
धनुर्भृतामग्रत एव रक्षिणां[2] जहार शक्रः किल गूढविग्रहः ॥ ३९ ॥

ततः परम् एकोनशतक्रतुप्राप्त्यनन्तरं **यज्वना** विधिनेष्टवता **तेन** दिलीपेन **पुनः** पुनरपि **मखाय** मखं कर्तुम् । ‘क्रियार्थोपपदस्य–’ इत्यादिना चतुर्थी । **उत्सृष्टं** मुक्तम् **अनर्गलम्** अप्रतिबन्धम् । अव्याहतस्वैरगतिमित्यर्थः । ‘अपर्यावर्तयन्तोऽश्वमनुचरन्ति’ इत्यापस्तम्बस्मरणात् । **तुरङ्गं धनुर्भृतां रक्षिणां** रक्षकाणाम् **अग्रतः एव शक्रः गूढविग्रहः** सन् । **जहार किल** । किलेत्यैतिह्ये ॥

विषादलुप्तप्रतिपत्ति विस्मितं कुमारसैन्यं सपदि स्थितं च तत् ।
वसिष्ठधेनुश्च यदृच्छयाऽऽगता श्रुतप्रभावा[3] ददृशेऽथ नन्दिनी ॥ ४० ॥

तत् [**कुमारसैन्यम्**] कुमारस्य सैन्यं सेना **सपदि** [**विषादलुप्तप्रतिपत्ति**] विषाद इष्टनाशकृतो मनोभङ्गः । तदुक्तम्—‘विषादश्चेतसो भङ्ग उपायाभावनाशयोः’ इति । तेन लुप्ता प्रतिपत्तिः कर्तव्यज्ञानं यस्य तत्तथोक्तम् । **विस्मितम्** अश्वनाशस्याकस्मिकत्वादाश्चर्याविष्टं सत् **स्थितं** तस्थौ **च** । **अथ श्रुतप्रभावा यदृच्छया** स्वेच्छया **आगता** । रघोः स्वप्रसादलब्धत्वादनुजिघृक्षयेति भावः । **नन्दिनी** नाम **वसिष्ठधेनुश्च ददृशे** । द्वौ चकारावविलम्बसूचकौ ॥

तदङ्गनिस्यन्दजलेन लोचने प्रमृज्य पुण्येन पुरस्कृतः सताम् ।
अतीन्द्रियेष्वप्युपपन्नदर्शनो बभूव भावेषु दिलीपनन्दनः ॥ ४१ ॥

सतां पुरस्कृतः पूजितो **दिलीपनन्दनः** रघुः **पुण्येन** तस्या नन्दिन्या यदङ्गं

---

[1] घनानां मघानां व्यपायो ध्वंसो यस्मिन्काले स कालः । शरत्समय इत्यर्थः । ‘सदुःसहः’ इत्यत्र ‘दुरासदः’ इति पा०. [2] ‘अतः,’ रक्षिणाम्—‘पश्यताम्’ इ० पा. [3] श्रुतः प्रभावो रघ्वपत्यवरप्रदानलक्षणो यस्याः सा । आकर्णितमाहात्म्येत्यर्थः । द्वौ चकारौ तुल्यकालतां गमयेते । इति चा० ।

तस्य निस्यन्दो द्रवः स एव जलम् । मूत्रमित्यर्थः । तेन [**तदङ्गनिस्यन्दजलेन**[1]] **लोचने प्रमृज्य** शोधयित्वा । **अतीन्द्रियेषु** इन्द्रियाण्यतिक्रान्तेषु । ' अत्यादयः क्रान्ताद्यर्थे द्वितीयया । ' इति समासः । द्विगुप्राप्तापन्नालंपूर्वगतिसमासेषु परवल्लिङ्गताप्रतिषेधाद्विशेष्यनिघ्नत्वम् । **भावेषु वस्तुषु अपि उपपन्नदर्शनः** संपन्नसाक्षात्कारशक्तिः **बभूव** ॥

स पूर्वतः पर्वतपक्षशातनं ददर्श देवं नरदेवसंभवः ।
पुनः पुनः सूतनिषिद्धचापलं हरन्तमश्वं रथरश्मिसंयतम् ॥ ४२ ॥

नरदेवसंभवः स पुनः पुनः [**सूतनिषिद्धचापलं**] सूतेन निषिद्धचापलं निवारितौद्धत्यं [**रथरश्मिसंयतं**] रथस्य रश्मिभिः प्रग्रहैः । ' किरणप्रग्रहौ रश्मी ' इत्यमरः । संयतं बद्धम् **अश्वं हरन्तं** [**पर्वतपक्षशातनं**[2]] पर्वतपक्षाणां शातनं छेदकं **देवम्** इन्द्रं **पूर्वतः** पूर्वस्यां दिशि **ददर्श** ॥

शतैस्तमक्ष्णामनिमेषवृत्तिभिर्हरिं विदित्वा हरिभिश्च वाजिभिः ।
अवोचदेनं गगनस्पृशा रघुः स्वरेण धीरेण निवर्तयन्निव ॥ ४३ ॥

रघुः तं अश्वहर्तारं **अनिमेषवृत्तिभिः**[3] निमेषव्यापारशून्यैः **अक्ष्णां शतैः हरिभिः** हरिद्वर्णैः । ' हरिर्वाच्यवदाख्यातो हरित्कपिलवर्णयोः । ' इति विश्वः । **वाजिभिः** अश्वैः **च हरिं** इन्द्रं **विदित्वा** । ' हरिर्वातार्कचन्द्रेन्द्रयमोपेन्द्रमरीचिषु ।' इति विश्वः । **एनं** इन्द्रं **गगनस्पृशा**[4] व्योमव्यापिना **धीरेण** गभीरेण **स्वरेण** ध्वनिनैव **निवर्तयन् इव अवोचत्** ॥

मखांशभाजां प्रथमो मनीषिभिस्त्वमेव देवेन्द्र सदा निगद्यसे ।
अजस्रदीक्षाप्रयतस्य मद्गुरोः क्रियाविघाताय कथं प्रवर्तसे ॥ ४४ ॥

हे **देवेन्द्र मनीषिभिस्त्वमेव मखांशभाजां** यज्ञभागभुजां **प्रथमः सदा निगद्यसे** । तथाऽप्यजस्रदीक्षायां नित्यदीक्षायां प्रयतस्य [**अजस्रदीक्षाप्रयतस्य**] **मद्गुरोः क्रियाविघाताय** क्रतुविघाताय । क्रियां विहन्तुमित्यर्थः । ' तुमर्थाच्च भाववचनात् ' इति चतुर्थी । **कथं प्रवर्तसे** ॥

त्रिलोकनाथेन सदा मखद्विषस्त्वया नियम्या ननु दिव्यचक्षुषा ।
स चेत्स्वयं कर्मसु धर्मचारिणां त्वमन्तरायो भवसि च्युतो विधिः ॥ ४५ ॥

---

१ ' स्वेदेन ' इति चा० । ' दुग्धेन ' इत्यपि केचित् । २ पुरा किल हिरण्याक्षमायया संजातपक्षान्स्वस्थानप्रचलितान् पर्वतान् लोकक्षयाय प्रवृत्तानालोक्येन्द्रो वज्रेण तेषां पक्षान् चिच्छेद । तदुक्तं हरिवंशे—कदाचित्तु सपक्षास्ते पर्वता धरणीधराः । प्रस्थिता धरणीं त्यक्त्वा नूनं तस्यैव मायया ॥...स्थैर्यहेतोर्धरण्यास्तु ज्ञात्वा त्वागस्कृतान्गिरीन् । स्वेषु स्थानेषु संस्थाप्य पर्वतानां पुरंदरः । चिच्छेद भगवान् पक्षान् वज्रेण शतपर्वणा ॥ सर्वेषामेव पक्षास्तु छिन्नाः शक्रेण धीमता । एकः सपक्षो मैनाकः सुरैस्तत्समयः कृतः ॥ इत्या० । ३ नास्ति निमेषेऽक्षिस्पन्दे वृत्तिः व्यापारो येषां तैः । निमेषशून्यत्वं हि देवानां लक्षणम् । ' सुरमत्स्यावनिमिषौ ' इत्यमरः । ४ ' गगनस्पृशा धीरेणेति भीत्यभावोक्तिः ' इति चा० ।

त्रयाणां लोकानां नाथस्त्रिलोकनाथः । 'तद्धितार्थ–' इत्यादिनोत्तरपदसमासः । तेन [त्रिलोकनाथेन] त्रैलोक्यनियामकेन **दिव्यचक्षुषा** अतीन्द्रियार्थदर्शिना **त्वया मखद्विषः** क्रतुविघातकाः **सदा निरस्याः ननु** शिक्ष्याः खलु । **स त्वं धर्मचारिणां कर्मसु** क्रतुषु **स्वयम् अन्तरायः** विघ्नः **भवसि चेत्** । **विधिः** अनुष्ठानं **च्युतः** क्षतः । लोके सत्कर्मकथैवास्तमियादित्यर्थः ॥

तदङ्गमग्र्यं मघवन्महाक्रतोरमुं तुरङ्गं प्रतिमोक्तुमर्हसि ।
पथः श्रुतेर्दर्शयितार ईश्वरा मलीमसामाददते न पद्धतिम् ॥ ४६ ॥

हे **मघवन् तत्** तस्मात्कारणात् **महाक्रतोः** अश्वमेधस्य **अग्र्यं** श्रेष्ठं **अङ्गं** साधनं **अमुं तुरङ्गं प्रतिमोक्तुं अर्हसि** । तथा हि । **श्रुतेः पथः दर्शयितारः** सन्मार्गप्रदर्शकाः **ईश्वराः** महान्तः **मलीमसां** मलिनां **पद्धतिं न आददते** न स्वीकुर्वते । असन्मार्गं नावलम्बन्त इत्यर्थः । 'मलीमसं तु मलिनं कच्चरं मलदूषितम् ।' इत्यमरः ॥

इति प्रगल्भं रघुणा समीरितं वचो निशम्याधिपतिर्दिवौकसाम् ।
निवर्तयामास रथं सविस्मयः प्रचक्रमे च प्रतिवक्तुमुत्तरम् ॥ ४७ ॥

इति रघुणा समीरितं प्रगल्भं वचः निशम्य आकर्ण्य । दिवौकसः स्वर्गौकसः । 'दिवं स्वर्गेऽन्तरिक्षे च' इति विश्वः । तेषां [**दिवौकसाम्**] **अधिपतिः** देवेन्द्रो रघुप्रभावात् **सविस्मयः** सन् । **रथं निवर्तयामास** । **उत्तरं प्रतिवक्तुं प्रचक्रमे च** ॥

यदात्थ राजन्यकुमार तत्तथा यशस्तु रक्ष्यं परतो यशोधनैः ।
जगत्प्रकाशं तदशेषमिज्यया भवद्गुरुर्लङ्घयितुं ममोद्यतः ॥ ४८ ॥

हे **राजन्यकुमार** क्षत्रियकुमार । 'मूर्धाभिषिक्तो राजन्यो बाहुजः क्षत्रियो विराट् ।' इत्यमरः । **यद्** वाक्यं **आत्थ** ब्रवीषि । 'ब्रुवः पञ्चानाम्–' इत्यादिनाहादेशः । **तत्तथा** सत्यम् । किं **तु यशोधनैः** अस्मादृशैः **परतः** शत्रुतः **यशः रक्ष्यम्** । ततः किमत आह–**भवद्गुरुः** त्वत्पिता **जगत्प्रकाशं** लोकप्रसिद्धं **अशेषं** सर्वं **मम तद्** यशः **इज्यया** यागेन **लङ्घयितुं** तिरस्कर्तुं **उद्यतः** उद्युक्तः ॥

किं तद्यश इत्याह—

हरिर्यथैकः पुरुषोत्तमः स्मृतो महेश्वरस्त्र्यम्बक एव नापरः ।
तथा विदुर्मां मुनयः शतक्रतुं द्वितीयगामी न हि शब्द एष नः ॥४९॥

---

१ अन्तर्मध्ये अन्तरस्य व्यवधानस्य वायनम् । अय् गतौ, इण् वा । घञ् प्रत्ययः अच् वा । २ अश्वं विनाश्वमेधस्यासंभवात् । ३ श्रुतेः–'स्वर्गकामोऽश्वमेधेन यजेत' इत्यादिरूपायाः । मलीमसाम्-मलोऽस्या अस्तीति नाम् । 'ज्योत्स्नातमिस्रा–' इति निपातितः । 'श्रुतेः' इत्यत्र 'शुचेः' इति व० दिनकरादयः पठन्ति । एतत्पाठे 'पथः' इति षष्ठ्यन्तं पदम् । ४ गूढविग्रहमपि मां कथमयमदिव्यः पश्यति निर्भयं सदर्पं च भाषते इति समुपजातविस्मयः इति भावः । ५ कर्मितुमुद्युक्तः । इज्या—'व्रजयजोर्भावे क्यप्' इति चा० ।

पुरुषेषूत्तम इति सप्तमीसमासः । ' न निर्धारणे ' इति षष्ठीसमासनिषेधात् । कर्मधारये तु ' सन्महत्परमोत्तमोत्कृष्टाः पूज्यमानैः ' इत्युत्तमपुरुष इति स्यात् । **यथा हरिः** विष्णुः **एक एव पुरुषोत्तमः स्मृतः** । यथा च **त्र्यम्बकः** शिवः **एव महेश्वरः** स्मृतः । **नापरः** अपरः पुमान्न । **तथा मां मुनयः शतक्रतुं विदुः** विदन्ति । ' विदो लटो वा ' इति झेर्जुसादेशः । **नः** अस्माकम् । हरिहरयोर्मम चेत्यर्थः । **एष** त्रितयोऽपि **शब्दः द्वितीयगामी न हि** । द्वितीयाप्रकरणे गमिगम्यादीनामुपसंख्यानात्समासः ॥

अतोऽयमश्वः कपिलानुकारिणा पितुस्त्वदीयस्य मयाऽपहारितः ।
अलं प्रयत्नेन तवात्र मा निधाः पदं पदव्यां सगरस्य संततेः ॥५०॥

यतोऽहमेव शतक्रतुः अतः **त्वदीयस्य पितुः अयं** शततमः **अश्वः कपिलानुकारिणा** कपिलमुनितुल्येन **मया अपहारितः** अपहृतः । अपहारित इति स्वार्थे णिच् । **तव अत्र** अश्वे **प्रयत्नेन अलम्** । प्रयत्नो मा कारीत्यर्थः । निषेध्यस्य निषेधं प्रति कारणत्वात्तृतीया । **सगरस्य** राज्ञः **संततेः** संतानस्य **पदव्यां पदं मा निधाः** न निधेहि । निपूर्वाद्धाञ्धातोर्लुङ् । ' न माङ्योगे ' इत्यडागमप्रतिषेधः । महदास्कन्दनं ते विनाशमूलं भवेदिति भावः ॥

ततः[3] प्रहस्यापभयः पुरंदरं पुनर्बभाषे[4] तुरगस्य रक्षिता ।
गृहाण शस्त्रं यदि सर्ग[5] एष ते न खल्वनिर्जित्य रघुं कृती भवान् ५१

ततः तुरगस्य रक्षिता रघुः **प्रहस्य** प्रहासं कृत्वा । **अपभयः** निर्भीकः सन् । **पुनः पुरंदरं बभाषे** । किमिति–हे देवेन्द्र **यदि एष** अश्वामोचनरूपः **ते** तव **सर्गः** निश्चयः । ' सर्गः स्वभावनिर्मोक्षनिश्चयाध्यायसृष्टिषु । ' इत्यमरः । तर्हि **शस्त्रं गृहाण** ।

---

१ पुरुषोत्तमादीनां निरुक्तिर्महाभारते यथा—' नराणामयनाच्चापि ततो नारायणः स्मृतः । पुराणात्सदनाच्चापि ततोऽसौ पुरुषोत्तमः ॥ ' ' निर्मथ्य देवा यदा चैनं भजन्ते भुवनेश्वरम् । द्यौरपः पृथिवी चैव त्र्यम्बकस्तु ततः स्मृतः ॥ नित्येन ब्रह्मचर्येण लिङ्गमस्य यदा स्थितम् । महानस्त्येष लोकाच्च महेश्वर इति स्मृतः ॥ ' इति । अनुरूपभाव एकादशसर्ग–अन्यदा जगति–इ. श्लो. ७३.
२ ' पुरा यज्ञाश्वमन्वेषयमाणाः सगरसुतास्तुरगापहारी अयमिति वदन्तः कपिलमुनिना व्यापादितास्तथा त्वमपि इति कपिलानुकृत्या सूचयति ' इति चा. । अत्रेयं कथानुसंधेया-पुरा किलेन्द्रः राक्षसीं तनुमास्थाय सगरस्य राज्ञो यज्ञियमश्वमपहृत्य पातालं निनाय । अथ सगरस्य षष्टिः सहस्राणि पुत्रास्तदन्वेषणपरा धरणीतलमवदार्य पातालं गताः कपिलस्य नातिदूरे विचरन्तमश्वं दृष्ट्वा तमेवाश्वापहारिणं मत्वाभ्यधावन् । कुपितस्य तस्य हुंकारेण भस्मीभूताश्च । (रामा. बा. का. ४० सर्गः). कपिला०—कपिलानुसारिणा; मा कृथाः—मानुगाः इति पा. ३ ततः प्रहस्याह पुनः पुरंदरं व्यपेतभीर्भूमिपुरंदरात्मजः । इ. दिनकरः पठति. ४ अत्र तृन्प्रत्ययरूपकृद्योगात् ' तुरगस्य ' इति कर्मणि षष्ठी । अशीलार्थे तृन् प्रत्ययः शीलार्थे षष्ठीनिषेधात् । रवेः प्रयोजनवशादश्वरक्षणे नियुक्तत्वात् । ५ ' सर्गः सगरसुतपदवीं नेष्यामीत्येवंरूपः ' इ. चा. । ' सर्गः ' इत्यत्र ' गर्वः ' इ. व. सु. पठतः । चा० अपीमं पाठमुद्धरति ।

भवान् रघुं माम् **अनिर्जित्य** । कृतमनेनेति **कृती** कृतकृत्यः **न खलु** । 'इष्टादिभ्यश्च' इतीनिप्रत्ययः । रघुमित्यनेनात्मनो दुर्जयत्वं सूचितम् ॥

स एवमुक्त्वा मघवन्तमुन्मुखः करिष्यमाणः सशरं शरासनम् ।
अतिष्ठदालीढविशेषशोभिना वपुःप्रकर्षेण विडम्बितेश्वरः ॥ ५२ ॥

स रघुः **उन्मुखः** सन् । **मघवन्तं** इन्द्रं **एवमुक्त्वा शरासनं** चापं **सशरं करिष्यमाणः** । आलीढेनालीढाख्येन स्थानभेदेन विशेषशोभिनातिशयशोभिना [**आलीढविशेषशोभिना**] **वपुःप्रकर्षेण** देहौन्नत्येन **विडम्बितेश्वरः** अनुसृतपिनाकी सन् । **अतिष्ठत्** । आलीढलक्षणमाह यादवः—' स्थानानि धन्विनां पञ्च तत्र वैशाखमस्त्रियाम् । त्रिवितस्त्यन्तरौ पादौ मण्डलं तोरणाकृति ॥ अन्वर्थं स्यात्समपदमालीढं तु ततोऽग्रतः । दक्षिणे वाममाकुञ्च्य प्रत्यालीढं विपर्ययः ॥ ' इति ॥

रघोरवष्टम्भमयेन पत्त्रिणा हृदि क्षतो गोत्रभिदप्यमर्षणः ।
नवाम्बुदानीकमुहूर्तलाञ्छने धनुष्यमोघं समधत्त सायकम् ॥ ५३ ॥

रघोः अवष्टम्भमयेन[2] स्तम्भरूपेण ।'अवष्टम्भः सुवर्णे च स्तम्भप्रारम्भयोरपि ' इति विश्वः। **पत्त्रिणा** बाणेन **हृदि** हृदये **क्षतः** विद्धः । अत एव **अमर्षणः** असहनः । क्रुद्ध इत्यर्थः । **गोत्रभिद्** इन्द्रः **अपि** ।'संभावनीये चौरेऽपि गोत्रः क्षोणीधरे मतः' इति विश्वः । नवाम्बुदानामनीकस्य वृन्दस्य मुहूर्तं क्षणमात्रं लाञ्छने चिह्नभूते [**नवाम्बुदानीकमुहूर्तलाञ्छने**] **धनुषि** । दिव्ये धनुषीत्यर्थः । **अमोघम्** अवन्ध्यं **सायकं** बाणं **समधत्त** संहितवान् ॥

दिलीपसूनोः स बृहद्भुजान्तरं प्रविश्य भीमासुरशोणितोचितः ।
अपावनास्वादितपूर्वमाशुगः कुतूहलेनेव मनुष्यशोणितम् ॥ ५४ ॥

भीमानां भयंकराणामसुराणां शोणिते रुधिरे उचितः परिचितः [**भीमासुरशोणितोचितः**] **स** इन्द्रमुक्तः **आशुगः**[3] सायकः **दिलीपसूनोः** रघोः **बृहद्** विशालं **भुजान्तरं** वक्षः **प्रविश्य** । **अनास्वादितपूर्वं** पूर्वमनास्वादितम् । सुप्सुपेति समासः । **मनुष्यशोणितं कुतूहलेन इव**[4] **पपौ** ॥

हरेः कुमारोऽपि कुमारविक्रमः सुरद्विपास्फालनकर्कशाङ्गुलौ ।
भुजे शचीपत्त्रविशेषकाङ्किते स्वनामचिह्नं निचखान सायकम् ॥५५॥

---

१ ' नामिता पूर्वजङ्घा च पश्चिमा प्रगुणा भवेत् । असमो मध्यकायः स्यादालीढस्य च लक्षणम् ' ॥ इ. चा. । कुमारसंभवेऽपि–स दक्षिणापाङ्गनिविष्टमुष्टिं नतांसमाकुञ्चितसव्यपादम् । इत्यालीढवर्णनम् । विडम्बितेति ' पुरा किल भगवान् त्रिपुरदिधक्षया दिव्यं वर्षशतमालीढविशेषेण स्थानाधिक्येन ऊर्ध्वमुखोऽतिष्ठत् ' । इ. द. उक्तं च भारते–' त्रिपुरस्य वधार्थाय स्थाणुः प्रहरतां वरः ।......स्थानं माहेश्वरं कृत्वा दिव्यमप्रतिमं प्रभुः । अतिष्ठत्स्थाणुभूतः स सहस्रं परिवत्सरान् ॥ ' इ. २ 'स्थैर्यरूपेण काञ्चनमयेन वा ' इ. चा० । ' अवष्टम्भप्रधानोऽवष्टम्भमयस्तेन रघोरभिमानमयेन पत्त्रिणा ' इ. व. । दिनकरोऽपि 'काञ्चनमयेन' इति व्याख्यायाह–प्रथमं काञ्चनमयप्रहारवर्णनं कविसमयाविरुद्धमिति केचिदाचक्षते । तन्मते अवष्टम्भमयेन स्थैर्यरूपेण । ३ आशु शीघ्रं गच्छतीति । गमेर्डः । ४ इव पपौ इत्यत्र उत्प्रेक्षालंकारः ।

कुमारस्य स्कन्दस्य विक्रम इव विक्रमो यस्य स तथोक्तः [**कुमारविक्रमः**]। 'सप्तम्युपमान–' इत्यादिना समासः । **कुमारः अपि** रघुरपि सुरद्विपस्यैरावतस्यास्फालनेन[1] कर्कशा अङ्गुलयो यस्य स तस्मिन् [**सुरद्विपास्फालनकर्कशाङ्गुलौ**] । शच्याः पत्रविशेषैः[2]रङ्किते **शचीपत्रविशेषकाङ्किते हरेः** इन्द्रस्य **भुजे स्वनामचिह्नं** स्वनामाङ्कितं **सायकं निचखान** निखातवान् । निष्कण्टकराज्यमा[3]सस्यायं महानभिभव इति भावः ॥

जहार चान्येन मयूरपत्रिणा शरेण शक्रस्य महाशनिध्वजम् ।
चुकोप तस्मै स भृशं सुरश्रियः प्रसह्य केशव्यपरोपणादिव ॥ ५६ ॥

अन्येन मयूरपत्रिणा मयूरपत्रवता **शरेण शक्रस्य** इन्द्रस्य **महाशनिध्वजं** महान्तमशनिरूपं ध्वजं **जहार** चिच्छेद **च** । **स** शक्रः **सुरश्रियः प्रसह्य** बलात्कृत्य केशानां व्यपरोपणादवतारणाच्छेदनाद् [**केशव्यपरोपणाद्**] **इव** । **तस्मै** रघवे **भृशं** अत्यर्थं **चुकोप** । तं हन्तुमियेषेत्यर्थः । 'क्रुधद्रुह–' इत्यादिना संप्रदानाच्चतुर्थी ॥

तयोरुपान्तस्थितसिद्धसैनिकं गरुत्मदाशीविषभीमदर्शनैः ।
बभूव युद्धं तुमुलं जयैषिणोरधोमुखैरूर्ध्वमुखैश्च पत्रिभिः ॥ ५७ ॥

जयैषिणोः अन्योन्यजयाकाङ्क्षिणोः **तयोः** इन्द्ररघ्वोः । गरुत्मन्तः पक्षवन्तः । 'गरुत्पक्षच्छदाः पत्रम्' इत्यमरः । आशिषि दंष्ट्रायां विषं येषां त आशीविषाः सर्पाः । पृषोदरादित्वात्साधुः । 'स्त्री त्वाशीर्हिताशंसाहिदंष्ट्रयोः' इत्यमरः । त इव भीमदर्शनाः । सपक्षाः सर्पा इव द्रष्टॄणां भयावहा इत्यर्थः । तैः [**गरुत्मदाशीविषभीमदर्शनैः**] **अधोमुखैः ऊर्ध्वमुखैः च** । धन्विनोरुपर्यधोदेशावस्थितत्वादिति भावः । **पत्रिभिः** बाणैरुपान्तस्थितास्तटस्थाः सिद्धा देवा इन्द्रस्य सैनिकाश्च रघोर्यस्मिंस्तत्तथोक्तं [**उपान्तस्थितसिद्धसैनिकम्**] **तुमुलं** संकुलं **युद्धं बभूव** ॥

अतिप्रबन्धप्रहितास्त्रवृष्टिभिस्तमाश्रयं दुष्प्रसहस्य तेजसः ।
शशाक निर्वापयितुं न वासवः स्वतश्च्युतं वह्निमिवाद्भिरम्बुदः ॥५८॥

वासवः अतिप्रबन्धेनातिसातत्येन प्रहिताभिः प्रयुक्ताभिरस्त्रवृष्टिभिः [**अतिप्रबन्धप्रहितास्त्रवृष्टिभिः**] **दुष्प्रसहस्य** । दुःखेन प्रसह्यत इति दुष्प्रसहं तस्य । दुःखेनाप्यसह्यस्येत्यर्थः । **तेजसः** प्रतापस्य **आश्रयं तं** रघुम् । **अम्बुदः अद्भिः स्वतः च्युतं** निर्गतं **वह्निमिव** । **निर्वापयितुं न शशाक** । रघोरपि लोकपालात्मकस्येन्द्रांशसंभवत्वादिति भावः ॥

ततः प्रकोष्ठे हरिचन्दनाङ्किते प्रमथ्यमानार्णवधीरनादिनीम् ।
रघुः शशाङ्कार्धमुखेन पत्रिणा शरासनज्यामलुनाद्बिडौजसः ॥ ५९ ॥

---

१ प्रोत्साहनेन ताडनेनेत्यर्थः । एवं कुमारेपि–ऐरावतास्फालनकर्कशेन हस्तेन पस्पर्श तदङ्गमिन्द्रः । इति । २ पत्राकारैः रचनाविशेषैः । 'शचीपत्रलताक्रियोचिते' इ. व. चा. दि. पठन्ति । ३ निष्कण्टकराज्ये तस्य इ. पाटः ।

ततः रघु हरिचंन्दनाङ्कित प्रकोष्ठे मणिबन्धे **प्रमथ्यमानार्णवधीरनादिनीं** प्रमथ्यमानार्णव इव धीरं गम्भीरं नदतीति तां तथोक्ताम् । वेवेष्टि व्याप्नोतीति विट् व्यापक-मोजो यस्य स तस्य **बिडौजसः** इन्द्रस्य । पृषोदरादित्वात्साधुः । **शरासनज्यां** धनुर्मौर्वी शशाङ्कस्यार्धः खण्ड इव मुखं फलं यस्य तेन [**शशाङ्कार्धमुखेन**] **पत्रिणा अलुनाद्** अच्छिनत् ॥

स चापमुत्सृज्य विवृद्धमत्सरः प्रणाशनाय प्रबलस्य विद्विषः ।
महीध्रपक्षव्यपरोपणोचितं स्फुरत्प्रभामण्डलमस्त्रमाददे ॥ ६० ॥

विवृद्धमत्सरः प्रवृद्धवैरः **स** इन्द्रः **चापं उत्सृज्य प्रबलस्य विद्विषः** शत्रोः **प्रणाशनाय** वधाय । महीं धारयन्तीति महीध्राः पर्वताः । मूलविभुजादित्वात्कप्रत्ययः । तेषां पक्षव्यपरोपणे पक्षच्छेदे उचितं [**महीध्रपक्षव्यपरोपणोचितं**] **स्फुरत्प्रभा-मण्डलम् अस्त्रं** वज्रायुधम् । **आददे** जग्राह ॥

रघुर्भृशं वक्षसि तेन ताडितः पपात भूमौ सह सैनिकाश्रुभिः ।
निमेषमात्रादवधूय तद्व्यथां सहोत्थितः सैनिकहर्षनिःस्वनैः ॥ ६१ ॥

रघुः तेन वज्रेण **भृशम्** अत्यर्थं **वक्षसि ताडितः** हतः सन् । सैनिकानामश्रुभिः [**सैनिकाश्रुभिः**] **सह भूमौ पपात** । तस्मिन्पतिते ते रुरुदुरित्यर्थः । **निमेषमात्रात तद्व्यथां** दुःखम् **अवधूय** तिरस्कृत्य सैनिकानां हर्षेण ये निःस्वनाः क्ष्वेडास्तैः [**सैनिक-हर्षनिःस्वनैः**] **सह उत्थितः** च । तस्मिन्नुत्थिते हर्षात्सिंहनादांश्चक्रुरित्यर्थः ॥

तथाऽपि शस्त्रव्यवहारनिष्ठुरे विपक्षभावे चिरमस्य तस्थुषः ।
तुतोष वीर्यातिशयेन वृत्रहा पदं हि सर्वत्र गुणैर्निधीयते ॥ ६२ ॥

तथाऽपि वज्रपातेऽपि शस्त्राणामायुधानां व्यवहारेण व्यापारेण निष्ठुरे क्रूरे । [**शस्त्र-व्यवहारनिष्ठुरे**] **विपक्षभावे** शात्रवे **चिरं तस्थुषः** स्थितवतः **अस्य** रघोः **वीर्यातिशयेन** वृत्रं हतवानिति **वृत्रहा** । ' ब्रह्मभ्रूणवृत्रेषु क्विप् ' । **तुतोष** । स्वयं वीर एव वीरं जानातीति भावः । कथं शत्रोः संतोषोऽत आह–**हि गुणैः सर्वत्र** शत्रु-मित्रोदासीनेषु **पदम्** अङ्घ्रिः **निधीयते** । गुणैः सर्वत्र संक्रम्यत इत्यर्थः । गुणाः शत्रू-नप्यावर्जयन्तीति भावः ॥

---

१ देवचन्दनचर्चालिप्ते । ' पञ्चैते देवतरवो......पुंसि वा हरिचन्दनम् ' इत्यमरः । यद्वा कुङ्कुममण्डिते । ' गोशीर्षे कुङ्कुमे देववृक्षे श्रीहरिचन्दनम् । ' इत्यर्धनारीश्वरः । २ विडतीति विडं भेदकमोजोऽस्येति वा । ३ तदुक्तं मत्स्यपुराणे–' त्रिशूलं चापि रुद्रस्य वज्रमिन्द्रस्य चाधिकम् । दैत्यदानवसंहर्तुः सहस्रकिरणात्मकम् ॥ ' इति । महीध्रेति–पर्वतपक्षच्छेदनवृत्तान्तस्तूक्तः । ४ उक्तं च उत्तररामचरिते–वीराणां समयो हि दारुणरसः स्नेहक्रमं बाधते ॥ इति । ५ ' गुणी गुणं वेत्ति न वेत्ति निर्गुणः ' इति न्यायेनेति शेषः । ६ अनुरूपाः श्लोकांशाः–' गुणाः प्रियत्वेऽधिकृता न संस्तवः ' इति किरातार्जुनीये । ' गुणाः पूजास्थानं गुणिषु न च लिङ्गं न च वयः । ' इति उत्तरराम० च । कुमारेऽपि–' स्त्री पुमानित्यनास्थैषा वृत्तं हि महितं सताम् ' इति ।

असङ्गमद्रिष्वपि सारवत्तया न मे त्वदन्येन विसोढमायुधम् ।
अवेहि मां प्रीतमृते तुरङ्गमात्किमिच्छसीति स्फुटमाह वासवः ॥६३॥

सारवत्तया अद्रिषु अपि असङ्गम् अप्रतिबन्धं **मे आयुधं** वज्रं **त्वदन्येन न विसोढम्**। अतः **मां प्रीतं** संतुष्टम् **अवेहि । तुरङ्गमाद् ऋते** तुरङ्गमं वर्जयित्वा । 'अन्यारादितरर्ते-' इति पञ्चमी । **किम् इच्छसि इति स्फुटं वासवः आह**। तुरङ्गमादन्यददेयं नास्तीति भावः ॥

ततो निषङ्गादसमग्रमुद्धृतं सुवर्णपुङ्खद्युतिरञ्जिताङ्गुलिम् ।
नरेन्द्रसूनुः प्रतिसंहरन्निषुं प्रियंवदः प्रत्यवदत्सुरेश्वरम् ॥ ६४ ॥

ततः निषङ्गात् तूणीराद् **असमग्रं** यथा तथा **उद्धृतं** सुवर्णपुङ्खद्युतिभिः रञ्जिताः अङ्गुलयो येन तं [**सुवर्णपुङ्खद्युतिरञ्जिताङ्गुलिम्**] **इषुम् प्रतिसंहरन्** निवर्तयन् । 'नाप्रहरन्तं प्रहरेत्' इति निषेधादिति भावः । प्रियं वदतीति **प्रियंवदः**। 'प्रियवशे वदः खच्' इति खच्प्रत्ययः । 'अरुर्द्विषद् –' इत्यादिना मुमागमः । **नरेन्द्रसूनुः** रघुः **सुरेश्वरं प्रत्यवदत्** । न तु प्राहरदिति भावः ॥

अमोच्यमश्वं यदि मन्यसे प्रभो ततः समाप्ते विधिनैव कर्मणि ।
अजस्रदीक्षाप्रयतः स मद्गुरुः क्रतोरशेषेण फलेन युज्यताम् ॥६५॥

हे **प्रभो** इन्द्र **अश्वं अमोच्यं मन्यसे यदि ततः** तर्ह्यजस्रदीक्षायां प्रयतः [**अजस्रदीक्षाप्रयतः**] **स मद्गुरुः** मम पिता **विधिना एव कर्मणि समाप्ते** सति **क्रतोः** यत्फलं तेन **फलेन अशेषेण** कृत्स्नेन **युज्यतां** युक्तोऽस्तु। अश्वमेधफललाभे किमश्वेनेति भावः ॥

यथा च वृत्तान्तमिमं सदोगतस्त्रिलोचनैकांशतया दुरासदः ।
तवैव संदेशहराद्विशांपतिः शृणोति लोकेश तथा विधीयताम् ॥६६॥

सदोगतः सदो गृहं गतस्त्रिलोचनस्येश्वरस्यैकांशतया [**त्रिलोचनैकांशतया**]। अष्टानामन्यतममूर्तित्वात् । **दुरासदः** अस्मादृशैर्दुष्प्राप्यः **विशांपतिः यथेमं वृत्तान्तं तव संदेशहराद्** वार्ताहराद् **एव शृणोति च** हे **लोकेश** इन्द्र **तथा विधीयताम्** ॥

---

१ असङ्गम्—अभङ्गं, असह्यम् इ.; अवेहि–अवैहि इ. पा. । स्फुटम्–'स्मितम्' (स्म तं :) इ. व०; 'वरं वृणीष्वेति तमाह' इ. चा०, 'वरं वृणीष्वेति तमादिदेश सः' इ. दिन० च पठन्ति । 'वरं वृणीष्वेति तमाह वृत्रहा' इ. पा. २ असमग्रनिःसृतम्, नरेन्द्र०—दिलीप०; प्रियंवदः—प्रियंवदम् इ. पा० ३ 'दीक्षितत्वात्त्रिलोचनस्यैकांशेन दुरधिगमः' इ. दिन. चा. । 'अष्टमूर्तित्वाद् यजमानलक्षणांशभावाद्दुरभिभवो दुराकलनीयः' इ. व० । 'दीक्षितमुग्रः प्रविशति' इ. आगमः । 'या च होत्री' इति शाकुन्तले च ।

तथेति कामं प्रतिशुश्रुवान्रघोर्यथागतं मातलिसारथिर्ययौ ।
नृपस्य नातिप्रमनाः सदोगृहं सुदक्षिणासूनुरपि न्यवर्तत ॥ ६७ ॥

मातलिसारथिः इन्द्रः **रघोः** संबन्धिनं **कामं** मनोरथं **तथेति** तथास्त्विति **प्रतिशुश्रुवान्** । 'भाषायां सदवसश्रुवः' इति क्वसुप्रत्ययः । **यथागतं**[1] **ययौ** । **सुदक्षिणासूनुः** रघुः **अपि** **नातिप्रमनाः** विजयलाभेऽप्यश्वनाशान्नातीव तुष्टः सन् । नञर्थस्य नशब्दस्य सुप्सुपेति समासः । **नृपस्य सदोगृहं** प्रति **न्यवर्तत** ॥

तमभ्यनन्दत्प्रथमं प्रबोधितः प्रजेश्वरः शासनहारिणा हरेः ।
परामृशन्हर्षजडेन पाणिना तदीयमङ्गं कुलिशव्रणाङ्कितम् ॥ ६८ ॥

हरेः इन्द्रस्य **शासनहारिणा** पुरुषेण **प्रथमं प्रबोधितः** ज्ञापितः । वृत्तान्तमिति शेषः । **प्रजेश्वरः** दिलीपः **हर्षजडेन** हर्षशिशिरेण **पाणिना कुलिशव्रणाङ्कितम्** तस्य रघोरिदम् **तदीयं अङ्गं** शरीरं **परामृशन्**[2] **तं** रघुम् **अभ्यनन्दत्** ॥

इति क्षितीशो नवतिं नवाधिकां महाक्रतूनां महनीयशासनः ।
समारुरुक्षुर्दिवमायुषः क्षये ततान सोपानपरंपरामिव ॥ ६९ ॥

महनीयशासनः पूजनीयाज्ञः **क्षितीशः इति** अनेन प्रकारेण । 'इति हेतुप्रकरणप्रकर्षादिसमाप्तिषु ।' इत्यमरः । **महाक्रतूनाम्** अश्वमेधानां नवभिरधिकां [**नवाधिकां**] **नवतिं** एकोनशतं **आयुषः क्षये** सति **दिवं** स्वर्गं **समारुरुक्षुः** आरोढुमिच्छुः सोपानानां परंपरां पङ्क्तिं [**सोपानपरंपराम्**] **इव ततान** ॥

अथ स विषयव्यावृत्तात्मा यथाविधि सूनवे
नृपतिककुदं दत्त्वा यूने सितातपवारणम् ।
मुनिवनतरुच्छायां देव्या तया सह शिश्रिये
गलितवयसामिक्ष्वाकूणामिदं हि कुलव्रतम् ॥ ७० ॥

अथ विषयेभ्यो[3] व्यावृत्तात्मा निवृत्तचित्तः [**विषयव्यावृत्तात्मा**] **स** दिलीपः **यथाविधि** यथाशास्त्रं **यूने सूनवे नृपतिककुदं** राजचिह्नम् । 'ककुद्वत्ककुदं श्रेष्ठे वृषाङ्के राजलक्ष्मणि ।' इति विश्वः । **सितातपवारणं**[4] श्वेतच्छत्रं **दत्त्वा तया देव्या** सुदक्षिणया **सह** मुनिवनतरोः छायां [**मुनिवनतरुच्छायां**] **शिश्रिये** श्रितवान् । वानप्रस्थाश्रमं स्वीकृतवानित्यर्थः। तथा **हि** । **गलितवयसां** वृद्धानां **इक्ष्वाकूणां** इक्ष्वाकोः गोत्रापत्यानाम् ।

---

१ येन मार्गेणायातस्तेनैव गतः इ. व० । 'न तु रघुं विजित्येति भावः इ. चा० ।
२ पुनः पुनः स्पृशन् । अभ्यनन्दत्—चुम्बनशिरोवघ्राणादिभिः संभावयामास । अनुरूपभावश्चतुर्दशे —'ते पुत्रयोर्नैर्ऋतशस्त्रमार्गानार्द्रानिवाङ्गे सदयं स्पृशन्त्यौ' इति । ३ विषयाः रूपरसगन्धस्पर्शशब्दाः । अस्य व्युत्पत्तिर्भट्टकारिकायाम्...विशब्दो हि विशेषार्थः सिनोतिर्बन्ध उच्यते । विशेषेण सिनोतीति विषयोऽतो नियामकः ॥ ४ सितच्छत्रस्य राजलक्ष्म्याः प्रधानाङ्गत्वाद्राजलक्ष्मीं दत्त्वेत्यर्थो लभ्यते । 'छत्रमातपवारणम्' इति हेमचन्द्रः ।

तद्राजसंज्ञकत्वादञो लुक् । **इदं** वनगमनं **कुलव्रतम्** । देव्या सहेत्यनेन सपत्नीकवानप्रस्थाश्रमपक्ष उक्तः । तथा च याज्ञवल्क्यः—'सुतविन्यस्तपत्नीकस्तया वाऽनुगतो वनम् । वानप्रस्थो ब्रह्मचारी साग्निः सोपासनो व्रजेत् ॥' इति । हरिणीवृत्तमेतत् । तदुक्तम्—'रसयुगहयैर्न्सौ म्रौ स्लौ गो यदा हरिणी तदा' इति ॥

इति महामहोपाध्यायकोलाचलमल्लिनाथसूरिविरचितया संजीवनीसमाख्यया व्याख्यया समेतो महाकविश्रीकालिदासकृतौ रघुवंशे महाकाव्ये रघुराज्याभिषेको नाम तृतीयः सर्गः ।

चतुर्थः सर्गः ।

शारदां शारदाम्भोजवदना वदनाम्बुजे ।
सर्वदा सर्वदाऽस्माकं सन्निधिं संनिधिं क्रियात् ॥

स राज्यं गुरुणा दत्तं प्रतिपद्याधिकं बभौ ।
दिनान्ते निहितं तेजः सवित्रेव हुताशनः ॥ १ ॥

स रघुः **गुरुणा** पित्रा **दत्तं राज्यं** राज्ञः कर्म प्रजापरिपालनात्मकम् । पुरोहितादित्वाद्यक् । **प्रतिपद्य** प्राप्य । **दिनान्ते** सायंकाले **सवित्रा** सूर्येण **निहितं तेजः** प्रतिपद्य **हुताशनः** अग्निः इव । **अधिकं बभौ** । 'सौरं तेजः सायमग्निं संक्रमते । आदित्यो वा अस्तं यन्नग्निमनुप्रविशति । अग्निं वा आदित्यः सायं प्रविशति' इत्यादिश्रुतिः प्रमाणम् ॥

दिलीपानन्तरं राज्ये तं निशम्य प्रतिष्ठितम् ।
पूर्वं प्रधूमितो राज्ञां हृदयेऽग्निरिवोत्थितः ॥ २ ॥

दिलीपानन्तरं राज्ये प्रतिष्ठितं अवस्थितं **तं** रघुं **निशम्य** आकर्ण्य **पूर्वं**

---

१ अत्र अण इति पाठः लेखकप्रमादात्स्यात् । तद्राजस्य बहुष्वित्यादिसूत्रेण तद्राजप्रत्ययानामेव लोपविधानात् ।। २ अनुरूपं श्लोकद्वयमष्टमे–अथ वीक्ष्य रघुः प्रतिष्ठितं प्रकृतिष्वात्मजमात्मवत्तया । विषयेषु विनाशधर्मसु त्रिदिवस्थेष्वपि निस्पृहोऽभवत् ॥ (१०) गुणवत्सुतरोपितश्रियः परिणामे हि दिलीपवंशजाः । पदवीं तरुवल्कवाससां प्रयताः संयमिनां प्रपेदिरे ॥ (११) इति. ३ तदुक्तं प्राक्–'वार्द्धके मुनिवृत्तीनाम्' इत्यत्र । ४ अत्र मनुसंमतिस्तूक्ता (प्र. स. अष्ट. श्लो. टि.) ५ शरत्कालोत्पन्नकमलवत्प्रफुल्लवदना शारदा वाग्देवी सर्वदा सर्वस्य दात्री सर्वदाऽस्माकं वदनाम्बुजे सतां मङ्गलानां निधिं शेवधिभूतं संनिधिं वसतिमित्यर्थः क्रियात् । ६ प्रथमद्वितीययोर्मध्ये—**न्यस्तशस्त्रं दिलीपं च तं च शुश्रुवुषां प्रभुं (पति) म् । राज्ञामुद्धृ (मुत्खा) तनाराचे हृदि शल्यमिवार्पितम्** ॥ इति पद्यं चा. दि. व. सु. पठन्ति ।

दिलीपकाले **राज्ञां हृदये** प्रकर्षेण धूमोऽस्य संजातः **प्रधूमितः अग्निः** संतापाग्निः **उत्थितः इव** प्रज्वलित इव । पूर्वेऽन्योऽधिकसंतापोऽभूदित्यर्थः । राजकर्तृकस्यापि निःश्वसनस्याग्नावुपचारान्न समानकर्तृकत्वविरोधः ॥

पुरुहूतध्वजस्येव तस्योन्नयनपङ्क्तयः ।
नवाभ्युत्थानदर्शिन्यो ननन्दुः सप्रजाः प्रजाः ॥ ३ ॥

पुरुहूतध्वजः इन्द्रध्वजः । स किल राजभिर्वृष्ट्यर्थं पूज्यत इत्युक्तं भविष्योत्तरे—'एवं यः कुरुते यात्रामिन्द्रकेतोर्युधिष्ठिर । पर्जन्यः कालवर्षी स्यात्तस्य राज्ये न संशयः ॥' इति । 'चतुरस्रं ध्वजाकारं राजद्वारे प्रतिष्ठितम् । आहुः शक्रध्वजं नाम पौरलोकसुखावहम् ॥' इति च । **पुरुहूतध्वजस्येव तस्य** रघोर्नवमभ्युत्थानमभ्युन्नतिमभ्युदयं च पश्यन्तीति **नवाभ्युत्थानदर्शिन्यः** । ऊर्ध्वं प्रस्थिता उल्लसिताश्च नयनपङ्क्तयो यासां ताः [**उन्नयनपङ्क्तयः**] **सप्रजाः** ससंतानाः **प्रजाः** जनाः । 'प्रजा स्यात्संततौ जने' इत्युभयत्राप्यमरः । **ननन्दुः** ॥

सममेव समाक्रान्तं द्वयं द्विरदगामिना ।
तेन सिंहासनं पित्र्यमखिलं चारिमण्डलम् ॥ ४ ॥

द्विरद इव द्विरदैश्च गच्छतीति **द्विरदगामिना**[६] । 'कर्तर्युपमाने' इति 'सुप्यजातौ—' इति च णिनिः । **तेन** रघुणा **समं** युगपद् **एव द्वयं समाक्रान्तं** अधि-

---

१ संजातधूमोत्पीड इत्यर्थः । २ तुमुन्क्त्वाल्यबादयः प्रत्ययाः समानकर्तृकत्वे भवन्ति । अत्र राज्ञो राजहृदयस्थिताग्नीनां चाधाराधेयभावतया परस्परसंबन्धादेकस्य कर्तृत्वेऽन्यस्यापि कर्तृत्वं लक्षणयोपपद्यते इत्यर्थः । वस्तुतस्तु तुमुनादिप्रत्ययानां समानकर्तृकत्वं नैकान्तिकं भिन्नकर्तृकस्यापि बहुलं प्रयोगेषु दर्शनात् ॥ प्रधूमितः—०ते इति चा. दि. व० सु० पठन्ति । ३ पुरु बहुलं हूतमाह्वानं यज्ञेष्वस्य । पुरूणि हूतानि नामान्यस्येति वा । पुरुहूतध्वजस्येव इन्द्रमहोत्सवस्येव । तथा हि—'गजाकारं चतुःस्तम्भं पुरद्वारे प्रतिष्ठितम् । पौराः कुर्वन्ति शरदि पुरुहूतमहोत्सवम्' इति व० । कालिकापुराणे च—'एवं यः कुरुते पूजां वासवस्य महात्मनः । स चिरं पृथिवीं भुक्त्वा वासवं लोकमाप्नुयात् ॥ न तस्य राज्ये दुर्भिक्षं नेतयो न्याय्यधर्मकृत् । स्थास्यन्ति मृत्युर्नाकाले जनानां तत्र जायते ॥' इत्यादि । अत्रेयं पौराणिकी कथा—पुरा किल दानवपरिभूता इन्द्रपुरःसरा देवाः क्षीरसागरशायिनं भगवन्तं शरणं वव्रजुः । तदा विष्णुर्दैत्यकुलसंहाराय दिव्यप्रभावं विचित्रं ध्वजमेकं महेन्द्राय प्रादात् । तत्प्रभावादिन्द्रः सर्वान्दानवाञ्जघान । इन्द्रदत्तं च तं ध्वजं पूजयित्वा वसुर्नाम चेदिनृपः परां सिद्धिं लेभे । ततः प्रीतो महेन्द्रो व्यादिदेश—'प्रीतो महेन मघवाः प्राहैवं ये नृपाः करिष्यन्ति । वसुवद्वसुमन्तस्ते भुवि सिद्धाज्ञा भविष्यन्ति ॥ मुदिताः प्रजाश्च तेषां भयरोगविवर्जिताः प्रभूतान्नाः । ध्वज एव चाभिधास्यति जगति निमित्तैः फलं सदसत् ॥' इत्यादि । विस्तरस्तु बृहत्संहितायां ४३ अध्याये द्रष्टव्यः । ४ 'गजारोहणादिकम् । अभिषिक्तो हि राजा गजेन्द्रमारुह्य पुरं प्रदक्षिणीकुर्यादित्याचारः ।' इति चा० । सप्रजाः—सुप्रजाः इ. चा. दि. व. सु. पठन्ति । ५ पैत्र्यमिति पा० ६ द्विरदेन गन्तुं शीलं यस्य तेन । अभिषिक्तो नृपो हस्तिनमारुह्य भ्रमतीति वृद्धाचारः इ. दि. । द्विरद इव गच्छतीति द्विरदगामी तेन । 'द्विरदमारुह्य पुरं प्रदक्षिणीकृतवता' इति व० ७ अत्र सिंहासनारोहणानन्तरमेवारिमण्डलाक्रमणेऽपि कार्यकारणयोः समकालत्वेन निर्देशादतिशयोक्तिनामालंकारः । 'कार्यकारणयोर्यश्च पौर्वापर्यविपर्ययः' इति काव्यप्रकाशोक्तेः ।

ष्ठितम् । किं तद् द्वयम् । पितुरागतं **पित्र्यम्** । 'पितुर्यत्' इति यत्प्रत्ययः । **सिंहासनम्** । अखिलं अरीणां मण्डलं राष्ट्रं [**अरिमण्डलं**] **च** ॥

अथ सिंहासनारोहणानन्तरं तस्य लक्ष्मीसंनिधानमाह—

छायामण्डललक्ष्येण तमदृश्या किल स्वयम् ।
पद्मा पद्मातपत्रेण भेजे साम्राज्यदीक्षितम् ॥ ५ ॥

अत्र रघोस्तेजोविशेषेण स्वयं संनिहितया लक्ष्म्या छत्रधारणं कृतमित्युत्प्रेक्ष्यते । **पद्मा** लक्ष्मीः । 'लक्ष्मीः पद्मालया पद्मा कमला श्रीर्हरिप्रिया ।' इत्यमरः । सा **स्वयं अदृश्या किल** । किलेति संभावनायाम् । सती **छायामण्डललक्ष्येण** कान्तिपुञ्जानुमेयेन । न तु स्वरूपतो दृश्येन । छायामण्डलमित्यनेनानातपज्ञानं लक्ष्यते । 'छाया सूर्यप्रिया कान्तिः प्रतिबिम्बमनातपः ।' इत्युभयत्राप्यमरः । **पद्मातपत्रेण**[1] पद्ममेवातपत्रं तेन कारणभूतेन **साम्राज्यदीक्षितं** साम्राज्ये साम्राज्यकर्मणि मण्डलाधिपत्ये दीक्षितमभिषिक्तं **तं भेजे** । अन्यथा कथमेतादृशी कान्तिसंपत्तिरिति भावः ॥

संप्रति सरस्वतीसांनिध्यमाह—

परिकल्पितसांनिध्या काले काले च बन्दिषु ।
स्तुत्यं स्तुतिभिरर्थ्याभिरुपतस्थे सरस्वती ॥ ६ ॥

सरस्वती च काले काले सर्वेष्वपि योग्यकालेषु । 'नित्यवीप्सयोः' इति वीप्सायां द्विर्वचनम् । **बन्दिषु परिकल्पितसांनिध्या** कृतसंनिधाना सती **स्तुत्यं** स्तोत्रार्हं तं रघुम् । **अर्थ्याभिः** अर्थादनपेताभिः । 'धर्मपथ्यर्थन्यायादनपेते' इति यत्प्रत्ययः । **स्तुतिभिः** स्तोत्रैः **उपतस्थे**[2] । देवताबुद्ध्या पूजितवतीत्यर्थः । देवतात्वं च 'ना विष्णुः पृथिवीपतिः' इति वा लोकपालात्मकत्वाद्वेत्यनुसंधेयम् । एवं च सति 'उपाद्देवपूजासंगतिकरणमित्रकरणपथिषु' इति वक्तव्यादात्मनेपदं सिध्यति ॥

मनुप्रभृतिभिर्मान्यैर्भुक्ता यद्यपि राजभिः ।
तथाऽप्यनन्यपूर्वेव तस्मिन्नासीद्वसुंधरा[3] ॥ ७ ॥

वसुंधरा मनुप्रभृतिभिः मन्वादिभिः **मान्यैः** पूज्यैः **राजभिः भुक्ता यद्यपि** । भुक्तेवेत्यर्थः । यद्यपीत्यवधारणे । 'अप्यर्थे यदिवार्थे स्यात्' इति केशवः । **तथाऽपि तस्मिन्** राज्ञि । अन्यः पूर्वो यस्याः साऽन्यपूर्वा । अन्यपूर्वा न भवतीति **अनन्यपूर्वा** अनन्योपभुक्ता **इव आसीत्** । तत्प्रथमपतिकेवानुरक्तवतीत्यर्थः ॥

अत्र कारणमाह—

स हि सर्वस्य लोकस्य युक्तदण्डतया[4] मनः ।
आददे नातिशीतोष्णो नभस्वानिव दक्षिणः ॥ ८ ॥

---

१ 'लक्ष्मीर्हि पद्मरूपेण छत्रेण सम्राजं सेवते इत्यागमः' इ० टि० । उत्प्रेक्षालंकारः । २ अत्रान्योन्यवैरभावाश्रिताभ्यामपि लक्ष्मीसरस्वतीभ्यां सेवाकरणाद्रघोः कोऽपि महिमातिशयः सूचितः । ३ सीद्धि मेदिनी इ० पा. ४ याकृद० .

हि यस्मात्कारणात् **स** रघुः **युक्तदण्डतया** यथापराधदण्डतया **सर्वस्य लोकस्य मनः आदत्ते** जहार । क इव । अतिशीतोऽत्युष्णो वा न भवतीति **नातिशीतोष्णः** । नञर्थस्य नशब्दस्य सुप्सुपेति समासः । **दाक्षिणः** दक्षिणदिग्भवः **नभस्वान्** वायुः **इव** । मलयानिल इवेत्यर्थः । युक्तदण्डतयेत्यत्र कामन्दकः–'उद्वेजयति तीक्ष्णेन मृदुना परिभूयते । दण्डेन नृपतिस्तस्माद्युक्तदण्डः प्रशस्यते[1] ॥' इति ॥

मन्दोत्कण्ठाः कृतास्तेन गुणाधिकतया गुरौ ।
फलेन सहकारस्य पुष्पोद्गम इव प्रजाः ॥ ९ ॥

तेन रघुणा **प्रजाः गुरौ** दिलीपविषये । सहकारोऽतिसौरभश्चूतः । 'आम्रश्चूतो रसालोऽसौ सहकारोऽतिसौरभः ।' इत्यमरः । तस्य [**सहकारस्य**] **फलेन पुष्पोद्गमे** पुष्पोदये **इव** । ततोऽपि **गुणाधिकतया** हेतुना **मन्दोत्कण्ठाः** अल्पौत्सुक्याः **कृताः** । गुणोत्तरश्चोत्तरो विषयः पूर्वं विस्मारयतीति भावः ॥

नयविद्भिर्नवे राज्ञि सदसच्चोपदर्शितम् ।
पूर्व एवाभवत्पक्षस्तस्मिन्नाभवदुत्तरः ॥ १० ॥

नयविद्भिः[2] नीतिशास्त्रज्ञैः **नवे** तस्मिन् **राज्ञि** विषये । तमधिकृत्येत्यर्थः । **सत्** धर्मयुद्धादिकं **असत्** कूटयुद्धादिकं **च उपदर्शितम्** । **तस्मिन्** राज्ञि **पूर्वः पक्षः एव अभवत्** । संक्रान्त इत्यर्थः । **उत्तरः** पक्षः **न अभवत्** । न संक्रान्त इत्यर्थः । तत्र सदसतोर्मध्ये सदेवाभिमतं नासत् । तदुद्भावनं तु ज्ञानार्थमेवेत्यर्थः[3] । पक्षः साधनयोग्यार्थः । 'पक्षः पार्श्वगरुत्साध्यसहायबलभित्तिषु ।' इति केशवः ॥

पञ्चानामपि भूतानामुत्कर्षं पुपुषुर्गुणाः ।
नवे तस्मिन्महीपाले सर्वं नवमिवाभवत् ॥ ११ ॥

पृथिव्यादीनां **पञ्चानां भूतानामपि गुणाः** गन्धादयः[4] **उत्कर्षम्** अतिशयं **पुपुषुः** । अत्रोत्प्रेक्षते—**तस्मिन्** रघौ नाम **नवे महीपाले** सति **सर्वं** वस्तुजातं **नवं इव अभवत्** । तदेव भूतजातमिदानीमपूर्वगुणयोगादपूर्वमिवाभवदिति भावः ॥

---

१ उक्तं च भारते—मृदुर्भवत्यवज्ञातस्तीक्ष्णादुद्विजते जनः । काले काले तु संप्राप्ते मृदुस्तीक्ष्णोऽथ वा भवेत् ॥ अनुरूपश्लोकोऽष्टमे—न खरो न च भूयसा मृदुः–इ० । किरातार्जुनीये च समवृत्तिरुपैति मार्दवं समये यश्च तनोति तिग्मताम् । अधितिष्ठति लोकमोजसा स विवस्वानिव मेदिनीपतिः ॥ इति । २ नयचक्षुर्भिः इ. पा. ३ उभे प्रज्ञे वेदितव्ये ऋज्वी वक्रा च भारत । जानन्वक्रां न सेवेत प्रतिबाधेत चागताम् ॥ इति भारते च । ४ 'पृथ्वी पञ्चगुणा तोय चतुर्गुणमथानिलः । त्रिगुणो द्विगुणो वायुर्वियदेकगुणं भवेत् ॥' इ० व० । ते च गुणा यथा––पृथिव्यां रूपरसगन्धस्पर्शशब्दाः पञ्च गुणाः । अप्सु रूपरसस्पर्शशब्दाश्चत्वारो गुणाः । तेजसि रूपस्पर्शशब्दास्त्रयो गुणाः । मरुति स्पर्शशब्दौ द्वौ गुणौ । व्योम्नि च शब्द एवैको गुणः । तदुक्तं प्रपञ्चसारे–शब्दाद्व्योम स्पर्शतस्तेन वायुस्ताभ्यां रूपाद्वह्निरेतै रसाच्च । अम्भांस्येतैर्गन्धतो भूधराद्या भूताः पञ्च स्युर्गुणानां क्रमेण ॥ इति ।

यथा प्रह्लादनाच्चन्द्रः प्रतापात्तपनो यथा ।
तथैव सोऽभूदन्वर्थो राजा प्रकृतिरञ्जनात् ॥ १२ ॥

यथा चन्दयतीत्याह्लादयतीति **चन्द्रः** इन्दुः । चदिधातोरौणादिको रप्रत्ययः । **प्रह्लादनाद्** आह्लादकरणाद् अन्वर्थः अनुगतार्थनामकः **अभूत्** । **यथा च** तपतीति **तपनः** सूर्यः । नन्द्यादित्वाल्ल्युप्रत्ययः । **प्रतापात्** संतापजननादन्वर्थः । **तथैव स राजा प्रकृतिरञ्जनाद् अन्वर्थः** सार्थकराजशब्दः **अभूत्** । यद्यपि राजशब्दो राजते-र्दीप्त्यर्थात्कनिन्प्रत्ययान्तो न तु रञ्जेस्तथाऽपि धातूनामनेकार्थत्वाद्रञ्जनाद्राजेत्युक्तं कविना ॥

कामं कर्णान्तविश्रान्ते विशाले तस्य लोचने ।
चक्षुष्मत्ता तु शास्त्रेण सूक्ष्मकार्यार्थदर्शिना ॥ १३ ॥

विशाले तस्य रघोः **लोचने कामं** कर्णान्तयोर्विश्रान्ते कर्णप्रान्तगते [**कर्णान्त-विश्रान्ते**] । **चक्षुष्मत्ता तु** चक्षुःफलं त्वित्यर्थः । सूक्ष्मान्कार्यार्थान्कर्तव्या-र्थान्दर्शयति प्रकाशयतीति **सूक्ष्मकार्यार्थदर्शिना शास्त्रेण** एव । 'शास्त्रं दृष्टिर्विवे-किनाम्' इति भावः ॥

लब्धप्रशमनस्वस्थमथैनं समुपस्थिता ।
पार्थिवश्रीर्द्वितीयेव शरत्पङ्कजलक्षणा ॥ १४ ॥

अथ लब्धस्य राज्यस्य प्रशमनेन परिपन्थिनामनुरञ्जनप्रतीकाराभ्यां स्थिरीकरणेन स्वस्थं समाहितचित्तं [**लब्ध[3]प्रशमनस्वस्थ**] **एनं** रघुं **पङ्कजलक्षणा** पद्मचिह्ना । श्रियोऽपि विशेषणमेतत् । **शरत्** । **द्वितीया पार्थिवश्रीः** राजलक्ष्मीः **इव** । **समुपस्थिता** प्राप्ता । 'रक्षा पौरजनस्य देशनगरग्रामेषु गुप्तिस्तथा योधानामपि संग्रहोऽपि तुल्या मानव्यवस्थापनम् । साम्यं लिङ्गिषु दानवृत्तिकरणं त्यागः समानेऽर्चनं कार्याण्येव महीभुजां प्रशमनान्येतानि राज्ये नवे ॥'

निर्वृष्टलघुभिर्मेघैर्मुक्तवर्त्मा सुदुःसहः ।
प्रतापस्तस्य भानोश्च युगपद्व्यानशे दिशः ॥ १५ ॥

---

१ एवं महाभारतेऽपि–रञ्जिताश्च प्रजाः सर्वास्तेन राजेति शब्द्यते । इति शान्तिप० । अन्वर्थः–'अर्थमनुगतोऽन्वर्थ इति कैयटः' इ० चा० । २ उक्तं च हितोपदेशे–'अनेकसंशयोच्छेदि परोक्षार्थस्य दर्शकम् । सर्वस्य लोचनं शास्त्रं यस्य नास्त्यन्ध एव सः ॥' इति । 'शास्त्रं चक्षुर्विवेकिनाम्' इति चान्यत्र । अत्र टीकास्थानीयं दशकुमारचरितवाक्यम्—आगमदीपदृष्टेन खल्वध्वना सुखेन वर्तत लोकयात्रा । दिव्यं हि चक्षुर्भूतभवद्भाविष्यत्सु व्यवहितविप्रकृष्टादिषु च विषयेषु शास्त्रं नामाप्रतिहतवृत्ति । तेन हीनः सतोरप्यायतविशाल-योर्लोचनयोरन्ध एव जन्तुरर्थदर्शनेष्वसामर्थ्यात् । इ० । कामम् इ०–'कामं कमलपत्राणां नेत्रे तस्यानुकारिणी' इ. दि. चा० पठतः । सूक्ष्मेति–सूक्ष्मकार्यार्थदर्शिनः इ. पा. ३ 'लब्धप्रश-मनं स्वस्थम्' इति चा. व. दयः पठन्ति ।

४ निर्वृष्टलघुभिर्मेघः सवितुस्तस्य चोभयोः ।
वर्धिष्णवो दिशां भागान्प्रतापा यत्र रेचिताः ॥

—इति दि. चा. पठतः ।

निःशेषं वृष्टाः निर्वृष्टाः । कर्तरि क्तः । अत एव लघवः । तैः [**निर्वृष्टलघुभिः**] **मेघैः मुक्तवर्त्मा** त्यक्तमार्गः । अत एव **सुदुःसहः** । **तस्य** रघोः **भानोः च प्रतापः** पौरुषमातपश्च । 'प्रतापौ पौरुषातपौ' इति यादवः । **युगपद् दिशः व्यानशे** व्याप ॥

वार्षिकं संजहारेन्द्रो धनुर्जैत्रं रघुर्दधौ ।

प्रजार्थसाधने तौ हि पर्यायोद्यतकार्मुकौ ॥ १६ ॥

इन्द्रः वर्षासु भवं **वार्षिकम्** । वर्षानिमित्तमित्यर्थः । 'वर्षाभ्यष्ठक्' इति ठक्प्रत्ययः । **धनुः संजहार । रघुः जैत्रं** जयशीलम् । जेतृशब्दात्तृन्नन्तात् 'प्रज्ञादिभ्यश्च' इति स्वार्थेऽण्प्रत्ययः । धनुः **दधौ । हि** यस्मात् **तौ** इन्द्ररघू प्रजानामर्थस्य प्रयोजनस्य वृष्टिविजयलक्षणस्य साधनविषये [**प्रजार्थसाधने**] पर्यायेणोद्यते कार्मुके याभ्यां तौ **पर्यायोद्यतकार्मुकौ** । 'पर्यायोद्यमविश्रमौ' इति पाठान्तरे पर्यायेणोद्यमो विश्रमश्च ययोस्तौ पर्यायोद्यमविश्रमौ । द्वयोः पर्यायकरणादक्लेश इति भावः ॥

पुण्डरीकातपत्रस्तं विकसत्काशचामरः ।

ऋतुर्विडम्बयामास न पुनः प्राप तच्छ्रियम् ॥ १७ ॥

[**पुण्डरीकातपत्रः**] पुण्डरीकं सिताम्भोजमेवातपत्रं यस्य स तथोक्तः । [**विकसत्काशचामरः**] विकसन्ति काशानि काशाख्यतृणकुसुमान्येव चामराणि यस्य स तथोक्तः । **ऋतुः** शरदृतुः । पुण्डरीकनिभातपत्रं काशनिभचामरं **तं** रघुं **विडम्बयामास** अनुचकार । तस्य रघोः श्रियं [**तच्छ्रियम्**] **पुनः** शोभां तु **न प्राप** । 'शोभासंपत्तिपद्मासु लक्ष्मीः श्रीरिव दृश्यते ।' इति शाश्वतः ॥

प्रसादसुमुखे तस्मिंश्चन्द्रे च विशदप्रभे ।

तदा चक्षुष्मतां प्रीतिरासीत्समरसा द्वयोः ॥ १८ ॥

प्रसादेन सुमुखे [**प्रसादसुमुखे**] **तस्मिन्** रघौ **विशदप्रभे** निर्मलकान्तौ **चन्द्रे च द्वयोः** विषये **तदा चक्षुष्मतां प्रीतिः** अनुरागः **समरसा** समस्वादा । तुल्ययोगेति यावत् । 'रसो गन्धे रसः स्वादे' इति विश्वः । **आसीत्** ॥

हंसश्रेणीषु तारासु कुमुद्वत्सु च वारिषु ।

विभूतयस्तदीयानां पर्यस्ता यशसामिव ॥ १९ ॥

हंसानां श्रेणीषु पङ्क्तिषु [**हंसश्रेणीषु**] । **तारासु** नक्षत्रेषु । कुमुदानि येषु सन्तीति कुमुद्वन्ति । 'कुमुद्वान्कुमुदप्राये' इत्यमरः । 'कुमुदनडवेतसेभ्यो ड्मतुप्' । तेषु

---

१ अयं दि. संमतः पाठः । अनुरूपो भाव उक्तः प्रथमे–'दुदोह गां स यज्ञाय–' इत्यत्र । अस्मात् श्लोकात्परमतिरिक्तं श्लोकमेकं सु० व० पठतः—

अधिज्यमायुधं कर्तुं समयोऽयं रघोरिति ।

स्वं धनुः शङ्कितेनेव संजह्रे शतमन्युना ॥ इति ।

२ विलसत्–इ. पा. ३ श्रेणिषु इ. पा. । ४ 'यशसि धवलता वर्ण्यते' इति कविसमयानुरोधादुत्प्रेक्षते—हंसानेति । क्रियोत्प्रेक्षा ।

[**कुमुद्वत्सु**] । कुमुदप्रायेष्वित्यर्थः । **वारिषु च तदीयानां** रघुसंबन्धिनां **यशसां विभूतयः** संपदः **पर्यस्ताः इव** प्रसारिताः किम् । इत्युत्प्रेक्षा । अन्यथा कथमेषां धवलिमेति भावः ॥

इक्षुच्छायनिषादिन्यस्तस्य गोप्तुर्गुणोदयम् ।
आकुमारकथोद्धातं शालिगोप्यो जगुर्यशः ॥ २० ॥

इक्षूणां छायेक्षुच्छायम् । 'छाया बाहुल्ये' इति नपुंसकत्वम् । तत्र निषण्णाः **इक्षुच्छायनिषादिन्यः** । 'इक्षुच्छायानिषादिन्यः' इति स्त्रीलिङ्गपाठे इक्षोश्छायेति विग्रहः । अन्यथा बहुत्वे नपुंसकत्वप्रसङ्गात् । शालीन्गोपायन्ति रक्षन्तीति **शालिगोप्यः** सस्यपालिकाः स्त्रियः । 'कर्मण्यण्' । 'टिड्ढाणञ्–' इत्यादिना ङीप् । **गोप्तुः** रक्षकस्य **तस्य** रघोः गुणेभ्य उदयो यस्य तद् **गुणोदयं** गुणोत्पन्नमाकुमारं कुमारादारभ्य कथोद्धातः कथारम्भः यस्य तत् [**आकुमारकथोद्धातम्**] । कुमारैरपि स्तूयमानमित्यर्थः । **यशः जगुः** गायन्ति स्म । अथ वा कुमारस्य सतो रघोर्याः कथा इन्द्रविजया आरभ्याकुमारकथम् । तत्राप्यभिविधावव्ययीभावः । आकुमारकथमुद्धातो यस्मिन्कर्मणि । गानक्रियाविशेषणमेतत् । 'स्यादभ्यादानमुद्धात आरम्भः' इत्यमरः । 'आकुमारकथोद्भूतम्' इति पाठे कुमारस्य सतस्तस्य कथाभिश्चरितैरुद्भूतं यद्यशस्तद्यश आरभ्य यशो जगुरिति व्याख्येयम् ॥

प्रससादोदयादम्भः कुम्भयोनेर्महौजसः ।
रघोरभिभवाशङ्कि चुक्षुभे द्विषतां मनः ॥ २१ ॥

महौजसः कुम्भयोनेः अगस्त्यस्य । 'अगस्त्यः कुम्भसंभवः' इत्यमरः । **उदयाद् अम्भः प्रससाद** प्रसन्नं बभूव । महौजसः **रघोः** उदयाद् **अभिभवाशङ्कि द्विषतां मनः चुक्षुभे** कालुष्यं प्राप । 'अगस्त्योदये जलानि प्रसीदन्ति' इत्यागमः ॥

मदोदग्राः ककुद्मन्तः सरितां कूलमुद्रुजाः ।
लीलाखेलमनुप्रापुर्महोक्षास्तस्य विक्रमम् ॥ २२ ॥

मदोदग्राः मदोद्धताः । ककुदेषामस्तीति **ककुद्मन्तः** । महाककुद इत्यर्थः । यवादित्वान्मकारस्य वत्वाभावः । **सरितां** कूलान्युद्रुजन्तीति **कूलमुद्रुजाः** । 'उदि

---

१ तस्य गोप्तुर्द्विरेफानां कर्णोत्पलनिपातिनाम् ।
स्वरसंवादिभिः कण्ठैः शालिगोप्यो जगुर्गुणान् ॥

इति सर्व एव श्लोकोऽन्यथा पठ्यते कैश्चित् । इक्षुच्छाय०–०च्छायानि० इति चा० व० सु० दि० । कथोद्धातम्–०कथोद्भूतम् इ. दि. सु०. २ अगस्त्यस्य कुम्भयोनित्वकथा यास्कनिरुक्ते—तयोरादित्ययोः सत्रे दृष्ट्वाऽप्सरसमुर्वशीम् । रेतश्चस्कन्द तत्कुम्भे न्यपतद्वासतीवरे ॥ तेनैव तु मुहूर्तेन वीर्यवन्तौ तपस्विनौ । अगस्त्यश्च वसिष्ठश्च तत्रर्षी संबभूवतुः ॥ बहुधा पतितं रेतः कलशे च जले स्थले । स्थले वसिष्ठस्तु मुनिः संबभूवर्षिसत्तमः ॥ कुम्भे त्वगस्त्यः संभूतो जले मत्स्यो महाद्युतिः । इति पद्मपु० सृष्टिखण्डे २२ अ. द्रष्टव्यः । ३ एवमग्रेऽपि 'तस्याविलाम्भःपरिशुद्धिहेतोर्भौमो मुनेः स्थानपरिग्रहोऽयम्' इति । अत्र वराहमिहिरः—उदये च मुनेरगस्त्यनाम्नः कुसुमायोगमलप्रदूषितानि । हृदयानि सतामिव स्वभावात्पुनरम्बूनि भवन्ति निर्मलानि ॥ इ० । अभिभवाशङ्कि–परिभवा० इ. पा.

कूले राजिवहोः ' इति खश्प्रत्ययः । ' अरुर्द्विष–' इत्यादिना मुमागमः । महान्त उक्षाणो **महोक्षाः** । ' अचतुर–' इत्यादिना निपातनादकारान्तः । **लीलाखेलं** विलाससुभगं **तस्य** रघोरुत्साहवतो वपुष्मतः परभञ्जकस्य **विक्रमं** शौर्यम् **अनुप्रापुः** अनुचक्रुः ॥

प्रसवैः सप्तपर्णानां मदगन्धिभिराहताः ।
असूययेव तन्नागाः सप्तधैव प्रसुस्रुवुः ॥ २३ ॥

मदस्येव गन्धो येषां तैः **मदगन्धिभिः** । ' उपमानाच्च ' इतीकारः समासान्तः । **सप्तपर्णानां** वृक्षविशेषाणाम् । ' सप्तपर्णो विशालत्वक्शारदो विषमच्छदः । ' इत्यमरः । **प्रसवैः** पुष्पैः **आहताः** तस्य रघोः नागा गजाः [**तन्नागाः**] । ' गजेऽपि नागमातङ्गौ ' इत्यमरः । **असूयया इव** आहतिनिमित्तया स्पर्धयेव **सप्तधा एव प्रसुस्रुवुः** मदं ववृषुः । प्रतिगन्धाभिमानादिति भावः । ' करात्कटाभ्यां मेढ्राच्च नेत्राभ्यां च मदस्रुतिः । ' इति पालकाप्ये । करान्नासारन्ध्राभ्यामित्यर्थः ॥

सरितः कुर्वती गाधाः पथश्चाश्यानकर्दमान् ।
यात्रायै चोदयामास तं शक्तेः प्रथमं शरत् ॥ २४ ॥

सरितः गाधाः सुप्रतराः **कुर्वती** । **पथः** मार्गान् **च आश्यानकर्दमान्** शुष्कपङ्कान्कुर्वती । ' संयोगादेरातो धातोर्यण्वतः ' इति श्यतेर्निष्ठातस्य नत्वम् । **शरत्** शरदृतुः **तं** रघुं **शक्तेः** उत्साहशक्तेः **प्रथमं** प्राग् **यात्रायै** दण्डयात्रायै **चोदयामास** प्रेरयामास । प्रभावमन्त्रशक्तिसंपन्नस्य शरत्स्वयमुत्साहमुत्पादयामासेत्यर्थः ॥

तस्मै सम्यग्घुतो वह्निर्वाजिनीराजनाविधौ ।
प्रदक्षिणार्चिर्व्याजेन हस्तेनेव जयं ददौ ॥ २५ ॥

वाजिनामश्वानां नीराजनाविधौ नीराजनाख्ये शान्तिकर्मणि [**वाजिनीराजनाविधौ**] **सम्यग्** विधिवत् **हुतः** होमसमिद्धः **वह्निः** । प्रगता दक्षिणम् प्रदक्षिणम् । तिष्ठद्गुप्रभृतित्वादव्ययीभावः।प्रदक्षिणं यार्चिर्ज्वाला तस्या व्याजेन [**प्रदक्षिणार्चिर्व्याजेन**] **हस्तेनेव तस्मै जयं ददौ** । उक्तमाहवयात्रायाम् —'इद्धः प्रदक्षिणगतो हुतभुङ् नृपस्य धात्रीं समुद्ररशनां वशगां करोति ' इति । वाजिग्रहणं गजादीनामप्युपलक्षणं तेषामपि नीराजनाविधानात् ॥

---

१ ' लीलया निरायासेन खेलं विसृत्वरम्' इ. चा. २ ' रघोर्विक्रममनुप्राप्ता अनुगताः । वृषपक्षे तु विक्रमो गतिविशेषः । रघुविक्रमोऽपि महोदयः ककुद् राजचिह्नं तद्युक्तः यात्रायां करितुरगादिखुराद्यभिघातेन सरितां कूलभेदको भवति । ' इति च चा. ३ आहतास्ताडिता उन्मादिता इति यावत् । उत्प्रेक्षालंकारः । ४ तालुवक्षःकपोलेभ्यः शङ्खकुम्भकरे तथा । रोमकुम्भकटिभ्यश्च दानं प्रक्षरति द्विपः ॥ इति सु० । ५ प्रेरयामास, नोदयामास इ. पा. ६ नीरस्य शान्त्युदकस्य अजनाक्षेपोऽस्मिन्निति नीराजना । 'गजाश्वमङ्गलाय राजानः प्रयाणसमये नीराजनाविधिं कुर्वन्तीत्यागमः' इ. सु. । नीराजनाविधिस्तु विस्तरश उक्त वराहमिहिरविरचितायां बृहत्संहितायां चतुश्चत्वारिंशेऽध्याये तत्रैव द्रष्टव्यः । ७ उत्प्रेक्षालंकारः ।

स गुप्तमूलप्रत्यन्तः शुद्धपार्ष्णिरयान्वितः ।
षड्विधं बलमादाय प्रतस्थे दिग्जिगीषया ॥ २६ ॥

गुप्तौ मूलं स्वनिवासस्थानं प्रत्यन्तः प्रान्तदुर्गं च येन स **गुप्तमूलप्रत्यन्तः** । **शुद्धपार्ष्णिः** उद्धृतपृष्ठशत्रुः सेनया रक्षितपृष्ठदेशो वा । **अयान्वितः** शुभदैवान्वितः । 'अयः शुभावहो विधिः' इत्यमरः । **स** रघुः **षड्विधं** मौलभृत्यादिरूपं **बलं** सैन्यम् । 'मौलं भृत्यः सुहृच्छ्रेणी द्विषदाटविकं बलम् ।' इति कोशः । **आदाय** दिशां जिगीषया जेतुमिच्छया [**दिग्जिगीषया**] **प्रतस्थे** चचाल ॥

अवाकिरन्वयोवृद्धास्तं लाजैः पौरयोषितः ।
पृषतैर्मन्दरोद्धूतैः क्षीरोर्मय इवाच्युतम् ॥ २७ ॥

वयोवृद्धाः पौरयोषितः तं रघुं प्रयान्तं **लाजैः** आचारलाजैः । **मन्दरोद्धूतैः पृषतैः** बिन्दुभिः **क्षीरोर्मयः** क्षीरसमुद्रोर्मयः **अच्युतं** विष्णुम् **इव** । **अवाकिरन्** पर्यक्षिपन् ॥

स ययौ प्रथमं प्राचीं तुल्यः प्राचीनबर्हिषा ।
अहिताननिलोद्धूतैस्तर्जयन्निव केतुभिः ॥ २८ ॥

प्राचीनबर्हिर्नाम कश्चिन्महाराज इति केचित् । प्राचीनबर्हिरिन्द्रः । 'पर्जन्यो मघवा वृषा हरिहयः प्राचीनबर्हिस्तथा ।' इतीन्द्रपर्यायेषु हलायुधाभिधानात् । तेन [**प्राचीनबर्हिषा**] **तुल्यः स** रघुः । अनिलेनानुकूलवातेनोद्धूतैः [**अनिलोद्धूतैः**] **केतुभिः** ध्वजैः **अहितान्** रिपून **तर्जयन्निव** भर्त्सयन्निव । तर्जिभर्त्स्योरनुदात्तेत्त्वेऽपि चक्षिङो

---

१ अत्र मनुः—कृत्वा विधानं मूले तु यात्रिकं च यथाविधि । *** ॥ संशोध्य त्रिविधं मार्ग षड्विधं च बलं स्वकम् । सांपरायिककल्पेन यायादरिपुरं प्रति ॥ इति । उक्तं च कामन्दकेन— पुरश्च पश्चाच्च यदा समर्थस्तदाभियायान्महते फलाय । पुरः प्रसर्पन्नविशुद्धपृष्ठः प्राप्नोति तीव्रं खलु पार्ष्णिभेदम् ॥ इति । अरिं प्रति निर्यातेन विजिगीषुणा येभ्यः पृष्ठवर्तिनृपेभ्यो देशाक्रमणाद्याशङ्कयेत तेषां संयमनं कार्यमिति मनुरप्याह—'पार्ष्णिग्राहं च संप्रेक्ष्य तथाक्रन्दं च मण्डले' इति । अयोपेतः—अत्र कामन्दकः—देवानभ्यर्च्य विप्रांश्च प्रशस्तग्रहतारकम् । षड्विधं तु बलं व्यूह्य द्विषतोऽभिमुखं व्रजेत् ॥ 'प्रशस्तग्रहतारकम्' इत्यत्र 'गुरुं च शुभवासरे' इति पठित्वा चारित्रवर्धनेनायेनद्वचनमुद्धृतम् । २ मूलाद्वंशपरंपरयागतम् । एतद् दृढभक्तित्वादुत्तमम् । द्विषत्—उत्कोचभेदादिभिरुपायैः शत्रुपक्षात्स्वपक्षमानीतम् । आटविकम्—एतत्परदेशप्रवेशे उपयुक्तम् । तदुक्तम्—'परदेशप्रवेशे च कुर्यादाटविकान्पुरः' इति । ३ नास्ति च्युतं स्वस्वभावात्स्खलनं यस्य । सच्चिदानन्दरूपमेकरसम् । उक्तं च भगवता 'यस्मान्न च्युतपूर्वोऽहमच्युतस्तेन कर्मणा' इति भागवते । ४ यद्वा प्राचीनबर्हिर्नाम हविर्द्धानपुत्रो महाप्रभावः प्रजापतिः । उक्तं च वह्निपुराणे—प्राचीनबर्हिर्भगवान्महानासीत्प्रजापतिः । हविर्द्धानाद् द्विजश्रेष्ठ येन संवर्धिताः प्रजाः ॥ प्राचीनाग्राः कुशास्तस्य पृथिव्यां विश्रुता मुने । प्राचीनबर्हिर्भगवान् ख्यातो भुवि महाबलः ॥ इ० ५ 'अन्योऽपि अङ्गुल्यादिना तर्जयति' इ० चारि०.

ङित्करणेनानुदात्तेत्त्वनिमित्तस्यात्मनेपदस्यानित्यत्वज्ञापनात्परस्मैपदमिति वामनः । **प्रथमं प्राचीं** दिशं **ययौ** ॥

रजोभिः स्यन्दनोद्धूतैर्गजैश्च घनसंनिभैः ।
भुवस्तलमिव व्योम कुर्वन्व्योमेव भूतलम्[1] ॥ २९ ॥

किं कुर्वन् । **स्यन्दनोद्धूतैः रजोभिः घनसंनिभैः** वर्णतः क्रियातः परिमाणतश्च मेघतुल्यैः **गजैश्च** यथाक्रमं **व्योम** आकाशं **भुवस्तलमिव भूतलं** च **व्योमेव कुर्वन्** । ययाविति पूर्वेण संबन्धः ॥

प्रतापोऽग्रे ततः शब्दः परागस्तदनन्तरम् ।
ययौ पश्चाद्रथादीति चतुःस्कन्धेव सा चमूः ॥ ३० ॥

अग्रे प्रतापः[3] तेजोविशेषः । ' स प्रभावः प्रतापश्च यत्तेजः कोशदण्डजम् । ' इत्यमरः । **ततः शब्दः** सेनाकलकलः । **तदनन्तरं परागः** धूलिः । ' परागः पुष्परजसि धूलिस्नानीययोरपि । ' इति विश्वः । **पश्चाद् रथादि** रथाश्वादिकं चतुरङ्गबलम् । ' रथानीकम् ' इति पाठे इतिशब्दाध्याहारेण योज्यम् । **इति** इत्थं **चतुःस्कन्धा इव** चतुर्व्यूहेव । ' स्कन्धः प्रकाण्डे कायेऽसे विज्ञानादिषु पञ्चसु । नृपे समूहे व्यूहे च ' इति हैमः । **सा चमूः ययौ** ॥

मरुपृष्ठान्युदम्भांसि नाव्याः सुप्रतरा नदीः ।
विपिनानि प्रकाशानि शक्तिमत्त्वाच्चकार सः ॥ ३१ ॥

स रघुः **शक्तिमत्त्वात्**[4] समर्थत्वात् **मरुपृष्ठानि** निर्जलस्थानानि । ' समानौ मरुधन्वानौ ' इत्यमरः । **उदम्भांसि** उद्भूतजलानि चकार । **नाव्याः** नौभिस्तार्याः **नदीः** ' नाव्यं त्रिलिङ्गं नौतार्ये ' इत्यमरः । ' नौवयोधर्मविषमूल-' इत्यादिना यत्प्रत्ययः । **सुप्रतराः** सुखेन तार्याश्चकार । **विपिनानि** अरण्यानि । ' अटव्यरण्यं विपिनम् ' इत्यमरः । **प्रकाशानि** निर्वृक्षाणि **चकार** । शक्त्युत्कर्षात्तस्यागम्यं किमपि नासीदिति भावः ॥

स सेनां महतीं कर्षन्पूर्वसागरगामिनीम् ।
बभौ हरजटाभ्रष्टां गङ्गामिव भगीरथः ॥ ३२ ॥

---

१ अस्मात् श्लोकात्परं चा. दि. वल्लभादयः श्लोकमेकं पठन्ति यथा—

परागैः कलुषास्तस्य सहप्रस्थायिभिः कृशाः ॥
पश्चात्प्रयायिभिः पङ्काश्चक्रिरे मार्गनिम्नगाः ॥ इति ।

२ कृष्णवर्णत्वाद्विशालत्वान्निर्घोषतुल्यबृंहितत्वान्मदवारिधारावर्षित्वाच्च गजानां घनसाम्यम् ।
३ इन्द्रजयादिरूपः । 'शत्रूणां भयजननवार्ता' इ. व० । ' परागः-' 'पुरोगाः' ' रथादीति-' ' रथानीकम् ' इ. चा. व. सु. दि. पठन्ति । ४ प्रशस्ता शक्तिर्विद्यतेऽस्येति शक्तिमांस्तस्य भावस्तस्मात् । ' अनिखननव्यापारेण ' इ. चा० ' प्रभूतकटसैन्यसामग्रीतः ' इ. सु० च व्याख्यातः । किं त्वेतद्व्याख्यानं न मनोरमम् । तथा व्याख्याने दिव्यप्रभावस्य रघोः प्राकृतनृपतुल्यत्वापत्तेः । कूपखननसेतुबन्धनादिलौकिकोपायानन्तरेण रघोर्दिव्यप्रभाववत्त्वादेव तत्तत्कार्यसिद्धिर्जाता इति केचित् ।

महतीं सेनां पूर्वसागरगामिनीं कर्षन् स रघुः । हरस्य जटाभ्यो भ्रष्टां [**हरजटाभ्रष्टां**] **गङ्गां** कर्षन् । सापि पूर्वसागरगामिनी । **भगीरथः इव बभौ** । भगीरथो नाम कश्चित्कपिलदग्धानां सागराणां नप्ता तत्पावनाय हरकिरीटाद्गङ्गां प्रवर्तयिता राजा । यत्संबन्धाद्गङ्गा च भागीरथीति गीयते ॥

त्याजितैः फलमुत्खातैर्भग्नैश्च बहुधा नृपैः ।
तस्यासीदुल्बणो मार्गः पादपैरिव दन्तिनः ॥ ३३ ॥

'फलं फले धने बीजे निष्पत्तौ भोगलाभयोः ।' इति केशवः । **फलं** लाभम् । वृक्षपक्षे प्रसवं च । **त्याजितैः** । त्यजेर्ण्यन्ताद् द्विकर्मकादप्रधाने कर्मणि क्तः । **उत्खातैः** स्वपदात् च्यावितैः । अन्यत्रोत्पाटितैः । **बहुधा भग्नैः** रणे जितैः । अन्यत्र छिन्नैः । **नृपैश्च** । **पादपैः दन्तिनः** गजस्य **इव तस्य** रघोः **मार्गः उल्बणः** प्रकाशः **आसीत्** । 'प्रकाशं प्रकटं स्पष्टमुल्बणं विशदं स्फुटम् ।' इति यादवः ॥

पौरस्त्यानेवमाक्रामंस्तांस्ताञ्जनपदाञ्जयी ।
प्राप तालीवनश्याममुपकण्ठं महोदधेः ॥ ३४ ॥

जयी जयनशीलः । 'जिदृक्षिविश्री–' इत्यादिना इनिप्रत्ययः । स रघुः **एवम्** । पुरो भवान् **पौरस्त्यान्** प्राच्यान् । 'दक्षिणापश्चात्पुरसस्त्यक्' इति त्यक्प्रत्ययः । **तांस्तान्** । सर्वानित्यर्थः । वीप्सायां द्विरुक्तिः । **जनपदान्** देशान् **आक्रामन्** तालीवनैः श्यामं [**तालीवनश्यामम्**] **महोदधेः उपकण्ठं** अन्तिकं **प्राप** ॥

अनम्राणां समुद्धर्तुस्तस्मात्सिन्धुरयादिव ।
आत्मा संरक्षितः सुह्मैर्वृत्तिमाश्रित्य वैतसीम् ॥ ३५ ॥

अनम्राणाम् । कर्मणि षष्ठी । **समुद्धर्तुः** उन्मूलयितुः **तस्माद्** रघोः सकाशात् । 'भीत्रार्थानां भयहेतुः' इत्यपादानत्वात्पञ्चमी । **सिन्धुरयात्** नदीवेगात् । **इव सुह्मैः**

---

१ भगीरथो नाम सूर्यवंश्यो राजा मर्त्यलोके गङ्गाप्रवर्तकः । स किल सगरपुत्रस्यासमञ्जस्य प्रपौत्रः । तथा च रामायणम्–सगरस्यासमञ्जस्तु असमञ्जादथांशुमान् । दिलीपोंऽशुमतः पुत्रो दिलीपस्य भगीरथः । इ० ॥ पुरा किल भगीरथः सगरस्य पुत्रानुद्दिधीर्षुर्गङ्गाया भुव्यवतरणं कारयितुं वर्षसहस्राणि तीव्रं तपस्तेपे । ततस्तुष्टो ब्रह्मा तस्मादभीष्टं वरं दत्त्वा गङ्गाधारणाय शिवं प्रार्थयितुमादिदेश । ततः स दुष्करेण तपसा शिवं पर्यतोषयत् । शिवोऽपि हिमाचलं गत्वा जटां विकीर्य पतेति गङ्गामब्रवीत् । शिवेन सह पातालं विशामीत्यवलेपाच्छिरसि पतिता सा तत्र संवत्सरं बभ्राम । पश्चाद्भगवान् भगीरथप्रार्थनया गङ्गामुत्ससर्ज । ततः स सगरसुतकृतखातेन तां पातालं नीत्वा तज्जलेन पूर्वपुरुषानुद्धारयांचकार । विशेषस्तु रामा. बा. ४२–४४ अध्यायेषु द्रष्टव्यः । २ एवं त्रयोदशेऽपि वर्णनम्–दूरादयश्चक्रनिभस्य तन्वी तमालतालीवनराजिनीला । इ० । उपकण्ठम्–उपगतः कण्ठं सामीप्यं कूलमिति यावत् । 'उपकण्ठान्तिकाभ्यर्णाभ्यग्रा अप्यभितोऽव्ययम्' इत्यमरः । ३ ब्रह्मदेशीयै राजभिः । इति सु० व० । 'यथा नदीवेगाद्वेतसा वृक्षा नम्रवृत्तिं कृत्वा नदीवेगादात्मानं रक्षन्ति तद्वत्तैः सुह्मैरात्मा रक्षितः । इ० सु० । शरणार्थिनस्ते महात्मना रघुणा नोन्मूलिताः । 'तृणानि नोन्मूलयति प्रभञ्जनो मृदूनि नीचैः प्रणतानि सर्वशः । समुच्छ्रितानेव तरून्प्रबाधते महान्महत्येव करोति विक्रमम् ॥' इति न्यायेनेति भावः ।

सुह्मदेशीयैः । सुह्मादयः शब्दा जनपदवचनाः क्षत्रियमाचक्षते । **वैतसीं** वेतसः संबन्धिनीं **वृत्तिम्** । प्रणतिमित्यर्थः । **आश्रित्य आत्मा संरक्षितः** । अत्र कौटिल्यः– ' बलीयसाऽभियुक्तो दुर्बलः सर्वत्रानुप्रणतो वेतसधर्ममातिष्ठेत् । ' इति ॥

वङ्गानुत्खाय तरसा नेता नौसाधनोद्यतान् ।
निचखान जयस्तम्भान्गङ्गास्रोतोन्तरेषु सः ॥ ३६ ॥

नेता नायकः **स** रघुर्नौभिः साधनैरुद्यतान्संनद्धान् [**नौसाधनोद्यतान्**] **वङ्गान्** राज्ञः **तरसा** बलेन । ' तरसी बलरंहसी ' इति यादवः । **उत्खाय** उन्मूल्य गङ्गायाः स्रोतसां प्रवाहाणामन्तरेषु द्वीपेषु [**गङ्गास्रोतोन्तरेषु**] । **जयस्तम्भान् निचखान** । स्थापितवानित्यर्थः ॥

आपादपद्मप्रणताः कलमा इव ते रघुम् ।
फलैः संवर्धयामासुरुत्खातप्रतिरोपिताः ॥ ३७ ॥

आपादपद्ममङ्घ्रिपद्मपर्यन्तं प्रणताः [**आपादपद्मप्रणताः**] । अत एवोत्खाताः पूर्वमुद्धृता अपि प्रतिरोपिताः पश्चात्स्थापिताः [**उत्खातप्रतिरोपिताः**] **ते** वङ्गाः **कलमा इव** शालिविशेषा इव । 'शालयः कलमाद्याश्च षष्टिकाद्याश्च पुंस्यमी । ' इत्यमरः । तेऽप्यापादपद्मं मूलपद्मपर्यन्तं प्रणताः । ' पादा बुध्ने तुरीयांशे शैलप्रत्यन्तपर्वते । ' इति विश्वप्रकाशः । उत्खातप्रतिरोपिताश्च । **रघुं फलैः** धनैः । अन्यत्र सस्यैः । **संवर्धयामासुः** । ' फलं फले धने बीजे निष्पत्तौ भोगलाभयोः । सस्ये ' इति केशवः ॥

स तीर्त्वा कपिशां सैन्यैर्बद्धद्विरदसेतुभिः ।
उत्कलादर्शितपथः कलिङ्गाभिमुखो ययौ ॥ ३८ ॥

स रघुर्बद्धा द्विरदा एव सेतवो यैस्तैः [**बद्धद्विरदसेतुभिः**] **सैन्यैः कपिशां** नाम नदीं **तीर्त्वा** । ' करभाम् ' इति केचित्पठन्ति । उत्कलै राजभिरादर्शितमार्गः [**उत्कलादर्शितपथः**] सन् **कलिङ्गाभिमुखः ययौ** ॥

स प्रतापं महेन्द्रस्य मूर्ध्नि तीक्ष्णं न्यवेशयत् ।
अङ्कुशं द्विरदस्येव यन्ता गम्भीरवेदिनः ॥ ३९ ॥

स रघुः **महेन्द्रस्य** कुलपर्वतविशेषस्य । ' महेन्द्रो मलयः सह्यः शुक्तिमानृक्षपर्वतः ।

---

१ ०द्धृतान् इ. पाठः । वङ्गानां नौनिर्माणकौशलं महाभारतादप्यवगम्यते । यथा–ततः प्रवासितो विद्वान्विदुरेण नरस्तदा । पार्थानां दर्शयामास मनोमारुतगामिनीम् ॥ सर्ववातसहां नावं यन्त्रयुक्तां पताकिनीम् । शिवे भागीरथीतीरे नरैर्विस्रम्भिभिः कृताम् ॥ इत्या० २ ' नगराणि जित्वा तत्र स्तम्भाः क्रियन्ते ' इत्यागमः । इ. सु० । ३ कलमादीनां जलपूर्णमूलेषु जलजपुष्पाणि जायन्ते । तथा हि भारविः—'तुतोष पश्यन्कलमस्य सोऽधिकं सवारिजे वारिणि रामणीयकम् ' इति । अत्र ' अन्यत्र मञ्जरीभारेण नम्राः कलमा बहु फलन्ति ' इ. चा० । अयं श्लोकः श्लिष्टः । ' प्रणताः ' इत्यत्र ' प्रवणाः ' इ. व० पठति । ४ उत्कलदेशीयास्तु संग्रामदिने एव रघुचरणयोर्न्यपतन् इत्यर्थः इ० चा० । 'उत्कलाद०'–उत्कलैर्दर्शि०, उत्कलादेशि० इ. पा. । कलिङ्गाभिमुखः– ०मुखम् इ. पा.

विन्ध्यश्च पारियात्रश्च सप्तैते कुलपर्वताः ॥ ' इति विष्णुपुराणात् । **मूर्ध्नि तीक्ष्णं** दुःसहं **प्रतापम्** । **यन्ता** सारथिः **गम्भीरवेदिनः द्विरदस्य** गजविशेषस्य मूर्ध्नि तीक्ष्णं निशितं **अङ्कुशमिव** । **न्यवेशयत्** निक्षिप्तवान् । ' त्वग्भेदाच्छोणितस्रावान्मांसस्य क्रथनादपि । आत्मानं यो न जानाति स स्याद्गम्भीरवेदिता ॥ ' इति राजपुत्रीये । ' चिरकालेन यो वेत्ति शिक्षां परिचितामपि । गम्भीरवेदी विज्ञेयः स गजो गजवेदिभिः ॥ ' इति मृगचर्मीये ॥

प्रतिजग्राह कालिङ्गस्तमस्त्रैर्गजसाधनः ।
पक्षच्छेदोद्यतं शक्रं शिलावर्षीव पर्वतः ॥ ४० ॥

गजसाधनः सन् **कालिङ्गः** कलिङ्गानां राजा । ' द्व्यञ्मगधकलिङ्ग–' इत्यादिना अण्प्रत्ययः । **अस्त्रैः** आयुधैः **तं** रघुम् । पक्षाणां छेद उद्यतमुद्युक्तं [**पक्षच्छेदोद्यतं**] **शक्रं शिलावर्षी पर्वत इव** । **प्रतिजग्राह** प्रत्यभियुक्तवान् ॥

द्विषां विषह्य काकुत्स्थस्तत्र नाराचदुर्दिनम् ।
सन्मङ्गलस्नात इव प्रतिपेदे जयश्रियम् ॥ ४१ ॥

काकुत्स्थः रघुः **तत्र** महेन्द्राद्रौ **द्विषां नाराचदुर्दिनम्** नाराचानां बाणविशेषाणां दुर्दिनम् । लक्षणया वर्षमुच्यते । **विषह्य** सहित्वा । सद् यथाशास्त्रं मङ्गलस्नातः [**सन्मङ्गलस्नातः**] **इव** विजयमङ्गलार्थमभिषिक्त इव **जयश्रियं प्रतिपेदे** प्राप । ' यत्तु सर्वौषधिस्नानं तन्माङ्गल्यमुदीरितम् । ' इति यादवः ॥

ताम्बूलीनां दलैस्तत्र रचितापानभूमयः ।
नारिकेलासवं योधाः शात्रवं च पपुर्यशः ॥ ४२ ॥

तत्र महेन्द्राद्रौ । युध्यन्त इति **योधाः** । पचाद्यच् । [**रचितापानभूमयः**] रचिताः कल्पिता आपानभूमयः पानयोग्यप्रदेशा यैस्ते तथोक्ताः सन्तः **नारिकेलासवं** नारिकेलमद्यं **ताम्बूलीनां** नागवल्लीनां **दलैः पपुः** । तत्र विजहुरित्यर्थः । **शात्रवं यशश्च** पपुः । जहुरित्यर्थः ॥

---

१ त्वग्भेदाद्रुधिरस्रावान्मांसस्य गल–(व्यथ–) नादपि । संज्ञां न लभते यस्तु विद्याद्गम्भीरवेदिनम् ॥ इति पालकाप्ये । इ० चा० २ अत्र गम्भीरवेदिसाम्यान्महेन्द्रस्य दुर्जयत्वं सूचितम् । ३ ' वरिचाणवारिवर्षणसहनानन्तरं रघुररीन् व्यजेष्ट । ' इ. चा. । अस्मात् श्लोकात्परं श्लोक एकः पठ्यते चा० दि० व० सु० आदिभिः । यथा–

' **वायव्यास्त्रविनिर्धूतात्पक्ष–(क्षा–) विद्धान्महोदधेः ।**
गजानीकात्स कालिङ्गं तार्क्ष्यः सर्पमिवाददे ॥ ' इति ।

४ आ संभूय पिबन्त्यत्रेति आपानं मद्यपानस्थानम् । आसवम्–अत्र आसूयते इति योगबलादासवशब्देन मद्यमात्रं गम्यते । भावप्रकाशे तु ' यच्च पक्वौषधाम्बुभ्यां सिद्धमन्नं स आसवः ' । इति विशेष उक्तः । माधवेनापि–शीधुरिक्षुरसैः पक्वैरपक्वैरासवो भवेत् । मैरेयं धातकीपुष्पगुडधानाम्लसंहितम् ॥ इति भेदः प्रदर्शितः ।

गृहीतप्रतिमुक्तस्य स धर्मविजयी नृपः ।
श्रियं महेन्द्रनाथस्य जहार न तु मेदिनीम् ॥ ४३ ॥

धर्मविजयी धर्मार्थं विजयशीलः **स नृपः** रघुः । गृहीतश्चासौ प्रतिमुक्तश्च गृहीतप्रतिमुक्तः तस्य [**गृहीतप्रतिमुक्तस्य**] **महेन्द्रनाथस्य** कालिङ्गस्य **श्रियं जहार** । धर्मार्थमिति भावः । **मेदिनीं तु न** जहार । शरणागतवात्सल्यादिति भावः ॥

ततो वेलातटेनैव फलवत्पूगमालिना ।
अगस्त्याचरितामाशामनाशास्यजयो ययौ ॥ ४४ ॥

ततः प्राचीविजयानन्तरं **फलवत्पूगमालिना** फलितक्रमुकश्रेणीमता । व्रीह्यादित्वादिनिप्रत्ययः । वेलायाः समुद्रकूलस्य तटेनोपान्तेन [**वेलातटेन**] **एव** अगस्त्येनाचरिताम् [**अगस्त्याचरिताम्**] **आशां** दक्षिणां दिशम् । **अनाशास्यजयः** अयत्नसिद्धत्वादप्रार्थनीयजयः सन् **ययौ** । ' अगस्त्यो दक्षिणामाशामाश्रित्य नभसि स्थितः । वरुणस्यात्मजो योगी विन्ध्यवातापिमर्दनः ॥ ' इति ब्रह्मपुराणे ॥

स सैन्यपरिभोगेण गजदानसुगन्धिना ।
कावेरीं सरितां पत्युः शङ्कनीयामिवाकरोत् ॥ ४५ ॥

स रघुः । गजानां दानेन मदेन सुगन्धिना [**गजदानसुगन्धिना**] । ' गन्धस्य—' इत्यादिनेकारादेशः समासान्तः । यद्यपि गन्धस्येत्त्वे तदेकान्तग्रहणं कर्तव्यमिति नैसर्गिकगन्धविवक्षायामेवेकारादेशः तथापि निरङ्कुशाः कवयः । तथा माघकाव्ये—' ववुरयुक्छदगुच्छसुगन्धयः सततगास्ततगानगिरोऽलिभिः' (६।५०); नैषधे च—' अपां हि तृप्ताय न वारिधारा स्वादुः सुगन्धिः स्वदते तुषारा ' (३।९३) इति । न कर्मधारयान्मत्वर्थीय इति निषेधादिनिप्रत्ययपक्षोऽपि जघन्य एव । सेनायां समवेताः । ' सेनायां समवेता ये

१ अत्र वल्लभव्याख्यानं यथा—धर्मविजयी लोभविजयी असुरविजयी चेति त्रिविधो राजा । यः शत्रुं निर्जित्य तदीयां श्रियं नीत्वा शत्रुं तस्मिन्नेव स्थाने स्थापयति स धर्मविजयी । यः शत्रुं निर्जित्य तदीयां श्रियं मेदिनीं च गृहीत्वा पाणैः न विकुरुते स लोभविजयी । यः शत्रुं हत्वा तदीयां श्रियं मेदिनीं च गृह्णाति सः असुरविजयी । २ अयं भावः—'गन्धस्येत् उत्पूतिसुसुरभिभ्यः' इति सूत्रेण बहुव्रीहावेवेभ्यः परस्य गन्धशब्दस्येकारोऽन्तादेशः स्यात् । तत्र ' गन्धस्येत्त्वे तदेकान्तग्रहणम् ' इति वार्त्तिकेण यत्र कस्यचिद् द्रव्यस्य स्वाभाविक एव गन्धोऽभिप्रेतो नागन्तुकस्तत्रैव उक्तादिपरस्य गन्धस्य समासान्त इकारादेशः स्यान्नान्यत्र । अत्र तु सैन्यपरिभोगस्य कश्चित्स्वाभाविको गन्धो नास्ति । गजदानरूपद्रव्यान्तरादेव स उत्पन्नः अत एव यद्यपि नात्र समासान्त इकारो युक्तस्तथापि महाकविप्रयोगात् नात्र कटाक्षः पातयितुमुचितः । तथा च शोभनः गन्धः सुगन्धः सोऽस्त्यस्येति गजदानसुगन्धी तेनेति साधुरिति पक्षोऽप्यनाश्रयणीयः । ' न कर्मधारयान्मत्वर्थीयः ' इति निषेधात् । सत्यां बहुव्रीहिसमासेनैवार्थसिद्धौ कर्मधारयात्परं पुनरपि मत्वर्थीयप्रत्ययकल्पनागौरवात् जघन्यपक्ष एव । एवं सत्यपि नैसर्गिक इत्यस्य भाष्ये वृत्तौ चादर्शनादेकान्त एकदेश इवाविभागेन लक्ष्यमाण इत्येव पक्षः साधीयान् ।

सैन्यास्ते सैनिकाश्च ते ' इत्यमरः । ' सेनाया वा ' इति ण्यप्रत्ययः । तेषां परिभोगेण [**सैन्यपरिभोगेण**] **कावेरीं** नाम सरितं **सरितां पत्युः** समुद्रस्य **शङ्कनीयां** न विश्वसनीयाम् **इव अकरोत्** । संभोगलिङ्गदर्शनाद्भर्तुरविश्वासो भवतीति भावः ॥

बलैरध्युषितास्तस्य विजिगीषोर्गताध्वनः ।
[2]मारीचोद्भ्रान्तहारीता मलयाद्रेरुपत्यकाः[3] ॥ ४६ ॥

विजिगीषोः विजेतुमिच्छोः **गताध्वनः तस्य** रघोः **बलैः** सैन्यैः । ' बलं शक्तिः बलं सैन्यम् ' इति यादवः । मारीचेषु मरीचवनेषूद्भ्रान्ताः परिभ्रान्ता हारीताः पक्षिविशेषा यासु ताः [**मारीचोद्भ्रान्तहारीताः**] । ' तेषां विशेषा हारीतो मद्गुः कारण्डवः प्लवः । ' इत्यमरः । **मलयाद्रेः उपत्यकाः** आसन्नभूमयः । ' उपत्यकाद्रेरासन्ना भूमिरूर्ध्वमधित्यका । ' इत्यमरः । ' उपाधिभ्यां त्यकन्- ' इत्यादिना त्यकन्प्रत्ययः । **अध्युषिताः** । उपत्यकासु उषितमित्यर्थः । ' उपान्वध्याङ्वसः ' इति कर्मत्वम् ॥

ससञ्जुरश्वक्षुण्णानामेलानामुत्पतिष्णवः ।
तुल्यगन्धिषु मत्तेभकटेषु फलरेणवः ॥ ४७ ॥

अश्वैः क्षुण्णानाम् [**अश्वक्षुण्णानाम्**] **एलानाम्** एलालतानां **उत्पतिष्णवः** उत्पतनशीलाः । ' अलंकृञ्- ' इत्यादिनेष्णुच्प्रत्ययः । **फलरेणवः** फलरजांसि **तुल्यगन्धिषु** समानगन्धिषु । सर्वधनीतिवदिन्नन्तो बहुव्रीहिः । मत्तेभानां कटेषु [**मत्तेभकटेषु**] **ससञ्जुः** सक्ताः । ' गजगण्डे कटः कटौ ' इति कोषः ॥

भोगिवेष्टनमार्गेषु चन्दनानां समर्पितम् ।
नास्रसत्करिणां ग्रैवं त्रिपदीछेदिनामपि ॥ ४८ ॥

चन्दनानां चन्दनद्रुमाणां **भोगिवेष्टनमार्गेषु** सर्पवेष्टननिम्नेषु **समर्पितं** सञ्जितं **त्रिपदीछेदिनां** पादशृङ्खलच्छेदकानाम् **अपि** । ' त्रिपदी पादबन्धनम् ' इति यादवः । **करिणाम्** । ग्रीवासु भवं **ग्रैवं** कण्ठबन्धनम् । ' ग्रीवाभ्योऽण्च ' इत्यण्प्रत्ययः । **न अस्रसत्** न स्रस्तमभूत् । ' द्युद्भ्यो लुङि ' इति परस्मैपदम् । पुषादित्वादङ् । ' अनिदिताम्- ' इति नकारलोपः ॥

---

१ सैन्यसंभोगचिह्ना कावेरी परपुरुषसंभोगाचिह्निता कामिनीव स्वभर्तुः शङ्कनीयपातिव्रत्या इवाभवदित्युत्प्रेक्षा । अस्मात् परं ' भयोत्सृष्ट- ' इति पद्यं (४.५४) चा० व० दि० सु० ध० आदयः पठन्ति ।

२ मरीचो०, हारीतोत्सृष्टमारीचाः इ. पा. ३ अस्मात्परं श्लोकमिममधिकं पठन्ति वल्लभादयः—

आजानेयखुरक्षुण्णपक्वैलाक्षेत्रसंभवम् ।
व्यानशे सपदि व्योम कीटकोशाविलं रजः ॥ इति ।

४ मारीचानां गन्धेन भक्षणेन वा उद्भ्रान्तास्त्रस्ता इतस्ततश्चलिता हारीताः पक्षिविशेषा अर्थात् शुका यासु ताः इ. धर्ममेरुः । ५ त्रयः पादा अस्या इति । ' त्रिपदीं छिन्दन्तीति त्रिपदीछेदिनस्तेषाम् । सुखावस्थात्यागिनामपि । सुखावस्थितस्य गजस्य पदत्रयावस्था त्रिपदी इत्युच्यते इति व० । एतन्मते सुखावस्थात्यागिभिरपि गजैः चन्दनसौरभ्यातिशयलोभात्स्वबन्धनानि न छिन्नानि इति भावः ।

दिशि मन्दायते तेजो दक्षिणस्यां रवेरपि ।
तस्यामेव रघोः पाण्ड्याः प्रतापं न विषेहिरे ॥ ४९ ॥

दक्षिणस्यां दिशि रवेरपि तेजो मन्दायते[1] मन्दं भवति । लोहितादित्वात्क्यष्प्रत्ययः । 'वा क्यषः' इत्यात्मनेपदम् । दक्षिणायने तेजोमान्द्यादिति भावः । **तस्यामेव** दिशि **पाण्ड्याः** । पाण्डूनां जनपदानां राजानः पाण्ड्याः । 'पाण्डोर्ड्यण्वक्तव्यः' । **रघोः प्रतापं न विषेहिरे** न सोढवन्तः । सूर्यविजयिनोऽपि विजितवानिति नायकस्य महानुत्कर्षो गम्यते[2] ॥

ताम्रपर्णीसमेतस्य मुक्तासारं महोदधेः ।
ते निपत्य ददुस्तस्मै यशः स्वमिव संचितम् ॥ ५० ॥

ते पाण्ड्यास्ताम्रपर्ण्या नद्या समेतस्य संगतस्य [**ताम्रपर्णीसमेतस्य**] **महोदधेः** संबन्धि **संचितं मुक्तासारं** मौक्तिकवरम् । 'सारो बले स्थिरांशे च न्याय्ये क्लीबं वरे त्रिषु ।' इत्यमरः । **स्वं** स्वकीयं संचितं **यशः इव** । **तस्मै** रघवे **निपत्य** प्रणिपत्य **ददुः** । यशसः शुभ्रत्वादौपम्यम् । ताम्रपर्णीसंगमे मौक्तिकोत्पत्तिरिति प्रसिद्धम् ॥

स निर्विश्य यथाकामं तटेष्वालीनचन्दनौ ।
स्तनाविव दिशस्तस्याः शैलौ मलयदर्दुरौ ॥ ५१ ॥
असह्यविक्रमः सह्यं दूरान्मुक्तमुदन्वता ।
नितम्बमिव मेदिन्याः स्रस्तांशुकमलङ्घयत् ॥ ५२ ॥

युग्ममेतत् । **असह्यविक्रमः स** रघुः **तटेषु** सानुषु **आलीनचन्दनौ** व्याप्तचन्दनद्रुमौ । 'गन्धसारो मलयजो भद्रश्रीश्चन्दनोऽस्त्रियाम् ।' इत्यमरः । स्तनपक्षे प्रान्तेषु व्याप्तचन्दनानुलेपौ । **तस्याः** दक्षिणस्याः **दिशः स्तनाविव** स्थितौ **मलयदर्दुरौ** नाम **शैलौ यथाकामं** यथेच्छं **निर्विश्य** उपभुज्य । 'निर्वेशो भृतिभोगयोः' इत्यमरः । उदकान्यस्य सन्तीत्युदन्वानुदधिः । 'उदन्वानुदधौ च' इति निपातः । **उदन्वता दूरान्मुक्तं** दूरतस्त्यक्तम् । 'स्तोकान्तिकदूरार्थकृच्छ्राणि क्तेन' इति समासः । 'पञ्चम्याः स्तोकादिभ्यः' इत्यलुक् । **स्रस्तांशुकं मेदिन्याः नितम्बम् इव** स्थितं **सह्यं** सह्याद्रिम् **अलङ्घयत्** प्राप्तोऽतिक्रान्तो वा[3] ॥

---

१ दक्षिणायने मेघावृतत्वात् शिशिरप्रादुर्भावाच्च रविर्मन्दतेजा भवति । मकरसंक्रममारभ्य मिथुनसंक्रमपर्यन्तं रविः किंचिद्वक्रगत्या उत्तराशां प्रयाति तदा भानोरुत्तरायणम् । तथा च यदा कर्कटकादारभ्य मकरपर्यन्तं दक्षिणाशां याति तदा दक्षिणायनम् । तदुक्तं सूर्यसिद्धान्ते—'भानोर्मकरसंक्रान्तेः षण्मासा उत्तरायणम् । कर्कादेस्तु तथैव स्यात् षण्मासा दक्षिणायनम् ॥' इति । २ अत्रोपमानात्सूर्यादप्युपमेयस्य रघुप्रतापस्याधिक्यवर्णनात् व्यतिरेकालंकारः । 'उपमानाद्यदन्यस्य व्यतिरेकः स एव सः' इति तल्लक्षणात् । ३ अत्र रघोः कामुकेन, दक्षिणाशायाः कामिन्या साम्यम् । एवमन्येषामप्यूह्यम् ।

संप्रति प्रतीचीं दिशमभिययावित्याह—

तस्यानीकैर्विसर्पद्भिरपरान्तजयोद्यतैः ।

रामास्त्रोत्सारितोऽप्यासीत्सह्यलग्न इवार्णवः ॥ ५३ ॥

अपरान्तानां पाश्चात्त्यानां जय उद्यतैरुद्युक्तैः [**अपरान्तजयोद्यतैः**] । ' अपरान्तास्तु पाश्चात्त्यास्ते च सूर्यरिकादयः । ' इति यादवः । **विसर्पद्भिः** गच्छद्भिः **तस्य** रघोः **अनीकैः** सैन्यैः । ' अनीकं तु रणे सैन्ये ' इति विश्वः । **अर्णवः** रामस्य जामदग्न्यस्या-स्त्रैरुत्सारितः [**रामास्त्रोत्सारितः**] **अपि सह्यलग्नः इव आसीत्** । सैन्यं द्वितीयोऽर्णव इवादृश्यतेति भावः ॥

भयोत्सृष्टविभूषाणां तेन केरलयोषिताम् ।

अलकेषु चमूरेणुश्चूर्णप्रतिनिधीकृतः ॥ ५४ ॥

तेन रघुणा भयेनोत्सृष्टविभूषाणां परिहृतभूषणानां [**भयोत्सृष्टविभूषाणां**] **केरलयोषितां** केरलाङ्गनानाम् **अलकेषु चमूरेणुः** सेनारजः चूर्णस्य कुङ्कुमादिरजसः प्रतिनिधीकृतः [**चूर्णप्रतिनिधीकृतः**] । एतेन योषितां पलायनं चमूनां च तदनु-धावनं ध्वन्यते ॥

मुरलामारुतोद्धूतमगमत्कैतकं रजः ।

तद्योधवारबाणानामयत्नपटवासताम् ॥ ५५ ॥

मुरला नाम केरलदेशेषु काचिन्नदी । ' मुरवीमारुतोद्धूतम् ' इति केचित्पठन्ति । तस्या मारुतेनोद्धूतमुत्थापितं [**मुरलामारुतोद्धूतं**] **कैतकं** केतकीसंबन्धि **रजः तद्योध-वारबाणानां** रघुभटकञ्चुकानाम् । ' कञ्चुको वारबाणोऽस्त्री ' इत्यमरः । **अयत्नपट-वासतां** अयत्नसिद्धवस्त्रवासनाद्रव्यत्वम् **अगमत्** । ' पिष्टातः पटवासकः ' इत्यमरः ॥

अभ्यभूयत वाहानां चरतां गात्रशिञ्जितैः ।

वर्मभिः पवनोद्धूतराजतालीवनध्वनिः ॥ ५६ ॥

चरतां गच्छतां **वाहानां** वाजिनाम् । ' वाजिवाहार्वगन्धर्वहयसैन्धवसप्तयः । '

---

१ ' कौङ्कणानाम् ' इ. व० । २ पुरा किल पितृवधामर्षितो भगवान् जामदग्न्यः त्रिःसप्तकृत्वः पृथिवीं निःक्षत्रियां कृत्वा क्षत्रियाणां रुधिरेण पितॄंस्तर्पयित्वा यज्ञे कश्यपायाखिलां महीं प्रतिपाद्य स्ववासार्थं शरैः समुद्रं दुरमपसार्य भूमिमुद्धार । तदुक्तम् महाभारते—' त्रिःसप्तकृत्वः पृथिवीं कृत्वा निःक्षत्रियां प्रभुः । दक्षिणामश्वमेधान्ते कश्यपायाददात्ततः ॥ स क्षत्रियाणां शेषार्थं करेणोद्दिश्य कश्यपः । स्रुक्प्रग्रहवता राजंस्ततो वाक्यमथाब्रवीत् ॥ गच्छ तीरं समुद्रस्य दक्षिणस्य महामुने । न ते मद्विषये राम वस्तव्यमिह कर्हिचित् ॥ ततः शूर्पारकं देशं सागरस्तस्य निर्ममे । सहसा जाम-दग्न्यस्य सोऽपरान्तमहीतलम् ॥' इति । ३ भयेनोत्सृष्टा विभूषा याभिः । चूर्ण०–' वासयोगस्तु चूर्णं स्यात् ' इति हैमः इ० चा० । ४ ' त्वगुशीरपत्रभागैः सूक्ष्मैलार्धेन संयुतश्चूर्णः । पटवासः प्रवरोऽयं मृगमदकर्पूरप्रबोधेन ॥ ' इ० वराह०

इत्यमरः । **गात्रशिञ्जितैः** गात्रेषु शब्दायमानैः । कर्तरि क्तः । 'गात्रसञ्जितैः' इति च पाठः । सञ्जतेर्ण्यन्तात्कर्मणि क्तः । **वर्मभिः** कवचैः । 'मर्मरः' इति पाठे गात्राणां गात्रशिञ्जितैर्गोत्रध्वानिभिरित्यर्थः । मर्मरः मर्मरायमाण इति ध्वनेर्विशेषणम् । पवनेनोद्धूतानां कम्पितानां राजतालीवनानां ध्वनिः [**पवनोद्धूतराजतालीवनध्वनिः**] **अभ्यभूयत** तिरस्कृतः ॥

खर्जूरीस्कन्धनद्धानां मदोद्गारसुगन्धिषु ।
कटेषु करिणां पेतुः पुंनागेभ्यः शिलीमुखाः ॥ ५७ ॥

खर्जूरीणां तृणद्रुमविशेषाणाम् । 'खर्जूरः केतकी ताली खर्जूरी च तृणद्रुमाः ।' इत्यमरः, स्कन्धेषु प्रकाण्डेषु । 'अस्त्री प्रकाण्डः स्कन्धः स्यान्मूलाच्छाखावधिस्तरोः ।' इत्यमरः । नद्धानां बद्धानां [**खर्जूरीस्कन्धनद्धानां**] **करिणां** मदोद्गारेण मदस्रावेण सुगन्धिषु [**मदोद्गारसुगन्धिषु**] । 'गन्धस्य--' इत्यादिनेकारः । **कटेषु** गण्डेषु **पुंनागेभ्यः** नागकेशरेभ्यः । पुंनागपुष्पाणि विहाय । ल्यब्लोपे पञ्चमी । **शिलीमुखाः** अलयः **पेतुः** । 'अलिबाणौ शिलीमुखौ' इत्यमरः । ततोऽपि सौगन्ध्यातिशयादिति भावः ॥

अवकाशं किलोदन्वान्रामायाभ्यर्थितो ददौ ।
अपरान्तमहीपालव्याजेन रघवे करम् ॥ ५८ ॥

उदन्वान् उदधिः **रामाय** जामदग्न्याय । **अभ्यर्थितः** याचितः सन् । **अवकाशं** स्थानं **ददौ किल** । किलेति प्रसिद्धौ । **रघवे** तु **अपरान्तमहीपालव्याजेन करं** बलिं ददौ । 'बलिहस्तांशवः कराः' इत्यमरः । अपरान्तानां समुद्रमध्यदेशवर्तित्वात्तैर्दत्ते करे समुद्रदत्तत्वोपचारः । करदानं च भीत्या न तु याच्ञयेति रामाद्रघोरुत्कर्षः ॥

मत्तेभरदनोत्कीर्णव्यक्तविक्रमलक्षणम् ।
त्रिकूटमेव तत्रोच्चैर्जयस्तम्भं चकार सः ॥ ५९ ॥

तत्र स रघुर्मत्तानामिभानां रदनोत्कीर्णानि दन्तक्षतान्येव । भावे क्तः । व्यक्तानि स्फुटानि विक्रमलक्षणानि पराक्रमचिह्नानि विजयवर्णावलिस्थानानि यस्मिंस्तं [**मत्तेभरदनोत्कीर्णव्यक्तविक्रमलक्षणम्**] तथोक्तं **त्रिकूटमेव उच्चैः जयस्तम्भं चकार** । गाढप्रहारात्त्रिकूटोऽद्रिरेवोत्कीर्णवर्णस्तम्भ इव रघोर्जयस्तम्भोऽभूदित्यर्थः ॥

पारसीकांस्ततो जेतुं प्रतस्थे स्थलवर्त्मना ।
इन्द्रियाख्यानिव रिपूंस्तत्त्वज्ञानेन संयमी ॥ ६० ॥

ततः स रघुः **संयमी** योगी **तत्त्वज्ञानेन इन्द्रियाख्यान्** इन्द्रियनामकान्

---

१ 'पुंनागः केशरोऽशोकः' इत्यभिधानचिन्तामणिः । 'नद्धानाम्'—बद्धानाम्. इ. पा० २ इयं कथोक्ता (श्लो. ५३). ३ त्रिकूटं सुवेलागिरिम् इ. व० अत्र गजदन्तोल्लेखचिह्नानि नामपराक्रमादिख्यापकाक्षरतुल्यानि जातानीति भावः ।

रिपूनिव । **पारसीकान्** राज्ञः जेतुं **स्थलवर्त्मना प्रतस्थे** । न तु निर्दिष्टेनापि जलपथेन । समुद्रयानस्य निषिद्धत्वादिति भावः ॥

यवनीमुखपद्मानां सेहे मधुमदं न सः ।
बालातपमिवाब्जानामकालजलदोदयः ॥ ६१ ॥

स रघुर्यवनीनां यवनस्त्रीणाम् । 'जातेरस्त्रीविषयादयोपधात्' इति ङीष् । मुखानि पद्मानीव मुखपद्मानि । उपमितसमासः । तेषां [**यवनीमुखपद्मानां**] मधुना मद्येन यो मदो मदरागः । कार्यकारणभावयोरभेदेन निर्देशः । तं [**मधुमदं**] **न सेहे** । कथमिव । अकाले प्रावृड्व्यतिरिक्ते काले जलदोदयः [**अकालजलदोदयः**] प्रायेण प्रावृषि पद्मविकासस्याप्रसक्तत्वाद् **अब्जानां** संबन्धिनं **बालातपमिव** । अब्जाहितत्वाद्ब्जसंबन्धित्वं सौरातपस्य ॥

संग्रामस्तुमुलस्तस्य पाश्चात्त्यैरश्वसाधनैः ।
शार्ङ्गकूजितविज्ञेयप्रतियोधे रजस्यभूत् ॥ ६२ ॥

तस्य रघोः **अश्वसाधनैः** वाजिसैन्यैः । 'साधनं सिद्धिसैन्ययोः' इति हैमः । पश्चाद्भवैः **पाश्चात्त्यैः** यवनैः सह । 'दक्षिणापश्चात्पुरसस्त्यक्' । सहार्थे तृतीया । शृङ्गाणां विकाराः शार्ङ्गाणि धनूंषि । तेषां कूजितैः शब्दैः । 'शार्ङ्गं पुनर्धनुषि शार्ङ्गिणः । जये च शृङ्गविहिते चापेऽप्याह विशेषतः ।' इति केशवः । अथ वा शार्ङ्गैः शृङ्गसंबन्धिभिः कूजितैर्विज्ञेया अनुमेयाः प्रतियोधाः प्रतिभटा यस्मिंस्तस्मिन् [**शार्ङ्गकूजितविज्ञेयप्रतियोधे**] **रजसि तुमुलः संग्रामः** संकुलं युद्धम् **अभूत्** । 'तुमुलं रणसंकुले' इत्यमरः ॥

भल्लापवर्जितैस्तेषां शिरोभिः श्मश्रुलैर्महीम् ।
तस्तार सरघाव्याप्तैः स क्षौद्रपटलैरिव ॥ ६३ ॥

स रघुः **भल्लापवर्जितैः** बाणविशेषकृत्तैः । 'स्नुहीदलफलो भल्लः' इति यादवः । **श्मश्रुलैः** प्रवृद्धमुखरोमवद्भिः । 'सिध्मादिभ्यश्च' इति लच्प्रत्ययः । **तेषां** पाश्चात्त्यानां **शिरोभिः** । सरघाभिर्मधुमक्षिकाभिर्व्याप्तैः [**सरघाव्याप्तैः**] । 'सरघा मधुमक्षिका' इत्यमरः । क्षुद्राः सरघाः । 'क्षुद्रा व्यङ्गा नटी वेश्या सरघा कण्टकारिका ।' इत्यमरः । क्षुद्राभिः कृतानि क्षौद्राणि मधूनि । 'मधु क्षौद्रं माक्षिकादि' इत्यमरः । 'क्षुद्राभ्रमरवटरपादपादञ्' इति संज्ञायामञ्प्रत्ययः । तेषां पटलैः संचयैः [**क्षौद्र**-

---

१ 'सिन्धुतटवासिनो म्लेच्छराजान्' इ० सु० । संयमिसादृश्येन रघोर्मनःस्थैर्यधैर्यादि, तत्त्वज्ञानसादृश्येन स्थलवर्त्मनः प्राशस्त्यं, इन्द्रियरिपुसादृश्येन पारसीकानां दुर्जयत्वं कुपथगामित्वं च सूचितम् । तत्त्वज्ञानं नित्यात्सच्चिदानन्दस्वरूपाद् ब्रह्मणोऽभिन्नोऽहमिति ज्ञानम् । २ युद्धयात्रासु इति शेषः । ३ 'यवनदेशीयक्षत्रियस्त्रीणामर्थात्तुरुष्कस्त्रीणाम्' इ. ध० । 'तासां यवनीनां पतयो बन्दिग्राहं गृहीता अथ वा प्राणैर्वियोजिता येन तन्मुखपद्मरागो विनश्येत् इति भावः' इ. सु० । ४ 'पाश्चात्त्याः श्मश्रून् स्थापयित्वा केशान्वपन्तीति तद्देशाचारोक्तिः । इ. चा० ।

पटलैः]। 'पटलं तिलके नेत्ररोगे छन्दसि संचये । पाटके परिवारे च' इति हैमः । **इव महीं तस्तार** आच्छादयामास ॥

अपनीतशिरस्त्राणाः शेषास्तं शरणं ययुः ।
प्रणिपातप्रतीकारः संरम्भो हि महात्मनाम् ॥ ६४ ॥

शेषाः हतावशिष्टाः **अपनीतशिरस्त्राणाः** अपसारितशीर्षण्याः सन्तः । 'शीर्षकम् । शीर्षण्यं च शिरस्त्रे' इत्यमरः । शरणागतलक्षणमेतत् । **तं शरणं ययुः** । तथा हि । **महात्मनां संरम्भः** कोपः । 'संरम्भः संभ्रमे कोपे' इति विश्वः । प्रणिपातः प्रणतिरेव प्रतीकारो यस्य स [**प्रणिपातप्रतीकारः**] **हि** । महतां परकीयमौद्धत्यमेवासह्यं न तु जीवितमिति भावः ॥

विनयन्ते स्म तद्योधा मधुभिर्विजयश्रमम् ।
आस्तीर्णाजिनरत्नासु द्राक्षावलयभूमिषु ॥ ६५ ॥

तस्य रघोर्योधा भटाः [**तद्योधाः**] आस्तीर्णान्याजिनरत्नानि चर्मश्रेष्ठानि यासु तासु [**आस्तीर्णाजिनरत्नासु**] द्राक्षावलयानां भूमिषु [**द्राक्षावलयभूमिषु**] । 'मृद्वीका गोस्तनी द्राक्षा स्वाद्वी मधुरसेति च ।' इत्यमरः । **मधुभिः** द्राक्षाफलप्रकृतिकैर्मद्यैः **विजयश्रमं** युद्धखेदं **विनयन्ते स्म** अपनीतवन्तः । 'कर्तृस्थे चाशरीरे कर्मणि' इत्यात्मनेपदम् । 'लट् स्मे' इति भूतार्थे लट् ॥

ततः प्रतस्थे कौबेरीं भास्वानिव रघुर्दिशम् ।
शरैरुस्रैरिवोदीच्यानुद्धरिष्यन्रसानिव ॥ ६६ ॥

ततः रघुः भास्वान् सूर्यः **इव शरैः** बाणैः **उस्रैः** किरणैः **इव** । 'किरणोस्रमयूखांशुगभस्तिघृणिरश्मयः ।' इत्यमरः । **उदीच्यान्** उदग्भवान्नृपान् **रसान्** उदकानि **इव उद्धरिष्यन् कौबेरीं** कुबेरसंबन्धिनीं **दिशम्** उदीचीं **प्रतस्थे** । अनेकेनेवशब्देनेयमुपमा । यथाह दण्डी—'एकानेकेवशब्दत्वात्सा वाक्यार्थोपमा द्विधा ।' इति ॥

विनीताध्वश्रमास्तस्य सिन्धुतीरविचेष्टनैः ।
दुधुवुर्वाजिनः स्कन्धाँल्लग्नकुङ्कुमकेसरान् ॥ ६७ ॥

सिन्धुर्नाम काश्मीरदेशेषु कश्चिन्नदविशेषः । 'देशे नदविशेषेऽब्धौ सिन्धुर्ना सरिति

---

१ अत्रोपमानोपमेययोर्बिम्बानुबिम्बित्वादेकधर्मवत्त्वं साधर्म्यम् । रमश्रुलत्वमरघाव्याप्तत्वयोर्धर्मयोरेककृष्णत्वादिगुणयोगादेकत्वम् । उक्तं च साहित्यदर्पणे—'एकरूपः क्वचित्क्वापि भिन्नः साधारणो गुणः । भिन्ने बिम्बानुबिम्बत्वं शब्दमात्रेण वा भिदा ॥' इति । २ अत्र कर्मपदस्य विजयश्रमस्य कर्तॄणां योधानां शरीरस्थत्वान्मूर्तिरहितत्वाच्चात्मनेपदमित्यर्थः । ३ 'औदीच्यान्' इ. पा० । अस्माच्छ्लोकात्परमतिरिक्तं श्लोकं पठन्ति दि० चा० सु० ध० वि० आदयः—

जितानजय्यस्तानेव कृत्वा रथपुरःसरान् ।
महार्णवमिवौर्वाग्निः प्रविवेशोत्तरापथम् ॥ इति ।

स्त्रियाम् ।' इत्यमरः । सिन्धोस्तीरे विचेष्टनैरङ्गपरिवर्तनैः [**सिन्धुतीरविचेष्टनैः**] **विनीताध्वश्रमाः तस्य** रघोः **वाजिनः** अश्वाः । लग्नाः कुङ्कुमकेसराः कुङ्कुमकुसुमकिञ्जल्का येषां तान् [**लग्नकुङ्कुमकेसरान्**] । यद्वा लग्नकुङ्कुमाः केसराः सटा येषां तान् । 'अथ कुङ्कुमम् । काश्मीरजन्म' इत्यमरः । 'केसरो नागकेसरे । तुरङ्गसिंहयोः स्कन्धकेशेषु बकुलद्रुमे । पुंनागवृक्षे किञ्जल्के स्यात्' इति हैमः । **स्कन्धान्** कायान् । 'स्कन्धः प्रकाण्डे कायेऽसे विज्ञानादिषु पञ्चसु । नृपे समूहे व्यूहे च' इति हैमः । **दुधुवुः** कम्पयन्ति स्म ॥

तत्र हूणावरोधानां भर्तृषु व्यक्तविक्रमम् ।
कपोलपाटलादेशि बभूव रघुचेष्टितम् ॥ ६८ ॥

तत्र उदीच्यां दिशि **भर्तृषु व्यक्तविक्रमम्** । भर्तृवधेन स्फुटपराक्रममित्यर्थः । **रघुचेष्टितं** रघुव्यापारः । हूणा जनपदाख्याः क्षत्रियाः । [जनपदाः तत्र राजानः इ० पा०] तेषामवरोधा अन्तःपुरस्त्रियः । तासां [**हूणावरोधानां**] कपोलेषु पाटलस्य पाटलिम्नस्ताडनादिकृतारुण्यस्यादेश्युपदेशकं [**कपोलपाटलादेशि**] **बभूव** । अथ वा पाटल आदेशी आदेष्टा यस्य तद्बभूव । स्वयं लक्ष्यायत इत्यर्थः ॥

काम्बोजाः समरे सोढुं तस्य वीर्यमनीश्वराः ।
गजालानपरिक्लिष्टैरक्षोटैः सार्धमानताः ॥ ६९ ॥

काम्बोजाः राजानः **समरे तस्य** रघोः **वीर्यं** प्रभावम् । 'वीर्यं तेजःप्रभावयोः' इति हैमः । **सोढुं अनीश्वराः** अशक्ताः सन्तः । गजानामालानं बन्धनम् । भावे ल्युटि 'विभाषा लीयतेः' इत्यात्वम् । तेन परिक्लिष्टैः परिक्षतैः [**गजालानपरिक्लिष्टैः**] **अक्षोटैः सार्धम् आनताः** ॥

तेषां सदश्वभूयिष्ठास्तुङ्गा द्रविणराशयः ।
उपदा विविशुः शश्वन्नोत्सेकाः कोसलेश्वरम् ॥ ७० ॥

तेषां काम्बोजानां सद्भिरश्वैर्भूयिष्ठा बहुलाः [**सदश्वभूयिष्ठाः**] **तुङ्गाः** द्रविणानां

---

१ 'वङ्क्षुतीर-' इ. पा. । 'वङ्क्षुनाम्नी नदी' इ. व० । 'वङ्क्षुर्नाम काश्मीरो नदः' इ. दि० । २ हूणास्तुरुष्कभेदाः इ. चा० । कपोलेति–हूणयोषितः कुचकपोलविदारणपूर्वं रुदन्तीति देशाचारः । इ. चा. । ३ 'पञ्चनदं समारभ्य म्लेच्छाद्दक्षिणपूर्वतः । कम्बोजदेशो देवेशि वाजिराजिपरायणः ॥' इति तन्त्रशास्त्रोक्तदेशभवाः । ते च प्रथमं क्षत्रिया आसन् । किं तु वैदिकक्रियालोपात्पश्चान्म्लेच्छतां गताः । सगरराजेन तेषां सर्वशिरोमुण्डनं कृतम् । तथा च हरिवंशे–'अर्धं शकानां शिरसो मुण्डयित्वा व्यसर्जयत् । यवनानां शिरः सर्वं काम्बोजानां तथैव च ॥' इति । ४ अङ्कोलैः इ. पा. ५ सहोक्तिरलंकारः । 'सा सहोक्तिः सहार्थस्य बलादेकं द्विवाचकम् ।' इति काव्यप्रकाशः । ६ विविशुस्तं कोशलेशं उदन्वन्तमिवापगाः; उपदा विविशुः शश्वत्समुद्रमिव निम्नगाः; विविशुस्तं विशां नाथं महार्णवमिवापगाः; शश्वत्–तं च इ. च पाठान्तराणि ।

हिरण्यानाम् । ‘ हिरण्यं द्रविणं द्युम्नम् ’ इत्यमरः । राशयः [**द्रविणराशयः**] एव **उपदाः** उपायनानि । ‘ उपायनमुपग्राह्यमुपहारस्तथोपदा । ’ इत्यमरः । **कोसलेश्वरम्** कोसलदेशाधिपतिं तं रघुं **शश्वद्** असकृद् **विविशुः** । ‘मुहुः पुनः पुनः शश्वदभीक्ष्णमसकृत्समाः । ’ इत्यमरः । तथापि **उत्सेकाः** गर्वास्तु **न** विविशुः । सत्यपि गर्वकारणे न जगर्वेत्यर्थः ॥

ततो गौरीगुरुं शैलमारुरोहाश्वसाधनः ।
वर्धयन्निव तत्कूटानुद्धूतैर्धातुरेणुभिः ॥ ७१ ॥

ततः अनन्तरम् । **अश्वसाधनः** सन्गौर्या गुरुं पितरं [**गौरीगुरुं**] **शैलं** हिमवन्तम् **उद्धूतैः** अश्वखुरोद्धूतैर्धातूनां गैरिकादीनां रेणुभिः । [**धातुरेणुभिः**] **तत्कूटान्** तस्य शृङ्गाणि । ‘ कूटोऽस्त्री शिखरं शृङ्गम् ’ इत्यमरः । **वर्धयन्निव** । **आरुरोह** । उत्पतद्धूलिदर्शनाद्गिरिशिखरवृद्धिभ्रमो जायत इति भावः ॥

शशंस तुल्यसत्त्वानां सैन्यघोषेऽप्यसंभ्रमम् ।
गुहाशयानां सिंहानां परिवृत्यावलोकितम् ॥ ७२ ॥

तुल्यसत्त्वानां सैन्यैः समानबलानाम् । गुहासु शेरत इति गुहाशयास्तेषां [**गुहाशयानां**] । ‘ अधिकरणे शेतेः ’ इत्यच्प्रत्ययः । ‘ दरी तु कन्दरो वा स्त्री देवखातबिले गुहा । ’ इत्यमरः । **सिंहानां** हरीणाम् । ‘ सिंहो मृगेन्द्रः पञ्चास्यो हर्यक्षः केसरी हरिः । ’ इत्यमरः । संबन्धि **परिवृत्य** परावृत्य **अवलोकितं** शयित्वैव ग्रीवाभङ्गेनावलोकनम् । कर्तृ । **सैन्यघोषे** सेनाकलकले संभ्रमकारणे सति **अपि असंभ्रमम्** अन्तःक्षोभविरहितत्वम् । नञः प्रसज्यप्रतिषेधेऽपि समास इष्यते । **शशंस** कथयामास । सैन्येभ्य इत्यर्थाल्लभ्यते । बाह्यचेष्टितमेव मनोवृत्तेरनुमापकमिति भावः । असंभ्रान्तत्वे हेतुस्तुल्यसत्त्वानामिति । न हि समबलः समबलाद्बिभेतीति भावः ॥

---

१ एतेन रघोर्धीरोदात्तनायकगुणवत्त्वं सूचितम् । ‘ महासत्त्वोऽतिगम्भीरः क्षमावानविकत्थनः । स्थिरो निगूढाहंकारो धीरोदात्तो दृढव्रतः ’ ॥ इति दशरूपके । २ ‘ विविशुस्तं विशांनाथमुदन्वन्तमिवापगाः ’ इति पाठान्तरे आपगा नद्य उदन्वन्तं समुद्रमिव विशां नाथं तं रघुं विविशुः । इत्यधिकं क्वचित् । ३ उद्धतैः इ. पा० ४ हिमालये धातुबाहुल्यादिदम् । हिमाचलस्य धातुबाहुल्यं वर्णितं कुमारसंभवे–‘ यश्चाप्सरोविभ्रममण्डनानां संपादयित्रीं शिखरैर्बिभर्ति । बलाहकच्छेदविभक्तरागामकालसंध्यामिव धातुमत्ताम् ॥ ’ इति । ५ ‘ अप्राधान्यं विधेर्यत्र प्रतिषेधे प्रधानता । प्रसज्यप्रतिषेधोऽसौ क्रियया सह यत्र नञ् ॥ ’ ‘ असंभ्रमं शशंस ’ इत्यत्र सत्यपि संभ्रमकारणे संभ्रमशंसनरूपस्य विधेरविवक्षितत्वादप्रधानत्वं, संभ्रमाभावरूपस्य निषेधस्यैवात्र विवक्षितत्वात्प्राधान्यम् । तस्य निषेधस्य चात्र ‘ शशंस ’ इति क्रियया संबन्धः । एवमत्र नञः प्रसज्यप्रतिषेधत्वं ज्ञेयम् । एवं सत्यपि विधेयाविमर्शदोषदुष्टतयायं समासपक्षो गौण एव । दिनकरस्तु एतद्दोषपरिहारायान्यथा व्याचष्टे–‘प्रकरणात् स रघुरित्यध्याह्रियते । स रघुरात्मना तुल्यं सत्त्वं येषां तादृशानां गुहासु स्थितानां सिंहानां सैन्यकोलाहलेऽप्यसंभ्रमं सधैर्यं यथा स्यात्तथा परिवृत्यावलोकनं शशंस अस्तौषीत ’ इति । वल्लभोऽपि ‘ असंभ्रमम् ’ इति ‘ अवलोकितम् ’ इत्यस्य विशेषणं कृत्वा दिनकरवद्व्याचष्टे ।

भूर्जेषु मर्मरीभूताः कीचकध्वनिहेतवः ।
गङ्गाशीकरिणो मार्गे मरुतस्तं सिषेविरे ॥ ७३ ॥

भूर्जेषु भूर्जपत्रेषु । 'भूर्जपत्रो भुजो भूर्जो मृदुत्वक्चर्मिका मता ।' इति यादवः । मर्मरः शुष्कपर्णध्वनिः । 'मर्मरः शुष्कपर्णानाम्' इति यादवः । अयं च शुक्लादिशब्दवद्गुणिन्यपि वर्तते प्रयोज्यते च—'मर्मरैर्गुरुधूपगन्धिभिः' इति । अतः **मर्मरीभूताः** । मर्मरशब्दवन्तो भूता इत्यर्थः । कीचकानां वेणुविशेषाणां ध्वनिहेतवः [**कीचकध्वनिहेतवः**] । श्रोत्रसुखाश्चेति भावः । **गङ्गाशीकरिणः** । शीतला इत्यर्थः । **मरुतः** वाताः **मार्गे तं सिषेविरे** ॥

विशश्रमुर्नमेरूणां छायास्वध्यास्य सैनिकाः ।
दृषदो वासितोत्सङ्गा निषण्णमृगनाभिभिः ॥ ७४ ॥

सैनिकाः सेनायां समवेताः । प्राग्वहतीयष्ठक्प्रत्ययः । **नमेरूणां** सुरपुंनागानां **छायासु** निषण्णानां दृषदुपविष्टानां मृगाणां कस्तूरीमृगाणां नाभिभिः [**निषण्णमृगनाभिभिः**] **वासितोत्सङ्गाः** सुरभिततलाः **दृषदः** शिलाः **अध्यास्य** अधिष्ठाय । 'अधिशीङ्स्थासां कर्म' इति कर्म । दृषत्स्वधिष्ठायेत्यर्थः । **विशश्रमुः** विश्रान्ताः ॥

सरलासक्तमातङ्गग्रैवेयस्फुरितत्विषः ।
आसन्नोषधयो नेतुर्नक्तमस्नेहदीपिकाः ॥ ७५ ॥

सरलेषु देवदारुविशेषेष्वासक्तानि यानि मातङ्गानां गजानां **ग्रीवासु भवानि ग्रैवेयाणि** कण्ठशृङ्खलानि । 'ग्रीवाभ्योऽण्च' इति चकाराद् ढञ्प्रत्ययः । तेषु **स्फुरितत्विषः** प्रतिफलितभासः [**सरलासक्तमातङ्गग्रैवेयस्फुरितत्विषः**] **ओषधयः** ज्वलन्तो ज्योतिर्लताविशेषाः **नक्तं** रात्रौ **नेतुः** नायकस्य रघोः **अस्नेहदीपिकाः** तैलनिरपेक्षाः प्रदीपाः **आसन** ॥

तस्योत्सृष्टनिवासेषु कण्ठरज्जुक्षतत्वचः ।
गजवर्ष्म किरातेभ्यः शशंसुर्देवदारवः ॥ ७६ ॥

तस्य रघोः उत्सृष्टेषूज्झितेषु निवासेषु सेनानिवेशेषु [**उत्सृष्टनिवासेषु**] कण्ठरज्जुभिर्गजग्रैवैः क्षता निष्पिष्टास्त्वचो येषां ते [**कण्ठरज्जुक्षतत्वचः**] **देवदारवः**

---

१ स. २ श्लो. १२ द्रष्टव्यः । गङ्गेति—अनुरूपभावो द्वितीये—'पृक्तस्तुषारैः' इ. श्लो. १३.
२ अनुरूपवर्णनं कुमारे—गणा नमेरुप्रसवावतंसा भूर्जत्वचः स्पर्शवतीर्दधानाः । मनःशिलाविच्छुरिता निषेदुः शैलेयनद्धेषु शिलातलेषु ॥ इति ॥ ३ अग्नौ ओषधिषु च तेजो निधाय रविरस्तं याति इत्यागमः । अत्रौषधीष्वारोप्यमाणस्य प्रदीपत्वस्य प्रकृतराधिव्यवहारोपयोगित्वात्परिणामालंकारः । तदुक्तम्—'आरोप्यमाणस्य प्रकृतोपयोगित्वे परिणामः ।' इति । तथा प्रदीपकारणतैलपूरणनिषेधादकारणकार्योत्पत्तिलक्षणा विभावना चेत्युभयोः संसृष्टिः । अनुरूपवर्णनं कुमारे—वनेचराणां वनितासखानां दरीगृहोत्सङ्गनिषक्तभासः । भवन्ति यत्रौषधयो रजन्यामतैलपूराः सुरतप्रदीपाः ॥ इति ।

किरातेभ्यः वनचरेभ्यो गजानां वर्ष्म प्रमाणम् [**गजवर्ष्म**]। ' वर्ष्म देहप्रमाणयोः ' इत्यमरः । **शशंसुः** कथितवन्तः । देवदारुस्कन्धलग्नक्षतैर्गजानामौन्नत्यमनुमीयत इत्यर्थः ॥

तत्र जन्यं रघोर्घोरं पर्वतीयैर्गणैरभूत् ।
नाराचक्षेपणीयाश्मनिष्पेषोत्पतितानलम् ॥ ७७ ॥

तत्र हिमाद्रौ **रघोः** । पर्वते भवैः **पर्वतीयैः** । ' पर्वताच्च ' इति छप्रत्ययः । **गणैः** उत्सवसंकेताख्यैः सप्तभिः सह । ' गणानुत्सवसंकेतानजयत्सप्त पाण्डवः । ' इति महाभारते । नाराचानां बाणविशेषाणां क्षेपणीयानां भिन्दिपालानामश्मनां च निष्पेषेण संघर्षेणोत्पतिता अनला यस्मिंस्तत्तथोक्तम् [**नाराचक्षेपणीयाश्मनिष्पेषोत्पतितानलम्**] । क्षेपणीयो भिन्दिपालः खड्गो दीर्घो महाफलः ।' इति यादवः । **घोरं** भीमं **जन्यं** युद्धं **अभूत्** । ' युद्धमायोधनं जन्यम् ' इत्यमरः ॥

शरैरुत्सवसंकेतान्स कृत्वा विरतोत्सवान् ।
जयोदाहरणं बाह्वोर्गापयामास किंनरान् ॥ ७८ ॥

स रघुः **शरैः** बाणैः **उत्सवसंकेतान्** नाम गणान् **विरतोत्सवान् कृत्वा** । जित्वेत्यर्थः । **किंनरान् बाह्वोः** स्वभुजयोः **जयोदाहरणं** जयख्यापकं प्रबन्धविशेषं **गापयामास** । ' गतिबुद्धि–' इत्यादिना किंनराणां कर्मत्वम् ॥

परस्परेण विज्ञातस्तेषूपायनपाणिषु ।
राज्ञा हिमवतः सारो राज्ञः सारो हिमाद्रिणा ॥ ७९ ॥

तेषु गणेषूपायनयुक्ताः पाणयो येषां तेषु [**उपायनपाणिषु**] सत्सु । **परस्परेण** अन्योन्यं **राज्ञा हिमवतः सारः** धनरूपो **विज्ञातः** । **हिमाद्रिणा** अपि **राज्ञः सारः** बलरूपः **विज्ञातः** । एतेन तत्रत्यवस्तूनामनर्घ्यत्वं गणानामभूतपूर्वश्च पराजय इति ध्वन्यते ॥

तत्राक्षोभ्यं यशोराशिं निवेश्यावरुरोह सः ।
पौलस्त्यतुलितस्याद्रेरादधान इव ह्रियम् ॥ ८० ॥

---

१ अनुरूपवर्णनं शिशुपालवधे–'वर्ष्म द्विपानां विरुवन्त उच्चकैर्वनेचरेभ्यश्चिरमाचचक्षिरे । गण्डस्थलाघर्षगलन्मदोदकद्रवद्रुमस्कन्धनिलायिनोऽलयः ॥' स० १२–६४. २ संग्रामः सह तैस्तत्र पार्वतीयैरभूद्रघोः इति. विमर्दः सह तैस्तत्र ... । ... नानलः ॥ इ० प्र० द्वि० पादयोः पा० । ३ पार्वतीयैः इति पाठे पर्वतीयानामिमे पार्वतीयाः गणास्तैः इति व्याख्येयम् । ४ उत्सवसंकेतादयः सप्त गणा हिमालये वसन्ति इति महाभारतेऽपि वर्णितम् । 'पौरवं युधि निर्जित्य दस्यून्पर्वतवासिनः । गणानुत्सव० ' इति । ५ 'यशो जयोदाहरणम् ' इति हैमः उ. चा०। प्रतापरुद्रस्तु--' येन केनापि तालेन गद्यपद्यसमन्वितम् । जयत्युपक्रमं मालिन्यादिप्रासविचित्रितम् । तदुदाहरणं नाम विभक्त्यष्टाङ्कसंयुतम् ॥ ' इति उदाहरणलक्षणमाचष्टे । किंनरान्--कुत्सिता नराः । तेषामश्वमुखत्वान्नरदेहत्वाच्च । एव किंपुरुषा इत्यादिकाः संज्ञाश्च । ६ उत्सवसंकेतानामित्यर्थः ।

स रघुः **तत्र** हिमाद्रौ **अक्षोभ्यं** अधृष्यं **यशोराशिं निवेश्य** निधाय । पौलस्त्येन रावणेन तुलितस्य चालितस्य [**पौलस्त्यतुलितस्य**] **अद्रेः** कैलासस्य **ह्रियं आदधानः** जनयन् **इव** । **अवरुरोह** अवततार । कैलासमगत्वैव प्रतिनिवृत्त इत्यर्थः । न हि शूराः परेण पराजितमभियुज्यन्त इति भावः ॥

चकम्पे तीर्णलौहित्ये तस्मिन्प्राग्ज्योतिषेश्वरः ।
तद्गजालानतां प्राप्तैः सह कालागुरुद्रुमैः ॥ ८१ ॥

तस्मिन् रघौ । तीर्णो लौहित्यो नाम नदी येन तस्मिन् **तीर्णलौहित्ये** सति । प्राग्ज्योतिषाणां जनपदानामीश्वरः [**प्राग्ज्योतिषेश्वरः**] । तस्य रघोर्गजानामालानतां [**तद्गजालानतां**] **प्राप्तैः कालागुरुद्रुमैः** कृष्णागुरुवृक्षैः **सह चकम्पे** कम्पितवान् ॥

न प्रसेहे स रुद्धार्कमधारावर्षदुर्दिनम् ।
रथवर्त्मरजोऽप्यस्य कुत एव पताकिनीम् ॥ ८२ ॥

स प्राग्ज्योतिषेश्वरः **रुद्धार्कम्** आवृतसूर्यम् । अधारावर्षं च तद्दुर्दिनं च [**अधारावर्ष-दुर्दिनम्**] धारावृष्टिं विना दुर्दिनीभूतम् । **अस्य** रघोः **रथवर्त्मरजः अपि न प्रसेहे** । **पताकिनीं** सेनां तु **कुत एव** प्रसेहे । न कुतोऽपीत्यर्थः ॥

तमीशः कामरूपाणमत्याखण्डलविक्रमम् ।
भेजे भिन्नकटैर्नागैरन्यानुपरुरोध यैः ॥ ८३ ॥

कामरूपाणां नाम देशानां **ईशः अत्याखण्डलविक्रमं** अतीन्द्रपराक्रमं **तं** रघुम् । भिन्नाः स्रवन्मदाः कटा गण्डा येषां तैः [**भिन्नकटैः**] **नागैः** गजैः साधनैः **भेजे** । नागान्दत्त्वा शरणं गत इत्यर्थः । कीदृशैर्नागैः । **यैः अन्यान्** रघुव्यतिरिक्तान् नृपान् **उपरुरोध** । शूराणामपि शूरो रघुरिति भावः ॥

---

१ पुलस्त्यस्य गोत्रापत्यं पुमान्पौलस्त्यः । एकदा कुबेरं जित्वा तत्पुष्पकमपहृत्य गच्छतो रावणस्य विमानं कैलासिकदेशं प्राप्य निश्चलमभूत् । अत्रान्तरे नन्दिनाऽऽगत्य ‘ अगम्यादस्माच्छंकरविहारशैलान्निवर्तस्व ’ इति स आदिष्टः । ‘ अचिन्तयित्वा स तदा नन्दिवाक्यं महाबलः । पर्वतं तु समासाद्य वाक्यमाह दशाननः । पुष्पकस्य गतिश्छिन्ना यत्कृते मम गच्छतः । तमिमं शैलमुन्मूलं करोमि तव गोपते ॥ * * * एवमुक्त्वा ततो राम भुजान् विक्षिप्य पर्वते । तोलयामास तं शीघ्रं स शैलः समकम्पत ॥ ’ इति रामायणकथाऽत्रानुसंधेया ॥

२ लौहित्यः—अयं नदः कैलासे लौहित्यसरस उत्पन्नत्वात् लौहित्यः ब्रह्मतेजःसंभूततया च ब्रह्मपुत्र इति प्रसिद्धिं गतः । परशुरामः किल कुठारेण पर्वतं भित्त्वा तन्मार्गेण नदमिमं पृथिव्यां प्रवर्तयामास । तथा प्रवर्तितः स कामरूपादिदेशमाप्लावयन्वहति । तदुक्तं कालिकापुराणे—जातसंप्रत्ययः सोऽथ तीर्थमासाद्य तं वरम् । वीथिं परशुना कृत्वा ब्रह्मपुत्रमवाहयत् । ब्रह्मकुण्डात्सुतः सोऽयं कासारे लोहिताह्वये । कैलासोपत्यकायां तु न्यपतद् ब्रह्मणः सुतः ॥ * * तस्य नाम विधिश्चक्रे स्वयं लोहितगङ्गकम् । लौहित्यात्सरसो जातो लौहित्याख्यस्ततोऽभवत् ॥ स कामरूपमखिलं पीठमाप्लाव्य वारिणा । गोपयन्सर्वतीर्थानि दक्षिणं याति सागरम् ॥ इति ॥ प्राग्ज्योतिषव्युत्पत्तिः कालिकापुराणे—अत्रैव हि स्थितो ब्रह्मा प्राङ् नक्षत्रं ससर्ज ह । ततः प्राग्ज्योतिषाख्येयं पुरी शक्रपुरीसमा ॥ ३ अतिक्रान्त आखण्डलस्य विक्रमो येन तम् ।

कामरूपेश्वरस्तस्य हेमपीठाधिदेवताम् ।
[1]रत्नपुष्पोपहारेण च्छायामानर्च पादयोः ॥ ८४ ॥

कामरूपेश्वरः हेमपीठस्याधिदेवतां [**हेमपीठाधिदेवताम्**] **तस्य** रघोः **पादयोः** **छायां** कनकमयपादपीठव्यापिनीं कान्तिं रत्नान्येव पुष्पाणि तेषामुपहारेण समर्पणेन [**रत्नपुष्पोपहारेण**] **आनर्च** अर्चयामास ॥

इति जित्वा दिशो जिष्णुर्न्यवर्तत रथोद्धतम्[2] ।
रजो विश्रामयन्राज्ञां छत्रशून्येषु मौलिषु ॥ ८५ ॥

जिष्णुः जयशीलः । 'ग्लाजिस्थश्च ग्स्नुः' इति ग्स्नुप्रत्ययः । स रघुः **इति** इत्थं **दिशः** **जित्वा** रथैरुद्धतं [**रथोद्धतं**] **रजः**। **छत्रशून्येषु** । रघोरेकच्छत्रकत्वादिति भावः । **राज्ञां** **मौलिषु** किरीटेषु । 'मौलिः किरीटे धम्मिल्ले चूडाकङ्केलिमूर्धसु ।' इति हैमः । **विश्रामयन्** । संक्रामयन्नित्यर्थः । **न्यवर्तत** निवृत्तः ॥

स विश्वजितमाजह्रे[3] यज्ञं सर्वस्वदक्षिणम् ।
आदानं हि विसर्गाय सतां वारिमुचामिव ॥ ८६ ॥

स रघुः सर्वस्वं दक्षिणा यस्य तं **सर्वस्वदक्षिणम्** । 'विश्वजित्सर्वस्वदक्षिणः' इति श्रुतेः । **विश्वजितं** नाम **यज्ञं** **आजह्रे** । कृतवानित्यर्थः । युक्तं चैतदित्याह—**सतां** साधूनाम् । **वारिमुचां** मेघानां **इव** **आदानम्** अर्जनं **विसर्गाय** त्यागाय **हि** । पात्रविनियोगायेत्यर्थः[4] ॥

सत्रान्ते सचिवसखः पुरस्क्रियाभि—
र्गुर्वीभिः शमितपराजयव्यलीकान् ।
काकुत्स्थश्चिरविरहोत्सुकावरोधा—
न्राजन्यान्स्वपुरनिवृत्तयेऽनुमेने ॥ ८७ ॥

काकुत्स्थः रघुः **सत्रान्ते** यज्ञान्ते । 'सत्रमाच्छादने यज्ञे सदादाने वनेऽपि च' इत्यमरः । सचिवानाममात्यानां सखेति **सचिवसखः** सन् । 'सचिवो भृतकेऽमात्ये' इति हैमः । तेषामत्यन्तानुसरणद्योतनार्थं राज्ञः सखित्वव्यपदेशः । 'राजाहःसखिभ्यष्टच्' । **गुर्वीभिः** महतीभिः । 'गुरुर्महत्याङ्गिरसे पित्रादौ धर्मदेशके ।' इति हैमः । **पुरस्क्रियाभिः** पूजाभिः शमितं पराजयेन व्यलीकं दुःखं वैलक्ष्यं वा येषां तान् [**शमितपराजयव्यलीकान्**] । 'दुःखे वैलक्ष्ये व्यलीकम्' इति यादवः । चिरविरहेणोत्सुका उत्कण्ठिता अवरोधा अन्तःपुराङ्गना येषां तान् [**चिरविरहोत्सुकावरोधान्**]। राज्ञोऽपत्यानि राजन्याः क्षत्रियास्तान् [**राजन्यान्**]। 'राजश्वशुराद्यत्' इत्यपत्यार्थे यत्प्रत्ययः । 'मूर्धाभिषिक्तो राजन्यो बाहुजः क्षत्रियो विराट्' इत्यमरः । स्वपुरं प्रति निवृत्तये प्रतिगमनाय [**स्वपुरनिवृत्तये**] **अनुमेने** अनुज्ञातवान् । प्रहर्षिणीवृत्तमेतत् । तदुक्तम्—'म्नौ ज्रौ गस्त्रिदशयतिः प्रहर्षिणीयम् ।' इति ॥

---

१ 'हेमपुष्पो०' इ. पा. २ 'रथोद्धतम्' इ. पा. ३ 'आरेभे' इ. चा० दि० मु० व० ध० दयः पठन्ति । ४ यथा जलदानां समुद्राज्जलग्रहणं विसर्गाय वृष्टये भवति तथा सज्जनानामपि । इ. सु० । ५ सीदन्त्यस्मिन्निति सत्रम् ।

ते रेखाध्वजकुलिशातपत्रचिह्नं
सम्राजश्चरणयुगं प्रसादलभ्यम् ।
प्रस्थानप्रणतिभिरङ्गुलीषु चक्रु-
र्मौलिस्रक्च्युतमकरन्दरेणुगौरम् ॥ ८८ ॥

ते राजानः । [**रेखाध्वजकुलिशातपत्रचिह्नं**] रेखा एव ध्वजाश्च कुलिशानि चातपत्राणि च । ध्वजाद्याकाररेखा इत्यर्थः । तानि चिह्नानि यस्य तत्तथोक्तम् । प्रसादेनैव लभ्यं **प्रसादलभ्यम्** । **सम्राजः** सार्वभौमस्य रघोः **चरणयुगं** प्रस्थाने प्रयाणसमये याः प्रणतयो नमस्कारास्ताभिः [**प्रस्थानप्रणतिभिः**] करणैः **अङ्गुलीषु** । मौलिषु केशबन्धनेषु याः स्रजो माल्यानि ताभ्यश्च्युतैर्मकरन्दैः पुष्परसैः । 'मकरन्दः पुष्परसः' इत्यमरः । रेणुभिः परागैश्च । 'परागः सुमनोरजः' इत्यमरः । गौरं गौरवर्णं [**मौलिस्रक्च्युतमकरन्दरेणुगौरं**] **चक्रुः** ॥

इति महामहोपाध्यायकोलाचलमल्लिनाथसूरिविरचितया संजीवनीसमाख्यया व्याख्यया समेतो महाकविश्रीकालिदासकृतौ रघुवंशे महाकाव्ये रघुदिग्विजयो नाम चतुर्थः सर्गः ।

पञ्चमः सर्गः ।

इन्दीवरदलश्यामामिन्दिरानन्दकन्दलम् ।
वन्दारुजनमन्दारं वन्देऽहं यदुनन्दनम् ॥

तमध्वरे विश्वजिति क्षितीशं निःशेषविश्राणितकोषजातम् ।
उपात्तविद्यो गुरुदक्षिणार्थी कौत्सः प्रपेदे वरतन्तुशिष्यः ॥ १ ॥

विश्वजिति विश्वजिन्नाम्नि **अध्वरे** यज्ञे । 'यज्ञः सवोऽध्वरो यागः' इत्यमरः । [**निःशेषविश्राणितकोषजातम्**] निःशेषं विश्राणितं दत्तम् । 'श्रण दाने' चुरादिः । कोषाणामर्थराशीनां जातं समूहो येन तं तथोक्तम् । 'कोषोऽस्त्री कुड्मले खड्गपिधानेऽर्थौघदिव्ययोः' इत्यमरः । 'जातं जनिसमूहयोः' इति शाश्वतः । एतेन कौत्सस्यानवसरप्राप्तिं सूचयति । **तं क्षितीशं** रघुं **उपात्तविद्यः** लब्धविद्यो वरतन्तोः शिष्यः [**वरतन्तुशिष्यः**] **कौत्सः** । 'ऋष्यन्धक–' इत्यण् । इञोऽपवादः । **गुरुदक्षिणार्थी** । 'पुष्करादिभ्यो देशे' इत्यत्रार्थाच्चासंनिहिते तदन्ताच्चेतीनिः । अप्रत्याख्येय इति भावः । **प्रपेदे** प्राप । अस्मिन्सर्गे वृत्तमुपजातिः ।

---

१ यदुक्तं सामुद्रके–यस्य पादतले पद्मं चक्रं वाऽप्यथ तोरणम् । अङ्कुशं कुलिशं छत्रं स सम्राड् भवति ध्रुवम् ॥ इति । अस्मात्परं श्लोकमेकं पठन्ति दि० व० सु० यादयः । यथा–

यज्ञान्ते तमवभृथाभिषेकपूतं सत्कारैः शमितपराजयव्यलीकाः ।
आमन्त्र्योत्सुकवनितानिरुद्धचित्ताः स्वानि स्वान्यवनिभुजः पुराणि जग्मुः ॥

२ इन्दीवरं नीलकमलं तस्य दलवत् श्यामम् । इन्दिरा लक्ष्मीस्तस्या आनन्दस्य कन्दलं विकासभूतम् । वन्दारुजनो भक्तजनस्तस्य मन्दारं कल्पवृक्षम् । एवंविधं यदुनन्दनं कृष्णमहं वन्दे । ३ अध्वरशब्दनिरुक्तिस्तूक्ता (स० १ श्लो० ३१). ४ उपात्ता अधीताः चतुर्दश विद्या येन । २१ श्लोके तथोक्तत्वात् । विद्या अपि तत्रैवोक्ताः टीकाकृता ।

तल्लक्षणं तु–'स्यादिन्द्रवज्रा यदि तौ जगौ ग उपेन्द्रवज्रा जतजास्ततो गौ । अनन्तरोदीरित-लक्ष्मभाजौ पादौ यदीयावुपजातयस्ताः ॥' इति ॥

स मृन्मये वीतहिरण्मयत्वात्पात्रे निधायार्घ्यमनर्घशीलः ।
श्रुतप्रकाशं यशसा प्रकाशः प्रत्युज्जगामातिथिमातिथेयः ॥ २ ॥

अनर्घशीलः अमूल्यस्वभावः । असाधारणस्वभाव इत्यर्थः । 'मूल्ये पूजाविधावर्घः' इति, 'शीलं स्वभावे सद्वृत्ते' इति चामरशाश्वतौ । **यशसा** कीर्त्या । प्रकाशत इति **प्रकाशः** । पचाद्यच् । अतिथिषु साधुः **आतिथेयः** । 'पथ्यतिथिवसतिस्वपतेर्ढञ्' इति ढञ् । **स** रघुः । हिरण्यस्य विकारो हिरण्मयम् । 'दाण्डिनायन–' आदिसूत्रेण निपातः । **वीतहिरण्मयत्वात्** अपगतसुवर्णपात्रत्वात् । यज्ञस्य सर्वस्वदक्षिणाकत्वादिति भावः । **मृन्मये** मृद्विकारे **पात्रे** । अर्घार्थमिदं **अर्घ्यम्** । 'पादार्घाभ्यां च' इति यत् । पूजार्थं द्रव्यं **निधाय** श्रुतेन शास्त्रेण प्रकाशं प्रसिद्धम् [**श्रुतप्रकाशं**] । श्रूयत इति श्रुतं वेदशास्त्रम् । 'श्रुतं शास्त्रावधृतयोः' इत्यमरः । **अतिथिं** अभ्यागतं कौत्सम् । 'अतिथिर्ना गृहागते' इत्यमरः । **प्रत्युज्जगाम** ॥

तमर्चयित्वा विधिवद्विधिज्ञस्तपोधनं मानधनाग्रयायी ।
विशांपतिर्विष्टरभाजमारात्कृताञ्जलिः कृत्यविदित्युवाच ॥ ३ ॥

विधिज्ञः शास्त्रज्ञः । अकरणे प्रत्यवायभीरुरित्यर्थः । मानधनानामग्रयायी अग्रेसरः [**मान-धनाग्रयायी**] । अपयशोभीरुरित्यर्थः । **कृत्यवित्** कार्यज्ञः । आगमनप्रयोजनमवश्यं प्रष्टव्य-मिति कृत्यवित् । **विशांपतिः** मनुजेश्वरः । 'द्वौ विशौ वैश्यमनुजौ' इत्यमरः । **विष्टर-भाजम्** आसनगतम् । उपविष्टमित्यर्थः । 'विष्टरो विटपी दर्भमुष्टिः पीठाद्यमासनम् ।' इत्यमरः । 'वृक्षासनयोर्विष्टरः' इति निपातः । **तं तपोधनं विधिवत्** विध्यर्हम् । यथाशास्त्रमित्यर्थः । 'तदर्हम्' इति वतिप्रत्ययः । **अर्चयित्वा आरात्** समीपे । 'आराद्दूरसमीपयोः' इत्यमरः । **कृताञ्जलिः** सन् **इति** वक्ष्यमाणप्रकारेण **उवाच** ॥

अप्यग्रणीर्मन्त्रकृतामृषीणां कुशाग्रबुद्धे कुशली गुरुस्ते ।
यतस्त्वया ज्ञानमशेषमाप्तं लोकेन चैतन्यमिवोष्णरश्मेः ॥ ४ ॥

कुशाग्रबुद्धे सूक्ष्मबुद्धे । 'कुशाग्रीयमतिः प्रोक्तः सूक्ष्मदर्शी च यः पुमान् ।' इति हलायुधः । **मन्त्रकृतां** मन्त्रद्रष्टॄणाम् । 'सुकर्मपापमन्त्र–' इत्यादिना क्विप् । **ऋषीणाम् अग्रणीः** श्रेष्ठः **ते** तव **गुरुः कुशली अपि** क्षेमवान्किम् । अपि प्रश्ने । 'गर्हासमुच्चयप्रश्नशङ्का-संभावनास्वपि ।' इत्यमरः । **यतः** यस्माद्गुरोः सकाशात् **त्वया अशेषं ज्ञानम् लोकेन उष्णरश्मेः** सूर्यात् **चैतन्यं** प्रबोधः **इव** । **आप्तम्** स्वीकृतम् ॥

---

१ तदुक्तं मनुना–संप्राप्ताय त्वतिथये प्रदद्यादासनोदके । अन्नं चैव यथाशक्ति सत्कृत्य विधि-पूर्वकम् ॥ २ 'चैतन्यमुग्रादिव दीक्षितेन' इ. हे० व० पटतः । वल्लभो व्याचष्टे च–यथा दीक्षितेन याज्ञिकेनोग्रादीश्वराच्चैतन्यमाप्यते ज्ञानं प्राप्यते इ० । 'चैतन्यम्–आलोकम्––अर्कादिव जीवलोकः' इति च पा०. ३ 'वेदसंहिताकारिणाम्' इति चा० । ४ सूर्यसाम्याद् गुरोर्ज्ञानतेजसोऽज्ञानतिमिर-ध्वंसः सूचितः । उक्तं च—'अज्ञानतिमिरान्धस्य ज्ञानाञ्जनशलाकया । चक्षुरुन्मीलितं येन तस्मै श्रीगुरवे नमः ॥' इति ।

कायेन वाचा मनसाऽपि शश्वद्यत्संभृतं वासवधैर्यलोपि ।
आपाद्यते न व्ययमन्तरायैः कच्चिन्महर्षेस्त्रिविधं तपस्तत् ॥ ५ ॥

कायेन उपवासादिकृच्छ्रचान्द्रायणादिना **वाचा** वेदपाठेन **मनसा** गायत्रीजपादिना **अपि**। करणेन। वासवस्येन्द्रस्य धैर्यं लुम्पतीति **वासवधैर्यलोपि**। स्वपदापहारशङ्काजनक-मित्यर्थः। **यत्** तपः **शश्वद्** असकृत्। 'मुहुः पुनः पुनः शश्वदभीक्ष्णमसकृत्समाः।' इत्यमरः। **संभृतं** संचितम् **महर्षेः** वरतन्तोः **त्रिविधं** वाङ्मनःकायजं **तत् तपः अन्तरायैः** विघ्नैरिन्द्रप्रेरिताप्सरःशापैः **व्ययं** नाशं **न आपाद्यते कच्चित्** न नीयते किम्। 'कच्चित्कामप्रवेदने' इत्यमरः ॥

आधारबन्धप्रमुखैः प्रयत्नैः संवर्धितानां सुतनिर्विशेषम् ।
कच्चिन्न वाय्वादिरुपप्लवो वः श्रमच्छिदामाश्रमपादपानाम् ॥ ६ ॥

आधारबन्धप्रमुखैः आलवालनिर्माणादिभिः **प्रयत्नैः** उपायैः। 'आधार आलवालेऽम्बुबन्धेऽधिकरणेऽपि च।' इति विश्वः। [**सुतनिर्विशेषम्**] सुतेभ्यो निर्गतो विशेषोऽतिशयो यस्मिन्कर्मणि तत्तथा। **संवर्धितानां श्रमच्छिदां वः आश्रमपादपानां वाय्वादिः**। आदिशब्दाद्दावानलादिः। **उपप्लवः** बाधकः **न कच्चित्** नास्ति किम् ॥

क्रियानिमित्तेष्वपि वत्सलत्वादभग्नकामा मुनिभिः कुशेषु ।
तदङ्कशय्याच्युतनाभिनाला कच्चिन्मृगीणामनघा प्रसूतिः ॥ ७ ॥

क्रियानिमित्तेष्वपि अनुष्ठानसाधनेष्वपि **कुशेषु मुनिभिः वत्सलत्वाद्** मृग-स्नेहाद् **अभग्नकामा** अप्रतिहतेच्छा। [**तदङ्कशय्याच्युतनाभिनाला**] तेषां मुनी-नामङ्क एव शय्यास्तासु च्युतानि नाभिनालानि यस्याः सा तथोक्ता। **मृगीणां प्रसूतिः** संततिः **अनघा** अव्यसना **कच्चित्**। अनपायिनी किमित्यर्थः। 'दुःखैनोव्यसनेष्वघम्' इति यादवः। ते हि व्यालभयाद्दशरात्रमङ्क एव धारयन्ति ॥

निर्वर्त्यते यैर्नियमाभिषेको येभ्यो निवापाञ्जलयः पितॄणाम् ।
तान्युञ्छषष्ठाङ्कितसैकतानि शिवानि वस्तीर्थजलानि कच्चित् ॥ ८ ॥

---

१ 'यद्वज्रिणो धैर्यविलोपि तप्तम्' इ० पा. २ इन्द्रप्रेरिताप्सरोभिः शापेन च इत्य०। इन्द्रस्य हि अन्यसमाधिभीरुत्वं कवयस्तत्र तत्र वर्णयन्ति। यथा कुमारे—'कनाभ्यसूयया पदकांक्षिणा ते नितान्तदीर्घैर्जनिता तपोभिः॥' अग्रेऽप्यष्टमसर्गे—'चरतः किल' इत्यादि। त्रयोदशे-'समाधिभीतेन किल' (३९) इत्या०, 'नालं विकर्तुम्' (४२) इ० च। अन्यस्मात्त्राणाभावे मुनयोऽन्तरायशान्त्यर्थं शापप्रयोगेन तपोव्ययं कुर्वन्ति। उक्तं च पञ्चदशे—'त्राणाभावे हि शापास्त्राः कुर्वन्ति तपसो व्ययम्' इति। ३ 'कच्चित् इष्टप्रियप्रश्ने' इत्यभिधानचिन्तामणिः। कोमलामन्त्रणे इ. ४ 'वृक्षकाणाम्' इति दि० पठति। तेऽप्यतिथिसंभावनया पुत्रवदुपकुर्वन्ति। यदुक्तं त्रयोदशे छायाविनीताध्वपरिश्रमेषु भूयिष्ठसंभाव्यफलेष्वमीषु। तस्यातिथीनामधुना सपर्या स्थिता सुपुत्रेष्विव पादपेषु॥ (४६) इति। ५ 'न हि व्यालभयाद्दशरात्रमङ्क एव धारयन्ति इति शान्तिदयोक्तिः' इ. हे०।

यैः तीर्थजलैः **नियमाभिषेकः** नित्यस्नानादि **निर्वर्त्यते** निष्पाद्यते। **येभ्यः** जलेभ्यः। उद्धृत्येति शेषः। **पितॄणां** अग्निष्वात्तादीनां **निवापाञ्जलयः** तर्पणाञ्जलयः। 'पितृदानं निवापः स्यात्' इत्यमरः। निर्वर्त्यन्ते। [**उञ्छषष्ठाङ्कितसैकतानि**] उञ्छानां प्रकीर्णोद्धृतधान्यानां षष्ठैः षष्ठभागैः पालकत्वाद्राजग्राह्यैरङ्कितानि सैकतानि पुलिनानि येषां तानि तथोक्तानि। **वः** युष्माकं **तानि तीर्थजलानि शिवानि** भद्राणि **कच्चित्**। अनुपप्लवानि किमित्यर्थः। 'उञ्छो धान्यांशकादानं कणिशाद्यर्जनं शिलम्।' इति यादवः। 'षष्ठाष्टमाभ्यां ञ च' इति षष्ठशब्दाद्भागार्थेऽन्प्रत्ययः। अत एवापूरणार्थत्वात् 'पूरणगुण-' इत्यादिना न षष्ठीसमासप्रतिषेधः। सिकता येषु सन्ति सैकतानि। 'सिकताशर्कराभ्यां च' इत्यण्प्रत्ययः॥

नीवारपाकादि कडंगरीयैरामृश्यते जानपदैर्न कच्चित्।
कालोपपन्नातिथिकल्प्यभागं वन्यं शरीरस्थितिसाधनं वः॥ ९॥

[**कालोपपन्नातिथिकल्प्यभागं**] कालेषु योग्यकालेषूपपन्नानामागतानामतिथीनां कल्प्या भागा यस्य तत्तथोक्तम्। वने भवं **वन्यम्**। शरीरस्थितेर्जीवितस्य साधनं [**शरीरस्थितिसाधनं**] **वः** युष्माकम्। पच्यत इति पाकः फलम्। धान्यमिति यावत्। **नीवारपाकादि**। आदिशब्दाच्छ्यामाकादिधान्यसंग्रहः। जनपदेभ्य आगतैः **जानपदैः**। 'तत आगतः' इत्यण्। **कडंगरीयैः**। कडंगरं बुसमर्हन्तीति कडंगरीयाः। 'कडंगरो बुसं क्लीबे धान्यत्वचि तुषः पुमान्।' इत्यमरः। 'कडंगरदक्षिणाच्छ च' इति छप्रत्ययः। तैर्गोमहिष्यादिभिः **न आमृश्यते कच्चित्**। न भक्ष्यते किमित्यर्थः॥

अपि प्रसन्नेन महर्षिणा त्वं सम्यग्विनीयानुमतो गृहाय।
कालो ह्ययं संक्रमितुं द्वितीयं सर्वोपकारक्षममाश्रमं ते॥ १०॥

किं च **त्वं प्रसन्नेन** सता **महर्षिणा सम्यग्विनीय** शिक्षयित्वा। विद्यामुपदिश्येत्यर्थः। **गृहाय** गृहस्थाश्रमं प्रवेष्टुम्। 'क्रियार्थोपपद-' इत्यादिना चतुर्थी। **अनुमतः अपि** अनुज्ञातः किम्। **हि** यस्मात् **ते** तव सर्वेषामाश्रमाणां ब्रह्मचर्यवानप्रस्थयती-

---

१ नियमेन नित्यकर्तव्यतया अभिषेकः। अत्र कात्यायनः–'यथाहानि तथा प्रातर्नित्यं स्नायादनातुरः।' इति। जाबालिश्च-'आचरेदुषसि स्नानं तर्पयेद्देवमानुषान्।' इति। २ अग्निष्वात्तादीनाम्। मरीचिपुत्रा देवपितरश्चाग्निष्वात्तसंज्ञाः। यथाह मनुः–विराट्सुताः सोमसदः साध्यानां पितरः स्मृताः। अग्निष्वात्ताश्च देवानां मारीच्या लोकविश्रुताः॥ ३ उञ्छषष्ठेत्यत्र हेमाद्रिः–मुनयो हि नृपोद्देशेन षष्ठं भागं तीरे क्षिपन्ति। यदुक्तम्—'यस्मादारण्यका अप्युञ्छषष्ठभागं निर्वापयन्ति।' इति श्रुतेः। योऽस्मान्पालयतीति। 'कुशूलकुम्भीधान्यो वा त्र्याहिकोऽश्वस्तनोऽपि वा। जीवेद्वाऽपि शिलोञ्छेन श्रेयानेषां परः परः॥' इति याज्ञवल्क्यः। मुनयो हि नृपोद्देशेन षष्ठं भागं तीरे क्षिपन्ति। योऽस्मान्पालयति तस्मै षष्ठोऽयं भागः। इति व०। उञ्छवृत्तौ मनुः—'शिलोञ्छमप्याददीत विप्रो जीवत्यतस्ततः।' इति। ४ अत्र हेमाद्रिव्याख्या यथा–पाकशब्दोऽल्पार्थः प्रशंसार्थश्च। तथा त्रयः पाकयज्ञा इत्यत्राश्वलायनगृह्यनारायणीयवृत्तौ–पाकयज्ञा अल्पयज्ञाः प्रशस्तयज्ञाश्च। अल्पप्रशस्तयोरुभयोः पाकशब्दः। योऽस्मात्पाकतर इत्यत्राल्पत्वे पाकशब्दः। तं पाकेन मनसाऽपश्यं यो मां पाकेन मनसेत्यत्र प्रशंसायामिति।

नामुपकारे क्षमं शक्तम् [**सर्वोपकारक्षमम्**] । ' क्षमं शक्ते हिते त्रिषु ' इत्यमरः । **द्वितीयं आश्रमं** गार्हस्थ्यं **संक्रमितुं** प्राप्तुं **अयं कालः** । विद्याग्रहणानन्तर्यात्तस्येति भावः । ' कालसमयवेलासु तुमुन् ' इति तुमुन् । सर्वोपकारक्षममित्यत्र मनुः–' यथा मातरमाश्रित्य सर्वे जीवन्ति जन्तवः । वर्तन्ते गृहिणस्तद्वदाश्रित्येतर आश्रमाः ॥ ' इति ॥

कुशलप्रश्नं विधायागमनप्रयोजनप्रश्नं चिकीर्षुराह—

तवार्हतो नाभिगमेन तृप्तं मनो नियोगक्रिययोत्सुकं मे ।
अप्याज्ञया शासितुरात्मना वा प्राप्तोऽसि संभावयितुं वनान्माम् ११

अर्हतः पूज्यस्य प्रशस्तस्य । ' अर्हः प्रशंसायाम् ' इति शतृप्रत्ययः । **तव अभिगमेन** आगमनमात्रेण **मे मनः न तृप्तं** न तुष्टम् । किंतु **नियोगक्रियया** आज्ञाकरणेन **उत्सुकं** सोत्कण्ठम् । ' इष्टार्थोद्युक्त उत्सुकः ' इत्यमरः । ' प्रसितोत्सुकाभ्यां तृतीया च ' इति सप्तम्यर्थे तृतीया । **शासितुः** गुरोः **आज्ञया अपि आत्मना** स्वतः **वा** । ' प्रकृत्यादिभ्य उपसंख्यानम् ' इति तृतीया । **मां संभावयितुं वनात् प्राप्तोऽसि** । गुर्वर्थं स्वार्थं वा आगमनमित्यर्थः ॥

इत्यर्घ्यपात्रानुमितव्ययस्य रघोरुदारामपि गां निशम्य ।
स्वार्थोपपत्तिं प्रति दुर्बलाशस्तमित्यवोचद्वरतन्तुशिष्यः ॥ १२ ॥

अर्घ्यपात्रेण मृन्मयेनानुमितो व्ययः सर्वस्वत्यागो यस्य तस्य [**अर्घ्यपात्रानुमितव्ययस्य**] **रघोः इति** उक्तप्रकारां **उदाराम्** औदार्ययुक्तां **अपि गां** वाचम् । ' मनो नियोगक्रिययोत्सुकं मे ' इत्येवंरूपाम् । ' स्वर्गेषुपशुवाग्वज्रदिङ्नेत्रघृणिभूजले । लक्ष्यदृष्ट्या स्त्रियां पुंसि गौः ' इत्यमरः । **निशम्य** श्रुत्वा **वरतन्तुशिष्यः** कौत्सः **स्वार्थोपपत्तिं** स्वकार्यसिद्धिं **प्रति दुर्बलाशः** मृन्मयपात्रदर्शनाच्छिथिलमनोरथः सन् **तं** रघुम् **इति** वक्ष्यमाणप्रकारेण **अवोचत्** ॥

सर्वत्र नो वार्तमवेहि राजन्नाथे कुतस्त्वय्यशुभं प्रजानाम् ।
सूर्ये तपत्यावरणाय दृष्टेः कल्पेत लोकस्य कथं तमिस्रा ॥ १३ ॥

हे **राजन्** त्वं **सर्वत्र नः** अस्माकं **वार्तं** स्वास्थ्यम् **अवेहि** जानीहि । ' वार्तं फल्गुन्यरोगे च ' इत्यमरः । ' वार्तं पाटवमारोग्यं भव्यं स्वास्थ्यमनामयम् । ' इति यादवः ।

---

१ यथाह मनुः–' वेदानधीत्य वेदौ वा वेदं वापि यथाक्रमम् । अविप्लुतब्रह्मचर्यो गृहस्थाश्रममाविशेत् । गुरुणानुमतः स्नात्वा समावृत्तो यथाविधि ॥ ' इति । अ. २. श्लो. ७७, ७८. अ. ६. श्लो. ८९, ९० द्रष्टव्याः । २ अनुग्रहेणाभिगमाश्रितेन तवार्हतस्तुष्य(स्तृप्य) ति मे न चेतः । इ. दि० पठति । ३ धातूनामनेकार्थत्वात् । प्रेयोनामालंकारः । तथा काव्यादर्शे–' प्रेयः प्रियतराख्यानम् ' इ. हे० । ४ ' तं प्रत्यवोचत् ' हे० व० । ' प्रत्याह कौत्सस्तमपेतकुत्सम् ' इ. दि० ध० वि० । ५ ' गुर्वाश्रमप्रभृतिषु ' इति दि० ।

न चैतदाश्चर्यमित्याह–नाथ इति । **त्वयि नाथे** ईश्वरे सति **प्रजानाम् अशुभं** दुःखं **कुतः** ? तथा हि । अर्थान्तरं[१] न्यस्यति–सूर्य इत्यादिना । **सूर्ये तपति** प्रकाशमाने सति **तमिस्रा** तमस्ततिः । 'तमिस्रं तिमिरे रोगे तमिस्रा तु तमस्ततौ । कृष्णपक्षनिशायां च' इति विश्वः । 'तमिस्रम्' इति पाठे तमिस्रं तिमिरम् । 'तमिस्रं तिमिरं तमः' इत्यमरः । **लोकस्य** जनस्य । 'लोकस्तु भुवने जने' इत्यमरः । **दृष्टेः आवरणाय कथं कल्पेत** । दृष्टिमावरितुं नालमित्यर्थः । क्रियेरलमर्थत्वात्तद्योगे 'नमःस्वस्ति–' इत्यादिना चतुर्थी । 'अलमिति पर्याप्त्यर्थग्रहणम्' इति भगवान्भाष्यकारः । [यद्वा] कथं कल्पेत संपद्येत । न कल्पेतेत्यर्थः । 'क्लृपि संपद्यमाने च' इति चतुर्थी ॥

'तवार्हतः–' (५।११) इत्यादिनोक्तं यत्तन्न चित्रमित्याह—

भक्तिः प्रतीक्ष्येषु कुलोचिता ते पूर्वान्महाभाग तयाऽतिशेषे ।
व्यतीतकालस्त्वहमभ्युपेतस्त्वामर्थिभावादिति मे विषादः ॥ १४ ॥

प्रतीक्ष्येषु पूज्येषु । 'पूज्यः प्रतीक्ष्यः' इत्यमरः । **भक्तिः** अनुरागविशेषः **ते** तव **कुलोचिता** कुलाभ्यस्ता । 'अभ्यस्तेऽप्युचितं न्याय्यम्' इति यादवः । हे **महाभाग** सार्वभौम **तया** भक्त्या **पूर्वान् अतिशेषे** अतिवर्तसे । [तु] किं तु सर्वत्र वार्तं चेत्तर्हि कथं खेदखिन्न इव दृश्यसेऽत आह–व्यतीतेति । **अहं व्यतीतकालः** अतिक्रान्तकालः सन् **अर्थिभावात् त्वाम् अभ्युपेतः इति मे** मम **विषादः** ॥

शरीरमात्रेण नरेन्द्र तिष्ठन्नाभासि तीर्थप्रतिपादितर्द्धिः ।
आरण्यकोपात्तफलप्रसूतिः स्तम्बेन नीवार इवावशिष्टः ॥ १५ ॥

हे **नरेन्द्र** [**तीर्थप्रतिपादितर्द्धिः**] तीर्थे सत्पात्रे प्रतिपादिता दत्ता ऋद्धिर्येन स तथोक्तः । 'योनौ जलावतारे च मन्त्र्याद्यष्टादशस्वपि । पुण्यक्षेत्रे तथा पात्रे तीर्थं स्याद्दर्शनेष्वपि ॥' इति हलायुधः । **शरीरमात्रेण तिष्ठन्** । आरण्यका अरण्ये भवा मनुष्या मुनिप्रमुखाः । 'अरण्यान्मनुष्ये' इति वुञ्प्रत्ययः । तैरुपात्ता फलमेव प्रसूतिर्यस्य स [**आरण्यकोपात्तफलप्रसूतिः**] **स्तम्बेन** काण्डेन **अवशिष्टः** । प्रकृत्यादित्वात्तृतीया । **नीवारः इव** । **आभासि** शोभसे ॥

स्थाने भवानेकनराधिपः सन्नकिंचनत्वं मखजं व्यनक्ति ।
पर्यायपीतस्य सुरैर्हिमांशोः कलाक्षयः श्लाघ्यतरो हि वृद्धेः ॥ १६ ॥

भवान् एकनराधिपः सार्वभौमः **सन्** । **मखजं** मखजन्यम् । न विद्यते किंचन यस्येत्यकिंचनः । मयूरव्यंसकादित्वात्तत्पुरुषः । तस्य भावस्तत्त्वं [**अकिंचनत्वं**] निर्धनत्वं **व्यनक्ति** प्रकटयति । **स्थाने** युक्तम् । 'युक्ते द्वे सांप्रतं स्थाने' इत्यमरः । तथा हि । **सुरैः**

---

१ एतत्प्राचां मतेन । अत्र द्वितीयार्धगतेन वाक्यार्थेन प्रथमार्धगतार्थस्य समर्थनादर्थान्तरन्यासालंकारः । तदुक्तं दण्डिना–'ज्ञेयः सोऽर्थान्तरन्यासो वस्तु प्रस्तुत्य किंचन । तत्साधनसमर्थस्य न्यासो योऽन्यस्य वस्तुनः ॥' इति । अनुरूपः श्लोकः शाकुन्तले–'कुतो धर्मक्रियाविघ्नः सतां रक्षितरि त्वयि । तमस्तपति घर्मांशौ कथमाविर्भविष्यति ॥' इति । २ दिनकरस्तु 'महाभागतया' इत्येकं पदं पठित्वा महाभागस्य भावो महाभागता तया उत्कृष्टभाग्यत्वेन–इति व्याचष्टे ।

देवैः पर्यायेण क्रमेण पीतस्य [**पर्यायपीतस्य**] **हिमांशोः कलाक्षयः वृद्धेः** उपचयात् **श्लाघ्यतरः हि वरः** खलु । 'मणिः शाणोल्लीढः समरविजयी हेतिनिहतो मदक्षीणो नागः शरदि सरितः श्यानपुलिनाः । कलाशेषश्चन्द्रः सुरतमृदिता बालवनिता तानिम्ना शोभन्ते गलितविभवाश्चार्थिषु नृपाः ॥' इति भावः । अत्र कामन्दकः–'धर्मार्थे क्षीणकोशस्य क्षीणत्वमपि शोभते । सुरैः पीतावशेषस्य कृष्णपक्षे विधोरिव ॥' इति ॥

तदन्यतस्तावदनन्यकार्यो गुर्वर्थमाहर्तुमहं यतिष्ये ।
स्वस्त्यस्तु ते निर्गलिताम्बुगर्भं शरद्घनं नार्दति चातकोऽपि ॥ १७ ॥

तद् तस्मात् **तावदनन्यकार्यः** । 'यावत्तावच्च साकल्येऽवधौ मानेऽवधारणे ।' इति विश्वः । प्रयोजनान्तररहितः । **अहं अन्यतः** वदान्यान्तराद् **गुर्वर्थं** गुरुधनं **आहर्तुम्** अर्जयितुं **यतिष्ये** उद्योक्ष्ये । **ते** तुभ्यं **स्वस्ति** शुभं **अस्तु** । 'नमःस्वस्ति–' इत्यादिना चतुर्थी । तथा हि । **चातकोऽपि** । 'धरणीपतितं तोयं चातकानां रुजाकरम्' इति हेतोरनन्यगतिकोऽपीत्यर्थः । निर्गलितोऽम्ब्वेव गर्भो यस्य तं [**निर्गलिताम्बुगर्भं**] **शरद्घनं न अर्दति** न याचते । 'अर्द गतौ याचने च' इति धातुः । 'याचनार्थे रणेऽर्दनम्' इति यादवः ॥

---

१ 'चन्द्रमा वा अमावास्यायामादित्यमनुप्रविशति । सोऽन्तर्धीयते । तं निर्जानन्ति ॥' इति ऐतरेयब्राह्मणम् । चन्द्रस्य किल षोडश कलाः । तासां पञ्चदश कलाः कृष्णपक्षे देवैः पर्यायेण पीयन्ते । एवं निपीत एकया कलयावशिष्टश्चन्द्रोऽमावास्यायां सूर्यं प्रविशति । स च तं शुक्लपक्षे कलाभिर्वर्धयति । इति पौराणिका मन्यन्ते । तथा च देवीपुराणे–'कलाः षोडश सोमस्य शुक्ले वर्धयते रविः । अमृतेनामृतं कृष्णे पीयते दैवतैः क्रमात् ॥ प्रथमां पिबते वह्निर्द्वितीयां पवनः कलाम् । विश्वेदेवास्तृतीयां तु चतुर्थीं तु प्रजापतिः । पञ्चमीं वरुणश्चापि षष्ठीं पिबति वासवः । सप्तमीमृषयो दिव्या वसवोऽष्टौ तथाष्टमीम् । नवमीं कृष्णपक्षस्य पिबतीन्द्रः कलामपि । दशमीं मरुतश्चापि रुद्रा एकादशीं कलाम् । द्वादशीं तु कलां विष्णुर्धनदश्च त्रयोदशीम् । चतुर्दशीं पशुपतिः कलां पिबति नित्यशः । ततः पञ्चदशीं चैव पिबन्ति पितरः कलाम् । कलावशिष्टो निष्पीतः प्रविष्टः सूर्यमण्डलम् । अमायां विशते यस्मादमावाशी ततः स्मृतः ॥' मतान्तरे यथा–'प्रथमां पिबते वह्निर्द्वितीयां पिबते रविः । विश्वे देवास्तृतीयां तु चतुर्थीं सलिलाधिपः ॥ पञ्चमीं तु वषट्कारः षष्ठीं पिबति वासवः । सप्तमीमृषयो दिव्या अष्टमीमज एकपात् ॥ नवमीं कृष्णपक्षस्य यमः प्राश्नाति वै कलाम् । दशमीं पिबते वायुः पिबत्येकादशीमुमा ॥ द्वादशीं पितरः सर्वे समं प्राश्नन्ति भागशः । त्रयोदशीं धनाध्यक्षः कुबेरः पिबते कलाम् ॥ चतुर्दशीं पशुपतिः पञ्चदशीं प्रजापतिः । निष्पीतः कलावशेषश्चन्द्रमा न प्रकाशते ॥ कला षोडशिका या तु अपः प्रविशति सदा । अमायां तु सदा सोम ओषधीः प्रतिपद्यते ॥ तमोषधिगतं गावः पिबन्त्यम्बुगतं च यत् । तत्क्षीरममृतं भूत्वा मन्त्रपूतं द्विजातिभिः ॥ हुतमग्निषु यज्ञेषु पुनराप्याय्यते शशी । दिने दिने कलावृद्धिः पौर्णमास्यां तु पूर्णता ॥' इति माधवीये कालनिर्णये । २ 'शुक्लप्रतिपदि सर्वे क्षीणमपि चन्द्रं नमस्कुर्वन्ति । यदुक्तं किराते–प्रणमन्त्यनपायमुत्थितं प्रतिपच्चन्द्रमिव प्रजा नृपम्' इ. सु० । एवं वृद्धचाणक्येऽपि–'गुणाः सर्वत्र पूज्यन्ते न महत्योऽपि संपदः । पूर्णेन्दुः किं तथा वन्द्यो निष्कलङ्को यथा कृशः ॥' इति ॥ ३ 'अपिशब्दश्चातकस्य जलदैकशरणत्वसूचनार्थः' इति चा. हे० । 'किं पुनर्विद्यमानोपायोऽहं त्वामित्यर्थः' इ. हे० । उक्तं च–'पयोद हे वारि ददासि वा न वा त्वदेकचित्तः पुनरेष चातकः । वरं महत्या म्रियेत पिपासया तथाऽपि नान्यस्य करोत्युपासनाम् ॥' इति । अर्थान्तरन्यासोऽलंकारः ।

एतावदुक्त्वा प्रतियातुकामं शिष्यं महर्षेर्नृपतिर्निषिध्य ।
किं वस्तु विद्वन्गुरवे प्रदेयं त्वया कियद्वेति तमन्वयुङ्क्त ॥ १८ ॥

एतावद् वाक्यम् **उक्त्वा** प्रतियातुं कामो यस्य तं **प्रतियातुकामं** गन्तुकामम् । 'तुम्काममनसोरपि' इति मकारलोपः । **महर्षेः** वरतन्तोः **शिष्यं** कौत्सं **नृपतिः** रघुः **निषिध्य** निवार्य । हे **विद्वन् त्वया गुरवे प्रदेयं वस्तु किं कियत्** किंपरिमाणं **वा** । **इति** एवं **तं** कौत्सम् **अन्वयुङ्क्त** अपृच्छत् । 'प्रश्नोऽनुयोगः पृच्छा च' इत्यमरः ॥

ततो यथावद्विहिताध्वराय तस्मै स्मयावेशविवर्जिताय ।
वर्णाश्रमाणां गुरवे स वर्णी विचक्षणः प्रस्तुतमाचचक्षे ॥ १९ ॥

ततो यथावद् यथार्हम् । अर्हार्थे वतिः । **विहिताध्वराय** विधिवदनुष्ठितयज्ञाय । सदाचारायेत्यर्थः । **स्मयावेशविवर्जिताय** गर्वाभिनिवेशशून्याय । अनुद्धतायेत्यर्थः । वर्णानां ब्राह्मणादीनामाश्रमाणां ब्रह्मचर्यादीनां च [**वर्णाश्रमाणां**] **गुरवे** नियामकाय । 'वर्णाः स्युर्ब्राह्मणादयः' इति, 'ब्रह्मचारी गृही वानप्रस्थो भिक्षुश्चतुष्टये । आश्रमोऽस्त्री' इति चामरः । सर्वकार्यनिर्वाहकायेत्यर्थः । **तस्मै** रघवे **विचक्षणः** विद्वान् **वर्णी** ब्रह्मचारी । 'वर्णिनो ब्रह्मचारिणः' इत्यमरः । 'वर्णाद् ब्रह्मचारिणि' इतीनिप्रत्ययः । **स** कौत्सः **प्रस्तुतं** प्रकृतम् **आचचक्षे** ॥

समाप्तविद्येन मया महर्षिर्विज्ञापितोऽभूद्गुरुदक्षिणायै ।
स मे चिरायास्खलितोपचारां तां भक्तिमेवागणयत्पुरस्तात् ॥ २० ॥

समाप्तविद्येन मया महर्षिः गुरुदक्षिणायै गुरुदक्षिणास्वीकारार्थं **विज्ञापितः अभूत्** । **स** च गुरुः **चिराय अस्खलितोपचारां तां** दुष्करां **मे भक्तिमेव पुरस्तात्** प्रथमं **अगणयत्** संख्यातवान् । भक्त्यैव संतुष्टः किं दक्षिणयेत्युक्तवानित्यर्थः । अथ वा भक्तिमेव तां दक्षिणामगणयदिति योज्यम् ॥

निर्बन्धसंजातरुषाऽर्थकार्श्यमचिन्तयित्वा गुरुणाऽहमुक्तः ।
वित्तस्य विद्यापरिसंख्यया मे कोटीश्चतस्रो दश चाहरेति ॥ २१ ॥

निर्बन्धेन प्रार्थनातिशयेन संजातरुषा संजातक्रोधेन [**निर्बन्धसंजातरुषा**] **गुरुणा** । **अर्थकार्श्यं** दारिद्र्यम् **अचिन्तयित्वा** अविचार्य **अहम्** । **वित्तस्य** धनस्य **चतस्रः**

---

१ 'अनूपसर्गेण सहितो युजिः पृच्छार्थः' हे० चा० २ स्मयस्यावेशस्तेन विवर्जिताय । गुरवे-क्रियाग्रहणमपि कर्तव्यमिति क्रियाग्रहणाच्चतुर्थी । तत्तद्धर्मप्रतिष्ठापकत्वाद्राजा वर्णाश्रमगुरुः रक्षणाच्च । तदुक्तं मनुना—'स्वे स्वे धर्मे निविष्टानां सर्वेषामनुपूर्वशः । वर्णानामाश्रमाणां च राजा सृष्टोऽभिरक्षिता ॥' इति । वर्णी-'वर्णः प्रशस्तिः' इति क्षीरस्वामी । विशेषस्तु किरा० टीकायां प्र. स. प्र. श्लो० व्याख्याने मल्लिनाथेनोक्तो द्रष्टव्यः । यद्वा तपोविद्याजन्या प्रशस्तिः वर्णोऽस्यास्तीति वर्णी । ३ अवाप्तविद्येन इ. दि. पठन्ति । ४ 'पादप्रक्षालनादिरुपचारः परिचर्या यस्यां सा तां तथोक्ताम् ।' हे० चा० । शुश्रूषाशून्यायोपदेशो न वक्तव्यः ॥ यथा मनुः-धर्मार्थौ यत्र न स्यातां शुश्रूषा वाऽपि तद्विधा ॥ तत्र विद्या न वक्तव्या शुद्धं बीजमिवोषरे । भगवद्गीतासु च—'इदं ते नातपस्काय नाभक्ताय कदाचन । न चाशुश्रूषवे वाच्यम्' इति । 'यथा खात्वा खनित्रेण भूतले वारि विन्दति । तथा गुरुगतां विद्यां शुश्रूषुरधिगच्छति ॥' इ. वृद्धचाणक्ये ।

दश च कोटीः चतुर्दशकोटीः **मे** मह्यम् **आहर** आनय **इति विद्यापरिसंख्यया** विद्यापरिसंख्यानुसारेणैव **उक्तः** । अत्र मनुः—' अङ्गानि वेदाश्चत्वारो मीमांसा न्यायविस्तरः । पुराणं धर्मशास्त्रं च विद्या ह्येताश्चतुर्दश ॥ ' इति ॥

सोऽहं सपर्याविधिभाजनेन मत्वा भवन्तं प्रभुशब्दशेषम् ।
अभ्युत्सहे संप्रति नोपरोद्धुमल्पेतरत्वाच्छ्रुतनिष्क्रयस्य ॥ २२ ॥

सोऽहं सपर्याविधिभाजनेन अर्घ्यपात्रेण **भवन्तं** प्रभुशब्द एव शेषो यस्य तं [**प्रभुशब्दशेषं**] **मत्वा** । निःस्वं निश्चित्येत्यर्थः । **श्रुतनिष्क्रयस्य** विद्यामूल्यस्य **अल्पेतरत्वाद्** अतिमहत्त्वात् **संप्रति उपरोद्धुं** निर्बन्द्धुं **न अभ्युत्सहे** ॥

इत्थं द्विजेन द्विजराजकान्तिरावेदितो वेदविदां वरेण ।
एनोनिवृत्तेन्द्रियवृत्तिरेनं जगाद भूयो जगदेकनाथः ॥ २३ ॥

द्विजराजकान्तिः चन्द्रकान्तिः । ' द्विजराजः शशधरो नक्षत्रेशः क्षपाकरः । ' इत्यमरः । ' तस्मात्सोमो राजा नो ब्राह्मणानाम् ' इति श्रुतेः । द्विजराजकान्तित्वेनार्थावाप्तिवैराग्यं वारयति । एनसः पापान्निवृत्ता इन्द्रियवृत्तिर्यस्य स [**एनोनिवृत्तेन्द्रियवृत्तिः**] **जगदेकनाथः** रघुः **वेदविदां वरेण** श्रेष्ठेन **द्विजेन** कौत्सेन **इत्थं आवेदितः** निवेदितः सन् । **एनं** कौत्सं **भूयः** पुनः **जगाद** ॥

गुर्वर्थमर्थी श्रुतपारदृश्वा रघोः सकाशादनवाप्य कामम् ।
गतो वदान्यान्तरमित्ययं मे मा भूत्परीवादनवावतारः ॥ २४ ॥

श्रुतस्य पारं दृष्टवान् **श्रुतपारदृश्वा** । ' दृशेः क्वनिप् ' इति क्वनिप् । **गुर्वर्थं** गुरुदक्षिणार्थं यथा तथा **अर्थी** याचकः । विशेषणद्वयेनास्यास्य प्रत्याख्येयत्वमाह । **रघोः सकाशात् कामं** मनोरथम् **अनवाप्य** अप्राप्य **वदान्यान्तरं** दात्रन्तरं **गतः** । ' स्युर्वदान्यस्थूललक्ष्यदानशौण्डा बहुप्रदे । ' इत्यमरः । **इति** एवंरूपः **अयं** परीवादस्य नवो नूतनः प्रथमोऽवतार आविर्भावः [**परीवादनवावतारः**] **मे मा भूत्** मास्तु । रघोरिति स्वनामग्रहणं संभावितद्योतनार्थम् । तथा च—'संभावितस्य चाकीर्तिर्मरणादतिरिच्यते' इति भावः ॥

स त्वं प्रशस्ते महिते[3] मदीये वसंश्चतुर्थोऽग्निरिवाग्न्यगारे ।
द्वित्राण्यहान्यर्हसि सोढुमर्हन्यावद्यते साधयितुं त्वदर्थम् ॥ २५ ॥

स त्वं महिते पूजिते **प्रशस्ते** प्रसिद्धे[4] **मदीये अग्न्यगारे** त्रेताग्निशालायां **चतुर्थः अग्निरिव वसन् द्वित्राणि** द्वे त्रीणि वा **अहानि** दिनानि । 'संख्ययाव्ययासन्नादूराधिक-

---

१ अनेन धार्मिकत्वमुक्तम् । अनुप्रासालंकारः । २ यतो रघवो यथाकामार्चितार्थिनः । तदुक्तं प्रथमसर्गे ' यथाकामार्चितार्थिनाम् । ' एकादशेपि ' अप्यसुप्रणयिनां रघोः कुले न व्यहन्यत कदाचिदर्थिता ' इति । ' अवतारावतरयोर्दीर्घह्रस्वव्यत्यासो चालिशानामिति वामनः ' इ. हे० । रघोः इ०—निःस्वेभ्यो दानं विद्यानुरूपमिति मनूक्त्या अप्रत्याक्षेपप्रीतिनिन्दाप्रतिषेधाद्रघोरात्मस्तुतिर्दोषः । तदाह—' गुरोरर्थमर्थयत ' इति हे० । अनवाप्य कामम् अनवाप्तकामः इ. पाठः । ३ ' महितः ' इ. पा० । ४ मनोहरे इति चा० । ५ पिता वै गार्हपत्योऽग्निर्माताऽग्निर्दक्षिणः स्मृतः । गुरुराहवनीयस्तु साग्नित्रेता गरीयसी ॥ इति मनुः ।

संख्याः संख्येये ' इति बहुव्रीहिः । ' बहुव्रीहौ संख्येये डजबहुगणात् ' इति डच्प्रत्ययः समासान्तः । **सोढुम् अर्हसि** । हे **अर्हन्** मान्य[1] **त्वदर्थं** तव प्रयोजनं **साधयितुं यावद् यते** यतिष्ये । ' यावत्पुरानिपातयोर्लट् ' इति भविष्यदर्थे लट् ॥

तथेति तस्यावितथं[2] प्रतीतः प्रत्यग्रहीत्संगरमग्रजन्मा ।

गामात्तसारां रघुरप्यवेक्ष्य निष्क्रष्टुमर्थं चकमे कुबेरात् ॥ २६ ॥

अग्रजन्मा[3] ब्राह्मणः **प्रतीतः** प्रीतः सन् **तस्य** रघोः **अवितथम्** अमोघं **संगरं** प्रतिज्ञाम् । ' अथ प्रतिज्ञाजिसंविदापत्सु संगरः । ' इत्यमरः । ' तां गिरम् ' इति केचित्पठन्ति । **तथेति प्रत्यग्रहीत्** । **रघुः अपि गां** भूमिम् **आत्तसारां** गृहीतधनां **अवेक्ष्य कुबेरात् अर्थं निष्क्रष्टुम्** आहर्तुं **चकमे** इयेष ॥

वसिष्ठमन्त्रोक्षणजात्प्रभावादुदन्वदाकाशमहीधरेषु ।

मरुत्सखस्येव बलाहकस्य गतिर्विजघ्ने न हि तद्रथस्य ॥ २७ ॥

वसिष्ठस्य यन्मन्त्रेणोक्षणमभिमन्त्र्य प्रोक्षणं तज्जात् [**वसिष्ठमन्त्रोक्षणजात्**] **प्रभावात्**[4] सामर्थ्याद्धेतोः । **उदन्वदाकाशमहीधरेषु** उदन्वत्युदधावाकाशे महीधरेषु वा । **मरुत्सखस्य**[5] । मरुतः सखेति तत्पुरुषः, बहुव्रीहौ समासान्ताभावात् । ततो वायुसहायस्येति लभ्यते । वारीणां वाहको बलाहकः । पृषोदरादित्वात्साधुः । तस्य [**बलाहकस्य**] **इव** मेघस्येव । **तद्रथस्य गतिः** संचारः **न विजघ्ने** न विहता **हि** ॥

अथाधिशिश्ये प्रयतः प्रदोषे रथं रघुः कल्पितशस्त्रगर्भम् ।

सामन्तसंभावनयैव धीरः कैलासनाथं तरसा जिगीषुः ॥ २८ ॥

अथ प्रदोषे रजनीमुखे । तत्काले यानाधिरोहणविधानात् । **प्रयतः धीरः रघुः** समन्ताद्भवः सामन्तः[6] राजमात्रमिति संभावनया [**सामन्तसंभावनया**] **एव कैलासनाथं** कुबेरं **तरसा** बलेन **जिगीषुः** जेतुमिच्छुः सन् । कल्पितं सज्जितं शस्त्रं गर्भे यस्य तं [**कल्पितशस्त्रगर्भम्**] **रथं अधिशिश्ये** । रथे शयितवानित्यर्थः । ' अधिशीङ्स्थासां कर्म ' इति कर्मत्वम् ॥

प्रातः प्रयाणाभिमुखाय तस्मै सविस्मयाः कोषगृहे नियुक्ताः ।

हिरण्मयीं कोषगृहस्य मध्ये वृष्टिं शशंसुः पतितां नभस्तः ॥ २९ ॥

---

१ ' अर्हन्तौ जिनसन्मान्यौ ' इति यादवः । २ ' अवितथप्रयत्नः ' इति पा० । ३ अग्रजन्मा-अग्रे जन्म यस्य । वर्णेषु मध्ये अग्रजातत्वात् । अग्रात्प्रधानाङ्गान्मुखाज्जातत्वात् । ' ब्राह्मणोऽस्य मुखमासीत् ' इति, यो ' ब्रह्माणं विदधाति पूर्वं यश्चास्मै प्रहिणोति वेदम् ' इति च श्रुतिः । तथा च ताण्ड्यमहाब्राह्मणे-' सोऽकामयत यज्ञं सृजेयेति स मुखत एव त्रिवृतमसृजत * * * * तस्मात्त्रिवृत्सोमानां मुखं......ब्राह्मणो मनुष्याणां...तस्माद् ब्राह्मणो मुखेन वीर्यं करोति मुखतो हि सृष्टः । ' इति । ४ अत्र रघोः कार्ये चित्तस्यानाकुलत्वमुक्तम् । उक्तं च माघकाविना-' आरभन्तेऽल्पमेवाज्ञाः कामं व्यग्रा भवन्ति च । महारम्भाः कृतधियस्तिष्ठन्ति च निराकुलाः ॥ ' इति । ५ बलाहकेन गत्यर्थं वायोरपेक्षितत्वान्मरुत्सखा यस्येति अभिमतः समासः । एवं सति ' राजाहःसखिभ्यष्टच् ' इति टच्प्रत्ययो न स्यात् तस्य तत्पुरुषेऽभिधानात् । अनश्चिन्त्यमेतत् । इति चा० हे० दि० । ६ ' कतिपयग्रामपतिः सामन्तः ' हे० ।

प्रातः प्रयाणाभिमुखाय तस्मै रघवे कोषगृहे नियुक्ताः अधिकृता भाण्डागारिकाः **सविस्मयाः** सन्तः **कोषगृहस्य मध्ये नभस्तः** नभसः । पञ्चम्यास्तसिल्प्रत्ययः । **पतितां हिरण्मयीं** सुवर्णमयीम् । 'दाण्डिनायन–' इत्यादिना निपातनात्साधुः । **वृष्टिं शशंसुः** कथयामासुः ॥

तं भूपतिर्भासुरहेमराशिं लब्धं कुबेरादभियास्यमानात् ।
दिदेश कौत्साय समस्तमेव पादं सुमेरोरिव वज्रभिन्नम् ॥ ३० ॥

भूपतिः रघुः । **अभियास्यमानात्** अभिगमिष्यमाणात **कुबेरात्लब्धम्** । वज्रेण कुलिशेन भिन्नं [**वज्रभिन्नं**] **सुमेरोः पादं** प्रत्यन्तपर्वतम् **इव** स्थितम् । 'पादाः प्रत्यन्तपर्वताः' इत्यमरः । 'शृङ्गं सुमेरोः' इति क्वचित्पाठः । **तं** भासुरं भास्वरम् । 'भञ्जभासमिदो घुरच्' । हेमराशिं [**भासुरहेमराशिम्**] **समस्तं** कृत्स्नम् **एव कौत्साय दिदेश** ददौ । न तु चतुर्दशकोटिमात्रमित्येवकारार्थः ॥

जनस्य साकेतनिवासिनस्तौ द्वावप्यभूतामभिनन्द्यसत्त्वौ ।
गुरुप्रदेयाधिकनिःस्पृहोऽर्थी नृपोऽर्थिकामादधिकप्रदश्च ॥ ३१ ॥

तौ अर्थिदातारौ **द्वौ अपि साकेतनिवासिनः** अयोध्यावासिनः । 'साकेतः स्यादयोध्यायां कोसला नन्दिनी च सा ।' इति यादवः । **जनस्य अभिनन्द्यसत्त्वौ** स्तुत्यव्यवसायौ **अभूताम्** । 'द्रव्यासुव्यवसायेषु सत्त्वमस्त्री तु जन्तुषु ।' इत्यमरः । कौ द्वौ । गुरुप्रदेयादधिकेऽतिरिक्तद्रव्ये निस्पृहः [**गुरुप्रदेयाधिकनिःस्पृहः**] **अर्थी** । **अर्थिकामाद्** अर्थिमनोरथाद् [**अधिकप्रदः**] अधिकं प्रददातीति तथोक्तः । 'प्रे दाज्ञः' इति कप्रत्ययः । **नृपः च** ॥

अथोष्ट्रवामीशतवाहितार्थं प्रजेश्वरं प्रीतमना महर्षिः ।
स्पृशन्करेणानतपूर्वकायं संप्रस्थितो वाचमुवाच कौत्सः ॥ ३२ ॥

अथ प्रीतमना महर्षिः कौत्सः संप्रस्थितः प्रस्थास्यमानः **सन्** । 'आशंसायां भूतवच्च' इति भविष्यदर्थे क्तः । उष्ट्राणां क्रमेलकानां वामीनां वडवानां च शतैर्वाहितार्थं प्रापितधनम् [**उष्ट्रवामीशतवाहितार्थं**] **आनतपूर्वकायम्** । विनयनम्रमित्यर्थः । **प्रजेश्वरं** रघुः **करेण स्पृशन् वाचम् उवाच** ॥

किमत्र चित्रं यदि कामसूर्भूर्वृत्ते स्थितस्याधिपतेः प्रजानाम् ।
अचिन्तनीयस्तु तव प्रभावो मनीषितं द्यौरपि येन दुग्धा ॥ ३३ ॥

---

१ कौत्साय–कौत्सस्य, पादम्–शृङ्गं, शैलम् इ. पा० । २ वाचमुवाच–अत्र हेमाद्रिः–विशेषणं विना वाक्शब्दप्रयोगश्चिन्त्यः । यद्वामनः–विशेष्यस्य च विशेषणप्रतिपन्यर्थमुक्तार्थस्य प्रयोगः । यद्वा काव्येषु संक्षेपानादरः । तथा काव्यादर्शे–अलंकृतमसंक्षिप्तं–काव्यमिति वक्ष्यमाणेन संबन्धः । काशिकावृत्तौ च—'समुच्चये सामान्यवचनस्येत्यत्र लौकिकशब्दव्यवहारे लाघवं नाद्रियते ' इति । 'येनाङ्गविकारः' इत्यत्र पाणिनीयमतदर्पणे च-'अक्षादिशब्देन विनापि देहः स्यादेव काणादिगुणप्रतीतेः । तथापि लोके गुरुलाघवं प्रत्यनादरात् शब्दमपि प्रयुङ्क्ते ॥' इति । चारित्रवर्धनोऽपि-'शुचिस्मितां वाचमवोचदच्युतः' इत्यादौ यथा शुचिस्मितामिति विशेषणं तथात्र वाचो विशेषणायोगात् 'वाचमुवाच' इति चिन्त्यम् ।

वृत्ते स्थितस्य । 'न्यायेनार्जनमर्थस्य वर्धनं पालनं तथा । सत्पात्रे प्रतिपत्तिश्च राजवृत्तं चतुर्विधम् ॥' इति कामन्दकः । तस्मिन्वृत्ते स्थितस्य **प्रजानां अधिपतेः** नृपस्य भूः कामान्सूते इति **कामसूः यदि** । 'सत्सूद्विषद्रुह–' इत्यादिना क्विप् । **अत्र** कामप्रसवने **किं चित्रम्** । न चित्रमित्यर्थः । किं तु **तव प्रभावः** महिमा **तु अचिन्तनीयः** । **येन** त्वया **द्यौः अपि मनीषितम्** अभिलषितं **दुग्धा** । दुहेर्द्विकर्मकत्वादप्रधाने कर्मणि क्तः । 'प्रधानकर्मण्याख्येये लादीनाहुर्द्विकर्मणाम् । अप्रधाने दुहादीनां ण्यन्ते कर्तुश्च कर्मणः ॥' इति स्मरणात् ॥

आशास्यमन्यत्पुनरुक्तभूतं श्रेयांसि सर्वाण्यधिजग्मुषस्ते ।
पुत्रं लभस्वात्मगुणानुरूपं भवन्तमीड्यं[2] भवतः पितेव ॥ ३४ ॥

सर्वाणि श्रेयांसि शुभानि **अधिजग्मुषः** प्राप्तवतः **ते** तव **अन्यत्** पुत्रातिरिक्तम् **आशास्यम्** आशीःसाध्यमाशंसनीयं वा **पुनरुक्तभूतं[3]** सर्वं सिद्धमित्यर्थः । किं तु **ईड्यं** स्तुत्यं **भवन्तं भवतः पिता इव आत्मगुणानुरूपम्** । त्वया तुल्यगुणमित्यर्थः । **पुत्रं लभस्व** प्राप्नुहि ॥

इत्थं प्रयुज्याशिषमग्रजन्मा राज्ञे प्रतीयाय गुरोः सकाशम् ।
राजाऽपि लेभे सुतमाशु तस्मादालोकमर्कादिव जीवलोकः ॥ ३५ ॥

अग्रजन्मा ब्राह्मणः । 'अग्रजन्मा द्विजे श्रेष्ठे भ्रातरि ब्रह्मणि स्मृतः ।' इति विश्वः । **इत्थं राज्ञे आशिषं प्रयुज्य** दत्त्वा **गुरोः सकाशं** समीपं **प्रतीयाय** प्राप । **राजा अपि** । **जीवलोकः** जीवसमूहः । 'जीवः प्राणिनि गीष्पतौ' इति विश्वः । **अर्कात् आलोकं** प्रकाशम् **इव** । 'चैतन्यम्' इति पाठे ज्ञानम् । **तस्माद्[4]** ऋषेः **आशु सुतं लेभे** प्राप ॥

ब्राह्मे मुहूर्ते किल तस्य देवी कुमारकल्पं सुषुवे कुमारम् ।
अतः पिता ब्रह्मण एव नाम्ना तमात्म[5]जन्मानमजं चकार ॥ ३६ ॥

तस्य रघोः **देवी[6]** महिषी **ब्राह्मे[7]** । 'तस्येदम्' इत्यण् । ब्रह्मदेवताकेऽभिजिन्नामके **मुहूर्ते किल** । ईषदसमाप्तं कुमारं **कुमारकल्पं** स्कन्दसदृशम् । 'ईषदसमाप्तौ'

---

१ यद्वा 'गुरोः पूजा घृणा शौचं सत्यमिन्द्रियनिग्रहः । प्रवर्तने हितानां च तत्सर्वं वृत्तमुच्यते ॥ इति हे० । २ ईड्यः' इ. पा. ३ पुनरुक्तमिव । इवार्थे भूतशब्दः 'मातृभूतः' 'पितृभूतः' इत्यत्र भूतशब्दस्येवोपमानार्थत्वमिति कैयटेन प्रत्यपादि । इति चा० । पुत्रमिति–एवं प्रथमसर्गे 'अविघ्नमस्तु'–इ. (श्लो. ९१); शाकुन्तलेऽपि–'पुत्रमेवंगुणोपेतं चक्रवर्तिनमाप्नुहि' इति । आत्मगुणानुरूपम्–अत्र हेमाद्रिव्याख्या यथा–'आत्मशब्देन राजा विवक्षितः अन्तरात्मा वा । श्रुतशौर्यादयो ह्यात्मगुणाः' इति । 'अनुरूपम्' इति 'अव्ययं विभक्ति–' इत्यादिना अव्ययीभावे क्लीबता स्यात् । अथ 'कुगतिप्रादयः' इति अनुगतो रूपमित्यनुरूप इति तत्पुरुषे कृतेऽपि 'परवल्लिङ्गं द्वंद्वतत्पुरुषयोः' इति स एव दोष इति चेन्न । 'द्विगुप्राप्तापन्नालंपूर्वगतिसमासेषु निषेधो वक्तव्यः' इति परवल्लिङ्गतानिषेधात् निष्कौशाम्बिरिव पुल्लिङ्गता भवति । तथा हि कुमारसंभवे–'आत्मानुरूपां विधिनोपयेमे ।' मेघदूते च–'मार्गं तावच्छृणु कथयतस्त्वत्प्रयाणानुरूपम्' इति । ४ आशिषः प्रयोगात् न तु मुनेः, ग्राम्योक्तिप्रसङ्गात् । हे० । केचन तस्माद् द्विजादिति व्याचक्षते तन्न ग्राम्यत्वात् । चा० । ५ अग्र्य-अग्र-जन्मानामिति पा०. ६ पट्टराज्ञी प्रभावती इ. हे० । ७ ब्राह्मे मुहूर्ते—'रात्रेश्च पश्चिमे यामे मुहूर्तो ब्राह्म उच्यते ।' इति पितामहोक्ते रात्रिशेषयामार्धस्थिते अरुणोदयकालात्प्राग्दण्डद्वयात्मके काले । 'शेषार्धप्रहरे ब्राह्मो मुहूर्तः' इति मदनपारिजाताच्च । तत्रापि सूर्योदयात्प्रागर्धप्रहरे द्वौ मुहूर्तौ तत्राद्यो ब्राह्मः, द्वितीयो रौद्रः, इति आह्निकतत्त्वम् । 'उत्तरघटिकात्रयं ब्राह्मो मुहूर्तः' इ. चा० । 'पश्चिमरात्रघटिकाद्वयम्' इति सु० । अस्मिन्मुहूर्ते

इत्यादिना कल्पप्प्रत्ययः । **कुमारं** पुत्रं **सुषुवे** । ‘कुमारो बालके स्कन्दे’ इति विश्वः । **अतः** ब्राह्ममुहूर्तोत्पन्नत्वात् **पिता** रघुः **ब्रह्मणः** विधेः **एव नाम्ना तं आत्मजन्मानं** पुत्रम् **अजं** अजनामकं **चकार**। ‘अजो हरौ हरे कामे विधौ छागे रघोः सुते ।’ इति विश्वः ॥

रूपं तदोजस्वि तदेव वीर्यं तदेव नैसर्गिकमुन्नतत्वम् ।
न कारणात्स्वाद्बिभिदे कुमारः प्रवर्तितो दीप इव प्रदीपात् ॥ ३७ ॥

ओजस्वि तेजस्वि बलिष्ठं वा । ‘ओजस्तेजसि धातूनामवष्टम्भप्रकाशयोः । ओजो बले च दीप्तौ च’ इति विश्वः । **रूपं** वपुः । ‘अथ रूपं नपुंसकम् । स्वभावाकृतिसौन्दर्यवपुषि श्लोकशब्दयोः ॥’ इति विश्वः । **तद्** एव पैतृकमेव । **वीर्यं** शौर्यं **तदेव** । **नैसर्गिकं** स्वाभाविकम् **उन्नतत्वं तदेव** । तादृशमेवेत्यर्थः । **कुमारः** बालकः **प्रवर्तितः** उत्पादितः **दीपः प्रदीपात्** स्वोत्पादकदीपात् **इव** । **स्वात्** स्वकीयात् । ‘पूर्वादिभ्यो नवभ्यो वा’ इति स्माद्भावो वैकल्पिकः । **कारणात्** जनकात् **न बिभिदे**[2] भिन्नः न अभूत् । सर्वात्मना तादृश एवाभूदित्यर्थः ॥

उपात्तविद्यं विधिवद्गुरुभ्यस्तं यौवनोद्भेदविशेषकान्तम्[3] ।
श्रीः सा[4]ऽभिलाषाऽपि गुरोरनुज्ञां धीरेव कन्या पितुराचकाङ्क्ष ॥३८॥

गुरुभ्यः[5] विधिवत् यथाशास्त्रम् । **उपात्तविद्यं** लब्धविद्यम् । यौवनस्योद्भेदादाविर्भावाद्धेतोर्विशेषेण कान्तं सौम्यं [**यौवनोद्भेदविशेषकान्तं**] **तम्** अजं प्रति **साभिलाषा अपि श्रीः धीरा** स्थिरान्नतचित्ता । ‘स्थिरा चित्तोन्नतिर्या तु तद्धैर्यमिति संज्ञितम् ।’ इति भूपालः । **कन्या पितुः इव** । **गुरोः अनुज्ञाम् आचकाङ्क्ष** इयेष । यौवराज्या[6]र्होऽभूदित्यर्थः । अनुज्ञाशब्दात्पितृपारतन्त्र्यमुपमासामर्थ्यात्पाणिग्रहणयोग्यता च ध्वन्यते ॥

जातस्य फलं कोष्ठीप्रदीपे —अतिसुललितकान्तिः संमतः सज्जनानां ननु भवति विनीतश्चारुकीर्तिः सुवेशः ॥ द्विजवरसुरभक्तो व्यक्तवाङ् मानवः स्यादभिजिति यदि सूतिर्भूपतिः स्वस्ववंशे ॥ इति । अत्र हेमाद्रिः—अष्टमो मुहूर्तो ब्राह्मः । ननु ‘ब्राह्मे मुहूर्ते चोत्थाय चिन्तयेदात्मनो हितम् ।’ इति रात्रेः पश्चिमयामे रूढिः । ‘पूर्वरात्रे महारात्रस्ततश्चापररात्रकः । ब्राह्मोऽन्त्येन क्रमाद्यामाः’ इति यादवप्रकाशः । तत्र हि ब्रह्मणो वेदस्याध्ययनप्रवृत्तिं निमित्तीकृत्य ब्रह्मशब्दः प्रयुक्तः । नाडिकाद्वयवाचिनो हि मुहूर्तस्य यामवाचकत्वे दोषः । स च मुहूर्तो ब्रह्मादिदेवतावाचकश्च न भवतीति तन्न । ते च मुहूर्ताः ज्योतिषरत्नमालायाम्—“रुद्राहिमित्रपितरो वसुवारिविश्वे वेधा विधिः शतमखः पुरुहूतवह्नी । नक्तंचरश्च वरुणार्यमयोनयश्च प्रोक्ता । दिने दश च पञ्च तथा मुहूर्ताः ॥” इति । “निशामुहूर्ता गिरिशाजपादाहिर्बुध्न्यपूषाश्वियमाग्नयश्च । विधातृचन्द्रादितिजीवविष्णुतिग्मद्युतिस्त्वाष्ट्रसमीरणाश्च ॥” इत्यपि । दैवज्ञवल्लभोऽपि—“ब्राह्मो मुहूर्तोऽभिजिदष्टमो यस्तस्मिन्नपाचीं ककुभं विहाय । प्रशस्यते यानमशेषदिक्षु सर्वाणि कार्याणि च यान्ति सिद्धिम् ॥” यद्यपि दिवा निशि च ब्राह्ममुहूर्तसद्भावः तथाप्यत्र दिवैव प्राशस्त्येति मन्तव्यम् । ‘नक्तं बुधो भौमशशाङ्कमन्दा गुर्वर्कशुक्रा दिनशक्तयः स्युः ।’ इति श्रीपतिपद्धत्युक्तेः । प्रकाशकग्रहसूर्यस्य शुभग्रहगुरुशुक्रयोश्च दिवा बलीयस्त्वात् । बलिषु श्रेष्ठग्रहेषु महाभाग्यत स्यात् । नारदीयसंहितायां च—“मध्यंदिनगते भानौ मुहूर्तोऽभिजिदाह्वयः । नाशयत्यखिलान् दोषान् पिनाकी त्रिपुरं यथा ॥” इति ।

१ समर्थितमेतदष्टमसर्गे ५ श्लोके । ओजस्वीत्यादिविशेषणान्युभयत्र योज्यानि । २ कर्मकर्तरि प्रयोगः । ३ ‘रम्यम्’ इ. पा. ४ गन्तुकामा—कामयाना इ. पा. । ५ बहूक्त्या नानाविद्याप्तिः इति हे० । ६ अत्र ‘विनयोपग्रहान्—’ इत्यादि कामन्दकवचनं नृ.स. ३५ श्लोकटीकायां टीकाकृतोद्धृतं दृश्यम् ।

अथेश्वरेण क्रथकैशिकानां स्वयंवरार्थं स्वसुरिन्दुमत्याः ।
आप्तः कुमारानयनोत्सुकेन भोजेन दूतो रघवे विसृष्टः ॥ ३९ ॥

अथ स्वसुः भगिन्याः **इन्दुमत्याः स्वयंवरार्थं** कुमारस्याजस्यानयन उत्सुकेन [**कुमारानयनोत्सुकेन**] **क्रथकैशिकानां** विदर्भदेशानाम् **ईश्वरेण** स्वामिना **भोजेन** राज्ञा **आप्तः** हितः **दूतः रघवे विसृष्टः** प्रेषितः । क्रियामात्रयोगेऽपि चतुर्थी ॥

तं श्लाघ्यसंबन्धमसौ विचिन्त्य दारक्रियायोग्यदशं च पुत्रम् ।
प्रस्थापयामास ससैन्यमेनमृद्धां विदर्भाधिपराजधानीम् ॥ ४० ॥

असौ रघुः **तं** भोजं **श्लाघ्यसंबन्धम्** अनूचानत्वादिगुणयोगात्स्पृहणीयसंबन्धं **विचिन्त्य** विचार्य **पुत्रं च दारक्रियायोग्यदशं** विवाहयोग्यवयसं विचिन्त्य **ससैन्यं एनं** पुत्रम् **ऋद्धां** समृद्धां विदर्भाधिपस्य भोजस्य राजधानीं पुरीं [**विदर्भाधिपराजधानीम्**] प्रति **प्रस्थापयामास** । धीयतेऽस्यामिति धानी । 'करणाधिकरणयोश्च' इत्यधिकरणे ल्युट्प्रत्ययः । राज्ञां धानीति विग्रहः ॥

तस्योपकार्यारचितोपचारा वन्येतरा जानपदोपदाभिः ।
मार्गे निवासा मनुजेन्द्रसूनोर्बभूवुरुद्यानविहारकल्पाः ॥ ४१ ॥

उपकार्यासु राजयोग्येषु पटभवनादिषु । 'सौधोऽस्त्री राजसदनमुपकार्योपकारिका' इत्यमरवचनव्याख्याने क्षीरस्वामी–उपक्रियत उपकरोति वा पटमण्डपादि राजसदनमिति । रचिता उपचाराः शयनादयो येषु ते तथोक्ताः [**उपकार्यारचितोपचाराः**] । जानपदानां जनपदेभ्य आगतानामुपदाभिरुपायनैः [**जानपदोपदाभिः**] । वन्या वने भवा इतरे येषां ते **वन्येतराः** अवन्या इत्यर्थः । 'न बहुव्रीहौ' इति सर्वनामसंज्ञानिषेधः । तत्पुरुषे सर्वनामसंज्ञा दुर्वारैव । **तस्य मनुजेन्द्रसूनोः** अजस्य **मार्गे निवासाः** वासनिकाः । उद्यानान्याक्रीडाः । 'पुमानाक्रीड उद्यानम्' इत्यमरः । तान्येव विहारा विहारस्थानानि तत्कल्पाः । तत्सदृशा इत्यर्थः । 'ईषदसमाप्तौ–' इति कल्पप्प्रत्ययः । [**उद्यानविहारकल्पाः**] **बभूवुः** ॥

स नर्मदारोधसि सीकरार्द्रैर्मरुद्भिरानर्तितनक्तमाले ।
निवेशयामास विलङ्घिताध्वा क्लान्तं रजोधूसरकेतु सैन्यम् ॥ ४२ ॥

विलङ्घिताध्वा अतिक्रान्तमार्गः **सः** अजः **सीकरार्द्रैः** । शीतलैरित्यर्थः । **मरुद्भिः** वातैः । आनर्तिताः कम्पिता नक्तमालाश्चिरबिल्वाख्यवृक्षभेदाः । 'चिरबिल्वो नक्तमालः करजश्च करञ्जके ।' इत्यमरः । यस्मिंस्तस्मिन् [**आनर्तितनक्तमाले**] । निवेश इं इत्यर्थः ।

---

१ 'क्रथकौशिकानाम्' इति पाठः । २ 'शीलवान्गुणसंपन्नो राजपुत्रः कुमारः' इ. हे० ३ तदुक्तं वृद्धचाणक्ये–'वरयेत्कुलजां प्राज्ञो विरूपामपि कन्यकाम् । रूपशीलां न नीचस्य विवाहः सदृशे कुले ॥' इति । ४ 'कीर्णान्तराः' इ. पा० ५ 'सैन्यं श्रमोत्फेनवनायुजाश्वम्' इति दि० सु० ध० पठन्ति ।

नर्मदाया रोधसि रेवायास्तीरे [**नर्मदारोधसि**] **क्लान्तं** श्रान्तं रजोभिर्धूसराः केतवो ध्वजा यस्य तत् [**रजोधूसरकेतु**] **सैन्यं निवेशयामास** ॥

अथोपरिष्टाद्भ्रमरैर्भ्रमद्भिः प्राक्सूचितान्तःसलिलप्रवेशः ।
निर्धौत[2]दानामलगण्डभित्तिर्वन्यः सरित्तो गज उन्ममज्ज ॥ ४३ ॥

अथ उपरिष्टात् ऊर्ध्वम् । ' उपर्युपरिष्टात् ' इति निपातः । **भ्रमद्भिः** मदलोभादिति भावः । **भ्रमरैः प्राक्** उन्मज्जनात्पूर्वं [**सूचितान्तःसलिलप्रवेशः**] सूचितो ज्ञापितोऽन्तःसलिले प्रवेशो यस्य स तथोक्तः । [**निर्धौतदानामलगण्डभित्तिः**] निर्धौतदाने क्षालितमदे अत एवामले गण्डभित्ती यस्य स तथोक्तः । ' दानं गजमदे त्यागे ' इति शाश्वतः । प्रशस्तौ गण्डौ गण्डभित्ती ; 'प्रशंसावचनैश्च' इति समासः । भित्तिशब्दः प्रशस्तार्थः । तथा च गणरत्नमहोदधौ—'मतल्लिकोद्भमिश्राः स्युः प्रकाण्डस्थलभित्तयः । ' इति । भित्तिः प्रदेशो वा । **वन्यः गजः सरित्तः** नर्मदायाः सकाशात् । पञ्चम्यास्तसिल्प्रत्ययः । **उन्ममज्ज** उत्थितः ॥

निःशेषविक्षालितधातुनाऽपि वप्रक्रियामृक्षवतस्तटेषु ।
नीलोर्ध्वरेखाशबलेन शंसन्दन्तद्वयेनाश्मविकुण्ठितेन ॥ ४४ ॥

कथंभूतो गजः । **निःशेषविक्षालितधातुनाऽपि** धौतगैरिकादिनापि । नीलाभिरूर्ध्वाभी रेखाभिस्तटाभिघातजनिताभिः शबलेन कर्बुरेण [**नीलोर्ध्वरेखाशबलेन**] । ' चित्रं किर्मीरकल्माषशबलैताश्च कर्बुरे । ' इत्यमरः । अश्मभिः पाषाणैर्विकुण्ठितेन कुण्ठीकृतेन [**अश्मविकुण्ठितेन**] **दन्तद्वयेन** । ऋक्षवान्नाम कश्चित्तत्रत्यः पर्वतः । तस्य [**ऋक्षवतः** [3]] **तटेषु वप्रक्रियां** वप्रक्रीडाम् । उत्खातकेलिमित्यर्थः । ' उत्खातकेलिः शृङ्गाद्यैर्वप्रक्रीडा निगद्यते । ' इति शब्दार्णवः । **शंसन्** कथयन् । सूचयन्नित्यर्थः । युग्मम् ॥

संहारविक्षेपलघुक्रियेण हस्तेन तीराभिमुखः सशब्दम् ।
बभौ स भिन्दन्बृहतस्तरङ्गान्वार्यर्गलाभङ्ग इव प्रवृत्तः ॥ ४५ ॥

संहारविक्षेपयोः संकोचनप्रसारणयोर्लघुक्रिये[4]ण क्षिप्रव्यापारेण । [**संहारविक्षेपलघुक्रियेण**] । ' लघु क्षिप्रमरं द्रुतम् ' इत्यमरः । **हस्तेन** शुण्डादण्डेन । ' हस्तो नक्षत्रभेदे स्यात्करेभकरयोरपि । ' इति विश्वः । **सशब्दं** सघोषं **बृहतः तरङ्गान् भिन्दन्** विदारयन् **तीराभिमुखः स** गजः । वारी गजबन्धनस्थानम् । ' वारी तु

---

१ ' अनेन सैन्यबाहुल्यं सूचितम् ' इति हे० । २ ' निर्धौत '–' निर्धूत ' इ. चा० दि० वि० ' निर्धूत–गल्लभित्तिः ' इ० हे० व०, ' निर्धूत–गण्डलेखः ' इ० मु० ध० च पठन्ति. ३ कुलपर्वतविशेषः । ' महेन्द्रो मलयः सह्यः शुक्तिमानृक्षपर्वतः । विन्ध्यश्च पारियात्रश्च सप्तैते कुलपर्वताः ॥' ४ लघुक्रियेण ' कुशलेन ' इ. दि० । वारी गजबन्धनस्थानं तस्यां बहिर्गमनरोधार्थं दत्तार्गला विष्कम्भस्तस्या भङ्गे प्रवृत्त इव । यद्वा वारि जलमेवार्गला तस्या भङ्गे प्रवृत्त इव । इति हे० ।

अत्र भिन्नरूपः श्लोक एकः पठ्यते चा० ध० दि० रादिभिः । स यथा–

स भोगिभोगाधिकपीवरेण संवेष्टितार्धप्रसृतेन [-तोर्ध्वप्रहरेण-तार्धप्रयुतेन] दीर्घान् । प्रतिक्षिपंस्तीरमुखः [-चिक्षेप तीराभिमुखः] सशब्दं हस्तेन वारिपारिधानिवोर्मीन् ॥

गजबन्धनी ' इति यादवः । वार्या अर्गलाया विष्कम्भस्य भङ्गे भञ्जने [**वार्यर्गलाभङ्ग**] **प्रवृत्तः इव बभौ** ॥

शैलोपमः शैवलमञ्जरीणां जालानि कर्षन्नुरसा स पश्चात् ।
पूर्वं तदुत्पीडितवारिराशिः सरित्प्रवाहस्तटमुत्ससर्प ॥ ४६ ॥

शैलोपमः स गजः **शैवलमञ्जरीणां जालानि** वृन्दानि **उरसा कर्षन् पश्चात्** तटमुत्ससर्प । **पूर्वं** तेन गजेनोत्पीडितो नुन्नो वारिराशिर्यस्य स [**तदुत्पीडितवारिराशिः**] **सरित्प्रवाहः तटम् उत्ससर्प** ॥

तस्यैकनागस्य कपोलभित्त्योर्जलावगाहक्षणमात्रशान्ता ।
वन्येतरानेकपदर्शनेन पुनर्दिदीपे मददुर्दिनश्रीः ॥ ४७ ॥

तस्य एकनागस्य एकाकिनो गजस्य **कपोलभित्त्योः** जलावगाहेन क्षणमात्रं शान्ता निवृत्ता [**जलावगाहक्षणमात्रशान्ता**] **मददुर्दिनश्रीः** मदवर्षलक्ष्मीर्वन्येतरेषां ग्राम्याणामनेकपानां द्विपानां दर्शनेन [**वन्यतरानेकपदर्शनेन**] **पुनः दिदीपे** ववृधे ॥

सप्तच्छदक्षीरकटुप्रवाहमसह्यमाघ्राय मदं तदीयम् ।
विलङ्घिताधोरणतीव्रयत्नाः सेनागजेन्द्रा विमुखा बभूवुः ॥ ४८ ॥

सप्तच्छदस्य वृक्षविशेषस्य क्षीरवत्कटुः सुरभिः प्रवाहः प्रसारो यस्य तं [**सप्तच्छदक्षीरकटुप्रवाहम्**] । ' कटुतिक्तकषायास्तु सौरभ्येऽपि प्रकीर्तिताः । ' इति यादवः । **असह्यं तदीयं मदं आघ्राय सेनागजेन्द्राः** । [**विलङ्घिताधोरणतीव्रयत्नाः**] विलङ्घितस्तिरस्कृत आधोरणानां हस्तिपकानां तीव्रो महान्यत्नो यैस्ते तथोक्ताः सन्तः । ' आधोरणा हस्तिपका हस्त्यारोहा निषादिनः । ' इत्यमरः । **विमुखाः** पराङ्मुखाः **बभूवुः** ॥

स च्छिन्नबन्धद्रुतयुग्यशून्यं भग्नाक्षपर्यस्तरथं क्षणेन ।
रामापरित्राणविहस्तयोधं सेनानिवेशं तुमुलं चकार ॥ ४९ ॥

स गजः । छिन्ना बन्धा यैस्ते छिन्नबन्धाः । द्रुताः पलायिताः । युगं वहन्तीति युग्या वाहा यस्मिन्सः । स चासौ शून्यश्च तं [**छिन्नबन्धद्रुतयुग्यशून्यम्**] । भग्ना अक्षा रथावयवदारुविशेषाः । ' अक्षो रथास्यावयवे पाशकेऽप्यक्षमिन्द्रियम् । ' इति शाश्वतः । येषां ते भग्नाक्षा अत एव पर्यस्ताः पतिता रथा यस्मिस्तं [**भग्नाक्षपर्यस्तरथम्**] ।

---

१ उरसा-' तरसा ' इ. पा. अत्र भिन्नरूपं श्लोकं पठन्ति चा० हे० व० भादयः । यथा—
कारण्डवोत्सृष्टमृदुप्रवालाः [प्रतानाः-प्रतान्ताः] पुलिन्दयोषाम्बुविहारकाञ्चीः ।
कर्षन् स शै(से)वाललता नदीष्णः प्रवाह(प्रौ-प्रो-हाव) लग्नास्तटमुत्ससर्प ॥
२ ' ह्रदा० ' इति चा० हे० व० दि० सु० ध० वि० पठन्ति ।
३ अत्र एकशब्दः संख्यार्थो मुख्यार्थो वा । ' एके मुख्यान्यकेवलाः ' इति हे० चा० । दुर्दिनशब्देन दानवर्षणमुच्यते इति हे०. ४ ' विमुखीबभूवुः ' इति बहुसंमतः पाटः ।
५ ' युगकीलकाः ' इ. वि० । यद्वा अक्षा रथचक्राणि । ' अक्षो ज्ञातार्थशकटव्यवहारेषु पाशके । * * * चक्रे कर्षे पुमान् ' इति मेदिनी ।

रामाणां स्त्रीणां परित्राणे संरक्षणे विहस्ता व्याकुलाः। 'विहस्तव्याकुलौ समौ' इत्यमरः। योधा यस्मिंस्तं [**रामापरित्राणविहस्तयोधम्**]। **सेनानिवेशं** शिबिरम्। **क्षणेन** **तुमुलं** संकुलं **चकार** ॥

तमापतन्तं नृपतेरवध्यो वन्यः करीति श्रुतवान्कुमारः।
निवर्तयिष्यन्विशिखेन कुम्भे जघान नात्यायतकृष्टशार्ङ्गः ॥ ५० ॥

नृपतेः राज्ञः **वन्यः करी अवध्यः इति श्रुतवान्** शास्त्राज्ज्ञातवान् **कुमारः** **आपतन्तं** अभिधावन्तं **तं** गजं **निवर्तयिष्यन्** न तु प्रहरिष्यन्। अत एव नात्या-यतमनतिदीर्घं यथा स्यात्तथा। नञर्थस्य नशब्दस्य सुप्सुपेति समासः। कृष्टशार्ङ्गः ईषदाकृष्ट-चापः [**नात्यायतकृष्टशार्ङ्गः**] सः। **विशिखेन** बाणेन **कुम्भे जघान**। अत्र चाक्षुषः—'लक्ष्मीकामो युद्धादन्यत्र करिवधं न कुर्यात्। इयं हि श्रीर्यत् करिणः' इति। अत एव 'युद्धादन्यत्र' इति द्योतनार्थमेव वन्यग्रहणं कृतम् ॥

स विद्धमात्रः किल नागरूपमुत्सृज्य तद्विस्मितसैन्यदृष्टः।
स्फुरत्प्रभामण्डलमध्यवर्ति कान्तं वपुर्व्योमचरं प्रपेदे ॥ ५१ ॥

स गजः **विद्धमात्रः** ताडितमात्रः **किल** न तु प्रहृतः तथापि **नागरूपं** गज-शरीरम् **उत्सृज्य**। तेन वृत्तान्तेन विस्मितैस्तद्विस्मितैः सैन्यैर्दृष्टः [**तद्विस्मितसैन्यदृष्टः**] सन्। स्फुरतः प्रभामण्डलस्य मध्यवर्ति [**स्फुरत्प्रभामण्डलमध्यवर्ति**] **कान्तं** मनोहरं **व्योमचरं वपुः प्रपेदे** प्राप ॥

अथ प्रभावोपनतैः कुमारं कल्पद्रुमोत्थैरवकीर्य पुष्पैः।
उवाच वाग्मी दशनप्रभाभिः संवर्धितोरःस्थलतारहारः ॥ ५२ ॥

अथ प्रभावेनोपनतैः प्राप्तैः [**प्रभावोपनतैः**] **कल्पद्रुमोत्थैः** कल्पवृक्षोत्पन्नैः **पुष्पैः** **कुमारं** अजं **अवकीर्य** अभिवृष्य **दशनप्रभाभिः** दन्तकान्तिभिः [**संवर्धितोरः-स्थलतारहारः**] संवर्धिता उरःस्थले ये तारहाराः स्थूलमुक्ताहारास्ते येन स तथोक्तः। वाचोऽस्य सन्तीति **वाग्मी** वक्ता। 'वाचो ग्मिनिः' इति ग्मिनिप्रत्ययः। स पुरुषः **उवाच**॥

मतङ्गशापादवलेपमूलादवाप्तवानस्मि मतङ्गजत्वम्।
अवेहि गन्धर्वपतेस्तनूजं प्रियंवदं मां प्रियदर्शनस्य ॥ ५३ ॥

अवलेपमूलात् गर्वहेतुकात्। 'अवलेपस्तु गर्वे स्याल्लेपने दूषणेऽपि च।' इति विश्वः। मतङ्गस्य मुनेः शापात् [**मतङ्गशापात्**] **मतङ्गजत्वं अवाप्तवान् अस्मि**। **मां** **प्रियदर्शनस्य** प्रियदर्शनाख्यस्य **गन्धर्वपतेः** गन्धर्वराजस्य **तनूजं** पुत्रम्।

---

१ 'कृष्टचापः' इति हे० वि० व० पठन्ति। २ विद्ध एव विद्धमात्रः। सुप्सुपेति समासः। ३ प्रभावो दिव्यसामर्थ्यम्। ४ तारहारः—'तारस्तु मुक्ताधौतमुक्तेऽतिदीप्तौ तारः इति विक्रमादित्योक्तिः' इ. चा०। ५ 'पुरा किलेश्वरसेवागमनेऽखर्वगर्वसंतापितेन जातमन्युना गजो भवेति शप्त इति वार्ता।' इ. चा० सु०।

'स्त्रियां मूर्तिस्तनुस्तनूः' इत्यमरः। 'तन्वादेर्वा' इत्यूङिति केचित्। **प्रियंवदं** प्रियंवदाख्यं **अवेहि** जानीहि। प्रियं वदतीति प्रियंवदः। 'प्रियवशे वदः खच्' इति खच्प्रत्ययः॥

स चानुनीतः प्रणतेन पश्चान्मया महर्षिर्मृदुतामगच्छत्।
उष्णत्वमग्न्यातपसंप्रयोगाच्छैत्यं हि यत्सा प्रकृतिर्जलस्य॥ ५४॥

स महर्षिः च प्रणतेन मया अनुनीतः सन् **पश्चात् मृदुतां** शान्तिं **अगच्छत्**। तथा **हि**। **जलस्य उष्णत्वम्** अग्नेरातपस्य वा संप्रयोगात्संपर्कात् [**अग्न्यातपसंप्रयोगात्**]। न तु प्रकृत्योष्णत्वम्। **यत् शैत्यं सा प्रकृतिः** स्वभावः। विधेयप्राधान्यात्सेति स्त्रीलिङ्गनिर्देशः। महर्षीणां[1] शान्तिरेव स्वभावो न क्रोध इत्यर्थः॥

इक्ष्वाकुवंशप्रभवो यदा ते भेत्स्यत्यजः कुम्भमयोमुखेन।
संयोक्ष्यसे स्वेन वपुर्महिम्ना तदेत्यवोचत्स तपोनिधिर्माम्॥ ५५॥

इक्ष्वाकुवंशः प्रभवो यस्य सः [**इक्ष्वाकुवंशप्रभवः**] **अजः यदा ते कुम्भम् अयोमुखेन** लोहाग्रेण शरेण **भेत्स्यति** विदारयिष्यति **तदा स्वेन** वपुषो महिम्ना [**वपुर्महिम्ना**] पुनः **संयोक्ष्यसे** संगंस्यसे **इति स तपोनिधिः मां अवोचत्**॥

संमोचितः सत्त्ववता त्वयाऽहं शापाच्चिरप्रार्थितदर्शनेन।
प्रतिप्रियं चेद्भवतो न कुर्यां वृथा हि मे स्यात्स्वपदोपलब्धिः॥ ५६॥

चिरं प्रार्थितं दर्शनं यस्य तेन [**चिरप्रार्थितदर्शनेन**] **सत्त्ववता** बलवता **त्वया अहं शापात् संमोचितः** मोक्षं प्रापितः[2]। **भवतः प्रतिप्रियं** प्रत्युपकारं **न कुर्यां चेन्मे स्वपदोपलब्धिः** स्वस्थानप्राप्तिः। 'पदं व्यवसितत्राणस्थानलक्ष्माङ्घ्रिवस्तुषु।' इत्यमरः। **वृथा स्यात् हि**। तदुक्तम्—'प्रतिकर्तुमशक्तस्य जीवितान्मरणं वरम्।' इति॥

संमोहनं नाम सखे ममास्त्रं प्रयोगसंहारविभक्तमन्त्रम्।
गान्धर्वमादत्स्व[3] यतः प्रयोक्तुर्न चारिहिंसा[4] विजयश्च हस्ते॥ ५७॥

हे **सखे**। सखिशब्देन समप्राणतोक्ता। यथोक्तम्—'अत्यागसहनो बन्धुः सदैवानुमतः सुहृत्। एकक्रियं भवेन्मित्रं समप्राणः सखा मतः॥' इति। प्रयोगसंहारयोर्विभक्तमन्त्रं [**प्रयोगसंहारविभक्तमन्त्रम्**]। **गान्धर्वं** गन्धर्वदेवताकम्। संमोह्यतेऽनेनेति **संमोहनं नाम मम अस्त्रं आदत्स्व** गृहाण। **यतः** अस्त्रात् **प्रयोक्तुः** अस्त्रप्रयोगिणः **अरिहिंसा न च विजयः च हस्ते**। हस्तगतो विजयो भवतीत्यर्थः॥

---

१ 'आमरणान्ताः प्रणयाः कोपास्तत्क्षणभङ्गुराः। परित्यागाश्च निःसङ्गा भवन्ति हि महात्मनाम्'॥ इति हितोपदेशे। मुनीनां क्रोधस्तु कुतश्चित्कारणात्संधुक्षितोऽप्यस्वभावत्वात्तत्क्षणं विनश्यति। शमस्तु प्रकृतिसिद्धत्वाच्चिरस्थायीत्यर्थः। २ अनेन शापविमोचनसामर्थ्यं प्रदर्शितम्। ३ आदत्स्व–'आधत्स्व;' प्रयोक्तुः –'प्रहर्तुः'; च हस्ते–'स्वहस्ते' इ. पा०। भवोऽपि श्लोकोऽन्यथोपलभ्यते क्वचित्। यथा–

'**गान्धर्वमस्त्रं तदितः प्रतीच्छ प्रयोगसंहारविभक्तमन्त्रम्।**
प्रस्वापनं नाम यतः प्रहर्तुर्न चारिहिंसा विजयः स्वहस्ते॥'

४ स्वास्त्रस्यास्त्रान्तरविलक्षणं गुणमाह–यत इति। न चारिहिंसा–'न हिंस्यात्सर्वाणि भूतानि' इति श्रुतेर्हिंसां विना विजयलाभ एव श्रेयस्कर इति भावः।

वधलज्जितः कथमस्त्रग्रहणपरः स्यामिति चेत्तत्राह—

अलं ह्रिया मां प्रति यन्मुहूर्तं दयापरोऽभूः प्रहरन्नपि त्वम् ।
तस्मादुपच्छन्दयति प्रयोज्यं मयि त्वया न प्रतिषेधरौक्ष्यम् ॥ ५८ ॥

किं च । **मां प्रति ह्रिया** प्रहारनिमित्तया **अलम्** । कुतः । **यत्** यतो हेतोः **त्वं मां प्रहरन् अपि मुहूर्तं दयापरः** कृपालुः **अभूः** । **तस्माद् उपच्छन्दयति** प्रार्थयमाने **मयि त्वया [प्रतिषेधरौक्ष्यम्]** प्रतिषेधः परिहारः स एव रौक्ष्यं पारुष्यं तत् **न प्रयोज्यं** न कर्तव्यम् ॥

तथेत्युपस्पृश्य पयः पवित्रं सोमोद्भवायाः सरितो नृसोमः ।
उदङ्मुखः सोऽस्त्रविदस्त्रमन्त्रं जग्राह तस्मान्निगृहीतशापात् ॥ ५९ ॥

ना सोमः चन्द्र[2] इव **नृसोमः** । उपमितसमासः । 'सोम ओषधिचन्द्रयोः' इति शाश्वतः । पुरुषश्रेष्ठ इत्यर्थः । **अस्त्र[3]विद्** अस्त्रज्ञः **सः** अजः **तथेति** सोम उद्भवो यस्याः सा तस्याः **सोमोद्भवायाः सरितः** नर्मदायाः । 'रेवा तु नर्मदा सोमोद्भवा मेखलकन्यका ।' इत्यमरः । **पवित्रं पयः उपस्पृश्य** पीत्वा । आचम्येत्यर्थः । **उदङ्मुखः** सन् **निगृहीतशापात्** निवर्तितशापात् । उपकृतादित्यर्थः । **तस्मात्** प्रियंवदात् **अस्त्रमन्त्रं जग्राह** ॥

एवं तयोरध्वनि दैवयोगादासेदुषोः सख्यमचिन्त्यहेतु ।
एको ययौ चैत्ररथप्रदेशान्सौराज्यरम्यानपरो विदर्भान् ॥ ६० ॥

एवं अध्वनि मार्गे **दैवयोगाद्** दैववशाद् **अचिन्त्यहेतु** अनिर्धार्यहेतुकं **सख्यं** सखित्वम् । 'सख्युर्यः' इति यत्प्रत्ययः । **आसेदुषोः** प्राप्तवतोः **तयोः** मध्ये **एकः** गन्धर्वः चैत्र[4]रथस्य कुबेरोद्यानस्य प्रदेशान् **[चैत्ररथप्रदेशान्]** । 'अस्योद्यानं चैत्ररथम्' इत्यमरः । **अपरः** अजः सौराज्येन राजन्वत्तया रम्यान् **[सौराज्यरम्यान्] विदर्भान्** विदर्भदेशान् **ययौ** ॥

तं तस्थिवांसं नगरोपकण्ठे तदागमारूढगुरुप्रहर्षः ।
प्रत्युज्जगाम क्रथकैशिकेन्द्रश्चन्द्रं प्रवृद्धोर्मिरिवोर्मिमाली ॥ ६१ ॥

नगरस्योपकण्ठे समीपे **[नगरोपकण्ठे] तस्थिवांसं** स्थितं **तम्** अजं तस्याजस्यागमेनागमनेनारूढ उत्पन्नो गुरुः प्रहर्षो यस्य सः **[तदागमारूढगुरुप्रहर्षः] क्रथकैशिकेन्द्रः** विदर्भराजः । **प्रवृद्धोर्मिः ऊर्मिमाली** समुद्रः **चन्द्रं इव** । **प्रत्युज्जगाम** ॥

---

१ 'वारणार्थालंयोगे तृतीयेन' इ० हे० सु० । 'अलं भूषणपर्याप्तिशक्तिवारणवाचकम् ।' इत्यमरः । तस्मादिति–अनुरूपा प्रार्थना द्वितीये–'तद्भूतनाथानुग–' (५८) इति । २ 'अत्रोभयोरानन्दकारित्वं साम्यम् । नर्मदाशब्देन सुखदातृत्वं व्यज्यते ' हे० । उदङ्मुखः–उत्तरास्यः । 'उदङ्मुखस्तु गृह्णीयात् ' इति स्मृतेः । यद्वा उदङ्मुख उपस्पृश्य । ' अन्तर्जानु शुचौ देशे उपविष्ट उदङ्मुखः । प्राग्वा ब्राह्मेण तीर्थेन द्विजो नित्यमुपस्पृशेत् ॥ ' इति याज्ञवल्क्यः । इति हे० ३ अस्त्रविद्–'अस्त्रविदः' इ. चा० दिनकरादिसंमतः पाठः । अस्त्रविदोऽस्त्रज्ञात् इति तस्यार्थः । निगृहीतशापात्–'निगृहीतशासी ' इति हे० दि० चा० पठन्ति । दि० व्याचष्टे च–' निःशेषेण गुरोः सकाशाद् गृहीतं विद्यादि शास्ति रक्षतीति तथा । ' ४ चित्ररथेन गन्धर्वराजेन निर्वृत्तं चैत्ररथम् ।

प्रवेश्य चैनं पुरमग्रयायी नीचैस्तथोपाचरदर्पितश्रीः ।
मेने यथा तत्र जनः समेतो वैदर्भमागन्तुमजं गृहेशम् ॥ ६२ ॥

एनम् अजम् अग्रयायी । सेवाधर्मेण पुरो गच्छन्नित्यर्थः । नीचैः नम्रः पुरं प्रवेश्य प्रवेशं कारयित्वा प्रीत्या अर्पितश्रीः तथा तेन प्रकारेण उपाचरद् उपचरितवान् [च] यथा येन प्रकारेण तत्र पुरे समेतः मिलितः जनः वैदर्भं भोजम् आगन्तुं प्राघूर्णिकं मेने । अजं गृहेशं गृहपतिं मेने ॥

तस्याधिकारपुरुषैः प्रणतैः प्रदिष्टां
प्राग्द्वारवेदिविनिवेशितपूर्णकुम्भाम् ।
रम्यां रघुप्रतिनिधिः स नवोपकार्यां
बाल्यात्परामिव दशां मदनोऽध्युवास ॥ ६३ ॥

रघुप्रतिनिधिः रघुकल्पः । रघुतुल्य इत्यर्थः । उक्तं च दण्डिना सादृश्यवाचकप्रस्तावे–‘ कल्पदेशीयदेश्यादि प्रख्यप्रतिनिधी अपि । ’ इति । सः अजः प्रणतैः नमस्कृतवद्भिः । कर्तरि क्तः । तस्य भोजस्याधिकारो नियोगस्तस्य पुरुषैः [अधिकारपुरुषैः] अधिकृतैरित्यर्थः । प्रदिष्टां निर्दिष्टां प्राग्द्वारस्य वेद्यां विनिवेशितः प्रतिष्ठापितः पूर्णकुम्भो यस्यास्ताम् [प्राग्द्वारवेदिविनिवेशितपूर्णकुम्भाम्] । स्थापितमङ्गलकलशामित्यर्थः । रम्यां रमणीयां नवोपकार्यां नूतनं राजभवनम् । ‘ उपकार्या राजसद्मन्युपचारचितेऽन्यवत् । ’ इति विश्वः । मदनः बाल्यात् परां शैशवादनन्तरां दशां इव । यौवनमित्यर्थः । अध्युवास अधिष्ठितवान् । तत्रोषितवानित्यर्थः । ‘ उपान्वध्याङ्वसः ’ इति कर्मत्वम् ॥

तत्र स्वयंवरसमाहृतराजलोकं
कन्याललाम कमनीयमजस्य लिप्सोः ।
भावावबोधकलुषा दयितेव रात्रौ
निद्रा चिरेण नयनाभिमुखी बभूव ॥ ६४ ॥

तत्र उपकार्यायाम् । स्वयंवरनिमित्तं समाहृतः संमेलितो राजलोको येन तत् [स्वयंवरसमाहृतराजलोकं] कमनीयं स्पृहणीयं कन्याललाम कन्यासु श्रेष्ठम् । ‘ ललामोऽस्त्री ललामापि प्रभावे पुच्छे ध्वजे । श्रेष्ठभूषापुण्ड्रशृङ्गपुच्छचिह्नाश्वलिङ्गिषु ॥ ’ इति यादवः । लिप्सोः लब्धुमिच्छोः । लभेः सन्नन्तादुप्रत्ययः । अजस्य भावावबोधे पुरुषस्याभिप्रायपरिज्ञाने कलुषा असमर्था [भावावबोधकलुषा]

---

१ तस्मिन्स्वयंवरे इ. हे । समेतः–‘ समस्तः ’ ‘ समग्रः ’ इ. पा० । २ पटकुटीम् इ. चा० सु० । ‘ प्राग् द्वारं यस्याः सा प्राग्द्वारा सा चासौ वेदिश्च तत्र निवेशितो हेम्नः कुम्भो यस्याः सा ताम् ।’ इति दि० व्याख्याति । ‘ इतो एकादश श्लोका वसन्ततिलकाछन्दसा । तल्लक्षणं च–‘उक्ता वसन्ततिलका तभजा जगौ गः ’ । इ. चा० । अधिकार०–‘अधिकारि० ’ पूर्ण०–‘ हेम ’ इ. पा. ३ मुग्धतयेति शेषः । यद्वा तस्येन्दुमतीगतमनस्कतया ‘ अन्यत्रानुसक्तोऽयमित्यभिप्रायवेदनेन कलुषा अप्रसन्ना ’ इ. चा० हे० । ईदृशी कान्ताऽपि पत्युर्विविधानुनयैश्चिरात्तदभिमुखी भवति । चिरेण इ०—बहुषु स्थितेषु मां वृणीत न वेत्याकुलत्वात् चिरेण निद्रामगमत् इ. हे० । ‘ केचित्तु निद्राकथनं शृङ्गारपोषकं न भवतीत्याहुः ’ इ. चा०

दयिता इव । रात्रौ निद्रा चिरेण नयनाभिमुखी बभूव । ' राजानं कामिनं चौरं प्रविशन्ति प्रजागराः । ' इति भावः । अभिमुखीशब्दो ङीषन्तश्च्व्यन्तो वा ॥

तं कर्णभूषणनिपीडितपीवरांसं
शय्योत्तरच्छदविमर्दकृशाङ्गरागम् ।
सूतात्मजाः सवयसः प्रथितप्रबोधं
प्राबोधयन्नुषसि वाग्भिरुदारवाचः ॥ ६५ ॥

कर्णभूषणाभ्यां निपीडितौ पीवरौ पीनावंसौ यस्य तम् [**कर्णभूषणनिपीडितपीवरांसम्**]। शय्याया उत्तरच्छदस्योपर्यास्तरणवस्त्रस्य विमर्देन घर्षणेन कृशो विरलोऽङ्गरागो यस्य तं [**शय्योत्तरच्छदविमर्दकृशाङ्गरागम्**] । न त्वङ्गनासङ्गादिति भावः । **प्रथितप्रबोधं** प्रकृष्टज्ञानं **तम्** एनमजं **सवयसः** समानवयस्काः **उदारवाचः** प्रगल्भगिरः **सूतात्मजाः** बन्दिपुत्राः । ' वैतालिकाः ' इति वा पाठः । ' वैतालिका बोधकराः ' इत्यमरः । **वाग्भिः** स्तुतिपाठैः **उषसि प्राबोधयन्** प्रबोधयामासुः ॥

रात्रिर्गता मतिमतां वर मुञ्च शय्यां
धात्रा द्विधैव ननु धूर्जगतो विभक्ता ।
तामेकतस्तव बिभर्ति गुरुर्विनिद्र-
स्तस्या भवानपरधुर्यपदावलम्बी ॥ ६६ ॥

हे **मतिमतां वर** । निर्धारणे षष्ठी । **रात्रिर्गता । शय्यां मुञ्च** विनिद्रो भवेत्यर्थः । विनिद्रत्वे फलमाह--धात्रेति । **धात्रा** ब्रह्मणा **जगतः धूः** भारः । ' धूः स्याद्यानमुखे भारे ' इति यादवः । **द्विधैव** । द्वयोरेवेत्यर्थः । एवकारस्तृतीयनिषेधार्थः । **विभक्ता ननु** विभज्य स्थापिता खलु । तत्किमत आह--**तां** धुरम् **एकतः** एककोटौ **तव गुरुः** पिता **विनिद्रः** सन् **बिभर्ति । तस्याः** धुरः **भवान्** । धुरं वहतीति धुर्यो भारवाही । तस्य पदं वहनस्थानम् । अपरं यद्धुर्यपदं तदवलम्बी [**अपरधुर्यपदावलम्बी**] । ततो विनिद्रो भवेत्यर्थः । न ह्युभयवाह्यमेको वहतीति भावः ॥

निद्रावशेन भवताऽप्यनवेक्षमाणा
पर्युत्सुकत्वमबला निशि खण्डितेव ।

---

१ अयं हे० चा० दि० व० संमतः पाठः । प्रथि०-' प्रतिबोधहेतोः ' इति दि० पठति । ' वैतालिकाः स्फुटपदप्रकटार्थबन्धनम् ', ' वैतालिका ललितबन्धमनोहराभिः ' इ. तृतीयपादपा० । २ मधुरगानेन हि प्रभूणां प्रबोधः क्रियते । तथा हि भोजः—मृदुभिर्मर्दनैः पादे शीतैर्व्यजनकैस्तथा । श्रुतौ वा मधुरैर्गानैर्निद्रान्तो बोधयेत्प्रभुम् ॥ इ. हे० ३ ताम्-' याम् ' । विनिद्रः-' वितन्द्रः ' इ. पा०

लक्ष्मीर्विनोदयति येन दिगन्तलम्बी
सोऽपि त्वदाननरुचिं विजहाति चन्द्रः ॥ ६७ ॥

चन्द्रारविन्दराजवदनादयो लक्ष्मीनिवासस्थानानीति प्रसिद्धिमाश्रित्योच्यते । **निद्रावशेन** निद्राधीनेन । स्त्र्यन्तरासङ्गोऽत्र ध्वन्यते । **भवता पर्युत्सुकत्वं अपि** । त्वय्यनुरक्तत्वमपीत्यर्थः । ‘ प्रसितोत्सुकाभ्यां तृतीया च ’ इति सप्तम्यर्थे तृतीया । अपिशब्दस्तद्विषयानुरागस्यानपेक्ष्यत्वद्योतनार्थः । **निशि खण्डिता** भर्तुरन्यासङ्गज्ञानकलुषिता **अबलेव** नायिकेव । ‘ ज्ञातेऽन्यासङ्गविकृते खण्डितेर्ष्याकषायिता । ’ इति दशरूपके । **अनवेक्षमाणा** अविचारयन्ती सती । उपेक्षमाणेत्यर्थः । **लक्ष्मीः येन** चन्द्रेण सह । त्वदाननसदृशत्वादिति भावः । **विनोदयति** विनोदं करोति । विनोदशब्दात् ‘ तत्करोति तदाचष्टे ’ इति णिच्प्रत्ययः । सादृश्यदर्शनादयो हि विरहिणां विनोदस्थानानीति भावः । **स चन्द्रः अपि दिगन्तलम्बी** पश्चिमाशां गतः सन् । अस्तं गच्छन्नित्यर्थः । अत एव **त्वदाननरुचिं विजहाति** । त्वन्मुखसादृश्यं त्यजतीत्यर्थः । अतो निद्रां विहाय तां लक्ष्मीमनन्यशरणां परिगृहाणेति भावः । अथ वा [‘ह्यनवेक्ष्यमाणा’ इति पाठे] निद्रावशेन भवताऽनवेक्ष्यमाणाऽनिरीक्ष्यमाणा । कर्मणि शानच् । लक्ष्मीः प्रयोजककर्त्री येन प्रयोज्येन चन्द्रेण पर्युत्सुकत्वं त्वद्विरहवेदनाम् । ‘ कालाक्षमत्वमौत्सुक्यं मनस्तापज्वरादिकृत् ।’ इत्यलंकारे । विनोदयति निरासयतीति योजना । शेषं पूर्ववत् । नाथस्त्वर्थोपपत्तिमपश्यन्निमं पक्षमुपेक्षिष्ट ॥

तद्वल्गुना युगपदुन्मिषितेन ताव-
त्सद्यः परस्परतुलामधिरोहतां द्वे ।
प्रस्पन्दमानपरुषेतरतारमन्त-
श्चक्षुस्तव प्रचलितभ्रमरं च पद्मम् ॥ ६८ ॥

तत् तस्माल्लक्ष्मीपरिग्रहणात् **वल्गुना** मनोज्ञेन । ‘ वल्गु स्थाने मनोज्ञे च वल्गु भाषितमन्यवत् ’ इति विश्वः । **युगपत् तावत् उन्मिषितेन** युगपदेवोन्मीलितेन **सद्यः द्वे**

---

१ यद्वा ‘ अपि ’ शब्दस्य ‘भवता’ इत्यनेनान्वयः । भवतापि त्वद्विषयकमपि । अत एवानपेक्षणीयं पर्युत्सुकत्वम् । २ अयं वल्लभसंमतः पाठः । तद्व्याख्या यथा—हे मतिमतां वर सोऽपि चन्द्रस्त्वदाननरुचिं तव मुखकान्तिं विजहाति परित्यजत्यस्तं व्रजाति विच्छायीभवतीत्यर्थः । कोऽसावित्याह । हि निश्चितम् । लक्ष्मीः श्रीर्भवता त्वयाऽनवेक्ष्यमाणाऽसेव्यमाना सती निशि रात्रौ येन चन्द्रमसा सह पर्युत्सुकत्वं विनोदयति रणरणकत्वमतिवाहयति । किंभूतेन त्वया । निद्रावशेन निद्रया वशीकृतेन । किंभूतश्चन्द्रः । दिगन्तलम्बी । केव लक्ष्मीः । खण्डिताऽबलेव । यथा खण्डिताऽबला निशि रात्रौ नार्यन्तरसङ्गाद्भर्त्रानवेक्ष्यमाणा सती कापि तत्प्रतिनिधिसुहृत्संनिधाने औत्सुक्यं विनोदयति इ. खण्डितालक्षणं वल्लभव्याख्याने—‘ निद्राकषायमुकुलीकृतताम्रनेत्रो नारीनखव्रणविशेषविचित्रिताङ्गः । यस्याः कुतोऽपि गृहमेति पतिः प्रभाते सा खण्डितेति कथिता कविभिः पुराणैः ॥’ इति । ‘ अनवेक्षमाणा ’ इत्यत्र ‘ अनपेक्षमाणा ’ इति दि० पठति ‘ अनभिलषन्ती ’ इति व्याचष्टे च । दि० तु श्लोकमिमं प्रक्षिप्तं मन्यते । अयं श्लोको भिन्नरूपः पठ्यते कैश्चित् । यथा—

निद्रावशं त्वयि गते शशिना कथंचिदात्मानमाननरुचा (चिः)भवतो वियुज्य विनाद्य ।
लक्ष्मीर्विभातसमयेऽपि हि [प्रिय] दर्शनेन पर्युत्सुका प्रणयिनी (यनी) निशि खण्डितेव

आपि **परस्परतुलाम** अन्योन्यसादृश्यम् **अधिरोहतां** प्राप्नुताम् । प्रार्थनायां लोट् । के द्वे । **अन्तः [प्रस्पन्दमानपरुषेतरतारम्]** प्रस्पन्दमाना चलन्ती परुषेतरा स्निग्धा तारा कनीनिका यस्य तत्तथोक्तम् । 'तारकाऽक्ष्णः कनीनिका' इत्यमरः । **तव चक्षुः** । अन्तः **प्रचलितभ्रमरं** चलद्भृङ्गं **पद्मं च** । युगपदुन्मेषे संपूर्णसादृश्यलाभ इति भावः ॥

> **वृन्ताच्छ्लथं हरति पुष्पमनोकहानां**
> **संसृज्यते सरसिजैररुणांशुभिन्नैः ।**
> **स्वाभाविकं परगुणेन विभातवायुः**
> **सौरभ्यमीप्सुरिव ते मुखमारुतस्य** [1] **॥ ६९ ॥**

विभातवायुः प्रभातवायुः **स्वाभाविकं** नैसर्गिकं **ते** तव **मुखमारुतस्य** [2] निःश्वासपवनस्य **सौरभ्यम्** । तादृक्सौगन्ध्यमित्यर्थः । **परगुणेन** अन्यदीयगुणेन । सांक्रामिकगन्धेनेत्यर्थः । **ईप्सुः** आप्तुमिच्छुः **इव** । 'आप्ज्ञप्यृधामीत्' इतीकारादेशः । **अनोकहानां** [3] वृक्षाणां **श्लथं** शिथिलं **पुष्पं वृन्तात्** पुष्पबन्धनात् । 'वृन्तं प्रसवबन्धनम्' इत्यमरः । **हरति** आदत्ते । **अरुणांशुभिन्नैः** तरणिकिरणोद्बोधितैः सरसि जातैः **सरसिजैः** कमलैः सह । 'तत्पुरुषे कृति बहुलम्' इति सप्तम्या अलुक् । **संसृज्यते** संगच्छते । सृजेर्दैवादिकात्कर्तरि लट् ॥

> **ताम्रोदरेषु पतितं तरुपल्लवेषु** [4]
> **निर्धौतहारगुलिकाविशदं हिमाम्भः ।**
> **आभाति लब्धपरभागतयाऽधरोष्ठे**
> **लीलास्मितं** [5] **सदशनार्चिरिव त्वदीयम् ॥ ७० ॥**

ताम्रोदरेषु अरुणाभ्यन्तरेषु **तरुपल्लवेषु पतितं** निर्धौताः या हारगुलिकाः मुक्तामणयस्तद्वद्विशदं [**निर्धौतहारगुलिकाविशदं**] **हिमाम्भः लब्धपरभागतया** लब्धोत्कर्षतया । 'परभागो गुणोत्कर्षे' इति यादवः । **अधरोष्ठे त्वदीयं सदशनार्चिः** दन्तकान्तिसहितं **लीलास्मितं इव आभाति** शोभते ॥

---

१ अस्मात्परं भिन्नरूपं श्लोकं पठन्ति सु० दि० रादयः—
मन्दं विवाति हिमसंभृतशीतभावः संसृज्यते सरसिजैररुणांशुभिन्नैः ।
सौरभ्यमीप्सुरिव ते मुखमारुतस्य यत्नो गुणान्प्रति निशापरिणामवायुः ॥
संसृज्यते—'संयुज्यते' इ. पा. २ उत्तमजातीयपुरुषस्य मुखमारुतः पद्मसुरभिर्भवति । प्रथमसर्ग श्लो. ४३ द्रष्टव्यः । ३ अनसः शकटस्याकं गतिं हन्तीति अनोकहः । ४ 'द्रुमपल्लवेषु' इ. पा० । निर्धौत०—'निर्धूतहारगुटिका—' इ. पा० । ५ लीलास्मितम्—लीलया स्मितं विलासान्मन्दहसितम् । उक्तं च साहित्यदर्पणे—'ज्येष्ठानां स्मितहसिते मध्यानां विहसितावहसिते च ।' इत्यादि । लब्धेति—अनुरूपभाववर्णनं कुमारे—'पुष्पं प्रवालोपहितं यदि स्यान्मुक्ताफलं वा स्फुटविद्रुमस्थम् । ततोऽनुकुर्याद्विशदस्य तस्यास्ताम्रौष्ठपर्यस्तरुचः स्मितस्य ॥' इति ।

यावत्प्रतापनिधिराक्रमते न भानु-
रह्नाय तावदरुणेन तमो निरस्तम् ।
आयोधनाग्रसरतां त्वयि वीर याते
किं वा रिपूंस्तव गुरुः स्वयमुच्छिनत्ति ॥ ७१ ॥

प्रतापनिधिः तेजोनिधिः **भानुः यावत् न आक्रमते** नोद्गच्छति । 'आङ उद्गमने' इत्यात्मनेपदम् । **तावत्** भानावनुदित एवेत्यर्थः । **अह्नाय** झटिति । 'द्राग्झटित्यञ्जसाऽह्नाय' इत्यमरः । **अरुणेन** अनूरुणा । 'सूर्यसूतोऽरुणोऽनूरुः' इत्यमरः । **तमः निरस्तम्** । तथा हि । हे **वीर त्वयि** आयोधनेषु युद्धेषु । 'युद्धमायोधनं जन्यम्' इत्यमरः । अग्रसरतां पुरःसरतां [**आयोधनाग्रसरतां**] **याते** सति **तव गुरुः** पिता **रिपून् स्वयम् उच्छिनत्ति किं वा** । नोच्छिनत्त्येवेत्यर्थः । न खलु योग्यपुत्रन्यस्तभाराणां स्वामिनां स्वयं व्यापारखेद इति भावः ॥

शय्यां जहत्युभयपक्षविनीतनिद्राः
स्तम्बेरमा[2] मुखरशृङ्खलकर्षिणस्ते ।
येषां विभान्ति तरुणारुणराग[3]योगा-
द्भिन्नाद्रिगैरिकतटा इव दन्तकोशाः ॥ ७२ ॥

उभाभ्यां पक्षाभ्यां पार्श्वाभ्यां विनीतापगता निद्रा येषां ते **उभयपक्षविनीतनिद्राः** । **अत्र** समासविषये उभशब्दस्थाने उभयशब्दप्रयोग एव साधुरित्यनुसंधेयम् । यथाह कैयटः—'उभादुदात्तो नित्यमिति नित्यग्रहणस्येदं प्रयोजनं वृत्तिविषये उभशब्दस्य प्रयोगो मा भूत् । उभयशब्दस्यैव यथा स्यात् । उभयपुत्र इत्यादि भवति' इति । [**मुखरशृङ्खलकर्षिणः**] मुखराण्युत्थानचलनाच्छब्दायमानानि शृङ्खलानि निगडानि कर्षन्तीति तथोक्ताः **ते** तव स्तम्बे रमन्त इति **स्तम्बेरमाः** हस्तिनः । 'स्तम्बकर्णयो रमिजपोः' इत्यच्प्रत्ययः । 'हस्तिसूचकयोः' इति वक्तव्यात् । 'इभः स्तम्बेरमः पद्मी' इत्यमरः ।

---

१ 'त्वयि संग्रामाग्रणीत्वं प्राप्ते सति' इ. हे० । अग्रसरताम्—अत्र हे० चा० व्याख्या यथा—'पुरोऽग्रतोऽग्रेषु सर्तेः' इति सूत्रे न्यासकृत्—'अग्रेसरः इत्येतद्रूपं सप्तम्या अलुकापि सिध्यत्येव । अग्रं सरतीत्यसप्तम्यन्त उपपदे अग्रेसर इत्यैतद्रूपं यथा स्यादित्येवमर्थमग्रेशब्दस्य एकारान्तत्वनिपातनमिति विज्ञेयम्' । अतः अग्रसरता इति प्रयोगश्चिन्त्यः । तथा—'पुरोगाग्रेसरप्रष्ठाग्रतःसरपुरःसराः' इत्यमरः । यथात्रैव षष्ठे सर्गे 'अग्रेसरैर्वाजिभिरुद्धतानि' । भर्तृहरिश्च 'किं जीर्णं तृणमत्ति मानमहतामग्रेसरः केसरी' इति । अथ वा अग्रे सरन्तः गच्छन्तः अग्रसरन्तः । तेषां सुभटानां मध्ये वीर इति वा । तदा त्वयि रिपून् याते इति । सरतीति सरः । 'पचाद्यच्' इति विशेषणसमासे साधुत्वमिति वा । 'यङोचि च' इति सूत्रे सर्वे धातवः पचाद्यन्तःपातिनः इति न्यासकृत् । तथात्रैव नवमे सर्गे 'सवरुणावरुणाग्रसरं रुचा' 'हरिहयाग्रसरेण धनुर्भृता' 'यूथं तदग्रसरगर्वितकृष्णसारं' इति ।
२ 'सेनागजाः' इ. पा० । ३ 'कान्ति' इ. पा०. ४ 'कैयटविवरणे च–'उभादुदात्तो नित्यमित्यत्रास्वरितत्वाद्द्वित्येतन्नानुवर्तते इति । तन्निवृत्त्यर्थं नित्यग्रहणम्' इति भावः ।' इ. हे०

तत्पुरुषे कृति बहुलम् ' इति सप्तम्या अलुक् । **शय्यां जहति** त्यजन्ति । **येषां** स्तम्बेरमाणाम् । दन्ताः कोशा इव **दन्तकोशाः** दन्तकुड्मलाः । **तरुणारुणराग-योगात्** बालार्कारुणसंपर्कात् **भिन्नार्द्रगैरिकतटाः इव विभान्ति** । धातुरक्ताः इव भान्तीत्यर्थः ॥

दीर्घेष्वमी नियमिताः पटमण्डपेषु
निद्रां विहाय वनजाक्ष वनायुदेश्याः ।
वक्त्रोष्मणा मलिनयन्ति पुरोगतानि
लेह्यानि सैन्धवशिलाशकलानि वाहाः ॥ ७३ ॥

हे **वनजाक्ष** नीरजाक्ष । ' वनं नीरं वनं सत्त्वम् ' इति शाश्वतः । **दीर्घेषु पट-मण्डपेषु नियमिताः** बद्धाः **वनायुदेश्याः** वनायुदेशे भवाः । 'पारसीका वनायुजाः' इति हलायुधः । **अमी वाहाः** अश्वाः **निद्रां विहाय पुरोगतानि लेह्यानि** आस्वाद्यानि **सैन्धवशिलाशकलानि** । ' सैन्धवोऽस्त्री सित(शीत)शिवं माणिमन्थं च सिन्धुजे । ' इत्यमरः । **वक्त्रोष्मणा मलिनयन्ति** मलिनानि कुर्वन्ति । उक्तं च सिद्धयोगसंग्रहे— ' पूर्वाह्णकाले चाश्वानां प्रायशो लवणं हितम् । शूलमोहविबन्धघ्नं लवणं सैन्धवं वरम् ॥ ' इत्यादि ॥

भवति विरलभक्तिर्म्लानपुष्पोपहारः
स्वकिरणपरिवेषोद्भेदशून्याः प्रदीपाः ।
अयमपि च गिरं नस्त्वत्प्रबोधप्रयुक्ता-
मनुवदति शुकस्ते मञ्जुवाक्पञ्जरस्थः ॥ ७४ ॥

[**म्लानपुष्पोपहारः**] म्लानः पुष्पोपहारः पुष्पपूजा म्लानत्वादेव **विरलभक्तिः** विरलरचनः **भवति । प्रदीपाः** च स्वकिरणानां परिवेषस्य मण्डलस्योद्भेदेन स्फुरणेन शून्याः [**स्वकिरणपरिवेषोद्भेदशून्याः**] भवन्ति । निस्तेजस्का भवन्तीत्यर्थः । **अपि च अयं मञ्जुवाक्** मधुरवचनः **पञ्जरस्थः ते** तव **शुकः** त्वत्प्रबोधनिमित्ते प्रयुक्तामुच्चारितां [**त्वत्प्रबोधप्रयुक्तां**] **नः** अस्माकं **गिरं** वाणीम् **अनुवदति** । अनुकृत्य वदतीत्यर्थः । इत्थं प्रभातलिङ्गानि वर्तन्ते । अतः प्रबोद्धव्यमिति भावः ॥

इति विरचितवाग्भिर्बन्दिपुत्रैः कुमारः
सपदि विगतनिद्रस्तल्पमुज्झांचकार ।

---

१ ' कोशस्तु कुड्मले पात्रे दिव्यखड्गपिधानयोः ' इति विश्वः । २ 'वनजेक्षण बाह्लि [बाह्लि]-देश्याः ' इ. ' वनायुजास्ते ' इ. पा० । ३ श्लोकद्वयस्य मालिनी वृत्तम् । ' ननमयययुतेयं मालिनी भोगिलोकैः ' इति तल्लक्षणम् । ४ ' विहत-विद्रुत-गलित-निद्रः ' इ. पा० ।

मदपटु निनदद्भिर्बोधितो राजहंसैः
सुरगज इव गाङ्गं सैकतं सुप्रतीकः ॥ ७५ ॥

इति इत्थं **विरचितवाग्भिः बन्दिपुत्रैः** वैतालिकैः । पुत्रग्रहणं समानवयस्कत्वद्योतनार्थम् । **सपदि विगतनिद्रः कुमारः । तल्पं** शय्याम् । 'तल्पं शय्याट्टदारेषु' इत्यमरः । **उज्झांचकार** विससर्ज । 'इजादेश्च गुरुमतोऽनृच्छः' इत्याम्प्रत्ययः । कथमिव । मदेन पटु मधुरं [**मदपटु**] **निनदद्भिः राजहंसैः बोधितः** [**सुप्रतीकः**] सुप्रतीकाख्यः **सुरगजः** ईशानदिग्गजः गङ्गाया इदं **गाङ्गं सैकतं** पुलिनम् **इव** । 'तोयोत्थितं तत्पुलिनं सैकतं सिकतामयम् ।' इत्यमरः । 'सिकताशर्कराभ्यां च' इत्यण्प्रत्ययः । सुप्रतीकग्रहणं प्रायशः कैलासवासिनस्तस्य नित्यं गङ्गातटविहारसंभवादित्यनुसंधेयम् ॥

अथ विधिमवसाय्य शास्त्रदृष्टं दिवसमुखोचितमञ्चिताक्षिपक्ष्मा ।
कुशलविरचितानुकूलवेषः[2] क्षितिपसमाजमगात्स्वयंवरस्थम् ॥ ७६ ॥

अथ उत्थानानन्तरमञ्चितानि चारूण्यक्षिपक्ष्माणि यस्य सः [**अञ्चिताक्षिपक्ष्मा**][3] अजः शास्त्रे दृष्टमवगतं [**शास्त्रदृष्टं**] **दिवसमुखोचितं** प्रातःकालोचितं **विधिम्** अनुष्ठानम् **अवसाय्य** समाप्य । स्यतेर्ण्यन्तात् ल्यप् । [**कुशलविरचितानुकूलवेषः**] कुशलैः प्रसाधनदक्षैर्विरचितोऽनुकूलः स्वयंवरोचितो वेषो नेपथ्यं यस्य स तथोक्तः सन् । **स्वयंवरस्थं क्षितिपसमाजं** राजसमूहम् **अगात्** अगमत् । 'इणो गा लुङि' इति गादेशः । पुष्पिताग्रावृत्तमेतत् । तल्लक्षणम्–' अयुजि नयुगरेफतो यकारो युजि च नजौ जरगाश्च पुष्पिताग्रा ।' इति ॥

इति महामहोपाध्यायकोलाचलमल्लिनाथसूरिविरचितया संजीवनीसमाख्यया व्याख्यया समेतो महाकविश्रीकालिदासकृतौ रघुवंशे महाकाव्ये अजस्वयंवराभिगमनो नाम पञ्चमः सर्गः ।

---

१ अस्मात्परमस्मात्प्राक्तिभिन्नं श्लोकं पठन्ति चा० इयः—

इति स विगतनिद्रस्तल्पमल्पेतरांशः सुरगज इव गङ्गासैकतं सुप्रतीकः ।
परिजनवनितानां पादयोर्व्यापृतानां वलयमणिविदिष्टं प्रच्छदान्तं मुमोच ॥

२ 'अनुरूपवेषः' इ. पा०. ३ अनेन सुलक्षणत्वोक्तिः । उक्तं च–' मुखमर्धं शरीरस्य सर्वं वा मुखमुच्यते । तत्रापि नासिका श्रेष्ठा नासिकायाश्च लोचने ॥' इ० चा०.

TRANSLATION.

———:0:———

CANTO I.

1. For the right comprehension of words and their senses, I salute Pârvatî (the mountain's daughter) and Parameśvara (the supreme lord), the parents of the universe, who are (perpetually) united like words and their meanings.

2. The (exalted) race sprung from the sun, and my intellect of limited scope (to describe it),—how unequal the two! It is under a delusion that I am desirous of crossing, by means of a raft, the ocean, so difficult to be crossed.

3. Dull (of intellect) and yet aspiring after a poet's fame, I shall expose myself to ridicule, like a dwarf, who, through greed, uplifts his hands for a fruit accessible (only) to the tall.

4. Or rather, I shall find entrance into this race (I may enter upon the task of describing this line of kings), to which the door of description has already been opened by poets of yore, as does a thread into a gem previously perforated by a diamond-pin.

5–9. I, who am such, will describe the line of the Raghus, though my powers of expression are scanty, being impelled to this inconsiderate act by their (transcendental) virtues coming to my ears:—the Raghus, who were pure from birth, who persevered in works until they bore fruit, who were lords of the earth bounded by the ocean, and the track of whose cars lay as far as the celestial regions (9,5); who offered oblations to the holy fires in accordance with the prescribed rules, who honoured supplicants (by gifts) according to their desires, who inflicted punishment in proportion to the crime, and who (woke up, or) were on the alert at the proper time (6); who amassed wealth for giving it away in charity, who spoke sparingly for the sake of truthfulness, who were desirous of conquest for fame (alone), and who consorted with their wives solely for the sake of offspring (7); who (again) spent their boyhood in the study of letters, who enjoyed pleasures in their youth, who led an anchorite's life in their old age, and who finally resigned their bodies by means of *yoga* (*i. e.* fixing their minds in meditation upon the supreme spirit). (8).

10. It behoves the learned who alone can discriminate what is good from what is bad (*lit.* who are the causes of the distinction

between good and bad) to listen to this (poem): for it is in fire alone that the purity or alloy of gold is tested.

11. There was a king, by name Manu, the son of Vivasvat, esteemed by the wise, who was the first of kings, as the sacred syllable *Om* is of the Vedas.

12. In this pure race was born a purer king, Dilipa by name, a supremely eminent monarch, just as the purer moon arose from the pure milky ocean.

13. Broad-chested, stout-shouldered (*lit.* having shoulders like those of a bull), tall as the *s'âla* tree, and massive-armed, he looked like the military virtue (heroism) appearing in a corporeal frame fitted for the discharge of its duties.

14. Like the mountain Meru, he stood occupying (dominating) the whole earth, with a frame that exceeded all in strength, outshone all in lustre and transcended all in majesty.

15. His intellect was commensurate with his bodily form, his knowledge with his intelligence, his undertakings with his knowledge, and his success with his undertakings.

16. By his kingly virtues which were both awe-inspiring and amiable, he was to his subjects, at once unapproachable and inviting, just as the ocean is on account of its monsters and gems.

17. Acting like the rim of a wheel under a skilful driver, the subjects of him, their guide, swerved not even to the width of a line from the path that had been trodden from the days of Manu.

18. He received taxes from his subjects only for the promotion of their welfare : for the sun sucks up water simply to give it back a thousand-fold (in the shape of rain).

19. His army was but an appendage to him ; his means of accomplishing his objects were only twofold–an intelligence that was unfoiled in (penetrated) the branches of learning, and the string stretched out on the bow.

20. His counsels being secret and his countenance and designs inscrutable, his measures, like the impressions (left on the mind by the good or evil deeds) of a prior existence, were to be inferred only from their results.

21. (Though) without fear, he protected his body ; unafflicted with disease, he performed religious rites ; unavaricious he amassed wealth ; and unaddicted he enjoyed pleasures.

22. His modest reserve, notwithstanding his knowledge; forbearance, in spite of power; and absence of boasting, in the presence of beneficence; thus virtues, from their association in him with others (of opposite nature), were, as it were, like brothers born of the same womb (linked in a tie of brotherhood).

23. He, who was not attracted by carnal pleasures, who had seen the very end of (mastered) the branches of knowledge, and who took delight in the discharge of his duty, had (all the perfection of) old age without being (actually) aged.

24. By reason of his educating, protecting, and maintaining his subjects, he was (virtually) their father; their (real) fathers were merely the sources (authors) of their birth.

25. He punished criminals for the preservation of order, and had married only for progeny, so that, even his pursuit of wealth and sensual pleasures was simply the (pursuit of) *Dharma* (the performance of duty).

26. He drained (collected tributes from) the earth for the performance of sacrifices, and Indra drained the heavens for (the growth of) crops; thus by an exchange of their wealth the two sustained the twin worlds.

27. Other kings, indeed, could not attain his fame for protecting people; for (the crime of) theft having turned away from men's property, survived only in the term (expressive of theft).

28. A good man, though unfriendly, was acceptable to him, just as (though distasteful) medicine is to the sick; and even a friend, if wicked, was to be discarded, like a finger bitten by a cobra.

29. Verily the Creator fashioned him with the ingredients of the five great elements: for all his qualities had solely the good of others (for their object).

30. He governed the earth as if it were a single city, having the shores of the seas for its line of ramparts and the seas themselves for its moats, and owning no other rule.

31. He had a wife, like Dakshiṇâ of Yajña, a princess of the royal line of the Magadhas, by name Sudakshiṇâ, a name grown out of her amiability (or generosity, benignity).

32. He, the lord of the earth, though he had a large harem, regarded himself as having a wife by her, a high-minded lady, and by the goddess of royal fortune,

33. (Ever) longing for the birth of a son from her, his worthy consort, he passed his days in hopes, the realization of which was long delayed.

34. With a view to perform some religious rite that he might obtain a son, he took down from his arms the heavy yoke of the world (withdrew himself from the heavy task of governing the world) and entrusted it to his ministers.

35. Then being purified, the two, husband and wife, worshipped the Creator of the world with the desire of obtaining a son, and then started for the hermitage of Vasishtha, their spiritual guide.

36. They drove in a single chariot which made a deep but agreeable sound, and (therefore) looked like Lightning and Airâvata riding a cloud of the rainy season.

37. That there should be no disturbance to the hermitage, they took a limited retinue with them ; but on account of their peculiar majesty they looked as if they were surrounded by an army.

38. They were fanned (as they passed on) by breezes of a pleasant touch, wafting the odour of the exudations of the *S'âla* trees, scattering about the pollen of flowers, and gently shaking the rows of the forest trees.

39. They listened to the notes, delightful to the mind, of peacocks that raised their necks at (on hearing) the rumbling of the wheels of the chariot, notes of a double kind and corresponding (in pitch) to the *Shadja* air.

40. They observed the similarity of each other's eyes in those of the couples of deer, that moved a little out of the way and had their eyes riveted on the gliding car.

41. Occasionally they raised their heads (attracted) by the cranes uttering sweet notes, and forming, as it were, as they flew in a row, a gateway-garland unsupported by posts.

42. On account of the favourableness of the wind betokening the fulfilment of their wish, the tresses of the queen and the turban of the king were not touched by the dust raised by the horses.

43. They smelt the highly-pleasing fragrance of the lotuses in the tanks, cool by its coming in close contact with the ripples and imitating (the fragrance of) their breath.

44. In the villages granted by themselves and marked with the sacrificial posts, they accepted, after they had received the offerings

of honour, the unfailing benedictions of the sacrificers (Brâhmaṇas who properly performed the sacrificial rites).

45. They inquired of the aged cowherds, that came to them with fresh butter, the names of the wild trees by the road-side.

46. As they journeyed on, clad in bright apparel, an indescribable beauty was visible in them, like that in the conjunction of the constellation *Chitrâ* with the moon, when freed from the mists of winter.

47. Engaged in showing this thing and that thing (*i. e.* the various curiosities of the road) to his spouse, the lord of the earth, of amiable appearance and worthy to be compared with Budha, was not even aware of the whole distance travelled over.

48. He (the king), of a fame unattainable (by any one else) and having the queen for his companion, reached, at dusk, with his steeds fatigued, the hermitage of the mighty sage who always practised self-control.

49. (The hermitage) which was (then) being filled by anchorites returning from other forests bringing with them sacrificial sticks, holy grass, and fruits, and welcomed back by the sacred fires advancing forward in an invisible form ;

50.—which was being crowded with deer accustomed to receive a share of the *nivâra* corn (wild rice) and blocking up the doors of the huts, as if they were the children of the wives of the hermits ;

51.—wherein the saplings were quitted by the hermits' daughters immediately after the watering was over, in order to inspire confidence in the birds accustomed to drink water from the basins round the roots of the trees ;

52.—where the antelopes were chewing the cud, squatting in the courtyards of the huts in which wild rice had been collected into heaps, at the decline of the evening sunshine.

53.—which was purifying the casual visitors coming towards it by the columns of smoke, indicating the blazing of fires, shaken up by the wind and charged with the odour of the offerings.

54. Then having ordered the charioteer to give rest to the horses, the King assisted his wife to alight from the car and himself also got down.

55. The hospitable saints, with their senses perfectly controlled, gave an honourable welcome to him, their worthy protector,

who was guided by the principles of justice, and to his royal consort.

56. When the evening rites were over, the King saw the treasure of penance (Vasishtha) with Arundhatî seated behind him, like the god of fire with the goddess *Svâhâ* sitting behind.

57. The king and the queen, the princess of Magadha, seized (touched) their feet in adoration, and the spiritual guide and his wedded spouse greeted (blessed) them with affection in return.

58. The sage asked him, who was a hermit in the hermitage of a kingdom, and whose fatigue caused by the jolting of the car had been removed by the act of hospitality, whether all was right with his kingdom.

59. Then, before the sage, the repository of the Atharva-lore, he, the lord of wealth, who had conquered the cities of the enemies, and was foremost among eloquent men, began (entered upon) a speech full of sense.

60. "Proper, indeed, it is that welfare should reign in all the seven elements of my state, of whose God-sent and man-caused calamities you are the averter.

61. My arrows which can hit only a visible mark, are, as it were, rendered futile by the spells, which discomfit enemies from a distance (even before they are seen), of you, the author of incantations.

62. O sacrificer, the oblation duly offered by you to the holy fires turns itself into rain for nourishing the crops, which, else, would wither by drought.

63. That my subjects live the full period of human life, that they are free from fears, and are never visited by public calamities, is all due to (the virtue of) your spiritual power.

64. When I am thus taken care of by you, my preceptor, the son of Brahman, and so am free from calamities, why should not my prosperity be uninterrupted ?

65. But, even the (sovereignty of the whole) earth, with all its islands, though the yielder of the precious products, does not please me, who have not seen a worthy offspring born of this your daughter-in-law.

66. Surely my departed ancestors, foreseeing the cessation of exequial offerings, after my death must not have been eating their fill at the S'râddha ceremony, being intent upon storing up the obsequial offerings (for future use).

67. Verily the libation of water, offered by me, is drunk, rendered lukewarm with their sighs, by my forefathers, thinking that it would be difficult to be obtained after my death.

68.' I, therefore, with my soul purified by the performance of sacrifices, but obscured by want of issue, am both shining and not shining like the mountain *Lokâloka* (which is lighted on one side and dark on the other).

69. Religious merit, resulting from the performance of penance and acts of charity, produces happiness in the next world; but offspring, of pure extraction, leads to bliss in the next, as also in this world.

70. How is it, O mighty sage, that you are not grieved to see me destitute of the same, like a sapling of the hermitage, watered personally through affection, bearing no fruit ?

71. Know then, O mighty one, that the last debt has been causing me unendurable pain, as the tie-post piercing the vitals, does to an elephant, deprived of the bath.

72. It behoves you, O father, to do that by which I may be released from it; for when an object is difficult of attainment to the descendants of Ikshvâku, the success depends upon you."

73. Thus respectfully informed by the king, the saint remained for a moment, with his eyes fixed in meditation, like a tank, with its fish asleep.

74. He whose soul was purified by ascetic exercises, discovered by meditation the cause of the stoppage of issue to the lord of the earth and then informed him thus :—

75. "On a former occasion, when you were returning to the earth, having waited upon Indra, *Surabhi* (the divine cow) was reposing under the shade of a *Kalpa*-(desire-granting) tree on your way.

76. Full of thoughts of this your queen, bathed after menstruation, being afraid to violate a sacred obligation (to her), you did not act properly towards her who deserved the honour (*lit.* act) of circumambulation.

77. (And) she cursed you thus :—'Since you have shown disrespect to me, no progeny shall be born to you unless you propitiate my daughter.'

78. Neither by you, nor by your charioteer, was the imprecation heard (being pronounced), as the stream of the Celestial

Ganges was then in tumultuous uproar on account of the elephants of the quarters sporting wantonly in it.

79. Know, then, that the attainment of your desire is barred by (that disrespect towards the cow); for omission of honour to those worthy of honour obstructs one's welfare.

80. That heavenly cow, however, is at present dwelling in the nether regions, the gates of which are blocked up (guarded) by serpents, for the supply of oblations in the prolonged sacrificial session which Varuṇa has instituted.

81. Do you then take the daughter of *Surabhi* as her representative, and with your wife, propitiate her in a state of purity; for she, when pleased, is a milker of (gratifies) desire."

82. Just as he was speaking thus there came back from the forest the cow, Nandinī by name, blameless and the source (provider) of oblations to that habitual sacrificer.—

83. Of a soft pink colour, like a (new) leaf, and bearing a slightly-curved mark of white hair (appearing on her forehead), just as the evening-sky (pale-red like the young shoot), bears the crescent of the new moon.—

84. With a large udder, and drenching the earth with a stream of tepid milk, which flowed at the sight of her calf and which was more sanctifying than even the ablution performed at the conclusion of a sacrifice.—

85. Imparting to the king the sanctity that arises from ablutions in a holy stream, by means of the particles of dust raised by her hoofs and coming from near in contact with his body.

86. Seeing her of holy appearance, the receptacle of asceticism (the sage), versed in reading omens, again addressed him (the king), whose officiating priest he was, and whose desire to gain his object was not to be barren (was sure to be fulfilled).

87. " Know for certain, O king, that the fulfilment of your wish is not far distant, since this blessed one has turned up the very moment her name was mentioned.

88. It behoves you (therefore) to propitiate this cow by unceasing attendance upon her, and living upon the products of the forest, just as one does (gains) knowledge by close application.

89. You should move on when she moves on, stand when she stands, sit down when she does so, and drink water when she has done the same.

90. And let this our daughter-in-law too, being pure and full of devotion, follow her, after she is worshipped, in the morning, as far as the bounds of the penance-grove, and also advance thither in the evening to receive her.

91. Thus be devoted to her service, until she is propitiated; may no obstruction overtake you; may you stand, like your father, at the head of those who are blessed with worthy sons !"

92. The disciple (of the sage), who knew the proper place and time, bowing accepted, in a pleased mood, with his queen, the command of his spiritual instructor, saying, " I will do so."

93. Then at night, the learned son of the Creator, who always spoke agreeable and truthful words, dismissed the king, of distinguished fortune (or of blazing radiance) to retire to bed.

94. Although possessed of the superhuman power due to ripe asceticism, the sage, learned in ritual, having regard for the vow (undertaken by the king), provided him with such accommodation as was suited to a forest life.

95. The king, accompanied by his wife free from pollution, occupied a hut pointed out by the *kulapati*, and (there) lying on a bed of *Kus'a* grass passed the night, the close of which was announced by the sage's disciples, chanting (aloud) the Veda.

CANTO II

1. Then at dawn, the lord of men, to whom his fame was a treasure, set free for (going out to) the forest the cow of the sage whose calf had been tied up after it had its suck and who was made to accept sandal, garlands of flowers &c. (by him) through his wife.

2. The lawful wife of the lord of men, worthy of being named at the head of chaste ladies, followed the path of the cow, the dust whereof was consecrated by the plantings of her hoofs, as (closely as) Smṛiti (remembered law) follows the sense of S ruti.

3. The kind-hearted monarch, lovely with glory, having asked his beloved spouse to return, (himself) began to guard the daughter of *Surabhi*, whose milk exceeded in quantity the waters of the four seas, as if he was protecting the earth itself, tranformed into a cow, with the four oceans turned into four teats.

4. By him following the cow as a vow, the rest of his retinue too was sent back; the protection of his body was not due to an

external source : for Manu's descendants were ever protected by their own valour.

5. By (giving her) savoury mouthfuls of grass, by scratchings, by keeping off flies, and by unobstructed rovings at will, thus did the supreme monarch became diligently engaged in her propitiation.

6. The lord of the earth followed her like a shadow—standing still whenever she stopped, proceeding on when she went on, patiently sitting down when she sat down, and drinking water when she drank it.

7. Possessing kingly fortune (or royalty) which, with its insignia cast aside, could be inferred from the super-eminence of majesty, he resembled a royal elephant, inwardly in condition of rut but without the lines of ichor manifested externally.

8. Marked with hair tied up with the tendrils of creepers, he, with his bow strung, wandered in the wood, as if wishing to discipline the ferocious beasts of the forest, under the pretext of guarding the sacrificial cow of the sage.

9. The trees on either side of the king, mighty like the god with the noose (Varuṇa), (as he passed on) unattended by servants, uttered, as it were, the exclamations of "Victory to the king : here he comes," by means of the notes of impassioned birds.

10. On him, bright as fire and worthy of adoration, the young creepers, agitated (urged) by the wind, showered their flowers, as he passed by their side, as the maidens of the city (*lit.* the daughters of citizens) would the customary *lâjâs* (fried paddy).

11. The female deer, gazing on his person declared to be full of feelings, tender with compassion, by their hearts remaining unaffected with fear though he wielded a bow, obtained the fruit of great expanse of their eyes.

12. He heard (as he went on) his own lofty glory, loudly carolled from the bowers by the sylvan nymphs, in a manner in which the purpose of (the accompaniment of the music of) flutes was served by singing bamboos, having their holes filled with wind.

13. The wind charged with the spray of the mountain streams, and bearing the fragrance of the gently shaken flowers of the trees, served (refreshed) him, who, purified by his righteous conduct, was oppressed by heat as he had no umbrella with him.

14. As he, the protector, entered the wood, the forest-conflagration became extinguished even without a shower (of rain) exuberant was the growth of fruits and flowers, and among animals the strong did not oppress the weak.

15. Having purified the spaces between the directions by their courses, at the close of the day the light of the sun, and the cow of the sage, both red like the tint of a (fresh) leaf, began each to return to their abode.

16. He, the protector of the middle world, followed her, who supplied to the sage the necessary articles for the rites due to gods, manes and guests ; and attended by him, esteemed by the good, she, too, looked like (as graceful as) faith incarnate, when accompanied by observance (also embodied).

17. He passed (returned), beholding the woods which were darkening up, in which herds of wild boars were emerging from the pools, in which peacocks were flying towards their roosting trees and where antelopes were squatting on the swards.

18. The cow (that had calved but once) on account of her exertion to bear the burden of her full udder, and the king by reason of his massive body, both decorated with their charming gaits the way back to the penance-grove.

19. His wife drank him in, from the skirt of the forest, as he returned following the cow of Vasishṭha, with winkless eyes, that had fasted long, as it were.

20. Placed in front, on the way, by the lord of the earth, and received by the king's wife (his associate in religious rites) advancing towards her, the cow shone between them, like twilight situated between day and night.

21. Sudakshiṇâ, with a pot of whole rice in her hands went round that milch-cow, keeping her on the right side, and, bowing, worshipped the broad space between her horns (the forehead), the very door as it were to the fulfilment of her wish.

22. They both (the king and queen) were delighted to see that the cow, though eager to meet her calf, patiently accepted the worship offered to her : for, verily the signs of pleasure of (venerable) beings of her type, manifested towards those full of (or, who approach them with) devotion, indicate the near fulfilment (of their wishes).

23. After having shampooed the feet of his preceptor and his wife and having finished his evening devotions, Dilîpa, who had

uprooted his foes by (the might of) his arms, again waited upon the milch-cow, as she sat down after the milking was over.

24. He, the protector, accompained by his wife, sat close after the cow, near whom were placed a lighted lamp and offerings of worship; and as gradually she slept he slept too, following her example, and rose in the morning when she awoke from sleep.

25. Three times seven days passed away, while he, of adorable fame and accustomed to deliver persons in distress, was thus engaged with his royal consort, in keeping the vow for the birth of a son.

26. On the following day, the cow that supplied to the sage materials for sacrificial offerings, desirous of testing the devotion of her follower, entered a cave of the mountain Himâlaya (*lit.* Gaurî's father) where tender grass had grown in (or, owing to) the vicinity of the fall of the Ganges.

27. A lion, it appeared, unobserved in his attack by the king, who had directed his eyes to the beauty of the mountain, confident that the cow was not assailable even in thought, by the beasts of prey, forcibly pulled her.

28. Her cry, deepened (or, prolonged) by its reverberations in the cave, drew back, by catching as it were in a noose of ropes, the sight of the king, the protector of the distressed, that was riveted on the King of mountains.

29. That eminent archer saw a lion, seated upon the rosy cow, like a full-blossomed *lodhra* tree, situated on the table-land of a mountain full of red minerals.

30. Then the king, who walked as undauntedly (or, proudly) as a lion (lord of brutes), who was the protector of the distressed, and who had by force extirpated his enemies, being thus affronted, wished to take out an arrow from his quiver to slay the lion, who merited death.

31. As he wished to strike, his right hand, with its fingers stuck fast to the haft of the arrow, the heron's feathers whereof were beautifully tinted by the lustre of its nails, remained with its action committed, as it were, to a picture.

32. With his rage increased by the paralysis of his arm, the king burnt within himself by the fire of his own energy, which could not touch the offender though very near, like a cobra with its power restrained by charms and herbs.

33. (Then) the lion, who had seized the cow, spoke in human accents to him, who was ever a partisan of the good, who was the most illustrious of Manu's race, and whose strength was as great as that of a lion,—thus astonishing him (all the more) already astonished at his own plight.

34. "Away, O astonished protector of the earth, with your effort; your weapon, though discharged against me, would prove of no avail; the fury of the storm, though (able) to uproot trees, has no effect upon a mountain.

35. Know me to be a servant of the eight-formed god (S'iva), Kumbhodara by name, the friend of Nikumbha, whose back is consecrated by the favour of his planting his foot upon it, when he wishes to mount his bull, white like the mountain Kailâsa.

36. You see the yonder Devadâru tree; it has been adopted as a son by S'iva (the bull-bannered good); and it has known the taste of the *payas* (water-milk) of Skanda's mother issuing out from her (maternal) breasts, in the form of gold pitchers.

37. On one occasion its bark was destroyed by a wild elephant scratching his temples against it; whereupon Pârvatî (*lit.* the mountain's daughter) grieved for it, as if it was Skanda (*lit.* the general of the divine forces) himself, wounded by the missiles of the demons.

38. From that day forth, I have been placed in this cave of the mountain, by Siva (the trident-holder) for scaring away the wild elephants, directing me to prey, as a lion, on (*lit.* making my condition as a lion depend for food on) animals coming within my reach.

39. For the gratification of me, thus situated and hungry, this feast of blood after fast, destined by the supreme lord for this time, and (therefore) coming to me, is enough; just as the nectar of the moon coming as a meal is to (the gratification of) the enemy of gods (Râhu).

40. Do you, therefore (*lit.* you who are thus made helpless), go back, casting off shame; you have shown your devotion, as a disciple, to your preceptor; where it is impossible to protect a charge by means of arms, it (inability to protect) does not damage the reputation of those who wield arms."

41. On hearning this bold (or, significant) speech of the king of beasts, the king of men (knowing that) his missile was foiled by the power of S iva slackened his disregard of himself.

42. And also (he) spoke in reply to him (the lion), being unsuccessful in his attempt to shoot an arrow, which for the first time knew what failure was, like the wielder of the thunderbolt (Indra) paralysed by the glance of S'iva, when about to discharge his weapon.

43. " O lord of beasts, laughable, indeed, is the speech, which I, whose actions are restrained, am going to utter; but you know the inward feelings of living beings, and therefore, I will say my say.

44. All adorable to me is that (S'iva), who is the cause of the creation, preservation and destruction of all things, animate and inanimate; I cannot also, on the other hand, allow this property of my preceptor to be destroyed before me (my eyes).

45. Be pleased, therefore, to make your subsistence on this my body, and let this cow of the great sage be liberated, whose young calf will be anxiously looking for her (return) at the close of the day."

46. On hearing these words, that attendant of S'iva (*lit.* the lord of beings) laughed a little and spoke once more to the king (*lit.* the lord of riches), rending into pieces the gloom of the mountain-caves by the gleam (rays) of his teeth.

47. " Sovereignty over the world marked by one imperial umbrella, prime youth, and this handsome form—you who wish to forego all these for the sake of a trifle, seem to me to be wanting in discernment.

48. If this be your compassion for living beings, this cow alone will be happy (saved) by your death. But if alive, O king of men, you, like a father, will ever protect your subjects from calamities.

49. Now if you dread your preceptor, who having an only cow, will be burning with anger at your offence, (like a blazing) fire, it is possible for you to pacify his wrath by presenting him with crores of cows with udders as big as pitchers.

50. Preserve, therefore, your mighty body, the enjoyer of blessings: for the wise say that a prosperous kingdom is identical with the heaven of Indra, only differing in that it is situated on the earth."

51. When the lord of beasts had ceased, having said this much, the mountain too, on account of the echo of his words resounding in the caves, seemed affectionately and loudly to say the very same thing to the king.

52. Having heard the words of the attendant of S'iva, the king of men spoke again, his compassion being excited all the more, being looked at with terror-smitten eyes by the cow in the grip of the lion.

53. "The noble name of *kshatra*, (the military caste) is verily known in the worlds as 'the one that protects from danger'; but to one who acts in opposition to this, of what use is a kingdom, or a life tarnished by infamy ?

54. And how is the pacification of (the anger of) the great sage possible by the gift of ordinary milch-cows ? Know that this cow is in no way inferior to *Surabhi* (the divine cow); that you have attacked her is only through the power of Rudra.

55. It is, therefore, proper that I should deliver this one from you by offering my own body as a ransom. Thus your meal-after-fast will not be obstructed, and the means of the sage's rites also will not be destroyed.

56. You, too, who are a servant, know this—for great is your care for the *Devadâru* tree—that it is not possible (for a servant) to stand before his employer, himself unhurt, after having allowed his charge to perish.

57. Or, if somehow you deem me not fit to be killed, be compassionate to my (other) body consisting of glory ; for in the case of people like me, there is utter want of regard for the necessarily perishable lumps of matter (the bodies).

58. They say that a friendly connexion has conversation for its cause ; and the same has been formed between us, (thus) met together in this forest tract ; hence, O follower of the lord of beings, it behoves you not to reject the request of me, your connexion."

59. To the lion, who said 'So let be,' Dilîpa, his hand released from restraint the very moment, offered, after laying down his weapons, his body, like (as if it were no better than) a lump of flesh.

60. At that moment upon the king (*lit.* the protector of the people) expecting, with his face downwards, the terrible leap of

the lion, there fell a shower of flowers discharged by the hands of the *Vidyâdharas*.

61. Hearing the words gladdening like nectar—' Rise, my child' uttered there, the king rising, beheld the cow standing before him like his own mother, with milk dripping down (from her udder) and not the lion.

62. The cow thus addressed the astonished king,—'O benevolent one ! Creating an illusion, you have been tested by me ; by virtue of the sage's power, not even the god of death can strike me ; much less other destructive animals.

63. My son, by your devotion to your preceptor and your compassion for me I am pleased (with you) ; ask a boon (of me) ; know me to be not only the producer of milk, but also a fulfiller of wishes when pleased.'

64. Then he, who had honoured supplicants and earned the title of Hero by the might of his arms, joined his hands, and asked for a son by Sudakshiṇâ, such as would be the founder of a dynasty and earn an undying reputation.

65. Having promised, by saying ' So be it,' the gift of the desire of the king who longed for progeny, the milch-cow commanded him thus—'My son, extract my milk in a vessel of leaves, and drink it.'

66. ' I wish to drink your milk, O mother, out of what will remain after the calf has sucked and after it has been used for the sacrificial rites, having received the sage's permission, just as I receive the sixth portion of the (produce of the) earth, protected by me.'

67. Thus addressed by the king, the cow of Vasishṭha became still more pleased, and followed by him, returned with an easy pace from the Himâlayan cave to the hermitage.

68. The lord of kings, with his face bright like the smiling moon (or his moonlike face smiling), informed his preceptor and then his beloved wife, of the favour of the cow, in words which seemed to be a repetition, as it was already inferred (by them) from the external signs of ecstatic joy.

69. He, of unblemished character, and kind to the virtuous, having been permitted by Vasishṭha, drank, with unslaked thirst the milk of Nandinî, that remained after the calf had been gratified and the offerings made, as if it were his own spotless fame embodied.

70. The next morning, the repast at the conclusion of the aforesaid vow being over, the self-restrained Vasishṭha, dismissed the (royal) couple to return to their own capital, after having pronounced on them the benediction proper at the time of departure (or, having performed the ceremony that was to ensure them a happy journey).

71. Having circumambulated the holy fire to which the offerings were made, and Arundhatî just after her husband, and then the cow too, together with her calf, the king started on his journey, his prowess being rendered mightier by the auspicious rites (performed at his departure).

72. The patient king, accompanied by his lawfully wedded wife, traversed the road, driving in a chariot, the sound of which was agreeable to the ear and which was comfortable on account of the absence of jolting, as if it was his own desire now fulfilled.

73. His subjects, in whom a longing (to see him) was produced on account of his absence, drank him in, as it were, whose form was emaciated, by the observance of the vow for progeny, with eyes ever unsatiated, just as they would the newly-risen moon (*lit.* the lord of plants), creating a longing (for his sight) and his body wasted (waned) by the vow (of being devoured from day to day), for (in the interest of) the creation.

74. He, with the splendour of Indra (*lit.* the Splitter of the demons' towns), entered the city decorated with flying banners, greeted with acclamations by the citizens, and once again placed the yoke of the earth on his arm whose sustaining strength equalled that of the serpent king (resumed the government).

75. Then (in course of time) for the well-being of the race of the king, the queen bore a fœtus, formed with the weighty essences of the guardians of regions, as the sky bore the luminary sprung from the tears of Atri, and as the divine river (Gaṅgâ) bore S iva's energy deposited by Agni (the fire-god).

CANTO III.

1. After that (conception) Sudakshiṇâ bore the evidence (signs) of pregnancy, which was (as it were,) the very desire of her husband, with its fulfilment approached which was (as gladdening) to the eyes of her female friends as the appearance of the moon-light, and which was again the cause of the perpetuation of Ikshvâku's race.

2. Not wearing all her ornaments on account of the attenuation of her body and with her face pale like the *lodhra* flower, she looked like the night bordering on dawn, with but a few stars displayed (therein) and marked by the moon shining dimly.

3. The king smelling, in private, her mouth fragrant with clay (that she would eat), never felt satisfaction, like an elephant smelling a small pond in a forest tract, sprinkled over with drops from the clouds, at the close of summer.

4. Her (future) son was to enjoy (the sovereignty of) the earth with his (conquering) chariot stopping only at the extremeties of the quarters, as the lord of the gods enjoys that of heaven ; hence it was that she (the queen) set her heart upon an object of that kind (clay) in preference to all other objects of taste.

5. "Through bashfulness the princess of Magadha does not tell me her wish ; what are the things that she has a craving for ?—" thus did the lord of the North-Kosalas constantly ask his wife's companions in loving concern.

6. Having reached the state painful on account of hankerings of pregnancy, whatever she asked for, she saw brought to her ; for there was nothing, which being desired by him, was unattainable to him, who had his bow strung, even if it were in heaven.

7. Gradually getting over the painful state of pregnancy-cravings, she appeared beautiful, as her limbs grew plump, like a creeper, which after the fall of the old leàves, is dressed in lovely foliage.

8. As days rolled on, her two breasts, growing exceedingly plump, and with nipples black all round, far surpassed the loveliness of a couple of well-formed lotus-buds with black bees perched upon them.

9. The monarch regarded the queen with child, as if she were the sea-girt earth holding within a hidden treasure, or the

S'amî tree with fire lying concealed inside, or the river Sarasvatî with its (stream of) water underground.

10. He performed, in due order, the ceremonies (attendant on pregnancy) beginning with *Puṃsavana*, in a style worthy of the love he bore to his beloved queen, of the loftiness of his mind, of the vast wealth he had acquired by the might of his arms from all quarters, and also of his great joy.

11. Whenever the king visited her apartment he was delighted to see how she, with tremulous glances, rose from her seat with difficulty on account of the heaviness of the fœtus with the portions of the mighty gods (infused therein), and also experienced languor even as she joined together her hands to make the customary bow.

12. Now, in due season, the development of the fœtus having been effected by trusty physicians, well versed in the treatment of infants, the husband saw, with a delighted mind, his beloved queen, about to be delivered, like the sky, over-hung with clouds, about to discharge a shower of rain at the close of summer.

13. Then she, comparable to S'achî, gave birth to a son, whose most exalted fortune was betokened by five planets in their (respective) ascendant high position, and not approaching the sun, just as regal power, arising from three agencies, produces inexhaustible wealth.

14. The very moment the quarters brightened; and the holy fire received the oblations with its flame turning to the right : (thus) everything indicated auspiciousness : for the birth of persons like him is for the good of the world.

15. Deprived of their lustre all of a sudden by the natural refulgence of the well-born babe, spreading around the bed in the lying-in-chamber, the midnight lamps became as if they were painted in a picture.

16. To the attendants of the inner apartments announcing the birth of a son, in words which rivalled nectar in sweetness, there were only three things which the king could not give, *viz.* his (imperial) umbrella bright as the moon, and the two *chauries* (being the insignia of royalty).

17. As the king was looking intently at (*lit.* drinking in) the lovely face of his son, with an eye as steady as a lotus in a breeze-

less spot, his intense joy could not be contained in himself, like the flood of the great ocean at the appearance of the moon.

18. When the entire natal ceremony was performed by the ascetic-priest coming from the penance-forest, the son of Dilîpa shone forth with additional brilliance (all the more), like a gem produced in a mine, after it has undergone the process of polishing.

19. The sounds of the auspicious musical instruments, pleasant to hear, accompanied by the delightful dances of the courtesans, went on, not only in the palace of him, the husband of the Magadha princess, but also in the regions of the denizens of heaven.

20. There was no prisoner—such a protector he was—whom, delighted at the birth of a son, he could release; only his own self was, on that occasion, liberated from the bond, called ' the ancestors' debt.'

21. Foreseeing that the boy would go to the end of all learning and also of his foes in battle (*i. e.* would extirpate them), the king, conversant with the meaning of words, named his son Raghu, taking into consideration the meaning ' to go ' of the root.

22. Under the care of the father, who was endowed with fortune of every kind, the boy developed, day by day, the graceful limbs of his body, just as the young moon waxes in size by the infusion of the rays of the sun (*lit.* he who drives green horses).

23. As Umâ and S'iva (*lit.* the bull-badged god) were delighted with Kártikeya (*lit.* one born in reeds), as S'achî and Indra (*lit.* the cleaver of the demons' cities) were delighted with Jayanta, so were the king and the Magadha princess, equal to them, pleased with their son, who was also like them (the two divine boys).

24. The love which existed mutually between the king and the queen and which had united together their hearts, like that of a pair of *Chakravâka* birds, increased (deepened) on the part of each towards the other, though now shared by their only son.

25. The boy lisped the words first uttered by the nurse, walked holding her finger, and bent low (bowed) by being taught to make obeisance; by these acts he added to the joy of his father.

26. Having placed on his lap the boy who seemed to be shedding ambrosia on his skin by means of the pleasurable sensation

generated by the contact of his body, the king, with his eyes closed at the corners, experienced the deliciousness of the touch of a son, after a long time (*i. e.* a long period of disappointment), or for a long time (or, cameto the state of knowing—became conscious of—the pleasure of the touch of his son after a long time—so much benumbed with joy he was).

27. And he, no transgressor of the prescribed bounds, considered his line as well perpetuated by him (his son) of exalted birth, a different form of his own person and the possessor of the foremost of merits, just as Brahmâ (*lit.* the lord of creation) considers his own creation well preserved by that other form of his own self (Vishṇu) working in combination with Satva, the best of the three qualities (that govern the world).

28. When his tonsure ceremony was performed, he, accompanied by the ministers' sons of the same age and with waving locks of hair, mastered properly the alphabet, and thereby entered the vast field of learning, as one enters the sea through the mouth of a river.

29. And, when he had been duly invested with the sacred thread, learned preceptors educated him, a favourite with preceptors (or, who loved his preceptors), and found their labours not wasted upon him ; for labour bestowed on a proper object (or, instruction imparted to a worthy recipient) is productive of fruit.

30. Gifted with a noble understanding, he by the force of all the excellences of intellect, got across (mastered), in succession, the four lores, comparable in vastness to the four oceans, as the lord of the directions (the sun) traverses the four quarters by means of his bay steeds, surpassing the wind in velocity.

31. Having put on the holy skin of the *ruru* (a kind of deer) he learnt the art of using missiles, together with their incantations, from his father himself ; for not only was his sire the sole sovereign on earth, but the sole archer also.

32. Like a young calf reaching the state of a full-grown bull, and the young elephant attaining the condition of a huge elephant, Raghu, whose childhood was gradually supplanted by youth, developed a frame charming by its gravity (dignity).

33. Then after the ceremony of the cutting of the hair had been performed, his father performed the marriage rite, and the daughters

of kings having found an excellent husband in him, shone like the daughters of Daksha married to the moon (*lit.* the god who chases away darkness.)

34. Young, with arms long as the yoke of a car, a chest broad like a folding-door, and a neck well-turned, Raghu surpassed his father by his physical excellence and yet looked lowly before him through humility.

35. Then the king wishing to lighten the exceedingly heavy burden of governing his subjects long sustained by himself, invested Raghu with the title of 'young king,' seeing that he was disciplined (fitted for it) both by nature and by education.

36. S'rî (the goddess of royal fortune) who always loves merits, went over partially from her original seat, the old king, to the new resting place called 'the young king,' just as the goddess of beauty passes from a lotus to a fresh blown one.

37. Like the fire by its associate the wind, like the sun by its ally the autumnal season (*lit.* in which there is the disappearance of clouds), and like the elephant by its auxiliary, the bursting of his temples, the king (Dilîpa) became most irresistible by his help.

38. Having appointed him, a pre-eminent archer, followed by (other) princes, to guard the sacrificial horse, he, comparable to Indra (*lit.* the performer of a hundred sacrifices) performed a hundred sacrifices short by one, without obstruction.

39. The horse let loose (to wander) unrestrained, after that, for another sacrifice, by that sacrificer, Indra in an invisible form, it is said, took off, even before the eyes of the guards armed with bows.

40. Then, just as the prince's army stood amazed, not knowing what to do in their bewilderment, there was seen Nandinî, Vasishtha's cow, of well-known power, coming accidentally.

41. The son of Dilîpa, honoured by the good, having cleansed his eyes with the holy water that flowed from her body (her urine), was endued with the power of seeing objects even beyond the ken of senses.

42. The prince (*lit.* the son of the king) descried, in the east, the cleaver of the wings of mountains (Indra), carrying away the horse, tethered by the traces of his car, with his restiveness repeatedly checked by the charioteer.

43. Recognizing him to be Indra, by his hundreds of winkless eyes, and also by his green steeds, Raghu addressed him in a deep voice that reached the vaults of heaven, forcing him to turn back, as it were, thereby.

44. "O lord of gods! you alone are described by sages as the first of those who enjoy shares at sacrifices; how do you then proceed to obstruct the sacrificial rites of my sire, purified for (engaged in) the constant performance of sacrificial vow?

45. The enemies of sacrifices ought, indeed, to be always checked (suppressed) by you, the lord of the three worlds, possessed of divine power of vision; but if you yourself stand in the way of the rites undertaken by the righteous, all pious work must be at an end!

46. Therefore, O Indra, it behoves you to set free the horse, the most essential part of the great sacrifice; great lords, who lead the paths pointed out by the Vedas, never adopt a sinful course."

47. On hearing these bold words spoken by Raghu, the lord of the denizens of heaven, astonished, turned back the chariot and began to return a reply.

48. "O son of a kshatriya, what you say is all true; but those who regard their fame as their wealth must protect it from their enemies; and your father, by his sacrifices, is bent upon eclipsing the same in its entirety of me, so well known in all the worlds.

49. As Hari alone is known by the name of Purushottama, as Tryambaka (the three-eyed god), and none else, is styled Mahes'vara, so do the sages know me as S'atakratu. This designation (respectively attached to us three) does not refer (belong) to a second.

50. Therefore has this horse of your father been carried away by me, imitating the sage Kapila; away with (nothing will be gained from) an effort in this matter; set not your foot upon the path pursued by Sagara's progeny (sons)."

51. Then the dauntless protector of the sacrificial horse laughed and again addressed Purandara:—"Take up your weapon, if this be your determination; you will never gain your object without conquering Raghu."

52. Having thus addressed Indra, he, with his face turned upwards, and wishing to fix an arrow on his bow, stood with his majestic form appearing to advantage in the attitude of *A'līḍha*

(the right leg advanced and the left one drawn in), thus imitating the god S'iva.

53. The resentful splitter of mountains (Indra) too, struck at heart by Raghu's shaft consisting of his defiant posture, (or, spirit) placed an arrow, that never failed to hit its mark, on his bow, which shows itself as the momentary signal of the fresh clouds (*i. e.* the rainbow).

54. The arrow of Indra, accustomed to drink the blood of terrific demons, entered (penetrated) the broad chest of the son of Dilîpa, and drank, out of curiosity as it were, the blood of a human being, never tasted before.

55. The prince also, with the prowess of Kumâra (Kârtikeya), planted an arrow, marked with his own name, into Indra's arm, whose fingers were roughened by patting Airâvata (the celestial elephant), and which bore the prints of S'achî's ornamental paintings.

56. And with another arrow, having peacock's feathers attached to it, he struck down Indra's great thunderbolt-banner; whereupon the god got mightily wroth with him, as if he had forcibly cropped off the hair of the deity presiding over the fortune of the celestials.

57. A fierce fight then ensued between the two, each intent on overcoming the other, by means of feathered shafts, as frightful as winged snakes, flying upwards and downwards, while the Siddhas on the one side and the soldiers on the other stood by (as silent spectators).

58. Even with showers of missiles poured in ceaseless succession, Indra was not able to extinguish him, the receptacle of exceedingly unbearable (irresistible) energy (power), as the cloud cannot extinguish by its waters the fire (of lightning) emitted from itself.

59. Then Raghu, by means of an arrow with a head shaped like the crescent of the moon, cut off the string of the Indra's bow, roaring deep, like an ocean that is being churned, on his fore-arm, besmeared with the sandal of heaven.

60. He, with his jealous anger intensified, threw aside the bow, and with a desire to slay his very powerful adversary, took up the thunderbolt, blazing with a circle of radiance and accustomed to clip off the wings of mountains.

61. Severely struck on the breast by that weapon, Raghu fell on the ground, along with the tears of his soldiers; shaking off in

an instant the pain caused thereby, he rose up, together with their acclamations of joy.

62. Even then, the slayer of Vṛitra (Indra) was pleased by the supreme valour of him who had long maintained a hostile position, cruel by the use of arms ; for a foot is set (an impression is made) everywhere by merit.

63. "By none but you, was ever withstood (borne the stroke of) my weapon, unobstructed in its operation, by reason of its inherent strength, even on mountains ; know me to be pleased ; excepting the horse what else would you have (from me) ?"—so said Vâsava to him in clear (unmistakable) terms.

64. Then the son of the lord of kings, putting back an arrow which was not entirely drawn out from the quiver, and which tinged his fingers with the lustre of the gold on its feathered haft, replied (now) speaking sweetly to the lord of gods.

65. "If you think, O lord, that the horse is not to be released, then let my sire, purified by the constant performance of sacrifices be endowed with the entire fruit of the sacrifice, as if it had been completed in due form.

66. Moreover, O lord of the worlds, be it so arranged that the lord of the people, seated in the (sacred) chamber and inaccessible, being a part of the three-eyed god, may hear of this incident from your own messenger."

67. Having promised to grant the wish of Raghu, with the words 'so it shall be', Indra (*lit.* the god having Màtali for his charioteer) went his way ; and the son of Sudakshiṇâ too, not much pleased at heart, returned to the council-hall of the king.

68. The lord of men, already informed by the messenger of Indra warmly received him touching his body marked with the wound of the thunderbolt, with a hand benumbed with joy.

69. Thus did the lord of the earth, of laudable rule, wishing to ascend heaven, at the close of his life, accomplish nine-and-ninety great sacrifices, as if he constructed a flight of steps.

70. And now he, with his mind turned away from the objects of sense, made over in due form to his young son the white umbrella, the emblem of royalty, and betook himself in company with his celebrated queen to the shade of a tree in a forest inhabited by hermits : for this, indeed, was the family vow (practice,) of the princes of Ikshvàku's race, when in the decline of their life.

CANTO IV.

1. Having obtained the kingdom made over by his sire, Raghu shone yet more brilliantly (than before), as does fire (*lit.* the feeder on oblations) on receiving the effulgence deposited with it by the sun at the close of the day.

2. On hearing that he was established on the throne after Dilîpa, the fire (of jealousy) which had long been thickly smoking in the hearts of (hostile) princes, now blazed forth, as it were.

3. His subjects with their children rejoiced to see with beaming rows of eyes his new rise (to the throne), as they would see, with uplifted rows of eyes, the flag hoisted in honour of Indra.

4. Two things were simultaneously brought under himself by him who walked with the gait of an elephant (or on elephant-back), *viz.* the paternal throne and the whole circle of his enemies.

5. Him, consecrated to the universal sovereignty, served Padmâ (the goddess of regal fortune), as it seemed, herself invisible, by holding over him a lotus-umbrella, discernible from the halo of radiance (that encircled him).

6. And the goddess of learning too, being present in the panegyrizing bards at stated hours, served him, worthy of praise, with eulogies, full of sense.

7. The earth, though enjoyed by estimable monarchs, with Manu at their head, appeared in his case like one that had no previous master (was not enjoyed by any one else before).

8. He, by the justice of his punishments, won the heart of all the people, like the southern breeze, which is neither very cold nor excessively hot (and therefore delightful to every one).

9. By his possessing superior virtues the people were made to long less for his father by him just as they are by the fruit of the mango tree for its blossoming.

10. By men versed in the political art, two courses, the fair and the unfair, were pointed out to the new king ; but the first alone was adopted by him and not the second.

11. Even the qualities of the five primary elements (now) attained a (fresh) excellence. Under his new regime everything became new, as it were.

12. As the moon by its power to delight is rightly called *Chandra*; and as the sun by its diffusing heat is correctly named *Tapana*; so he, by pleasing his subjects, was justly styled *Rájá*.

13. Granted that his eyes were large, extending to the ears; but the function of (real) eyes was discharged in his case by (his knowledge of) the S'ástras, pointing out to him the minute details of his regal duties (or the subtle purposes to be accomplished).

14. Now as he was at ease (happy) by the pacification of (establishment of order and peace in) his kingdom, there came to him like a second goddess of wealth, autumn, marked by lotuses.

15. His exceedingly unbearable prowess and the intolerable heat of the sun simultaneously pervaded all the quarters of heaven, their path being cleared by the clouds, lightened by this contents being discharged.

16. Indra withdrew *his* pluvial bow and Raghu took up *his* victorious one; for they both took up their respective bows in turn for the good of the people.

17. The (autumnal) season, with its umbrella of white lotuses and with its *chauries* of the opening Kás a flowers, imitated Raghu with his lolus-like umbrella and his *chauries* resembling, the blooming Kás'a flowers, but could not attain his regal splendour.

18. At that time the delight of those who had eyes was of equal flavour (or, ardour) at the sight of him with a sweet smiling face, and of the moon of bright lustre.

19. The affluence of his fame seemed to be distributed among the rows of geese, among the starry spheres, and in waters abounding in (white) lillies.

20. Women keeping watch over the fields of paddy corn seated in sugar-cane shades, sang the fame of him, the protector, springing from his merits, beginning from his heroic deeds as a boy (or whereof a beginning was made by even children).

21. At the rise of him sprung from a pitcher (the star of Agastya), of great splendour, water became clear (pure and pellucid); at that of Raghu, of great might, the heart of his enemies apprehensive of defeat, got muddled (roiled).

22. Huge bulls with massive humps, fierce with fury and rending up (battering down) the banks of rivers, imitated the prowess of Raghu, which had much the grace of sport.

23. Wounded (in their vanity, or excited) by the rut-scented flowers of the *saptaparṇa* trees, Raghu's elephants poured forth, as if in emulation, ichor in all the seven ways (*i.e.* from all the seven parts of their body).

24. Making the rivers fordable and the roads with their mud dried up, Autumn incited him to an expedition of conquest, before his personal energy (inspired him to do it).

25. At the lustration ceremony of his horses, the sacrificial fire, fed with oblations duly offered, gave him (the blessing of) victory with his own hand, as it were, in the form of the flame turning towards the right (and thus betokening victory).

26. Having his capital and the frontier forts well-guarded, and the rear cleared of his foes (or with his rear well protected), and attended with good luck, he marched out with a sixfold force for the conquest of the quarters.

27. The women of the city, advanced in age, scattered over him fried rice, as the waves of the milky ocean deluged Achyuta with the drops thrown up by Mandara.

28. He, Indra's peer (in valour), first marched towards the east, menacing, as it were, his foes with his flags waved by the wind.

29. And turning, as it were, the sky into the earth's surface and the earth's surface into the sky by means (respectively) of the clouds of dust raised by his chariots and of his elephants resembling clouds.

30. His prowess in the van, then the uproar, thereafter the dust, and last of all the chariots and the rest ; thus did the army (of Raghu) march forward, consisting of four divisions (corps) as it were.

31. By reason of his being possessed of power or (resources), he turned deserts into well-watered tracts, the navigable rivers into easily fordable ones, and the forests into open plains (spaces).

32. Leading his mighty army marching towards the eastern sea, he looked like Bhagîratha, leading the broad Gaṅgá fallen from the matted hair of S'iva and flowing towards the eastern sea.

33. His path was conspicuous by the (hostile) kings made to part with their acquisitions (wealth), dethroned and variously

routed, like that of a tusker, which is marked by trees, shorn of their fruits, uprooted and destroyed in various ways.

34. Thus overruning the kingdoms in the east the victor came to the shore of the great ocean, dark with the forests of *tàli* trees.

35. From him the uprooter of all that did not bend before him, as from the current of a river, the Suhmas saved themselves by following the course of cane-plants (adopting the policy of submission).

36. Having by his power uprooted the Vaṅga kings, who had resisted him by means of their ships, he, the leader, planted (memorial) pillars of victory in the intervals of (*i. e.* the islets between) the streams of the Ganges.

37. Like the *Kalama* plants which bend low to (or to the lotuses at) their roots and yield a rich harvest after having been first uprooted and then transplanted, they, first uprooted and then reinstated, bowed down to his lotus-like feet and honoured him by gifts of riches.

38. He crossed the river Kapis'â with his troops by means of a bridge formed of the elephants and marched towards Kaliṅga, the way being led by the Utkala (Orissa) princes.

39. He planted his mighty prowess (made it keenly felt) on the head (peak) of the mountain Mahendra, just as a driver does his sharp goad in the head of a *Gambhîravedi* (not easily sensitive to pain) elephant.

40. The king of Kaliṅga, strong in his war elephants, received him with showers of missiles, as a mountain, showering stones, would (receive) Indra, prepared to cut its wings.

41. Having borne a heavy shower of the enemies' iron-arrows, the descendant of Kakutstha won the goddess of victory, as if after having taken an auspicious bath.

42. There, his soldiers, having prepared places for wassail, quaffed in (cups of) betel leaves cocoanut-wine, and also the glory of their enemies.

43. The king, a righteous conqueror, took away the wealth and not the territory of the lord of Mahendra first made a captive but afterwards released.

44. Then marching along the sea-coast, lined with betel-nut trees bearing fruit, he, to whom victory was not a thing to be

sought after, marched towards the quarter resorted to by Agastya (the south).

45. By reason of her enjoyment by his army, redolent of (marked by) by the sweet scent of elephants' ichor, he made Kâverî (the river) suspectable (an object of suspicion), as it were, to the lord of the rivers (the Ocean).

46. By the forces of him bent on conquest after he had travelled the day's distance, were occupied the adjoining grounds of the mountain Malaya, where the Hârîta birds (parrots of a particular kind) were flying about in the forests of peppers.

47. The dust of the fruits of the cardamom plants pounded by (the hoofs of) his horses, flying up, clung to (settled on) the temples of the infuriated elephants, exhaling a similar smell.

48. The neck-chains of the elephants powerful enough to break down even the foot-chains, did not slip off, being tied round the lines of grooves (depressions) made by the coilings of snakes into the sandal trees.

49. Even the splendour (heat) of the sun is dimmed (mitigated) when in the southern quarter; but in that very quarter the Pâṇḍya princes could not bear the burning prowess of Raghu.

50. Bowing down (at his feet) they presented to him the finest pearls found at the place where the Tâmraparṇî falls into the great ocean, their own accumulated glory, as it were.

51-52. Having enjoyed to the satisfaction of his wish the mountains Malaya and Dardura, with sandal trees covering their skirts, as if they were the breasts of the quarter with sandal paste applied to their sides, he, of irresistible prowess, crossed (or, reached) the Sahya mountain, far left off by the sea, the rump of the earth, as it were, with its vesture slipped off.

53. On account of his forces marching along, prepared to conquer the countries of the west, the sea, though far removed by the missile of Paras'urâma, seemed to be connected with the mountain Sahya.

54. The dust raised by the army was placed by him, as a substitute for the hair-powder, on the curls of the Kerala ladies who had given up personal decorations in terror.

55. The pollen of the Ketaka flowers, wafted by breezes from the Muralâ, served as a scented powder obtained without effort for the armours of his warriors.

56. The rustling of the large palm forests shaken by the wind was drowned by the clank of armours on the bodies of his warhorses moving about.

57. The black bees deserting the Punnâga trees fell upon the temples scented with the flow of the ichor of elephant tied to the trunks of the date trees.

58. History has it that the ocean gave space to Ráma on being requested by him ; but to Raghu, it gave tribute under the disguise of the western kings.

59. There he turned the trikûta itself into a lofty pillar of victory, bear as it did the distinct record of his military valour in the form of the incisions of the tusks of his infuriated elephants.

60. Thereafter he set out by a land-route to conquer the Persians, as a man possessed of self-control proceeds, with the help of the knowledge of truth, to subdue the foes known as the senses (passions.)

61. He did not bear the flush imparted by liquor to the lotuslike faces of the Yavan dames, just as an untimely rise of clouds does not (bear *i. e.* intercepts) the morning sunlight on (tinging) the lotuses.

62. A fierce battle took place between him and the Yavanas of the west, whose army consisted of cavalry, in the midst of dust (raised by the armies) so (dense) that the opposing warriors could know each other simply by the twang of their bows.

63. He strewed the earth with their bearded heads, severed by means of Bhallas (arrows having board blades) as if with so many honey-combs covered with bees.

64. The rest (*i. e.* survivors) took off their helmets and sought his protection ; for the wrath of the high-minded is appeased by humble submission (*lit.* has submission for its remedy).

65. His soldiers removed the fatigue of victory by means of wine, in vine-yards (*lit.* grounds covered with bowers of vine) with the finest deer-skins spread thereon.

66. Then Raghu marched towards the quarter of Kubera (the north) with the desire of uprooting, by means of his arrows, the northern king just as the great luminary (sun) passes northwards in order to suck up moisture with his rays.

67. His horses having the fatigue of their journey relieved by rolling on the bank of the Sindhu, shook their shoulders to which were adhering the filaments of saffron (or, the manes of which had safforn sticking to them).

68. There the exploits of Raghu, the prowess whereof was displayed on the husbands of the Hûṇa ladies, became a teacher of ruddiness in the cheeks to them (or came to have the redness of their cheeks for a record).

69. The Kâmboja princes, unable to stand his valour in battle, bent low (before him) together with the walnut trees strained injured all round by the fastening (or fastening-chains) of his elephant.

70. Lofty (stupendous) heaps of riches, abounding in noble steeds, reached the lord of the Kosalas every day ; but not their boastful manners (or, 'but pride never touched him').

71. Then he ascended the mountain Himâlaya (Gaurî's father) with his cavalry augmenting, in size, as it were, its peaks by the mineral dust raised up (by his horses).

72. The gaze, by turning back (their necks), of the lions lying in their dens and of equal might (with the army), indicated absence of agitation (or fear) on their part (their intrepidity) even in the midst of the din (tumult) of the army.

73. Breezes, rustling among the birch trees, the cause of the musical sounds of the singing bamboos, and charged with the spray of the Ganges, ministered to (fanned) him on the way.

74. His soldiers took rest under the shade of the Nameru trees sitting on stone-slabs with their surfaces perfumed with the navel (musk) of the musk-deer squatting upon them.

75. The lustrous herbs with their light reflected from the iron neck-chains of the elephants tied to the Sarala trees, served, at night, as lamps (that burnt) without oil, to him, the leader of the forces.

76. In the halting places left by him, the *devadaru* trees, the bark of which was rubbed off by the neck-ropes (with which the elephants were tied to them) indicated to the *Kiratas* the height of his elephants.

77. There a fierce battle took place between him and the mountain tribes, in which fire flashed forth as the iron darts and the stones flung by means of slings clashsd together.

78. Having made the Utsavasaṅketas destitute of their festivities by means of his arrows, he caused the Kiṃnaras to sing the songs descriptive of the victory of (won by) his arms.

79. When they approached (him), presents in hand, these came to be mutually known, Himavat's strength (wealth) by the king and the King's strength (prowess) by Himâdri (the snowy mountain).

80. Having established there the unshakeable (or irrefragable) mass of his glory, he descended (from the mountain), causing shame, as it were to the mountain that was balanced (being uplifted) by Paulastya (Râvaṇa)—*i.e.* Kailâsa.

81. When he crossed the Lauhityâ the lord of the Prâgjyotishas quaked (with fear), as also did the black aloe-wood trees got to the condition of (used) as tie-posts for his elephants.

82. He could not bear even the dust raised from the track of his chariots, which hid the sun and which looked like a cloudy day, (atmosphere) without a shower; how could he face his army ?

83. The King of the Kâmarûpas waited upon him whose valour exceeded that of Indra himself, with those very elephants, with ripped ichor-shedding temples, with which he had resisted (or repulsed) others.

84. The lord of Kâmarûpas adored the lustre of Ragu's feet, the presiding goddess of the golden foot-stool, with offerings of flowers in the form of gems.

85. Having thus conquered all the quarters, the conqueror turned back, making the dust raised by his chariots rest on the heads of the kings (now) stripped of the regal umbrellas.

86. He performed the *Vis'vajit* sacrifice in which one's entire wealth is given away as *Dakshiṇâ* ; for of the good as of clouds, acquisition is for distribution.

87. At the end of the sacrifice, the descendant of Kakutstha (Raghu), assisted by his ministers of state, allayed the wounded feelings of the defeated kings by honouring them with marks of great respect, and permitted them to go back to their capitals, where their wives were longing (for their return) owing to their long absence.

88. They, at the time of their departure, bowed down to the emperor's pair of feet bearing linear marks of banners, swords, and

royal umbrellas, and accessible by his favour alone, and made them yellowish white at the toes, with the pollen and honey that dropped from the garlands on their heads.

CANTO V.

1. Then there came to the monarch (Raghu) who had given away, so as to leave no remainder, his wealth of every kind (or his whole treasure) in the *Vis'vajit* sacrifice, Kautsa, the disciple of Varatantu, who had acquired learning (finished his education) and whose purpose it was to get money to pay his teacher (as tuition fees; or seeking to obtain money for remunerating his preceptor).

2. On account of the (stock of his) gold vessels being exhausted, he, of priceless (inestimable, noble) character, bright with glory, and hospitable, having placed the materials of worship in an earthen pot, went forth to receive the guest radiant (illustrious) with his Vedic knowledge.

3. The lord of men, adept (or versed) in duty and the rules of action (prescribed by the S'âstras) and foremost among those to whom honour is wealth, having worshipped, in the proper form, the guest, who regarded penance as his wealth and who, sitting on a seat, thus addressed him with joined palms, remaining close by.

4. " O you of acute intellect (*lit.* whose intellect is as acute as the sharp end of a blade of Kus'a grass), is it all well with your preceptor, the foremost of the sages, the composers (or recipients) of the Vedic hymns, from whom you have acquired complete knowledge, as the world derives its animation (or vitality) from the sun ?

5. I hope the threefold penance of the great sage, which has long been treasured up (by him) by (the exercise of) his body, speech, and mind, and which disturbs (or shakes off) the stability of Indra's mind, suffers no diminution (is not spent up) by impediments (requiring its use).

6. I hope no calamity, such as a hurricane, visits (befalls) the trees of your hermitage, which beguile fatigue and which have been reared up without distinction with (just like) your sons with efforts, such as the construction of water-basins and others.

7. Are those offsprings of the female deer all right, whose desire to eat the Kus'a grass, the hermits, from affection, do not foil (*i. e.* indulge) even though it is necessary for sacred rites and

whose umbilical cords drop down on their laps serving (the fawns) as beds ?

8. I hope it is all right with your sacred waters wherein your daily ablutions are performed, from which handfuls of libations are presented to the manes, and whose sandy banks are marked with the sixth part of the gleanings (gleaned corn).

9. I hope the ripe *nîvâra* and other corn, the sylvan means of the sustenance of your bodies, out of which portions are allotted to the guests coming in time, is not eaten up by country cattle (accustomed to eat chaff).

10. Has the great sage, being pleased after he had well educated you, permitted you to lead the house-holder's life ? For it is now time for you to enter on the second stage of life which is capable of benefiting all the other three (or which enables one to oblige every body).

11. My mind is not satisfied by the (mere) coming of you, adorable one, (but) it longs to execute some command (of yours); is it at your preceptor's bidding or of your own accord that you have come to honour me (do me the honour of a visit) from the forest ?"

12. Although he heard the noble words of Raghu, whose gift (or expenditure) of his whole wealth was inferred from the vessel containing the materials of worship, the disciple of Varatantu, having but a feeble hope of success in his object, thus addressed him.

13. "Know, O king, it is all well with us in all respects. How can woe betide the subjects while you are king (or, their protector) ? How can the dark night (or a dense mass of darkness) obstruct the sight of men while the sun is shining ?

14. Reverence for (or attention to) those worthy of honour is customary with your race (or is the hereditary possession of your dynasty) ; but, O illustrious one (or O great monarch), you outdo your ancestors in that. I, however, have come to you as a suitor out of (the proper) time, and hence my regret.

15. O lord of men, having bestowed all your wealth on worthy recipients, you appear with your body only remaining to you, like a *nîvâra* plant having its corn appropriated by foresters (forest-living ascetics) and its stalk (or culm) only left to it.

16. It is but proper (or creditable to you, or becoming in you) that you, though a paramount king, should exhibit poverty (*lit,*

a state of having nothing) born of (the result of) a sacrifice ; for the waning of the moon (whose nectar is) drunk in their turns by gods is more to her praise than her waxing.

17. I, therefore, who have no other business in view, will strive to obtain money for my preceptor from some other source ; may you fare well. Even the *châtaka* bird troubles not (with its petitioning) the autumnal cloud whose watery contents are all discharged."

18. Dissuading (from going) the disciple of the great sage, who was desirous of going away, after having said this much, the king asked him, " Learned sir ! What thing and how much of it is to be presented by you to your preceptor ? "

19. Then to the ruler of the (four) classes and the stages of life, who had duly performed a sacrifice and who was entirely free from the influence of vanity, the learned ascetic (thus) expressed his purpose (immediate business)—

20. " The great sage was requested by me, when I had completed my course of study, to accept from me preceptor's fee. He, however, counted (regarded) foremost (held more important than, or considered the best, fee) my long and unswerving devotion to him of that kind (so difficult to be performed).

21. Incensed at my importunities, my preceptor, without taking into consideration the scantiness of my means, said to me : ' Bring me four-and-ten crores of money (gold coins) corresponding to the number of lores (studied) by you.'

22. Thus circumstanced I, concluding from your vessel of offerings that you have only the title of sovereign remaining to you, have not the mind to constrain you at present, on account of the price of my learning being other than (far from) low (*i. e.*, very exorbitant or heavy)."

23. Thus informed by the twice-born (Brâhmaṇa), the best of Vedic scholars, the sole lord of the world, fair as the moon, and with the propensities of his senses restrained from sin, once more spoke to him.

24. " 'A certain suitor who asked money for his preceptor and who had seen the end (was master) of learning, went to another donor, not obtaining his object from Raghu'—let there not be this new (or for the first time) reproach on my name.

25. You, therefore (*lit.* thus circumstanced), O venerable one, be pleased to wait, like a fourth fire, in my well-known and revered

sanctuary of (holy) fires, for two or three days, in which time I will endeavour to fulfil your object."

26. With the words 'Be it so' the Brâhmaṇa, being delighted, accepted his unfailing promise. Raghu, on his part, seeing that the earth was drained of all its wealth, wished to wrench (thought of procuring by force) money from Kubera.

27. By virtue of the miraculous power accruing from Vasishṭha's sprinkling accompanied by holy incantations (at the time of his coronation), the course of his chariot, like that of a cloud assisted by the wind, was not obstructed, whether on the sea, or in the sky, or on the mountains.

28. Then in the evening Raghu, firm-minded and pious, slept in his chariot in the interior of which weapons were arranged, desirous of conquering the lord of Kailâsa (Kubera) by his prowess, looking upon him as (as if he were no better than) a mere feudatory prince.

29. At dawn, officers, employed in the treasury, full of wonder, reported to him, about to set forth, a shower of gold fallen from the sky into the treasury-house.

30. The king gave to Kautsa the whole of that glittering heap of gold which was obtained from Kubera, who was about to be attacked, and which looked like an adjoining hill of the (mountain) Sumeru detached by Indra's thunder-bolt.

31. Both of them, the suitor who would not take (*lit.* who had no desire to accept) more than what was to be given to his preceptor, and the king who gave more than what was asked by the suitor, had the greatness of their mind (or their conduct) greatly praised by the people inhabiting Sâketa (Ayodhyâ).

32. Then at his departure, the great sage Kautsa, delighted in the mind, touched by the hand the king who had caused his treasure to be transported (or conveyed) by hundreds of camels and mares, as he bent the forepart of his body before him, and addressed him (this) speech—

33. "What wonder is there (*i. e.* it is no wonder) if the earth yields the desires of a monarch who abides by his duty ? But incomprehensible is your power, since by you even heaven itself was milked (made to grant) your desired object.

34. Any other benediction (than that of issue) would be a repetition (superfluous) to you who have attained all blessings,

May you obtain a son worthy of your excellences, as your father obtained your praiseworthy self."

35. Having thus conferred a blessing upon the king, the Brâhmaṇa returned to his preceptor. The king, too, soon after, obtained a son from it (by virtue of it, *scil.* the blessing) as the world of the living receives light from the sun.

36. At the hour presided over by Brahmâ, history records (किल), his queen gave birth to a son like Kumâra. On that account the father made (called) his son Aja, after the name of Brahmâ himself.

37. His majestic (or resplendent) form was the same, the valour the same, and the natural sublimity (or nobleness of nature) also the same; the new-born prince did not differ from his generating cause (father) as a lamp lighted from another (does not differ from it).

38. The goddess of royalty, though she had a yearning after him when he had duly received his education from his preceptors and was looking all the more charming (or peculiarly charming) by reason of his blooming youth, waited for her master's (or his sire's) permission, as a discreet, noble-minded daughter does for her fathers.

39. About this time, a trusty messenger was sent to Raghu by Bhoja, lord of the Kra'hakais'ikas, who was ardently desirous of bringing the prince (Aja) for (to be present at) the ceremony of the self-election-marriage of his sister Indumatî.

40. Considering him to be one with whom a connexion was desirable and (further) that his son had arrived at a marriageable age, he sent him with an army to the flourishing (or wealthy) capital of the king of the Vidarbhas.

41. The halting stations on the way of him, a king's son, in which accommodations of all kinds were provided in tents of royal state, and which, on account of the presents brought by the villagers, appeared other than (the reverse of) sylvan, were almost like places of amusement in gardens.

42. When he had gone over some way (certain distance) he encamped his wearied army, with its banners sullied with dust, on the bank of the Narmadâ, the *naktamâla* trees on which were made to dance a little (gently shaken) by the breezes charged with spray (or moist with the drops of water).

43. Just then there emerged from the river a wild elephant, whose plunge (*lit.* entrance) into the water had already been indicated by black bees hovering above (over the surface of the water) and whose expansive cheeks were clean, as the ichor had been entirely washed off—

44. Who betrayed his butting-sports on the skirts of the Rikshavat mountain by means of his two rock-blunted tusks, which were checkered with blue lines running upwards, although completely washed of all mineral dust.

45. As he faced the bank and cut (his way) with (loud) noise (through) the large waves with this trunk quick in its contractions and protrusions, he looked as if engaged in breaking asunder the bolts of his stall.

46. The mountain-like elephant dragging with him by his breast the meshes of moss (*s'aivala*) reached the bank afterwards, the current of waters violenty agitated by him having reached it first.

47. The darkish splendour of the ichor flowing from the broad cheeks of that one (single of its kind, chief &c.) elephant, which had been stopped for a moment by his plunge into water, shone forth afresh at the sight of tame (*lit.* other than wild) elephants.

48. On smelling his unbearable rut whose flow was as strong-smelling (or fragrant) as the milky exudation of the *saptachchhada* (seven-leaved) tree, the huge elephants in the army turned back (shied), notwithstanding (or defying) the strenuous efforts of their drivers.

49. In a moment he threw the encampment into utter confusion, cleared of horses which tore their bonds and fled, with the chariots fallen to the ground, their axles being broken and with the warriors perplexed in protecting the ladies.

50. The prince, who knew (from the S'āstras) that a king ought not to kill a wild elephant, not drawing his horn-made-bow to any great length, struck the rushing elephant on the forehead with an arrow, (merely) wishing to make him turn back.

51. The moment he was wounded, as history tells us, he quitted the form of an elephant, and assumed the lovely figure of a heavenly being, encircled with a flashing halo of light, and looked at by the army astonished at the (curious) occurrence.

52. Then having showered on the prince the flowers of the heavenly trees that came to him through his superhuman power,

the eloquent one (thus) spoke, enhancing with the lustre of his teeth the (brightness of the) necklace of large pearls pendant on his bosom.

53. " I was reduced to the state of an elephant by the curse of Mataṅga, incurred by my own arrogance. Know me to be Priyaṃvada, the son of Priyadars'ana, king of the Gandharvas.

54. The great sage, however, being supplicated by me falling at his feet, relented afterwards ; for the hotness of water is due to its contact with fire or solar heat ; what is coldness is but the nature (natural property) of water.

55. 'When Aja, sprung from the family of Ikshvâku, will split thy frontal globe with his iron-pointed shaft, then shalt thou be united with (restored to) thy magnificent form '--so spoke that repository of penance (the great sage) to me.

56. I have been liberated from the curse by you endowed with might, whose sight had long been earnestly wished for by me. If I do you no good in return, my restoration to my proper position is all to no purpose.

57. Accept, therefore, O friend, this missile of mine, 'Saṃmohana (the stupifier)' by name, which has a Gandharva for its presiding deity, and has separate incantations for its discharge and withdrawal whereby the discharger has victory in his hand (sure in his possession) and yet has not to kill enemies.

58. You should not be ashamed ; for, though striking me, you were moved (for a moment) with compassion ; let not the rudeness of a refusal be shown to me who am beseeching you."

59. With the words 'Be it so' the eminent (*lit.* the moon among men) prince, skilled in the use of weapons, having sipped the holy water of the river sprung from Soma (Narmadâ) and turned his face towards the north, received (learned) the incantations of (connected with) the missile from him who was freed from the curse.

60. Of them two, who, by a strange chance, had thus formed on the way, a friendship (originating) from some unknown cause, one went to the regions of Chaitraratha and the other to the country of Vidarbha delightful on account of the good government (it enjoyed).

61. The lord of the Krathakais ikas filled with ecstatic joy went forth to receive him who had halted in the vicinity of the

city, as the ocean with its swelling waves goes forth to receive the moon.

62. Walking in the front he led him into the city, and having presented to him his wealth, waited upon (ministered to) him with humility, in such a way that the people assembled there considered Aja to be the host (*lit.* the lord of the palace) and the king of the Vidarbhas to be the guest.

63. He, the representative of Raghu, occupied the delightful new pavilion into which he was shown by the officers of king Bhoja, bending low (before him), and in which vessels filled with water were placed on a dais near its eastern entrance, as Madana (Cupid) occupies the state (age) next to childhood.

64. There, like a loved spouse unable to read (understand) the feelings (of her husband), (or, clouded—displeased by her divination of the mental attitude—affection for a rival), sleep came late at night towards the eyes of Aja, longing to win the captivating gem of a damsel, by whom a host of kings was caused to be assembled at her self-choice-marriage.

65. At dawn, the sons of bards, of equal age (with Aja), and eloquent in speech, awakened, with their panegyrical songs, him, of reputed scholarship, whose stout shoulders were pressed by his ear-ornaments and the sweet unguents applied to whose body were almost effaced by his rollings on the bed sheet.

66. "O you, best of talented men, the night is gone; quit your bed; surely the burden of the world has been divided into two parts only, by the Creator: your vigilant father bears it at one end and your honour is the supporter of the other (*lit.* that borne by the other bearer).

67. The moon by (looking at) whom the goddess of beauty (Lakshmî) was diverting herself at night, like a woman offended by her husband, (somehow) disregarding even her longing for you under the influence of sleep;—he, too, now resting on the extremity of the western horizon, is giving up (losing) the splendour of your face.

[Or, with the reading अनवेक्ष्यमाणा, (see notes):—The moon by (looking at) whom the goddess of beauty, though neglected by you under the influence of sleep, was, like a woman offended by her husband, beguiling her love-longing, even he &c.]

68. Let, therefore, the two, by their beautiful simultaneous unfolding, obtain mutual similtude: *viz.* your eye with the

lively-(*lit.* other than rough) pupil rolling about within and the lotus with a black bee moving inside.

69. The morning breeze, as if desirous of obtaining, by means of borrowed properties, the natural fragrance of the breath of your mouth, bears away the loosened flowers of trees from their stalks and comes in contact with lotuses opened by the rays of the morning sun Aruṇa).

70. The dew-drops, white like the well-cleansed pearls of a necklace, fallen on the tender leaves of trees with their interiors red, resemble, on account of the position of advantage thus gained by them (or their increased excellence), your sportive smile fallen on your lip, brightened by the splendour of your teeth.

71. While the sun, the store of radiant heat, does not rise, even before that, darkness has been, all at once, dispelled by Aruṇa; when, O hero, you have taken the lead in battles, will (why should) your sire himself extirpate the foes?

72. Your elephants, with their sleep shaken off from both sides, are leaving their beds, pulling at their clanking chains: the elephants whose bud-like tusks seem as if they had pierced the red-mineral-skirts of a mountain, on account of their having come in contact with the rosy tints of the morning sun.

73. O lotus-eyed one, the horses of the breed of the Vanâyu country (Persian horses), tied in spacious tents, having given up their sleep, are soiling with the warm breath (vapour) of their mouth the pieces of rock-salt placed before them for being licked.

74. The flower-offering, being withered, has become loose in texture; the lamps are void of the throbbing circles (halo) of their light; and this your sweet-speaking parrot resting in its cage imitates our speech employed to rouse you."

75. The prince, his sleep dispelled by the young bards singing their songs in this strain, instantly left his bed, just as the heavenly elephant, Supratîka, awakened from sleep by the royal swans cackling sweetly under excitement, leaves the sandy beach of the Ganges.

76. Then, having finished the rites proper for day-break, as prescribed in the S'âstras, the prince, with beautiful eyelashes, after his toilet was finished in a fitting style by experts (in that art), repaired to the assembly of kings gathered in the hall of the self-election-marriage.

NOTES.

CANTO I.

रघुवंशः—रघूणां वंशो रघुवंशः the race of the Raghus, the solar dynasty of kings; and then by उपचार (transference of an epithet) तदाख्यः प्रबन्धः the composition which describes रघुवंशः; and since the word प्रबन्ध is in the *mas.* gender we get the form रघुवंशः. That the poet intended to designate his work by some *mas.* title appears from his line 'तं सन्तः श्रोतुम्' &c. where Malli. supplies the word 'प्रबन्धम्' as referred to by the demonstrative pronoun तम्.

The authority for forming the titles of literary works is the Sûtra 'तदधिकृत्य कृते ग्रन्थे' (Pâṇ. IV. 3. 87) and the Vârt. on it, *viz.*, लुबाख्यायिकाभ्यो बहुलम्. But the Sûtra and the Vârttika do not apply in the present case. Nor can we add अण् by कृते ग्रन्थे (IV. 3. 116); for then we shall get राघुवंशः. The title, therefore, ought to be explained like 'शारीरकम्' the name of the venerable Śaṅkarâchârya's *Bhâshya* on the Vedânta-Sûtra of Bâdarâyaṇa. In trying to explain this, Bhaṭṭoji Dikshita remarks—शारीरकं भाष्यमिति त्वभेदोपचारात् "the word शारीरक which means 'the soul' signifies the *Bhâshya* by transference of an epithet." 'कुमारसंभव,' 'रत्नावली' and other similar names ought to be explained similarly.

Agreeably to the canon of poetics which lays down that "Every poetic composition should open with (a verse or verses expressive of) a blessing pronounced on its readers or a salutation by the author to his favourite deity, or the hinting of the subject-matter,"* the Raghuvaṁśa opens with a salutation by the poet to Śiva and Pârvatî who, according to the verse from the Vâyupurâṇa, quoted in his introduction by Malli., ought to be invoked by those desirous of poetic fame.

Sl. 1. †वागर्थाविव is a compound word and not, as some might be led to think, two words. 'वागर्थौ' by itself cannot be syntactically connected either with वन्दे or with पितरौ, and Malli. rightly considers the two words वागर्थौ and इव as forming an adverbial compound (अव्ययसमास) modifying the sense of संपृक्तौ (कथं संपृक्तौ वागर्थाविव).

---

*आशीर्नमस्क्रियावस्तुनिर्देशो वापि तन्मुखम् । Daṇḍin.

†वाक् चार्थश्च वागर्थौ । According to the general rule the word अर्थ ought to precede वाक्. But since the word is classed under the राजदन्तादि group we have वागर्थौ. According to the Vṛittikâra अर्थवाचौ is also correct.

The text of Malli.'s com. on this word wherein we find इवेन सह नित्यसमासः &c. seems to be corrupt; for Malli., in explaining the comp. quotes the Bhâshya of Patañjali. Now Patañjali says 'इवेन सह समासो विभक्त्यलोपः पूर्वपदप्रकृतिस्वरत्वं च वक्तव्यम्' and not नित्यस० as appears in Malli.'s com. in the existing editions of the Raghu. Secondly, there are numerous instances in the Raghuvamsa itself which show that the comp. with इव is optional and not *Nitya* (obligatory); *e. g.*, उद्बाहुरिव वामनः (वामन इव); प्रणवश्छन्दसामिव &c. The text of Malli., therefore, has been corrected accordingly. संपृक्तौ —*Cf.* तमर्थमिव भारत्या सुतया योक्तुमर्हसि । Kum. VI. 79.

वागर्थप्रतिपत्तये—अर्थ is of three kinds. वाच्य or expressed, लक्ष्य or indicated, and व्यङ्ग्य or suggested. Vide K.-P. II. पार्वतीपरमेश्वरौ—Note the formation of the comp. explained by Malli. The Com. Vijayagani has—परा उत्कृष्टा मा शक्तिर्यस्यासौ परमः । ईष्टे असौ ईश्वरः । परमश्चासौ ईश्वरश्च परमेश्वरः । *Cf.* also ईशे एत्राहमत्यर्थं न च मामीशते परे । ददामि च यदैश्वर्यमीश्वरस्तेन कीर्तितः ॥ Some commentators give fanciful renderings of this—*e. g.* पार्वतीं पाति रक्षतीति पार्वतीपो रुद्रः । रमाया लक्ष्म्या ईश्वरः रमेश्वरः । पार्वतीपश्च रमेश्वरश्च पार्वतीपरमेश्वरौ तौ हरिहरौ । यद्वा पार्वतीं पिपर्ति पालयति इति पार्वतीपरः । पृपालनपूरणयोरिति धातुत्वात् । मायाः पद्माया ईश्वरः मेश्वरो विष्णुः । तौ वन्दे । इत्यस्मिन्पक्षे वागर्थाविवेत्युपमाया भिन्नलिंगत्वं न दोषाय । न लिंगवचने भिन्ने इत्या° see foot-note 4, p. 11. *Cf.* प्रभाकराविव संपृक्तौ भवभीतिनिवृत्तये । रक्षितारौ त्रिजगतो लक्ष्मीनारायणौ भजे ॥ fr. दिव्यसूरिचरित, as quoted by Nandar.

Kâlidâsa has opened almost all his works with a verse or verses either invoking a blessing of the God Siva, or containing a salutation to him—a fact which might point to the conclusion that he was a devotee of the God. It is not, however, to be inferred from this that he was a bigoted Saiva. For in the tenth canto of the present work, and in Kum. II., he assigns to Vishnu and Brahman respectively the highest attributes, which properly apply to Brahman (*neu.*); while in one place (Kum. VII. 44) he speaks of all these three as one. All this shows that he regarded Brahman, Vishnu and Siva, as each identical with the supreme Brahman viewed in its different capacities of creating, protecting, and finally resolving into itself, the universe.

Sl. 2. अल्पविषया—विषय proper province, range. दुस्तरम्—difficult to be crossed (even in a ship). Malli. who says 'तरितुमशक्यम्' seems to connect it with उडुपेन (उडुपेन दुस्तरमपि सागरमुडुपेनैव तितीर्षुरस्मि). मोहात्—through a wrong conception of my true powers; through inability to judge of my true powers. उडुप lit. what protects (प)

on water (उडु); a boat, a raft. सागरम्—सागरः (गरेण विषेण सह जातः सगरः। सगरस्यायं सगरेण कृतो वा)—from Sagara, a king of the solar race, whose 60,000 sons, while in search of the sacrificial horse of their father, enlarged the bounds of the sea, which thenceforth came to be called 'Sâgara.' For further particulars see III. 50, XIII. 3 and the notes thereon; also Râmâyaṇa I. 40. Nandar. quotes क्व दिव्यसूरिचरितं क्व च मे मन्दशेमुषी। नियन्तुकामोस्मि गजं साहसाद्बिसतन्तुना ॥ दिव्यसूरिचरित I. 2. (which is undoudbtedly based on this).

"It is curious to note that there is still to the south of the delta in the Bay of Bengal a spot which has not yet been sounded and is supposed to be unfathomable. That mysterious phenomenon known as the 'Burrisaul Guns,' is supposed by some to emanate from the hollow of this unfathomable cavern". Prof. Ray's note.

The figure of speech here is निदर्शना; see foot-note.

Śl. 3. कवियशःप्रार्थी—कवियशःप्रार्थनाशीलः (Malli.), persistingly striving after a poet's fame. Or the compound may be expounded thus : प्रकृष्टोर्थः प्रार्थः, कवियश एव प्रार्थोऽसंनिहितोऽस्य by the Vârttikas 'अर्थाच्चासंनिहिते' and 'तदन्ताच .' यशस्–fr. अश् to pervade : अश्नुते व्याप्नोतीति यशः, the अ of अश् is changed to य before the Uṇâdi aff. असुन् (अस्).

With these two ślokas wherein the poet modestly speaks of his inability to complete the task he has set to himself, may be compared the last of Báṇa's introductory verses to his Kád. and the passage in the Har.-Cha. बाणस्तु विहस्याब्रवीत् * * * क्व परिमाणुपरिमाणत्रुदहृदयम् &c. which, it is quite likely, Báṇa might have modelled on these verses of Kálidása.

Śl. 4. अथवा—or rather; I need not be discouraged. अस्मिन्—The pron. इदम् refers to what is near, तत् to what is not perceived owing to its distance. See Gr. § 72. Here the poet refers to the race by इदम् since it is present to his mind. On such points Bhaṭṭoji Dîkshita remarks–'विप्रकृष्टस्यापि बुद्ध्या सन्निधापितस्य बहुशः सम्बोधनदर्शनात्' what is far removed is often pictured to the mind as near and so addressed.

पूर्वसूरिभिः—by Vâlmîki and other Paurāṇic writers. सूरिः—सूते सूयते वा he who gives birth to new ideas, &c.; hence a poet; it also means a 'philosopher' as in the S'ruti 'सदा पश्यन्ति सूरयः' The sage Chyavana is said to have described the solar race before Vâlmîki—*cf.* वाल्मीकिनादश्च ससर्ज पद्यं जग्रन्थ यन्न च्यवनो महर्षिः। चिकित्सितं यच्च चकार नात्रिः पश्चात्तदात्रेय ऋषिर्जगाद ॥ Budd. I. 48. वज्रसमुत्कीर्णे–वज्र is a steel instrument with a diamond pin for perforating precious stones. वंशे मे

गतिः—this ought to be understood only metaphorically, the race being reprsented as a house.

S'l. 5. S'lokas 5–9 are to be construed together and form what is technically called a *Kulaka*; see ft.-note. सोऽहम्—that I, I as described above, *i. e.*, पूर्वसूरिभिः कृतेन वाग्द्वारेण लब्धप्रवेशः who have obtained entrance through the door opened by ancient poets; *cf.* V. 22; XIV. 66· When be we are speaking of something already described the correlative may omitted, as in the present case.

आजन्म &c.—in all these attributes the particle आ implies limit both inceptive as well as conclusive (see Malli.). आसमुद्रम्—Visva-nâth remarks that for the sake of emphasis this should not have been compounded. आनाक &c.—see note on S'l. 75. and *cf.* V. 27. नाकः-कं happiness न कं अकं; न अकं यत्र स नाकः स्वर्गः. Here न is not changed to अन्; *fc.* नाको नवेदा नकुलश्च नक्रो नासत्यनक्षत्रनपाच्च नभ्राट्। नपुंसकं वै नमुचिर्नखं च नादेशमेतेषु वदन्ति धीराः॥ See Pâṇ. VI. 3. 75.

S'l. 6. यथाविधिहुताग्नीनाम्—This refers to the three sacred fires दक्षिण, गार्हपत्य and आहवनीय (see Manu. II. 321) which a *Dvija* (twice-born, *i. e.*, a Bráhmaṇa, a Kshatriya and a Vais'ya) is enjoined to consecrate and keep up. *Cf.* अग्निहोत्रं च जुहुयादाद्यन्ते द्युनिशोः सदा। दर्शेन चार्धमासान्ते पौर्णमासेन चैव हि॥ Manu. VI. 25; for the विधि see Manu. IV. 21–32. Châr. and Vijay. also dissolve as यथाविधि हुतमग्निभिः इति वा; remarking वैयधिकरण्येपि.... ..गमकत्वाद्वा समासः। The kings of the solar race had a special house built for the purpose; see *infra* V. 25. The three fires are collectively called त्रेता; in Manu III. 100, 185, five holy fires are mentioned, two more सभ्य and आवसथ being added to the list.

यथाकालप्रबोधिनाम्—The term इन् shows habit. This may mean who were in the habit of (1) waking up at the proper time, *i. e.* ब्राह्मे मुहूर्ते (see Manu. IV. 92); or (2) knowing in detail (प्र) and taking action. The latter is better. Who knew everything in time, such as the secret movements of their enemies, &c. and provided for emergencies; who woke, in time, to the proper sense of danger whenever it threatened their subjects and protected them from it. See Malli. (प्रजापालनसमय &c.) and *Cf.* XVII. 51.

S'l. 7. त्यागाय, सत्याय &c., see Malli. and Gr. § 687. गृहमेधिनाम्—Mallinâtha's explanation of this seems to be quite correct and S. P. Pandit's remarks on it quite out of place. Mr. Pandit would derive the word fr. गृहमेध a kind of sacrifice to be performed in a house, and गृहमेधिन् according to him is simply a householder. But this does not seem to be intended by the poet at least here. See s'l. 25, where the poet clearly says परिणेतुः प्रसूतये. The गृहमेध of Mr. Pandit has nothing to do with प्रजा or 'progeny.' Manu's statement 'अग्नौ प्रास्ताहुतिः &c.' applies to the welfare of the people in general, resulting from the performance of sacrifices. Char., Din. and Sumat. have गृहमेधो विवाहः सोऽस्त्येषां, and Valla. says गृहं कलत्रं मेधन्ते सेवन्त इति.

S'l. 8. विषयैषिणाम्—विषज्यन्ते इंद्रियाणि येषु इति विषयाः those on which the senses are set, *i. e.*, the objects of pleasure; विषयान् इच्छन्तीति विषयैषिणः. *Cf.* 'रूपं शब्दो गन्धरसस्पर्शाश्च विषया अमी' Amar. मुनिवृत्तीनाम्- मुनि fr. मन् to think+इन् before which the अ of मन् is changed to उ. वृत्तीनां—A Vyadhikarana Bah. comp.; मुनीनामिव वृत्तिर्येषाम्.

According to the Mahábháshya the comp. ought to be dissolved thus:—मुनीनां वृत्तिर्मुनिवृत्तिः, मुनिवृत्तिरिव वृत्तिर्येषाम्, in accordance with the rule सप्तम्युपमानपूर्वपदस्योत्तरपदलोपश्च वक्तव्यः,' If dissolved otherwise there would be no उपमानपद. Malli., when he says मुनीनां वृत्तिः इव, means मुनिवृत्तिरिव; see his com. on वृषस्कन्धः s'l. 13 further on. But Vámana and many other later grammarians do not seem to like to stick to the verbal rigour of the Bhâshya in such cases. Thus Vâmana, in his Kâs'iká says उष्ट्रस्य मुखमिव मुखं यस्य स उष्ट्रमुखः and not उष्ट्रमुखमिव मुखं यस्य as in the Bhâshya. Malli. evidently follows the Bháshya.

योगेन—*i. e.* they practised *yoga* or contemplation (see VIII. 19, 20) and when they became adepts in that they caused thier soul to merge into the Supreme soul by contemplation. The four epithets in this s'l. imply the four stages of life of a twice-born; see com.

S'l. 9. 'रघूणाम्—Here by लक्षणा Raghus means 'the kings of the race of Raghu;' रघूणामन्वयम्......इति तु तदपत्ये लक्षणया. For the defi. of लक्षणा see K.-P. II. 'लक्षणा शक्यसंबन्धस्तात्पर्यानुपपत्तितः' | Bhâ. Pari.

अन्वयम्—अन्वियन्ति परस्परं सम्बन्धं गच्छन्ति अस्मिन्नित्यन्वयः a connected line, genealogy. तनुवाग्विभवोऽपि-though my powers of expression are scanty or very poor; though possessed of a limited power of description. चापलाय see note on वनाय II. 1.

N. B. All these attributes of the Raghus will be found illustrated in the present work; see ft.-note.

S'l. 10. सन्तः—सत् properly 'what exists' (pres. p. of अस्); and as goodness alone endures for a long time, it secondarily means-good, a good man. सदसद्व्यक्तिहेतवः—see Malli. Here असत् does not imply negation of good, but has a positive sense; 'what is opposed to good.' *Cf.* Mâl. II. 10, quoted in the foot-note, where the idea nearly recurs.

Śl. 11. वैवस्वतो मनुः—There are 14 Manus in a Kalpa. For their names see foot-note. विवस्वत्—the sun, is variously derived; विविधं वस्ते आच्छादयति इति; or विवो रश्मिः (fr. विवस् + क्विप्), अस्यास्तीति. It is also derived from वस् with वि Ved. 6. P. to shine forth, to dawn (व्युच्छति); the brilliant one.

The Manu referred to here is the 7th of the 14 Manus, sometimes called सत्यव्रत from his purity. He is considered to be the son of विवस्वत् 'the sun,' and is regarded as the progenitor of the present race of living beings. He is also described as the brother of Yama, who, as son of Vivasvat, is also called *Vaivasvata*. This Manu is regarded as the founder and first king of Ayodhyâ. His daughter Ilá married Budha, son of the Moon, the two great solar and lunar races being thus united. This Manu was preserved from a great flood, according to another account, by Vishṇu in the form of a fish, and has been compared in this respect to Noah of the Old Testament.

मनीषिणाम्—Malli. takes this as a comp. of the पृषोदरादि class; मनस् ईषिन्=मन् + ईषिन्; like पृषत् + उदर=पृष + उदर, the अस् of मनस् being irregularly dropped; in this he follows the Bhâshya and Kaiyata. Bhaṭṭoji Dîkshita includes this under the शकन्ध्वादि गण; मनस + ईषिन् like शक + अन्धु=शकन्धु; there being पररूपसन्धि, see Gr. § 15. मनीषिन्—one who goes to everything by his mind, *i. e.* intellect; wise.

महीक्षितां—Read in the com. महीं क्षयन्तीति as क्षि in the sense of 'to rule' is of the भ्वादि class. *Cf.* ईष्टे वा गच्छतीत्यर्थे क्षयतीत्यादिकं भवेत् । पृथिव्यां क्षियतीत्यादौ निवासार्थः प्रकीर्तितः ॥ See note on महीक्षितः I. 85. प्रणवः-is the sacred syllable ओम्, so called from its being repeated in the beginning of Vedic verses (fr. प्र + नु 'to praise') "According to some accounts the mystic प्रणव was the source of all the Vedas. A passage in the Aitareya Bráhmaṇa, however, makes the प्रणव arise from the Vedas. See Ai.—Br. V. 31." S. P. Pandit's note.

A Brâhmaṇa must repeat the holy syllable ओम् at the beginning and end of the recital of a Vedic passage; for unless the syll. ओम् precedes, his learning will slip away from him; unless it follows nothing will be long retained by him. (Vide Manu. quoted in the foot-note). It appears for the first time in the Upanishads (Vide the Mâṇḍûkya and the Chhândogya Upanishads) as a mystic monosyllable and is there set forth as the object of profound religious meditation, the highest spiritual efficacy being attributed to it. "All rites ordained in the Vedas, solemn sacrifices and others," says Manu "pass away; but that which passeth not away is the imperishable Om." Om is also regarded as a mystic name for the Trinity of the Godhead, the three sounds अ, उ and म् representing Vishṇu, Śiva ahd Brahman respectively:—अकारो विष्णुरुद्दिष्ट उकारस्तु महेश्वरः । मकारेणोच्यते ब्रह्मा प्रणवस्तु त्रयो मताः ॥ Vide Manu. II. 74–84. Also Gough's Upanishads pp. 69–73.

Sl. 12 प्रसूतः—Malli. translates this by जातः, meaning thereby that the root सू should be taken here as used intransitively. Unless we suppose so it is difficult to justify the use of the word with दिलीप. A transitive root may be used intransitively, when the कर्म is अविवक्षित, *i. e.*, not meant to be expressed; so we may say देवी कुमारं सुपुत्रे or देवी सूता or प्रसूता (*cf.* सद्यः प्रसूता प्रिया Bhav.) the कर्म in the latter case being suppressed and the affix क्त used कर्तरि वाच्ये। But it is not easy to understand an expression like पुत्रः प्रसूतः unless we supply तन्मात्रा. राजेन्दुः—By उपमितं व्याघ्रादिभिः सामान्याप्रयोगे Pāṇ. II. I. 56. *i. e.*, a noun expressing the *object* of comparison is compounded in a Tat. (कर्मधारय) with a noun expressive of the *standard* of comparison, such as व्याघ्र, when the common attribute is not mentioned; here इन्दु implies excellence.

इन्दुः क्षीरनिधाविव—This refers to the churning of the milky ocean by the gods and demons. The moon was one of the fourteen gems rescued from the churned ocean. For further particulars, see Mb. Ádip. 14. इन्दुः—उनत्ति अमृतेन चान्द्रिकया वा भुवनमिति; from उन्द् to wet, to bathe, and the Uṇâdi affix उः the उ being irregularly changed to इ.

The word इन्दु is frequently found in the Rigveda and is said to mean either (1) a bright drop of the Soma juice, or (2) the Soma juice itself. *Cf.* सुतास इन्दवः Rv. I. 16. 6. The word then came to signify a 'globule or a round little body' and finally became a name of the moon. See note on ओषधीनाथम् II. 73.

Sl. 13. व्यूढोरस्कः—क is necessarily added to a Bah. ending in उरस्; see com शालप्रांशुः—has also a technical meaning, for which see ft.-note. महाभुजः—Some understand by महत् 'reaching as far as the knees, From Dilipa's hugeness of form which enabled him to discharge the noble functions of heroism, such as the protection of the weak, &c., the poet infers that he was, as it were, heroism incarnate. आत्मकर्मक्षमं &c. *Cf.* क्षात्रो धर्मः श्रित इव तनुं ब्रह्मकोषस्य गुप्त्यै। Uttar. VI. 2.

Sl. 14. सर्वातिरिक्तसारेण—Malli. does not expound this but simply gives the meaning. Dissolve सर्वेषामतिरिक्ततरः सर्वातिरिक्तः (Gr. § 135. 3) सारो यस्य; or अतिरिक्तः सारो यस्य सोऽतिरिक्तसारः, सर्वेभ्योतिरिक्तसारतरः सर्वातिरिक्तसारः। सर्वतेजोभिभाविना--see Malli.; or better dissolve सर्वं च तत्तेजः सर्वतेजः, तदभिभूतवान्; Up. comp.; or तस्याभिभावी. According to Vámana the root भू with अभि takes इन् in the sense of the p. tense.

सर्वोन्नतेन--सर्वेभ्य उन्नततरस्तेन। मेरुरिव-- According to the geography of the Purāṇas, the mountain Meru forms the central point of the worlds, all the planets revolving round it, and is in shape like the cup or seed-vessel of a lotus, all the *Dvipas* spreading round it like petals. It is formed of gold, and is 84,000 *Yojanas* in height, 16,000 of which are below the surface of the earth. The Ganges falls from heaven on its peak and thence flows to the sea. Its summit is the residence of Brahman, and the meeting-place of the gods, *Rishis*, Gandharvas, &c. *Cf.* Kâl-P. मेरुर्मध्ये भुवनानां च भर्ता &c.; also Mat.-P. मेरुस्तु ब्रह्मभे दिव्यो राजवत्समधिष्ठितः । आदित्यतरुणाभासो विधूम इव पावकः । योजनानां सहस्राणि चतुरशीतिरुच्छ्रितः । प्रविष्टः षोडशाधस्तादष्टात्रिंशतिविंशतिः । विस्तारात्त्रिगुणस्तस्य परिणाहः समन्ततः । * * * स तु मेरुः परिवृतो भुवनैर्भूतभावनैः । &c. &c.

The words of Manu अष्टाभिश्च &c. quoted by Malli. apply to all kings in the true sense of the term. But here they apply to Dilipa alone, since he was pre-eminently the king who ruled over the other kings, as if they were no better than mere subjects when compared with him. See Sl. 30.

S'l. 15. प्रज्ञया सदृशागमः—This is grammatically inaccurate, if not wrong. The word प्रज्ञा cannot be in the instrumental case, unless it be connected with सदृश. Consequently all the three words ought to have been compounded together (प्रज्ञासदृशागमः) or सदृश and आगम should not have been compounded in a Bah., such a compound not being allowed except in the case of a संनिधिपद. The poet, however, may be defended by supposing the तृतीया to be used हेतौ; and the clause consequently, to mean 'his study of the S'ástras was such as would do credit to him by reason of his (acute) intellect. The same may be said of आगमैः सदृशारम्भः ।

आगम—According to Malli. आगम in सदृशागम means the study or the acquisition of the knowledge of the S'ástra (*cf.* बहुधाप्यागमैर्भिन्नाः *infra* 26) while in आगमैः it means the knowledge so acquired. For this latter sense, *cf.* आगमवृद्धसेवी *infra* VI. 41; and Kir. II. 28. सुकृतः परिशुद्ध आगमः कुरुते दीप इवार्थदर्शनम् ॥; *cf.* also for the curious derivation of the word.—आगतं शिववक्त्रेभ्यो गतं च गिरिजाश्रुतौ । मतं च वासुदेवस्य तस्मादागममुच्यते ॥

S'l. 16. भीमकान्तैः—may also be dissolved as a Dv. Comp. अनुजीविनाम्—The Gen. is used by the rule 'कृत्यानां कर्तरि वा'। उपजीविनो न धर्षयन्त इति उपजीविनामधृष्यः । पक्षे तृतीया । For the two epithets अधृष्य and अभिगम्य, *cf.* the quotations given in the foot-note अधृष्यः not to be approached or slighted. *Cf.* S'âk. अहो दीप्तिमतोपि विश्वसनीयतास्य (राज्ञो) वपुषः ।

S'l. 17. In this sl. the poet very happily compares Dilipa to a skilful charioteer driving the car of social and state affairs, the subjects to the circumference of the wheels and the line of conduct laid down by Manu to the track of the wheels.

क्षुण्णात् (*a*) practised; (*b*) beaten. नियन्तुः—(*a*) restrainer, guide; (*b*) charioteer. नेमिवृत्तयः—see note on मुनिवृत्तीनाम् Sl. 8.

S'l. 18. भूत्यर्थम्—भूतये इति: 'भूत्या अर्थाय' given by Malli. is the explanation and not the dissolution of the comp.; for the Mâhâbhâshya remarks 'नित्यः समासो नित्यसमासो यस्य विग्रहो (*i. e.* in terms of its own members) नास्ति ।' बलिम्—षष्ठांशरूपं करम् । Malli. Vide Manu. VII. 128–132. आदत्ते—The root दा to give (3 cl.) takes either pada; but when preceded by आ it is Âtm. in any other sense than that of 'opening the mouth', by 'आङो दोऽनास्यविहरणे' Pâṇ. I. 3. 20. For other particulars, see Gr. p. 406. हि रसं रविः—रूयते स्तूयते रवते गच्छतीति वा रविः; fr. रु and उणादि aff. इ (added to roots ending in a vowel); *cf.* पवि, कवि, अरि, अलि &c. *Cf.* canto X. 58. For the repetition of the thought, see IV. 86.

S'l. 19. सेना—सह इनेन प्रभुणा a leader, वर्तते इति. परिच्छदः—Here परिच्छद is related as विधेय to सेना. सेनापरिच्छदः may as well be taken as one comp. word (सेना परिच्छदः यस्य) in the Gen. case qualifying तस्य. परिच्छद (छद्) is what covers or surrounds a person, external appendage, paraphernalia--something more for show than for use. So great was the personal vigour of the king combined with his thorough knowledge of the political and military tactics, that his enemies dared not oppose him and his army remained merely hanging upon him like his paraphernalia, scarcely having occasion to go to war. *Cf.* IX. 10. द्वयम्-द्वाववयवावस्य । fr. द्वि + तय optionally changed to अय by the Sûtra 'द्वित्रिभ्यां तयस्यायज्वा ।' Hence we have the two forms द्वय and द्वितय; similarly त्रय and त्रितय.

S'l. 20. संवृतमन्त्रस्य—*Cf.* XVII. 50. गूढाकारेङ्गितस्य-आकार external features or the expression of the face, as giving a clue to one's inward thoughts or mental disposition. *Cf.* अशङ्किताकारमुपैति शङ्कितः Kir. I. 14. इङ्गित—inward thoughts, secret aims or purposes. *Cf.* अगूढसद्भावमितीङ्गितज्ञया &c. Kum. V. 62. For other particulars see Saṃjîvanî and foot-notes.

संस्काराः प्राक्तना इव—The word संस्कार is used in different senses in different places by Kâli.; *e.g.*, III. 18 where it means polishing; XV. 76 and Kum. I. 28, where it means grammatical purity; III. 35 and Kum. VII. 74, where it means education, mental culture, &c. Here it is used in the sense of the impressions produced by the good or bad works performed by an individual in a previous life. Such impressions are called Saṃskâras because they remain clinging to the soul of the individual who performed the works like the smell (वासना) of a thing like musk, which, though itself separated, yet remains in cloth. The new-born infant proceeding, untaught, to suck the mother's breast, is a case in point. According to the Nyáya philosophy the moral merit and demerit are qualities of the immortal soul, imperceptible but inferred from reasoning. According to the Vedánta philosophy, the soul has nothing to do with them but it is the astral body (लिङ्गदेह) which passes from one corporeal existence to another accompanied by the fruits of the good or evil actions man performs in a life which influence his actions in a future life. Vide Sâr.-Bhâsh. on Br.-Sût. III. 1. 8. Vide also Su. Nî. I. 45-52. Nearly the same thought is repeated in 'मनो हि जन्मान्तरसंगतिज्ञम्' VII. 15.

Note:—It will be seen that the etymological sense of the word Saṃskâra underlies the various senses given above. The word is formed fr. सम्...कृ...घञ् (अ). स is prefixed to the root कृ by the rules संपरिभ्यां करोतौ भूषणे । समवाये च (Pâṇ. VI. 1, 137-8), *i. e.* after the prepositions सम् and परि, when it means to ornament or to collect together. The Saṃskâras may in one sense be said to adorn a man, inasmuch as all that he does depends upon them, and which therefore are of prime importance. Or संस्कार may mean a collection; and since no other collection is more important than that of good or bad deeds done by a man in a previous life as affecting his present life, it may pre-eminently and of all other collections be said to be his *Saṃskâra*.

Sl. 21. जुगोप &c.-He took care of his body, as required by the śâstra; see foot-note. He did it, however, without employing body-guards like other kings (see Kir. I. 14-विधाय रक्षान् परितः परेतरान्); for he did not require these (see *infra* II. 4). अनातुरः—For, while in the enjoyment of good health, a man does not generally think of God and his religious duties, but when attacked by a disease he turns his eyes to these; cf. रोगी च देवताभक्तः अगृध्नुः &c.—see footnote. *Cf.* Bg. XVIII. 26:—मुक्तसंगोऽनहंवादी धृत्युत्साहसमन्वितः । सिद्ध्यसिद्ध्योर्निर्विकारः कर्ता सात्त्विक उच्यते ॥ 'That agent is called good, who has cast off attachment, who is free from egotistic talk, who is possessed of courage and energy, and unaffected by success or ill-success.' *K. T. Telang's Translation.*

अत्रस्तः, अनातुरः &c.—The negative particle नञ् (अ) in these is emphatic, being meant to distinguish Dilîpa from other princes. He protected his body not because he was in fear like other kings, but because it was his religious duty to do so. See Saṃ., and foot-notes.

This S'l. is quoted in the K.-P. VII. 3 to show that though the नञ् in अत्रस्त &c. is compounded there is no अविमृष्टविधेयांशदोष (*i. e.*, a fault of composition which consists in not expressing the predicate at all or in assigning to it a subordinate or wrong position) here. 'अत्रात्रस्ततावनुवादेनात्मगोपनादेर्विधेयत्वात्पर्युदासोपि नाविमृष्टविधेयांशत्वदोषः' remarks the *Udâharaṇachandrikâ*.

Writers on rhetorics explain two kinds of negation (नञ्), *viz.* प्रसज्यप्रतिषेध and पर्युदास. 'अप्राधान्यं विधेर्यत्र प्रतिषेधे प्रधानता । प्रसज्यप्रतिषेधोसौ क्रियया सह यत्र नञ् ॥' The नञ् is called प्रसज्यप्रतिषेध (emphatic) when the negation instead of the affirmation is prominent, and the नञ् is expressed with the verb. Again, प्रधानत्वं विधेर्यत्र प्रतिषेधेऽप्रधानता । पर्युदासः स विज्ञेयो यत्रोत्तरपदेन नञ् ॥' The नञ् is called पर्युदास (unemphatic) when the affirmation is more prominent than the negation, the नञ् being compounded.

The author of the K.-P. and his commentators seem to take the negation in अत्रस्त &c. as पर्युदास or unemphatic, by the general principle, that if a word enters into a compound it is subordinated and cannot, therefore, be emphasized (समासे गुणीभूतत्वादप्राधान्यम्). But this takes largely from the beauty of the śloka. The नञ् here must be taken as emphatic, since in the negation of these attributes lies the superiority of Dilîpa over other princes. The general principle explained above does not hold good in every case. Páṇ. himself is often found compounding an emphatic नञ्, and Vâmana while commenting on Páṇ. III. 3. 19, remarks प्रसज्यप्रतिषेधेपि समासोस्ति । The नञ् here, therefore, ought to be taken as प्रसज्यप्रतिषेध and not as पर्युदास.

Sl. 22. ज्ञाने—Knowledge of the secret doings of others (Malli.). What is meant is this:-Even though the king knew of the actions of men done in a spirit hostile to him, he did not give utterance to words calculated to give them pain, but silently adopted measures to thwart their object, &c. In connexion with this the following śl. from Kám. may be quoted: हृदि विद्ध इवात्यर्थं यया संतप्यते जनः । पीडितोपि हि मेधावी न तां वाचमुदीरयेत् ॥ ज्ञान may also be taken to mean knowledge in general. ज्ञाने, शक्तौ &c.—the Loc. here is अनादरे; 'notwithstanding knowledge,' *i. e.* he attached greater importance to observing silence than to displaying his knowledge, &c. त्यागे &c.—Because of the precept न दत्त्वा परिकीर्तयेत् । गुणा०-अनुबध्नन्तीत्यनुबन्धिनस्तेषां भावः अनुबन्धित्वं; now see Samj. सप्रसवाः—A difficulty arises in solving such compounds Malli. says सह प्रसवो येषां ते सप्रसवाः; but it is very difficult to see what authority he has for this. This comp. is of the nature of सपक्ष, साधर्म्य, सजातीय &c. But there is no Sûtra of Páṇ. satisfactorily explaining these. Vâmana in his Káśiká gives a very simple solution of the difficulty. While commenting on the Sûtra 'समानस्य छन्दस्यमूर्धप्रभृत्युदर्केषु' he observes that the portion 'समानस्य' should be detached from this and considered as a separate Sûtra by itself, so that it may explain the above-mentioned cases. Bhaṭṭoji Dîkshita conforms to this opinion of Vámana, but, following Haradatta, suggests that the स in compounds like सपक्ष may not be substituted for समान but for सह meaning 'like to,' as in the case of ससखि (अथवा सहशब्दः सदृशवचनोऽस्ति । सदृशः सख्या ससखीति यथा ।), and that the comp. may be called Bah., the word सह not occurring in the विग्रहवाक्य (तेनायमस्वपदविग्रहो बहुव्रीहिः ।). We must therefore dissolve either as समानः प्रसव एषाम्, or following the Sid.-Kau., as सदृशः प्रसवो येषां सप्रसवाः, or सहप्रसवाः, सह being optionally changed to स by the rule वोपसर्जनस्य; and not as Malli. has it (सह प्रसवो येषाम्). It will thus be seen that it is difficult to find a defence for Malli. unless we suppose (not without warrant; see notes on I. 1) सह to be wrongly put in for सदृश by some meddlesome copyist.

Śl. 23. त्रिषयैः—for der. see notes to Śl. 8. विद्यानां पारदृश्वनः—पारं दृष्टवान्पारदृश्वा (दृश्+क्वनिप् Páṇ. III. 2. 94) one who has seen the other side. दृश्वन् is used at the end of a comp. (see V. 24). Words of similar derivation are राजयुध्वन्, राजकृत्वन् &c. विद्यानाम्—According to some there are four *Vidyâs* (see the Śl. quoted in foot-note), *viz.* (1) आन्वीक्षिकी logic and metaphysics; (2) त्रयी the three Vedas ऋक्, यजुस् and सामन्; (3) वार्ता the practical arts such as agriculture, commerce &c. (see XVI. 2); and (4) दण्डनीति the science of government or politics (see XVIII. 46). To these Manu adds a fifth, *viz.* आत्मविद्या the philosophy of the soul (vide Manu. VII. 43). According to others the *Vidyâs* are fourteen (vide Saṃ. on V. 21 and Manu. quoted therein); while there are others still who add four more *Vidyâs* to the above list, making up the number eighteen आयुर्वेदो धनुर्वेदो गान्धर्वश्चेति ते त्रयः । अर्थशास्त्रं चतुर्थं च विद्या ह्यष्टादशैव तु ॥ Pr. Tat.

Śl. 24. विनयाधानात्—विनय good morals, discipline; here, education in general; cf. III. 29 (विनिन्युः); आधान—infusing, inculcating; रक्षणात्, भरणात् all these are ablatives showing the हेतु of Dilîpa's being the father of his subjects. A noun denoting हेतु may take the Abl. or the Instr. See Sid.-Kau. on Pâṇ.

II. 3. 26. स पिता &c.—for the repetition of the same thought, see II. 48; XIV. 23. *Cf.* also त्वयि तु परिसमाप्तं बन्धुकृत्यं प्रजानाम् । Śák. V. 8. केवलं जन्महेतवः—a peculiar construction, though not rare in the writings of Kálidása. केवलं is an *adv.* qualifying the verb जन् in जन्म. *Cf.* न केवलं यो महतोपभाषते &c. Kum. V. 83.

S'l. 25. स्थित्यै—the Dat. here is तादर्थ्ये; 'for the purpose of' preserving social order. दण्डयतः—Malli. renders this by शिक्षयतः chastising. The root दण्ड् also means 'to fine'; *e. g.* गर्गान् शतं दण्डयति । This seems to be the meaning intended by the poet here. *Cf.* 'अस्वाल लोकस्थितये स राजा' Bk. I. 4; Kir. I. 13. परिणेतुः—परि+नी 'to take round,' hence to marry; the root has this meaning probably because the husband takes the bride *round* the sacrificial fire at marriage. प्रसूतये—This strengthens the statement प्रजायै गृहमेधिनाम् । I. 7.

अप्यर्थकामौ &c.—even the attainment of the two objects अर्थ (wealth) and काम (sensual pleasure) was to him the attainment of the third, *viz.* धर्म, *i. e.*, he attained the two objects as a part of the third. His sense of his religious and temporal duties was so great that he attached special importance to धर्म and subordinated to it the consideration of अर्थ and काम. See the gist of the line given by Malli. अर्थकामसाधनयोः &c. S. P. Pandit's remark on this passage which purports to say that the king did not employ separate means to attain धर्म but attained this as the result of the attainment of the other two, does not seem to be correct; for we are already told in the 23rd Śl. that the king took care to do his religious duties (धर्मरतेः). The poet simply means to say that the king did not extort money from his subjects to swell his treasury, nor did he give himself up to sensual pleasures, in such a way as to infringe scriptural law. For the recurrence of the same thought, see XVII. 57.

Note:—Since words falling under the धर्मादि group may be compounded in any order (धर्मादिष्वनियमः) we may have either अर्थकामौ or कामार्थौ; similarly धर्मार्थौ or अर्थधर्मौ, शब्दार्थौ or अर्थशब्दौ &c.

S'l. 26. दुदोह—Mark the use of दुह् which means 'to milk' in the first instance and then to drain or empty of the best part; and the pun on गो which means a cow and also earth. For this sense of दुह्, *cf.* दुदुहुर्धरित्रीं Kum. I. 2. गां दुदोह—This does not mean that he deprived the people of their money, but simply this, that he spent the greater part of the state-revenue in the performance of sacrifices as there were no wars to be carried on. मघवन्—मह्यते पूज्यते असौ मघवा; irregularly derived from मह् to adore and the Uṇádi affix

कनिन् (अन्) and augment वुक् (व्). There are twelve other words similarly derived; श्वन्, उक्षन्, पूषन्, प्लीहन्, क्लेदन्, स्नेहन्, मूर्धन्, मज्जन्, अर्यमन्, विश्वप्सन्, परिज्मन्, and मातरिश्वन् (by the Sûtra श्वन्नुक्षन् &c. Uṇâ. I. 157).

दुधतः—Properly this should be in Âtm. by the rule 'कर्तरि कर्मव्यतिहारे' 'the Âtm. should be used to express exchange of action' (see Gr. § 662); but since the poet does not wish to convey the idea of 'exchange of action (क्रिया),' but expressly that of 'exchange of wealth (संपद्विनियम)' the Sûtra does not apply and we have the Par. भुवनद्वयम्—*Cf.* Bg. III. 10-12 and S'âk. VII. 34 quoted in the foot-note.

S'l. 27. किल—indeed, verily; or it may be used ऐतिह्ये in the sense of 'history informs us &c.' अनुययुः—other kings of course could not attain his fame of protection; for had they imitated him, that would have been a kind of theft; but theft did not exist in his kingdom. परस्व is a noun and not a pronoun here. See Gr. § 150. तस्करता–तस्कर derived fr. तत्+कर (तत्करोति); by the Gaṇa-Sûtra VI. 1. 157. 'तद्बृहतोः करपत्योः, [चौरदेवतयोः सुट् तलोपश्च]'; तत् and बृहत् when followed by कर and पति drop the final त् and insert स् instead, provided the words mean चौर and देवता respectively; तस्कर, बृहस्पति. श्रुतौ—*i. e.* in the term expressive of theft (वाचकशब्दे); *i. e.* the word theft only remained; it did not exist in practice. See Malli. Or theft exerted itself (operated on) श्रुति, *i. e.*, the word theft was forgotten. This is more poetical.

S'l. 28. द्वेष्यः—one deserving to be hated; here used as equivalent to द्विषत् a foe. शिष्टः—Malli. seems to take it as an *adj.*; it may as well be taken as a substantive. शिष्टः द्वेष्योपि &c.; this better harmonizes with औषध. उरगः—उरसा गच्छतीति । The स् of उरस् is dropped by 'उरसो लोपश्च' Vârt. on Pâṇ. III. 2. 48.

S'l. 29. वेधाः—According to the Sid.-Kau. this word is derived fr. धा with वि, and the affix असु; विदधाति इति वेधाः he who creates; वेध being substituted for विधा by विधाञो वेध च Uṇâ. IV. 224. Some derive it fr. विध् 6 P. to rule, to govern, विधतीति. महाभूतसमाधिना—समाधि is 'what is collected together,' materials. The five great or primary elements are—earth (पृथ्वी), water (अप्), fire. (तेजस्), air (वायु), and ether (आकाश). For a similar idea see Kum. I. 49. तथाहि—and hence, owing to which. परार्थैकफलाः—*Cf.* 'गुणवत्तापि परप्रयोजना' *infra* VIII. 31.

S'l. 30. अनन्यशासनाम्—अन्यस्य शासनमन्यशासनम्; अविद्यमानमन्यशासनं यस्यास्ताम् । By the Vârt. नञोऽस्त्यर्थानां बहुव्रीहिर्वा चोत्तरपदलोपो वक्तव्यः

"the negative particle नञ् in combination with a word having the sense of 'there is' may enter in a Bah. comp. and the word following it be dropped optionally." 'विद्यमान' may optionally be dropped, and thus we may get the two forms अविद्यमानान्यशासनां, and अनन्यशासनाम्. उर्वीम्—lit. 'the wide one,' the earth; *fem.* fr. उरु irregularly derived fr. ऊर्णु-ऊर्णोति ऊर्णूयते वा (Uṇá. I. 31).

The presence of the word वलय which usually means 'a bracelet,' in वेलावप्रवलयाम् suggests a side-meaning. The earth is the spouse of the king who wears a bracelet in the shape of the वेला, a waist-zone in the form of the sea, and who is solely obedient to her husband's will. See Malli. on I. 32.

S'l. 31. दाक्षिण्यरूढेन—दक्षिणस्य भावो दाक्षिण्यं gentleness, winning manners, attention to the wants of others; (see Malli.). Some derive it from दक्षिण (right-hand,) right-handed, skilful, knowing how to please everybody; तस्माद्रूढेन sprung from, celebrated, grown familiar with everybody. मगधवंशजा—born in the family of the Magadha kings.

" Magadha was the ancient name of Southern Behar, or that part of Behar which is to the South of the Ganges, between Bengal and the Karmanáśá, and watered by the lower Śoṇa and the numerous little streams flowing towards the east in a parallel direction. Magadha was once the seat of several most clebrated dynasties of ancient Indian kings. It was also here that Buddhism first took its origin. Pâṭaliputra, the capital of Magadha, was situated near the confluence of the S'oṇa with the Ganges." S. P. Pandit's note. Its ancient capital was गिरिव्रज or राजगृह (identified with Râjgir, which is about seven miles to the south of Nalanda or Baragaon). Magadha was Kíkaṭa in later literature.

पत्नी—Fem. of पति; by the rule पत्युर्नो यज्ञसंयोगे, पति takes the augment न before the fem. aff. ई (ईप्) when participation in a sacrifice is implied. The use of this word shows that of all wives of Dilîpa she alone was धर्म्या *i. e.* had the right of joining him in religious rites.

अध्वरस्येव दक्षिणा —अध्वरः–The word is variously derived. (1) न ध्वरा हिंसा यस्मिन् that in which there is no sinful killing (that being the belief of the Mîmâṃsakas. Vide Manu. V. 44). Sâyaṇa in his com. on the Rigv. derives it as (2) न ध्वरतीत्यध्वरः हिंसारहितः free from molestation by the Rákshasas. See Sáyaṇa and Yáska quoted in the ft. note. Later writers derive it thus: (3, अध्वानं राति ददातीत्यध्वरः that which opens up a good path (*i e.*, the path which leads to bliss or heaven) for its performer; and lastly (4) न ध्वरः कुटिलः, न ध्वरति कुटिलो भवतीति

या that which never proves crooked, never fails to give its reward. The poet evidently uses it in the last two etymological senses.

दक्षिणा—(See Malli.). The donation to Brâhmaṇas at a sacrifice is personified as a goddess. She is said to be the author of *Rg*. X. 107. She is sometimes regarded as a daughter of *Prajàpati*, रुचि by name, or as the wife of Yajña or Sacrifice. She ought to be highly adored, else the sacrifice would be fruitless. Vide Bhâg.-P. IX. 1. The Br.-V.-P. thus accounts for the name:—कार्तिकीपूर्णिमायां तु रासे राधामहोत्सवे । आविर्भूता दक्षिणांशात्कृष्णस्य तेन दक्षिणा ॥

Note:—The points of similarity on which the simile is based are these–the king was very munificent and granted the desires of every one and so was like *Adhvara* which does the same. The *Dakshiṇâ* gladdens the Bráhmaṇas at a sacrifice and so *Sudakshiṇâ* pleased everybody by her conduct. The appropriateness of the simile might have been better understood in times when the sacrifices were in vogue than now. The particle सु, which indicates excellence, perhaps shows, as Prof. Ray thinks, that Dilîpa's wife was even superior to the wife of *Adhvara*, only who was *Dakshiṇâ*, and not *Su-dakshiṇâ*.

S'l. 32. अवरोधे—अवरुध्यत इत्यवरोधः the wives of a king taken collectively. See IV. 68, 87; VI. 48; XVI. 58, &c. The Loc. here is अनादरे (Pâṇ. II. 3. 38), *i. e.* conveying the idea of disregard. मनस्विन्या—प्रशस्तं noble मनोस्या अस्तीति, high-minded. Here the aff. विन् shows प्राशस्त्य or excellence. For the various additional senses in which affixes showing possession are used, see Gr. p. 209, *ft.-note*.*

कलत्रवन्तमात्मानमवरोधे महत्यपि । तया मेने मनस्विन्या लक्ष्म्या च वसुधाधिपः—Malli., who remarks 'वसुधाधिप इत्यनेन वसुधया चेति गम्यते' 'the epithet lord of the earth,' indicates that he considered himself कलत्रवान्, by the earth also,' takes लक्ष्मी as a distinct wife of the king. But लक्ष्मी is not generally spoken of by poets as wife of kings. It is वसुधा (the earth) that is mentioned in numerous passages as the only *Kalatra* (wife) of kings except the wedded Queen, and not Lakshmî. *Cf.* वसुमत्या हि नृपाः कलत्रिणः VIII. 83; परिग्रहबहुत्वेपि द्वे प्रतिष्ठे कुलस्य मे । समुद्ररशना चोर्वी सखी च युवयोरियम् । S'âk. III. 17. Lakshmî can, therefore, be spoken of as 'wife' of kings only through वसुधा, (*cf.* III. 36; 38) and we think the epithet 'वसुधाधिपः' is used by the poet with that intention. In support of Mallinátha's remark, however, we may quote VI. 20, where the words of the poet त्वमेव कल्याणि तयोस्तृतीया show that the poet speaks of the lord of the Aṅgas as the *Nàyaka* of *S'ri* and *Sarasvati*; also XIV. 86, and Kir. I. 44.

S'l. 33. तस्याम्—of course refers to Sudakshiṇá, as she is principally mentioned in the previous śl. आत्मानुरूपायाम्—अनुगतं रूपमस्या

अनुरूपा, आत्मनोऽनुरूपात्मानुरूपा तस्याम् । आत्मजन्मसमुत्सुकः—*Cf.* Malli. on the etymology of the word जाया (II. 1) and the Smṛiti quoted by him there. मनोरथः—करणे तृतीया 'by means of;' मनोरथ lit. 'the car of the mind,' hence a desire &c.

S'l. 34. संतानार्थाय—संतन्यत इति संतानः (संतन्+घञ् *i. e.* अ). संतान may have the sense of (1) progeny, and (2) continuation; as the affix घञ् is added in the sense of करण or भाव. Both the senses (though principally the first) seem to have been intended by the poet. See II. 64, and XVIII. 52.

धुः—(derived fr. धुर्व् I. P.) धुर्वति हिनस्ति वाहानिति धुः । 'that which injures the animals yoked,' hence a yoke. But as the weight of the carriage or plough (as the case may be) presses heavily upon the animals at the yoke, it is sometimes used in the secondary sense of 'weight, a heavy task, &c.,' in which sense it is used here. See notes to I. 91. निक्षेप is what one deposits with another in trust, and with the object of taking it back; *cf.* Kum. V. 13 (निक्षेप इवार्पितं द्वयम्).

S'l. 35. अभ्यर्च्य विधातारम्—Brahmà, as the lord of creation, is worshipped by those desirous of progeny. The poet could have as well said 'अथ ब्रह्माणमभ्यर्च्य' but he purposely uses the word विधातृ. It means he who ordains everything (विदधातीति), he upon whose will the birth of a child depends, and is very appropriate here. The use of the word Brahman would have destroyed the beauty of the śloka. पुत्रकाम्या—पुत्रकाम्या is derived fr. the nomi. verb पुत्रकाम्यति 'he wishes for a son' fr. पुत्र+काम्य (काम्यच्) added in the sense of 'wishing for that which is denoted by the base.' Similar verbs are यशस्काम्यति, सर्पिष्काम्यति, &c.

दम्पती—This word may be properly derived fr. दम् (दम) 'a house' and पति 'the lord of,' the dual दम्पती meaning 'the two masters of the house,' the husband and the wife. The word दम in the Veda means 'a house' and the word दम्पति is often used in the sing. in the Veda; *e. g.* 'समानं दम्पतिं भुजे' Rgv. I. 127. 8; 'तं त्वा सुशिप्र दंपते स्तोमैर्वर्धन्त्यग्नयः ।' V. 22. 4, &c. The word, however, is never found used in the sing. in classical Sanskrit; and grammarians, Páṇ. included, derive it fr. दम् irregularly substituted for जाया, and पति; जाया च पतिश्च जायापती, जम्पती, दम्पती.

This word is classed as one of the group राजदन्तादि; and as reference is made to this group several times in the com. or in the foot-notes we explain it here. राजदन्तादि is a class of words, in which what ought to appear first in a comp. appears last. By the rule 'अभ्यर्हितं पूर्वम्' the compound should have been पतिजाये, the word पति preceding जाया inasmuch as the husband has preference over the wife, when we are speaking of them with reference to the relation existing between them. But since the form जायापती occurs in language, it is classed under राजदन्तादि.

N. B.—When the relation of husband and wife that exists between a man and woman is not directly and prominently meant to be expressed, it is the woman that generally precedes; इन्दुमत्यजयोः &c.

Note:—The king goes accompanied by his wife, because the wife ought to join her husband, as enjoined by the S'âstra, in the performance of every religious rite.

S'l. 36. स्यन्दनम्—स्यन्दते इति that which moves on quickly; hence a chariot. It also means 'that which pours down,' a cloud. प्रावृषेण्यं—this epithet is used to account for स्निग्ध &c.; for an autumnal cloud is not so. पयोवाहम्—this epithet is used to keep up the pun implied in स्यन्दन; for a cloud is that which contains and also pours water. विद्युदैरावती इव—an instance where इव is not compounded (see our note on वागर्थाविव; for, if it were compounded, the comp. would qualify आस्थितौ and प्रावृषेण्यं पयोवाहम् would be disconnected and thereby rendered meaningless. ऐरावतः—In Pauràṇic literature, the elephant of Indra produced at the churning of the milky ocean, and the prototype of the elephant race (see Bg. X. 27); also considered as the elephant of the eastern quarter.

The earliest conception of Indra regards him as the lord of the atmosphere, the dispenser of rain and the governor of the weather. The elephant he rides can, therefore, be no other than a kind of cloud. *Cf.* the etymology of the word given by Malli. and Dakshiṇâvarta quoted in the ft.-note; for other particulars, see *ft.-notes.*

एकं स्यन्दनं &c.—According to the ancient custom of India, kings and Queens did not drive in one and the same carriage. See Mallinàtha's consequent remarks on this.

S'l. 37. मा भूदाश्रमपीडेति—*Cf.* तपोवनवासिनामुपरोधो मा भूत्। अत्रैव रथं स्थापय यावदवतरामि। विनीतवेषेण प्रवेष्टव्यानि तपोवनानि नाम। S'àk. I. परिमेय—lit. 'what can be measured,' hence a limited or small number of. अनुभावः अनुगतो भावोऽनुभावः। a *Pràdi Samàsa.* अनु is not an *Upasarga* here; for in that case भू will not take the affix घञ् (अ), by the rule श्रीनीभुवोऽनुपसर्गे (Pàṇ. III. 3. 21), 'the roots श्री, नी and भू take घञ् only when not preceded by a preposition'. Or it may be derived as अनुभावयतीति। पचाद्यच् (Pàṇ. III. 1. 134). The majesty or awe-inspiring splendour of their mien or general bearing.

S'l. 38. सुखस्पर्शैः—सुख is an *adj.* here, and means 'pleasant.' This implies that the breezes were cool. शालनिर्यासगन्धिभिः—शालानां निर्या-

सततस्य गन्धो विद्यते एषामिति गन्धिनस्तैः । ०रेणूत्करैः—Wafting, bearing away. *Cf.* निनाय सात्यन्तहिमोत्किरानिलाः Kum. V. 26. ०त्करैः *v. l.* where उत्कर means 'a collection; a cluster.'

An over-scrupulous critic may find fault with the epithet सुखस्पर्शैः. For, that is considered excellent poetry which is suggestive—it must suggest ideas which are striking and capable of pleasing and impressing the mind. Here the idea of सुख or pleasantness is the काङ्क्षितार्थ or the meaning intended to be conveyed by the poet, and should not, therefore, have been actually expressed, but left to be inferred from something like 'भागीरथीनिर्झरशीकराणां वोढा' which leads to the inference that the breeze was cool and therefore pleasing (in Kum. I. 15 where the description of the wind is certainly more poetical than here). Also, the idea of fragrance suggested by पुष्परेणूत्करैः is repeated in 'शालनिर्यासगन्धिभिः' which again spoils the beauty of the Sl. Perhaps the object of the poet is not so much to give us poetry as to describe the natural state of things by a स्वभावोक्ति. The epithet शाल &c. seems to show that the strong smell of the exudations of the *S'âla* trees overpowered that of other flowers; while पुष्परेणूत्करैः is intended to suggest an exuberance of flowers peculiar to the forest.

S'l. 39. मनोभिरामाः—अभिरमते जन आसु इति अभिरामाः । मनसोभिरामा मनोभिरामाः ravishing, delightful, to the mind.

षड्जसंवादिनीः—संवादो विद्यते आसामिति संवादिन्यः; now see Samj. षड्ज—The first of the seven primary notes of the Indian gamut. The seven notes in order of pitch are षड्ज, ऋषभ, गान्धार, मध्यम, पञ्चम, धैवत and निषाद abbreviated into स, रि, ग, म, प, ध, and नि. For deriv. see Malli. According to Nárada it is called षड्ज because the other six notes proceed from it, *i. e.* are based on it; यमाश्रित्य प्रजायन्ते ऋषभाद्याः षडेव तु । तस्मात्षड्ज इति प्रोक्तः । इ०.

द्विधा भिन्नाः—Disinguished in two ways; *i. e.* peculiar to each sex स्त्रीपुंसभेदेन Din.; स्त्रीपुंसभेदात् Chá.; Chá. also observes—महाजनदर्शनजनितविस्मयभयाभ्यां द्विधा भिन्नाः । विस्मयात्स्रवति स्निग्धो भयाद्दीर्घ उदाहृतः । इति दन्तिलः । Mallinátha's explanation is perhaps more scientific. Shadja is of two kinds, शुद्ध and विकृत. It is called S'uddha when it consists of the four श्रुतिs (tones or vibrations तन्त्रीजातो नादः) *viz*, तीव्रा, कुमुद्वती मन्द्रा and छन्दोवती (तीव्रा कुमुद्वती मंदा छंदोवत्यस्तु षड्जगाः ।); otherwise it is called विकृत. It is further subdivided into two kinds, च्युत and अच्युत. च्युतोऽच्युतो द्विधा षड्जो द्विश्रुतिर्विकृतो भवेत् the sound which appears in its last component part (छंदोवती) is called अच्युत; when otherwise, च्युत. केकाः—For deriv. see Malli. The Loc. term. in के is retained by the rule 'तत्पुरुषे कृति बहुलम्' 'In a Tatpurusha the Loc. term. is often retained when a कृत् affix is added.'

S'l. 40. परस्पराक्षिसादृश्यम्—अक्ष्णोः सादृश्यमक्षिसादृश्यम्। By 'कर्मव्यतिहारे सर्वनाम्नो द्वे वाच्ये' 'समासवच्च बहुलम्' (Vârttikas on Páṇ. VIII. 1. 12), a pronoun is always doubled and in many cases compounded (*i. e.* the case-termination of the first member may be dropped and the two words joined together as in a comp. to express interchange of action. To express the interchange of action here we must have परस्य परस्य अक्षिसादृश्यम्। But a comp. is not allowed in the case of पर and अन्य, as remarked by Bhaṭṭoji Dîkshita (बहुलग्रहणादन्यपरयोर्न समासवत्). Then by the Vârt. 'असमासवद्भावे पूर्वपदस्थस्य सुपः सुर्वक्तव्यः' when uncompounded, the case-term. of the first word is changed to सु, the term. of the nom. sing.; so we have परः परस्य and by the rule 'कस्कादिषु च' (see Gr. § 43, *d*) we have परस्परस्य. Now compounding this with अक्षिसादृश्यम् we get परस्पराक्षिसादृश्यम्. But here another difficulty arises. Since परस्परस्य becomes the first member of the new comp., सु of the first पर must be dropped by the general rule. Bhaṭṭoji Dîk., therefore, regards this as an irregularity (बाहुलकबलेन समाधेयम्). See Sid.-Kau. on Páṇ. VIII. 1. 12.

अदूरोज्झित &c.—Cf. विश्वासोपगमादभिन्नगतयः शब्दं सहन्ते मृगाः &c. S'âk. I. This shows that the benign appearance of the king and his queen easily inspired confidence in the herds of the deer. Vide II. 11.

S'l. 41. तोरणस्रजम्—सृज्यते इति सृजन्तीति वा स्रक् lit. 'that which is made or that which people make easily;' and as nothing is made more easily, and charms more when made, than a garland, it means a garland. तोरणम्—तुरन्त्यत्रेति, स्तुवन्ति रणन्त्यत्रेति वा where people gather with exclamations of joy; or तुतुराति मङ्गलार्थं त्वरन्तेऽत्र where people go in haste for auspicious purposes. तोरण usually means the outer gate of a palace or city, or an arched doorway. It also means 'a temporary ornamental arch,' which is the meaning here. When kings and other great personages go out on a tour it is customary for people to exhibit their joy by raising ornamental arches with garlands suspended over them and the cranes here, as it were, did the same.

As for Mallinâtha's remark 'उत्प्रेक्षाव्यञ्जक' &c. see Sáh.-Dar. quoted in the *ft.-note* to the 13th s'l. When words like इव, मन्ये &c. are omitted, the उत्प्रेक्षा is called गम्या, व्यङ्ग्या or प्रतीयमाना.

S'l. 42. अनुकूलत्वात्—अनुगतः कूलमनुकूलः 'running along the current' and not in a contrary direction; hence, favourable; *cf.* शान्तानुकूल-

पवनः, S'ák. IV. 11. रजोभिरस्पृष्टालक &c.—The नञ् in अस्पृष्ट is emphatic (प्रसज्यप्रतिषेध). See note to s'l. 21. As अस्पृष्ट is connected with रजोभिः the whole should either be अरजःस्पृष्टालकवेष्टनौ or अस्पृष्ट should not be compounded. See note on प्रज्ञया सदृशागमः s'l. 15.

S'l. 43. अरविन्दानाम्—Lit. 'those which have petals resembling the spokes of a carriage-wheel' (see *ft.-note*). अरविन्द has an exceedingly pleasing fragrance and is considered as one of the arrows of the God of love (see *ft.-note*). It is a day-lotus. *Cf.* 'मयूखैरिवभिन्नमिवारविन्दम्' Kum I. 32. आमोदे—fragrance exceedingly gratifying; आ समन्तात् मोदयति इत्यामोदः; मुद् cau. with आ + अ (अच्); or आमोदन्ते जना अनेन; with घञ् (अ) करणे.

S'l. 44. यूपचिह्नेषु—Having the sacrificial posts for their distinguishing marks. This shows that the pious Bráhmaṇas constantly performed sacrifices and thus used the revenue of the villages for the legitimate purpose for which they were granted to them. यज्वनां—Mark the meaning of यज्वन्; वन् is similarly added to सु, सुत्वन्. अर्घ्यानुपदम् &c. -पदस्य पश्चात् (see com.); here पश्चात् is the meaning of the preposition अनु. For मध्य see V. 2 *infra*

S'l. 45. हैयंगवीनम् -दुह्यते इति दोहः, गवां दोहः गोदोहः, ह्यः yesterday; ह्योगोदोहस्य विकारो हैयंगवीनं नवनीतम् (Sid.-Kau.), हियङ्गु being irregularly substituted for ह्योगोदोह and the affix अ addeded. Vide Pán. V. 2. 23; III. 1. 134. The Mb. has घृतम्, but on this the Manoramâ remarks -यद्यपि भाष्ये वृत्तौ च घृतमित्युक्तममरेणापि 'तत्तु हैयंगवीनं यद् ह्योगोदोहोद्भवं घृतम्' इत्युक्तं तथापि नवनीतमेव तत्र विवक्षितमिति हरदत्तादयः। It means 'fresh butter.' आदाय—The cow-herds brought butter with them, because one should never approach a king empty-handed. घोषवृद्धान्-घोषन्ति गावोऽत्रेति घोषः a place inhabited by cow-herds; घोषे वृद्धाः घोषवृद्धाः comp. सह सुपा; old men of the villages of cow-herds. Or the word घोष may mean a cow-herd (घोषन्ति गवामाह्वानाय शब्दायन्ते इति घोषाः) in which case the comp. will have to be dissolved as वृद्धा घोषा घोषवृद्धाः; the word घोष, being one of the कडारादि class, optionally takes पूर्वनिपात. नामधेयानि—By the rule भागरूपनामभ्यो धेयः (Vârt. on Pâṇ. V. 4. 25) the affix धेय is added to रूप, नाम and भाग without change of meaning.

Note—This sl. bears testimony to the magnanimity of the royal pair. They condescend to enter into conversation with the herdsmen on topics quite familiar to them.

S'l. 46. कापि—The pron. किम् in conjunction with अपि expresses the idea of indescribability. व्रजतोः—applies to चित्रा and चन्द्रमस् also, they too being in their diurnal motion. शुद्धवेषयोः—when applied to चित्राचन्द्रमसौ means 'of pure or bright (शुद्ध) appearance' *i. e.* light (especially on the full-moon day of Chaitra). आसीत्—According to Vis'vanātha the simile here is vitiated by the fault कालक्रमभङ्ग. The beauty of Chitra and the moon, when in conjunction, being always visible, the past tense (आसीत्) is inapplicable to it. See *ft.-notes.*

S'l. 47. तत्तत्—'that and that,' 'this thing and that thing', *i. e.* everything, all that struck him as beautiful. By the rule नित्यवीप्सयोः a *pada* may be repeated to denote frequency or universality; *e. g.* वृक्षं वृक्षं सिञ्चति *i. e.* all trees. प्रियदर्शनः—Malli. says प्रियं दर्शनं स्वकर्मकं यस्य, whose sight was agreeable. We may rather say स्वकर्तृकं and explain प्रियं (an agreeable task) दर्शनं showing things यस्य. बुधोपमः—may also be dissolved as बुधेन सदृशः as a nitya-samâsa, उपमा having the sense of सदृश when used as the latter part of a comp.; *cf.* स्युरुत्तरपदे त्वमी। निभसंकाशनीकाशप्रतीकाशोपमादयः। Amara. This epithet is used in order to indicate that the king was a lover of natural scenery and was able to see beauty in everything. बुध is thus described in the Matsya-P.:—ततः संवत्सरस्यान्ते द्वादशादित्यसंनिभः। दिव्यपीताम्बरधरः पीताभरणभूषितः॥ सर्वार्थशास्त्रविद्विद्वान्हस्तिशास्त्रप्रवर्तकः। राज्ञः सोमस्य पुत्रत्वात्सौम्यो राजसुतः स्मृतः॥

S'l. 48. दुष्प्रापयशाः—*cf. supra* 27. संयमिनः—Of pre-eminent asceticism or self-control (प्रशस्तः संयमोऽस्य); the affix इन् shows 'excellence'. Vasishṭha's self-control and patience are well known. He is described by poets as the receptacle of all knowledge and the greatest of self-restrainers. *Cf.* Bhaṭṭi;. यतिर्वसिष्ठो यमिनां वरिष्ठः &c. I. 15. महिषीसखः—Note this comp. which must be dissolved as a Gen. Tat. according to Páṇ. V. 4. 91. Were it not for this technical necessity of grammar it would be more natural to dissolve it as a Bah. and understand by it 'who had the queen for his companion.' The poet does not intend to imply सखित्व but merely साहचर्य. *Cf.* सचिवसखः IV. 87; सीतालक्ष्मणसखः: XII. 9; besides, all other compounds of a similar import are rendered as Bah. *Cf.* 'प्रयतपरिग्रहद्वितीयः' I. 95; गृहिणीसहायः II. 24.

N. B.—Mark the alliterative recurrence of identical syllables of which there are numerous instances in this Canto. See the preceding s'l.

S'l. 49. वनान्तरात्—अन्यद्वनं वनान्तरं तस्मात्। This is a Karm. of the मयूरव्यंसकादि class. See Gr. §228. As the comp. is नित्य (obligatory) it can have no dissolution (नित्यः समासो नित्यसमासो यस्य विग्रहो नास्ति Mb.) but only its meaning, which is here expressed by the words अन्यस्माद्वनात्. अन्तरशब्दोऽत्र भिन्नवाची Manoramâ. Here अन्तर is used to show that the place the sages lived in was also a forest. पूर्यमाणं—Pres. p. pass. of पूर् or पॄ अदश्याग्नि &c.—According to the S'ruti quoted by Malli. the holy fires go forth, in invisible forms, to meet their worshippers as they return from the forest in the evening laden with sacrificial sticks, &c. See note on यथाविधिहुताग्नीनाम् śl. 6.

S'l. 50. उटजद्वाररोधिभिः—द्वारं रोद्धुं शीलं येषाम्; now see Samj. They gathered there in numbers to get their share of the Nîvára corn. अपत्यैः—न पतन्ति पितरोऽनेन that by which the manes do not go to hell; hence, a child, a son; *cf.* 'शश्वत्पुत्रेण पितरोऽत्यायन्बहुलं तमः' Ait. Bráh. Pañch. VII. It may also be derived fr. अप and त्य 'that which springs from the stock.' Both these etymologies are countenanced by Yàska; see *ft.-note. Cf.* कृतासु नीवारविभागवृत्तिषु स्वकीयमग्रं मृदुहस्तसम्पुटैः। हरन्निरालोहितगण्डमण्डलैः प्लवंगमैः सेवितशैलकन्दरम्॥ Ján. V. 3.

S'l. 51. सेकान्ते मुनिकन्याभिः—So in S'ák. I. also we find the daughters of the hermits watering the trees of the hermitage. तत्क्षणोज्झित &c.—स क्षणस्तत्क्षणः Karm. comp.; ह्रस्वा वृक्षा वृक्षकाः; now see Samj. मुनिकन्याभिः takes तृतीया in connexion with उज्झित which therefore ought better not to have been compounded. वृक्षकं—The young trees were watered; so in the S'ák. त्वत्तोपि तातकाश्यपस्याश्रमवृक्षकाः प्रियतराः &c. p. 19. विहङ्गानाम्—विहायसा गच्छन्तीति विहङ्गाः or -ङ्गमाः Pân. III. 2. 47; and Várttikas on III. 2. 38. विश्वासाय—विश्वासमुत्पादयितुम्। see Gr. § 828.

S'l. 52. मृगैर्वर्तितरोमन्थम्—मथ्नातीति मन्थः, रोगाणां मन्थः रोमन्थः or रोगान्मथ्नातीति रोमन्थः। पृषोदरादित्वात्साधुः; rumination; this habit being indispensable to digestion and health in the case of certain quadrupeds. मृगैः may either be अनुक्ते कर्तरि तृतीया by poetical license, or इत्थंभूतलक्षणे तृतीया, *i. e.*, indicating a particular state of the hermitage (वर्तितरोमन्थ). वर्तित is appropriate with रोमन्थ as Pâṇ. has used it in the Sûtra 'कर्मणो रोमन्थतपोभ्यां वर्तिचरोः।' रोमन्थं वर्तयति रोमन्थायते.

S'l. 53. अतिथीन्—अतिथि lit. he who always goes; or he who does not stay for a second day at a place. See *ft.-notes. Cf.* तिथिपर्वोत्सवा सर्वे त्यक्ता येन महात्मना। सोतिथिः सर्वभूतानां शेषानभ्यागतान् विदुः॥ आश्रमोन्मुखान्-उद्गतं मुखं यस्यासौ उन्मुखः one with his face uplifted; and since a person who anxiously expects another, often raises his head to see if he is coming, raising up the head is a sign of anxiety, or eagerness, and hence the word has often the secondary sense of 'anxious' or 'eager for.' *Cf.* VIII. 12; XII. 26; Kum. VI. 34. Here it simply means 'coming or advancing towards'. *Cf.* II. 17.

आहुतिगन्धिभिः—आहुतीनां गन्ध एषां विद्यत इत्याहुतिगन्धिनः(आहुतिगन्ध + इन्); see Samj. *Cf.* VII. 26 and XIII, 37 where the purifying power of the sacrificial smoke is again referred to.

S'l. 54. यन्तारम्—He who checks the horses, *i. e.* guides their motion; hence, a charioteer. विश्रामय—Properly विश्रमय; श्रम् being one of the roots designated as मित्. See Samj.; but such forms as विश्रामयति, संक्रामयति occur and the वृत्तिकार says that such forms are to be explained by supposing optionality to exist in the rule मितां ह्रस्वः (*i. e.* these roots may not lengthen their penultimate) in certain fixed cases. मितां ह्रस्व इति सूत्रे वा चित्तविकारे इत्यतो वेत्यनुवर्त्य व्यवस्थितविभाषाश्रयणात्.

S'l. 55. तस्मै—The Dat. may be by कर्मणा—यमभिप्रैति स संप्रदानम्; the कर्म (अर्हणा) is done with reference to the king and so तस्मै. सभ्याः–'those who know how to act well in an assembly,' hence, courteous, polite. This shows that the hermits were acquainted with the ways and manners of the world and knew how to welcome high personages like Dilîpa and his queen.

गुप्ततमेन्द्रियाः—अतिशयेन गुप्तानि गुप्ततमानीन्द्रियाणि येषाम्; who had perfect mastery over the senses. This is an additional reason why they were allowed to appear before the queen. The word इन्द्रिय is curiously derived. इन्द्रस्य आत्मनो लिङ्गमिन्द्रियम्—that which is a sign (*i. e.* which leads to the inference) of the soul. Pâṇ. has इन्द्रियमिन्द्रलिङ्गमिन्द्रदृष्टमिन्द्रसृष्टमिन्द्रजुष्टमिन्द्रदत्तमिति वा (V. 2. 93); on which Vàmana thus comments:—(1) इन्द्रस्य लिङ्गमिन्द्रियम्। इन्द्र आत्मा। स चक्षुरादिना करणेनानुमीयते। नाकर्तृकं करणमस्ति। (2) इन्द्रेण दृष्टम्। तृतीयासमर्थात्प्रत्ययः। आत्मना दृष्टमित्यर्थः।(3) इन्द्रेण सृष्टम्। आत्मना सृष्टम्। तत्कृतेन शुभाशुभकर्मणोत्पन्नमिति कृत्वा। (4)इन्द्रेण जुष्टम्। आत्मना जुष्टं सेवितम्। तद्द्वारेण विज्ञानोत्पादनात्। (5) इन्द्रेण दत्तम्। आत्मना विषयेभ्यो दत्तं यथायथं ग्रहणाय। Also इन्द्रेणात्मना दुर्जयम् (Sid.-Kau.). नयचक्षुषे—नयति तत्त्वमिति नयः शास्त्रम्। *Cf.* IV. 13. The rhetorical figure here is अनुप्रास (वर्णसाम्यमनुप्रासः 'recurrence of similar sounds' Kav.-Pra.).

S'l. 56. सायंतनस्य—Pertaining to the evening time; the Tad. affix तन is added to सायं and other adverbs of time, such as ह्यः, श्वः, दिवा, दोषा, चिरं &c. in the sense of 'pertaining to'; ह्यस्तन &c. अन्ते—Because a Bràhmaṇa ought not to be saluted, while engaged in religious service. तपोनिधिम्—this epithet is used to signify that the sage had the power to grant the king's wishes. *Cf.* I. 94. अन्वासितम्—'attended upon.' आस् becomes a trans. verb by virtue of the preposition अनु. *Cf.* II. 24; also सखीभ्यामन्वास्यते S'ák. III. स्वाहया—स्वाहा is the exclamation used at the time of throwing an offering into the fire, afterwards personified into a wife of Agni.

It is very difficult to know what the original meaning of स्वाहा was, whether it was an oblation that could be well relished by the gods

(स्वादतेऽनेन), or whether it was an exclamation used to attract the deities (सुष्ठु आहूयतेऽनेन), or something else. The loss of its true etymology soon associated it with several other mystical exclamations connected with the sacrifices. *Cf.* 'स्वाहा देवहविर्दाने श्रौषट् वौषट् वषट् स्वधा' Ak. The utterance of the exclamation so invariably attended the throwing in of every offering into the sacred fire, that in aftertimes it came to be personified into a wife of Agni (the fire-god) and goddess presiding over burnt offerings. Her body is said to consist of the four Vedas and her limbs are the six *aṅgas*(minor works of) the Vedas. The Brah.-Vai.-P. has this on Svâhâ—प्रकृतेः कलया चैव सर्वशक्तिस्वरूपिणी । बभूव दाहिका शक्तिरग्नेः स्वाहा स्वकामिनी ॥ ऋषयो मुनयश्चैव ब्राह्मणा दक्षिणादयः । स्वाहान्तं मन्त्रमुच्चार्य हविर्ददति नित्यशः ॥ अपि च ब्रह्मोवाच—त्वमग्नेर्दाहिका शक्तिर्भव पत्नी च सुन्दरी । दग्धुं न शक्तस्त्वकृती हुताशश्च त्वया विना ॥ त्वन्नामोच्चार्य मन्त्रान्ते यो दास्यति हविर्नरः । सुरेभ्यस्तत्प्राप्नुवन्ति सुराः स्वानन्दपूर्वकम् ॥ अग्नेः सम्पत्स्वरूपा च श्रीरूपा सा गृहेश्वरी । देवानां पूजिता शश्वन्नरादीनां भवाम्बिके ॥ From this it appears that स्वाहा was originally an offering of clarified butter which made the fire burn more briskly and look cheerful, as it were, like a man in the company of his wife.

इव हविर्भुजम्—This simile is suggested by the mention of the सायंतनविधि and is very appropriate here both in time and place, as the evening sacrifice was then just performed and Agni and Svâhâ were brought together.

S'l. 57. तयोः &c.—जगृहतुः—The use of the dual shows that the king and queen performed the salutation jointly. When an action is done by several agents jointly the verb is plural, and when separately, it is sing. *Cf. infra* XIII. 27 and note thereon.

प्रीत्या प्रतिननन्दतुः—greeted or welcomed them with pleasure in return. प्रीत्या is added here to show that their joy at the sight of the royal pair was genuine and not feigned. Chari. quotes दृष्ट्वा हृष्येत्प्रसीदेच्च प्रतिनन्देच्च सर्वशः । Manu. II. 54, in support of this; in Manus., however, this is said in connexion with food (अशनं).

S'l. 58. आतिथ्य &c.—This *adj* is used to show that the king was able, now that his exhaustion was removed, to enter into conversation with the sage who was also now free, his evening prayers being done. राज्याश्रममुनिम्—राज्याश्रमः a रूपककर्मधा°, तस्य तस्मिन्वा मुनिम् a comp. सह सुपा. The epithet is used to account for the form of question put to the king (see Malli.). The following s'loka fr. the S'âk. is a good commentary on the word राज्याश्रममुनि-अध्याक्रान्ता वसतिरमुनाप्याश्रमे सर्वभोग्ये रक्षायोगादयमपि तपः प्रत्यहं संचिनोति । अस्यापि द्यां स्पृशति वशिनश्चारणद्वंद्वगीतः पुण्यः शब्दो मुनिरिति मुहुः केवलं राजपूर्वः ॥ See Malli.'s remarks on कुशलं and राज्ये.

S'l. 59. अथर्वनिधेः—The treasure of the knowledge of Atharva (*i. e.* the magical spells and rites contained therein, which is necessary for averting coming evils, rendering innocuous evil omens, &c.) Hence the king could lay his grievance before him as one able to remove it.

अथर्व—अथर्वणा (See अथर्वन् Apte's Dic.) प्रोक्त आम्नायः अथर्वः आथर्वणो वा. It is also derived fr. अथ a particle expressing auspiciousness, ऋ to go and aff. वन् 'that which leads to good or bliss.' Vasishtha is himself the author of a number of incantations and spells contained in the Atharva Veda. *Cf.* Mitá. quoted in the *ft.-note*, which says that the Purohita of a king ought to be well-versed in the Atharva Veda; see com. and note on IV. 1; also VIII. 4. अर्थपतिः—The lord of riches or master of polity, *i. e.* the king. We have here *Anuprása* again.

S'l. 60. उपपन्नं—Proper, as it should be; *cf.* नैतत्त्वय्युपपद्यते Bg. II. 3. It is used in various senses; *cf.* II. 16, 22, III. 41, &c. सप्तस्वङ्गेषु—The seven essential constituents of government, according to Indian writers on politics, are:—(1) sovereign; (2) ministry; (3) allies; (4) treasury; (5) kingdom; (6) fortresses; and (7) army. All these contribute to the prosperity of government, and the loss of any one of these renders the whole imperfect. Vide Kám. IV. 1, 2; and Manu. IX. 224. यस्य—The correlative तस्य may be omitted when यस्य occurs in the second part of a sentence (see V. 4) 'यच्छब्दस्योत्तरवाक्यगतत्वेनोपादाने सामर्थ्यात्तत्पूर्ववाक्ये तच्छब्दस्यार्थत्वम् ' Sah.-Dar. दैवीनां &c.—See Kám. quoted in the Sañj., आयुक्तकेभ्यः in the com. means-ministers, royal officers.

S'l. 61. मन्त्रकृत्—One who *has* made *mantras*, and not one who makes or will make them (Sid.-Kau.); see note on अथर्व above. दूरात्प्रशमित॰—a comp. word. See Gr. §209. c. ०रिभिः a Bah. प्रत्यादिश्यन्ते —'are ordered back' (as superfluous and useless), rendered futile. See Malli.; or 'are excelled;' for the *mantras* are अदृष्टलक्ष्यभिदः, while the arrows are only दृष्टलक्ष्याभिदः. प्रति has here the sense of 'opposition or contrariety,' and not of 'repetition.' *Cf.* VI. 39; X. 68.

S'l. 62. विधिवत्-विधिमर्हतीति 'according to rules,' by the rule तदर्हम्. सस्यानाम्—The Gen. for the Dat., which is allowed in the Vedas. अवग्रहाविशोषिणाम्—which (else) would dry up in a drought. The words अवग्रह and अवग्राह mean the same thing, one is derived by the affix अप् the other by घञ्. The king means that Vasishtha constantly performed sacrifices and prevented his territories from being smitten by famines.

S'l. 63. पुरुषायुषं &c.—पुरुषस्यायुः पुरुषायुषं the full period of human life. अ is added to आयुस at the end of a Tat. by Pán. V. 4. 77. Other instances are निश्चितं श्रेयो निःश्रेयसम्, द्व्यायुषम्, वाङ्मनसे &c. निरातङ्काः—निरस्त आतङ्को यासाम् free from fear or distress. आतङ्क is derived fr. तञ्च् to contract, with आ. which gives it the special significance of coagulating. Hence आतङ्क properly means bodily distress, torment; and then that which causes distress, mental disquietude &c. आतञ्चन which means 'butter-milk' is derived fr om the same root. निरीतयः—for the six scourges see Sañj. स्वब्रह्मवर्चसम्—ते ब्रह्म० would have been more forcible. अ is added to वर्चस् after ब्रह्म and हस्तिन्; see com.; so हस्तिवर्चसम् .

S'l. 64. चिन्त्यमानस्य-taken care of, looked after. *Cf.* मातृभिश्चिन्त्यमानानां Uttar. I. 19. ब्रह्मयोनिना—Vasishtha is regarded as one of the ten mind-born sons of Brahman. See the Sans. note. सानुबन्धाः—अनुबध्यत इत्यनुबन्धः (अनु+बन्ध्+घञ्) that which is fastened on in succession, hence an uninterrupted succession, continuous flow &c. अनुबन्धेन सह वर्तमानाः सानुबन्धाः Bha. comp. (irregular, as there is no तुल्ययोग here). निरापदः may also be construed with सम्पदः.

S'l. 65. वध्वाम्—since Vasishtha was in the place of father to Dilipa, being his *Guru*, Sudakshiṇá was his daughter-in-law. अवति—अव् (Latin *avere*) means originally *to be gratifited, to rejoice*; it 'then acquires the force of a transitive verb, and means *to gratify, to please. Cf. infra* XI. 75. The more frequent signification of the root met with in classical Sanskrit, *viz.* that of protecting, is only a derived one from that of pleasing or favouring. ' S. P. Pandit. More than twenty other meanings are assigned to this root in the Dhà.-P. See Malli.

सद्वीपा—द्विर्गता आपः अत्रेति द्वीपम् (द्वि+अप्, by Pân. VI. 3. 97, 'द्व्यन्तरुपसर्गेभ्योऽप ईत्,' 'the अ of अप् becomes ई when following द्वि, अन्तर or a prep.; so द्वीप् and द्वीप by Pân, V. 4. 14.) द्वीपैः सह वर्तते सद्वीपा. For the number of *dvipas*, see Sans. note on VI. 38. रत्नसूः—रत्नानि (रत्न means the best thing of every class; जातौ जातौ यदुत्कृष्टं तद्रत्नमिति कथ्यते ।) सूतेऽसौ, according to modern grammarians. See Malli. मेदिनी—मेदोऽस्त्यस्यामिति मेदिनी. According to the Purâṇas, when the demons मधु and कैटभ were slain, their fat and flesh covered the whole earth which was thenceforth called *medinî*, मधुकैटभयोस्त्रासीन्मेदमांसपरिप्लुता । तेनेयं मेदिनी देवी प्रोच्यते ब्रह्मवादिभिः ॥

S'l. 66. पिण्डविच्छेद०—पिण्डस्य विच्छेदं पुनः पुनः पश्यन्तीति again and again seeing &c.; इन् shows repetition. See I. 42. श्राद्धे—श्रद्धा अत्रास्तीति

श्राद्धं; श्रद्धा + अ (णः). स्वधा &c.—As स्वाहा means an oblation offered to the gods, so स्वधा means food offered to the spirits of the departed ancestors. This is irregularly derived fr. स्वद्, स्वद्यतेऽनेन and is, like स्वाहा, an exclamation uttered at the time of offering food to the manes. तत्परं प्रधानं येषां ते तत्पराः; now see Sañj.

S'l. 67. *Cf.* Śâk. VI. 24; see *ft.-notes.* कवोष्ण-कोष्णं below; Śl. 84.

S'l. 68. सोहम्-see note on I. 5. इज्या &c.--Dissolve विशुद्ध आत्मा यस्य स विशुद्धात्मा इज्यया विशुद्धात्मा इज्याविशुद्धात्मा, and not as इज्यया विशुद्धः आत्मा यस्य in which case इज्यया cannot be compounded with विशुद्ध. This attribute shows that Dilîpa is internally bright (pure), his soul being purified by sacrifices. प्रजालोप &c.—but gloomy externally, because he has no son to continue his race—a thing external, as noticed by others. And so प्रकाशः (internally bright) and अप्रकाश externally gloomy.

लोकालोकः--See Malli. The लोकालोक, according to the Paurâṇic geography, is a belt or chain of mountains surrounding the outermost of the seven seas, (the sea of fresh water which itself surrounds *Pushkara*, the last of the seven continents) and dividing the visible world from the region of darkness. Since the sun and the whole firmament of stars roll within this circle, these mountains are lit up on one side and shrouded in perpetual darkness on the other. 'परेण पुष्करस्याथ आवृत्यावस्थितो महान्। स्वादूदकसमुद्रस्तु स समन्तादवेष्टयत् ॥ स्वादूदकस्य परितः शैलस्तु परिमण्डलः । प्रकाशश्चाप्रकाशश्च लोकालोकः स उच्यते ॥ आलोकस्तत्र चार्वाक्च निरालोकस्ततः परम् ।' Mat.-P. Ch. CXXII. स्वादूदकस्य पुरतो दृश्यते लोकसंस्थितिः । द्विगुणा काञ्चनी भूमिः सर्वजन्तुविवर्जिता ॥ लोकालोकस्ततः शैलो योजनायुतविस्तृतः । उच्छ्रायेणापि तावन्ति सहस्राण्यचलो हि सः ॥ Vish.-P. II. 4. *Cf.* also Pad.-P. लोकालोको गिरिर्यस्तु लोकान्ते वर्तते महान् । आवृणोति स तेजांसि सूर्यादीनामपि द्विज ॥ तमतिक्रम्य तेजांसि क्षमन्ते न प्रवर्तितुम् । इ० । According to the Bhâg.-P. it is so called because it is situated in the middle of the enlightened and unenlightened, or inhabited and uninhabited, regions.

The Lokâloka is really the wall of clouds that bound our horizon all round, conceived by the ancients to be a chain of mountains. As the sun and the other heavenly bodies were seen dipping into the sea within this wall of clouds, it was naturally supposed that the world of living beings was within it, its outer side being exposed to perpetual darkness. To this misconception are also due all the legends about Indra's clipping the wings of mountains.

S'l. 69. सुख—सुखयतीति सुखं (पचाद्यच्). सन्ततिः—सन्तन्यते वंशोऽनया । शुद्ध०—This shews how anxious the Hidu Aryans were to keep their blood pure.

S'l. 70. विधातः—This epithet is very significant. It implies neglect (unintentional though it be) on the part of Vasishtha, since he has the power to bless the king with progeny. See Malli. and notes on I. 35. सिक्तं स्वयमिव &c. वृक्षकं, अनुकम्पितो वृक्षः वृक्षकः—The simile is very appropriate here as being drawn from the daily scenes of life and therefore perfectly familiar to sages. The Rishis considered the trees of the hermitage as their children (see V. 6) and so the king could very well rouse the mercy of Vasishtha by comparing himself to a tree reared up by the sage but bearing no fruit.

S'l. 71. भगवन्—properly an epithet of the Supreme Being. It means 'one who posssesses all kinds of excellences.' ऐश्वर्यस्य समग्रस्य धर्मस्य यशसः श्रियाः। वैराग्यस्याथ मोक्षस्य षण्णां भग इतीरणा ॥ (भगो विद्यते अस्य भगवान्।) उत्पत्तिं च विनाशं च भूतानामगतिं गतिम्। वेत्ति विद्यामविद्यां च स वाच्यो भगवानिति। अन्त्यमृणम्–'the last debt', *i. e.* the debt due to the ancestors. According to the Hindu Sâstras, everyone that is born has three debts to pay off, *viz.* to sages, to gods and to the departed forefathers. He frees himself from these respectively by studying the Vedas, offering the daily and other sacrifices, and by having a son. *Cf.* VIII. 30 and the Śruti quoted by Malli. in his com. *ad loc.*

अरुन्तुदम्—fr. अरुस् + तुद् ; for the change of स् to म् see Pâṇ. VI. 3. 67. आलानम्—Here Malli. is quite right in understanding by आलान the post to which an elephant is tied and not a chain or rope, as some would have it. That the simile should be quite appropriate, आलानम् must mean something that inflicts mental, and not actual bodily pain. The elephant would be as glad to enjoy a cool bath with a chain round his neck as without one. *Cf.* 'सोढुं न तत्पूर्वमवर्णमीशे आलानिकं स्थाणुमिव द्विपेन्द्रः' XIV. 38; also IV. 81. That the force of the simile should be fully understood, construe: (1) अरुन्तुदं मे अन्त्यम् ऋणमनिर्वाणस्य दन्तिनः अरुन्तुदमालानमिव असह्यपीडम् अवेहि, or (2) असह्यपीडं मे अन्त्यम् ऋणम् अनिर्वाणस्य दन्तिनः अरुन्तुदम् आलानमिव अवेहि।

S'l. 72. इक्ष्वाकूणाम्—इक्ष्वाकोः राज्ञः अपत्यानि पुमांस इक्ष्वाकवः *p. l.* of ऐक्ष्वाकः the aff. अञ् (अण् in the com. is probably an oversight) being dropped when the word is used in the plural and not in the fem.; see Pân. II. 4. 62. Ikshváku was the son of Vaivasvata Manu and father of Vikukshi. He was the first king of the solar dynasty in Ayodhyâ. He was born from the nostril of Manu, as he happened to sneeze. *Cf.* Bhâg.-P. 'क्षुवतस्तु मनोर्जज्ञ इक्ष्वाकुर्घ्राणतः सुतः।' इक्ष्वाकूणां may also be construed with सिद्धयः.

त्वदधीनाः—त्वयि अधि त्वदधीनाः। The comp. being optional, the uncompounded form will be त्वयि अधि सिद्धयः; अधि necessarily takes the term. ख (ईन) when it is the latter member of a comp.: 'अषडक्षाशितङ्ग्वलंकर्मालंपुरुषाध्युत्तरपदात्खः' Pân. V. 4. 7. For a similar idea, *cf.* सिद्ध्यन्ति कर्मसु महत्स्वपि यन्नियोज्याः &c. S'ak. VII. 4.

S'l. 73. इति thus. विज्ञापितः—respectfully addressed or informed.

N. B.—The verbs आज्ञापय् and विज्ञापय् are technical terms of addressing a person, without any idea of actual command or request. Thus when a person addresses one who is his superior in rank or dignity, the verb विज्ञापय् is used, while in the case of one addressing another who is inferior in rank or dignity to him, आज्ञापय् is the verb used.

ध्यानस्तिमितलोचनः—This indicates that the functions of all the external senses were suspended. *Cf.* the description of the contemplation of S'iva, in Kum. III. 48, 'अवृष्टिसंरम्भमिवाम्बुवाहम्' &c. क्षणमात्रम्—Here मात्र is used to emphasize क्षण; a moment only. This shows that Vasishtha was a master of *yoga*, who could put himself in a contemplative mood (समाधि) in a moment, and set in operation the inner apparatus for discovering unknown things.

सुप्तमीन इव ह्रदः—Mark the use of the word मीन which is deliberate. This shows how scrupulous the Poet is in selecting proper words to express his similes. Vasishtha, who is the repository of harmless thoughts and actions, can with propriety be compared to a ह्रद having nothing in it but such harmless creatures as fish. With this *cf.* VII. 30 where the princes looking pleased when really angry are described as ह्रदाः प्रसन्ना इव गूढनक्राः, where गूढमीनाः would not have suited.

S'l. 74. प्रणिधानेन—Malli. takes this with भावितात्मा, it should rather be construed with अपश्यत्. प्रणिधान 'close application', concentration of the mind upon one thing. भावितात्मा—भावय् properly means to steep, as a medicine, into a liquid that it should imbibe its properties and be free from the inherent impurities it is desired to be cleared off. Hence भावित means completely pervaded or imbued by. भावितात्मन् therefore means one whose mind is purged of all impurities forming its rust by its being imbued with spiritual knowledge by constant meditation. See Pat. Yog. I. 30, Ved. Sára. 32 (Nir. Ed.)

एनं प्रत्यबोधयत्—The optional forms एनम् &c. of the pronouns इदम् and एतद् are used when there is अन्वादेश or a subsequent assertion; see Gr. § 137. The first assertion here is भावितात्मा सः अस्य भुवो भर्तुः &c; and then the second is introduced by अथ, अथैनं प्रत्यबोधयत्. For the acc. एनं see Sañj. and Gr. § 808

S'l. 75. शक्रम्—शक्नोतीति शक्रः he who is able to do everything. Indra is regarded in the Vedas as the mightiest of all gods, though in the Purâṇas he occupies a position subordinate to Vishṇu, Brahman and S'iva उपस्थाय—स्था with उप is trans.; *cf.* IV. 6, X. 13. The kings of the solar race are represented as often visiting *Svarga* to assist Indra in his wars with the demons. See VI. 71, 72. This supports the assertion आनाकरथवर्त्मनाम्, *supra* s'l. 5.

कल्पतरुच्छायाम्—कल्पः संकल्पितोर्थः what is desired; तत्फलकः तरुः, or कल्पस्य तरुः। जन्यजनकभावसम्बन्धे षष्ठी। In either case the comp. is शाकपार्थिवादिः *i.e.* उत्तरपदलोपी. See Gr. § 229. See, however Malli. on VI. 6 infra. Dissolve कल्पतरोश्छाया कल्पतरुच्छाया ताम् and not कल्पतरूणां as the comp. will be neu. in that case. See Gr. § 245 (*e*).

S'l. 76. इमां स्मरन्—According to the M.-Bh. the root स्मृ governs the gen. only when there is शेषविवक्षा of the *karma, i. e.* when a person or thing is not directly brought to the mind, but is remembered through the instrumentality of something else; *e. g.* मातुः स्मरति गुणैः; here the good qualities of the mother are principally brought to the mind and then (through them) the mother. But when the मातृ is directly remembered the acc. should be used (यदा कर्म विवक्षितं भवति तदा षष्ठी न भवति Mah.-Bhâ.), as in the present instance; मातरं स्मरति. प्रदक्षिणक्रियार्हायाम्—प्रगता दक्षिणं प्रदक्षिणं Pan. II. 1. 17; प्रदक्षिणस्य क्रिया प्रदक्षिणक्रिया तस्या अर्हा योग्या ताम्। तस्यां—सा as the आधार of the आचरणक्रिया takes the loc. *Cf.* अयमाचरत्यविनयं मुग्धासु तपस्विकन्यासु S'âk. I. 25 उपकारिणि विश्रब्धे शुद्धमतौ यः समाचरति पापम् H. 1.

S'l. 77. प्रसूतिम्—प्रसूयत इति प्रसूतिः offspring, issue. अनाराध्य—indec. p. p. of राध् with आ; by the rules of syntax the subject of the absolutive and of the main verb must be the same; here प्रजा is not the subject of the आराधनक्रिया; Malli. therefore, takes आराध्य in the causative sense, since he renders it by असेवयित्वा-प्रजा (त्वया) मत्प्रसूतिमनाराध्य न भविष्यति (*i. e.* मत्प्रसूत्याराधनसापेक्षा भविष्यति।) without having my child propitiated by you. Or we may explain मत्प्रसूतिमनाराध्य स्थितस्य तव प्रजा &c.

S'l. 78. सारथिना -सारयति अश्वानिति सारथिः; fr. सृ cau. and Uṇadi अथि (अथिन्; सर्तेर्णिच); or रथेन सह सरथः (Bah.) तस्यापत्यं (सरथ + इञ्). आकाशगङ्गा—This is really the galaxy or the milky way. दिग्गजे—There are eight elephants belonging to the eight regents of the cardinal points who assist them in the defence and protection of the directions. (1) Indra's elephant at the East is ऐरावत; (2) Agni's at the S.-East is पुण्डरीक; (3) Yama's at the South is वामन; (4) Sûrya's at the S.-West is कुमुद; (5) Varuṇa's at the West is अञ्जन; (6) Vâyu's at the N.-West is पुष्पदन्त; (7) Kubera's at the North is सार्वभौम; and (8) Soma's at the N.-East is सुप्रतीक. See ft.-note.

S'l. 79. ईप्सितं—P. p. p. of the desid. of आप्; see. com. सार्गलम् — अर्गलेन सह वर्तमानम्; with impediment or obstruction; see सानुबन्ध above 64. here अर्गल means (metaphorically) obstruction. Sumati. quotes— अपूज्या यत्र पूज्यन्ते पूज्यापूज्यव्यतिक्रमः। दुर्भिक्षं मारिरोगाश्च भवन्त्येव न संशयः॥

S'l. 80. हविषे—Malli. seems to take this as तादर्थ्ये चतुर्थी; see Gr. § 827. दीर्घसत्रस्य—सीदन्त्यत्र इति सत्रम् that in which priests sit down, a sacrificial session. The period of time required for a *Satra* varies between one year and a thousand years. See Bhág-P. I. 1. 4. The distinction between an ordinary sacrifice and a *dirgha satra* is this; in the former the merit arising from the sacrifice belongs wholly to the Yajamâna, the priests getting only the *dakshina*, while in the latter the merit is shared by the Yajamâna, and the sixteen priests. Vide Âs'v. Sû. Adh. XII. सा च—Here च is पक्षान्तरे—but she; she again. भुजङ्गपिहितद्वारम्—भुजेन कुटिलगत्या गच्छतीति भुजङ्गः, भुज+गम्+अ (खच् before which a nasal is added to the word); also भुजङ्गम and भुजग with ड (अ) added. पिहित=अपिहित that on which any thing is placed; hence hidden, concealed. The word is generally used with reference to the closing or concealing the mouth of a pit or hole. Accoring to the grammarian Bhaguri, अव and अपि used as उपसर्गs drop their अ optionally; अवगाहः वगाहः, अपिधानं पिधानम् &c.

S'l. 81. सुरभेः—Abl. case, though the meaning is that of the gen., by the deduction from the rule 'प्रतिनिधिप्रतिदाने च यस्मात्,' on which Nâgesabhaṭṭa remarks 'अस्मादेव निपातनात्षष्ठ्यर्थे पञ्चमी।' प्रतिनिधि- is always *mas.*

S'l. 82. S'lokas 82—85 form what is called a *kalâpaka*, being syntanctically connected; see ft.-note p. 3. इति वादिनः एवास्य—एव is used in the sense of अवधारणा, 'just as he uttered the words and before he could utter any more.' वादिनः is a gram. inccuracy, it being used in the sense of वदतः. For the root वद् takes इन् either when it denotes habit or when it implies impropriety, neither of which is possible here.

होतुराहुतिसाधनम्—होतुः ought to be construed with आहुतिसाधनम्, as Malli. does, and not with वादिनः as suggested by S. P. Pandit. The तृ in होतृ implies habit. See Malli. Vasishtha was habitually a sacrificer: (अग्निहोत्रिन्), and, therefore, habitually in need of घृत, necessary for sacrifice. आहुतिसा०—This is emphatic and as such retains its gender. The cow was kept by Vasishtha not because he cared to have milk for luxury, but because he wanted घृत for sacrificial purposes. The cow was thus आहुतिसाधनम् and not पयःसाधनम्. The two words, therefore, ought to be construed together; otherwise they will lose their force. Strangely enough, Mr. Nandargikar also, following S. P. Pandit, says—' अस्य होतुः may also be taken and perhaps more correctly with वादिनः, and be construed as its subject, rather than with the phrase आहुतिसाधनम्.'

S'l. 83. The simile here is one of the most beautiful and perfect similes for which our poet is famous. It is appropriate both in point of time and place. It was evening time and the cow visited the hermitage in the evening like संध्या with the moon on her forehead. ललाटोदयम्—ललाट means the forehead, and also by implication the western sky, where the new moon is seen at the evening time. उदय means (1) appearance; and (2) rise. आभुग्नम्--both were a little curved. पल्लवस्निग्धपाटला—The cow was of a स्निग्ध *i. e.* pleasing (mild) pink colour. The *Saṃdhyà* is also of this colour owing to the slanting rays of the sun falling upon the evening clouds. नवम्—This attribute is used to account for the crescent shape of the moon and also to leave out of sight the stain, that the resemblance with the curved white tuft of hair on the forehead of the cow should be complete.

S'l. 84. कोष्णेन—कु as the first member of a Karm. Comp. substitutes for itself का, कव and कत्, when meaning ईषत् or little. See Gr. § 224, (b). कुण्डोध्नी—derived fr. कुण्ड a pitcher and ऊधस् (changed to ऊधन् in a Bah. Comp. before ई) an udder; Gr. § 328; 'having a pitcher-like, *i e.* full udder.' " ऊधन् has originally, like अहन्, two crude forms, *viz.* ऊधन् and ऊधर् (sometimes ऊधस्). The न in कुण्डोध्नी is, therefore, radical, and not extraneous, as the grammarians have it. *Cf.* also ऊधन्य 'milk'." S. P. P. मेध्येनावभृथादपि—मेध्य lit. 'that which is fit to be killed or sacrificed;' hence, holy, sacred; अवभृथ a purificatory bath taken at the end of a sacrifice. Vide Tait. Br. II. 6.6. Also a minor sacrifice performed at the close of a principal sacrifice. 'दीक्षान्तोऽवभृथो यज्ञः' Amar. Here the former sense, of course, is intended. See IX. 23. and notes thereon मेध्येन. and अपि—as the excess of holiness is expressed by अपि the purpose of the affix तर is served and we have मेध्येन, instead of मेध्यतरेण, which also means द्वयोरतिशयेन मेध्येन.

S'l. 85. अन्तिकात्—from their vicinity (being raised from the ground near the king). महीक्षितः—See Samj.; according to Bopadeva

महीं क्षयति; see also note on महीक्षितां I. 11. Here reference is made to a kind of bath technically known as Vâyavya. In the Kûrma. P. six kinds of baths are mentioned; ब्राह्ममाग्नेयमुद्दिष्टं वारुणं दिव्यमेव च। वायव्यं यौगिकं तद्वत्षोढा स्नानं प्रकीर्तितम् ॥.

S'l. 86. पुण्य—is an adj. here and means 'sanctifying.' It is also a noun; see s'l. 69. निमित्तज्ञः—'Versed in omens,' *i. e.* who knew what were good omens and what were bad. See Bhg. II. 31. Here the opportune appearance of the cow is an auspicious omen indicating the near fulfilment of the King's wishes. याज्यम्—See Samj. The king is the *Yajamâna*; Vasishtha is the *Yâjaka*. राजा यजति, वसिष्ठस्तं याजयति, इति राज्ञो याज्यत्वम्। आशंसिता°—may also be explained as आशंसिता (indicated) अवन्ध्या प्रार्थना यस्य whose desire was thus indicated as sure to be fulfilled. Some take आशंसिता separately, as the Nom. sing. of आशंसितृ qualifying तपोनिधि, but without propriety. *Cf.* for a similar idea हरत्यघं सम्प्रति हेतुरेष्यतः शुभस्य पूर्वाचरितैः कृतं शुभैः। शरीरभाजां भवदीयदर्शनं व्यनक्ति कालत्रितयेऽपि योग्यताम् ॥ S'is'. I. 26, where Nârada's appearance is similarly described as sanctifying at the time, and indicating future good fortune

S'l. 87. अदूरवर्तिनीम्—Here the नञ् has the sense of opposition. For the various senses in which नञ् is used, see foot-note and Gr. §375. सिद्धिम्—according to Malli. is used for कार्यस्य सिद्धिम्. *Cf.* तद्गच्छ सिद्ध्यै Kum. III. 18; and आवेदयन्ति हि प्रत्यासन्नमानन्दमग्रपातीनि शुभानि निमित्तानि। Kâd. विगणय--*Cf.* Eng. 'count upon.'

S'l. 88. वन्यवृत्तिः—may also be interpreted as वने भवा वन्या मुनयस्तेषां वृत्तिः मुनिवृत्तिः सा इव वृत्तिर्यस्य । 'leading the life of an anchorite or hermit.' शश्वत् *Indec.* qualifies आत्मानुगमनेन. आत्मानुगमनेन—by personal attendance, by following her in person. प्रसादयितुमर्हसि—अर्ह् used with the inf. in the second person (and sometimes in the third) expresses a mild command, or a courteous request, and should be translated by 'pray' 'be pleased to,' &c.; see V. 25.

S'l. 89. प्रस्थितायां प्रतिष्ठेथाः &c.—By these injunctions the sage implies that the king is to be absolutely guided in all his actions by those of the cow; *i. e.* he is not to move until she has moved, he is not to cease moving before the cow has done so, and so on.

S'l. 90. वधूः—Sudakshiṇâ is previously spoken of as the daughter-in-law of the sage by the king (I. 65), and so Vasishtha here calls her वधू. But she is to worship the cow as the wife of the king and therefore Malli. translates it by जाया.

अर्चितामन्वेतु—Let her follow the cow worshipped (already by her), *i. e.* let her worship the cow and then follow her (see II. 1). This is one of those constructions so common in synthetical languages. प्रयता—This means नियमवती सती leading an ascetic's life (like the king). सायं प्रत्युद्व्रजेदपि—अपि shows that Sudakshiṇá is to go forth to meet the cow and worship her also in the evening. (See II. 21).

S'l. 91. इति—in this manner. परिचर्यापरः—परिचर्या formed irregularly fr. चर् with परि + अ (श) fem.; words similarly derived are परिसर्या, मृगया and अटाट्या. See Várt. on Páṇ. III. 3. 101. पर—Solely. परिचर्या एव परं केवलं यस्य. अविघ्नम्—Absence of impediment. This is a नित्यसमास and therefore Malli. does not expound it but simply gives the meaning. धुरि—See note on II. 2. पुत्रिणाम्—इन् is used प्राशस्त्ये; see Samj.; 'those having noble sons.'

S'l. 92. प्रीतिमान्—shows that the King undertook to carry out the instructions of the sage willingly and not under compulsion. सपरिग्रहः-परि साकल्येन गृह्यते इति परिग्रहः. fr. परिग्रह् + अप् (अ); wife; see S'ák. III. 20. परिग्रहेण सह वर्तते इति । तुल्ययोगे बहुव्रीहिः, there being equal participation in acting up to the injunctions of the sage. देशकालज्ञः—See Mallinâtha's remarks on this. See also Chár. quoted in the ft.-note.

S'l. 93. अथ—a particle frequently used to introduce a change of subject. See notes on II. 1. प्रदोषे—प्रारब्धा दोषा यस्मिन् lit. that in which the night has its beginning. See also ft.-note. दोषा adv. meaning 'at night' is a different word. दोषज्ञः—दोषं जानातीति one able to know mistakes or faults; hence, a learned man. This epithet is very significant here. Vasishṭha knew that it would be a दोष on his part to keep the king long engaged in conversation with him after the fatigue of a day's journey and so asked him to go to bed, just in the first part of the night. This attribute also supports the use of the epithet सूनृतवाक्. संवेशाय—The dat. here ought to be explained as used तादर्थ्ये. We cannot explain it as संवेष्टुं विससर्ज; for this will mean 'the sage dismissed the king in order that he, and not the king, may go to bed', the inf. being used when both the verbs have the same subject (समानकर्तृकेषु तुमुन्); the rules, क्रियार्थोपपदस्य &c. and तुमर्थाच्च भाववचनात् are, therefore inapplicable. विशांपतिम्—This word is generally understood to be अलुक् षष्ठीसमास, and seems to be used as a संज्ञा like राजा in many places. *Cf.* III. 66, V. 33 &c. And Malli. who translates it by मनुजेश्वरं seems to take it as such.

But there is nothing in Pâṇ. or his commentators countenancing such a supposition; while the passage further on अथ तस्य विशां पत्युः &c. (X. 50) seems to go straight against it; for had विशांपति been an *aluk* comp. we should have expected विशांपतेः and not विशां पत्युः । See also Ján. II. 18.

सूनृतवाक्—सूनृतं-सुष्ठु नृत्यत्यनेन what is true and agreeable. We know that Vasishṭha had just addressed a speech to Dilîpa which was at once pleasing and true. उदितश्रियम्—Some editions read ऊर्जितश्रियम्; ऊर्जिता अधिका great, excellent श्रीः fortune यस्य. But the reading उदितश्रियम् seems to be preferable, as reference is made here to the king's fortune which consists in his being soon blessed with a son and which is therefore उदित now. श्री may also mean 'brightness.' The king's countenance which was depressed so long now looked bright with joy. 'ऊर्जित' has no special propriety here. प्रभुः सन्—implies that the sage had the power to overcome all the obstacles to the king's successful performance of the vow of propitiating the cow and to the consequent birth of a son to him. Mark the alliterations in this and in the following s'lokas.

S'l. 94. सत्यामपि &c.—The loc. is अनादरे. The phrase means सतीमपि तपःसिद्धिमनादृत्य deliberately not bringing into operation his power of asceticism. This he did ' नियमापेक्षया ' having regard to the vow, *i. e.* that he should perform the vow properly. For an illustration of the power of penance to call into being the desired things, *cf.* वस्त्रान्नपानं शयनं च नाना कृत्वावकाशे रुचिसंप्रक्लृप्तम् । तान्प्रीतिमानाह मुनिस्ततः स्म निवध्वमाध्वं पिबतात्त शेध्वम् ॥ Bhaṭṭi. III. 44; also, 42, 43. कल्पवित् &c.—who knew the proper ritualistic procedure or mode of performing a religious rite; on this Chár. remarks: यद्यपि तपोमाहात्म्यात्नाना-विधानि भक्ष्यभोज्यानि सुकराणि तथापि शास्त्रप्रतिपादितप्रयोगाभिज्ञो मुनिर्भूपस्य व्रतविषयनियमार्थं वन्यामेव वृत्तिं कृतवानिति तात्पर्यम् ।

S'l. 95. कुलपतिना—See ft.-note. Kulapati is a sage who feeds and instructs ten thousand *Munis*. पर्णशाला—पर्णनिर्मिता शाला. The comp. is of the शाकपार्थिवादि class. प्रयत—self-restrained, (and also pure in body). तच्छिष्याध्ययन &c.—Sanskrit poets always represent kings as awakened in the morning by the songs of bards accompanied by music; and even when the usual appendages of royalty are not present, they imagine something as serving that purpose. Thus the noise of the pupils of the sage reading early in the morning is made here to serve the purpose of the morning songs of bards to rouse the king from his slumber.

CANTO II.

S'l. 1. अथ—has here the sense of आनन्तर्य; 'then,' 'afterwards'; see Malli. It has also here the additional sense of 'auspiciousness, which it does not express directly, but conveys by its very utterance. *Cf.* 'अर्थान्तरप्रयुक्त एव अथशब्दः श्रुत्या मङ्गलप्रयोजनो भवति' S'à. Bhá.; also ओंकारश्चाथ शब्दश्च द्वावेतौ ब्रह्मणः पुरा । कण्ठं भित्त्वा विनिर्यातौ तस्मान्माङ्गलिकावुभौ' ॥ Tait. Prát. The particle is here used to indicate the future blessing of the cow.

जाया &c.—See Mallinàtha's remarks on the word जाया. Expound—गन्धा गन्धद्रव्याणि धूपचन्दनादीनि । The word is mas. and in the pl. number according to the Manoramá which remarks—"अस्ति च गन्धशब्दो द्रव्यवचनः । 'वहति जलमियं पिनष्टि गन्धानियमियमुद्ग्रथते स्रजो विचित्राः' इति दर्शनात् । गन्धस्तु सौरभे नृत्ये गन्धके गर्वलेशयोः । स एव द्रव्यवचनो बहुत्वे पुंसि च स्मृतः ॥' इति कोशाच्च ।" गन्धाश्च माल्यं च गन्धमाल्ये । Now see Saṃj. By whom perfumes and garlands were caused to be accepted by (through) his Queen. Some grammarians, who differ from Páṇ., class the root ग्रह् among verbs which govern two accusatives. But it will be difficult to expound this comp. according to them. For, in this case we get जायया धेनुर्गन्धमाल्ये प्रतिग्राहिता which is not compoundable. Remarks the Manoramá—"ग्राहेर्द्विकर्मकत्वं यद्यपि सुधाकरादीनां सम्मतं तथापि बहुनामसंमतम् । * * * ग्राहेर्द्विकर्मकत्वे हि जायाप्रतिग्राहितगन्धमाल्यामित्यत्र केन प्रयोज्याया धेनोरभिधानं स्यात् । ण्यन्ते कर्तुश्च कर्मण इत्युक्तेः । ततश्च जायया गन्धमाल्ये प्रतिग्राहितामिति स्यात् । सिद्धान्ते तु प्रतिग्राहिते गन्धमाल्ये ययेति विग्रहः । जायानिष्ठप्रेरणाविषयभूतं गन्धमाल्यकर्मकं यत्प्रतिग्रहणं तत्कर्त्रीमित्यर्थः । " माला एव माल्यम् चातुर्वर्ण्यादित्वात्स्वार्थे ष्यञ् (य).

वनाय—Malli. explains datives like 'चापलाय' I. 9, 'वनाय,' 'गृहाय,' V. 10 &c. by the rule 'क्रियार्थोपपदस्य च कर्मणि स्थानिनः' Pâṇ. II. 3. 14, which means 'when an action is done with a view to a second, the कर्म of the second takes चतुर्थी, if the second act be not explicitly expressed;' *e. g.* in फलान्याहर्तुं the गमनक्रिया is accomplished with a view to आहरणक्रिया; hence when the आहरणक्रिया is not expressly mentioned, we may say फलेभ्यो याति; so चापलाय प्रचोदितः means चापलं कर्तुं प्रचोदितः, वनाय मुमोच means वनं गन्तुं मुमोच. Here the rule 'समानकर्तृकेषु तुमुन्' may not be insisted upon, since the inf. is not directly used. See Sid.-Kau. on the same (Páṇ. III. 3. 158). If it be insisted upon, it will be necessary to explain the first as तादर्थ्ये चतुर्थी and the 2nd by the general rule कर्मणा यमभिप्रैति स संप्रदानम् । Páṇ. I. 4. 32, where according to the Mb. it is not necessary to understand the कर्म *of* the root दा alone, as Vâmana and Dîkshita do; Kaiyaṭa commenting on the passage in Mb., remarks:—कैश्चिदन्वर्थसंज्ञाविज्ञानाद्दाति-विषय एव संप्रदानसंज्ञेत्यभ्युपगतम् । दानं च स्वत्वनिवृत्तिः परस्वत्वापत्तिपर्यन्ता इति प्रत्यज्ञायि । तदुभयमप्ययुक्तमन्यत्रापि भाष्यकारेण संज्ञाया अभ्युपगमात् ।

पीतप्रतिबद्धवत्साम्—पीत is made up of 'पीतं drink' and the possessive affix अ, meaning 'that had its fill or drink.' See Saṃj. on this. For further discussion on the subject, see Mallinátha's remarks on 'विदित' Kir. I. 1. आदौ पीतः पश्चात्प्रतिबद्धः पीतप्रतिबद्धः Karm. Comp.; 'the calf that had first its fill of milk and then was tied.' **यशोधनः**—For the force of this epithet see Saṃj. More probably this is intended by the poet to foreshadow the King's chivalrous rescue of the cow from the grip of the lion to be subsequently described.

S'l. 2. **पांसु**—mark the different meanings of this word in this śl. Note that the affix ल (लच्) denotes 'possession'; *cf.* अंसल, वत्सल &c. See Gr. p. 213. **धुरि** 'at the head of.' धुर् properly means the yoke of a carriage; and as it is the yoke of an approaching carriage that prominently attracts attention, being in the front, it sometimes has the secondary sense of 'the first place or the front.'

धर्मपत्नी—Gen. Tat., see Saṃj. and ft.-notes; wife for ceremonials at the performance of religious rites.

श्रुतेरिवार्थम् &c.—This refers to the doctrine that the Smṛitis, in laying down their injunctions, absolutely follow the S'rutis, from which they derive their authority. And when a precept is found in the Smṛitis, for which there is no express authority in the Veda, the difficulty is obviated by supposing that the Vedic passage which once authorized the Smṛiti in question is now lost. *Cf.* Manu. II. 10. Smṛiti is defined as 'अनुमेयश्रुतिमूलं मन्वादिशास्त्रम्.' The simile is appropriate as it suggests that Sudakshiṇâ not only followed the cow close upon her heels physically, but mentally also, *i. e.* with a devout mind. S. P. Pandit (followed by Mr. Nandargikar) is unable to see the appropriateness of the simile and hazards the remark 'now and then he (Kâlidasá) used similes which seem to be objectionable on this ground that the object to which any thing is compared is less intelligible or vivid than the thing itself,' forgetting that Kàlidása wrote at a time when S'ruti and Smṛiti were everything to the Hindus and the relation between the two was more vivid and better understood than now. Even now the simile is perfectly intelligible to those Hindus, who have not yet lost their regard for the authority of the Vedas, and the Smṛitis based on them. For the rhetorical figure, see Saṃj. and the ft.-notes.

Śl. 3. दयालुः—from दय् + आलु (आलुच्) which indicates habit; *cf.* स्पृहयालु, शयालु, निद्रालु &c. सौरभेयीं सुरभिः—the use of the epithet सुरभि for the king and सौरभेयी for the cow suggests maternal care in the king. मातेव रक्षेति ध्वनिः—Prof. Ray.

पयोधरीभूत &c.—This is called a च्विकरण(*chvi*-formation).Such formations are classed as prepositional Tat. compounds. Vide Gr. §§ 234, 343 (Sec. III.). Mark the play on the word पयस् which means both water as well as milk. गोरूपधराम्—Possibly there is an allusion here to the Earth's having assumed the form of a cow and her being milked by gods, sages, mountains &c , as directed by Pṛithu, the son of Vena. See notes to Kád. p. 11; Kum. I. 2 and Malli. thereon. इवोर्वीम्—The simile here serves a double purpose. It refers to the huge form of the cow (see śl. 29, where the cow is again compared to the table-land of a mountain), and also suggests that the king though engaged in tending the cow seemed nevertheless to exercise the functions of a ruler of the earth.

Śl. 4. व्रताय न्यषेधि—This gives the reason why Dilîpa ordered his servants not to accompany him. He followed the cow for the performance of a vow, which he was desired by Vasishṭha to do all alone. Vide I. 81. ०रक्षा-रक्षणं fr. रक्ष् + अ भावे by the rule गुरोश्च हलः (a root ending in a consonant and having a long syll. takes अ; so, ईहा). प्रसृति-see com.;from सृ + ति(क्तिन्);for different senses see 63belew.X.53,56,&c.

Śl 5. स्वैरगतैः—स्व ईरः प्रेरणमस्मिन्स्वैरम् । The Vṛiddhi vowel is substituted here by the Vart. 'स्वादीरेरिणोः' । See Gr. § 23 Exc. (c) स्वैराणि गतानि स्वैरगतानि तैः. सम्राट्—सम्यग्राजतेऽसौ । See Samj. and G. § 36. The epithet brings out the high sense of duty of Dilîpa. Himself a great king—served by other kings—he became devoted to the service of the cow. समाराधनम्—सम्यगाराधनम्. Gati Samása.

Śl. 6. निषेदुषीम्—निषेदिवस् Perf. part. of सद् with नि. The Perf. participles are generally used in the sense of the Aorist, *i. e.*, in the sense of 'who or what has or has been done.' See G. §§ 875, 677. आसनबन्धधीरः—आस्यतेऽनेनेत्यासनं तस्य बन्धस्तस्मिन् धीरः । Patiently seating himself down, remaining firm in his seat. The word धीर primarily means one who is considerate (धियं thought राति possesses इति) one who bestows proper thought upon a thing; hence, sticking fast to a purpose. And as a considerate man always acts wisely, *i. e.*, by taking into account all possible difficulties &c., it has also acquired the secondary sense of 'wise, learned.'

छायेव—an appropriate simile. Since the word छाया is *fem.* the Upamá is faulty according to श्रीभोज and some other later rhetoricians, but not so according to Vâmana, Daṇḍin and other ancient writers. See ft.-note.

S'l. 7. अन्तर्मदावस्थः—Here अन्तः has the sense of अन्तर्गता. According to a s'l. quoted by Vallabha, there are four species of elephants of which the one referred to here is of the Bhadra kind. द्विपेन्द्रः—द्वाभ्यां पिबतीति द्विपः। One who drinks with two, *scil.* first with the proboscis and then with the mouth; an elephant. इन्द्र in compounds like मनुजेन्द्र, नरेन्द्र &c. means a king and is added here to द्विप that it should better compare with Dilîpa, who was himself a *Manuja-indra.* See ft.-note. द्विपानामिन्द्र उपचाराद्राजा द्विपेन्द्रः। द्विप इन्द्र इव द्विपेन्द्रः। उपमितसमासः। Pâṇ. II. 1. 56; or द्विपेषु इन्द्रः।

S'l. 8. लताप्रतान &c.—This is a characteristic of the forester. When one intends to enter a forest for hunting &c., he is described as tying up his hair by means of tendrils or the like so that they may not be entangled in thorns and brambles. *Cf.* IX. 51. Thus the tying up of the hair being a sign (लक्षण) of one about to enter a forest (इत्थंभूत) the Sûtra quoted by Malli. applies. अधिज्यधन्वा—अधिगता ज्यानेन, अधिकृता ज्यास्य, ज्यामधिगतं वाधिज्यम्; मुनिहोमधेनुः—होमस्य धेनुः होमधेनुः। अश्वघासादिवत्तादर्थ्ये षष्ठीसमासः। See Sid.-Kau. on Pâṇ. II. 1. 36. मुनेः होमधेनुः मुनिहोमधेनुः।

Now the poet describes, in a poetical way of course, in s'lokas 9-13(see Mallinátha's introductory remark to these)how the king was received with usual formalities in the forest. When a monarch enters a town, his servants run on both sides shouting 'Prosperity to the king; here comes he,' &c.;this is done here by the trees(mark the *mas.*gender of द्रुमthat represents males). As on such occasions the town-damsels throw fried rice on the king and elderly ladies hurry to have a look at him, so the young creepers strew flowers upon the king and the female deer stand gazing upon him(10-11). Again songs in praise of the visitor are sung everywhere in the town, and so the glory of the king is here sung by the forest Dryads (12). Chauries are waved over him to remove perspiration, and that is done here by the gentle breezes (13).And lastly, as the royal visit is marked by some gracious act on the part of the monarch, so is described in s'l. 14 the good done to the forest by the presence of the king.

S'l. 9. विसृष्टपार्श्वानुचरस्य—*Cf.* above (s'l. 4); पार्श्वयोरनुचराः पार्श्वानुचराः। पर्शूनां समूहः पार्श्वम्। The word पार्श्व is derived from पर्शु (a contracted form of परशु) which means a rib-bone. पर्शु or परशु also means an axe, which sense it probably acquired from a sharp crooked rib-bone having been originally used as an axe. पाशभृता समस्य—The king, as chastiser of the wicked, is comparable to Varuṇa, the god armed with the noose, who also discharges a similar function. (नियमनादुभयोः साम्यम्); *cf*. IX. 6—समतया वसुवृष्टिविसर्जनैर्नियमनादसतां च नराधिपः । अनुययौ यमपुण्यजनेश्वरौ सवरुणावरुणाग्रसरं रुचा ॥ See note to this s'l.

आलोकशब्दम्-See Vallabha quoted in the ft.-note. आलोकशब्द is the set formula of words which one must utter on seeing a king. It also means the panegyric cry of attendants which they utter when a king moves about, in order to clear the way. उदीरयामासुः—A happy idea. Vrauṇa, as the lord of water, is the sustainer of the vegetable kingdom. *Cf*. Ṛig. VII. 49. 3. यासां (अपां) राजा वरुणो याति मध्ये सत्यानृते ऽवपश्यञ्जनानाम्' । The king resembled Varuṇa in every respect even in that he had with him the noose in the shape of his bow-string. Hence, naturally enough, the poet fancies, the trees expressed their reverence for the king, whom they mistook for Varuṇa (by means of the loud carollings of the birds living thereon.)

S'l. 10. मरुत्सखाभम्—For dissolution and the force of the epithet, see Saṃj. The king, by his resplendent body, resembled fire, the friend of the wind. This gives the reason why the creepers were मरुत्प्रयुक्ताः. आरादभिवर्तमानम्—passing by, approaching near. बाललताः—here बाल is used to preserve similarity with कन्या. प्रसून—fr. सू 4th cl. with प्र. Here प्र indicates 'excellence,' and as flowers are the most lovely production of nature, the term is restricted to *flowers* only. आचारलाजैः—see ft.-note.

S'l. 11. धनुर्भृतः—धनतीति धनुः that which kills; a bow. This shows that the female deer had cause for fear. अपि has here the sense of गर्हा or contempt; notwithstanding the king's having a bow, the weapon of destruction, in his hand. दयार्द्रभावम्—Malli. takes भाव in the sense of 'feeling, intention;' it may also be taken in the sense of चेष्टा or action. See Amara. quoted in the Saṃj. अन्तःकरणैः-अन्तःकरणं the internal sense, the mind. There are eleven senses, called करणs or the instruments of communication with the external world of the inner man. Of these the five ज्ञानेंद्रियs and the five कर्मेन्द्रियs are external, while the mind, which is उभयात्मक is internal; pl. is used with reference to the number of the female deer. आख्यातम्—p. p. p. of चक्ष् and not of ख्या. According to Dîkshita who refers to the Mb. for support, the root ख्या cannot take an Ardhadhátuka term. (अयं सार्वधातुकमात्रविषयः), and hence cannot take क्त. *Cf*. for a nearly similar idea न मृगः खलु कोऽप्ययं जिघांसुः स्खलति ह्यत्र तथा भृशं मनो मे । विमलं कलुषीभवच्च चेतः कथयत्येव हितैषिणं रिपुं वा ॥ Kir. XIII. 6.

वपुः—उप्यन्ते देहान्तरभोगसाधनबीजीभूतानि कर्माण्यत्र । अक्ष्णाम्—अश्नुते व्याप्नोति (अनेन वा) इत्यक्षि, derived from अश् 5th Atm. or अश् 1. P. and इ (Uṇâdi). हरिण्यः—mark the use of the fem Gen.; the exclusion of हरिण *m.* is intentional. See introductory note to s'l. 9.

Śl. 12. कीचकैः--चीकति चीकयते वा that which produces a sound; a singing *bamboo*; der. fr. चीक् the letters being interchanged by the rule चीकयतेराद्यन्तविपर्ययश्च । Uṇâdi V. 36. मारुत &c.—मारुत the wind. The Râmâyaṇa thus accounts for the name:--When all the sons of Diti were killed in a fierce battle by Aditi's sons, the former implored her husband, Kaśyapa, to bless her with a son that could kill Indra in a fight. To this Kaśyapa consented and ordered her to observe strict purity for two thousand years. While वायु was thus in the womb, Indra, the step-son of Diti, got jealous of the superior prowess of the forthcoming child, and watching his opportunity, entered the womb when his mother was asleep (with her head towards the wrong end of the bed and thus in an impure state) and began dissecting the fœtus. The child cried with pain, when Indra, fearing lest its cries should rouse his mother, whispered out ' मा रुद ' 'do not cry'. Diti was roused and requested Indra to spare the child that was already hewn into seven pieces. Bâlakâṇḍa. Chap. 46. The child was saved and was called मारुत from मा रुद. *Cf.* त्वत्कृतेनैव नाम्ना वै मारुता इति विश्रुताः । &c. Chap. 47. See also Bhâg. P. VI. 18. आपादित &c.--*Cf.* Kum. 1. 8. उद्गीयमानम्--see ft.-note.

Śl. 13. पृक्तः &c.—This shows that the breeze was cool and therefore gladdening. अनोकहा &c.--This epithet is used to show that the breeze was gentle and fragrant. अनोकहः--अनसः शकटस्याकं वेगं हन्तीत्यनोकहः an Upapada Tat.; that which impedes the motion of carriage, hence a tree. The direct mention of गन्ध is not very poetical. See note on I. 38. अनातपत्रं--आतपात् त्रायते इति आतपत्रं; fr. त्रै+क (अ); अविद्यमानमातपत्रं यस्य तम्. आतपक्लान्तमनातपत्रम्--These two epithets show how much the king was in need of some refreshing agencies, while the third आचार supplies the reason why he was served even by the wind (the purifying element; mark the significance of पवन). See Samj. आचारपूतम्--Pure by his conduct, which was in strict accordance with scriptural rules and established custom.

Śl. 14. विशेषा--See Samj.; also विगतः शेषोऽस्याः that which is complete, perfect. फलेति--फलानि च पुष्पाणि च फलपुष्पं Sam. Dv. तस्य वृद्धिः । With the description here compare that of the hermitage of Vishwamitra : क्षुद्रा अत्र जक्षुर्हरिणान्मृगेन्द्रा विशश्वसे पक्षिगणैः समन्तात् । नमस्यमानाः फलदि-

त्सयेव चकाशिरे तत्र लता विलोलाः ॥ Bhatti. II. 25. गोप्तरि—He was the protector of all; and he proved to be so here also; for the trees and creepers were protected from fire and the weaker animals from the stronger ones, and the unusual growth of fruits and flowers kept the foresters out of want.

Śl. 15. दिगन्तराणि—*i. e.* all the space between the quarters traversed by the sun and the cow respectively. The sun's purifynig power is well known. The cow being a celestial being had also such power; *cf.* खुरन्यासपवित्रपांसुं *supra* II. 2. निलयाय—Dat. or the Acc. by गत्यर्थकर्मणि द्वितीयाचतुर्थ्यौ चेष्टायामनध्वनि (Páṇ. II. 3. 12) when a root having the sense of motion implies effort on the part of the agent, its कर्म, if it does not mean a road, takes the Acc. or the Dat. But in मनसा हरिं व्रजति where there is no effort implied or in अध्वानं गच्छति the Acc. is imperative. पल्लव &c.—ताम्रो गुणोऽस्या अस्तीति ताम्रा । the मतुप् affix is dropped by the Vârt. गुणवचनेभ्यो मतुपो लुगिष्टः । now see Samj.; *cf.* पल्लवाग्निरम्यपाटला I. 38. च-here means *also, as well,* and not *and*; hence the verb is in the *sing.*

Śl. 16. देवता &c:—This applies to both धेनु and श्रद्धा; in one case अर्थ means प्रयोजन or purpose, in the other, विषय or province. अन्वक्-अनु अञ्चति गच्छतीति an *ind.* or अव्यय used in the sense of अनुसरन्. [This line is important inasmuch as it settles the meaning of the ambiguous words of Amara. quoted by Malli. Had अन्वक् not been an अव्यय we should have expected here अन्वङ् instead of अन्वक् and तस्याः instead of ताम् । See Pâṇ. II. 3. 65; 3. 69; 4. 82]. मध्यम--मध्ये भवः मध्यमः । The earth is called मध्यमलोक as it stands midway between the heaven above and the nether regions below.

सतां मतेन—(*a*) esteemed by; (*b*) approved of or practised by. For construction see Samj. मतिबुद्धि &c. श्रद्धा—श्रद् is a prep. meaning 'faith'. It gets the उपसर्गसंज्ञा by the Vârt. 'श्रच्छब्दस्योपसंख्यानम् ।' *Cf.* श्रद्धस्मै धत्त Ṛig. II. 22. 5. विधि—is properly a scriptural injunction; it secondarily means 'the performance of a religious rite in obedience to such an injunction.' The simile here is very significant. It first suggests that Dilîpa had implicit faith in the cow and so he minutely followed out the details of worship as enjoined by Vasishṭha; and secondly that as such faith when accompanied by such practice is sure to be rewarded with its proper fruit, the king was sure to be blessed with the fulfilment of his desire soon.

Śl 17. आवास &c.—आवासाय वृक्षाः । सह सुपेति समासः । आवासस्य वृक्षा वा; see Samj श्यामायमानानि—Malli. supposes that the epithets पल्लवा-

चीर्ण &c. are intended to describe how the forest was becoming dark all over; and he is perfectly happy in this. When the king began to return, it was just the approach of evening. The light of the sun was a little dimmed, but the shades of night had not yet begun to close upon the forest; but within the forest the gloom caused by the approach of the eve and the spreading branches of the trees was deepened by the dark-skinned boars that now left the puddles and were spreading in all directions; by the expanded plumages of the peacocks that were now winging their way to their roosting trees, and by the agitated glances of the antelopes that were now gathering on the grass plots. In connexion with the last, *cf.* तत्प्रार्थितं जवनवाजिगतेन राज्ञा तूणीमुखोद्धृतशरेण विशीर्णपंक्ति । श्यामीचकार वनमाकुलदृष्टिपातैर्वातेरितोत्पलदलप्रकरैरिवार्द्रैः ॥ *infra* IX. 56. पश्यन्—This is emphatic. Though armed with a bow, and though he had such attractive games all round, he went only *looking* at them, without the least idea of shooting at them. How much kings are fond of shooting at good game like the boars, the deer and the peacocks, will appear from IX. 55. 59, 67, This corroborates the statement धनुर्भृतोप्यस्य दयार्द्रभावम् &c. II. 11.

Śl. 18. आपीन—That which is distended on all sides; hence, an udder. ०प्रयत्नात्—सुप्सुपेति समासः. गृष्टिः—A cow that calves but once, and whose milk, therefore, never fails. अञ्चित—That which is worshipped or respected; and as things of a charming appearance only can be conceived as deserving respect or worship, it means secondarily what is charming. तपोवनावृत्तिपथम्—Malli. who expounds तपोवनादावृत्तेः पन्थाः seems to take आवृत्तिपथ in the sense of 'the way which led from and back to the penance-grove'. The cow was an unfailing source of milk and her udder was always full, unlike that of ordinary cows, which is full in the evening only; also the king's massive frame had nothing particular added to it in the evening; so that there is no reason why we should not suppose that the way was graced as the cow and the king walked from and back to the penance-grove in the morning and evening. But if it be insisted upon that आवृत्ति must mean 'return' (see next s'loka) then dissolve तपोवन आवृत्तिः । सह सुपेति समासः । तस्याः पन्थाः the way back to the penance forest. S. P. Pandit and Mr. Nandargikar following him, both seem not to have grasped the correct meaning of Malli. and hence their difficulty to give तपोवन a meaning.

S'l. 19. अनुयायिनम्—अनुयानं व्रतमस्य तम् । वनिता—a woman is not a वनिता unless she has excessive love for her husband. *Cf.* Amara.

'वनिता जनितात्यन्तानुरागायां च योषिति'। वनान्तात्-from the skirt of the forest. This may also be construed with पपौ. Sudakshiṇá stood intently looking at her husband at the border of the penance-grove whither she had gone to recieve the cow in the evening, following the precept of the saint—'सायं प्रत्युद्व्रजेदपि.' Notice then se of पा with नयन or कर्ण in the sense of to look or listen to intently; *cf.* further on II. 79, III. 17, XI. 36, &c.

Śl. 20. पार्थिव and धर्मपत्नी—For derivation see Samj. दिनक्षपा &c. —क्षपयति चेष्टामिति क्षपा। The simile is appropriate here in point of time. The poet compares here the bright splendour of the king to the brightness of the day, the soft beauty of the queen to the moon-lit night, and the tawny colour of the cow to the rosy appearance of the twilight. The cow has already been compared to संध्या at I. 82. See ib.-note.

Śl. 21. प्रदक्षिणीकृत्य—प्रगतो दक्षिणं प्रदक्षिणम्। अप्रदक्षिणं प्रदक्षिणं कृत्वा प्रदक्षिणीकृत्य Gati Samása. This seems to be irregular. प्रदक्षिणं being a word of the तिष्ठद्गु class cannot enter into a compound with other words. पयस्विनीम्-Here the affix विन् is used प्राशस्त्ये *i. e.* to indicate goodness, both as regards quantity and quality. साक्षतपात्रहस्ता—अक्षतानां अक्षतायुक्तं वा पात्रमक्षतपात्रं तेन सह वर्तेते इति साक्षतपात्रौ; now see Samj. The comp. may also be expounded as अक्षतैः सह वर्तमानं साक्षतमेवंविधं पात्रं हस्तयोर्यस्याः। this would clearly indicate the presence of अक्षता in the vessel; but Malli. prefers the other way as the compound, in this latter case, will be हस्तसाक्षतपात्रा by the rule 'सप्तमीविशेषणे बहुव्रीहौ' an attributive and a noun in the Loc. should be placed first in a Bah. Comp. अक्षता—न क्षतं येषां ते lit. those that are not injured or bruised; whole grains of unhusked and well cleansed rice, which are offered after being washed and sometimes mixed with red powder, to images and other objects of worship.

The word does not mean *fried rice* generally, nor *barley*, both of which senses are given in the St. Petersburg Dict.; nor is the word understood in these senses at least in India at present. The word is always *mas.* and pl.

शृङ्गान्तरं द्वारम्—The expansive horns of the cow, looking like pillars and bending towards each other at the top looked very much like an arched gateway and easily suggested the idea of a door.

Śl. 22. वत्सोत्सुका-वदति स्नेहसामर्थ्यमिति वत्सः। fr. वद् + स Un. III. 62. वत्से उत्सुका वत्सोत्सुका। सपर्या—der. from सपर् a word of the कण्ड्वादि class meaning worship, and the affix. यक्; सपर्य + अ; स्त्रियां भावे सपर्या। उपपन्नेषु

युक्तेषु Malli. *Cf. supra* II. 16. तद्विधानां प्रसादचिह्नानि—The Comp. is to be defended like देवदत्तस्य गुरुकुलम् । पुरः फलानि—पुरः फलं येषाम् । which have their reward before them, *i. e.* at hand. Bah. Comp. by the Vârt. अव्ययानां बहुव्रीहिर्वक्तव्यः; *e. g.* उच्चैर्मुखाः &c.

S'l. 23. सदारस्य—The der. of दार is very amusing. दारयन्ति पतिं भ्रातृभ्य इति दाराः । A wife is called दाराः because she *estranges* her husband from his brothers. एव—is better construed with दोग्ध्रीं and not with पुनः as Mr. S. P. Pandit does. दोग्ध्रीमेव भेजे—attended upon the cow; did not attend to anything else. The use of the word दोग्ध्री suggests that she might milk the king's desire. भुजोच्छिन्नरिपुः—see below, notes to s'l. 25.

S'l. 24. गोप्ता—This keeps up the idea suggested by भुजोच्छिन्न-रिपुः । Also see note to s'l. 25. गृहिणीसहायः—a Bah. both logically and grammatically. क्रमेण—Here the Inst. is हेतौ, क्रम being the cause of the succession of the actions. Here क्रमेण indicates the succession of the actions of the cow herself, and अनु shows the king's following them so that there is no tautology. See Saṃj. अनु—is a कर्मप्रवचनीय and governs the acc. by अनुर्लक्षणे *i. e.* when अनु denotes a sign (an attendant circumstance, &c.);it has the force of 'after, in consequence of' &c. He slept *after*, *i. e*, slept because she had slept. उदतिष्ठत्—awoke and rose up. Here the idea of rising up must also be included; otherwise we shall get the form उदतिष्ठत instead of उदतिष्ठत् as स्था when preceded by उत् takes the Âtm. if it does not mean an upward action (उदोनूर्ध्वकर्मणि Pâṇ. I. 3. 24.).

Śl. 25. धारयतः—practising with ease. To defend the Par. the idea of ease must be included. A Causal verb takes the A'tm. when the action benefits the agent. Here the व्रतधारण is for Dilîpa's benefit and so we should expect the Âtm. But by the rule 'इङ्धार्योः शत्रकृच्छ्रिणि' Pâṇ. III. 2. 130, (on which Nâgeśhbhaṭṭa remarks, 'अकृच्छ्रिणीत्यनायासेन क्रियानिवर्तके'), the roots इ and धृ can take शतृ (अत्) when they imply absence of difficulty in the agent. See Gr. § 667 (*d*). *Cf.* धारयन्मरकरिव्रतम् Bhaṭṭi. V. 63. महिष्या—महिषः derived fr. मह् to worship, to honour (मह्यते पूज्यते इति) with the aff. इष (टिषच्) and means a crowned king, and महिषी the queen coronated with him. त्रिगुणानि—गुण properly means a string, then that part of a string which forms its fold when doubled; hence त्रिगुण means having three folds, threefold.

In s'lokas 23-25 the poet has used the four epithets (1) भुजो-च्छिन्नरिपुः; (2) गोप्ता; (3) महनीयकीर्तिः; and दीनोद्धरणोचितस्य; and they have their peculiar significane herce. For the poet is now about to describe an event which will call into requisition and tax to their utmost these respective attributese of the king. A शत्रु of Nandinî will presently appear whom the गोप्ता will try to destroy (उच्छिद्) with the power of his arm (भुज); but failing to do this the king will set a higher value upon his fame कीर्ति than upon his body and will finally achieve the उद्धरण of the cow in distress (दीना).

S'l. 26. अन्येद्युः—अन्यस्मिन्नहनि. On the next, *i. e.* the 22nd day; एद्युः is substituted for अहन् by Pân. V. 3. 22. जिज्ञासमाना--Pre. P· of the desid. of ज्ञा, 'wishing to know,. गङ्गा &c.-This may also be explained as अन्ते प्रान्ते विरूढानि शष्पाणि यस्य तदन्तविरूढशष्पम् गङ्गाप्रपातेनान्तविरूढशष्पं गङ्गा० near which tender grass had grown owing to the fall of the Ganges. This epithet is intended to show that the act of the cow looked quite natural and aroused not the least suspicion in the mind of the king.

S'l. 27. दुष्प्रधर्षा—दुःखन प्रधृष्यत इति । अपि expresses a hyperbole. She was unassailable *even* mentally. हिंस्रैः—The word दुष्प्रधर्षा is formed from दुस्+प्र+धृष्+the affix खल्; so the Gen. हिंस्राणां cannot be used owing to the prohibition 'न लोकाव्ययनिष्ठाखलर्थतृनाम्'—but not in connexion with the affixes ल, उ, उक, an अव्यय, a खलर्थ affix and the affixes निष्ठा (त of the p. p.) and तृन्. सिंहः–from हिंस to kill, the consonants being interchanged; see foot—note. किल—According to Malli.. this is used here अलीके *i. e.* showing that this was a fiction; 'as it appeared'.

S'l. 28. आर्तसाधुः—Kind or doing good to the distressed. रश्मिष्विव &c.—The idea is that the cry of distress of the cow drew back the glance of the king with that suddenness and certainty with which one pulls away a thing by catching it in a noose of ropes. For the Loc. see ft.-note. Châr. who remarks 'यथा प्रग्रहैः कश्चित् पुरुषो घोटकायन्यतो यातमाकृष्य निवारयति तथा गोक्रन्दितं राज्ञो दृष्टिं निवारितवदिति भावः' seems to take इव as a sign of उपमा; but in this case there is nothing in the sight corresponding to reins by which to catch it. रश्मि is derived fr. अश् 5 cl. Atm. wits the affix मि; अश्नुते अनेन वा । The अ is changed to र by अश्नोते रश्च, Uṇádi IV. 46. नगेन्द्रसक्ताम्—न गच्छन्तीति नगाः or अगाः । Nañ.-Tat. नगानां or नगेषु इन्द्रः or नग इन्द्र इव । See द्विपेन्द्र II. 7. Himálaya was the actual crowned king of mountains. Kum. I. 17.

S'l. 29. तस्थिवांसम्—A Vaidika form but used ordinary language also. See Sid.-Kau. on Páṇ. III. 2. 107. 'तं तस्थिवांसं नगरोपकण्ठे' इत्यादि

छान्दसा अपि भाषायां भवन्ति । Manoramâ. धनुर्धरः—Gen. Tat. Comp.; this implies that he had a bow ready in his hand for use and was thus able to punish the offender. केसरिणम्—This word is used here in preference to other words for a lion with the intention that the lion *with the mane* should better resemble the *loddhra* tree *with the flowers*. केसरिपदेन प्रफुल्लत्वात्साम्यम् Châr. and Din. अधित्यका—seems to be used here merely in the sense of an upland. धातुमय्याम्=is added to complete the resemblance with the cow who is described as पल्लवरागताम्रा । See also ft.-note. लोध्रद्रुमम्—द्रुम is derived as follows: द्रवति ऊर्ध्वं गच्छतीति द्रुः a tree and by the maxim 'समुदाये वृत्ताः शब्दा अवयवेष्वपि वर्तन्ते' it secondarily means 'a branch;' द्रवोऽस्य सन्तीति द्रुमः (द्रु+म) by the rule द्युद्रुभ्यां मः, Pân. V. 2. 108. सानुमतः—सानु 'a peak or a level plot of ground on a mountain'+मत्.

Sl. 30. मृगेन्द्रगामी—Who walked (habitually) with the majesty or fearlessness of a lion (under such circumstances). Prof. Ray thinks that the rapidity with which the King turned caused his movement to resemble that of the lion and takes the इन् (णिनि) कर्तरि उपमाने. But the poet does not seem to use the epithet with reference to the present act of the King. Again the poet does not describe a lion as turning round rapidly when disturbed, but only calmly; *cf. infra.* IV. 72. The epithet is meant to imply that he faced the lion like a lion. वधाय-the Dat. by 'तुमर्थाच्च भाववचनात्' Pân. II. 3. 15. Gr. § 828 (*a*). 'वध्यस्य'—The epithets शरण्य and जाताभिषङ्ग explain why the lion deserved death. जाताभिषङ्गः—who felt himself insulted. The King was the protector of the distressed and yet in his very presence the lion ventured to attack the cow, the same on whom he had rested his hopes of issue, and thus gravely insulted the King, forfeiting his life thereby. अभिषङ्ग—lit. that which sticks to the heart, and is not easily discarded; hence an insult that is keenly felt. *Cf.* तीव्राभिषङ्गप्रभवेण वृत्तिं &c. Kum. III.13. निषङ्गात्-नितरां सज्जन्त्यस्मिन् शरा इति । प्रसभोद्धृतारिः—see Malli. This indicates power in the king to punish the offender. If प्रसभ be taken to mean 'an act done without giving thought to it,' 'unhesitatingly' (प्रगता सभा विचारो यस्मात्), then this will mean-'who readily uprooted his foes.'

Śl. 31. वामेतरः—The use of the word here seems to be intentional, a pun being intended on the word वाम which means left as well as perverse, inimical. The right hand got stuck and refused to strike because it was also intuitively friendly (the lion being unreal). प्रहर्तुः—of him who was about to strike. The Pre. used in the sense of immediate futurity. 'कङ्कपत्रे—Ancient warriors used to furnish the hafts of their arrows with heron's feathers to regulate their motion. सक्ताङ्गुलिः—this goes with पुंखे; the hand remained stuck to the haft of the arrow; but then the two words should have been compounded as पुंखसक्ताङ्गुलिः; since they are not, it is a case of सापेक्षत्वेपि गमकत्वात्समासः. Some propose the construction करः सक्ताङ्गुलिः सन् सायकपुंखे एव अवतस्थे. But in this case the आकांक्षा of सक्त still remains :—where was it stuck ? चित्रार्पित &c.—Here आरम्भ means an action (क्रिया); *cf.* I. 15; Megh. I. 55. The hand of Dilîpa involuntarily stuck to the root of the arrow, looked like a painted hand in the act of drawing out an arrow. अवतस्थे—स्था is A'tm. when preceded by सम्, अव, प्र and वि (समवप्रविभ्यः स्थः Pâṇ. I. 3. 23).

S'l. 32. अभ्यर्णम्—P. p. p. of अर्द् with अभि; the other form is अभ्यर्दित (distressed). Malli. takes it as an indec. (अव्यय); it may be taken as an *adj.* meaning 'standing near,' qualifying आगस्कृतं. आगस्कृत्—आगः कृतवानित्यागस्कृत्; सहसा एति इति आगः crime, sin, fr. इ to go and the Uṇâdi aff. अस्. स्वतेजोभिः—तेजस् is that inborn spirit or sense of self-respect which does not allow one to put up with an insult at any cost; see ft.-note. भोगिन्—भोग the hood (or, body) of a serpent + इन् ' one having. ' मन्त्रौषधि &c.—It is a well-known fact, at least in India, that the cobra is reduced to a helpless condition, being made a prisoner within a charmed circle, by serpent-charmers by means of spells and the roots of herbs. *Cf.* तवाभिधानाद्व्यथते नताननः सुदुःसहान्मन्त्रपदादिवोरगः । Kir. I. 24.

S'l. 33. आर्यगृह्य—a partisan of the good, *i. e.* one who always stands by the good, (such as Vasishtha's cow in the present instance). See Sanj. and ft-note. *Cf.* अर्जुनगृह्य. मनुवंशकेतुम्—केतु is properly a flag, and since a flag prominently attracts attention and is the most important factor in an army, it means 'the most prominent or chief thing in a class.'

विस्माययन्—Pre. p. of the Cau. of स्मि. On the reading विस्मापयन् Malli. remarks as follows —With the reading विस्मापयन् we have only the प coming in; but this may be questioned. For when we change स्मि to स्मा by the rule नित्यं स्मयतेः, Pâṇ. VI. 1. 57, the wonder is understood to be due to the हेतु (causative agent) and not to a करण or instrument. But by the rule 'भीस्म्योर्हेतुभये' Pâṇ. I. 3. 68, we must have the Âtm. and the reading becomes विस्मापयमानः। Therefore, taking मनुष्यवाक् as the करण of the विस्मय we get विस्माययन्. See Sanj. and ft.-notes. Bhattoji Dîkshita also thinks that विस्माययन् is the poet's reading. He, however, finds out a defence for the reading विस्मापयन्—'यद्वा मनुष्यत्वाकृ प्रयोज्यकर्त्री विस्मापयते । तया सिंहो विस्मापयन्निति ण्यन्ताण्णौ (*i. e.* taking the cau. of विस्मापयते) शतेति व्याख्येयम् ।' Sid.-Kau. on Pâṇ. VI. 1. 57. सिंहोरुसत्त्वम्—This epithet is used to show that Dilîpa was not at all unnerved in his helpless condition. The epithets आर्यगृह्य &c. show why the celestial lion condescended to speak to the mortal king.

Ś1. 34. महीपाल—महीं पालयतीति; यद्वा पालयतीति पालः, मह्याः पालो महीपालः । श्रमेण—on the Instr. here Malli. observes—Here श्रम is the करण of the साधनक्रिया which is understood, and therefore takes तृतीया. For it is remarked in Nyâsoddyota—a क्रिया which is understood, implies instrumentality just as well as one actually mentioned; so श्रमेण अलं is equivalent to श्रमेण साध्यं नास्ति; साध्याभावात् श्रमो न कर्तव्यः—you are not to make an effort, for you cannot achieve your object. रंहः—*neu.* velocity, force. मूर्च्छति—prevails or has power against. *Cf.* VI. 9; IX. 79; XII. 57; also VIII. 89.

Ś1. 35. कैलास—a mountain in the vicinity of Himâlaya, formed of crystals, the site of Kubera's capital and the favourite abode of Śiva. *Cf.* Megh. II. 52. उत्तरतः कैलासो हिमवान्गिरिर्धनुष्मांश्च । Br.-Saṃ. अलका समया चैष कैलासः शंकरालयः । Kâś'. K. XIII. For its description see H. V. 217. वृषम्—वर्षति फलमिति वृषः । अष्टमूर्तेः—For the eight forms of Śiva see Saṃj. and the invocatory stanzas of the Śâk. and Mâlav. Here by referring to the pre-eminence of Śiva, the lion indirectly suggests his own greatness, as the follower of such a mighty master. निकुम्भमित्रम्—It is not clear whether this Nikumbha is one of celestial beings (गणs) attending on Śiva, or Pârvatî's lion, as Vallabha has it. This latter, however, is probable as कुम्भोदर is a lion.

Ś1. 36. पश्यसि—'इति काकुः'—By this Malli. means that the word पश्यसि ought to be uttered in such a tone as to emphasize it. *Cf.* S.-D. quoted in the com. पुत्रीकृतः—न पुत्रोऽपुत्रः । अपुत्रः पुत्रः कृतः । वृषभध्वजः—ध्वज means a standard; and since it is the marks on and the shape of a flag that distinguish one king from another, it means a distinguishing mark; hence वृषभध्वज means the God who has the bull for his distinguishing mark; Śiva; *cf.* मकरध्वज, धूमध्वज, मीनकेतन &c.

हेमकुम्भ &c.—Malli. remarks 'स्कन्धपक्षे हेमकुम्भ इव स्तनः;' in this case however, the com. will be स्तनहेमकुम्भ and not हेमकुम्भ &c ; for by thep rule 'उपमितं व्याघ्रादिभिः'—Pâṇ. II. 1. 56, the उपमित ought to precede. But such an inaccuracy is allowable in the case of Ślesha. It is not necessary, however to take it with स्कन्द. स्कन्दस्य &c.—This is used to show that the *devadâru* tree was in every way Gaurî's child, like Skanda. Mark the play on the word पयस् in this respect, which means water as well as milk. The Mah.-Bhár. thus accounts for the name Skanda—'स्कन्नत्वात्स्कन्दतां प्राप्तो गुहावासाद्गुहोऽभवत्' इति ।

S'l. 37. वन्यः—वने भवः । अथ—आनन्तर्ये 'then;' this implies that what preceded was the cause of what followed. सेनान्यम्—Skanda was called सेनानी because, just as he was born, he was appointed the General of the divine army that was to march against Târaka. See Kum. III. 15. आलीढम्—licked from all sides; hence, wounded. *Cf.* अश्वज्वालावलीढ &c. Veṇî. III. 7. असुरास्त्रैः—असुर is variously derived:—(1) न सुरा असुराः, Nañ-Tat., the नञ् indicating विरोध. (2) According to the Râmá. those who partook of the heavenly drink (सुरा, otherwise called अमृत) were called 'सुराः' while those who obtained no share of it were designated 'असुराः' । सुरापरिग्रहाद्देवाः सुरा इत्यभिविश्रुताः । अप्रतिग्रहणात्तस्या दैतेयाश्चासुरास्तथा ॥' (3) The Nirukta derives the word thus—अस्ताः प्रच्याविता दैवैः स्थानेभ्यः । असुरताः स्थानेषु न सुष्ठु रताः स्थानेषु चपला इत्यर्थः । Or असुः प्राणस्तेन तद्वन्तो भवन्ति । रो मत्वर्थे । सोः (प्रशस्तादात्मनः प्रदेशात्) देवानसृजत तत्सुराणां सुरत्वम्, असोरसुरानसृजत तदसुराणामसुरत्वम् ।

In the oldest parts of the Rigveda, the term *Asura* is used in the sense of 'a god' or 'divine'; (lit. one full of spirit, life, or created from the breath of Prajâpati; see Nir. quoted above); and is several times applied to Indra, Varuṇa and Agni; and sometimes it is used even for the Supreme Spirit. Now after the Persians, who had borrowed from their neighbours, the Hindu Áryas, the term *Asura* to designate their Supreme Deity (Ahura), quarrelled with the Hindus, they called their *devas* devils and the latter in retaliation said 'Your *Ahura* (asura) is a demon.' Thus the word *asura* which had so long signified 'a god,' came to signify 'a demon' with the Áryas; and their fertile genius easily led them to coin a word '*sura*' for 'a god,' from the very term *asura* (which now meant 'not a god') by eliminating अ from it, as if it were a negative particle. *Cf.* सित derived from असित meaning 'black,' which was an original word and not a compound of अ and सित.

S'l. 38. वनद्विपानाम्—वनभवा द्विपाः वनद्विपाः, a Comp. of the शाकपार्थिवादि class. त्रासार्थम्—is a Nitya Samása and as such has no विग्रहवाक्य. कुक्षि—properly means 'a cavity,' 'a hollow'; hence, here, a cavern. शूलभृता—The reference to शूल is probably intended to strike terror into the heart of the king who was going to meddle in the matter. अङ्कागत &c.—here वृत्ति means food, or means. *Cf. supra*, I. 88.

This implies that Śiva had so ordained it that the lion should get animals supplied to him for his subsistence, without his having to go in search of them. See next Śl. and 44.

Śl. 39. तृप्त्यै—See A. G. § 67. Valla. takes अलं with क्षुधितस्य and उपस्थिता as the predi., see ft.—note. प्रदिष्टकाला—This implies that the king ought not to attempt her rescue. शोणितपारणा—by the mention of शोणित the lion seems to keep out of sight the गोत्व of नन्दिनी. पारणा is a dinner, generally a sumptuous one, at the end (on the second day) of a fast; *e. g.* on the 12th day of each half of a lunar month. *Cf.* पारणं पावनं पुंसां सर्वपापप्रणाशनम् । उपवासाङ्गभूतं च फलदं यद्विकारणम् ॥ Bra. V. P. सुरद्विषः—of Ráhu, who is populary supposed to devour the moon at an eclipse. राहु and केतु are properly the names given in Hindu astronomy to the points of intersection of the ecliptic and the moon's orbit, *i. e.* the nodes, or rather to the shadows of the earth and the moon respectively. For the Pauránic account of Râhu, see Apte's Dic. चान्द्रमसी सुधेव—This shows that the lion was to get his meals at stated times, just as the enemy of the gods gets them. There is an allusion here to the extraction of nectar from the milky ocean and Râhu's betrayal by the sun and the moon. See note to Kád. Intro. Śl. 7. On this Śl. Prof. Ray remarks:—

" This Śloka shows good knowledge of astronomy on the part of the poet. This will be obvious if we examine the simile. Here the lion constantly watching the देवदारु *without moving from his place*, is compared to सुरद्विट् *i. e.* राहु, which we have seen is the name given to the *nodes* of the path of the moon. Hence the poet implies that राहु is fixed, and *does not hunt after the moon* to devour her. Indeed this is evident from the epithets प्रदिष्टकाला and उपस्थिता. The cow had her time to become a meal of the lion ordained beforehand, and she appeared at the appointed hour, just as the moon has her time, and appears before राहु accordingly. There is a limited area (अङ्क) within which the animal must be, in order to be seized upon by the lion, just as there is a limit, on both sides near the node, within which the moon must be for the eclipse to be possible. This is the astronomical theory of eclipse (ग्रहण). The cow was copper-coloured (पल्लवरागताम्रा) and the moon also becomes copper-coloured after entering the penumbra, just before actual eclipse takes place. "

Śl. 40 स त्वम्—'that you' *i. e.* who are made powerless by S'iva. This is the reason why he should not be ashamed of his inability to save the cow. रक्ष्यम्—यस्य रक्षा कर्तव्या तम् that which ought to be protected, being committed to one's care; object of protection.

Śl. 41. प्रगल्भम्—intelligent, full of sense; and not 'proud' as some take it. *Cf.* 'प्रगल्भः प्रतिभान्विते' Amar.; 'प्रगल्भवाक्' Kum. V. 30. पुरुषाधिराज—अधिराज is a Prádi Samása. मृगाधिराजस्य—The word अधिराज though used for alliteration further shows that there was a sort of equality between the two. प्रत्याहतास्त्रः—प्रत्याहत is what is struck back or repelled by being hit, as a missile by an enemy's missile, or some other force operating upon it. Hence, here, what is rendered futile and useless (although not actually struck back). गिरिशः—Swâmi derives it as गिरौ शेते इति। This is a Vaidic form. In ordinary language the form will be गिरिशयः by 'अधिकरणे शेतेः' Páṇ. III. 2. 15. Bhaṭṭoji Dîkshita includes गिरि under the लोमादि class and consequently it may take the possessive affix श; so we may explain गिरिराश्रयत्वेनास्यास्तीति गिरिशः. Chár. also derives it in this way.

Śl. 42. तत्पूर्वभङ्गे—'of which that was the first failure or repulse.' भङ्ग does not necessarily mean 'defeat,' but has often the sense of 'a mere failure in doing a thing.' Some read सङ्ग (which is found in some MS. copies of Malli.'s com. also) but it is difficult to see how सङ्ग means a 'hindrance' here. The Sanskrit Dictionaries, Vâch. included, do not give this meaning to सङ्ग. True that this sense of the word is given in Apte's Dic. But there it is probably based on the variant here and on III. 63, where the word has this meaning by लक्षणा. वितथप्रयत्नः—विगतं तथा सत्यं यस्मादिति वितथमनृतम्. *Cf.* Amar. 'वितथं त्वनृतं वचः'। And since words which have no truth in them often fail to bear their fruit, the word has the secondary sense of 'what is fruitless.' जडीकृतः—अजडो जडः कृतः।

त्र्यम्बकवीक्षणेन—त्र्यम्बक is a name of Śiva. Kâli. sometimes uses the Vaidic form त्रियम्बक. See Kum. III. 44. The word is variously derived: see Samj. and ft.-note; तिस्रोऽम्बा अस्य having three mothers. *Cf.* Kâli. P.—देवास्तिसृणामम्बानां गर्भे जातो यतो हरः। अतस्त्र्यम्बकनामासौ देवलोके च गीयते॥ In the Veda the term is applied to the father of the three deities, Brahmá, Vishṇu and Śiva. त्रयाणां ब्रह्मविष्णुरुद्राणां पितरं यजामहे &c. Sây. on Rig. VII. 29. 12.

The allusion here refers to the story given in the Mah.-Bhâr. See ft.-note. Once upon a time the gods being harassed by the demons, secure within their three cities, applied to Mahâdeva for deliverance, who, in compliance with their request, began to burn the three cities of the demons. To witness the scene of destruction there came the goddess Durgâ, bearing in her arms a child of wondrous effulgence. Indra, getting jealous of the child, raised his thunderbolt for its destruction, when strangely enough, the arm of Indra became motionless, being paralysed by the glance of the child. In this plight Indra saw Brahmâ, who told him to propitiate the child, which was no other than Śiva himself, who had assumed that form to please Durgâ. Thereupon Indra, accompanied by all the gods, went to the child and propitiated it with prayers and had his arm released from the paralysis.

Śl. 43. कामम्—an *indecl.* meaning an 'assent given with reluctance.' 'अकामानुमतौ कामम्' Amar.; granted that, admitting for the sake of argument that. अन्तर्गतम्—Acc. Tat. Comp. हि is used here हेतौ; because; for this reason. भवान्वेद—And so you will see that I do not mean to overreach or mislead you. वेद pres. 3rd per. sing. of विद्, optional form, वेत्ति being the other. अतः &c.—What the king means is that now, powerless as he was, any proposal that he might make to the lion would simply seem ridiculous to him after he had expressed his desire to eat up the cow. But since the lion knew the inward thoughts of men, he (the king) could freely speak them out. See, however, Saṃj.

Śl. 44. स्थावरज°—See ft.-note. स्थावर fr. स्था+वर means 'what always remains fixed by habit.' जङ्गम means the opposite of this; that which is constantly in motion. The यङ् (य of the Frequentative) here must be taken as भृशार्थे, *i. e.* denoting frequency of action. सर्ग &c.—Here Śiva is identified with the Supreme Brahman, though the part usually assigned to him is the last of the three mentioned here, *viz.* the destruction of the world. आहिताग्नेः—This epithet is used to show that Vasishtha is constantly in need of offerings supplied by the cow, and consequently he cannot afford to lose the cow. See Saṃj. On the other hand the order of Śiva is inviolable. So the king finds himself in a dilemma. The solution of the difficulty is proposed in the next s'l.

Śl. 45. स त्वम्—See Saṃj., and śl. 40 above; you who are such, *i. e.* ordered by Śiva to feed upon the animals coming within your reach. शरीर—lit. that which is subject to decay; शीर्यते इति from शॄ+ईरन् Uṇá. प्रसीद—What the king means is this: since the cow and he entered the cave together it was left to the option of the lion to make his meal either upon the cow or on himself. In either case his act would be within the meaning of Śiva's command. So he should be pleased to release the cow, and seize him instead. दिनावसान &c.—Here the word बाल is used to excite pity in the lion; since the calf would be helpless if its mother were not to return in the evening. According to Châr. the loss of the cow would also mean the destruction of the calf (and so the lion would incur the sin of killing the calf for nothing).

Śl. 46. अन्धकारं शकलानि कुर्वन्—A very pregnant construction. शकलानि being the विधेय of अन्धकार is not required to be necessarily in the sing. This is more forcible than शकलीकुर्वन्. The meaning is this:—Each cave of the mountain was enveloped in a mass of darkness. Now the rays of the lion's teeth, as they shot forth, dispelled the darkness from the places where they fell and thus split up the mass in each cave into a number of pieces, as it were. दंष्ट्रा—दश्यते अनया इति; fr. दंश् and the aff. ष्ट्र (ष्ट्रन् करणे). विहस्य—The lion laughed at the absurd proposal of the king. अर्थपतिम्—This epithet is very appropriate here. The king was the master of अर्थ or sense, *i. e.* a speech full of sense; and we shall see him finally succeeding in persuading the lion to accept his proposal.

Śl. 47. एकातपत्रम् &c.—Now the lion points out the advantages which the king is about to forego. For आतपत्र, see *supra* II. 13. An imperial king alone could wear a white silken umbrella; see *infra* III. 16. वयः—वयत इति fr. वी to go. अल्पस्य हेतोः—When the word हेतु is actually mentioned, the Genitive ought to be used instead of the usual Abl. or Inst.; see Saṃj. However, by the Vârt. 'निमित्तकारणहेतुषु सर्वासां प्रायदर्शनात्' a pronoun takes all cases, and words other than a pronoun take all except the Nom. and the Acc. when used with the words निमित्त, कारण, हेतु &c.; so अल्पेन हेतुना, अल्पाय हेतवे, अल्पात् हेतोः are also correct.

Śl. 48. चेत्—'If', 'on the other hand'. 'पक्षान्तरे चेद्यदि च' Amar. This shows a shifting of the point from which the question is viewed. स्वस्तिमती—happy by being saved. स्वस्ति is often found used like a substantive in the Veda. उपप्लवेभ्यः—उपप्लव der. fr. उप+प्लु+अप्; lit. that which passes over, and since nothing which passes over a man is felt more heavily than a calamity, it means 'a calamity or misfortune.' So the root उपप्लु means to cause affliction or calamity. *Cf.* X. 5; Kum. II. 32. प्रजाः—The pl. is used for the sake of contrast. Dying you save a single cow; but living you save numerous individuals. पितेव—The word पितृ is derived by some fr. पा to protect and the Uṇâdi affix तृ (डितृच्); by others irregularly fr. पा

and नृ (नृप्); lit. one who protects. Here the literal sense is meant to be prominent. The lion points out that it is emphatically the duty of the king to protect his subjects, not so much to save the cow.

Śl. 49. अपराधचण्डात्--अपराधे अपराधाद्वा चण्डात्। बिभेषि—see Sanj. If on the other hand you fear, then your fear is out of place; for, &c. शक्यः &c.—This is pass.; the active cons. will be भवानस्य मन्युं विनेतुं शक्नुयात्. As the idea of मन्यु is intended to be prominent here. the pass con. is used. See Apte's G. § 178-9. कृशानुः—कृश्यति तनूकरोति इति: fr. कृश्+आनु (क्). प्रतिमः—see Malli.; or प्रतिमाति imitates इति प्रतिमः, fr. मा+क (अ); कृशानोः प्रतिमः कृशा०. कोटिशः—Here the affix शस् shows repetition (वीप्सायां). 'A Koṭi at a time, in Koṭis.'

Śl. 50. कल्याणपरंपराणां—the word परंपरा appears to be formed from पर repeated; and Wilson indeed derives it as such. But it seems to be wrong. According to Bhaṭṭoji Díkshita this word has no derivation (परंपराशब्दस्त्वव्युत्पन्नं शब्दान्तरं स्त्रीलिङ्गम्). ऊर्जस्वल--ऊर्जस् takes वल and also विन; so ऊर्जस्विन् also. महीतल &c.--Expound महीतलस्पर्शनं प्रमाणमस्यासौ महीतलस्पर्शनमात्रो भेदः। तेन भिन्नम्। We must not say महीतलस्पर्शनमेव महीतलस्पर्शनमात्रम्; for in that case the Comp. becomes one of the मयूरव्यंसकादि class, and further compounding is precluded. ऋद्धं—p. p. p. of ऋध् 4. 5 P. to prosper, to flourish; see V. 40. राज्यम् —राज्ञो भावः कर्म वा।

Śl. 51. प्रतिस्वनेन—प्रतिनिधिः स्वनः प्रतिस्वनः a Prádi Comp. We must not dissolve it as an Upa. Comp., as we shall get प्रतिस्वान and not प्रतिस्वन as it cannot take अप्. अभाषत—भाष् is a root governing two objects, being a synonym of ब्रू. In explaining this Malli. quotes a Káriká from the Mah.-Bhásh. which means:—That which is the निमित्त (cause or origin) of उपयोग (what is desired e. g. पयः) with respect to the roots दुह्, याच् &c. and also that for whom is intended the subject-matter of the roots ब्रू and शास्, is, unless directed otherwise by special rules, called अकीर्तित i. e. अकथित 'what is not defined by the Sûtrakára.' In the present case, अर्थ is the subject-matter of अभाषत and is intended for क्षितिपाल; wherefore क्षितिपाल is अकथित. And by the rule 'अकथितं च' Pâṇ. I. 4. 51, क्षितिपाल is कर्म of अभाषत

Śl. 52. मनुष्यदेवः--The king of men, मनुष्याणां देवः राजा. Cf. Amar. राजा भट्टारको देवः। or मनुष्यो देव इव. There is a pun on the word देव which means a king and also a god, intended to show the excellence of Dilipa over the lion who is only a देवानुचर. तदध्यासित &c.—We may also dissolve तेनाध्यासिता तदध्यासिता। तदध्यासिता चासौ

कातराक्षी च तया । Malli. says तेन instead of तस्य as here the कर्तृता is emphasized. See Patañjali's remarks on the Vârt. 'नपुंसके भावे उपसंख्यानम्' । सुतराम्—from सु, an *indecl.*, meaning 'what is exceedingly proper, much' &c.; and, as the excess expressed here by the Tad. affix तर belongs to दयालुता (the दयनक्रिया) and not to the king, we have सुतराम्. The king was fitly all the more moved.

Śl. 53. This is a reply to ślokas 47, 48, 50. क्षतात्—from destruction, peril, &c; see ft.-note. किल—is used here वार्तायाम् । किल-शब्दस्तु वार्तायाम्—इति विश्वः. 'Such is the traditional history of the word. See foot-note. त्रायते &c.—What the poet gives is the meaning and not the derivation of the term क्षत्त्र, for which see Saṃj. उदग्रः—उन्नतमग्रं यस्य lit. whose point is raised above the general level or over the surface; hence, prominently attracting attention; and finally, what is renowned, noble. *Cf.* IV. 22, VI. 32. रूढः—On this Malli. remarks (see Saṃj.):—"The word does not mean 'the Kshatriya race' by mere convention, like the word अश्वकर्ण which means 'a Śála tree', but is योगरूढ, *i. e.* has its etymological sense restricted to a particular class, just as the term पङ्कज means 'a lotus' to the exclusion of every other thing growing in mud." *Cf.* the word आतपत्र and the English word *parasol*. Words have three kinds of meanings—यौगिक or etymological, as पाचक, &c.; रूढ or established by convention, as गो, अश्वकर्ण &c.; and योगरूढ or etymological as well as conventional, as पङ्कज. The Naiyâyikas recognize a fourth meaning, यौगिकरूढ; as उद्भिद्. See Muktâvalî on Bhâ. Par. 87. उपक्रोश—Ignominy, reproach; fr. क्रुश् with उप and aff. घञ् (अ). मलीमस—मल एषामस्तीति मलीमसाः; fr. मल+ईमस a possessive affix; tarnished; foul. वा—used in the sense of च '*and*.' *Cf.* Kir. quoted in the ft.-notes.

Śl. 54. This is a reply to śl. 49. नु—is interrogative, involving some doubt or uncertainty; *cf.* Kir. V. 1. कथं नु—How possibly; by no means. शक्य—is not generally used independently as here, but with the *inf.*; see *infra* 56. अनुनयः—Lit. leading one after; hence propitiation, pacification of anger. It has a slightly different sense in VI. 2. सुरभेः—may also be taken as षष्ठी and explained by the Sûtra 'तुल्यार्थैरतुलोपमाभ्यां तृतीयान्यतरस्याम्'। Páṇ. II. 3. 72; Apte's G. § 117. रुद्रौजसा—The name रुद्र is variously explained:—रोदयत्य-सुरान् इति रुद्राः । *Cf.* the Śruti—सो रोदीयदरोदीत्तद् रुद्रस्य रुद्रत्वम् । Also रोदनात्तव रुद्रेति नामधेयं भविष्यति । Kûrma-P.; and रुजः सर्वगता यस्मात् द्रावयामि जगत्त्रये । रोदनं हन्मि यस्माच्च रुद्रस्तस्मादहं प्रिये ॥ Skanda-P. प्रहृतम्—see Malli.; or त्वया अस्यां रुद्रौजसा प्रहृतं प्रहारः कृतः (न तु स्वबलेन).

Śl. 55. निष्क्रय—Here means निष्क्रयदान as अर्पण is a क्रिया, the body being the ransom paid in exchange; for the meaning 'ransom' *cf. infra* XV. 55; and व्यापत्तिं ज्ञातमस्य स्वतनुमहमिमां निष्क्रयं कल्पयामि । Mud. VI. 21. For the meaning 'price' *cf.* V. 22. विहता--obstructed. The root हन् with वि is generally used to express the violation of a sacred duty. The पारणा is as much enjoined as a fast itself by the Śâstras.

Śl. 56. अपि—is used here समुच्चये indicating equal participation in the knowledge by both *i. e.* the king and the lion. परवान्-परः (a master) अस्त्यस्य. स्वयमक्षतेन--स्वयं is used in the sense of the Inst. and is equivalent to आत्मना (with one's body). अक्षतेन is emphatic. Want of a wound on the body indicates neglect on the part of the रक्षितृ and supplies the reason why it is impossible for a servant to stand &c.

Śl. 57. किमपि—is used here पक्षान्तरे; see com; 'if, on the other hand.' The king finding the lion averse to cruelty seeks to move him from another stand-point. किमपि may also be construed with अहिंस्यः as suggested by S. P. Pandit, though not with equal propriety, and be translated as 'for some reason (best known to you, after what I have said to you),' owing to some indefinable cause. एकान्त &c.—एकमेवान्तं स्वरूपं यस्य तदेकान्तम् । 'of one form,' never changing,' *i. e.* sure to perish; or एकः अन्तः निश्चयः यस्मिन्कर्मणि एकान्तं यथा तथा विध्वंसितुं शीलं येषां तेषु । *Cf.* Hit. यदि नित्यमनित्येन निर्मलं मलवाहिना । यशः कायेन लभ्येत तन्न लब्धं भवेन्नु किम् ॥; also Kir. II. 19; Veṇ. III. 6 last two lines; and Bhag. II. 34—संभावितस्य चाकीर्तिर्मरणादतिरिच्यते । पिण्डेषु—The use of the word पिण्ड (a lump or mass of) shows the extreme insignificance of the body when compared with यशस्. अनास्था-Tne नञ् here though compounded, is emphatic. भौतिकेषु—formed of the elements; fr. भूत + ठक् (इक). See com.

Śl. 58. आभाषणपूर्वम्—पूर्व lit. 'what precedes,' and since is it the cause that precedes effect, it may be taken here to mean 'cause'. Good men are said to become friends very easily, even if they take seven steps together or exchange seven words in conversation. *Cf.* Hit. and Kum. V. 39 quoted in the ft.-note. वनान्ते—in this tract of the forest; or simply वने; *cf. supra* śl. 19.

Śl. 59. गाम्—गो speech, see V. 12. Chár. seems to have read गां (धेनु) मुक्तवते who released. सद्यः—The very moment; irregularly formed from समान + अहन् (समानेऽहनीति). पिण्ड—a lump *Cf.* the meaning of the same word in s'l. 57. आमिषस्य—This shows the indifference with which the king offered his body to the lion. For a different meaning, see VII. 31.

Śl. 60. पालयितुः प्रजानाम्—The use of this peraphrastic epithet without any reference to the king's proper name is intentional, and is very appropriate here. This shows that the king amply merited the title as was shown by his present act. उत्पश्यतः—Lit. looking upwards; hence, expecting, looking for; mark how the sense of उत् is quite lost; he was अवाङ्मुखः. अवाङ्मुखस्य-अव निम्नमञ्चतीत्यवाङ् । अवाक् (*neu.*) मुखं यस्य. विद्याधर &c.—विद्यायाः of secret arts (गुटिकाञ्जनादिकायाः) धरः विद्याधरः. The Vidyádharas are a class of demigods. The mountain Himálaya is supposed to be their favourite haunt. They are described as wandering in the air and showering down heavenly flowers whenever they notice any act of extraordinary merit performed by mortals. See also ft.-note.

Śl. 61. अमृतायमानम्—Pres. p. of the denom. from अमृत; नास्ति मृतमनेनेत्यमृतम् । अमृतमिवाचरतीत्यमृतायते । Formed with the aff. क्यङ्; see ft.-note. अग्रतः—here the affix तस् is used in the sense of the Loc. प्रस्नविणीम्—प्रकृष्टः स्नवः प्रस्नव. । a Prádi Comp. सोऽस्या अस्तीति ताम् । The flowing of milk generally takes place at the sight of the offspring. *Cf.* I. 84. This shows that the cow looked upon Dilîpa as her own offspring, and hence the poet says 'जननीमिव.' सिंहम्—See ft.-note p. 34. This word is used here to make the contrast more glaring. Instead of a cruel monster, the king saw before him a loving mother.

Śl. 62. साधो—साध्नोति साध्यति वा धर्मं परकार्यं वेति । साधुः—lit. one who is always devoted to his duty or to the work of another; hence, this is the fittest epithet that the cow could have used after witnessing the self-sacrifice of the king. मायाम्—माया is illusion, a delusive fantom. According to some the word is derived fr. मय the originator of the magical art. उद्भाव्य—Like the *inf.*, the absolutive also can sometimes be used passively. परीक्षितः—well put to test. परीक्ष् properly means to look at a thing all round, hence to carefully examine, &c. ऋषिप्रभावात्—प्रकृष्टो भावः प्रभावः Prádi Comp. अन्तकः—अन्तति बध्नाति प्राणिन इति । अन्तयति नाशयतीति वा अन्तकः । किमुत—much less. See Apte's G. § 267 (*a*).

Śl. 63. प्रीतास्मि—प्रसन्नास्मि । ते-तुभ्यम् 'with you.' The dat. by the Várt. (see com.) 'the person for whom an action is done is also the संप्रदान of that action;' but this is unnecessary according to the भाष्यकार as the case is covered by कर्मणा यमभिप्रैति स संप्रदानम्. पुत्र वरम्—Some commentators take this as one word, not with good taste, however, and explain पुत्ररूपं वरम् । न केवलानाम् &c.—See ft.-note. प्रसूतिं-the producer or source of; for this sense *cf.* प्रसूतिमेनःप्रणुदां श्रुतीनां Kir. III. 4.

Śl. 64. मानितार्थी—This epithet is used for the sake of effect. The king who always granted the wishes of suitors was now a suitor himself. स्वहस्तार्जित &c.—Dilīpa had earned for himself the title of 'hero' in all its aspects by the power of his arms. That he was a युद्धवीर, दानवीर and धर्मवीर is described in the first Canto. And here he proves himself to be a दयावीर also like जीमूतवाहन. सुदक्षिणायाम्—Suda. being the आधार of the जन्मक्रिया of the child is put in the Loc. case. तनयम्—तनोति वंशमिति तनयः; fi. तन् and अय (कयन्) Upād.IV.99.

Śl. 65. संतानकामाय—Upa. Tat. Comp.; see Samj. राज्ञे—The Dat. by the rule प्रत्याङ्भ्यां श्रुवः पूर्वस्य कर्ता । In the case of श्रु with प्रति or आ meaning to 'promise,' the person to whom something is promised, after request, is put in the Dat. case. दुग्ध्वा &c.—The cow wished to impart a peculiar efficacy to her milk which would undo the effect of the curse of her mother and remove the childlessness of the king. The king was वन्यवृत्ति and had not tasted her milk as yet.

Śl. 66. वत्सस्य—This means by लक्षणा, वत्सपीतस्य । अनुज्ञामधिगम्य—This is necessary as the sage had desired him to live on the products of the forest alone. औधस्यं—milk; lit. that produced in the udder (ऊधस्). षष्ठांशम् &c.—According to Manu, a sixth of the produce of the earth was due to the king from his subjects. See ft.-note; and *cf.* V. 8. The cow is here again compared to the earth; see II. 3. Here Châr. notices a different reading, *viz.* वत्साग्निकार्यव्यतिरिक्तमन्यद्... । स्तन्यं रसं वशिम वोपभोक्तुं षष्ठांशं &c. and remarks—रसस्य नपुंसकत्वाभावान्मत्वर्थविकल्पनं वा । Nandargikar.

Ś'l. 67. क्षितीशेन—क्षियन्ति निवसन्ति प्राणिनोऽस्यामिति क्षितिस्तस्या ईशः । The force of the epithet is this :—Dilīpa was a king and so could have done anything he liked. Yet he awaited the order of the sage to drink the cow's milk. This humility in the king pleased the cow. वसिष्ठधेनुः—The reference to Vasishtha here is not out of place. Though the king was ordered to drink the milk there and then, he declined to do so. And yet the cow was not offended. This was because Dilīpa wished to take the permission of Vasishtha, her revered master. प्रीततरा for she was already प्रीत (see 63 above). च—shows that the two actions expressed by प्रीततरा बभूव and प्रत्याययौ took place simultaneously. अश्रमेण—because both of them were in a pleased mood, and so did not feel the fatigue of the journey.

Ś'l. 68. प्रसन्नेन्दुमुखः—Ere this Dilīpa's face was overspread with a sort of gloom caused by his childless state. It now wore away and his face shone bright like the autumnal moon freed from the clouds. प्रहर्ष &c.—We might dissolve प्रकृष्टो हर्षः प्रहर्षः स एव चिह्नमनुमापकं तस्य वा चिह्नानि तेन तैर्वाङ्कितमितस् । पुनरुक्तया—पुनरुक्त must be taken here in the sense of 'repeated' and not 'superfluous' (which meaning also it has; see V. 34), as the word इव is used. If we take the latter meaning, the figure will be faulty, whether we take इव as the sign of an उपमा or उत्प्रेक्षा, in both of which the two things compared ought to be distinct, since Dilīpa's words were actually superfluous and not *like to* or *as if* superfluous.

Śl. 69. अनिन्दितात्मा, सद्वत्सलः—These two epithets, though apparently they seem to be used for the sake of alliteration, have a meaning here. The king's recent self-sacrifice had now proved that he was pre-eminently सद्वत्सल or kind to the good, and being blessed by the cow, he was free from the ban of sonlessness. Thus he was peculiarly सद्वत्सल and अनिन्दितात्मा now. For the meaning and der. of वत्सल, see Saṃj. and notes on V. 7. पपौ—drank, received in. To 'drink' fame seems to be a queer expression; but it is the Sanskrit idiom, meaning 'to receive in a fresh accession or addition of fame.' *Cf.* VII. 63, where the idea is repeated. शुभ्रं यशो मूर्तमिव—मूर्तम्—p. p. p. of मूर्च्छ्, incarnate, having a bodily existence.

On this S. P. Pandit observes:—"That renown or good fame should be conceived to be as white, *i. e.* clear or bright, as the shine of the full moon, free from all approach of obscuring clouds, or as any other perfectly white substance as pure milk, is intelligible enough. But when things of actual existence and of established whiteness like milk, snow, &c., are compared to renown, we leave the region of metaphor or simile as such, and step into the region of what may perhaps be called unreal similes."

But this criticism seems to be based either on a misunderstanding of the force of इव, or on an ignorance of the distinction between an उपमा and an उत्प्रेक्षा. The fig. of speech here is उत्प्रेक्षा and not उपमा, the इव indicating संभावना and not साधर्म्य, as is clear from the presence of the word मूर्त in the line. The उत्प्रेक्षा requires that the उपमान should be unreal. What is a fault in an उपमा is the essential condition of, and constitutes the beauty in, an उत्प्रेक्षा. See K. P. X. All that the poet means here is, that Dilīpa's sonlessness, which had so long hung like a dark cloud obscuring his otherwise spotless fame, was now removed, so that it seemed he was drinking in, not a quantity of milk, but was receiving in, as it were, a new fund of spotless fame (of having a child).

Śl. 70. यथोक्त &c.—उक्तस्यानतिक्रमो यथोक्तं Avya. Comp. यथोक्तमस्यास्तीति यथोक्तम्; यथोक्त+अ (अच्), an affix showing possession and added to the words of the अर्शआदि class by the rule 'अर्शआदिभ्योऽच्'. now see Saṃj; यथोक्तं व्रतं यथोक्तव्रतं तस्य पारणाया अन्ते. प्रास्थानिकम्—from प्रस्थान+इक (ठञ्); see com.; customary at the time of setting out. According to the words of the Vṛittikâra, quoted by Malli., words expressing time, even by लक्षणा, may take the affixes added to words expressive of time. Here the word प्रस्थान means by लक्षणा the प्रस्थानकाल and hence it takes ठञ्. स्वस्त्य°—स्वस्ति कल्याणं, an indec.; स्वस्ति अयनं स्वस्त्ययनं. राजधानीम्—धीयतेऽस्यामिति धानी। राज्ञो धानी राजधानी। fr. धा and aff अन (ल्युट्) with ई. वशी—Self-controlled. Here the word is peculiarly happy. Vasishṭha would certainly have liked to keep the king for a day or two with him and to entertain him sumptuously; but he knew that an immediate return to his capital would please the king more than a feast, now that his object was gained, and so checking his desire sent him away.

Śl. 71. प्रदक्षि° हुतं हुताशम्—Such was the custom; *cf.* वत्से इतः सद्योहुतानग्नीन्प्रदक्षिणीकुरुष्व Śák. IV. p. 140 Mark the difference between the meanings of हुत in हुतम् and हुताशम्. In one case it means 'propitiated with offerings', from हु to please; in the other 'what is offered,' fr. हु to offer. सन्मङ्गल &c.—सन्ति मङ्गलानि सन्मङ्गलानि; तैः अतिशयेनोदग्र उदग्रतरः (more mighty or pre-eminent) प्रभावो यस्य. Here प्रभाव rather means (though we have translated it by 'prowess') dignity, majestic appearance, as in प्रभाववान् इव लक्ष्यते Śák. I. p. 36 उदग्र means prominent, bright. He was no longer प्रजालोपनिमीलित. His face had its usual majestic splendour; the maṅgalas made it brighter. Dinakara explains this as सतां मङ्गलेन प्रीतवह्निगोब्राह्मणप्रदक्षिणीकरणेनोदग्रतरो महीयान् प्रभावो यस्य । See ft.-note. *Cf.*—धेनूर्वत्सप्रयुक्ता वृषगजतुरगान्दक्षिणावर्तवह्निं दिव्यस्त्रीपूर्णकुम्भद्विजनृपगणिकापुष्पमालापताकाः । सद्योमांसं घृतं वा दधि मधु रजतं काञ्चनं शुक्लधान्यं दृष्ट्वा श्रुत्वा पठित्वा फलमिह लभते मानवो गन्तुकामः ॥ According to Vallabha, सन्मङ्गल refers to the auspicious appearance of birds and the manifestation of other signs at Dilîpa's departure.

Śl. 72. श्रोत्राभिराम &c.—अभिरमत इत्यभिरामः श्रोत्रयोरभिरामस्तेन । सहिष्णुः—सोढुं शीलमस्य; fr. सह+इष्णु (च्); similarly अलंकरिष्णु, वर्धिष्णु; see Pâṇ. III. 2. 136. This is said with reference to his successful performance of the गोसेवाव्रत he had undertaken. अनुद्घातसुखेन—अविद्यमान उद्घातोऽस्मिन्नित्यनुद्घातः; not tossed up and down; free from jolting. Now see Saṃj. मनोरथेन—मनसो रथो मनोरथः । The desire carries the mind from one object to another just as a car does a man; so the desire is called the car of the mind. The epithets श्रोत्राभिरामध्वनिना and अनुद्घातसुखेन apply to मनोरथ as well. In this case ध्वनि means 'the sound of the desire being pronounced aloud' which was pleasing now that its fulfilment was certain; and अनुद्घात means 'the removal of obstacles'.; see Samj.

Śl. 73. आहित—lit. placed in the heart; produced; उत्सुकस्य भावः औत्सुक्यं eager longing, yearning. प्रजार्थे &c.—When referring to the moon प्रजा means 'the people, the world.' The moon also observes a sort of vow, *viz.*, of allowing the gods to drink of him for the good of the world, and gets emaciated. See ft.-note. नेत्रैः पपुः—*Cf.* मदविभ्रमासकलया पपे पुनः स पुरस्त्रियैकतमयैकशा दशा। Śis. XIII. 40; and *supra* II. 19. नाथमिवौषधीनाम्—See ft.-note. The moon is called the lord of plants, as moonlight is essential to their growth. *Cf.* Rig. X. 85. 2–'सोमेनादित्या बलिनः सोमेन पृथिवी मही। अथो नक्षत्राणामेषामुपस्थे सोम आहितः' Where Sáyaṇa explains अमृतसेकेनौषध्याभिवृध्या पृथिव्या बलवत्त्वम्'। Hv. XXV.—ततस्तस्मै ददौ राज्यं ब्रह्मा ब्रह्मविदां वरः। बीजौषधीनां विप्राणामपां च जनमेजय॥ &c.; and Kàs. K. XIV.—तस्य यत्प्लावितं तेजः पृथिवीमन्वपद्यत। तेनौषध्यः समुत्पन्ना याभिः संधार्यते जगत्॥ * * * बीजौषधीनां तोयानां राजाभूद्द्विजन्मनाम्। &c. See also Vàyu. P.-XXVIII. 12. 16. S. P. Pandit has the following note on the history of the word:--

"Properly speaking, ओषधीनां नाथः or the king of plants,' is the Soma plant, which being largely used in sacrifices, naturally came to be regarded as the highest plant, and be styled 'the king of plants.' The key to the fact of ओषधीपतिः meaning both the Soma plant and the Moon seems to lie in the word इन्दु. This word is frequently found in the Rig-veda, but always in the sense of(1) a drop of the Soma juice, and(2)the Soma juice itself. It apppears that the word इन्दु, coming then to signify a globule, or a round little body, very naturally became a name of the full Moon. Now according to a very common principle that has had such a prominent influence on the development of the Sanskrit vocabulary,— *viz.* that whenever a vocable that signifies two things has other synonyms, those other synonyms also become each expressive of the same two things,—the word Soma acquired the additional sense of the Moon. Then, as is very common in the growth of mythology, the conceptions, attributes &c. connected with the original personified or rather deified concept, Soma, *viz.* that of the plant, became attached to the new concept, *viz.* that of the Moon. Thus the whole derivation may be put in the following pseudo-logical form. 'The word इन्दु meant both a drop of the juice of the sacrificial plant, (or the juice itself) and the Moon; a synonym of इन्दु in the first sense is the word

सोम; therefore सोम meant both the plant and the Moon. Now because Soma, '*the plant,*' was developed into a personification by certain attributes, therefore, Soma, the Moon, acquired also the same attributes. And thus it is that the Moon also came to be described as the King or Lord of the plants."

S'l. 74. पुरंदरश्रीः—Puraṃdara or 'the destroyer of the enemies' cities, is a name of Indra, because he is described in the hymns of the Ṛigveda as having destroyed the cities of his enemies, *i. e.* the clouds. In the Purâṇas, however, he is described as often being driven out of his heaven by the demons, but as always re-entering his capital on all such occasions, after having finally overcome his foes, and restring order to the universe. Here the poet probably refers to this when he says that Dilîpa, entering his capital and once more resuming the government of the earth, had the grace of Indra. भुजगेन्द्र &c.—The lord of serpents is Śesha regarded as the emblem of eternity, whence he is also called Ananta. He is represented as supporting the entire world on his head. *Cf.* Vishṇu-Purâṇa 'पातालानामधश्चास्ते विष्णोर्या तामसी तनुः। शेषाख्या यद्गुणान्वक्तुं न शक्ता दैत्यदानवाः॥ योऽनन्तः पठ्यते सिद्धैर्देव-देवर्षिपूजितः। तस्यैषा सकला पृथ्वी फणामणिशिखारुणा। आस्ते कुसुममालेव कस्तद्वीर्यं वदिष्यति॥ &c.; and Kum. III. 13. Hence the comparison. आससञ्ज—Here सञ्ज् must be taken as used in the cau., as it is intransitive by itself (अन्तर्भावितण्यर्थः).

S'l. 75. अत्रेर्नयनसमुत्थं &c.—Atri is a celebrated sage and author of many Vedic hymns. He is one of the sons of Brahmá. According to the Váyu-P., the essence of Soma or Moon dropped down in the streams from the eyes of Atri, while he was absorbed in meditation. The presiding goddesses of the ten quarters, at the command of Brahmâ, bore the foetus, and the moon was born. For a fuller account, see Hv. quoted by Malli. Wilson's Vishṇu-P. p. 392, and Padma-P. Svargakhaṇḍa. सुरसरिदिव &c.—For the allusion see Saṃj.; also Mah.-Bhâr. Anu. Parva, 84, 85, Vâmana-P. 54, Kum. IX. and X. Wilson's Megh., note 79.

लोकपालानुभावैः—The Lokapálas are the guardian-deities presiding over the eight quarters. For their names see note on दिग्गज I. 78. *Cf.* Amar. इन्द्रो वह्निः पितृपतिर्नैर्ऋतो वरुणो मरुत्। कुबेर ईशः पतयः पूर्वादीनां दिशां क्रमात्॥ अनुभाव seems to be used here in the sense of मात्रा or अंश 'a portion of.' *Cf.* III. 11. Vallabha quotes the following s'l. on this: इन्द्रात्प्रभुत्वं तपनात्प्रतापं क्रोधं हरादैश्रवणाच्च वित्तम्। आह्लादकत्वं च निशाधिनाथादादाय राज्ञः क्रियते शरीरम्॥ *Cf.* Manu. V. 96, quoted by Malli. and ft.-note. आपन्न—On this Malli. remarks—The Queen simply bore the fœtus, meaning thereby, that she took no part in its development (as it was formed of divine energies). In support of this he quotes Âśvalâyana. The word **आधान** is used in various senses by Kâlidâsa. See I. 24, 85; VII. 20; Megh. I. 3, 10, &c.

The two similes here contain in them the promise of tender and warlike virtues in the future child, besides being complimentary to the magnanimity and the sanctity of the king and the queen.

CANTO III.

Śl. 1. **उपस्थितोदयं भर्तुरीप्सितम्**—This is in apposition with **दौर्हृद-लक्षणं** 'outward marks of being with child', which were the very wish of her husband with its fulfilment at hand. **आप्तुमिष्टमीप्सितं**–here used substantively. Pandit thinks that Vallabha has explained it better by taking it as an *adj.* qualifying **दौर्हृदलक्षणं**, and meaning **अभिमतं**, 'wished for;' but **दौर्हृद०** was not the **ईप्सित** of the king, but the birth of a son **सखीजन** &c.—**सखीनां जनः सखीजनः ।** In such cases **जन** means, 'a collection or multitude;' *cf.* **पौरजनस्य** VI. 7; **बन्धुजनः** Kum. I. 26. **उद्वीक्ष्यत एभिरित्युद्वीक्षणानि**, eyes; now see Saṃj. **कौमुदी०**–The first gleam of moonlight, to be soon followed by the moon. **०महं** –*v. l.* refers to the festival celebrated on the full-moon-night of Áśvina; *cf.* **बन्धुताहृदयकौमुदीमहः** &c., Mâl.-Mâdh. IX. 21.

निदानम्—The root, chief cause. **दौर्हृदलक्षणम्—दौर्हृदस्य गर्भस्य लक्षणम् ।** On this Malli. has the following remark :—A pregnant woman is said to be **द्विहृदया** or one who has two hearts, her own, and that of the fœtus. And the fœtus, in connexion with that, is called **दौर्हृद**, while the woman in relation to it is called **दौर्हृदिनी ।** See Saṃj. *Cf.* **तस्माच्चतुर्थे गर्भस्तु नाना वस्तूनि वाञ्छति । तत्र द्विहृदया यस्यान्नारी दौर्हृदिनी मता ॥** Suśruta. **दौर्हृद**, therefore, is irregularly derived from **द्वि + हृद्** , to be explained like **पृषोदर**; or it may be derived from **दुर् + हृद्**, also irregularly (the regular form being **दौर्हार्द**); **दुष्टं हृद् हृदयमस्या इति दुर्हृद् गर्भिणी तस्याः संबन्धीदम् । हृच्छब्दोपि प्रकृत्यन्तरमस्तीति वृत्तिकारः ।** Some read **दौहृद**, which, though irregular, may be explained like **सौहृद** , for which see Uttar. I. 45 and our note *ad loc.* The best way to avoid all these irregularities is to adopt the reading '**दोहदलक्षणम्**' which appears to be the reading of the poet also; see Ślokas 6, 7.

Śl. 2. **०सादः**—fr. **सद् + अ (घञ्)**; wasting away, emaciation, of the body (and the consequent weakness). For a different sense see VIII. 58. असमग्र—सञ्जातमग्रमस्येति समग्रं lit. having the end attached, hence, complete; न समग्रमसमग्रं भूषणं यस्याः। मुखेन—Malli. takes this as इत्थंभूतलक्षणे तृतीया; Prof. Ray thinks that it will be better to take this and शशिना as हेतौ तृतीया. See his note. लोध्रपाण्डुना—From this it seems that the Lodhra has flowers of a palish white colour; *cf.* the simile in II. 29. In literature we often find the *lodhra* flower mentioned to convey the idea of paleness. See Śis'. VI. 64. विचेयतारका—विचेयाः which are to be searched for; hence, few. प्रभातकल्पा—प्रारब्धं भातमस्यां प्रारब्धा वा भातुमिति प्रभाता। See Saṃj. कल्प added to nouns and adjectives means 'a little less than, nearly equal to', &c. शर्वरी—शृणाति चेष्टा इति। Uṇá. II. 121. For the external signs of pregnancy see Vâgbhaṭa quoted by Malli. *Cf.* also Bhâvaprakâs'a:—अवसादः पिपासा च ग्लानिः......। स्तनयोर्मुखकार्ष्ण्यं स्याद्रोमराज्युद्गमस्तथा। अक्षिपक्ष्माणि चाप्यस्याः संमील्यन्ते विशेषतः॥ अकामतश्छर्दयति गन्धादुद्विजतेऽशुभात्। प्रसेकः सदनं चैव गर्भिण्या लिङ्गमुच्यते॥ &c.

Śl. 3. मृत्सुरभि—Having an earthy fragrance, smelling of earth; applies to both आनन and पल्वल. Some pregnant women eat baked earth; Sudakshiṇâ also did it and had an earthy fragrance about her lips. The king welcomed it for its significance. See the next s'loka. रहसि-(*a*) in private; (*b*) in a sequestered spot. पयोमुचां &c.—The poet in several places refers to the earthy fragrance issuing forth from dry ground during the first showers of rain after summer; see XIII. 21

Śl 4. मरुत्वान्—मरुतो देवाः सन्त्यस्यानुचरत्वेनेति मरुत्वान्। He who is followed by the gods; Indra. In the Veda the Maruts are described as the gods of the air. दिगन्त०—Dissolve दिशामन्तः दिगन्तः। दिगन्ते विश्रान्तः दिगन्तविश्रान्तः; दिगन्तविश्रान्तः रथः यस्य। विश्रान्त—The root श्रम् with वि means generally to rest or to relieve fatigue; see I. 54, IV. 74; and also, though less often, to stop moving, to cease, in which sense it is used here; *cf.* for this sense विश्रान्तविग्रहकथः Rat. I. 8; विरोधो विश्रान्तः Uttar. VI. 11.

Śl. 5. अनुवेलम्—वेलायां वेलायामनुवेलम्; constantly; here अनु has the sense of 'वीप्सा' or repetition. उत्तरकोसलेश्वरः—उत्तरकोसलानामीश्वरः। उत्तरकोसल being a संज्ञा has no विग्रहवाक्य. The country of Kosala, according to the Râmâyaṇa, was situated along the banks of Sarayù, the river Gogra of modern times. Its capital Ayodhyâ is described in the fifth chapter of the Âdikâṇḍa and said is to have been twelve *Yojanas* in length and three in breadth. It was also called Sâketa; one of its principal suburbs was नन्दिग्राम staying where Bharata ruled the kingdom during the absence of Râma. Kosala was divided into 'Uttara

Kosala' and 'Dakshiṇa Kosala.' In the Matsya Purâṇa, the former is called Ganda, a district still known by the same name, and occurring in the Mah.—Bhâr. after Pañchâla among the conquests of Bhîma. See Mah.-Bhár. Sabh. Parva Chap. XXX. It is certain, therefore, that the country north of Ayodhyá comprising Ganda and Baraitch was known as Uttara-kosala. Aja, Das'aratha &c. are said to have ruled over this province. At the time of Râma's death, his two sons Kuśa and Lava reigned respectively at Kus'âvatî in Southern Kosala in the defiles of the Vindhyas, and at Śrávastî in Northern Kosala. For fuller information see Anandoram Borooah's Ancient Geography of India, pp. 86–90, paras 93–96.

Śl. 6. दोहद &c.—दुःखयतीति दुःखम् । दुःखं शीलं स्वभावो यस्य तस्य भावो दुःखशीलता (the pain-causing condition); now see Saṃj. दोहनं दोहः । दोहमाकर्षं ददातीति दोहदः the qualms or hankerings of pregnancy; दोहद also means the fœtus. On this Śus'ruta has the following:—तस्माच्चतुर्थे गर्भस्तु &c., quoted before; *supra* sl. 1. दौर्हृदावमानया कुब्जं कुणिं षण्ढं च वामनम् । विकृताक्षमनक्षं वा पुत्रं नारी प्रसूयते ॥ यतः स्त्री दौर्हृदं प्राप्य वीर्यवन्तं चिरायुषम् । पुत्रं प्रसूयते तस्मात्तस्यै वाञ्छितमर्पयेत् ॥ इन्द्रियार्थानसौ यान्यान्भोक्तुमिच्छति गर्भिणी ॥ गर्भबाधाभयात्तांस्तान्भिषगाहृत्य दापयेत् ॥ &c. शारीरस्थान तृ॰.

त्रिदिवः—is curiously derived, from त्रि three *i. e.* the gods ब्रह्मा, विष्णु and शिव, and दिव् to sport; *lit.* the place where the three gods take divine pleasure. त्रिसृष्टप्यत्रस्थास्तु त्रयो ब्रह्मविष्णुरुद्रा वा दीव्यन्त्यत्रेति । हलश्चेति घञ् । संज्ञापूर्वकत्वान्न गुणः । Or ब्रह्मवैष्णवरौद्रभेदेन सात्त्विकराजसतामसभेदेन वा त्रिविधो दीव्यति व्यवहरति प्रकाशते वेति । This is free from any grammatical irregularity. Or त्रितीया द्यौः । त्रिदिवं *neu.* is also correct.

अधिज्यधन्वनः—इति हेतुगर्भं विशेषणं (*i. e.* which explains why nothing was अनासाद्य to him).

Śl. 7. निस्तीर्य—Having got over. च—is used here पक्षान्तरे.—'But when she had got over' &c. दोहदव्यथां—*i. e.* the painful period of (owing to depraved cravings, nausea, loss of appetite, languor, &c; see com. on s'l. 2.). प्रचीयमाना॰—Pres. p. of चि with प्र, pass; *cf.* for this sense चीयते बालिशस्यापि सत्क्षेत्रपतिता कृषिः । Mud. I. 3; क्षीणोऽप्युपचीयते चन्द्रः । Bh. पुराण—पुराभवं पुरातनं or पुरानत्रं formed irregularly. अनन्तरम्—here indicates nearness in point of time.

Śl. 8. दिनेषु—The period of gestation; 'as days passed' *i. e.* as she advanced in pregnancy. तिरश्चकार—तिरस्कृत properly means, what is hidden from view and therefore not noticed; hence, secondarily, what is not noticed even though not hidden. Thus when one of two things by its superior excellence prominently draws attention to itself, diverting it from the other, the second thing is said to be तिरस्कृत,

i. e. excelled by the other. **अभिलीनयोः**—**ली** is here transitive, though it is generally used intransitively. **सुजातयोः**—well-formed or developed; corresponds to **नितान्तपीवर**. See VIII. 37. **श्रियं**—see IV. 17.

Śl. 9. **निधान** &c.—**निधीयतेऽनेनेति निधानं निधिः**, a treasure. This epithet indicates the mighty fortune of the forthcoming babe. **सागराम्बराम्**—**सागरः अम्बरं** (a garment) **यस्याः** the sea is more often spoken of as the waist-band of the earth; *cf.* XV. 1 (**रत्नाकरमेखला**). Malli. takes this as a **संज्ञा**. *Cf.* '**भूतधात्री रत्नगर्भा विपुला सागराम्बरा**' **इति कोषः।** Vâmana, however, cites this as an instance of an attribute alone being used for the corresponding substantive when the meaning is plain; **विशेषणमात्रप्रयोगो विशेष्यप्रतिपत्तौ......यथा—'निधानगर्भामिव सागराम्बराम्'। अत्र हि पृथिव्या विशेषणमात्रमेव प्रयुक्तम् । एतेन 'क्रुद्धस्य तस्याथ पुरामरातेर्ल्ललाट-पट्टादुदगादुदर्चिः'। 'गिरेस्तडित्वानिव तावदुच्चकैर्जवेन पीठादुदतिष्ठदच्युतः' । इत्यादयः प्रयोगा व्याख्याताः । शमीम्**—fire is believed to reside in the Śamî tree, a rod of which is used to produce fire by friction for holy purposes. See ft.-note. By this epithet **प्रताप** or prowess in the child is indicated. **नदीमिव** &c.—This indicates purity in the child to be born. **अन्तःसलिलां—अन्तर्गतं सलिलं यस्याः सा अन्तःसलिला ताम्. सरस्वतीम्**—The river Sarasvatî flows near Thâṇeshvara (**स्थाण्वीश्वर**). Its modern name is Sarasvatî or Caggar. Anandoram Boroosh says—"Two other junctions are mentioned which are borne out by the map, *viz.* of the Kaus'ikî and the Dṛishadvatî on the west and of the Aruṇa with the Sarasvatî below Thâṇeshvara. Near the first is Vyâsasthalî, the modern Basthali. Not far from the junctions of the two combined streams, (Sarasvatî and Dṛishadvatî) is the modern Kaithal, which is probably Kapishṭhala of the Vanparvan. The Sarasvatî which loses itself in the sandy desert is supposed by the poets to flow under the surface of the earth, and join ultimately the ocean." The Ṛigveda represents it as flowing into the sea. But later legends make it disappear under ground and join the Gangá and Yamunâ at Prayâga. Pilgrims yet speak of a river in Bihar having a dry bed but giving water within a few inches of its sandy surface, which they call Falgu-Gangá and consider almost as sacred as Gangâ itself. The Mah.-Bhár. thus accounts for its disappearance—Varuṇa once carried off Bhadrâ, the beautiful spouse of a Brâhmaṇa named, Utathya, and would not yield her up. The Brâhmaṇa then addressed himself to the countries and the river Sarasvatî, saying, 'O goddess, Sarasvatî, vanish into the deserts and let this land, deserted by trees, become impure.' When the country had been thus turned into a desert, Varuṇa restored his wife to Utathya.

सत्त्वाम्—सत्त्वेन गर्भरूपेण सह वर्तत इति। The fig. of speech here according to Chár. is मालोपमा; see K.-D. II. 42.

Śl. 10. मनःसमु०—The loftiness, magnanimity of the mind; *cf.* मनसः शिखराणां च सदृशी ते समुन्नतिः। Kum. VI. 66. पुंसवनादिकाः—पुंसवन is the first ceremony performed on a woman's showing distinct signs of conception with a view to the birth of a male child. This is performed in the 2nd or 3rd month when the moon is in conjunction with some male star. *Cf.* Gobbhila:—तृतीयस्य गर्भमासस्यादिमदशे पुंसवनस्य कालः। Śaunaka-व्यक्ते गर्भे तृतीये तु मासे पुंसवनं भवेत्। गर्भेऽव्यक्ते तृतीये चेच्चतुर्थे मासि वा भवेत्॥ and Vasishṭha-कुर्यात्पुंसवनं प्रसिद्धविषये गर्भे तृतीयेऽथवा मासि स्फीततनौ तुषारकिरणे पुष्येऽथवा वैष्णवे। हित्वा कर्कटकं नृयुग्ममबलामन्येष्वरिक्ते तिथौ शुद्धे नैधनधाम्नि शुक्रशशभृद्विन्मन्त्रिणां वासरे॥ See Saṃj. धीरः—Wise, patient (and not agitated by the loss of money); hence he did all that; *cf.* स तुल्यपुष्पाभरणो हि धीरः। *infra* XVI. 74. सदृशी—समान इव पश्यतीति सदृशः सदृक् वा; though thus derived, the idea of 'seeing' is not present in these words; they have a meaning established by usage (viz., that of similar to, or worthy of).

Śl. 11. सुरेन्द्र &c.—सुरेषु इन्द्रा लक्षणया श्रेष्ठाः सुरेन्द्रास्तेषां &c; *cf.* II. 75. उपचाराञ्जलि &c.—उपचर्यते इति उपचारः। (act of honouring or worshipping, homage) भावे घञ्; or उपचर्यते अनेन। करणे घञ् by which respect is shown; *cf.* न तेऽङ्गानि उपचारमर्हन्ति। Śâk. III. 18; now see Saṃj. This shows how feeble सुदक्षिणा had grown when advanced in pregnancy. It is a duty enjoined on every Hindu woman to rise and join hands to show respect when her husband approaches her. *Cf.* अभ्युत्थानमुपागते गृहपतौ तद्भाषणे नम्रता तत्पादार्पितदृष्टिरासनविधिस्तस्योपचर्या स्वयम्। सुप्ते तत्र शयीत तत्प्रथमतो जह्याच्च शय्यामिति प्राच्यैः पुत्रि निवेदितः कुलवधूसिद्धान्तधर्मागमः॥ पारिप्लव &c.-परिप्लवते इति परिप्लवम्। 'That which moves all round,' hence, unsteady; परिप्लवमेव पारिप्लवम्। पारिप्लवनेत्रत्व has nothing to do with pregnancy in particular. It is a sign of natural timidity which is a characteristic of woman in general. *Cf.* त्रस्तैकहायनकुरङ्गविलोलदृष्टेः &c. Uttar. III. 28; चकितहरिणीप्रेक्षणा Megh. II. 22. It also refers to physical movement; *cf.* XIII. 30.

Śl. 12. कुमारभृत्याकुशलैः—Kumárabhrityâ is the name given by Suśrûta to one of the eight branches of medical science which deals with the proper development of the fœtus, taking care of the mother during the latter days of her pregnancy, and of the babe when born, &c. कौमारभृत्यं नाम कुमारभरणधात्रीक्षीरदोषसंशोधनार्थं दुष्टस्तन्यग्रहसमुत्थानां च व्याधीनामुपशमार्थम्। Susrûta. कुमारभृत्या गर्भिण्याः परिचर्योच्यते। Hárâvalî. कुशलैः-कुशान् लातीति कुशलः lit. one who plucks the blades of Kus'a grass; but as it requires great skill to pluck the sharp blades of Kus'a grass, without hurting one's fingers, it has come to mean 'one who is skilful'. गर्भभर्मणि—The development of the fœtus. According to the Sid.-Kau. the affix is मनिन् and not मनिच्. प्रतीतः—हृष्टः Malli. *Cf.* V. 26. It may also mean 'confident.' काले—has a double sense—(1) in the tenth month; (2) at the advent of the rains.

S'l. 13. ग्रहैः—गृह्णन्ति भाविशुभाशुभफलयोजनया स्वायत्तीकुर्वन्तीति ग्रहाः । गृह्यन्ते रविरश्मिभिराहृत्य तिरस्क्रियन्त इति वा । उच्चसंश्रयैः—उच्चः संश्रयोऽवस्थानं येषां occupying a high position; in the ascendant. Malli. seems to have read उच्चसंस्थितैः. This and the other *adj.* असूर्यगैः have been fully explained in the Samj. and the foot-notes. The s'l. 'अजवृषभ' &c. quoted by Malli. means:—तुङ्ग is the technical term for 'high, in the ascendant.' If a राशि be divided into 30 equal parts, then the seven planets रवि, सोम, मङ्गल, बृहस्पति, शुक्र and शनि are said to be in the ascendant when they are each in the following zodiacal signs respectively: मेषः (aries), वृषभ (taurus), मृग (cervus), अङ्गना (virgo), कर्क (cancer), मीन (pisces), and तुला (libra); and particularly so when in the 10th, 3rd, 28th, 15th, 11th, 27th, and 20th division respectively of each. A low position is at the end of the diameter through a high position, *i. e.* the 7th sign from the high position. असूर्यगैः—The नञ् here, though compounded, is emphatic. Close proximity with the sun forms the setting (अस्तमय) of the planets, and their separation from the sun is their rise. (See Samj.). This indicates that the glory of the child to be born would be ever in the ascendant. सूचित &c.—संपद् excellence, exuberance. One planet in the ascendant at the time of one's birth foretells happiness, two, great achievement, three, a king-like position, four a throne, and five, a divine position. Raghu was foreshown by five such planets to be a divine being. Only a divine incarnation is said to be favoured by five planets. *Cf.* the account of Ráma's birth:—उच्चस्थे ग्रहपञ्चके सुरगुरौ सेन्दौ नवम्यां तिथौ लग्ने कर्कटके पुनर्वसुदिने मेषं गते पूषणि । निर्दग्धुं निखिलाः पलाशसमिधो मेध्यादयोध्यारणेराविर्भूतमभूदपूर्वविभवं यत्किंचिदेकं महः ॥ Champurámá. I. 29 त्रिसाधना शक्तिः—the efficiency which combines in itself the three agencies or powers, *viz.*, (1) प्रभुशक्ति or the power arising from the resources at the command of and the pre-eminent position of the king; (2) उत्साहशक्ति or that arising from the king's personal energy or enthusiasm; and (3) मन्त्रशक्ति or that arising from good counsel.

S'l. 14. दिशः &c.—These are the signs that attend the birth of a great benefactor of the world. *Cf.* with this Kum. I. 23 quoted in the ft.-note; तथापि पापीयसि निर्जिते गते दिशः प्रसेदुः प्रबभौ निशाकरः । दिवो निपेतुर्भुवि पुष्पवृष्टयो रराज योषेव विकल्मषा निशा ॥ Bud. ch. XIII. 73; and परं प्रसादं ककुभः प्रपेदिरे गुणैः कुमारस्य सहोत्थितैरिव । Vikra.-Ch. II. 86.

S'l. 15. अरिष्टशय्याम्—A comp. सह सुपा; see com.; नास्ति रिष्टमत्र, न रिष्यते स्म हिंस्रैः (by evil-doers) इति वा अरिष्टम् , (from रिष् I. IV. P. to hurt, to harm.). S. P. Pandit says that अरिष्ट is one of those many words in Sanskrit which bear senses quite opposed to each other. अरिष्ट originally meant *unhurt, safe, certain.* And then it means, in classical Sanskrit, *unhappy, unfortunate, dangerous. Cf.* आरात् near, at a distance; यु to join, to disjoin; असला a chaste, and an unchaste woman. It is quite possible that this should arise from a later generation misunderstanding the language of their ancestors, especially in regard to words which, though once clear as daylight, have become somehow obscure to them. हतत्विषः &c.—*Cf. infra* X. 68; and स हि स्वगात्रप्रभयोज्ज्वलन्त्या दीपप्रभां भास्करवन्मुमोष । Bud.-Ch. I. 35.

Śl. 16. शुद्धान्त—शुद्धा उपधाशुद्धाः (of tried continence जितेन्द्रियाः) रक्षका अन्ते समीपेऽस्येति शुद्धान्तः । or शुद्धः अन्तः the border, surrounding part यस्य, no objectionable person being allowed to enter it. अमृत &c.—न म्रियते अनेन इति अमृतं, fr. न+मृ with त (तन् Uṇâdi.); अमृतस्य संमितानि अक्षराणि यस्य तत् । अदेयम्—दानस्य योग्यं देयं न देयमदेयम् । त्रयं—त्रयोऽवयवा अस्य; see note on द्वय, *supra* 1. 19. भूपतेः—By 'कृत्यानां कर्तरि वा' the agent of the action expressad by the pot. p. p. is optionally put in the gen., so भूपतिना also. शशिप्रभं &c.—For, this was the chief emblem of universal sovereignty; see IV. 17.

Śl. 17. निवात &c.—निरुद्धो निवृत्तो वा वातोऽस्मात्प्रदेशादिति निवातः । See Saṃj. *Cf.* यथा दीपो निवातस्थो &c. Bg. VI. 19. सुताननम्—Here the compounded form is better than सुतस्य आननम् as it brings prominently the idea of सुत before the mind, the idea of आनन being subordinate in the compound and consequently makes the joy due to the face being that of his child. In the other case कान्तं would qualify आनन directly, so the joy would be due to the loveliness of the face, which is not so good as the first. आत्मनि प्रबभूव—See Saṃj. *Cf.* युगान्तकालप्रतिसंहृतात्मनो जगन्ति यस्यां सविकाशमासत । तनौ ममुस्तत्र न कैटभाद्विषस्तपोधनाभ्यागमसंभवा मुदः ॥ Śis'. I. 23; also Kum. VI. 59.

Śl. 18. जातकर्मन्—A ceremony performed at the birth of a child before the scission of the navel string. It is thus summarized by S. P. Pandit from Nârâyaṇabhaṭṭa's Prayogaratna:—

"The moment the birth of a son is announced the father shall see his face, and shall bathe in a river with his face turned towards the east, or if that is not possible, shall bathe at home in cold water mixed with hot water, brought (from a river) during daytime, and purified by a bit of gold being thrown in it. Then having sipped water, he shall besmear himself with sandal and wear garlands of flowers, and before the scission of the navel-stalk, and before the baby is touched by any one except the midwife, he shall cause it to be placed on the lap of its mother, with its face turned to the east, and say **ममास्य कुमारस्य गर्भाम्बुपानजनितसकलदोषनिर्हरणायुर्मेधाभिवृद्धिबीजगर्भसमुद्भवैनोनिबर्हणद्वारा श्रीपरमेश्वरप्रीत्यर्थं जातकर्म करिष्ये.** He then shall perform a *S'ra'ddha* to the nine ancestors, and shall throw oblations of clarified butter in the sacred fire, kindled for the purpose, in honour of Agni, Indra, Prajâpati, the Vis'vedevas, and Brahmá. He shall then mix a little honey and clarified butter together, in unequal proportions, and put up the compound on a flat piece of stone, and shall rub a bit of gold on it till some portion of it shall have been mixed with honey and clarified butter and with the same bit of gold he shall take the mixed honey and put it in the baby's mouth, with this *Mantra*: **ॐ प्र ते ददामि मधुनो घृतस्य वेदं सवित्रा प्रसूतं मघोनाम् । आयुष्मान्गुप्तो देवताभिः शतं जीव शरदो लोके अस्मिन् ।** He shall then wash clean the bit of gold and putting it on the right ear of the baby, he shall bring his own mouth close to the baby's and shall say: **ॐ मेधां ते देवः सविता मेधां देवी सरस्वती । मेधां अश्विनौ देवावाधत्तां पुष्करस्रजौ ।** Putting again the piece of gold on the left ear of the baby he shall repeat the same verse. He shall then lightly touch with the span of his right hand both the shoulders of the baby at the same moment, and repeat thus : **अश्मा भव परशुर्भव हिरण्यमस्तृतं भव । वेदो वै पुत्रनामासि स जीव शरदः शतम् । ॐ इन्द्र श्रेष्ठानि द्रविणानि धेहि चित्तिं दक्षस्य सुभगत्वमस्मे । पोषं रयीणामरिष्टिं तनूनां स्वाद्मानं वाचः सुदिनत्वमह्नाम् । ॐ अस्मे प्रयन्धि मघवन्नृजीषिन्निन्द्र रायो विश्ववारस्य भूरेः । अस्मे शतं शरदो जीवसे धा अस्मे वीराञ्छश्वत इन्द्र शिप्रिन् ॥** Then, to secure well-being and long life for the new-born, he shall say : **अङ्गादङ्गात्संभवसि हृदयादधि जायसे । आत्मा वै पुत्रनामासि स जीव शरदः शतम् ।** And with this he shall thrice smell the head of the baby. And having returned to the sacrifice, he shall complete it. Then with cold water, he shall wash the right breast of the mother, and shall make her suckle the babe with this *Mantra*: **ॐ इमां कुमारो जरां धयतु दीर्घमायुः प्रजीवसे । अस्मै स्तनौ प्रयुञ्जाना आयुर्वर्चो यशो बलम् ।** He shall then give cows, lands, *tila* corn, and gold to Brâhmaṇas as presents."

पुरोधस्—**पुरो धीयत इति पुरोधाः । आकरोद्भवः**—**आकुर्वन्त्यत्र, आकीर्यन्ते धातवोऽत्र इति वा आकरः** a mine. **आकर उद्भवः अस्य**; in its original or in its originae or uncut state. प्रयुक्तसंस्कार—(1) With the purificatory ceremonies performed; (2) subjected to grinding or the polishing process. *Cf. infra* VI. 32; संस्कारोल्लिखितो महामणिः Śâk. VI. 5.

Śl. 19. सुखश्रवाः—सुखयतीति सुखः now see com. वारयोषिताम्—वार a multitude, वारस्य योषितः; or वार a day; a woman that can be had for a day. दिवौकसाम्—Malli. takes this as a comp. of दिव् and ओकस् and so has to justify it by referring it to the पृषोदरादि class. The comp., however, will be regular if we analyse it as दिवमोको येषां ते; दिव *neu.*; 'मन्दरः सैरिभः शक्रभवनं खं दिवं नभः' इति त्रिकाण्डशेषः । Malli. himself seems to take it thus elsewhere; see śl. 47 *infra*. मागधीपतेः—The reference to मागधी is significant; the poet does not say तस्य भूपतेः; the king's joy was all the greater as the son was born of सुदक्षिणा as desired by him; see I. 65.

Śl. 20. न संयतः &c.—On the custom of liberating prisoners on the birth of a son and heir to the throne, and on other joyous occasions; *cf.* Hem. quoted in the ft.-note; and *infra* XVII.19-20 रक्षितुः—This explains why there were no prisoners whom he might set free. पितृणाम्—According to the Hindu *S'âstras*, a man remains indebted to his ancestors as long as he gets no son. Hence the compulsory character of the marriage rite among the Hindus. See note to I. 71.

Śl. 21. श्रुतस्य—श्रूयते इति श्रुतं-knowledge gained by means of the ear; hence the various Śâstras; see V. 2. युधि &c.—It will be seen from the 4th canto that this expectation of the king was also fulfilled. अर्भकः—ऋध्यते वृद्धिं प्राप्यत इति । परेषाम्—पूर्व, पर &c. are pronouns when they imply व्यवस्था *i. e.*, denote mere relation in time, space or person, and are not class names. See Pâṇ I. 1. 43. Thus पर properly means 'one who stands in a specified relative order of space to another; hence is 'different from him.' It is through this meaning of 'different' that the meaning 'enemy or adversary' is obtained by उपचार. *Cf.* Manoramá—देशवाचितया व्यवस्थाविषययोरेव परापरशब्दयोरुपचारात्प्रतिवादिनि च प्रयोगः &c. अवेक्ष्य धातोः &c.—This der. is of course poetical. See, however, Saṃj.

Śl. 22. शरीरावयवैः—अवयव (*a*) limbs; (*b*) digits. हरिदश्वः—The sun he has seven horses, all of green colour, harnessed to his chariot, called by the name हरित्. दीधितेः—The ray referred to here is called सुषुम्ण. It is one of the principal rays of the sun which causes the moon to wax; *cf.* सूर्यरश्मिः सुषुम्णो यस्तर्पितस्तेन चन्द्रमाः । कृष्णपक्षेऽमरैः शश्वत्पीयते वै सुधामयः ॥ Vishṇu-Purâṇa. चन्द्रमाः—चन्द्रं कर्पूरं सादृश्येन माति तुलयतीति चन्द्रमाः Uṇâ. IV. 228; or चन्द्रमाह्लादं मिमीते निर्मिमीते इति । or कालं मिमीते इति माः । the maker of time; माश्चासौ चन्द्रश्च

राजदन्तादिः । or चन्द्रश्चासौ माः । The pleasant maker of time. The sun and the moon are both the keepers of time; *cf.* ये द्वे कालं विधत्तः Śâk. I. 1; but the moon is called the pleasant time-maker as her rays do not hurt the eye. *Cf.* Kum. I. 25 quoted in the ft.-note.

Śl. 23. उमा—For a poetic account of the name, *cf.* उ मेति मात्रा तपसो निषिद्धा पश्चादुमाख्यां सुमुखी जगाम Kum. I. 26; ओर्महेशस्य मा लक्ष्मीरिति वा । वृषाङ्कः-वृषः अङ्कः यस्य; see वृषभध्वज II. 36. शरजन्मना-Kártikeya, so called because he was born in the *S ara* grass and reared there by the six divine Krittikâs. See foot-note and Malli. on II. 75.

Śl. 24. रथाङ्ग &c.-रथस्याङ्गं चक्रं नाम यस्यासौ रथाङ्गनामा । Now see Samj. भावबन्धनम्—Malli. takes भाव in the sense of हृदय and he is supported in this by Bhavabhuti's lines 'अन्तःकरणतत्त्वस्य दम्पत्योः स्नेहसंश्रयम् । आनन्दग्रन्थिरेकोऽयमपत्यमिति बध्यते ॥' अन्तःकरण is given as one of the senses of भाव in the Vâchaspatya where it is derived fr. भू चिन्तायाम्+करणे अच् । Châr. Vall. and others understand by भाव, चेतोविकार a particular feeling or emotion produced by affection or love; in this case भावबन्धन may mean 'that which strengthens or steadies affection;' or which is founded on love. For this sense of भाव *cf.* VI. 36; Kum. III. 35. Either of these meanings will suit the context. परस्पराश्रयम्--which had each of them for its आश्रय or support रथाङ्गनाम्नोरिव-Poets suppose that the very separation of the Chakravâka birds creates longing in each for the other and thus it ever increases their love for each other. See *infra* VIII. 56.

पर्यचीयत--Imperf. 3rd pers. sing. of the passive of चि 5th conj. with परि.

Śl. 25. नम्र--See note on अजस्र below, s'l. 44. तेन--The sing. shows that the king's joy was due to each of his son's actions separately, and not necessarily to all these taking place simultaneously. अर्भक--See VII. 67. This s'l. is quoted in the Sâh.-Dar. as an instance of वत्सलरस. See ft.-note.

Śl. 26. शरीरयो०--शरीरस्य (नृपशरीरेण) योगः शरीरयोगस्तस्माज्जायन्ते तैः. उपान्त &c.—उपान्ते स्थितौ ययोः or उपगतावन्तमुपान्तौ &c.; see Samj.; 'with eyes closed at the extremities.' This is the sign of extreme pleasure, a spontaneous action of the body, being the result of a thrill of joy, rather than a wilful action, as S. P. Pandit's note seems to suggest. *Cf.* शृङ्गेण च स्पर्शनिमीलिताक्षीं मृगीमकण्डूयत कृष्णसारः । Kum. III. 36. चिरात् &c.-after or for a long time. जानातीति ज्ञः सुतस्पर्शरसस्य ज्ञः सुतस्पर्शरसज्ञस्तस्य भावस्तत्ता ताम् । Knew (experienced) after a long time (*i. e.* a period of unrealized longing) the deliciousness of the touch of a son;

know that he was enjoying the touch of a son after a long time, so benumbed was he with joy; or it may mean 'attained, for a long time, to the condition of enjoying &c.'; see ft.-note. Also *cf.* Śák. VII. 17.

Śl. 27. परार्ध्य &c.—परस्मिन्नर्धे भवं परार्ध्यम् । and as it is the upper half of any thing that is high up and more important, परार्ध्य means 'the best' (उत्कृष्ट). See ft.-note, and *infra* VI. 4. स्थितेरभेत्ता—not the transgressor, *i. e.* the preserver, of proper conduct (the social order). This he did by keeping himself within the limits of his own duties and not allowing each individual to violate his. *Cf. supra* I. 17. स्वमूर्तिभेदेन—applies both to Raghu and Vishṇu; see ft.-note. गुणाग्र्य० &c.—अग्रे भवमग्र्यं गुणेषु अग्र्यं गुणाग्र्यं तेन &c; see Saṃj. पतिः प्रजानाम्—This is purposely left uncompounded that it may apply to the king as well.

Śl. 28. वृत्तचूडः—वृत्ता चूडा यस्य । चूडा is the ceremony of cutting the hair on the head of a child, leaving only one lock on the crown of Bráhmaṇa boys and five in the case of Kshatriyas; see Uttar. V. 2 (चञ्चत्पञ्चचूडः &c.). The ड here is changed to ल for the sake of alliteration; for a similar change *cf.* IX. 46. See Manu quoted in the Saṃj. For this ceremony see Nârâyaṇabhaṭṭa's Prayogaratna, under that heading. काकपक्षकैः—काकपक्ष इवेति काकपक्षकः (looking like a crow's wing), locks of hair left on either side of the head after tonsure, so called. अमात्य—अमा समीपे भवः । "means originally a companion at home, a follower". S. P. Pandit. सवयोभिः—समानं वयो येषां तैः । समान becomes स when followed by वयस्; see Pâṇ VI. 3. 85; lit. 'one of the same age'; it however means technically 'a friend of thes ame age;' see the quotation in Saṃj. यथावद्ग्रहणेन—यथा यादृशमर्हतीति यथावत् । Here वत् has the sense of 'as is proper for one'; see Pâṇ V. I. 117. वाङ्मयं—वाचः विकारः; the science of words, literature. समुद्रम्—समुनत्तीति; fr. उन्द् and the Uṇádi aff र; or समीचीना उद्रा जलचरविशेषा यस्मिन्निति, सह मुद्रया मर्यादया वर्तत इति वा ।

Śl. 29 उपनीतम्—उपनयन lit. 'leading near' *i. e.* either to the Guru for instruction in the Veda, or to the Veda, which is done after investiture with the sacred thread; hence the thread-ceremany. विपश्चितः-वि प्रकृष्टं निश्चिनोति चिन्तयति चेतति वा विपश्चित्, पृषोदरादिः । विनिन्युः—विनि means to train, to instruct; and is Par. in this sense. *Cf.* II. 8, V. 10, X. 76; for its Âtm. use *cf.* IV. 65 गुरुप्रियं—may also be taken as a Bah. (see ft.-note)–"to whom his preceptors were dear" *i. e.* who loved them. क्रिया &c.—an action directed to or an effort bestowed upon; here, instruction. For various senses *cf.* I. 58, 76, 10, 44; V. 7. 11, 45 &c. For parallel passages see ft.-note. हि—may also be taken in the sense of अवधारण, प्रसीदत्येव. वस्तु—the proper material; a fit object.

Śl. 30. धियः गुणैः—The following qualities of the intellect are enumerated in the s'l. quoted by Malli. from Kâm.—(1) Desire to hear, hence earnest desire for knowledge; (2) Attention; (3) Comprehension or proper understanding; (4) Retention; (5) Ratiocination or consideration of the pros and cons; (6) Grasping the correct sense and (7) Knowledge of truth or correct knowledge. Or ऊह (inference) and अपोह (rejection), may be taken separately. उदारधीः—उदारा excellent, of the first class धीः यस्य; explains how he had all the qualities of धी. चतस्रः विद्याः—see Samj. and note to I. 23. चतुरर्णवोपमाः—an instance of त्रिपदबहुव्रीहि. This indicates the immensity of the four lores. पवनातिपातिभिः—पवनमतिलङ्घ्य पतितुं शीलमेषामिति तथोक्तास्तैः, qualifies हरिभिः and गुणैः. The qualities of Raghu's intellect penetrating the various regions of thought, with a rapidity unkuown to the wind, and the horses of the sun journeying through the sky with an enormous velocity, are fitly compared with each other. It should also be noted that the sun has seven horses and the qualities are also seven. The sun's horses bear him through the four regions of space; and the qualities of Raghu's intellect carried him through the four lores. The ध्वनि here is this:—As the sun moves lighting up places where his rays penetrate, so Raghu by virtue of his keen intellect threw light on many an obscure passage in the *S'âstras.*

Śl. 31. रौरवीं—*Cf.* कार्ष्णरौरववास्तानि चर्माणि ब्रह्मचारिणः । Manu. II. 41 अस्त्रं—अस्यते what is thrown इति; fr. अस् 4 P.; or अस 1. P. to shine and त्र (ष्ट्रन् Uṇâdi); a missile, distiugnished from शस्त्र which is taken in the hand (as a sword). मन्त्रवत्—*Mantras* are the magical spells which endow the arrows with peculiar virtue; see V. 57. धनुर्धरः—धरतीति धरः, धनुषो धरः.

Śl. 32. वत्सतरः—तनुः वत्सः वत्सतरः । The तर is added by 'वत्सोक्षाश्वर्षभेभ्यश्च तनुत्वे' Pâṇ. V. 3. 91; lit. a calf in which there is very little (तनु) of वत्सत्व or the first stage of development, *i. e.* which has just entered she second stage of development. प्रथमवया वत्सस्तस्य तनुत्वं द्वितीयवयःप्राप्तिः । &c. Vámana. Here the 3rd stage उक्षता is left out. यौवन &c.—यौवनेन भिन्नं 'broken off, obscured', (*i. e.* left bhind) शैशवं (शिशोर्भावः) यस्य; who has just ceased to be a boy and arrived at the stage of youth. See ft.- notes. गाम्भीर्यमनोहरं—गाम्भीर्यं depth or steadiness of character; it is defined as भीशोकक्रोधहर्षाद्यैर्गाम्भीर्यं निर्विकारता। S.-Dar. III. 52 (the being unaffected by fear, grief, anger, joy &c.)

Śl. 33. गोदानविधेः—गोदान is the ceremony of cutting the hair performed in the 16th or 18th year, when a youth is shaved for the first time shortly before marriage. See ft.-note, and Nârâyaṇa. bhaṭṭa's Prayogaratna. Some derive it from गो having its usual sense of 'a cow', cows being given to Brâhmaṇas as presents on such occasions. विवाहदीक्षाम्—the vow of marriage. "दीक्षा is the assumption of a particular observance or observances during the performance of a ceremony. A sacrificer is said to take the यज्ञदीक्षा i. e. the vow to observe particular rules of conduct till the end of the sacrifice. So the young prince taking up the विवाहदीक्षा, binds himself to live in the condition of a married man until he should enter the Vânaprasthâśrama." (Pandit's note). तमोनुदं--तमः नुदति dispels इति तमोनुद् (fr. नुद्+क्विप्). दक्षसुताः--दक्ष is one of the *Prajâpatis*, and a son of Brahmâ, being born from his right thumb, as his wife was from the left. Daksha had 28 daughters of whom 27 were married to Chandra and the youngest (सती) to Śiva; see Kum. I. 21. The 27 daughters are the 27 constellations of stars in the 12 lunar mansions. According to other accounts he had 50, 60, or 44 daughters, out of whom thirteen, or according to some seventeen, or even eight according to others, became the wives of Kaśyapa, and became by him the mothers of Gods, demons, men &c.;

Śl. 35. अंसलः—having muscular shoulders. The affix ल (लच्) here denotes strength. It will be more grammatical to expound the Comp. as अंसो बलमस्य विद्यते इत्यंसलः। According to the Vṛittikâra, अंस in its proper sense cannot take ल; अंसौ अस्य स्तः will be अंसवान्. कपाटवक्षाः--कं वातं शिरो वा पाटयते इति कपाटः । कर्मण्यण्। the leaf or panel of a door, or a door; कपाटमिव वक्षः यस्य सः। परिणद्ध०--परिणद्धा (full-developed, well-rounded) कन्धरा neck यस्य; कं शिरो धारयति। खच्। or कं शिरो धरतीति। अच्। कन्धरा. वपुःप्रकर्षात्--प्रकर्ष excellence, due to muscular development. Prof. Ray is right in thinking that this sloka ought naturally to precede s'l 33.

Śl. 35. नितान्तगुर्वी--Heavy because of the responsibilities of government long sustained (Châr.). लघयिष्यता—This he would do by delegating to his son some of his regal functions. धुरं—*Cf.* V. 66. निसर्ग &c.--S. P. Pandit thinks that by a zeugma the word 'विनीत' means 'modest' when taken with *Nisarga*, and 'disciplined' when with *Saṃskâra*. इति--expresses हेतु (reason) here. युवराजशब्दभाक्-युवा चासौ राजा च युवराजः। युवराज इति युवराजस्य वा शब्दः युवराजशब्दः now see com.

It appears to have been an ancient custom in Asiatic monarchies, for the heir-apparent to be solemnly recognized as such in the life-time of his father by being formally installed in the regal dignity, and admitted to a share in the administration. The object of this custom appears to have been threefold. In the first place, it settled the succession, and prevented any civil war between rival claimants for throne which might arise at the death of the sovereign. Secondly, it furnished an aged or infirm ruler with a youthful coadjutor, who might relieve him of all the more active duties of Government, military as well as civil. Finally, it familiarized the young Prince with the administration of Justice and other branches of Government, and enabled him on the death of the father to fulfil with efficiency all the duties of sovereignty. Under such circumstances an heirapparent on attaining his majority would be solemnly installed as Râjâ, and henceforth he would receive the title of Yuvarâja, or 'Young Râjâ,' and would be presumed to act in subordination to his father, who would still retain the title of Mahârâja, or Great Râjâ. The installation of a Yuvarâja would naturally be regarded throughout the Râj as an important political event, since the accession of a young and promising Prince would be expected to result in such an infusion of new blood into the administration as would materially affect the interests of both chieftains and the people. The eldest son, properly educated, naturally occupied the position of a Yuvarâja. (See Wheeler's History of India, Vol. II. Chap. VI.).

Śl. 36. अनन्तरम्--अविद्यमानमन्तरं दूरता यस्य तत्; सन्निहितम्; for this sense *cf*. VII. 21. अनन्तरम् may also be taken as an *adv*. (after Raghu was installed as युवराज). आस्पदम्--आत्मनः पदं given by Malli. is the meaning and not the विग्रहवाक्य of आस्पदम्; आपद्यते अस्मिन्नित्यास्पदम्। 'आस्पदं प्रतिष्ठायामिति साधुः'। Pâṇ. VI. 1. 146. तत्—may also be taken as not compounded. गुणाभिलाषिणी--Malli. seems to add here णिनि in the sense of the agent (कर्तरि) by the rule 'नन्दिग्रहिपचादिभ्यो ल्युणिन्यचः' Pâṇ. III. 1. 134. But the root लष् is not to be found among the roots of the ग्रहादि class. It may be derived as गुणानभिलषितुं शीलमस्याः। by the general rule 'सुप्यजातौ णिनिस्ताच्छील्ये,' Páṇ. III. 2. 78. But according to some the root लष् ought to take उक (उकञ्) in this sense by Pâṇ. III. 2. 154. The best way to avoid all difficulties of grammar will be to derive it as गुणेषु अभिलाषोऽस्या अस्तीति गुणाभिलाषिणी। नवावतारम्—अवतरति आविर्भवत्यनेनेत्यवतारः an incarnation. The poet here supposes the old lotus to reappear in the shape of the bud. This also applies to Raghu; for according to the Hindu notion, the father takes a new birth in the form of this son.

Śl. 37. विभावसु—विभा वसु धनं यस्य whose wealth is light; refers to the sun and fire; here, the latter. It sometimes means 'the moon' also. सारथिना—here सारथि has the secondary meaning of 'a helper.' घनव्यपायेन—घनानां व्यपायः (the passing away or disappearance of) यस्मिन् सः the autumnal season; तेन। गभस्तिमान्—गः ज्ञेयवर्गः (knowable things) तं बभस्ति दीपयति इति गभस्तिः a ray, fr. भस् 3. Par.; गभस्तयः अस्य सन्तीति।

Śl. 38. होमतुरङ्गः—तुरेण त्वरया गच्छतीति तुरगः or तुरङ्गः or तुरङ्गमः। होमस्य तुरङ्गः। तादर्थ्ये षष्ठीसमासः। There is a reference here to the अश्वमेध, for which see note on VI. 61. शतक्रतूपमः--शतं क्रतवो यागा अस्येति शतक्रतुः। Strictly speaking the comp. शतक्रतुः should not be expounded, as it is a संज्ञा. According to western scholars क्रतुः in the Ṛigveda invariably means power, either mental or physical, *i. e.* wisdom or strength; and Indra is the god of hundred wisdoms or powers, *i. e.* whose wisdom and power are infinite. It has never in the Veda the sense of 'a sacrifice' which was attributed to it in post-Vedic times. 'It is quite possible' remarks S. P. Pandit, 'that the Vedic epithet शतक्रतु may have been misunderstood by the prosaic minds of the post-Vedic ages, and may have given rise to the current myth of Indra having performed one hundred sacrifices before he became the leader of the gods.' See note to the next s'l. क्रतूनाम्--करोति क्रियते वा इति क्रतुः; fr. कृ+अतु (क्रतु Uṇâdi 1. 77). *Cf.* Greek *Kratos*; Zenda *Khratu.*

Śl. 39. यज्वना—See I. 74. अनर्गलम्—अविद्यमानमर्गलं यस्य। अर्गल or अर्गला properly the bar or wooden bolt thrown across a door when closed; hence restraint, obstruction. The custom was to allow the sacrificial horse to go unchecked wherever it liked. The duty of the guards was simply to see that it was not captured by any one. अहार--According to the Paurâṇic accounts Indra is always alarmed whenever any mortal performs unusual religious austerties or tries to complete a hundred sacrifices, fearing lest he should lose his own position being superseded by his mortal rival; and his jealousy being excited interposes various obstacles in the way of his supposed rival in order to thwart his object. *Cf.* VI. 74; XIII. 29. शक्रः-शक्नोतीति lit. the powerful one. किल--as the story goes, as we hear. *Cf.* I. 27; II. 27; IV. 5 &c.

Śl. 40. विषाद०--विषाद dejection or disappointment; प्रतिपत्ति the adoption of proper measures, course of action; for a different sense see VIII. 65. च-च. The repetition of च indicates that the two actions, the guards remaining paralysed with wonder, and Nandinî's appearance--were simultaneous. श्रुतप्रभावा--whose (superhuman) power was well known. This prepares the reader for the help she was to give in the matter.

Śl. 41. निस्यन्द—Chár., followed by Vall. and Din., understands by निस्यन्द, स्वेद. पुरस्कृतः सताम्—If पुरस्कृत means पूजित, as Malli. takes it, then सतां is subjective Gen. by 'क्तस्य च वर्तमाने' Páṇ. II. 3. 67, but if it means अग्रतः कृतः *i. e.* 'chief of, foremost among,' then the Gen. is specific, by the rule 'यतश्च निर्धारणम् ।' The latter meaning seems preferable. अतीन्द्रिय-*Prádi* comp.: see Saṃj. भावेषु—things, objects of perception. Châr. translate भाव by प्रमेय and Vall. by पदार्थ, which means the same as वस्तु. For other meanings *cf.* infra V. 64, VI. 36, VIII. 52, &c. उपपन्न०—come to have, produced. See notes on II. 16. This conferring on Raghu of the power of perception of the imperceptible is an exhibition of Nandini's divine power (प्रभाव).

Śl. 42. पूर्वतः—Here तस् has the sense of the Loc. पर्वतपक्ष-शातनम्—शातयति इति शातनः, now see Saṃj.; or पर्वतपक्षाणां शातनं यस्मात् । The mountains had wings in ancient times, with which they flew about and grew very troublesome and refractory. On seeing this Indra cut off their wings with his thunderbolt, when hundreds of them flew to the sea for shelter; see XIII. 7. Only Maināka is said to have escaped the fate which overtook others. See Kum. I. 20. It is said that the demon Hiraṇyáksha, by virtue of his magical power, endowed the mountains with wings. See Harivaṃs'a quoted in the ft.-note. For the real nature of these mountains with wings, see not on लोकालोक I. 68. ददर्श देवम्—On this Prof. Ray thus remarks :—

"This sudden introduction of Nandinî may appear at first sight rather childish on the part of the poet. But it should be remembered that Indra was here trying his best to remain concealed, and it would not have been well for the prestige of the Lord of Gods if a mortal could discover him by mortal means alone. So the intervention of supernatural agency was necessary. If so, it was better that help should come from one whose gift Raghu was, and who was in a manner already interested in the cause of Raghu."

Śl. 43. अक्ष्णां शतैः—*i. e.* ten; hence Indra is called सहस्राक्ष. The refrence here is to Indra's amours with Ahalyá, the wife of the sage Gautama. On one occasion Indra, enamoured of her beauty, assumed the form of her husband and ravished her in his absenca. According to one account Ahalyâ knew the god in disguise, but in the wantonness of her heart yielded to his desire. Gautama returning from ablution saw the god runnin gaway in disguise, and understanding at once what had happened, cursed him to be covered with a thousand sores which he afterwards changed into eyes; and also cursed his spouse to be petrified.

अनिमेष &c.—**निमेषरूपा वृत्तिः निमेषवृत्तिः । अविद्यमाना निमेषवृत्तिर्येषां तैः ।** It is a characteristic of gods that they do not wink. **हरिभिः**—See Saṃj. But according to the Śálihotra, this word has a technical meaning: **स्वकेशबाललोमानि सुवर्णाभानि यस्य तु । हरिः स वर्णतोऽश्वस्तु पीतकौषेयसुप्रभः ॥** **एनम्**—To justify the use of the form here, we must have **अन्वादेश** which it is difficult to get here. Probably '**एवम्**' is the poet's reading. **धीरेण**—**धीर** as applied to voice means 'deep and powerful', stentorian; *cf.* **नवनीलनीरधरधीरगर्जित** Uttar. VI. 17. This shows that Raghu was not at all daunted, but addressed Indra in a steady voice actually stopping him.

Śl. 44. **मनीषिभिः**—See note on **मनीषिन्** I. 11. **अजस्र** &c.—**न कदापि जस्यति** (allows no break) **इति अजस्रं सन्ततम् ।** By **नमिकम्पि** &c. Pâṇ. III. 2. 167, **र** is added to the roots **नम्, कम्प्** &c., to indicate habit (**कर्तरि ताच्छील्ये**); **जासिर्नञ्पूर्वः क्रियासातत्ये वर्तते**; Sid.-Kau.; so we have **नम्र, कम्प्र, स्मेर, अजस्र, कम्र, हिंस्र** and **दीप्र. क्रियाविघाताय**—**क्रिया** here means the sacrifices and other ceremonies connected therewith.

Śl. 45. **त्रिलोकनाथेन**—Malli. expounds this as a **त्रिपदतत्पुरुष** which is objectionable according to Páṇ. The Manoramá has this observation on this-'**कथं तर्हि त्रिलोकनाथेन सता मखद्विषः' इति कालिदासः । त्रिलोकशब्दस्यासंज्ञात्वात् । न च समाहारे द्विगुः । द्विगोरिति ङीप्प्रसङ्गात् । न च पात्रादित्वं कल्प्यम्** (It should not be considered as one of the **पात्रादि** class) '**यदि त्रिलोकीगणनापरः स्यात् ' इति प्रयोगविरोधात् । न चोत्तरपदसमासः त्रिपदतत्पुरुषस्येह दुर्लभत्वात् । उच्यते-लोकशब्दोऽत्र लोकसमुदायपरः । त्रयवयवो लोकस्त्रिलोकः शाकपार्थिवादिः । एतच्च ' द्विगोर्लुगनपत्ये ' इति सूत्रे भाष्य एव स्पष्टम् ।" त्रिलोकस्य नाथस्त्रिलोकनाथस्तेन ।** *Cf.* **त्रिलोकरक्षी महिमा हि वज्रिणः ।** Vik. 1. 5. **नियम्याः**—On this Din. has the following discussion:-Though by the general rule '**पोरदुपधात्** ' a root ending in a letter of the labial class and having **अ** for its penultimate can take **यत्**, yet by the exception '**गदमदचरयमश्चानुपसर्गे** ' the root **यम्** cannot take it when preceded by an **उपसर्ग**. How do you defend the form then ? We reply-We first add the affix and then prefix the **उप०**. Or we defend it by **ज्ञापकप्रमाण**; for Kátyâyana says '[**यस्य हि शो नियमः सुदि नैतत्तेन**] **न तत्र भवेद्विनियम्यम्** '। and he cannot use a wrong form. Or we may explain as **नियमे साधवो नियम्याः**: by Páṇ. IV. 4. 98. Or **नियमनमर्हतीति यत् । धर्मचारिणाम्**—**धर्मं चरितुं शीलं येषां तेषाम् । स चेत्स्वयं** &c.—for a similar thought *cf.* **भवादृशाश्चेदधिकुर्वते रतिं निराश्रया हन्त हता मनस्विता ।** Kir. I. 43.

Śl. 46. अङ्गं—a requisite or implement of. महाक्रतोः—A horse-sacrifice which could be performed only by a universal sovereign; also called क्रतुराट्. See VI. 61. पथः—is Acc. pl. श्रुतेः दर्शयितारः—those whose duty it is to point out the ways of, *i. e.* the rites and ceremonies enjoined by, the Vedas. This is said in conformity with the belief that the Vedas are eternal and therefore older than Indra. Some read श्रुचेः for श्रुतेः । ईश्वराः—Malli. means by महान्तः 'mighty,' 'powerful' (*cf.* महान्महत्स्येव करोति विक्रमं) as it makes the remark more sarcastic. पद्धतिम्—पादाभ्यां हन्यत इति पद्धतिः । fr. पाद+हन्+क्ति (ति); what is trodden over; hence a foot-path; a course of behaviour. पाद becomes पद् when followed by हिम, काषिन् and हति by the rule हिमकाषिहतिषु च । Pāṇ. VI. 3. 54.

Śl. 47. प्रगल्भम्—bold and intelligent. It is generally applied to a speech addressed to a person superior in rank by one inferior to him when it is uttered with confidence and without any feeling of nervousness, which he is not expected to do. *Cf.* II. 41; VI. 20. उत्तरम्—उत्तीर्यतेऽनेन । That by which one gets over. When one urges forward an argument it is a sort of barrier to his adversary and since the reply he makes in order to refute the argument takes him, as it were, over this barrier, it is termed as उत्तर.

Śl. 48. राजन्य—राज्ञो अपत्यं राजन्यः क्षत्रियः. कुमार—By thus addressing the prince Indra shows that he treats him like an ordinary Kshatriya. तथा—just so, true. तु—But, on the other hand (पक्षान्तरे). रहस्यं—See II. 40. जगत्प्रकाशम्—जगत्सु प्रकाशम् ।

Śl. 49. पुरुषोत्तमः—Mallinâtha's expounding of this seems to be objectionable. 'वाक्येन संज्ञानवगमान्निरयसमासोयम् । अत एव पुरुषेषु उत्तम इति स्वपदविग्रहोऽसंगत इत्यवोचाम' । Tb. Better to expound as पुरुषा आत्मानः । आत्मनात्मभ्यो वा उत्तम इत्यर्थे समासः (अस्वपदविग्रहः) नित्यसमासः । As Indra wishes here to emphasize the संज्ञात्व of the three words पुरुषोत्तम, महेश्वर and शतक्रतु we must take them as Nitya Compounds having no स्वपदविग्रह; so महेश्वरः--श्रेष्ठः स्वामीत्यर्थेऽस्वपदविग्रहे नित्यसमासः; also मखानां शतं विद्यते कर्तृत्वेनास्येति 'शतक्रतुः' नित्यसमासः; । द्वितीयगामी--गमिष्यतीति गामी द्वितीयं गामी द्वितीयगामी । See Samj.; or द्वितीयं गन्तुं शीलमस्य । ०गामी न-'will not refer to or indicate'.

Here the ridiculousness of Indra's argument is quite clear. He puts forth this argument as he has no better defence to give. For if शतक्रतु is a संज्ञा it could have denoted him in spite of Dilîpa's performing a hundred sacrifices, as the term हिमालय still denotes the mount Himâlaya though there are other mountains which are the abodes of snow. If it be admitted for argument that शतक्रतु is not a संज्ञा, then the best course for Indra to adopt, in order to defeat Dilîpa, would have been to perform two hundred sacrifices, or more if necessary, a thing quite within the competence of the Lord of gods.

Śl. 50. अतः—*i. e.* in order to prevent another man from becoming Śatakratu. कपिलानुकारिणा—कपिलस्यानुकारोस्यास्तीति कपिलानुकारी तेन। Kapila is an ancient sage, of whom mention is made in the Śrutis, and who is often spoken of as an incarnation of Vishṇu. According to the Sârîrakabhâshya, the Vaidic sage Kapila ought not to be confounded with Kapila the author of the Sâṃkhya Sûtras. Here it should be remembered that it was Indra himself who had stolen the horse of सगर and left it by the side of Kapila. But Indra purposely conceals the fact and makes mention of Kapila in order to strike terror into Raghu's heart by implying that he will destroy him as Kapila had done the sons of Sagara. सगरस्य-सगरः—a king of the solar race, son of Bâhu by Yádavî, who was driven out of his kingdom by the Haihayas. Poison was given to his mother by a rival wife of his father, by virtue of which the fœtus remained in the womb for seven years. After this Báhu died, and his wife was delivered of a prince who was named Sagara (born with poison-गरेण सहितः) by the sage और्व. He vanquished the Yavanas and made them shave their heads entirely. See Vâyu-P. Vol. II. Chap. 26. For an account of Kapila's taking away the sacrificial horse of Sagara and reducing to ashes his sixty thousand sons, see ft.-note and note on भगीरथ IV. 32. See also Vish.-Puráṇa Vol. II. XXVI. 146-147.

Śl. 51. पुरन्दरम्—see *supra* note on पुरन्दरश्रीः II. 74. सर्गः—means here 'determination;' for this sense *cf. infra* XIV. 42, and Śiś. XIX. 38. रघुम्-the mention of the name indicates Raghu's self-confidence and chivalrous spirit. कृतिन्—may also be derived as कृतमस्यास्तीति। प्राशस्त्यार्थे इन्।

Śl. 52. उन्मुखः—Raghu stood with his face turned up in order to observe the movements of his adversary. शरासनम्—शरा अस्यन्ते अनेन। आलीढ &c.—विशेषेण शोभितुं शीलमस्येति विशेषशोभी। Now see Saṃj. आलीढ—See ft.-note and comp. Kum. III. 70, quoted therein. According to the lexicon quoted by Malli., there are five postures which archers assume when fighting. They are;—(1) वैशाख in which the feet are separated sideways by three Vitastis (about 24 inches); (2) मण्डल when the feet are so stretched that the part of the body from the waist appears like a gateway; (3) समपद when both the feet are placed evenly; (4) आलीढ in which the right foot is advanced and the left bent back; and (5) प्रत्यालीढ which is the reverse of आलीढ. Vallabha mentions eight postures, substituting कूर्म for मण्डल and adding पद्मासन, दुराकार and गरुडक्रम. वपुःप्रकर्षेण—see 34, *supra.* विडम्बितेश्वरः—the root विडम्ब् is used when the imitation is not exact, though much like the original. *Cf. infra* IV. 17: and विडम्बितकिरातनृपतिवपुषा: Kir. XII. 38. The allusion here is to the destruction of Tripura (the three cities of gold, copper and iron, respectively built by Maya for the *asuras* in the sky, in mid-space, and on earth) by Śiva, who had to wait for a thousand years in the आलीढ posture with his face upturned to watch for the moment when the three cities would meet, which was the right time for shooting the arrow, the cities being at other times invulnerable. See ft.-note.

Śl. 53. अवष्टम्भमयेन—S. P. Pandit translates this by 'with an arrow consisting of a post' *i. e.* 'as big as a post'; but this does not seem to be the meaning here. Not because there is anything impossible about it; for the Mâh.-Bhâr. tells us that Bhîshma's bow was as long as a tâla tree (तालध्वजं धनुर्धुन्वन्), while the arrows discharged by many of the warriors of those times were as big as a yoke or a pole; see Bh. P. 49, 35; but because the context does not justify it. It is decidedly better, as remarked by the late Prof. Apte in his Dic., to translate this by ' with an arrow consisting of his defiance' *i. e* the challenge thrown out, and the bold front presented, by him to Indra. Châr. and Vall. give this sense of the word, and Mallinâtha's rendering 'स्तम्भरूपेण' though somewhat ambiguous, seems to favour this meaning. It certainly brings out more forcibly the heroic conduct of Raghu if we suppose that he contented himself with a mere challenge and waited for his enemy to commence fighting. हृदि-मर्मणि struck at his heart. This clearly shows that अवष्टम्भ means ' defiance '. Raghu's defiance wounded Indra's pride. A real arrow would have struck him on the chest (वक्षसि and not हृदि). गोत्रभिद्—गां पृथिवीं त्रायन्त इति गोत्रास्तान् भिनत्तीति । Indra so called on account of his having lopped off the wings of mountains. नवाम्बुदानीक &c.—The standard of new clouds *i. e.* the rainbow (इन्द्रधनुः). अनीक—properly an army; hence a multitude of. समधत्त बाणम्—This shows that Indra did not wait to be struck first, but fitted an arrow and even discharged it. The reason for this overhastiness is supplied by the epithet ' अमर्षणः'.

Śl. 54. भुजान्तरं—the chest; *cf.* शृङ्गान्तरम् II. 26, *supra.* भीमासुर०—For असुर see note on असुराश्रैः II. 37; भीमासुराणां शोणिते उचितः

(accustomed to drink). अनास्वादित०—न आस्वादितमनास्वादितम्, पूर्वमनास्वादितमनास्वादितपूर्वम्; a comp. सह सुपा. पूर्व takes परनिपात (comes latter in the comp.) as suggested by Pán.'s *Sûtra* भूतपूर्वे चरट् आशुगः—आशु quickly गच्छति इति: an arrow. It also means 'the wind;' 'आशुगौ वायुविशिखौ' इत्यमरः।

Sl. 55. कुमारविक्रमः—विशेषेण कामत्यनेनेति विक्रमोऽतिशक्तिता excessive prowess; कुमारस्येव विक्रमो यस्य। See, however, note on 'मुनिवृत्तिनाम्' I. 8. कुत्सितः मारः मदनः यस्य: or कौ on earth मारयति दुष्टान् (fr. कु+मृ cau.) पचाद्यच्। इति कुमारः. According to Svámî he is so called because of his perpetual celibacy. The Váyu-P., however, refers to देवसेना as the wife of Kárttikeya. सुरद्विपास्फालन &c.—*Cf.* Kum. III. 22. This shows that Indra was no carpet-warrior with whom Raghu had to deal. *Cf.* Din. सुरद्विपेत्यादिविशेषणद्वयेन शक्रस्य वीरत्वं सुकुमारत्वं चोक्तम्। भुजे—*i. e.* the left arm, which served Sachî as her pillow. *Cf.* रामबाहुरुपधानमेष ते। Uttar. I. 37. शचीपत्र &c.—पत्राकारं विशेषकं पत्रविशेषकं a Karm. of the शाकपार्थिवादि class; शच्याः पत्रविशेषकं शचीपत्रविशेषकम्। ०षकैरङ्किते, which was marked with a print of the ornamental leaf-like figures traced by Śachî on her forehead, or cheeks. Raghu planted his arrow exatly in the place where Śachi much liked to rest her forehead. This gives the reason why the insult was unbearable to Indra. स्वनामचिह्नम्—It was customary with ancient warriors to engrave their names on their arrows. *Cf.* VII. 38; Vik. V. 7.

Sl. 56. मयूर—मयते मध्यामतिशयेन रौतीति वा मयूरः। जहार &c.—This was the greatest offence that Raghu could have given to Indra. Even to this day the loss of the standard is considered the greatest disgrace that an enemy can inflict upon the other party. See Samj.

Sl. 57. उपान्तस्थित &c.—अन्तस्य समीपमुपान्तम्। Avy. Comp; उपान्तं स्थिता उपान्तस्थिताः। Now see Samj. सिद्धः—The Siddhas are semi-divine beings characterized by eight superhuman powers called *Siddhis*; (अणिमादिसिद्धाः Malli. on Kum. I 5). They are eighty-eight thousand in number, of subdued passions, continent and pure, not subject to death, and free from all worldly desires. See Wilson's Vish. P. p. 227. गरुत्मदाशीविष &c.—गरुतः पक्षा विद्यन्त एषामिति गरुत्मन्तः winged; the addition of this is necessary to make the serpents resemble the feathered arrows. आशिषि विषं येषामित्याशीविषाः। पृषोदरादित्वात्साधुः। So the c mentators on Amar. According to some it is a regular form; अ यां विषं येषां ते। आशी being a word by itself. तुमुलं—ताम्यन्ति वीरा अत्र: पोदरादिः: wherein the warriors shout vehemently; see also note on तुमुल *infra* IV. 62.

Śl. 58. अतिप्रबन्ध &c.—अतिशयितः प्रबन्धोतिप्रबन्धः । Uninterrupted succession, close continuity. वासवः–The commentators on Amara derive this word in three ways: (1) वसवो देवा वसूनि धनान्यस्य वा सन्तीति; (2) वसोरपत्यमिति वा; (3) वासं देव्यानां वातीति वा । Of these the second is not supported by the Purāṇas. Indra is the son of कश्यप who is not a Vasu. Of the other two, the third seems better, being in accordance with Indra's character. स्वतश्च्युतम्—This applies to Raghu also. Raghu who was formed out of the energies of the *Lokapālas* of whom Indra was the greatest, may be said to have sprung from Indra. See II. 75; III. 11.

Śl. 59. प्रकोष्ठे—प्रकोष्ठ is the part between the elbow and the wrist. हरिचन्दन—हरेरिन्द्रस्य चन्दनम् । The celestial sandal tree; it is one of the five trees of heaven—पञ्चैते देवतरवो मन्दारः पारिजातकः । सन्तानः कल्पवृक्षश्च पुंसि वा हरिचन्दनम् । Ak.; here, its paste. प्रमथ्य &c.—धीरं नादितुं शीलमस्या धीरनादिनी । प्रमथ्यमानार्णव इव धीरनादिनी ताम् । or प्रमथ्यमानार्णवस्य धीरनादः प्रमथ्यमानार्णवधीरनादः सोस्त्यस्या इति ताम् । The story of the churning of the milky ocean for *Amṛita* by the gods and the demons under the guidance of Vishṇu is well known; see Bhág. P. VIII. 7, 8. शशाङ्का०—शशाङ्कस्य अर्धः a part शशाङ्कार्धः; here अर्ध does not mean 'a half'; for in that case अर्ध is neu. and the comp. will be अर्धशशाङ्क by the rule अर्धं नपुंसकम्; स इव मुखमस्य. बिडौजसः—According to Bhânujî Dîkshita बिडति भिनत्तीति बिडं भेदकम् । बिडमोजो यस्य । This leaves no irregularity in the Comp. Châr. also derives it thus.

Śl. 60. विवृद्धमत्सरः—मत्सर vehement anger; it was increased because Raghu a mortal kept him at bay. विद्विषः—विशेषेण द्वेष्टि इति विद्विट् तस्य. महीध्र &c.—महीं धरन्तीति महीधाः । Malli. has धारयन्ति which is probably a slip. The allusion has been already explained. See Râm. Sun. Kâṇḍa, I. 115-119. स्फुरत्प्रभा०—स्फुरन्ति प्रभामण्डलानि यस्य तत्. अस्त्रम्—This is the thunderbolt, the peculiar weapon of Indra. It is said to have been fashioned out of the bones of the age दधीच (or दधीचि) by *Vis'vakarman*, for the destruction of Vṛitra. It is sometimes described as circular, like Vishṇu's *chakra*, or shaped like a quoit, but with a broader circumference and a smaller central hole, and when hurled against an enemy, the fire of lightning is said to issue forth in destructive flames from its perifery.

Śl. 61. सैनिक—सेनायां समवेताः सैनिकाः । सह &c.—Raghu's fall was the cause; the tears shed by his soldiers the effect. But so imperceptible was the interval between the two that they might be said to have taken place simultaneously. निमेषमात्रात्—निमेषणं निमेषः

the act of winking once; निमेष एव निमेषमात्रम् । By the rule 'सप्तमीपञ्चम्यौ कारकमध्ये' the Abl. or the Loc. may be used to express the time or space between two actions. Hence निमेषमात्रात्० or मात्रे० will do सैनिक०—हर्षजा निस्वना हर्षनिस्वनाः, a comp. of the शाकपार्थिवादि class.

Sl. 62. शब्दव्यवहार &c.—व्यवहारः—वि नानार्थेऽव संदेहे हरणं हार उच्यते । नानासंदेहहरणाद्व्यवहार इति स्मृतः ॥ इति कात्यायनः । So व्यवहार primarily means 'what removes all doubts'; and since *all* doubts are not removed unless we put into practice or use the knowledge we aquire, it secondarily means '*use*'. This is the meaning here. विपक्षः—विरुद्धः पक्षोऽस्येति विपक्षः । वृत्रहा—The killer of Vṛitra; Indra. Vṛitra was the chief of certain tribes of the demons known as the Kâlakeyas. Endowed with terrible prowess he discomfited the gods with Indra and drove them out of heaven. Whereupon the gods applied to Brahmâ for redress. The deity said—"Ye gods, go to sage Dadhîcha and solicit from him his bones. With them prepare a mighty weapon called *Vajra*, endowed with six sides and of terrible roar. With that weapon Indra would be able to kill Vṛitra." See above, note on अत्र s'l. 60. The gods accordingly repaired to the sage who, for the good of the three worlds, renounced his body. Viśvakarmà fabricated the thunderbolt and with it Indra killed Vṛitra and routed the *Asuras*.

In the Veda, Vṛitra is the personification of an imaginary malignant influence, the demon of darkness and drought, supposed to take possession of the clouds, making them obscure the sky and keep back the waters. He is variously designated as Vṛitra, Ahi, Śambara, Namuchi, Bala &c. Indra is represented as battling successfully with this influence and letting loose the pent-up waters to the delight of the world. The clouds are also poetically pictured as the castles or towns of the demons which he shatters with his thunderbolt.

पदं हि &c.—See ft.-note. Virtues set foot-step in, *i. e.* prevail, everywhere; or virtues make impression (पदं) everywhere.

Sl. 63. असक्तम्—lit. 'not sticking' *i. e.* cutting through; hence unimpeded. Din. reads अभग्नम् 'not repulsed', which is certainly the best reading, being the easiest; see note on 'तत्पूर्वभङ्गे' *supra* II. 42, स्फुटम् 'distinctly.' 'For at first he felt only pleased secretly (तुतोष) at the manifestation of valour by the prince, but had not given expression to his feeling'. S. P. Pandit. आह—is here used in the sense of उवाच. Strictly speaking this use of it is ungrammatical, since according to the best authorities it has never the sense of the past tense. In this respect the reading 'किमिच्छसीति स्म तमाह वासवः' is better, as it removes the difficulty of grammar.

Śl. 64. सुवर्ण &c.--सुवर्णनिर्मितः पुंखः सुवर्णपुंखः; शाकपार्थिवादित्वात्कर्मधारयः. Arrows of a superior class are described as having gold hafts. It is not easy to see why gold was needed. It was probably used for the sake of beauty; perhaps it added to the efficacy of some kind of charms (*Mantras*) with which arrows were charmed. Ordinary arrows were probably made of hard wood or steel. Or सुवर्ण may mean 'of golden, beautiful yellow colour.' प्रियंवदः--Some (including S. P. Pandit and Mr. Nandargikar) read 'प्रियंवदम्' । But the reading ' प्रियंवदः' qualifying Raghu, is certainly preferable. We know that Raghu said what was desired by Indra *i. e.* he was प्रियंवद to Indra. But what Indra said (ऋते तुरंगमात् &c.) to Raghu was not pleasing to him. We shall see further on Raghu returning home *not much* peased (नृपस्य नातिप्रमनाः &c. 67); so Indra cannot be said to have been प्रियंवद to Raghu.

Śl. 65. प्रभो—This is to imply that Indra has the power to grant his request. ततः &c.—This may also be construed as ततः अविधिना (मुख्याङ्गस्याश्वस्याभावात्) एव कर्माणि समाप्ते सति &c. अजस्र &c.—This shows that Dilîpa had taken a vow to be engaged in sacrifices without cessation for a certain peroid of time.

Śl. 66. त्रिलोचनैकांशतया—Because Śiva is said to enter the body of a sacrificer who, during the time he is under the sacrificial vow, is considered as a form of Śiva. See ft.-notes; *cf.* S'ák I. 1. Śiva is then called उग्र. Vallabha, commenting on चैतन्यमुग्रादिव दीक्षितेन V. l. V. 4. quotes--भवो जले क्षितौ शर्वो रुद्रोऽर्केऽग्नौ पशोः पतिः। दीक्षिते उग्र इत्युक्तो महादेवो निशाकरे । आकाशे भीमनामा च ईशानाख्यः समीरणे। इत्यष्टौ रुद्रनामानि कथ्यन्तेऽष्टसु मूर्तिषु ॥ दुरासदः--See VIII. 4. सदोगतः--Seated in the assembly of sacrificial priests. The sacrificer or यजमान when duly initiated for the performance of the sacrifice, is on no account to leave the sacrificial hall, or to attend to any other busines than that connected with the sacrifice. So Dilîpa was surrounded by learned Brâhmaṇas; and probably the prince, out of modesty, did not like to announce personally his own success to the king, in their presence. शृणोति--is here equivalent to शृणुयात् ।

Śl. 67. यथागतम्—आगतस्य योग्यं यथागतम् । Just as he had come *i. e.* vanished from the sight of Raghu's men as suddenly as he had come, when the sacrificial horse was stolen. On this Chár. remarks—Indra went back as he had come, *i. e.* without conquering Raghu. नातिप्रमनाः--प्रहृष्टं मनोऽस्येति प्रमनाः। अत्यन्तं प्रमनाः अतिप्रमनाः। न अति०

अतिप्रमनाः नातिप्रमनाः । The comp. here is not with नञ्, in which case it would have been 'अनतिप्रमनाः,' but with the word न which is different from नञ्, but has the same meaning; *cf.* नशयानेन Mud. I. &c. सदोगृहम्-The house where sacrificial priests sit; hence, the sacrificial house. *Cf.* अन्यगार V. 25; and the word सदस्य. न्यवर्तत—Here Malli. supplies प्रति. Kàli. seems to use the root वृत् with नि as a transitive verb. *Cf.* IX. 14.

Śl. 68. अभ्यनन्दत्—Congratulated, hailed with marks of affection. See ft.-note. शासन०—शासनं (order, message) हर्तुं शीलमस्य इति ०हारी a messenger तेन. हर्षजडेन—Moving slowly on account of joy. Malli. translates जड by शिशिर, meaning thereby that the hand was benumbed, as it were, with joy. कुलिश &c.-कुलिशात्कुलिशेन वा व्रणाः कुलिशव्रणाः तैराङ्कितम् । See ft.-note.

Śl. 69. महाक्रतूनाम्—*i. e.* the *As'vamedha* sacrifices. सोपानं-स सह विद्यमानः उप उपरि आनो गमनमनेन इति । सोपानानां परम्परा सोपानपरम्परा ताम् । The word परम्परा has no derivation. See note on tha word, II. 50. This is probably suggested by आरुरुक्षुः । ततान—'stretched out, constructed'; तन् to stretch, to spread successively; hence *to perform* (as a sacrifice).

Śl. 70. विषयव्या०—विषिण्वन्ति पुरुषं इन्द्रियाणि वा बध्नन्ति इति विषयाः तेभ्यः व्यावृत्त आत्मा (mind) यस्य. The reason is supplied by गलितवयसां इ० कुलव्रतम्. नृपतिककुदम्—Acc. case in apposition with सितातपत्रारणम् । नृपतेः ककुदं नृपतिककुदम्; the emblem or *insignia* of royalty. ककुद is properly the hump which distinguishes the full-grown Indian bull. Hence any distinguishing mark. According to Amara and Medini, the word is *mas.* and *neu*; our poet, however, seems always to prefer the *neu.* gender. *Cf.* VI. 71. मुनितरु &c.—मुनितरुनतरोश्छाया and not तरूणाम् । First because if we take the plu. the comp. will be 'तरुच्छायम्' by the rule 'छाया बाहुल्ये' Pán. II. 4. 22; secondly because anchorites have their habitation fixed under the shade of some one tree. देव्या तया—with his renowned or famous queen. See ft.-notes. गलितव०.-कुलव्रतम्-*cf. supra* I. 8 (वार्धके मुनिवृत्तीनां) and *infra,* VIII. 10, 11.

CANTO IV.

Sl. 1. राज्यं—The kingdom with the full responsibility of government, sovereignty. दिनान्ते—In the case of Raghu means 'at the close of Dilipa's days of sovereignty'. सवित्रा—सुवति प्रेरयति प्राणिनो विषयेषु इति सविता । It may also be derived from सू 'to give birth to', though not so preferably. In the Rigv. the sun (सवितृ) is very often spoken of either as 'the impellor', he who impels men to active work, or as 'the producer, since when he rises in the morning, he produces afresh, as it were, the creation, swallowed up by nocturnal darkness See Ṛigv. II. 38. In the Veda, the sun-god is represented by four deities, *viz*., सूर्य, सवितृ, पूषन्, and मित्र, being sometimes identified, at others separated, with slightly varying functions assigned to each. According to the Purāṇas, the seven rays of the sun, सुषुम्ण, हरिकेश, विश्वकर्मन्, विश्वकार्य, सम्पद्वसु, अर्वावसु and स्वराज, supply heat severally to चंद्र, the नक्षत्रs, and to बुध, शुक्र, मङ्गल, गुरु and शनि. *Cf.* Vàyu-Puráṇa Vol. II. Chap. LIII. s'l. 7–13. If we take सवितृ as an *adj.* it may also refer to Dilîpa, meaning the father of Raghu. For a similar idea, *cf.* रुचिधाम्नि भर्तरि भृशं विमलाः परलोकमभ्युपगते विविशुः । ज्वलनं त्विषः कथमिवेतरथा सुलभोऽन्यजन्मनि स एव पतिः ॥ S'is'. IX. 13.

S'l. 2. पूर्वम्—During the time of Dilipa; Malli. It may refer to the time of Raghu's यौवराज्य as well. अग्निरिवोत्थितः—अग्नि here refers to the feeling of jealousy and heart-burnings of the kings conquered by Dilipa. Raghu was known to be mightier even than his father; and his accession to the throne was as unbearable to them as the flame of a long-smouldering fire. Or, ever since the advancement of the prince to the यौवराज्य, the fire of jealousy had already been consuming the hearts of the tributary princes, as he had to force them to acknowledge his supremacy as guardian of Dilîpa's sacrificial horses. See *supra* III. 38. But now that he actually occupied the throne, it took flame as it were. On this Malli. remarks—Though the असमापिका क्रिया 'निशम्य' has for its Nom. राजानः, and the समापिका क्रिया 'उत्थितः' अग्निः, yet by transference of epithets (उपचार) the hoaring may be attributed to Agni, and so समानकर्तृत्व established; see however, foot-note.

This s'l. seems to be quite out of place here. It is connected neither with the preceding nor with the succeeding s'l. If it is genuine, its proper place is either after s'l. 15 or 20.

S'l. 3. पुरुहूतध्वजस्य—A festival in honour of Indra was held for five days, from the 8th of the bright half of Bhādrapada to the 12th. Its chief feature was the erection of a post with a flag attached to it. For its size and other particulars, see ft.-note. It has been referred to by Bhása—राजसे रज्जुभिर्बद्धः शक्रध्वज इवोत्सवे । Madh. Vyá. I. 47, and by S'ûdraka in his Mṛich. X. 7. पुरुहूत lit. he who is invoked by many, either for protection or in sacrifices; Indra. पुरुहूतध्वज originally meant the rain-bow (इन्द्रधनुः) which being the standard of fresh or retiring clouds was worshipped to show honour to Indra, the god of rain. The custom of worshipping Indra's banner, referred to by our poet here, is no longer observed now, at least in the Deccan. उन्नयन &c.—When applied to Raghu उल्लसिता नयनपंक्तयो यासां with eyes wide open through joy; when applied to इन्द्रध्वज, ऊर्ध्वं नयनपंक्तयो यासां with eyes turned upwards. अभ्युत्थान-(b) elevation, prosperity; (b) rising up. ननन्दुः-*Cf.* ft.-note (मुदिताः प्रजाश्च तेषां &c.). सप्रजाः—(b) because people take their children with them when going out to see sights.

Sl. 4. सममेव-See ft.-note. For the thought differenty expressed *Cf.* XVII. 37. द्विरदगामिना—द्विरद इव गच्छति stepping as majestically as, when taken with reference to सिंहासन, and द्विरदैर्गन्तुं (marching accompanied by) शालमस्य when aken with reference to अरिमण्डल. सिंहासनम्—सिंहाकारं सिंह इव वा आसनम्; it is made of gold; when set with jewels, not being made of gold, it is called नृपासन or भद्रासन. *Cf.* Amara-'नृपासनं तु यद्भद्रासनं सिंहासनं तु तत्। हैमम्'। ०मण्डलं—the multitude or territory of.

S'l. 5. छायामण्डल—(a) The halo or circular orb of splendour; (b) circular shade. The word छाया has a double meaning here. Raghu's royal person was so majestic that an orb of glow was always visible about him. This the poet explains by supposing that Lakshmî, the goddess of fortune, attended upon him in an invisible form and her presence endowed him with unusual splendour, which was visible in the form of a halo of light round him. Again, when an umbrella is held over a person a छायामण्डल (circular shadow) is seen about him. And this छायामण्डल (note the pun on छाया which in this case means splendour) was seen round Raghu. So the poet fancies that Lakshmî held an umbrella over him. And when Lakshmî is made to serve the king with the umbrella, the only umbrella she could use would be the lotus-umbrella, the lotus being her special favourite. किल—indicates उत्प्रेक्षा, 'methinks,' 'as it seemed.' साम्राज्यदीक्षितम्—who had entered upon the vow of discharging the duties of an emperor. For दीक्षित see note on विवाहदीक्षाम् III. 33.

S'l. 6. परिकल्पितसान्निध्या—परिकल्पितं सन्निधिरेव सान्निध्यं यया; here ष्यञ् (य) is added to सन्निध, स्वार्थे by the Vârttika चातुर्वर्ण्यादीनां स्वार्थे उपसंख्यानम्. अन्वर्थाभिः—lit. not departing from अर्थ, *i. e.*, full of meaning, true. As a general rule much of the praise bestowed upon monarchs is flattery and is therefore meaningless. But as Raghu possessed virtues of every kind, anything said in praise of him was but simple truth. उपतस्थे—served with reverence. worshipped; Sarasvatî worshipped Raghu, because a king is supposed to be a divine being. For the senses in which स्था with उप is Âtm. see Samj., and H. S. Gr. Chapter XI.

S'l. 7. मनुप्रभृतिभिः--मनु *i. e.* Vaivasvata Manu; see *supra* I. 11 and note thereon. मान्यैः—beloved and esteemed. This is used to indicate the superior excellence of Raghu. वसुन्धरा—the earth, *i. e.* the people. Raghu's subjects were so much attached to him that their attachment seemed to be the first of the kind, the attachment of their predecessors for such worthy and excellent kings as Manu &c., not being comparable with it. Here the word वसुन्धरा is used, as the earth is metaphorically spoken of as the wife of a king; *cf.* वसुमत्या हि नृपाः कलत्रिणः । VIII. 83.

S'l. 8. हि—Malli. takes this हेतौ. It may also be taken अवधारणे । सर्वस्य हि of one and all, of all, people without exception. युक्तदण्डतया—युक्तो दण्डो यस्य तस्य भावस्तत्ता तया । नातिशीतोष्णः—शीतं च उष्णं च गुणौ शीतोष्णे । अत्यन्तं शीतोष्णे अतिशीतोष्णे । ते अस्य स्त इति अतिशीतोष्णः। See *supra* note on ताम्रा II. 15. न अतिशीतोष्णो नातिः;० a comp. सह सुपा. In the case of Raghu this means 'neither too kind nor too severe'. See VIII. 9, and ft.-note. नभस्वान्—नभोऽस्त्याश्रयत्वेनास्य । अधिष्ठातृत्वेन वा । वायुर्हि नभःस्वामी । तथा च वायुपु०—'शब्दाकाशबलानां च वायुरीशस्तथा कृतः ।' इ०

S'l. 9. गुणाधिकया—अधिकस्य भावोऽधिकता गुणानामधिकता तया । सहकारस्य—सह कारयति मेलयति द्वंद्वम् । A mango-tree. It is difficult to see how the word has acquired this meaning. The mango tree is so called probably because its leaves are used in the marriage-ceremony to cover the auspicious pots &c. Or poets represent it as the favourite resort of lovers on account of its constant association with the lovely *Mádhaví* creeper; hence (*i. e.* for bringing lovers together) it may have acquired that name.

S'l. 10. नयविद्भिः—The word नय is formed irregularly (बाहुलकात्) from नी+अच् ; for by the rule 'श्रीण्भुवोऽनुपसर्गे' the proper affix for नी without a preposition is घञ् (अ) which gives the form नायः । नयं नीतिशास्त्रं विदन्तीति नयविदः । सत्—right policy, fair means; असत् crooked policy, foul means. उत्तरः—अतिशयेनोद्गत उत्तरः lit. higher; but since what is higher is reached later, it secondly means 'latter.'

S'l. 11. पञ्चानाम् &c.—The five elements are पृथ्वी, 'earth,' अप् 'water', तेजस् 'fire', वायु 'air' and आकाश 'ether'. Their qualities are:—शब्द of आकाश, शब्द and स्पर्श of वायु, शब्द, स्पर्श and रूप of तेजस् ; शब्द, स्पर्श, रूप and रस of अप्; and शब्द, स्पर्श, रूप, रस, and गन्ध of पृथिवी, the additional quality in each case being its special quality. See foot-note. नवं—possessed of fresh *i. e.* unprecedented vigour, prosperity &c.,

S'l. 12. चन्द्र—From चन्द् to be glad; see com.; according to those who treat the root as trans. चन्दतीति. अन्वर्थः—अनुगतोऽर्थमनुगतोऽर्थो येन

वा । Prâdi Samâsa; or Bah. राजा—राजते रञ्जयतीति । The poet here supposes राज् to mean 'to please', by poetical license. See Samj.

S'l. 13. कामम्—an *ind.* implying 'unwilling assent.' अकामानुमतौ कामम *Amaru.* चक्षुष्मत्ता—चक्षुषी अस्य स्त इति चक्षुष्मान् । तस्य भावः । तु-is here used भेदे, *i. e.* to show the difference between the two pairs of eyes he possessed. That Raghu had his physical pair of eyes, the poet has to admit. But these were not his real eyes. His true eyes were the *S'âstras* (the knowledge and wisdom obtained by a study of these); these assisted him in settling intricate questions and accomplishing great ends. शास्त्रेण—The Instrumental is either अभेदे (शास्त्र being identified with चक्षुः) or हेतौ. सूक्ष्म &c.—कार्याश्च ते अर्थाश्च कार्यार्थाः । सूक्ष्माः कार्यार्थाः सूक्ष्मकार्यार्थास्तान्दर्शयितुं शीलमस्येति तेन । See footnote.

S'l. 14. लब्ध &c.—Here लब्ध is a noun (the kingdom obtained from his father). प्रशमन giving stability to what is obtained, by the conciliation or removal of opponents; see com. स्वस्मिन् तिष्ठतीति स्वस्थः at ease. प्रशमन may also mean 'the measures of pacification,' प्रशम्यन्ते एभिरिति प्रशमनानि । See the s'l. quoted by Malli. लब्धानि प्रशमनानि येन स लब्धप्रशमनः । आदौ लब्धप्रशमनः पश्चात्स्वस्थः । 'Who was at ease after he had adopted proper measures to give peace to his kingdom.' पङ्कजलक्षणा—The lotuses are one of the characteristics and not a special sign, of the autumn. But the poet makes special mention of these here, probably because of the idea of worship expressed in उपस्थिता. We are already told that the goddess of royal fortune waited upon Raghu with a lotus umbrella (s'l. 5); and now the goddess of autumnal beauty comes to worship him with actual lotuses. This is explained by 'पार्थिवश्रीर्द्वितीयेव' &c.; *cf. infra* IX. 14.

S'l. 15. मुक्तवर्त्मा—Malli. takes this as the cause of सुदुःसहः । It is better to take this with व्यानशे. The प्रताप (heat in the case of the sun, and prowess in the case of Raghu) was already सुदुःसह, but the world was screened from it by the intervening clouds. But since the clouds became light now, they moved away from its route and fled, so that it spread through all quarters without obstruction. The meaning is that now that the rainy season passed off and autumn came, the other princes became uneasy, dreading every moment an expedition of conquest by Raghu.

S'l. 16 जैत्रम्—जेतुं शीलमस्य जेतृ ; तदेव जैत्र by adding अण् स्वार्थे; see com. प्रजार्थसाधने—Indra by his rainbow produced rain and thereby brought prosperity to the people. Raghu after the lapse of the monsoons undertook an expedition of conquest and thereby brought wealth and prosperity to the people; he also performed sacrifices with that wealth and propitiated the gods who in their turn sent down rain. *Cf.* I. 26.

S'l. 17. पुण्डरीकातपत्रः—The lotuses bloom in autumn and are here poetically spoken of as the umbrella of शरद्. The white lotus is here chosen because the royal umbrella is of that colour. विकसत्काशचामरः—The Kás'a flowers look very much like chauries and are also white. *Cf.* Rit. III. 1, 2. विडम्बयामास—imitated, mimicked; see note on विडम्बितेश्वरः III. 52. पुनः—'but,' showing भेद.

S'l. 18. तदा—During *that* time, then only. The poet suggests by a hyperbole that Raghu's face was always pleasant to look at, while the moon was not so during the whole of the rainy season. It was *now* on the clearing up of the sky that the moon became as delightful to look at as Raghus's face. प्रसादसु०—may also mean delightful-faced on account of his benignity.

S'l. 19. विभूतयः—विशेषा भूतिर्विभूतिः affluence, excess. Fame is described by Sanskrit poets as white; and here the poet supposes the whiteness of geese, stars, &c. to be due to the excess of Raghu's white *i. e.* spotless fame. Geese, bright-shining stars, and lotus-abounding waters marked the advent of autumn. Whence, if not from Raghu's spotless fame, did they derive this whiteness? See Samj.

S'l. 20. इक्षुच्छाय &c.—इक्षुच्छाये (see Samj.) निषत्तुं शीलमेषामिति। Malli. notices and explains the reading 'इक्षुच्छायानिषादिन्यः' but Dîkshita's explanation of this seems better. For he remarks—इक्षूणां छाया इक्षुच्छायम् इक्षुच्छायेषु आ समन्तान्निषादिन्यः sitting round the fields &c. This is perhaps the better reading. It is usual with cultivators of all times to grow round corn-fields, in two or three rows, such useful plants as the sugar-cane &c., which are not shady enough to screen the sun from the corn-fields and yet form a fence of sufficient strength round them. Village girls appointed to keep watch over the fields pass the noon-day hour in singing merrily, seated under the scanty shade afforded by sugar-canes, &c. Now so wide-spread was Raghu's fame and so deeply was he loved that the female guardians would every day sing in his praise. गोप्तुः—This supplies the reason why he was so much beloved. गुणोदयम्—A Vyadhikarana. Bah.; see Samj.; such a Bah. though not directly sanctioned by Pâṇ. is often used by poets, but Vâmana remarks—'अत्रज्यों हि बहुव्रीहिर्व्यधिकरणो जन्माद्युत्तरपदः'—A Vya. Ba., is, indeed, unavoidable when the last member of the comp. is a word like जन्म, वृत्ति &c. *Cf.* 'आत्मजन्मानम्' V. 36. आकुमार &c.--कुमारं युवराजमारभ्याकुमारम्। also see Saṃj. The whole is either an *adv.* modifying जगुः or an *adj.* qualifying यशः (the narrative of which was commenced even by boys).

Śl. 21. उदयात्--has a double sense here; rise and spread of power. कुम्भयोनेः--This is the celebrated sage Agastya, who is said to have been born in a water jar. For the account of his birth along with Vashishṭha from the divine Mitra and Varuṇa, see ft.-note and Sâyaṇa on Ṛg. VII. 33. 11. Agastya is said to rest in the heavens in the form of the star 'Canopus' belonging to the constellation Argo Navis, *i. e.* the lunar mansion कुम्भ. Agastya begins to rise at sunset when the sun is in सिंह (Leo), *i. e.* in August, from the latter half of Śrâvaṇa, just before the commencement of शरद् or autumn. महौजसः—Here there is a reference to the power of Agastya. See VI. 61 and note thereon. Agastya had once drunk off the whole sea. So dreading his power, as it were, water cleared up. See XIII. 36. चुक्षुभे &c.--At the approach of autumn, water lost its turbidity; it was transferred, as it were, fancies the poet, to the hearts of Raghu's foes. For they trembled to think that that was the season for him to set out on his conquering expedition.

Śl. 22. मदोदग्र—उद्गतमग्रमेषामिति उदग्राः *lit.* prominent; hence formidable; मदेन उदग्राः मदोदग्राः. कूलमुद्रुजाः—Upapada Tat.; the roots रुज् and वह् take the affix खश् (अ) when preceded by उत्, and कूल in the Acc. as their उपपद; similarly कूलमुद्वहः. Words ending in a vowel, and the words अरुष् and द्विषत्, take मुम् (म्) , when an affix, dropping ख, follows. See Saṃj. लीलाखेलम्—खेलतीति खेलः लीलया खेलः लीलाखेलस्तं; gracefully sportive. Here the poet, by means of three epithets, describes the changes worked in the bulls by autumn. The bulls had lost their flesh and their humps had dwindled away before the rains set in for want of pasture and the hard work they had to do in the rainy season. But now at the advent of autumn, all things being favourable, they grew in flesh and regained their spirits, and so began their butting sports, when grazing by the riverside.

Śl. 23. मदगन्धिभिः--मदस्येव गन्धो येषां ते मदगन्धयः तैः. आहताः--struck, incited. असूयया—असूया गुणेषु दोषाविष्करणम्। Sid.-Kau. The *Saptaparṇa* trees naturally sent forth the rut-like scent from their flowers (*i. e. one* part) only; but the elephants, thinking that they did it to provoke them, as if in jealous emulation, poured ichor from the *seven* parts of their body. The autumn is the season when the elephants are in rut. For the seven parts of the elephant's body from which inchor exudes, see Samj. and ft.-note.

Śl. 24. **आश्यान**--P. p. of **श्यै** with **आ**; roots beginning with a conjunct consonant and ending in **आ** and containing **य् व् र्** or **ल्** change the **त** of the p. p. p. to **न**. See com. **यात्रायै नोदयामास**--The autumn held out before Raghu peculiar facilities for carrying on a compaign and thus actuated him, as it were, to undertake an expedition. The beasts of burden (the bulls especially) were now in full vigour, the war-elephants in their ruttish condition were eminently fitted for fighting, the rivers had become fordable and the roads being dried up would afford easy passage to Raghu's troops.

Śl. 25. **वाजिनीराजनाविधौ—नीराजना** see ft.-note; it may also be derived fr. **राज्** with **निर्** with the aff. **अन (युच्)** added भावे; the act of decoration. It is a kind of military and religious cermony performed by kings on the 9th of A'śvina, or on the 8th, 12th or 15th day of the bright half of Kârttika, before taking the field. It consists in the general purification of the king's *Purohita*, the ministers and all the various component parts of the army, together with the arms and implements of war, by offering oblations to the sacred fire, waving lights before idols, &c., and reciting the sacred *mantras*. **वाजि** here stands for both a horse and an elephant, possessed of auspicious signs. The ceremony is called '**वाजिनीराजना**' because the lustration of the horse and the elephant is its essential part. *Cf.* लक्षणयुक्तं तुरगं द्विरदवरं चैव दीक्षितं स्नातम् । अहतसिताम्बरगन्धस्रग्धूपाभ्यार्चितं कृत्वा । आश्रमतोरणमूलं समुपनयेत्सान्त्वयन् शनैर्वाचा । — + यद्यानीतास्तिष्ठेद्दक्षिणचरणं हयः समुत्क्षिप्य । स जयति तदा नरेन्द्रः शत्रूंश्चिराद्विना यत्नात् ॥ &c. Varâhamihira's Br.-Sam., chap. 44. See ft-note. The five kinds of नीराजना are--पञ्चनीराजनं कुर्यात्प्रथमं दीपमालया । द्वितीयं सोदकाब्जेन तृतीयं धौतवाससा । चूताश्वत्थादिपत्रैश्च चतुर्थं परिकीर्तितम् । पञ्चमं प्रणिपातेन साष्टाङ्गेन यथाविधि ॥ For other particulars See Pad. P. उत्तर०. chap. 107; Agni. P. chap. 267. **प्रदक्षिणार्चि** &c.—प्रगता दक्षिणा दिग्यया सा प्रदक्षिणा; by the rule प्रादिभ्यो धातुजस्य &c., Várt. on Páṇ. II. 2. 24. **प्रदक्षिणा अर्चिः प्रदक्षिणार्चिः**. this is auspicious; see above III. 14. **सैव व्याजस्तेन । विशेषेणाजन्ति क्षिपन्ति** (outwit, deceive) **अनेनेति व्याजः**; under the disguise of the flame moving to the right. Expounding the comp. thus is free from any grammatical difficulty.

Śl. 26. **मूलप्रत्यन्तः—मूल** the metropolis or capital; **प्रत्यन्त** the border forts protecting the city. **शुद्धपार्ष्णिः—पार्ष्णि** the rear. He had taken adequate measures to guard his capital and the frontier forts, and so feared no attack from behind or attack on his capital in his absence.

श्रयान्वित:—Accompanied by good fortune. This was because he had propitiated the gods before starting. See ft.-note. षड्विधं—See Saṃj. and foot-note. The six kinds of soldiers are :—(1) *Maulas or* those that are well-born and hereditary servants of the king; (2) *Bhṛityas* or those paid by the king; (3) *Suhṛits* or those who belong to his allies, or those who are well-disposed towards him, *i. e.*, on whom he has no claim such as tie of blood or service; (4) *S'renis* or forces levied on occasions of war; mercenaries; (5) *Dvishads* or the forces of the kings inimically disposed towards his enemy; (6) and *Âṭavikas* or the foresters. These last are cruel, rapaceous and hardy, and therefore best suited to lead an attack. See Hit. III. 96 and Kám. Nît. VIII. 23.

S'l. 27. वयोवृद्धाः—The elderly women with husbands living (and not young girls as in II. 10, as this was not an ordinary tour) scattered fried rice over him by way of expressing good wishes, as they alone could do it. लाजैः—is *mas.* and pl. क्षीरोर्मयः—The waves of the milky ocean. The word ऊर्मि is both *mas.* and *fem.*; but it is preferable to have it here in the *fem.* that it may compare well with पौरयोषितः। The allusion here is to the churning of the milky ocean, when Vishṇu supported and kept in position the mount Mandâra by his arms. See Bhág. P. VIII. 7. 12.

S'l. 28. प्राचीम्--प्र प्रथममञ्चति प्राप्नोति सूर्यमिति प्राची। प्राचीनबर्हिषा-- Raghu was Indra's equal; so he commenced by making the east feel his power. See ft.-note. तर्जयन्—Pres. p. of तर्ज् which belongs to the 1st and the 10th classes. The former is Par. and the latter Âtm., so that the one would give तर्जन् and the other तर्जयमानः। To defend the form तर्जयन् (see also XII. 41) Malli. quotes Vâmana who remarks—"Roots which are अनुदात्तेत् may be Par., because Pâṇ- when he says 'चक्षिङ् व्यक्तायां वाचि' himself indicates that mere अनुदात्तेत्त्व does not always give the A tm. For the root चक्ष्, though it has an अनुदात्त इ, has an additional indicatory ङ to give it the Âtm. Hence तर्ज् and भर्त्स् may be Par." Bhaṭṭoji's explanation is decidedly better. He takes तर्जयन् as the pre. p. of the causal of तर्ज्; केतवस्तर्जन्ति, 'the flags menace', and Raghu went on causing them to menace (केतुभिस्तर्जयन्ययौ). *Cf.* 'तर्जितः परशुधारया मम' XI. 78.

S'l. 29. घनसन्निभैः—सन्निभ properly means that which appears or shines; while the meaning wanted here is 'equal or like to.' Amara says that words like निभ, संकाश &c. express this meaning when they form the latter mĕmbers of compounds स्युरुत्तरपदे त्वमी। निभसंकाशनीकाश- प्रतीकाशोपमादयः॥ So this is a नित्यसमास which has no स्वपदविग्रह. We must, therefore, explain घनानां तुल्यैः । See Malli. on 'प्रफुल्लतापिच्छनिभैः' S'is'. I. 22. Malli. says the elephants resembled the clouds वर्णतः (in colour), क्रियातः by their action, *i. e.* by their pouring down the rain of rut, and परिमाणतः *i. e.* in size (the hugest of the lot being chosen for war service). भूतलम्--तल is both *mas.* and *neu.*; here it is *neu.* as it will compare better with व्योम.

S'l. 30. प्रताप:—technically means 'the pre-eminent majesty' of the king due to his having ample resources at command. This makes his enemies dread him; *cf.* प्रतापावनतसमस्तसामन्तचक्रः Kâd. p. 1. According to Vall. it means here the report of Raghu's approach which struck terror into his enemies' hearts. चतुःस्कन्धा—चत्वारः स्कन्धा यस्याः सा । चतुःस्कन्धेव may also be taken as a Comp. word. The four divisions meant here are those poetically given by the poet (the first three having done the work of striking terror into the hearts of the enemies like the fourth), and not the usual four divisions of any army. चमूः—The ancient army consisted of four divisions (1) chariots; (2) elephants;(3) horsemen; and (4) foot-soldiers. A चमू consists of 729 elephants, as many chariots, 2,187 horse-warriors and 3,645 foot-soldiers. But this technical meaning is not intended here. 'चमूः सेनाविशेषे च सेनामात्रे च योषिति' इति मेदिनी ।

S'l. 31. मरुपृष्ठानि—म्रियन्ते भूतान्यस्मिन्निति मरुः a waterless place, an arid tract or desert. मरूणां पृष्ठानि (surfaces) मरुपृष्ठानि । उदम्भांसि—उद्गतानि अम्भांसि येषु तानि with waters springing or spouting up. शक्तिमत्त्वात्--on account of his having the power and means to do it. Some take शक्ति in the sense of योगबल 'superhuman power'--Raghu did all this without having had to use human efforts, such as digging out wells, building bridges &c.; see ft.-note.

S'l. 32. पूर्वसागर &c.—पूर्वस्यां दिशि भवः पूर्वः । पूर्वः सागरः पूर्वसागरस्तमवश्यं गच्छतीति पूर्वसागरगामिनी तां; or गमिष्यतीति गामिनी पूर्वसागरं गामिनी पूर्वसागरगामिनी ताम् ।

गङ्गामिव भगीरथः--भगीरथ may be called the Indian Hercules. Sagara, an ancient king of the solar race, determined on performing 100 *As'vamedha* sacrifices. When he commenced the 100th sacrifice, the horse that was let off was carried away by Indra. The 60,000 sons of Sagara being commanded by their father, searched throughout the world for the horse but in vain. At length they excavated the earth, entered the nether regions and found the horse grazing by the side of the sage Kapila. Upon this they rashly charged him with having stolen the horse, whereupon the sage at once reduced them to ashes with the fire of his wrath. Subsequently Sagara came to know that his sons could only obtain salvation by being purified with the water of Gaṅgâ, who then watered the plains of heaven alone. Now it was no easy task to induce Gaṅgâ to come down to the humbler regions of the earth. So Sagara, his son Asamañjasa, and his grandson and great-grandson Aṃśumân and Dilîpa, all died without being able to effect the descent of the celestial river and the sons of Sagara, all the time, continued to be mere heaps of ashes. At length Bhagîratha, his great-great-grandson, succeeded, by his long-continued austerities, in propitiating Brahmâ, who told him to propitiate Śiva, since he alone was able to sustain on his head the current of the heavenly river. Śiva also was pleased with the penance of Bhagîratha, granted him his prayer, and called upon Gaṅgâ to descend upon his head. Gaṅgâ, imagining in her pride that she would bear down even Śiva, fell upon his head with tremendous force, but had to wander through the labyrinths of Śiva's matted hair for one year. At length being liberated by Śiva at the entreaties of Bhagîratha, the river descended upon the earth, and all the gods and other divine beings came to behold the wondrous sight. After this Bhagîratha directed his chariot towards the sea and the Ganges followed him as far as the *Sagar Kunda* and thence entering the Pâtâla watered the ashes of Sagara's sons, who were at one purified by the holy water and their souls ascended to heaven. The whole story is given in Râm. I. 35–44.

Śl. 33. Raghu's march through the eastern kingdoms is herein compared to the passage of an elephant through a forest. As an elephant marches straight on, smashing the trees that come in his way, so Raghu marched on, subduing ordinary kings and uprooting those that had the daring to defy him. The eastern kings, it seems, had given special offence to Raghu. For his treatment of other kings was marked with generosity and leniency; they were उत्खातप्रतिरोपित and not उत्खात alone. त्याजितैः—Some grammarians include roots like त्यज्, मुच् &c. in the list of the द्विकर्मक roots on the authority of च in Pâṇ.'s अकथितं च। And Kâli. uses the root त्यज् as such; *cf.* XV. 58; Kum. VII. 14; Meg. II. 36. Others do not hold this view. Kaiyata says गवा पयस्त्याजयति। *Cf.* also Bhaṭṭi—संत्याजयांचकाराथ सीतां त्रिंशतिबाहुना। फलम्—(*a*) profits *i. e.* the treasure; (*b*) fruits. उत्खातैः—(*a*) dethroned; (*b*) uprooted. भग्नैः—(*a*) defeated; (*b*) destroyed. उल्बण—clear; well-marked.

Śl. 34. पौरस्त्यान्—The Mat. P. mentions the following as the countries situated in the east: 'अङ्गा वङ्गा मद्गुरका अन्तर्गिरि बहिर्गिरि। प्राग्ज्योतिषाश्च पुंड्राश्च * * * *। सुह्मोत्तराः प्रविजया मार्गवागेयमालवाः॥ Adhyáya 113; see also Máh. Bhár. Sabh. P. Adh. 30. जयी—This shows that being always victorious he reached the sea-coast without having sustained a single defeat. उपकण्ठम्—उपगत. कण्ठमुपकण्ठः (Prádi Samâs.) तम्। महोदधेः—उदकानि धीयन्तेऽस्मिन्निस्युदधिः। महानुदधिर्महोदधिः।

Śl. 35. अनम्राणां समु०–The fate of some of the eastern kings served as a warning to the Suhmas; it showed that Raghu was the समुद्धर्ता of the अनम्र alone. सुह्मैः—The people of the Suhma country which was situated to the west of Vaṅga. It was so called after Suhma, the fourth son of Bali. Its capital ताम्रलिप्त, also called तामलिप्त, दामलिप्त, ताम्रलिप्ती and तामलिनी (see Hem. IV. 45) has been long identified with the modern Tumlook, on the right bank of the Cossya (here called Rûpanárâyaṇa) which is the Kapiśá of Kàlidâsa. In ancient times it was situated closer to the sea than at present, and was a place of considerable maritime trade. In the Máh. Bhâr., however, Tâmralipta is mentioned as a separate country from Suhmades'a (see Sabh. P. XXX.24, 25), which, therefore, seems to have included western Midnapur only. But in later times its extent was undoubtedly greater, as Tâmralipta is mentioned by many writers as its capital. According to the commentator of the Mahábhárata, the Suhmas were also called Râdhas (*Vide.* Sabh. P. XXX. 16), which is the name of Western Bengal and from which the Râdhi Brâhmaṇas take their name. It probably included Bardwân, (Vardhamâna) Bankoora (Mallabhûmi), and Beerbhoom (Vîrabhumi) as no separate mention is made of these districts in early works. Vall. and Sum. explain सुह्मैः as सुह्मदेशीयैः राजभिः. वृत्तिम्--वर्तते अनयेति वृत्तिः; behaviour, the action. वैतसीम्—The Suhmas lived in a country abounding in the cone-plants growing along the banks of the Ganges. Thus they had every day an opportunity to see how big trees resisting the force of the current were borne down by the river while the supple cane was spared, and to learn thereby the safest course of action in case of an invasion by a more powerful enemy. The simile is therefore appropriate in this respect. See ft.-note.

Śl. 36. वङ्गान्—The kings of the Vaṅga country. See Saṃj. on सुह्मैः. and ft.-note. The country of Vaṅga or Eastern Bengal lay to the west of Tipperah. It must not be confounded with Gauḍa (गौड) or Northern Bengal. In the Mâdhavachampû the two countries are clearly distinguished and Vaṅga is described to be that country through which the Padmâ and the Brahmaputrâ flow. And this will be clear to us if we remember that the main channel of the Brahmaputrâ originally flowed through Mymensing. The passage is important inasmuch as it introduces the word Vaṅga from which Bengal is derived, and which is applied as a nickname by Calcutta people to the people of Eastern Bengal. Kálidása here speaks of the branches of the Ganges, so it seems that Vaṅga included the sea-coast of Bengal. It is also called *Samatata* or plains. The word occurs in

Varáhasamhitâ, XIV. 6 along with Odra (Orissa) and Prâgjyotisha (Kamroop), but without any indication of its position. Hiouen Thsang does not make mention of Vaṅga, but in its place speaks of *samatata*. And we know that the Gangetic doab (Kuru Pâñchâla) was known by a similar name, Samasthalî. So it seems beyond doubt that Samatata was Vaṅga. The principa lold towns of this province are the early Mahomedan capital Suvarṇagrâma (Sonârgaum) or 'the golden village' near Painam, and Vikramapura or 'the capital of Vikrama', now the name of a Purganah. Vaṅga in old Sanskrit means 'tin,' and it occurs in this sense in literature. Now tin is not found in Bengal, but in Malaya, Pegu, China and especially in the island of Banka in the East Indies. It is probably so called because it was known to the Hindoos through Vaṅga or Eastern Bengal. Hence it must have had a considerable maritime trade from the earliest times. नेता—साधु नयति सेनामिति–a skilful general. Because he was always victorious in land fights as well as in naval fights. नौसाधनोद्यत-उद्यत 'prepared to offer resistance.' जयस्तम्भान्–जयसूचकाः स्तम्भा जयस्तम्भाः। 'pillars commemorating victory.'

Śl. 37. आपादपद्मप्रणता.—(*a*) पादः पद्मामिव पादपद्मं तन्मर्यादीकृत्य आपाद-पद्मं प्रणताः bending low as far as his lotus-like feet; (*b*) पादस्थं पद्मं पादपद्मं आ पादपद्मं प्रणताः bending low (by the weight of their ears) to the lotuses at their roots. The paddy fields are covered over with water during the rains and often abound in lotuses. *Cf.* Kir. IV. 4 'तुतोष पश्यन्कलमस्य सोऽधिकं सवारिजे वारिणि रामणीयकम्' । उत्खातप्रतिरोपिताः--applies both to ते and to कलमाः। The paddy is a kind of corn first sown in चैत्र or वैशाख in burnt soil and after a month or two transplanted to a softer soil, full of water. When thus transplanted the paddy has a luxuriant harvest. To understand the appropriateness and force of the simile we must suppose that the princes were replaced on their thrones by Raghu after they were defeated and dethroned. Then struck by the magnanimity of the victor and overcome by gratitude, they came to him with presents, and prostrating themselves before him, offered them. The simile here is appropriate both as regards time and place. The paddy flourished in water and so did the Vaṅgas, who were great navigators (नौसाधनाः) and Raghu attacked them at a time when the paddies were probably bent low on account of the weight of corn.

Śl. 38. कपिशाम्—See note on Śl. 35. उत्कल—The country of Utkala or Odra (Orissa) lay to the south of Tâmralipta, and from the present Śl. seems to have extended up to the river Kapiśá. Odra is probably the ancient name representing the aboriginal tribes of the country. It is mentioned in the Mâhâbhârata among the Indian provinces along with Videha and Támralipta and in the list of the southern conquests of Sahadeva. In the Bṛih. Saṃ., however, it is mentioned as a different country from Odhra. The chief town of this province 'Cuttak' is said to have been founded by Nṛipa-Kesarî in the tenth century. It was probably better known as Padmávatî. Jajpur (Yajñapura) on the borders of the Balsor (Baleśvara) district, and the city of the celebrated temple of Bhuvaneshvara in the Purî district, are said to be the older capitals of the district. The most important place, however, from a Hindoo point of view, is the town of Purî, the site of the far-famed temple of Jagannâtha. Its celebrity, however, dates from comparatively recent times as no notice of it is found in the Mahábhárata or the earlier Purâṇas. उत्कलादर्शितपथः—This shows that the Utkalas easily yielded to Raghu and assisted him in his passage towards Kaliṅga. कलिङ्गाभिमुखः—The country of Kaliṅga lay to the south of Odra and extended to the mouths of the Godávarî. In the time of the Mah. Bhár. it seems to have included Odra, as the river Vaitaraṇî, which runs by Jajpur, is clearly stated in one place to be in Kaliṅga. It did not generally extend beyond the Godâvarî, as its mouths are mentioned to have been in the possession of the Ándhras. According to Daṇḍin its capital Kaliṅganagara was at some distance from the sea-coast, inasmuch as he says that the king of Kaliṅga went out to pass some days at the seaside, when he was taken captive with his daughter by the king of Ándhra (see Dk. VII. 7). The capital was, therefore, not at Kaliṅgapattaṇa, on the north, nor probably at Vizagapattam (Vijayapattaṇa) but at Rájamahendrî on the south, as it is at some distance from the sea and borders on Ándhra-deśa. The Kaliṅgas are described as having sprung from Kaliṅga, the son of Dîrghatamas, and his wife Sudeshṇâ. It is thus described in the Tantras—जगन्नाथात्पूर्वभागे गङ्गातीरान्तगः शिवे । कलिङ्गदेशः संप्रोक्तो वाममार्गपरायणः ॥

Śl. 39. महेन्द्रस्य—This may mean by लक्षणा the lord of Mahendra or the mountain itself, since the humiliation suffered by the mountain was also suffered by its lord. By Mahendra is meant the chain of mountains that extends from Utkala or Orissa and the Northern Circars to Gond-vana. See Willson's Vish. P. p. 174. It is one of the seven principal mountain chains of India. General Cunningham (see his Ancient Geography of India p. 516) identifies this mountain with Mahendra Mâle which divides Ganjam from the valley of Mahánadî. According to Anadoram Borooah, however, it included the whole of the eastern Ghâṭs between the Mahânadî and the Godâvari. Kâlidása calls the king of Kalinga 'lord of Mahendra,' and Kalinga was not limited to the country about Ganjam but extended upto the Godávarí. The present town of Rájamahendrí on the Godâvari probably originally represented the capital of the Lord of Mahendra. तीक्ष्णम्—(*a*) unbearable (प्रताप); (*b*) sharp (अङ्कुश). न्यवेशयत्—(*a*) stamped; (*b*) drove in. यन्ता—may also refer to Raghu 'the controller,' *i. e.* chastiser of the haughty. गम्भीरवेदिनः—गम्भीरे वेदितुं शीलमस्य। This is a technical name for a king of elephants. According to a Śl. quoted by Châr. from the Pâlakápya (see ft.-note), and another quoted by Malli. from the Râjaputrîya a Gambhîravedî elephant is one who is not easily sensible to wounds, cutting of flesh or actual spilling of blood from his body. According to another quotation given by Malli., an elephant who is slow in understanding even well-understood signs is called गम्भीरवेदी.

Śl. 40. प्रतिजग्राह—प्रतिग्रह् usually means 'to accept;' here it means 'to oppose, to meet or receive in hostile spirit.' The root occurs again in this senes in VII. 36. कालिङ्गः—the king of the Kalingas. As this signifies one individual, the अण् is retained.

पक्षच्छेदोद्यतम्—For allusion see *supra* III. 60. This epithet also applies to Raghu. पक्ष means the allies, 'the forces on the side of the enemy;' पक्षाणां अरिमित्राणां छेदः &c. For the recurrence of the same thought, *cf.* 'शमितपक्षबलः शतकोटिना' &c. IX 12. शिलावर्षी—शिलाः rocks hillocks. Kalinga was like a mountain of yore. For he fought with huge elephants who resembled in colour, size and strength, the hillocks thrown by the mountains upon Indra. *Cf.* VI. 54.

Śl. 41, काकुत्स्थः—ककुत्स्थस्य गोत्रापत्यं पुमान्काकुत्स्थः। The descendant, of Kakutstha. For the allusion, see VI. 71-73 and note under 71; also the quotation from Bhág. P. given in the ft.-note, p. 146; also Hariv. Chap. X. नाराचदुर्दिनम्—नराणां समूहो नारम्। नारमाचामतीति नाराचः। an arrow made wholly of iron or steel (and therefore surely killing by entering deep into the body). दुर्दिनम्—means by लक्षणा a shower. This answers the purpose of a bath. सन्मङ्गलस्नातः—मङ्गलाय स्नातः म०; or मङ्गलेन मङ्गलद्रव्यमिश्रेण जलेन सर्वौषधिजलेन वा (see Samj.) स्नातः मङ्गलस्नातः। सत् यथाविधि मङ्गलस्नातः सन्मङ्गलस्नातः। It is necessary according to the Śástras to take an auspicious bath before taking possession of श्री. The poet fancies that this was furnished in the present case by the shower of iron arrows (a bath quite befitting a warrior).

S'l. 42. दलैः—by means of leaves, i. e. drinking bowls or vessels made of the leaves. This ought to be construed with पपुः and not रचित, as S. P. Pandit would have it. आपानभूमयः—आ समन्तात्संभूय वा पिबन्त्यत्रेति आपानम् । आपानस्य भूमयः &c. This is a technical name for a drinking place. शात्रवं च पपुर्यशः—The fact that Raghu's soldiers had their carousings there without the least molestation from the enemy shows that they had inflicted a crushing defeat upon their foes. So that, thinks the poet, along with the wine they quaffed there, they also drank off the fame of the enemy; i. e. by defeating the enemy they deprived him of his fame as a skilful warrior. Or शात्रवं may mean 'शत्रुजयोत्पन्नम्.' They drank in the fame springing from their defeat of the enemy, i. e. got additional fame. Cf. II. 69, VII. 60. Bhattoji Dîkshit and Jñânendrabhikshu read व for च (शात्रवं व पपुर्यशः), and Bhattoji remarks that this is quoted as the poet's reading by the old commentators of Amara. Here व stands for इव 'like' (though Kâli. is not likely to use it thus). शात्रवं यश इव पपुः, the likeness lying in the purity of the two—the wine they drank was simply unfomented cocoanut-juice, which was therefore clear and transparent; and the fame they obtained was also pure i. e. not sullied by defeat. Cf. Med. 'व प्रचेतासि जानीयादिवार्थे तु तदव्ययम्' । This reading is better inasmuch as it gives a more beautiful meaning.

S'l. 43. धर्मविजयी—A conqueror for religious purposes, i. e. for the sake of offering sacrifices &c. Three kinds of conquerors are mentioned by Sanskrit writers: (1) धर्मविजयी or a 'righteous conqueror' is one who takes the wealth of a conquered king but raises him to his throne again; (2) the conqueror who deprives him of his wealth and royalty as well, but spares his life is लोभविजयी; (3) and one who robs him of all these three is असुरविजयी. See ft. note. नृपः—The protector of men. An epithet peculiarly happy, as it comes after धर्मविजयी. न तु मेदिनीम्—Mallinâtha's remark on this seems to be unnecessary, as the reason of this is given by the poet himself by describing Raghu as धर्मविजयी.

Sl. 44. वेलातटेन—वेला is the land covered by the waters of the sea at high tide. तटेन—by the coast-line of the sea. फलवत्पूगमालिना—फलवतां पूगानां मालास्त्यस्येति तेन । अगस्त्याचरिताम्—आचरिता सेविता resorted to. Cf. for this sense, 'श्वापदाचरिते वने' Mah. Bhâr.; 'परेताचरितां दिशम्' Râma. अनाशास्यजयः—अनाशास्यो जयो यस्य 'to whom victory was not a thing to be sought after,' *i. e.* to whom victory came of itself. See Samj. It may also mean 'over whom victory was not to be hoped for', आशास्य is derived from शास् with आ Âtm., to wish for. [The rule 'शास इदङ् हलोः' Pâṇ. VI. 4. 34.—the root शास् changes its आ to इ when followed by अङ् or by an affix beginning with a consonant and having an indicatory क् or ङ्—applies to शास् Paras. meaning 'to introduce, to order' &c., from which we have the form आशिष्यः].

Śl. 45. सैन्यपरिभोगेण—The army enjoyed a cool bath in the river and the water bore scent of the rut of the elephants in the army as they plunged into it. Now the rivers are poetically considered as the wives of the sea (*Cf.* XIII. 9) and as such must be faithful to their lord. But here Kâverî bore marks of her sporting with others and so made the sea suspicious, as it were, of her virtue. गजदानसुगन्धिना—Malli. holds a long discussion on this and considers the form ०सुगन्धि a poetic license. According to the Várt. quoted and interpreted by him the smell must be natural to have the समासान्त इ; and since the दानगन्ध, referred to here, is not the natural smell of water the form should have been सुगन्धः। The supposition that we have the मत्वर्थीय affix इन् here, will also not do, because a मत्वर्थीय is prohibited after a Karm. See Samj. The word नैसर्गिक, however, is not to be found in the Mahâ-Bhâshya or the Vṛitti, and grammarians like Kaiyaṭa, Bhaṭṭoji, Nageśabhaṭṭa, &c. do not hold such a view. Mallinátha's criticism, though he has on his side Bhaṭṭi who says आघ्रायिवान्गन्धवहः सुगन्धस्तेनारविंदव्यतिषङ्गवांश्च' II. 5. seems therefore to be out of place. See ft.-note and Gr. § 256(c). कावेरी—A river of Southern India. It rises in the Western Ghauts and falls into the Bay of Bengal.

Śl. 46. विजिगीषुः—Simply means 'the conqueror,' 'one who had set out on a tour of conquest,' and does not imply that he longed for victory. See śl. 44. मारीचोद्भ्रान्त &c.—मरीचानां विषयो मारीचः the land of मरीच the black-pepper creepers; हारीताः—हारीत is a kind of parrot (the wood-pigeon, according to some) feeding on the leaves of the pepper-creepers; *cf.* पञ्चत्रिके भोजय मरीचापपल्लवाःलानि भवनहारीतान्। Kád. p. 281. मलयाद्रेः—मलयाख्यो मलयश्चासावद्रिश्चेति वा तस्य। The mountain which forms the southern Part of the western Ghâts. See below śl. 51, note on मलयदर्दुरौ. Malaya especially abounds in sandal trees and is famous for its cool breezes; the place, therefore, was a pleasant one for the jaded army to halt. उपत्यकाः—the adjoining sites.

Śl. 47. तुल्यगन्धिषु—Malli. defends this by referring to the Várt. 'सर्वादेश्च'; but the accuracy of his defence may be questioned as this does not begin with सर्व, while the instances given in the Bháshya all begin with सर्व. We may, therefore, expound तुल्यस्य गन्धस्तुल्यगन्धः स एषामस्तीति तुल्यगन्धिनस्तेषु । मत्तेभ—मत्त is used to indicate the presence of ichor on the temples of the elephants. ससञ्जुः—shows the great size and number of his elephants. The dust of cardamom seeds was raised by the hoofs of the horses, but so great was the obstruction caused by the compact line of his huge elephants, that it could not escape into the sky, but got stuck to the wet temples of the elephants.

Śl. 48. भोगिवेष्टन &c.—Serpents are supposed to coil round the sandal trees, being attracted by their sweet smell. अस्रसत्—स्रंस though A'tm. is Paras. when it takes the 2nd variety of the Aorist. ग्रैवम्—ग्रीवासु भवं ग्रैवम् tied round (not born on) the neck; the metal neck-chains round the neck. 'ग्रीवाशब्दो धमनीवचनस्तासां बहुत्वाद्बहुवचनम् । (सत्ता भवत्यर्थो गृह्यते न जन्म'). Vṛittikâra. त्रिपदीछेदिनाम्—त्रयः पादा अस्या इति त्रिपदी (the foot-chain), formed irregularly like कुम्भपदी according to the Sid.-Kau. which includes त्रिपदी under the कुम्भपदी list. According to the Vṛittikára we have two forms त्रिपाद् and त्रिपादी. See ft.-note.

'The poet means that elephants, who were so strong that they would have broken their foot-chains, were kept on their spots by the mere ropes tied round their necks, because the ropes were very firmly tied to the sandals on account of the grooves being so well-adapted to them; and because the odoriferous exhalations given out by the sandal trees were so charming to the elephants that they did not tear off neck-ropes.' S. P. Pandit.

Śl. 49. दिशि मन्दायते &c.—अमन्दं मन्दं भवति मन्दायते becomes dim; Malli. derives this with the affix क्यष् which takes the Âtm. optionally; so according to him the form मन्दायति will also be correct. But according to the Bhâshya, which is followed by Kaiyata, Bhattoji and others, क्यष् is to be affixed to लोहित and words with the affix डाच् (*i. e.* आ) and क्यङ् to the other words found in the list लोहितादि. Hence क्यङ् is the only correct affix and मन्दायते is the only correct form. रवेरपि—Even of the sun. When in the winter solstice the sun apparently moves from the north towards the south, the heat is mitigated. So the poet fancies the southern quarter to be invincible, since even the heat of the sun is subdued in that quarter. तस्यामेव—in the very quarter the Pândyas found Raghu's प्रताप unbearable *i. e.* it did not diminish. पाण्ड्याः—The derivation of the word given in the com. seems to be an interpolation. For ड्यण् being a तद्राज affix ought to disappear in the plural by 'तद्राजस्य बहुषु—' Pâṇ. II. 4. 62. Malli. has correctly applied the Sûtra in other places and he could not have misapplied it here. It may be derived after Bhaṭṭoji—पाण्डूनां राजा पाण्ड्यः पाण्ड्ये साधवः (well-disposed towards) पाण्ड्याः the partisans of Páṇḍya *i. e.* his people (warriors)—कथं तर्हि-तस्यामेव रघोः पाण्ड्या इति । पाण्ड्ये साधव इति समाधेयम् Sid. Kau. Páṇḍya is the name of a country in the extreme south of India and lying to the south-west of Chola-des'a. The mountain Malaya and the river Támraparṇî fix its position indisputably; *cf.* Bâl. Râm. III. 31. In the time of Kâlidâsa it must have extended from the banks of the Kâverî to the shores of the Indian ocean, as he says that its capital was 'Serpent town' (VI. 59) which must be the same as Negapattam (Nágapaṭṭana), 160 miles south of Madras. The town of Madhurá was founded some centuries after by king Kulaśekhara. The holy island of Rámeśvara belonged to this kingdom. The Mah. Bhár. speaks of Kumáris in this country which evidently seems to refer to Cape Comorin and shows that the principality at one time included part of the Malabar Coast, as independently testified by a Greek writer. In the same work we also find mention made of a mountain, Ṛishabha, in it. It is very likely a summit of the Malaya mountains.

Śl. 50 ताम्रपर्णीसमेतस्य—Támraparṇi is a small but celebrated river flowing past Pallamcotta and falling into the gulf of Mânár near the small town of Punakail. The place where it joins the sea is famous for its pearl-fisheries. Here the poet speaks of the union of the sea and the river, his wife, leading to the production of pearly treasures, which constitutes the glory of the land. मुक्तासारम्—see Malli.; or मुक्ता एव सारः स्थिरांशस्तम् । यशः स्वमिव—The point of similarity is whiteness—real in one case and fancied in the other.

Śl. 51. निर्विश्य—*i. e.*, having enjoyed their scenes and productions. स्तनाविव—The simile here is bad as far as Raghu is concerned since he was never given to lust. दिश स्याः—*i. e.* of the South. मलयदर्दुरौ—The two mountain chains in the country of the Pâṇḍyas. They are the southern portions of the western Ghâts. The Malaya is also reckoned to be one of the seven Kulaparvatas. The Rag. and the Mv. tell us that the slopes of the Malaya mountain are encircled by the river Káverî. In the Bál. Rám. the mountain is said to abound in cardamoms, pepper, sandal and betelnut trees, which are all found in abundance in most southerly India. We can therefore safely identify it with the southern portion of the Ghâts running from the south of Mysore and forming the eastern boundary of Travancore. Kálidása in this Śl. calls the mountains Malaya and Dardura the breasts of the earth, and Daṇḍin describes the southerly breeze as cool with the embrace of sandals on the sides of the mountain Dardura. The two mountains are also spoken of in one connexion in the Mârk. P. Dardura, therefore, must be that portion of the Ghâts which forms the south-eastern boundary of Mysore. The sources of four rivers are placed in this chain, *viz.* Kṛitamâlá, Tâmraparṇi, Pushpajá and Utpalâvatî.

Śl. 52. **असह्यविक्रमः**—सोढुमशक्योऽसह्यः विक्रमो यस्य । **सह्यम्**—One of the seven principal chains of mountains in India. It is still known as Sahyádri and is the same as Western Ghâts, as far as their junction with the Neilgherries north of the Malaya. **अलंघयत्**—reached or crossed. The two Ślokas form a युग्म.

Śl. 53. **अनीकैः**—"अनीक is originally the face; and meaning then the edge of any sharp weapon, it signifies, like the Latin *acies*, the sharp edge or edgelike appearance of an army in march *i. e.* a row. In classical Sanskrit the word only bears one signification derived from the last, *viz.*, that of 'multitude' or *army*." S. P. Pandit. **विसर्पद्भिः**—marching. **अपरान्तः**—अपरोन्तः अपरान्तः-the other side, *i. e.* the West (said with reference to the East). **अपरान्ताः**-the westerners (कौंकणाः Vall.). Konkan is the name of the strip of land between Sahya mountains and the sea, particularly the portion lying between Daman on the North and Goa on the South. **रामास्त्रोत्सारितः**—The Râma referred to here is Paraśuráma. He destroyed the Kshatriyas twenty one times and then made a gift of the earth, which was his by the right of conquest, to Kaśyapa, as *dakshiṇá* in a sacrifice. After this Paraśuráma wished to practise religious austerities. But now he found himself in a fix, for no merit accrues fiom penance practised on another's ground, and all the land then available in the world belonged to Kaśyapa. So he applied to the ocean for space. The ocean told him to raise land by removing the water if he could. This was no difficult task for a warrior like Paraśurâma. He took up his bow and shot an arrow, with the result that the waters of the sea receded from the vicinity of Sahyâdri, relinquishing the maritime district, named Surpâraka, according to the Mah. Bhâr. See also the passage quoted from the Mah. Bhâr. in the foot-note.

The traditions of the Peninsula ascribe the formation of the coast of Malabar to this origin and relate that Paraśurâma compelled the ocean to retire and introduced Brâhmṇas and colonists from the north into

Kerala or Malabar. According to some accounts he stood on the promontory of Delhi and shot his arrows to the South over the site of Kerala. It seems likely that we have proof of the local legend being at least as old as the beginning of the Christian era, as the Mons Pyrrhus of Ptolemy is, probably, the mountain of Paraśu or Paras'uráma. (See Wilson's Vishṇu Purâṇa p. 404, Note 21).

Śl. 54. भयोत्सृष्ट &c.—The women were struck with terror at the sudden appearance of Raghu's vast army and gave up decorating their persons. केरलयोषिताम्—Kerala is the ancient name of the whole tract comprising the districts of Cochin, Canara, and Travancore. Daṇḍin says (see Dk. Ull. 8th) that the king of Aśmaka or hilly country incited the kings of Kuntala, Konkaṇa, Vanavâsi, Murala, Richîka, and Nâsikya, to rise in a general revolt against the king of Vidarbha, and it will appear that Murala is the name of Kerala. The positions of all these countries except As'maka are definitely known and cover all southern India except Trâvancore. Hence it is clear that As'maka must be the old name for Trâvancore. This is confirmed by the fact that it is called Kûṭa by some Mahomedan writers, which means the same thing as Aśmaka. The principal rivers in this tract are the Netravatî on which Mangalore stands, the Sarasvati on which is situated Honawar, and the Kálînadî on which Śadâsivagad is situated. As the first two rivers have their distinctive names, the last must be the same as the Muralâ referred to by Kâlidâsa in the next Śl. and by Bhavabhûti in his Uttar. III. This is the principal river in Kerala and hence the people were sometimes called Muralas. From the description in the Raghuvams a and the Kathâsaritsâgara, it appears that Kerala meant the strip of land between the Western Ghâts and the sea north of the Kâverî. Popular opinion also fixes its northern boundary on the south of Konkan. In Hemachandra's glossary Urga is given as a synonym of Kerala.

अलकेषु—अलक seems to mean the locks of soft, curly hair flowing on either side of the female face. *Cf.* VI. 23, VIII. 52, 55. चूर्णप्रतिनिधिः—प्रतिनिधीयते इति प्रतिनिधिः । चूर्णात्प्रतिनिधिः चूर्णप्रतिनिधिः । We may take this as an Ab. Tat. because Pâṇ. says प्रतिनिधिः प्रतिदाने च यस्मात् । which shows that he prefers the Ab. with प्रतिनिधि. अचूर्णप्रतिनिधिश्चूर्णप्रतिनिधिः सम्पद्यमानः कृतश्चूर्णप्रतिनिधीकृतः। The remark of Malli. on this एतेन योषितां पलायनं &c. seems to be an interpolation. Hindu warriors are never described as pursuing women, far less frightened women; and Malli. who himself gives the prohibition नायुधव्यसनप्राप्ते &c. in his com. on VII. 49, is not likely to make such a remark. What is meant is this—So vast was the cloud of dust raised by the army that it spread over the whole country of Kerala and the dust settling on the heads of the women in it served the purpose of scented powder which women apply to their hair.

Śl. 55. मुरला &c.—For Muralá see note on केरलयो॰, preceding s'l. This implies that the breeze was cool and fragrant. वारबाणानाम्—वारयन्तीति वाराः (which ward off or resist); बाणानां वाराः वारबाणाः the armours; the appearance of वार first in the Comp. is to be accounted for by referring it to the मयूरव्यंसकादि class which is an आकृतिगण and by reference to which, according to the Vrittikára, any Tat., not actually explained by the rules given, may be explained. अयत्नपटवासताम्—पटो वास्यतेऽनेन, *lit.* that by which a garment is scented; a kind of fragrant powder of a yellowish-red colour; *cf.* प्रकीर्णपटवासपुञ्जपिञ्जरित &c. Rat. I. p.14. अविद्यमानो यत्नो यस्मै अयत्नः । अयत्नः पटवासस्तस्य भावस्तत्ता ताम् । For the component parts of पटवास, according to the Br. Sam., see ft.-note.

Śl. 56. वाहानाम्—उह्यत एभिरिति वाहाः horses. चरताम्—Malli. translates this by गच्छताम् which must be understood in the sense of 'moving about' and not 'marching on for battle.' For the poet seems to describe here a halt and not a march, as is clear from the next s'l. and the word शिञ्जित which is a gentle sound. It may better be translated by 'grazing.' The horses, of course mailed, were ' t off to graze by the riverside or so. पत्रनोद्भूत &c.—ताळीनां राजानो राजताल्यः probably a kind of gigantic palm; a comp. of the राजदन्तादि or मयूरव्यंसकादि group. अभ्यभूयत—This implies the vastness of Raghu's cavalry. For the rustling noise produced by the forests of gigantic palms was drowned by the jinglings of the armours caused by the gentle motion of the horses, whose number, therefore, must have been proportionately great.

Śl. 57. खर्जूरीस्कन्ध—स्कन्ध properly means that part of the trunk of a tree where it branches off. But the date tree being a kind of palm does not branch off but has a stalk and leaves. So this pobably here means 'the top of.' This shows that Káli. did not know the south personally; for the date tree does not grow in the Konkan. मदोद्गारसुगन्धिषु—उद्गार fr. उद्+गॄ+घञ् (भावे) the pouring out of. Here it refers to the act of pouring and not to the thing proured out. For in the latter case it will be difficult to account for the इ at the end of the compound, the rut being separable from the temples. See note on s'l. 45. पुन्नागेभ्यः—Dr. Roxbury thinks that the Punnâga tree is a native of the Coromandal Coast. It seems also to be a native of the opposite coast. शिलीमुखाः—शिली शल्यं मुखमेषां lit. 'needle-mouthed;' bees.

S'l. 58. अवकाशम्—अवकाशत इत्यवकाशः open space. किल—may be taken ऐतिह्ये; so it is related. Or we may place किल last-रघवे करं ददौ किल-taking it as a sign of उत्प्रेक्षा. रामाय-See the allusion under Śl. 53 (रामास्त्रोत्सारित &c.). अपरान्त &c.--The Inst. here is करणे. As the sea could not have given the tribute in person some such disguise was necessary.

Śl 59. मत्तेभ &c.—See Samj.; or मत्तेभरदनैः उत्कीर्णानि (noun) व्यक्तविक्रमलक्षणानि यस्मिन्। On which the cuts made by the tusks of infuriated elephants were the distinct marks of prowess (*i. e.* a writing commemorating his victory). Or we may take उत्कीर्ण as the p. p. and translate:—'On which the visible marks of victory were engraved by the tusks &c.;' or again, विक्रमो लक्ष्यतेऽनेनेति विक्रमलक्षणः, the indicator of prowess; व्यक्तो विक्रमलक्षणः व्यक्तविक्रमलक्षणः। मत्तेभरदनोत्कीर्णत्वात् एव व्यक्तविक्रमलक्षणः स तथोक्तः 'which was a distinct indicator of prowess because marked by' &c. त्रिकूटम्—*lit.* a mountain with three peaks. The one referred to here must be a hill in the territory of Trávancore. Kúṭa or Aśmaka is the ancient name of Trávancore, and hence it is possible that Trikúṭa may be one of the mountains in that country. This is distinct from the Trikùṭa on the top of which Laṅkâ is described to have been situated, though Vall. paraphrases this by 'सुवेलागिरिम्.'

Śl. 60. पारसीकान्—These are supposed to be the ancient Persians or inhabitants of that part of Persia which lies nearest to the Indus. See Wilson's Vish. P. p. 176 note 3. तत्त्वज्ञानेन—by the knowledge of the real nature of the individual soul and its relation to the supreme soul and of the cosmos and the Supreme spirit. This alludes to the Hindu doctrine that मोक्ष or final emancipation is not possible without *Tattvajnâna*. स्थलवर्त्मना—Malli. says that Raghu preferred the land-route because a voyage by sea is prohibited. This does not seem to be the correct explanation. The simile seems to suggest the true reason. A man can overcome his foes, the passions, only when he has तत्त्वज्ञान. So Raghu knew where the Persians were really weak (*i. e.* had तत्त्वज्ञान of their weakness). He might have thought that he could more easily defeat them on land and so undertaken a march by the perilous and circuitous land-route.

Sl. 61. यवनीमुखपद्मानाम्—The Gen. here is emphatic. He did not suffer the glow because it belonged to the lotus-like faces of the

Yavana ladies. Since Káli. applies the term *yavana* to the ancient Persians (and the other tribes on the North-west of India) it is clear that the term was not restricted to the Greeks or Ionians as some Western scholars suppose. मधुमदम्—The flush imparted by liquor. The invasion of Raghu struck terror into the hearts of the Persian ladies, who, though they were habitual drinkers, gave up drinking wine, so that their cheeks lost the usual glow of liquor. बालातपम्—the young, *i. e.*, the morning sun. This is added because it is the morning sun that gives the reddish glow to the lotuses. This serves to bear up resemblance with the red flush imparted by wine. अकाल &c.—out of the proper (the rainy) season *i. e.* in summer, when a sudden appearance of clouds is not expected. Raghus' invasion, too, took place at a time (*i. e.* early in summer) when the Yavana women were in their best spirits and did not at all expect an invasion. For a similar idea, *cf.* दैत्यस्त्रीगण्डलेखानां मदरागविलोपिभिः। हेतिभिश्चेतनावद्भिरुदीरितजयस्वनम् ॥ X. 12.

Sl. 62. तुमुलः—तौतीति, irregularly derived from तु 'to become full, to move, to injure', + मुक; 'tumultuous.' पाश्चात्यैः—पश्चाद्भवास्तैः। अश्वसाधनैः The special feature of the army of the Persians was their cavalry; and so they are spoken of here as अश्वसाधनाः, like the king of the Kalingas who is described as गजसाधन in Sl. 40, and the Vangas as नौसाधनोद्यत in Sl. 26. There is a distinct reference to the cavalry of the Persians as being their speciality in the Mudrâ. मेघाक्षः पञ्चमोस्मिन्पृथुतुरगबलः पारसीकाधिराजः &c. I. 20; see also *infra* V. 73. In fact the Yavanas, inhabiting the North-western frontier of India, were strong in their horse; *cf.* यः निरर्गलस्तुरगो विमुद्रः स सिन्धोर्दक्षिणरोधसि चरनश्वानीकेन यवनानां प्रार्थितः। Mâl. V. p. १९२. शार्ङ्गकूजित &c.—शार्ङ्ग see Samj. विज्ञातुं योग्या विज्ञेयाः। प्रतियुध्यन्त इति प्रतिगता योधा वा प्रतियोधाः; warriors on the other side, *i. e.* the Persians. This seems to show that though clouds of dust were raised here Raghu's skilful marksmen could still hit their enemies, while the Persians were confused, being blinded.

S'l. 63. भल्लापवर्जितैः—भल्लते इति भल्लः that which injures or kills; a kind of arrow with a crescent-shaped blade, generally made, of steel. भल्लैरपवर्जितानि तैः। श्मश्रुलैः—श्मश्रूणि सन्त्येषु इति तैः। Malli. explains this by referring it to the सिध्मादि class, but the word is not found in that list. We may therefore explain—श्मश्रूणि लान्तीति श्मश्रुलानि having beards. सरघा—सरं गतिमन्तं घातयतीति सह रघेण गत्या वर्तत इति वा। क्षौद्रपटलैरिव—The bearded heads of the fair-skinned Persians, with the scalp clean shaved, well resembled the honey-combs with a clustering swarm of bees over them.

Śl. 64. अपनीत &c.—This indicates that they did not wish to continue the fight. तं शरणं ययुः—approached him as their protector. A Sanskrit idiom which means 'sought his protection.' हि—See Samj. Or we may take it अवधारणे—'certainly,' and construe महात्मनां संरम्भः प्रणिपातप्रतिकारो हि। महात्मनाम्-here आत्मन् may mean 'soul', high-souled men; or 'effort', men of mighty efforts. It is impossible to resist such men, and therefore submission is the safest course. *Cf.* 'आत्मा यत्नो धृतिर्बुद्धिः स्वभावो ब्रह्म वर्ष्म च' Amara.

Śl. 65. विनयन्ते—नी with वि is Atm. when its object is in the body of the agent and not a part of the body, by the rule कर्तृस्थे &c. Pâṇ. I. 3. 37. See Samj. Thus here श्रम being in the body of the कर्ता or agent, and not a part of his body, we get विनयते. For further discussion of this point see Sid-Kau. on the Sûtra. अजिनरत्नाद्य-अजिनेषु रत्नानि अजिनरत्नानि best kinds of skins. *Cf.* जातौ जातौ यदुत्कृष्टं तद्रत्नमिति कथ्यते। *cf.* पुरुषरत्न, स्त्रीरत्न, अश्वरत्न &c. ०वलय—वलं यातीति वलयः a circle; a bower of. The regions to the North-west of India are still known for their luscious grapes and other fruits. क्वचित् 'वलजभूमिषु' इति पाठः। तत्र वलजं क्षेत्रम्। वलजे क्षेत्रपूर्द्वारे इत्यमरः। Châr.

Śl. 66. In this śl. Raghu is compared to the sun, his arms to the solar rays, and the kings he dethroned to the moisture sucked up by the rays of the sun. कौबेरीम्—(the quarter) presided over by Kubera, *i. e.* the north. वसुभिः—वसन्ति रसा अस्मिन्नित्युद्यः। The rays of the sun are compared to the bright arrows shot by Raghu in a battle. This indicates the agility with which Raghu discharged his arrows, as well as their immensity. उदीच्यान्—By this the poet refers to the whole tract including the north-west, the north and the north-east. उद्धरिष्यन्—The idea of lifting up is involved in both the instances. It is supposed that in the summer solstice (उत्तरायण) the sun goes towards the north to dry up moisture with his rays, and in the winter solstice (दक्षिणायन) he goes towards the south in order to pour the absorbed moisture in the form of rain. *Cf.* śl. 39.

Śl. 67. अध्वश्रमं--अध्वनोऽध्वजो वा श्रमः। सिन्धु—This may not necessarily be the Indus, but some river in Kashmere; as remarked by Malli. Châr. reads वङ्क्षु for सिन्धु (while Sum. reads वेक्षु) and remarks that it is a a pond in the country of Kashmere, which is a mere guess. वङ्क्षु has been conclusively proved to be the Oxus by Prof. Pathak (see Ind. Ant. Nov. 1912, p. 266) and is probably the older reading विचेष्टनैः—by rolling on their sides and stretching their limbs. It is thus that horses are relieved of their fatigue. कग्रकुङ्कुमकेसरान्—(1) To which filaments of saffron were sticking or (2) to the manes of which saffron was sticking. If however, the reading be—केशरान् the first sense alone is possible. For either केसर or केशर is correct when the meaning is 'pollen' or filaments of flowers; but when the meaning is 'the mane of a lion' (or horse) केसर alone is the correct form. This Śl. shows that the horses were quite refreshed and were now ready for fight again. The horses are especially mentioned here because Raghu had to make use of his cavalry in fighting with the Persians who were also अश्वसाधन and so the horses were hard-taxed.

Śl. 68. हूणावरोधानाम्—the white Huns or Indo-Scythians who were established in the Punjab and along the Indus at the commecement of the Christian era. See Wilson's Vish. P. Vol. II. p. 135. They evidently belonged to that nomadic tribe of the Huns who lived for some centuries in the plains of Tartary and were a great scourge to the Chinese and Roman possessions. कपोल &c.—आदेशुं शीलमस्येत्यादेशि; see Samj. The Hûṇa ladies had given up drinking which used to impart a red flush to their cheeks. But now that their husbands were killed in battle, they slapped their faces through grief which reddened their cheeks again. Thus Raghu ordered back, as it were, the red flush on their cheeks. Malli. suggests the alternative construction—पाटल आदेशी आदेष्टा यस्य of which the red hue was an indicator *i. e.* it became as it were a writing to keep up the memory of Raghu's valour.

Śl. 69. काम्बोजाः—In the Sab. P. of the Mah. Bhár. (XXVII. 22-3) the Kâmbojas are said to have been conquered by Arjuna along with the Daradas, after the conquest of Balkh. They must have inhabited the Hindukusha mountain which separates the Giljit valley from Balkh and the adjoining country, as its Kâfirs according to Elphinstone, still call themselves Kamoj, and probably extended upto Little Thibet and Ladak. Their country was famous for handsome horses and shawls made of goats', rats', and dogs' wool, and abounded in walnut trees. In the great war of Kurukshetra they are said to have fought on the side of the Kauravas. According to the Purâṇas they were originally Kshatriyas but degraded by the omission of the necessary rites. आनताः-(1) the trees bent down being pulled down by the elephants; (2) the kings bowed in submission to Raghu.

Śl. 70. सदश्व—Horses of the best breed. तुङ्गाः—high. It will be better to take तुङ्ग as compounded with द्रविणराशयः and read तुङ्गद्र०; the whole word would then qualify उपदाः (presents including lofty heaps of gold coins) and will thus improve the sense. उपदाः—उपदीयते इत्युपदा what is presented respectfully; complimentary presents; see V. 41 उत्सेकाः—pride, arrogance. The root सिच् with उद् means 'to be puffed up with pride.' Compare the use of the root in XVII. 43, न तस्योत्सिषिचे मनः । The poet means to say that though Raghu got wealth from every quarter he did not feel proud or conceited.

Śl. 71. अश्वसाधनः—He marched only with his cavalry, as it would have been very inconvenient for him to take the cars &c. with him on the mountain. वर्धयन्निव—This shows the vastness of his cavalry. उद्धूतैः—*i. e.* by the horses' hoofs. The mass of dust raised from the mineral soil was so great that it seemed to augment as it were the size of the peaks as it rose above them.

Śl. 72. तुल्यसत्त्वानाम्—सत्त्व properly means that quality of the mind which does not allow it to be flurried or perplexed in times of difficulties or dangers; hence, fortitude, courage; or सत्त्व may mean व्यवसाय, deeds of valour, exploit. The lions were equal in valour with the army and were not frightened at all. सैन्यघोष—The din and bustle of the army. असंभ्रमम्—The idea of negation is prominent here (असंभ्रमं शशंस being equivalent to संभ्रमो नास्तीति) though the नञ् is compounded. See note on I. 21. अवलोकितम्—is used here in the sense of 'a glance'. Châritravardhana and Dinakara interpret the passage differently. Dinakara says प्रकरणात्स इत्यध्याह्रियते । स रघुरात्मना तुल्यं सत्त्वं येषां तादृशानां गुहासु स्थितानां सिंहानां सैन्यकोलाहलेऽप्यसम्भ्रमं सधैर्यं यथा तथा परिवृत्यावलोकनं शशंसास्तौषीत्. He praised the bold glance cast by the lions turning round &c. Vallabha also construes the passage like Din. but takes असंभ्रमं as qualifying अवलोकितम्. This way of taking the passage is better no doubt, but then the difficulty is about the subject. We cannot get it from the context as Châr. and Dinakara proposes to do, since there is no attribute referring to रघु in this śl. For nearly the same thought *cf.* Śiś. XII. 52.

Śl. 73. मर्मरीभूताः—मर्मर is a rustling sound. This indicates that the breezes were gentle. *Cf.* VI. 57. कीचक &c.—This epithet shows that the breezes wafted musical sounds. गङ्गाशीकरिणः—implies coolness in the wind.

Śl. 74. वासितोत्सङ्गाः—उत्सजन्त्यस्मिन् इति उत्सङ्गः fr. सञ्ज्+अ (घञ्) अधिकरणे. उत्सङ्ग lit. means 'the lap'; see *infra* XIII. 31; Meg. II. 26. hence the surface. वासित properly means 'to which other qualities are imparted;' hence, here, scented. With their surfaces scented. नाभि-musk (in the navels). These two ślokas show that Raghu's soldiery had all the comforts there that might be desired.

Śl. 75. **ग्रैवेय**—ग्रीवासु भवानि स्थितानि वा ग्रैवेयाणि; see *supra* Śl. 48. **ओषधयः**—The other form is **औषधि**. **नक्तम्**—at night. **अस्नेह दीपिकाः**—न विद्यते स्नेहः यासां ता अस्नेहाः; दीपयन्तीति दीपिकाः; अस्नेहाश्च ता दीपिकाश्च अस्नेहदीपिकाः lamps requiring no oil. The mountain Himâlaya is said to have on it potent herbs endowed with the power of emitting light at night.. See Kum. I. 10. The herbs here served as watch-fires to Raghu's soldiers.

Śl. 76. **तस्योत्सृष्टनिवासेषु**—The presence of the word **उत्सृष्ट** shows that even the hardy and ferocious Kirâtas had fled away through fear when Raghu approached them. They ventured forth from their lurking places only when they found that Raghu had left. Since the word is emphatic it should not have been compounded. **गजवर्ष्म**—the height of the elephants. For a similar idea compare—Śiś. XII. 64. quoted in the foot note.

किरातेभ्यः—The word is derived as **किरं पर्यन्तभूमिमतति गच्छतीति किरात** one who lives on the borders of hills or mountains, a barbarian. *Cf.* **पर्यन्ताश्रयिभिर्निजस्य सदृशं नाम्नः किरातैः कृतम्** । Rat. II. 3. The Kirâtas are hillmen living by hunting and clad in a dress made of peacock's feathers. See Kum. I. 6, 15. In the Purâṇas they are mentioned along with Mlechchhas, and are described to be of a dark complexion, dwarfish in stature, with short arms and legs, projecting chin, broad, flat nose, red eyes and tawny hair. In the Sab. Par. of the Mah. Bhâr. (XXX. 15), Bhîma is said to have conquered seven Kirâta chiefs from Videha which included Darabhangá and part of Eastern Nepâl. In another passage they are said to be ferocious bow-men clad in hides and living upon fruits and roots. The Kirátas therefore seem to be a tribe of mountaineers inhabiting the sub-Himâlayan regions.

Sl. 77. **पर्वतीयैः**—With the mountain tribes. For derivation see Malli. Bhaṭṭoji Dîkshita prefers the reading **पार्वतीयैः** and explains **पर्वते भवाः पर्वतीयाः पार्वतीयानामिमे पार्वतीयाः** । **गणैः**—refers to the seven tribes (that inhabited the northern slopes of the Himálaya). See next Śl. and notes. **नाराच**—steel arrows. **०क्षेपणीयाश्म** &c.—shows the great skill of the mountaineers in throwing stones with slings.

Śl. 78. **उत्सवसंकेतान्**—The Utsavasaṃketas were a hill-tribe living in Ladak (its Sanskrit name is Hâśaka), north of Káśmere or in the north-east region of Ladak which is watered by the Kooner, and which is said to be the mythological abode of the Kimpurushas, the Kiṃnaras and other semi-divine beings. According to the Mahâbhárata, Arjuna, at the time of the *Rajasûya* sacrifice performed by Yudhishthira, conquered these barbarous tribes who are said to have been divided into seven classes *Cf.* पौरवं युधि निर्जित्य दस्यून्पर्वतवासिनः । गणानुत्सवसंकेतानजयत्सप्त पाण्डवः ॥ Mah. Bhár. Sab. P. Adh. XXVII. विरतोत्सवान्—implies that they were vanquished. जयोदाहरणम्—आह्रियतेऽस्मिन्नित्याहरणं; a connected account. उदाहरण is the loud narration of a connected account. Chá. and Din. take it simply in the sense of 'songs declaratory of glory.' According to some it has its technical meaning here, *viz.* a panegyric song beginning with such words as जयति &c., full of alliteration and composed in the Mâlinî or other similar metre, &c. See Pratâparudra quoted in the foot-note. किन्नरान्—कुत्सिता नराः a Nityasamâsa. They are so called because they have a deformed body—the face of a horse with a human body. See Wilson's Vish. P. Vol. I. pp. 82, 87.

Śl. 79. परस्परेण-परेण परेणेति परस्परेण. ज्ञातः-By the rule 'मतिबुद्धिपूजार्थेभ्यश्च' the affix त is added in the sense of the present tense. And when so added it governs the Gen. case. Following this reasoning, many commentators adopt the reading परस्परस्य. But there seems to be no necessity for changing the reading. The rule alluded to above does not always prevent the त from being added in the past tense; *e. g.* पूजितो यः सुरासुरैः । We have a ज्ञापकप्रमाण for this. See Pán. IV. 3. 115 उपायनपाणिषु—उपायनानि पाणिषु येषां तेषु । Malli. dissolves as उपायनयुक्ताः पाणयो येषां probably to avoid the application of the rule 'सप्तमीविशेषणे बहुव्रीहौ' forgetting that पाणि is treated as an exception in the Bháshya. सारः—(1) riches; (2) power.

Śl. 80. अक्षोभ्यम्—क्षोभमनर्हः अक्षोभ्यः not to be shaken off *i. e.* imperishable. पौलस्त्य—पुलस्त्यस्य गोत्रापत्यं पुमान् । This alludes to the story of Râvana's lifting up the mountain Kailâsa. Once while Rávaṇa was passing in his aerial car (called Pushpaka) which he had taken by force from Kubera, its motion was suddenly arrested as he approached that part of the mountain Kailása where lived Śiva and Párvatî. He was told by Nandî to leave the mountain. But Rávaṇa in anger uplifted it with his arms. Thereupon Śiva pressed the mountain with the little finger of his left foot and compelled Rávaṇa to relinquish his hold upon the mountain. See Râm. Utt. K. पौलस्त्यतुलित &c.--Here the poet gives the reason why the mountain had to be ashamed of itself. Raghu thought it beneath his dignity to advance against Kailâsa as the mountain was once overcome by Rávaṇa who was a *Bráhmaṇa*, and therefore was not worthy of his superior prowess as a *Kshatriya.*

Śl. 81. तीर्णलौहित्ये—Lauhityâ is the ancient name for the Brâhmaputrâ. Raghu crossed the river and re-entered India by the North-eastern frontier where lay the kingdom of Prágjyotisha. The ancient capital of Kámarûpa was at **Prâgjyotishapura** situated on the Lauhityâ. **प्राग्ज्योतिषेश्वरः**—The lord of Prâgjyotisha or *the City of eastern stars*. See Kâli. P. quoted in the foot-note. Prágjyotisha is identified with the eastern-most part of India comprising Western Bhootan and Eastern Assam. **कालागुरुद्रुमैः**—**कालान्यगुरूण्येव द्रुमाः कालागुरुद्रुमाः ।** As Raghu's elephants were tied to the trees they quaked and simultaneously with them trembled also the king of the land with fear. For a similar idea *cf.* Śl. 69.

Śl. 82. **अधारावर्ष &c.**—**धाराणां वर्षः धारावर्षः अविद्यमानः धारावर्षः यस्मिन् तदधारावर्षम् । अधारावर्षं च तद् दुर्दिनं च** a cloudy gloom without rainfall (caused by the dust raised by the moving chariots). **पताकिनी**—**पताकाः विद्यन्ते अस्यां** that in which there are flags displayed; hence, an army.

Śl. 83. **कामरूपाणाम्**—An important kingdom said to have extended from the banks of the Karatoyâ or Sadánîrâ to the extremities of Assam. Its king Bhagadatta plays a conspicuous part in the Mahábhârata. In the Sabháparva he is said to have fought with Arjuna for eight days with an army of 'Kirátas, Chînas, and seafaring men.' And in the Udyogaparva he is said to have assisted Duryodhana with an army of the Kirátas and Chînas. From these references it is clear that his kingdom must have extended upto the Himálaya on the north and the borders of China on the east. Further, Kâlidása speaks here of elephants which are still found in the jungles of Upper Assam and the Dooars, and of the aloe-wood tree which, according to Dr. Roxburgh, is a native of the eastern frontier; and this fact also leads to the same inference. **अत्याखण्डल &c.**—**आखण्डयति परबलमित्याखण्डलः** the destroyer of the enemies' army; Indra. **अत्याक्रान्त आखण्डलविक्रममत्याखण्डलविक्रमः** Prâdi. Comp.; or **अतिगत आखण्डलविक्रमो येन** a Bah. The reference to the prowess of Raghu as superior even to that of Indra is very pertinent. It shows how Raghu's very name struck terror into the heart of the king of Kâmarûpa. **भिन्नकटैः**—With the temples split open *i. e.* elephants in rut. See *supra* Śl. 47.

Śl. 84. —**हेमपीठाधिदेवताम्**—**हेमनिर्मितं पीठं हेमपीठं** an Uttarapadalopi Comp.; **अधिष्ठिता देवता अधिदेवता** the presiding deity; **हेमपीठस्याधिदेवता ताम् । छायाम्**—The orb of the splendour (of Raghu's feet). **रत्नपुष्पोपहारेण**—As Raghu's feet rested on the golden foot-stool their lustre spread all round. The poet considers the orb of lustre as the presiding goddess of the foot-stool and the gems that were presented to him as the offering of flowers made to that deity.

Śl. 85. इति—in this manner. जिष्णुः—a habitual conqueror. See Saṃj.; this may refer to Raghu by the maxim 'विशेषणमात्रप्रयोगो विशेष्यप्रतिपत्तौ,' or may qualify सः understood, as Malli. would have it. छत्रशून्येषु—destitute of the umbrellas i. e. of the white umbrellas. The white umbrella is an emblem of royalty and independence. Since the kings were conquered by Raghu and made his vassals they lost their independence and could no longer use the white umbrella. रजो विश्रामयन्—This and the preceding epithets indicate the undisputed universal sovereignty of Raghu. See note on विश्रामय I 54.

Śl. 86. विश्वजितम्—विश्वं जयतीति विश्वजित् तम् । The best of all sacrifices or a sacrifice for the universal conqueror. This is a kind of sacrifice in which the sacrificer has to give as *Dakshiná* all his wealth to the officiating priests and in which the immolation consists of five or two goats. आ जह्रे–It was natural that Raghu should perform a sacrifice at the termination of his successful campaign to please the Brahmaṇa class. He had advanced and honoured the chief Kshatriya warriors by his conquest; opened facilities for trade and so pleased the Vaishyas; and by acquring new lands for cultivation gratified the Śûdras; and it now remained for him to please the Bráhmaṇas whose blessings he must have received when starting.

हि—is used here in the sense of एव. विसर्गाय—The dative may be explained as 'तुमर्थाच्च भाववचनात्' *i. e.* equivalent to विस्रष्टुं; or तादर्थ्ये, विसर्गार्थम्. आदानं &c.—a proverbial saying. *Cf.* अगृध्नुराददे सोर्थं I. 21.

Śl. 87. सत्रान्ते—सीदन्त्यत्रानेन वेति सत्रम् । a sacrifice. सचिवसखः—सचिवानां सखा । Mallinâtha says that the king is here called the friend of the ministers to indicate that he and his ministers always acted in perfect accord. See Saṃj. *Cf.* सदानुकूलेषु हि कुर्वते रतिं नृपेष्वमात्येषु च सर्वसंपदः । Kir. I. 5. This shows that the king and his ministers were equally careful in attending to the kings. पुरस्क्रियाभिः—पुरस्क्रिया lit. placing in the front; hence, honouring; respectful treatment. ०पराजयव्यलीकान्—अलीक is what is not liked; hence, a feeling of dissatisfaction; विशेषेणालीकं व्यलीकम् । पराजयस्य व्यलीकं &c.; or, as Malli. takes it, पराजयेन (हेतुना) व्यलीकं, the comp. being सह सुपा.

चिरविरहो०—चिरं विरहः चिरविरहः; अवरुध्यन्ते इत्यवरोधाः; (those restricted within a limited area, the harem); now see Saṃj.; 'whose wives had become anxious on account of their long absence.' This indicates that the sacrificial session continued for many days. राजन्यान्—राज्ञोऽपत्यानि राजन्याः the vanquished princes. Here the poet uses this word instead of राज्ञः as their royalty did not deserve prominent mention along with that of Raghu. See Saṃj.

Śl 88. रेखाध्वज &c.—The linear marks of flags, umbrellas, &c. on the palms of the hands and the soles of feet indicate royalty. *Cf.*

the śl. from Sámudraka quoted in the foot-note. The marks on the hands of a universal sovereign are given in the following śl.:—अतिरक्तः करो यस्य ग्रथिताङ्गुलिको मृदुः । चापाङ्कुशाङ्कितः सोपि चक्रवर्ती भवेद् ध्रुवम् ॥ सम्राजः—A सम्राट् (mark the Saṃdhi) is one who rules over vassal kings and has performed a Rájasùya sacrifice. See Malli. on II. 4. प्रस्थानप्रणति—obeisance at the time of parting. मौलिस्रक् &c.—Malli. dissolves as मकरन्दश्च रेणवश्च &c.; the comp. should have been रेणुमकरन्द &c. by the rule 'अल्पाच्तरम्;' but the rule is often disregarded. Raghu's feet became yellow at the toes on account of the particles of honey and the pollen dropped down from the garlands on the heads of kings. This implies that a vast number of kings prostrated themselves at Raghu's feet.

CANTO V.

Śl. 1. तम्—To him (the conqueror of the four quarters as described in the fourth Canto). अध्वरे—See note on I. 31. विश्वजिति—See note on the word IV. 86. निःशेष &c.—निर्गतः शेषोऽस्मादस्य वेति निःशेषम्. Now see Saṃj. उपात्तविद्यः—For the fourteen *vidyas* see below (śl. 21) गुरुदक्षिणार्थी—गुरोर्दक्षिणा गुरुदक्षिणा । तादर्थ्ये षष्ठीसमासः । सैवार्थः गुरुदक्षिणार्थोऽसंनिहितोस्य । प्रपेदे—For this sense *cf.* Kum. I. 21; Bhaṭṭi. IV. 1, &c. The śloka begins with the syllable त which indicates the fulfilment of one's wishes. *Cf.* Bṛihaspati—तकारे सर्वसिद्धिश्च प्राप्यते विपुलं धनम् । सर्वश्रेयो भवेत्तस्य सुस्थितं चोपजायते ॥

Śl. 2. हिरण्मय—formed irregularly fr. हिरण्य + मय; see Saṃj. अर्घ्यम्—what is intended for worship (अर्घ); see com.; a respectful offering to gods, venerable men &c., consisting of flowers, water, rice, &c. According to the *tantras* it comprises eight articles, which are—आपः क्षीरं कुशाग्रं च दधि सर्पिः सतण्डुलम् । यवः सिद्धार्थकश्चैव अष्टाङ्गोऽर्घः प्रकीर्तितः ॥ The Devî—P. mentions these somewhat differently—रक्तबिल्वाक्षतैः पुष्पैर्दधिदूर्वाकुशैस्तिलैः । सामान्यः सर्वदेवानामर्घोयं परिकीर्तितः ॥ अनर्घ०—अविद्यमानः अर्घः यस्य तदनर्घं, अनर्घं शीलमस्य अनर्घशीलः. यशसा प्रकाशः—These two epithets explain why Raghu did not hesitate to expose his poverty before Kautsa. Indeed Kautsa reveres him all the more for this. See further on (śl. 16). श्रुतप्रकाशम्—This shows that Kautsa deserved the worship. अतिथिम्—See note on I. 53.

Śl. 3. विधिज्ञः—This may be an उपपदसमास (विधिं जानातीति by adding क *i. e.* अ by the rule आतोऽनुपसर्गे कः) or a षष्ठीत० (जानातीति ज्ञः विधेर्ज्ञः)। विशां पतिः—See note under I. 13. विष्टरभाजम्—विस्तीर्यते

(that which is spread) इति विष्टरः, when meaning 'a seat that is spread on the ground ' (for pious Brâhmaṇas or ascetics who do not sit on any other seat). विस्तरः is the form when referring to speech (a detailed description); as in अलं विस्तरेण. The स्त is changed to ष्ट by Páṇ. VIII. 3. 93. See Saṃj.

Śl. 4. अग्रणीः—अग्रं the front नयतीति; a leader, the foremost of. 'मन्त्रकृताम्—Those who arranged the Mantras or Vedic hymns; or rather those to whom the hymns were revealed; *cf.* Sáyaṇa—'न हि वेदस्य कर्तारो द्रष्टारः सर्व एव हि' । Or the Mantras referred to here may be those of the Atharva Veda, in which case we may translate—'of those who are the authors of the mantras'; *cf.* I. 61. कुशाग्रबुद्धे—कुशाग्रमिव बुद्धिर्यस्य । one whose intellect is as sharp as the blade of Kuśa grass, very acute or sharp. गुरुः—'स गुरुर्यः क्रियां कृत्वा वेदमस्मै प्रयच्छति'; 'he is called a Guru who performs the initiatory ceremonies (उपनयन) and teaches the Veda.' (Yâj.). There are eleven Gurus (not taken in this technical sense) mentioned by Devala—आचार्यश्च पिता ज्येष्ठो भ्राता चैव महीपतिः । मातुलः श्वशुरस्त्राता मातामहपितामहौ ॥ वर्णज्येष्ठः पितृव्यश्च पुंस्येते गुरवो मताः ॥ चैतन्यम्—चेतनस्य भावश्चैतन्यम् । The simile here is peculiarly appropriate. As the world of living beings is wholly and solely indebted to the sun for all its activity, its very life, so the disciple was fully indebted to his preceptor for the whole stock of his knowledge,—knowledge on which his future life depended. The King's question here is in accordance with the precept 'ब्राह्मणं कुशलं पृच्छेत्' &c.

Śl. 5. अपि—'*and*'. अन्तरायः—अन्तरं व्यवधानमयते गच्छत्यन्तरस्य वा अयः अयनं from इ and aff. घञ् or the root अय् and अच्. कच्चित्—asks a question mixed with hope, the expected answer being 'yes or no' according to the form of the question, and is translated by 'I hope that' &c.; see A. G. § 263. त्रिविधम्—तिस्रो विधा यस्य । The saint would be exhausting the store of his penance if he had to use his power of imprecation in removing obstacles or subduing temptations ; and hence the question of the king. (See ft.-note 5). For ancient kings considered it their duty to protect sages from all sorts of disturbances. *Cf.* Kir. II. 48, स क्षत्रियस्त्राणसहः सतां यः &c.; Śâk. I. 13, V. 14.

Śl. 6. आधार &c.—आधारस्य बन्ध आधारबन्धः । प्रगतो मुखं प्रमुखः (प्रादिस०) आधारबन्धः प्रमुखो येषाम् ॥ यद्वा प्रकृष्टं मुखं प्रमुखम् । आधारबन्धाः प्रमुखे येषाम् । विशेषः—Malli. takes this in the sense of अतिशय; but the meaning भेद ('difference') will do here. उपप्लवः--see note on उपप्लवेभ्यः II. 48. पादपानाम्—पादैः पिबतीति पादपः that which sucks up moisture by its roots, hence, a tree.

Śl. 7. वत्सलत्वात्—वत्से पुत्रादिस्नेहपात्रेऽभिलाषोऽस्यास्तीति वत्सलस्तस्य भावस्तत्त्वं तस्मात् । The मतुप् affix ल is added to वत्स and अंस in the sense of 'love for' and 'strength' respectively. 'वत्सांसाभ्यां कामबले' Páṇ. V. 2. 98. So वत्स when it takes ल loses its proper meaning and has a technical signification. चूडाल and चूडावान् have the same meaning; but वत्सल is not the same as वत्सवान्; the one means 'fond, compassionate,' the other 'one who has a child.' इत्तिविषये वत्सांसशब्दौ स्वभावात्कामबलयोर्वर्तमानौ तद्वति प्रत्ययमुत्पादयतः न ह्यत्र वत्सार्थः अंसार्थो वा विद्यते । Vâmana. ०नाभिनाला—नाभिस्थानि नालानि नाभिनालानि । अनघा--अविद्यमानमघं harm, a mishap यस्याः; *cf.* further XIV. 75; and मृगवधूर्यदा अनघप्रसवा भवति Śâk. V. p. 105.

Śl. 8. नियमाभिषेकः—नियमस्य नियमार्थो वाभिषेकः । Properly a bath preliminary to the discharge of daily duties; hence the daily bath. निवाप—न्युप्यते इति, निवपनं वा; fr. वप् with नि+अ (घञ्) added कर्मणि or भावे. It is a technical term applied to the oblations consisting of water, sesamum &c. offered to the souls of departed parents or other relatives. See *infra* VIII. 86, Mudr. IV. 5. पितॄणाम्—The deceased ancestors, as well as a class of divine beings known as the Pitṛis, to whom every Bráhmaṇa has to offer oblations every day.

The Pitṛis are supposed to be the progenitors of mankind. They inhabit celestial regions of their own. The original Pitṛis are divided into seven orders:-(1) वैराजाः; (2) अग्निष्वात्ताः; (3) बर्हिषदः; (4) सुकालाः; (5) आङ्गिरसः; (6) सुस्वधाः; and (7) सोमपाः । Of these the first three orders are without form (अमूर्तयः) *i. e.* composed of spiritual, not elementary substance, and they can assume any form they please; the other four are corporeal. *Cf.* Hv. सप्तैते जरतां श्रेष्ठ सर्वे पितृगणाः स्मृताः । चत्वारो मूर्तिमन्तो वै त्रय एषाममूर्तयः ॥ According to a legend given by the Vâyu P. and the Hv., the gods once offended Brahmâ by neglecting to worship him, and were cursed to be fools. Upon their repenting they were directed to apply to their sons for instruction. Being taught accordingly the rites of expiation and penance by them, the gods addressed them as fathers, whence the sons of gods became the first Pitṛis.

उञ्छषष्ठाङ्कित—The sixth parts of the rice collected by the ascetics due from them to the king were placed on the bank of the river to be taken away by the royal officers. See *supra*, षष्ठांशमुर्व्याः &c. II. 66, and foot-note thereon. Malli. justifies the षष्ठीतत्पु० in उञ्छषष्ठ thus—Here षष्ठ is not an ordinal numeral, but means 'the sixth part' and so there is no difficulty about compounding. The affix अन् is here added in the sense of a part (भागार्थे) and not पूरणार्थे by the rule षष्ठाष्टमाभ्यां ञ च Pâṇ. V. 3. 50. The Sûtra 'पूरणगुण'-(Pâṇ. II. 2. 11) forbids a Gen. Tat. with पूरणप्रत्ययान्त (an ordinal numeral) and not with an अन्प्रत्ययान्त. According to Bhattoji Dikshita, however, many (who take उन्त्रुषड as a Gen. Tat.) consider this as a slip of the poet. He suggests two alternatives:—(1) उन्छेषु षड उन्छषड: Loc. Tat.; (2) उन्छात्मकः षडः उन्छषडः शाकपार्थिवादिः । See Manoramá on 'पूरणगुण—.' सैकतानि—For der. see Saṃj. The word सिकता is generally used in the plural. तीर्थजलानि—Holy waters; तीर्थ water used by sages; निपानागमयोस्तीर्थमृषिजुष्टे जले गुरौ । इत्यमरः । Or तीर्थ a flight of steps for reaching water called a *ghát*; and as such *tírthas* are constructed at different places along the banks of holy rivers in India. तीर्थ also signifies holy water. तीर्थं शास्त्रेऽध्वरे क्षेत्रोपायोपाध्यायमन्त्रिषु । योनौ जलावतारे च । इति हलायुधः ।

Śl. 9. नीवारपाकादि—नीवारस्य पाकः नीवारपाकः स आदिर्यस्य तत् । See also ft.-note. कडंगरीयैः—गिरतीति गरः । कडस्य भक्षणीयस्य गरः कडंगरः the nasal comes in irregularly (Pâṇ. V. I. 69). कडंगरः—that which contains the grain *i. e.* chaff, husks. यद्वा कडति मदं करोतीति कड । कड च तदङ्गं च तद्गातीति कडंगरः । and by adding छ (ईय) in the sense of 'deserving to feed on,' we get कडंगरीय; see Saṃj. Vámana, Haradatta and Bhaṭṭoji reject the reading कडङ्गर and adopt कडङ्कर instead; so it will be preferable to read कडङ्करीयैः here. कडङ्कर—that which causes intoxication (कड) or distraction; properly, 'what appears perfect outwardly but has no grain within and thus becomes food for cattle only.' It takes this name probably because it has got the property of causing slight intoxication. आमृश्यते—is eaten up. The more general meaning of this root is 'to touch superficially, to handle roughly' &c.; *cf.* Kir. IV. 14; Śiś. IX. 34; Kum. III. 36. It also means 'to seize by force,' as in Kum. II. 31. जानपदैः—For it was the duty of villagers to see that their cattle did not trespass on holy grounds. कालोपपन्ना° &c.—It is the duty of every householder to wait for some time, before taking his meal, to see if a guest is coming. *Cf.* आचम्य च ततः कुर्यात्प्राज्ञो द्वारावलोकनम् । मुहूर्तस्याष्टमं भागमुद्वीक्ष्यो ह्यतिथिर्भवेत् ॥ Márk. P. शरीरस्थिति—feeding or sustenance of the body; for this sense *cf.* शरीरस्थितिमकरोत् Kâd. नीवारपाकादि may also be taken as an adj. qualifying शरीरस्थितिसाधनं which may be regarded as जातौ एकवचनम् । 'I hope the wild नीवार corn and the other wild sources of the nourishment' &c.

Ś'l. 10. विनीय—See III. 29. गृहाय—see note on II. 1. हि—हेतौ. This gives the reason for asking the question 'Have you been permitted' &c. सर्वोपकारक्षमम्—which enables one to oblige every body; which affords the amplest scope to charity of every kind. Or according to Malli. 'which is the upholder of the other three

Âs'ramas or on which the other *Âs'ramas* depend.' See Manu quoted by Malli. in support of his meaning. We may also quote 'गृहस्थ उच्यते श्रेष्ठः स त्रीनेतान्बिभर्ति हि' । 'यथा नदीनदाः सर्वे सागरे यान्ति संस्थितिम् । तथैवाश्रमिणः सर्वे गृहस्थे यान्ति संस्थितिम् ॥' Manu. VI. 89, 90. आश्रमम्—The religious life of a Brâhmaṇa is divided into four stages:-(1) ब्रह्मचर्य or the period of celibacy, which he ought to pass at his Guru's house in Vedic studies; (2) गार्हस्थ्य or the married life, which he leads as a house-holder; (3) वानप्रस्थ्य or the life of an anchorite, in which he retires to the forest with or without his wife (see Manu. VI. 3) which is meant as an initiative (see Manu. VI. 33) to—(4) संन्यास or the last stage, in which, all his passions being properly subdued, he may fix his mind on *Moksha.*

Ṡl. 11. अर्हतः—of one deserving of honour, respectable. नियोगक्रिया—नियोगस्य क्रिया—the execution of a command. उत्सुकम्—The words प्रसित and उत्सुक govern the Instr. or the Loc. case. मां संभावयितुम् &c.—The fig. of speech here according to Hem. is 'प्रेयः,' प्रेयः प्रियतराख्यानं; see Kâv. D. II. 275. In asking these queries Raghu's observance of propriety is worthy of note. He first chooses the most important person in the hermitage, *viz.*, the saint and inquires first after the welfare of his body and mind, then after his ascetic exercises and lastly after the well-being of everything connected with the hermitage of the sage. He next directs his inquiries to Kautsa himself, first with reference to his person and then to his purpose. The first line may also be translated as—"my mind, eager for the execution of some command from you, is not satisfied by the mere arrival of you."

Ṡl. 12. अपि—has here the force of गर्हा or disregard. Though Kautsa heard the noble words of Raghu, he placed more faith in the visible evidence of his poverty, disregarding his words; and so he was दुर्बलाश &c. स्वार्थोपपत्तिं प्रति—with respect to the attainment of his object. This way of restricting a general statement (here दुर्बलाशः) is called इत्थंभूताख्यान. प्रति is a कर्मप्रवचनीय in this sense—लक्षणेत्थंभूताख्यानभागवीप्सासु प्रतिपर्यनवः *i. e.* प्रति, परि and अनु are कर्म° in the sense of indication, limitation, share and repetition; see Sid.-Kau. on Pâṇ. I. 4. 90.

Ṡl. 13. वार्तम्—welfare; वृत्तिरस्त्यस्मिन् (Vârt. on Pâṇ. V. 2. 101); *cf. infra* XV. 41 (स पृष्टः सर्वतो वार्तमाख्यद्राज्ञे न संततिम्); स्वजनस्य वार्तमयमन्वयुङ्क्त च । Ṡis'. XIII. 68. अशुभम्—Here नञ् has the sense of opposition. Hence अशुभ means all that is opposed to शिव and not merely absence of शिव. तमिस्रा—तमो बहुलमस्त्यस्याम् । This word is irregularly formed, like ज्योत्स्ना and others given in Pâṇ. V. 2. 114. It means 'a dark night' or 'a mass of darkness.' तमिस्राच तमस्ततिः Viśvakośa. तमिस्रम् *V. l.*—This reading, which is also noticed by Malli., is perhaps preferable as it agrees with अशुभ in gender. सूर्ये &c.—The fig. of speech here according to Malli. is अर्थान्तरन्यास. This is after the older writers on Rhetoric, according to whom whenever one thing is cited in support of another, the fig. is अर्थान्तरन्यास. *Cf.* Daṇḍin quoted in the ft.-note. According to modern writers, however, a general fact must support a particular one or *vice versa* to constitute an अर्थान्तरन्यास. According to them the fig. here will be a दृष्टान्त and not अर्थान्तरन्यास. For a parallel passage, see ft.-note; also *cf.* तमांसि तिष्ठन्ति हि तावदंशुमान्न यावदायात्युदयाद्रिमौलिताम् ॥ Mâl.

Śl. 14. प्रतीक्ष्येषु--lit. those who are fit to be waited upon, to be treated with consideration; hence venerable, respectable. पूर्वान्--*cf.* अनुकारिणि पूर्वेषां युक्तरूपमिदं त्वयि । Śâk. II. 16. महाभाग—glorious or illustrious one; *cf.* महाभागः कामं नरपतिरभिन्नस्थितिरसौ । Śák. V. 10. Malli. translates this by सार्वभौम; so he takes the word भाग to mean 'a portion of the world,' महाभाग meaning 'one who possesses a very large portion of the world' *i. e.* a kingdom. भाग may also mean a portion of virtues, such as दया, दाक्षिण्य &c., or of good fortune. Some take महाभागतया as one word, 'by your magnanimity.' अर्थिभावात्—अर्थिनः भावः (the position or condition of) अर्थिभावस्तस्मात्, as 'a suitor.'

Śl. 15. शरीरमात्रेण—शरीरमेव शरीरमात्रम्; a *nitya samása*. According to Bhaṭṭoji मयूरव्यंसकादित्वात्समासः । नरेन्द्र--These two words are purposely placed side by side with each other in order to make the contrast more glaring. तीर्थ--note the different senses of this word. See śl. 8. Some take तीर्थ to mean, 'a sacrifice.' आरण्यक०--may also mean forest-dwelling ascetics; *cf.* तपः षड्भागमक्षय्यं ददत्यारण्यका हि नः । Śâk. II. 34. स्तम्ब--a stack. नीवार—*i. e.* the stalk with the grain on.

Śl. 16. स्थाने--This should rather be taken as an *adv.* qualifying व्यनक्ति; 'well or very properly do you' &c. Some take it as qualifying the whole sentence अकिंचनत्वं व्यनक्ति इति यत्तत् स्थाने &c. This makes स्थाने an *adj.*; *cf. infra* VII. 13, Kum. VI. 67. एकनराधिपः—एकोऽद्वितीयो नराधिपः a paramount king. पर्यायपीतस्य—see ft.-note. The word पीत is here used because the moon is supposed to be a watery mass. *Cf.* सलिलमये शशिनि रवेर्दीधितयो मूर्च्छितास्तमो नैशम् । Varâhamihira; रसात्मकस्योडुपतेश्च रश्मयः, Kum. V. 22; पुष्णामि चौषधीः सर्वाः सोमो भूत्वा रसात्मकः । Bg. XV. 13. हिमांशोः—हिमो गुणो विद्यते येषां ते हिमाः । The possessive affix is dropped after words expressive of qualities (by the Vârt. गुणवचनेभ्यो मतुपो लुगिष्टः); हिमा अंशवोऽस्य तस्य ।

In the case of the word हिमवान्, हिम means 'snow' which is a द्रव्य and not a गुण. For the reverence in which the new moon is held see II. 73, VI. 31; Kir. II. 11.

Śl. 17. तावत्--may either be taken साकल्ये (entirely, without any other object in view) as Malli. seems to do, or अवधारणे and construed with अहम्. अनन्यकार्यः--अविद्यमानमन्यत्कार्यं यस्य. गुर्वर्थम्--गुरोरर्थः--a Gen. Tat. like अश्वघास; or गुरवे देयोऽर्थः । निर्गलित &c.—निःशेषं गलितो निर्गलितः; अम्बु एव गर्भोऽम्बुगर्भः । निर्गलितोऽम्बुगर्भो यस्य। शरद्घनम्—A Gen. or a Loc. Tat. चातकः—A bird often referred to in Sanskrit poetry as entirely depending on clouds for water to drink. *cf.* तृषाकुलैश्चातकपक्षिणां कुलैः। Rit. II. 3

The *Châtaka* is not a fabulous bird, and what Káli. says here is a fact. It is a migratory bird which is seen in India in the rainy season and disappears in the autumn. It has a shrill but not unpleasant note, which is of the same pitch as that of the cuckoo, and very much resembles the word for 'a cloud' pronounced as vocative. Hence the bird is supposed to invoke the clouds for a shower, that it may intercept a few drops to quench its thirst. S. P. Pandit in his notes to Vik. II. thus describes the bird that is seen in Western India--'It is a small bird, smaller than the smallest dove, has a long tail and combines in itself the black, the yellow and the white. It has a long crest on its head, of the shape of a bow with an arrow stretched on it, which is supposed to prevent it from bending its head by coming opposite the back and thereby to prevent it from drinking water lying on the ground-or any water to drink which the beak is to be lowered.'

अपि--For the force of this see Samj. and ft.-note. The fig. of speech here is अर्थान्तरन्यास according to Dandin. Bhoja &c., and दृष्टान्त according to modern writers on Rhetoric.

Śl. 18. एतावत्--एतत् परिमाणमस्य । प्रतियातुकामम्--The nasal of the *inf.* is dropped before काम and मनस्; see Samj. "प्रतियातु is properly a substantive from प्रतिया with the affix तु. What is used in classical Sanskrit as the infinitive mood is only the acc. sing. of a mas. substantive ending in तु. In the Veda we meet with the Abl. Gen. and Dat. sing. of the so-called infinitive; *e. g.* गन्तवे, गन्तोः &c." Pandit. *Cf.* 'रे हस्त दक्षिण मृतस्य शिशोर्द्विजस्य जीवातवे विसृज शूद्रमुनौ कृपाणम् ।' Uttar. II. 10. त्वया—By the rule 'कृत्यानां कर्तरि वा' the agent takes Gen. or inst. in connexion with तव्य, अनीय, य &c.; so both त्वया and तव are admissible.

Śl. 19. यथावत्--यथा यादृशमर्हतीति यथावत् । यथावत् विहितः यथावद्विहितः अध्वरः येन तस्मै. The Dat. here is significant. It shows that Kautsa gives the details to Raghu, because he wished to know them. It is a reply to Raghu's question. **Had** it been the primary object of Kautsa to acquaint the king with the facts by way of a prayer we should have expected **तम्** instead of **तस्मै** by the rule '**कर्तुरीप्सिततमं कर्म**' । The Dat. here may be explained either as **तादर्थ्ये**; or by '**क्रियार्थोपपद—**' **रघुं प्रीणयितुम्**; or by '**कर्मणा यमभिप्रैति**'—**रघुमभिप्रेत्य. स्मयावेशः—स्मयस्य** vanity **आवेशः** touch or influence. **वर्णाश्रमाणाम्**—The **वर्ण**s are the four classes of men *viz.* the Brâhmaṇas, Kshatriyas, Vaiśyas and Śu'dras. For the *Âs'ramas* see note on '**आश्रमम्**'. Śl. 10. **वर्णी—वर्णः प्रशस्तिरस्यास्तीति वर्णी** । a Brahmachârin **प्रशस्ति** means 'moral excellence,' which is explained as absolute abstaining from eight kinds of sensual pleasures, for which see Malli. on **वर्णिलिङ्गी** Kir. I. 1. The affix **इन्** showing possession is added to this word in this sense alone; in other cases we shall have **वर्णवान्** । *Vide* the Káś. on '**वर्णाद्ब्रह्मचारिणि** Páṇ. V. 2. 134. **विचक्षणः—विशेषेण चष्टे इति विचक्ष्+अन** (**युच्**); wise, learned, clever. **प्रस्तुतम्**—used as a noun. It properly means 'what is brought on or introduced by **प्रस्ताव** (occasion or opportunity)' what is introduced with relevancy, there being a fit opportunity for it; hence what is pertinent or to the point, as opposed to **अप्रस्तुत** which means 'for which there is no proper opportunity' *i. e.* which does not refer to the subject under discussion, irrelevant.

Śl. 20. **चिराय**—*indec.* used in the sense of the Acc. by the rule '**कालाध्वनोरत्यन्तसंयोगे**' Pâṇ. II. 3. 5. **अस्खलितोपचाराम्**—see ft.-note **उपचार (उपचर्यते । अनेन वा)** may mean here service (**सेवा**) or materials of worship.' **अस्खलित उपचारः यस्याम्** in which the service I rendered him was without a flaw, was unswerving; or **अस्खलिता उपचारा यस्याम्** in which no materials of worship were wanting *i. e.* I ministered fully to all his wants. **पुरस्तात्**—indec. der. fr. **पूर्व+अस्तात्, पूर्व** being changed to **पुर्**; in the first place, or foremost, *i. e.* above fees.

Śl. 21. **अर्थकार्श्यम्—अर्थस्य** of wealth **कार्श्यं** scantiness. We may have the Gen. Tat. here, as the prohibition '**पूरणगुण**' &c. is not obligatory in the case of a word expressive of quality. *Cf.* Sid. Kau. **अनित्योयं गुणेन निषेधः । 'तदशिष्यं संज्ञाप्रमाणत्वात्' इत्यादिनिर्देशात् । तेनार्थगौरवं बुद्धिमान्द्यमित्यादि सिद्धम् । विद्यापरिसंख्या**—For the 14 *vidyas* see Saṃj. The six *aṅgas* are **शिक्षा कल्पो व्याकरणं निरुक्तं ज्योतिषां गतिः । छन्दो विचितिरित्येष षडङ्गो वेद उच्यते ॥**

Śl. 22. **सोहं**—I thus circumstanced, *i. e.* whose sole object is to procure money. **सपर्या**—fr. the root **सपर् पूजायां**—of the **कण्ड्वादि** class to which **य** is added (**सपर्यति**)—by adding **अ** to it **भावे (आ** fem.) **अल्पेतरत्वात्—अल्पादितरः अल्पेतरः तस्य भावः अल्पेतरत्वं तस्मात्. 0निष्क्रयस्य**—the price of (**श्रुतस्य नि0**); *cf.* II. 55.

Sl. 23. द्विजेन—द्विज the twice-born; a term which though applying to the first three classes, specially applies to the Brâhmaṇas; *cf.* मातुरग्रेऽधिजननं द्वितीयं मौञ्जिबन्धने । Manu. II. 169. द्विजराजकान्तिः—द्विजानां राजा द्विजराजः तस्य इव कान्तिर्यस्य । A Vya. Bah. The moon is considered to be the lord of *dvijas* or Brâhmaṇas. The epithet indicates that as the moon, although stripped of light, borrows it from the sun, and again illumines the world at night, so Raghu too, though now penniless, would procure money from Kubera, and so Kautsa had no reason to be disappointed. See Saṃj.

द्विजराज—an epithet which originally properly belonged to *Soma* the plant, so universally used in sacrificial offerings in ancient days, with reference to which alone the *S'ruti* quoted by Malli. 'तस्मात्सोमो' &c. is to be understood. Afterwards, however, by a confusion of terms, all the epithets of Soma, the plant, were transferred to Soma, the moon. Soma, the moon, is also called the king of plants or *vanaspatis*, while it was *Soma*, the plant, that was originally so called. See our note on ओषधीनां नाथम् II. 73.

वेदविदाम्—वेदान् विदन्तीति वेदविदस्तेषाम् । एनोनिवृत्तेन्द्रिय &c.—वृत्ति operation or exercise; *cf.* तीव्राभिषङ्गप्रभवेण वृत्तिं मोहेन संस्तम्भयतेन्द्रियाणाम् । Kum. IV. 73. This epithet which is purposely used here, shows how scrupulous the poet is in not allowing his hero's fame to be tarnished even indirectly. Raghu was द्विजराजकान्ति no doubt, but he was by no means a sinner like *dvijarâja*. The allusion here is to the Paurâṇic legend according to which चन्द्र carried off Târá, the wife of Bṛihaspati, his preceptor, for which he was cursed by the wronged husband to be indelibly marked with the stain, visible to this day. The student will notice the alliterations in this s'l.

Sl. 24. गुर्वर्थमर्थी—गुरवे इदं गुर्वर्थम् । गुरोरर्थो यस्मिन्कर्मणीति वा; *adv.* modifying the अर्थक्रिया implied in अर्थी (अर्थयत इति) गुर्वर्थं यथा तथार्थिभावेन वर्तमानः । coming as a suitor, seeking money for his preceptor; this is the chief reason why such a request could not be refused. श्रुतपारदृश्वा:—who had seen the other end of the *S'âstras*, *i. e.* thoroughly mastered them. रघोः—The mention of his name by the king shows, according to Malli., his high sense of personal honour, and the unbearableness of the reproach in connexion with it. See Saṃj. and Bg. quoted therein. Indeed, the reproach that 'the king of Kosala refused the request of a suitor' would not be so great as the one that 'Raghu refused the request of a suitor.' The lesson taught here by Raghu was not lost upon his descendants. *Cf.* XI. 2; see ft.-note. वदान्यान्तरम्—मां याचस्व इति वदतीति वदान्यः । Un. III. 104; अन्यः वदान्यः वदान्यान्तरम् । *Nityasamasa.* मा भूत्—Here the Aorist is used in the sense of the Future by the rule माङि लुङ्

the Aorist with the augment अ dropped is used with the prohibitive particle माङ् in all the tenses; *cf.* मा मुमुहत्खलु भवन्तमनन्यजन्मा मा ते मलीमसविकारघना मतिर्भूत् । Mâl.-Mâd. I. 32. परीवाद—or परिवाद by उपसर्गस्य घञि अमनुष्ये बहुलम् । Páṇ. VI. 3. 122.

Śl. 25. स त्वं—*i. e.* you, whose request cannot be refused चतुर्थोऽग्निरिव—Because there were three fires already. The three sacred fires, which a householder is enjoined to perpetuate and worship, are (1) गार्हपत्य, that which the गृहपति or the lord of the house receives from his father and transmits to his son in his turn, and from which fires for sacrificial purposes are lighted; (2) आहवनीय, that which is lighted from 'the perpetual fire' and into which all the offerings are made; (3) दक्षिणाग्नि, the southern fire, sometimes called अन्वाहार्यपचन. *Cf.* गार्हपत्यादाहवनीयं ज्वलन्तमुद्धरेत् । पिता वा एषोऽग्नीनां यद्दक्षिणः पुत्रो गार्हपत्यः पौत्र आहवनीयः । Âśvalâyana. See notes on I. 6. द्वित्राणि—द्वे वा त्रीणि वा । सोढुं—to bear (the delay of); hence, wait for. यावत्—See com.; it may also be taken here निश्चये (अवधारणे); 'निपातावेतौ निश्चयं द्योतयतः' Sid. Kau. 'And I will surely try' &c.

Śl. 26. अवितथम्—not always coming true, unfailing; a fact which accounts for his delight. अग्रजन्मा—see ft.-note. आत्तसारं—आत्त p. p. p. of दा with आ 3rd conj.; सार-wealth. कुबेरात्—Kubera is the son of Vis'ravas by Iḍáviḍá, and thus the half-brother of Râvaṇa. He is the lord of wealth and master of nine inestimable treasures (निधि). He is the regent of the North, his capital is situated on the mount Kailâsa and he is the king of Yakshas, Kiṃnaras and other inferior deities. The name कुबेर is expressive of his deformity, being derived fr. कु vile, ugly, and बेर body; *cf.* Vâyu P. 'कुत्सायां क्विति शब्दोऽयं शरीरं बेरमुच्यते । कुबेरः कुशरीरत्वान्नाम्ना तेन च सोऽङ्कितः' ॥ He is described as having three legs, only eight teeth and a yellow mark in place of one eye. No images of him occur, nor is any particular worship paid to him. In these respects there is a considerable analogy between him and the Grecian Plutus. Plutus is described as blind, malignant and cowardly and seems to have received but very slender homage from Greek or Roman devotion. कुबेर is also derived fr. कुब् to cover *i. e.* to protect: the protector of wealth. उक्षण—sprinkling with water, fr. उक्ष् 1. P. to sprinkle.

Śl. 27. वसिष्ठमन्त्र &c.—consecrated by mantras. Vasishtha was a master as well as the composer of charms. See I. 61. For the repetition of the idea, see VIII. 4. उदन्वत्—उदकानि सन्त्यत्र । उदक is changed to उदन् before मत् and धि when the Comp. forms a name of the sea; see Páṇ. VIII. 2. 13. But उदकवान् घटः, a jar containing water. मरुत्सखस्य—From the remark of Malli., and the synonym वायुसहायस्य given by him, it appears that he would have preferred to take this as a Bah. were it not for a technical difficulty of grammar. But the Tat. will better suit here. For, though सखित्व implies mutual affection, yet मरुतः सखा recognizes affection in मरुत्, while मरुत् सखा यस्य (बलाहकस्य) implies affection in बलाहक. The former better explains why मरुत् should be the helper of the cloud of its own accord. बलाहकस्य—a comp. of the पृषोदरादि class.

Śl. 28. प्रयतः—Pure in mind and body, *i. e.*, having bathed and observed the rules of conduct, such as restraining the passions, &c., as he had to attack a divine person. See I. 90. प्रदोषे—See *supra* I. 93. सामन्तसम्भावनया—सम्यगन्तः समन्तः border, frontier; तत्र भवः सामन्तः a frontier-king; a tributary prince. सामन्त इति सम्भावना सामन्तसम्भावना तया considering or treating him as a mere frontier-chieftain or tributary prince. एव—The force of एव is that Raghu considered Kubera to be no better than a tributary prince and therefore easy to be conquered. Raghu was the conqueror of Indra, the strongest of the *lokapâlas* and therefore, more than a match for Kubera, an ordinary *lokapâla*. Again we saw in canto IV., how Raghu turned back from the mountain Himâlaya, having established his sovereignty there when on his expedition of universal conquest. Evidently he, as conqueror of Himâ., treated the lord of Kailâsa, a mountain inferior to Himâ., as Sâmanta. See IV. 80.

Śl. 29. प्रयाणाभिमुखाय—अभिगतं मुखमस्याभिमुखः *Lit.* with one's face turned towards, facing; hence preparing for, about to start; प्रयाणस्याभिमुखः प्रयाणाभिमुखः. मध्ये—inside the treasury. This was the cause of astonishment. Here the poet very ingeniously extricates Raghu from the difficulty he was in. It would not have looked decent to make a *lokapâla*-like Kubera bend before a mortal like Raghu, nor to bring back his hero unsuccessful from his expedition. He, therefore, devises a third alternative which makes his hero achieve his object and spares Kubera the humiliation of a defeat at the hands of a mortal king.

S'l. 30. अभियास्य०—Fut. pass. p. of या with अभि. पादम्—A skirt-hill. सुमेरोः—Sumeru is the same as Meru, for which see notes on I. 14. दिदेश—gave; *cf. infra* XI. 2, XVI. 72; and बाणमत्र भवते निजं दिशन् Kir. XIII. 68.

Śl. 31. साकेत—The name of Ayodhyâ; see note on कोसल III. 5. जनस्य अभिनन्द्यसत्त्वौ—Here जन takes the Gen. कर्तरि in connexion with अभिनन्द्य which, therefore, ought not to have been compounded with सत्त्व as it is. The Comp., however, may be defended by the general maxim 'सापेक्षत्वेपि गमकत्वात्समासः, or the Gen. may be taken सम्बन्धे. सत्त्व—The strength of the mind, mental calibre; here the nobility or greatness of the mind, as Malli. takes it.

Śl. 32. इष्ट &c.—ग्राहितः अर्थो येन स वाहितार्थः, see Samj. प्रजेश्वरम् स्पृशन् करेण—*i. e.* on the head (as a sign of blessing). आनतपूर्वकायम्-These two epithets show the magnanimity of Raghu's character. He was the lord of *subjects* and yet he was so humble in his dealing with Kautsa, who was also a *subject*. वाचम्—Commentators find fault with the poet for having used this superfluous word; and this is cited by rhetoricians as an instance of अधिकपदत्वदोष—'अत्र वाचमित्यधिकमुवाचेत्यनेनैव कृतार्थत्वात्' । Sâh.-Dar. वाचम्—Cannot be used with उवाच unless there is an *adj.* to qualify it, as observed by Vâmana-विशेषणस्य च विशेष्यप्रतिपत्यर्थमुकार्थस्य प्रयोगः । See ft.-note. But one must not be so fastidious in small matters. Prof. Ray however, finds a defence for the poet by proposing to read अवाचं (qualifying प्रजेश्वरं)—'speechless, through excessive modesty.'

Śl. 33. वृत्ते—वृत्त *lit.* what is well-rounded; hence, one's proper sphere of duties. According to Kâm. quoted by Malli. the duty of a king is fourfold. See Samj. For वृत्त or proper conduct, as commonly understood, see ft.-note मनीषितम्—मनसा ईषितं what is reached by the mind, *i. e.* a desire. To be explained with reference to the पृषोदरादि or शकन्ध्वादि class. See note on मनीषिणाम् I. 11.

Śl. 34. आशास्यं—Pot. p. used as a noun; a blessing or benediction; *cf.* आशास्यचिन्तास्तिमितो बभूव । Kum. VII. 87. पुनरुक्तभूतम्—पुनः उक्तं पुनरुक्तम् । Avyaya Samâsa. भूत means सम or equal; see Amara. III. 3. 78. पुनरुक्तेन भूतं पुनरुक्तभूतम्, the Comp. being सह सुपा; 'equal to that which is repeated' *i. e.* superfluous. Châr. takes भूत in the sense of 'इव'. अधिजग्मुषः—poetical license, these forms being used only in the Veda. See note on तस्थिवांसम् II. 29. आत्मगुणानुरूपम्—अनुगतं रूपमस्येत्यनुरूपः । आत्मगुणानामनुरूपस्तम् ।

Śl. 35. तस्मात्—From him *i. e.* the sage (the benediction pronounced by him) was the cause (हेतु) of Raghu's getting a son so soon. Our poet is very careful to show that pious deeds are sure to be rewarded in this world. आलोकमर्कात्—अनेन रघुपुत्रस्यापि जगद्दुःखहारि किमपि पावनं तेजः सूचितम् ।

Śl. 36. ब्राह्मे मुहूर्ते—The Muhûrta presided over by Brahmâ; the last four (according to some two) *ghatikâs* of the night. For further information and the advantages accruing to a child born at this hour, see ft.-note. ०कल्पम्—See Samj. ईषदसमाप्तौ कल्पब्देश्यदेशीयरः. The affixes कल्प, देश्य and देशीय are added to a noun or verb in the sense of 'a little less than,' 'almost equal to;' so त्रिद्वदेश्यः पचतिकल्पम्. आत्मजन्मानम्—आत्मनः जन्म यस्य; see note on 'गुणोदयम्, IV. 20; for the idea *cf.* अङ्गादङ्गात्संभवसि हृदयादधिजायसे । आत्मैव पुत्रनामासि स जीव शरदः शतम् ॥ Manu.

Śl. 37. रूपम्—The symmetrical bodily make, as Malli. gives, or beauty. तत्—The very same. ओजस्वि—resplendent or muscular, well-built. नैसर्गिकम्—निसर्गेण निर्वृत्तम् natural, as disinguished from that which is acquired by training. उन्नतत्वम्—Magnanimity, high-mindedness; or height, the bodily stature. कारणात्—The root भिद् having the sense of 'अन्य' governs the abl. by 'अन्यारादितर--' Páṇ. II. 3. 39. प्रदीप—is a powerful lamp. The word दीप and प्रदीप are very happily selected. *Cf.* VIII. 5.

Śl. 38. उपात्तवि०—See *supra* sl. 1. गुरुभ्यः—The pl. shows that a separate Guru, adept in a particular branch of science, was engaged to teach him that branch. गुरोः—*i. e.* the person fit to give her away as in marriage. श्री was now in love with Aja, and it was in Raghu's power to bestow her upon him by making him a युवराज. Raghu is, therefore, fitly called the गुरु of श्री. Śrî is always represented as ceasing to look upon a king as her lord as soon as he abandons the throne in favour of his son. *Cf.* VIII. 14, where श्री is called the daughter-in-law of Raghu. धीरा—This may refer to श्री also. Further on we shall see our poet attributing the fickleness of Lakshmî to the faults of the person to whom she attaches herself for the time being. *Vide.* VI. 41.

Śl. 39. अथ—'Then', *i. e.* when Aja had reached his youth. The particle implies a blessing and is probably used here as the auspicious subject of the prince's marriage is about to be introduced. क्रथकैशिकानाम्—क्रथकैशिक is a class of Kshatriyas, said to be derived originally from Kratha and Kaisika, who were the sons of Vidarbha—a king who ruled over the province of the same name. The name क्रथकैशिक thus came to be used synonymously with Vidarbha. For this latter name, see note on विदर्भ śl. 60 क्रथकैशिकानां निवासो जनपद क्रथकैशिकास्तेषाम् । स्वयंवरार्थं—स्वयंवरायेदं स्वयंवरार्थं; adv. qualifying आनयनक्रिया. For स्वयंवर see notes, śl. 64 *infra*. आप्तः—हितः Malli.; *i. e.* one who would take interest in the matter and persuade Raghu to send his son in case of a refusal. The meaning of 'trusty' will also do. भोजेन—The king of the country is meant; see *infra* śl. 62. 'The Bhojas were a branch of the Yádavas. They were one of the greatest and mightiest peoples of ancient India. At different times they are represented to have occupied different parts of central and southern India.' S. P. Pandit.

Śl. 40. तम्, असौ, एनम्—By these three pronouns the poet refers to Bhoja, Raghu and Aja. Bhoja is altogether absent (परोक्ष) to him and so he refers to him by तद्; of the remaining two Aja is संनिकृष्ट to him being the object of immediate description and so he refers to him by इदम्, and Raghu being विप्रकृष्ट by अदस्. *Cf.* इदमस्तु संनिकृष्टं समीपतरवर्ति चैतदो रूपम्। अदसस्तु विप्रकृष्टं तदिति परोक्षे विजानीयात्॥ दाराक्रिया &c.—दाराणां (दारार्था) क्रिया। तादर्थ्ये समासः। तस्या योग्या दशा age, stage of life यस्य।

Śl. 41. उपकार्या—उपक्रियते इति उपकार्या। कर्मणि 'ऋहलोर्ण्यत्'। ('उप करोति' in the Samj. explaining उपकारिका।) उपकार्या is a tent or a temporary house prepared for the reception or residence of royal or other great personages when they go out on a journey or on an excursion of pleasure. उपचारः—articles of comfort and decorations. वन्येतराः—A Bah; if taken as a Tat. (वन्येभ्य इतरे) we shall have वन्येतरे; or, as Hemadri says—वन्यानि इतरयन्ती इति ण्यन्तात्पचाद्यच्। इतरयन्तीति सुब्धातुः। मार्गे निवासाः—haltings or stations on the way. Malli. seems to take the two words as an Aluk Comp. by the rule हलदन्तात्सप्तम्याः संज्ञायाम् or तत्पुरुषे कृति बहुलम्। Pâṇ. VI-3-9, 14. We may, however, take the two words as uncompounded, निवास meaning residence, halting, उद्यानविहारकल्पाः—उद्यन्ति वृक्षा अत्र इति उद्यानं a garden; fr. उद्+या। अन (ल्युट्); विहरन्ति एषु इति विहाराः विहारस्थानानि, घञ् being added अधिकरणे। Now see Samj.; it will be, however, preferable to analyse the Comp. as उद्याने विहाराः as better corresponding with the comp. मार्गेनिवासाः। If we take मार्गे and निवासा separately, विहार will mean 'sporting', घञ् being added भावे. Hemâdri suggests another construction, taking उपकार्या separately and as the subject: रचितोपचारा उपकार्या...मार्गे निवासा बभूवुः।

Śl. 42 सीकाराद्रैः &c.—The breezes were cool, fragrant, gentle and therefore highly pleasant. This explains why a halt there was desirable. विलङ्घिताध्वा—The day's journey being accomplished.—क्लान्तं, रजोधूसरकेतु, all these give the reason why the halt was necessary.

Śl. 43. उपरिष्टात्—ऊर्ध्वायां दिशि इत्युपरिष्टात्; from ऊर्ध्व irregularly changed to उप+रिष्टात्। भ्रमरैः—भ्रमतीति भ्रमरः fr. भ्रम्+अरच्। Uṇ. III. 128. The presence of two *rakâras* in this word has given rise to another name for the bee, *viz.* द्विरेफ. प्राक्सूचित &c.—अन्तःसलिल may be explained in two ways:—सलिलस्यान्तः अन्तःसलिलम्, राजदन्तादि; or अन्तःस्थितं सलिलम्, शाकपार्थिवादि.

Śl. 44. नीलोर्ध्व &c.—The blackish-dust firmly settled in the cracks in the tusks was not washed off and so it served as a clear evidence of his वप्रक्रीडा or the sport of butting against the skirts. See Meg. I. 5. ध्वंसन् उन्ममज्ज—This shows the simultaneity of the two actions, emerging from water, and the indication of वप्रक्रिया. ऋक्षवत्—(*lit.* possessed of bears) is one of the Kulaparvatas, or the seven principal mountain-chains, for which see ft.-note. It has been identified with the mountains of Gondavana. तटेषु—at different places of its sides.

Śl. 45. लघुक्रियेण—लघ्वी क्रिया यस्य of quick action. Dinakara translates by 'कुशलेन.' वार्यर्गला &c.—वारी 'an elephant's stall or fold.' When an elephant gets infuriated, huge trunks of trees are placed horizontally in his stall to serve as bolts. It is these that are compared to the waves obstructing the elephant's progress every moment. Some understand by वारी, 'a chain,' but it is difficult to understand how a chain can be fitly compared to a wave.

Śl. 46. शैलौपमः—उपमातीत्युपमः। शैलस्य उपमः; शैल उपमा उपमाने यस्येति वा or शैलेन सादृश्यं यस्य; a *nitya* samâsa.

Śl. 47. एकनागस्य—Here एक has the secondary sense of 'peerless,' exceptionally huge, as Châr. and Hem. suggest. Unless we understand it in this sense, it will be difficult to see why a whole host of tame elephants turned tail at the very scent of his rut. कपोलभित्त्योः—See Malli. on गण्डभित्ती śl. 43 *supra*. जलावगाह &c.—क्षणः मात्रा प्रमाणमस्य कालस्येति क्षणमात्रः; (and not क्षण एव क्षणमात्रं as the comp. will be of the मयूरव्यंस° class and there will be no further compounding) क्षणमात्रं शान्ता क्षणमात्रशान्ता। now see Saṃj. अनेकप—न एकः अनेकः अनेकाभ्यां पिबतीति। मददुर्दिनश्रीः—दुर्दिनं वर्षं (See IV. 41) तस्य श्रीः. दिदीपे—Shone forth *i. e.* the rut gushed out at once.

Śl. 48. कटु—bitter; strong-smelling ('agreeable,' Malli.). आधोरण—आधोरयन्ति गतिचातुर्यं कुर्वन्तीत्याधोरणाः, elephant-drivers. तीव्र—arduous, great.

Śl. 49. छिन्नबन्ध &c.—आदौ छिन्नबन्धाः पश्चाद् द्रुताः छिन्नबन्धद्रुताः। ते च ते युग्याः (see com.) छिन्नबन्धद्रुतयुग्याः (Karm.) तैः शून्यम्। Malli. takes the first as a Bah. and combines it with शून्य; but the सेनानिवेश was not quite शून्य; it was only शून्य so far as horses (and probably oxen) were concerned. This meaning is brought out by explaining the comp. as given above. विहस्त—विक्षिप्तः (badly or helplessly thrown about) or विगतः हस्तोऽस्य (one without hands as it were); hence, at a loss to know what to do; शोकादिभिरितिकर्तव्यताशून्यः (Bhânuji Dîkshita on Amara.). सेनानिवेश—see VII. 2.

Śl. 50. आपतन्तम्—rushing, charging (at the army). वन्यः—Kings are prohibited from killing elephants except in battles (see Samj.); and since wild elephants are never brought to battle, the prohibition includes them. कुम्भे–the temple (of an elephaant) कुं भुवमुम्भतीति कुम्भः । शकन्ध्वादिः. जघान—Here we see with what masterly skill the poet keeps out of view the warriors in the army and makes Aja himself strike, which is necessary for the subsequent development of the events representing the whole thing as a natural consequence of things.

Śl. 51. विद्धमात्रः—The *mas.* is irregular. For, विद्ध एव becomes विद्धमात्रम् । (See Vârt. on Páṇ. V. 2. 37) and no other term is available to explain the *mas.* form. किल—It is related. तत्—*i. e.* his assuming a divine form. व्योमचर—व्योम्नि चरतीति; fr. चर् + अ (ट) by चरेः टः (चर् takes ट when a word expressive of अधिकरण precedes).

Śl. 52. प्रभावो°—प्रभाव is the superhuman power which heavenly beings possess; *cf.* प्रभावनिर्मितेन भूर्जपत्रेण संपादितोत्तरा भवितुमिच्छामि । Vik. II. p. ११२. कल्पद्रुमोत्थैः—for कल्पद्रुम see notes, I. 75; कल्पद्रुमेभ्य उत्तिष्ठन्तीति कल्पद्रुमोत्थानि तैः । संवर्धित &c.—प्रशस्तमुर उरःस्थलम् । The word स्थल like भित्ति indicates excellence. See Samj. on भित्ति s'l. 43. तारहारः—तार big or bright, shining (the pearls being flawless) See Malli. on Meg. I. 33. वाग्मिन्—eloquent, a clever speaker; ग्मिन् is added to वाच् in a good sense, as आट or आल is added in a bad sense (वाचाट or वाचाल).

Śl. 53. मतङ्गशापात् See ft.-note. अस्मि—may be taken as a verb, or ind. equivalent to अहम्. मतङ्गजत्वम्—मतङ्गादृषेर्जातः मतङ्गज (Bhánuji Dîkshit) an elephant. It is difficult to see how the sage मतङ्ग was the producer of elephants. Probably he was the first person to tame elephants and show their utility to the world and hence the name. Târânâtha in the Vâch. derives the word thus–मतङ्गो मेघ इव जायते इति मतङ्गजस्तस्य तदाकारत्वात् । प्रियंवद—see III. 64.

Śl. 54. अनुनीतः—conciliated (by entreaty); *cf.* अनुनय II. 54. सत्ववता—by you, the powerful one (for he–Aja.–could split open the temple of such a powerful elephant as he was with an arrow shot with a slight force). च--on the other hand. उष्णत्वम्—उष्णो गुणः अस्यास्तीति उष्णस्तस्य भावस्तत्त्वम् । Explain similarly शैत्यम्; शैत्यं हि यत्—what is known as coldness.

Śl. 55. इक्ष्वाकु°—प्रभवत्यस्मादिति प्रभवः कारणमुत्पत्तिस्थानमित्यर्थः । अयोमुखेन—अयसो विकारः अयोविकारः । स मुखमस्य । Bah., the word विकार being dropped by the Vârt. समुदायविकारषष्ठ्याश्च बहुव्रीहिरुत्तरपदलोपश्चेति वक्तव्यम् । Or अयो लक्षणया अयोविकारः मुखमस्य । तपोनिधिः—indicates power in him to undo what had been done. ०महिम्ना—महतो भावः महिमा तेन.

Śl. 56. प्रतिप्रियम्—प्रतिकृतं प्रियं प्रतिप्रियम् । प्रतिप्रीणातीति वा । कुर्यां-स्यात् The potentials show futurity.

Śl. 57. संमोहनम्—causing sleep, hypnotic. प्रयोग &c.—Here प्रयोग and संहार do not mean merely the shooting or the thrusting back into the quiver of an arrow. प्रयोग means the repetition of a certain *mantra* to endow the arrow with a peculiar virtue which enables it to assume a particular form or to bring about a certain result; while संहार means the repetition of the counter-*mantra* which takes away from the arrow the peculiar virtue it was endowed with and it becomes again an ordinary arrow. See also note on III. 64. विभक्त०—The Mantra for which has two parts; one for its employment, the other for its withdrawal. आदत्स्व—दा with आ is Âtm. except in the sense of 'opening'; see Sid. Kau. on Pan I. 3.-20. न चारिहिंसा—Slaughter (हिंसा), except where absolutely necessery, was looked upon with horror long before the teachings of Buddha and was prohibited by the Śastra. See ft.-note. The repetition of च indicates the simultaneous existence of the two, *viz.* विजय and अहिंसा.

Śl. 58. मां प्रति—Malli. takes this with ह्रिया. He seems to emphasize 'माम्'. 'You need not feel ashamed in *my* presence' (*i. e.* of me to whom you have been kind). We may also say with Châri., and perhaps preferably, मां प्रति दयापरः । दयापरः—दया परा आश्रयणीयत्वेन प्रेक्षा यस्य । अपि—used here to express a hyperbole. You showed kindness to me *even* at a time when it is impossible to show it. उपच्छन्दयति मयि—now that I am entreating you; छन्द् with उप 10th conj. to entreat. प्रयोज्यम्—प्रयोक्तुं शक्यम् । capable of being employed; by the rule 'प्रयोज्यनियोज्यौ शक्यार्थे'-the words प्रयोज्य and नियोज्य are formed only in the sense of capability or practicability. Malli. has 'न कर्तव्यम्' but then we shall get the form प्रयोग्यम् and not प्रयोज्यम् । The sense is—You who were kind to me even when you *struck* cannot be unkind to me *now* when I am entreating you.

Śl. 59. उपस्पृश्य—उपस्पृश् has a technical meaning *viz.* that of touching the cavities of the eye or performing the *Āchamana*. सोमोद्भवायाः—सोमाल्लक्षणया सोमवंशजात्पुरूरवस उद्भवतीति । यद्वा सोमोऽमृतमु-द्भवत्यस्याः । or after Malli, उद्भवत्यस्मादिति उद्भवः कारणं; now see com. तेनावतारितत्वात् The river Narmadâ is so called because a channel was opened to it by king Purûravas of the lunar race. नृसोम—implies that he was always a delight-giver. उदङ्मुखः—उदगतं

सुखमस्य. [Properly उदीच्यां दिशि इति, उदीची+अस्ताति (अस्तात्); the affix अस्ताति which has the sense of the Loc. and which is added स्वार्थे (see Páṇ. V. 3. 27) is dropped by the rule 'अञ्चेर्लुक्' Pâṇ. V. 3. 30; and we have उदीची which again becomes उदक् by the rule 'लुक्तद्धितलुकि' when a Taddhita affix disappears, the *fem.* affix also disappears;' and finally we have उदग्गतं सुखमस्य ।] अस्त्रमन्त्रम्—The sing. because the *mantra* of प्रयोग and that of संहार formed but parts of one *mantra*.

Śl. 60. व्योगात्—through the combination or intervention of; hence as the result of; *cf.* रक्षायोगादयमपि तपः प्रत्यहं संचिनोति । Śak. II. 14. आसेदुषोः—Gen. dual of आसेदिवस्; perf. p. of सद् with आ. The perf. participles in वस् of the roots सद्, वस् and श्रु only are used in ordinary language. Paṇ. III. 2. 108. सौराज्यरम्यान्—सु शोभनो राजा येषां ते सुराजानः (not सुराजाः, the rule 'राजाहः'—applying only to Tat. Comp.) तेषां भावाः सौराज्यम् । विदर्भान्—विदर्भाणां क्षत्रियाणां निवासो जनपद विदर्भाः । The name is derived from वि without and दर्भ the Kusha grass, which is supposed not to grow in Vidarbha, because the son of a saint died there of a wound inflicted by the sharp blade of the grass.

Vidarbha, the modern Berar, but a far more extensive kingdom than its modern representative, lay on the north of Kuntala, extending from the banks of the Kṛishṇa to about the banks of the Narmadá. On account of its great size the country was also called Mahârâshṭra. *Cf.* Bál.-Râm, X. 14, where two names are applied to the same country It lay to the South of Narmadá as Aja crossed the river before entering it. Its people were called Krathakaiśikas (see note on that word, śl. 39). Kuṇḍinapura, sometimes called Vidarbha, was its capital, which is probably the modern Bedar. It was the seat of Bhîma, father of Damayantî and of Bhîma, father of Rukmiṇî. According to the Màlav., king Agnimitra divided Vidarbha into two parts, separated by the river Varadâ (Warda) which, in its Payne Ganga branch, separates the Assigned Districts of Berar from the Nizam's Dominions. Amarâvati (Oomarâvati) in Berar seems to have been the capital of the northern and Pratishṭhana (Paithan) on the Godâvarî that of the southern division. This was the land of the Bhojas, who are said to be descendants of Druhyu. They were not, however, confined to this province, as there are several Bhojapuras in different parts of India. They had different clans such as the Kuntî-Bhojas to whom Kunti belonged and the Mârtikâvatas or Bhojas of Mṛittikâvata whose chief fought at Kurukshetra on the side of Duryodhana. The celebrated king Bhojaraja who reigned at Dhárâ in the beginning of the tenth century, was evidently a descendant of these Bhojas.

Śl. 61. नगरोप०—उपगतः कण्ठं उपकण्ठः Pradi Tat.; who is near; now see com. क्रथकैशिकेन्द्रः—The lord of the Krathakaiśikas. See notes on Śl. 39. प्रवृद्धोर्मिः—प्रवृद्धाः begun to swell (क्तः आदिकर्मणि) ऊर्मयो यस्य. The joy of the king rising every moment as he advanced to receive the prince is aptly compared to the swelling waves of the ocean at moon-rise. ऊर्मिमाली—ऊर्मीणां माला अस्यास्तीति । For a similar idea see III. 17, VII. 19, X. 82, XII. 36, XVI. 27; and also Kum. III. 67.

Śl. 62. एनम्—Aja is referred to by तत् (तं तस्थिवांसं &c.) in the previous śloka, so the use of एनम् here is a poetical licence, एन not being allowed to be substituted for तद्. अग्रयायी—A poetic licence again; इन् is not added to या unless habit is implied. उपाचरत्—served, waited upon. *Cf.* 'गिरिशमुपचचार प्रत्यहं सा सुकेशी' Kum. I. 60. वैदर्भ—विदर्भाणां राजा वैदर्भः । fr. विदर्भ + अ (अञ्) आगन्तु —आगच्छतीति—; fr. आगम् with तु (तुन् Uṇadi) a guest.

Śl. 63. प्राग्द्वार &c.—प्राक्स्थितं द्वारं प्राग्द्वारम् । प्राग्द्वारस्था प्राग्द्वारस्य वा वेदिः &c.; see Sañj. Din. explains this differently for, which see ft.-note. The placing of a pot (of copper or silver) full of water on the *vedi* (a quadrangular raised spot) near the front door is considered auspicious even to this day. रघुप्रति०—प्रतिनिधीयते इति प्रतिनिधिः fr. प्रति + धा + इ (कि) added कर्मणि–the roots दा and धा take this aff. when a preposition precedes, in the sense of भाव or any Kâraka except the agent (कर्तृ). मुख्यसदृशः प्रतिनिधिः–a representative or deputy of. Raghu being the sole lord of the world, special reception was accorded to his representative. बाल्यात्परां &c.—The simile is appropriate both in point of time and place. Aja was now lodged in such a delightful place and at such a time, that being at ease there, he could not but have felt within himself the influence of love, as indicated in the next śl.

Śl. 64. स्वयंवर &c.—स्वयं व्रियतेऽस्मिन्निति, स्वयं वरणमिति वा स्वयंवरः । This form of marriage in which the bride chose her own husband seems to have been very popular in ancient India and was addopted specially by the Kshatriyas. स्वयंवरे स्वयंवरेण वा समाहृतो राजलोको येन । राज्ञां लोको राजलोकः । कन्याललाम—ललामन् (also ललाम *m. n.*) means 'the best'; कन्यासु ललाम कन्याललाम । कमनीयम्—कामयितुं योग्यम् । desirable, covetable. भावावबोधकलुषा—According to Malli. unable to know the mind (of her husband)', *i. e.*, who hesitates lest her approach might displease him. Some take भाव in the sense of 'love for another', offended or jealous because conscious of her husband's love for another. But Mallinâtha's meaning seems to be preferable.

The woman is दयिता dearly loved by her husband, and though unable to read his thoughts, (*i. e.* to know whether he is really longing for her), yet makes a tardy approach towards him of her own accord (अभिमुखीभवति), which an offended lady does not do. See below, śl. 67. The simple idea so poetically expressed by the poet is, that Aja being absorbed in thoughts about Indumatî could not get sleep for a long time. The report of Indumatî's unparalleled charms had attracted such a crowd of kings there, that, pitted against these, Aja could well feel misgivings within himself. It is said that Kâlidâsa had a strong desire to finish the canto before going to bed that day. But sleep overpowered him at this stage and he had to put down this pen. The Goddess of learning, however, wishing to gratify the wish of her favourite son, wrot e down for him the following Slokas, and the poet to his astonishment found the canto completed when he woke up the next morning. True or not, the anecdote shows how exquisitely beautiful the following verses are.

Śl. 65. कर्णभूषण &c.—The ear-ornament meant is the Kuṇḍala worn round the ear, which is made of gold, and is long and heavy enough to leave an impression upon the shoulder when the head is bent sufficiently either side in a mood of anxiety or care. शय्योत्तर० &c.—उत्तरच्छद—the bed-sheet. Indumatî had such hold on Aja's mind that disturbed by thoughts about her, he restlessly moved in his bed, so that the sandal-marks on his body were worn off and his shoulders bore traces of hard pressure. सूतात्मजाः—*i. e.* young bards. सवयसः—This implies equality of age and intimacy. उषसि—*i. e.* at the hour presided over by Brahmâ ब्राह्म (मुहूर्त) when it was the duty of kings to rise. वाग्भिः प्राबोधयन्—It was customary to rouse kings from their slumber by means of songs accompanied by gentle music; see ft.-note.

Śl. 66. On this and the following ślokas S. P. Pandit thus remarks :—"These 'awakening verses' have no special reference to the present time and place, but form what the bards used to recite in the Prince's own crpital." But the remark does not seem to be correct. The poet's description of the bards as उदारवाचः scarcely leaves us room to suppose that they sang on this occasion the same stale and hackneyed song which they were wont to sing in the capital. On the contrary, the contents of the verses show that they are meant peculiarly to suit the present occasion. For the bards begin with early morn, first describing how the moon gradually loses her splendour and how the lotuses are about to bloom and then how they actually bloom at the first peep of the morning sun. Next they describe how the rays of the morning sun tinge the tusks of the elephants which were within their sight, and conclude by describing how, as the sun progresses a good way over the horizon, his rays penetrate the tents and overpower the light of the lamps there. So the description here, on the whole, seems to apply to one residing in a tent surrounded by the stables of horses and elephants &c., and not in his palace, as well as to one who is a late riser, which Aja, a scion of the solar race, could not have been (*cf.* **यथाकालप्रबोधिनाम्** I.6) had he been in his capital and not troubled by distracting thoughts as he was on the present occasion.

मतिमतां वर—This is meant to indicate that the prince would readily do his duty on being reminded of that. **द्विधा**-in two parts. **धूः**—The pressure and not the load itself. **एव, ननु**—both are used **अवधारणे**, 'indeed', 'surely;' **धूर्विभक्ता ननु** indeed the burden is divided; but **द्विधैव विभक्ता** it is divided into two parts only (so that you cannot expect a third person to help your father). **विनिद्रः**—(your father) has quitted his bed (and is in his place) This may also qualify **भवान्**—and your royal self having left the bed &c. **अपरधुर्ये**—you are to take the place of the other bearer. What is meant is this—your father is up by this time and attending to his duties; and you as *yuvarâja* ought to do the same. *Cf.* **येनेदं ध्रियते विश्वं धुर्यैर्यानमिवाध्वनि ।** Kum. VI. 76.

Śl. 67. Chāritravardhana and Dinakara, though in their usual manner they give a full com. upon this śl., consider it to be an interpolation, but without giving reasons. There seems to be, however, nothing in it that would warrant such a supposition, and Malli. who is always scrupulous in detecting spurious ślokas, regards it as quite genuine.

भवताप्यनवेक्षमाणा—This śl. seems to have perplexed some commentators and annotators. But all difficulty about its correct interpretation would vanish if one were to understand correctly the commentary of Malli. **अपि** ought to be construed with **पर्युत्सुकत्वं** as Malli. very properly has done, and not with **भवता** as suggested by Pandit. The meaning of the poet is very well brought out in the com. Indian poets describe three places as the favourite resorts of Lakshmî (the goddess of beauty), *viz.*, the lotus, the moon and the most lovely face in the world (as that of a prince or a princess). The last is generally represented as her most favourite haunt. *Cf.* **चन्द्रं गता पद्मगुणान्न भुंक्ते पद्माश्रिता चान्द्रमसीमभिख्याम् । उमामुखं तु प्रतिपद्य लोला**

द्विसंभवां प्रीतिमवाप लक्ष्मीः ॥ Kum. I. 43. The poet here describes Lakshmî as the wife of Aja. As such she approaches him, but finds Aja fast in the enjoyment of sleep (personified as a female). This is too offensive a sight for Lakshmî to bear, who is मानिनी. Great is her longing for Aja; but in her wounded pride she disregards even this. अपि shows the extreme difficulty of doing so. Inwardly, however, she is restless and does not know how to beguile her love-sickness due to the Prince's action. She discovers that the moon makes the nearest approach to Aja's beautiful face. Thither therefore in her helpless condition she bends her gaze and somehow manages to beguile her longing for Aja (पर्युत्सुकत्व). But even the moon is now parting with the beauty of Aja's face, and the condition of Lakshmî will be really miserable. She cannot herself approach Aja, and even the moon from whom she derived some consolation is fast sinking down. Hence the earnest appeal of the bards to Aja, on behalf of Lakshmî, to get up and gladden her.

अनवेक्षमाणा—Not taking into consideration, not caring for; पर्युत्सु०--anxious longing for; note the use of this with the instr. भवता. खण्डिता—a woman offended with her husband on account of his infidelity to her and full of self-pride. See ft.-note. विनोदयति—diverts, amuses herself with; *cf.* XIV. 77; also Śâk. VI. लतासु दृष्टिं विनोदयामि । दिगन्तलम्बी—दिशोऽन्तो दिगन्तः; लम्बनं लम्बः दिगन्ते लम्बः दिगन्तलम्बः सोऽस्यास्तीति ।

The reading अनवेक्ष्यमाणा, however, noticed and commented upon by Malli., seems to be preferable as it yields a much better sense by making the appeal more touching and therefore better calculated to excite pity in Aja. भवतापि—'by you too'. Lakshmî was already repulsed by lotuses. So her hopes entirely rested upon you. But you too being under the influence of sleep refused to look after her. She was therefore utterly helpless and compelled to beguile her yearning for you by being with the moon. It was not a wilful act on her part and you need not, therefore, be jealous of her. विनोदयति is the Cau. of विद्यद्. चन्द्रः पर्युत्सुकत्वं विद्यदति the moon diverts her anxiety. लक्ष्मीः चन्द्रेण पर्युत्सुकत्वं विनोदयति Lakshmî causes the moon to ally her anxiety. See Sanj. If we read हि instead of अपि, हि may be taken in the sense of अवधारण. The meaning in this case will present no difficulties. If the object of the poet be to represent Lakshmî not so much as an object of compassion to Aja as a मानिनी नायिका, the reading in the text ought to be preferred.

Sl. 68. तत्—'therefore', *i. e.* because Lakshmî is helpless as the moon, her nightly resort, is giving up splendour. Malli. says

लक्ष्मीपरिग्रहणात् connecting तत् with वल्गु; but there does not seem to be any propriety of this when applied to the lotuses. For in the previous śl. the appeal for the परिग्रहण of Lakshmî is to Aja and not to the lotuses. वल्गुना—refers to both—the opening of Aja's eyes and the blooming of lotuses. युगपदुन्मिषितेन—If the poet means that the beauty lies in the simultaneous opening of the two, then it will be better to take this as a Comp. word as Prof. Ray suggests. पक्ष्मेतरा—पक्ष्मायाः इतरा or पक्ष्मा I यस्याः । The idea here is this—The moon is going down; the otuses have begun to bloom, you should therefore (तत्) wake etimes and prevent the lotuses from taking sole possesion of Lakshmî in the absence of any other rival in beauty. प्रबलितभ्रमरं—Bees are prescribed as being held up in lotuses when closed up at the approach of night and remaining there till sun-rise; *cf.* Ratn. I. 25, (लीयन्ते मुकुलान्तरेषु &c. and *infra* VII. 55.

Śl. 69. अनोकहानाम्—see II. 8. सरसिजैः-Aluk. Comp.; see Saṃj. भिन्नैः—भिन्न opened; *cf.* करैरिन्दोरन्तश्छुरित इव संभिन्नमुकुलः, Veṇi. I. 1. परगुणेन—परेषां of others (*i. e.* borrowed) गुणेन. इव—indicates उत्प्रेक्षा.

Śl. 70. निर्धौतहार &c.—गुलिका by लक्षणा (उपचार) means here 'a pearl.' परभाग—परः श्रेष्ठः भागः परभागः । A position of great advantage. तया—being most. advantageously placed. अधरोष्ठे-—अधरौष्ठः is an optional form. See ft.-notes. In this and the foregoing ślokas the excellence of Aja's breath and his lustrous teeth illumined by his beautiful smile are described in a poetic style. Vall. notices the reading संलक्ष्यते दशनचन्द्रिकयानुविद्धं बिम्बाधरलब्धपरभागमिव स्मितं ते ।

Śl. 71. प्रतापनिधिः—The treasure, the source, of heat which causes ताप. वीर—one who causes ताप to his foes. The two epithets are used to keep up the resemblance. अरुणेन—Aruṇa is the charioteer of the Sun, and the elder brother of Garuḍa. He is अनूरु (without thighs) having been prematurely brought out of the egg by his mother. See A. Dic. Here Aruṇa and Raghu are compared. Raghu having the same relation with respect to Aja which Aruṇa has with respect to the sun. Aruṇa precedes the Sun and Raghu precedes Aja. Each is the precursor of the other. आयोधनाग्रसरताम्—आयुध्यन्ते अस्मिन्नित्यायोधनं युद्धम् । अग्रे सरतीति अग्रसरः, formed irregularly according to some. By the rule 'पुरोऽग्रतोऽग्रेषु सर्तेः' सृ when preceded by पुरस्, अग्रतस्, and अग्रे takes टच् (अ) to express कर्ता or the agent. Hence the proper form should be अग्रेसरः. [This is according to the

Vrittikâra who supposes अग्रे to be the word used in the Sûtra. He is followed by Bhaṭṭoji, and Jñânendra Bhikshu. Patañjali gives no comm. on this Sûtra. Nâgeśabhaṭṭa, however, differs and supposes अग्रसर to be the correct form, अग्रेसर being obtained by the rule 'तत्पुरुषे कृति बहुलम्'। Kâli. uses both the forms. Cf. अग्रेसरैर्वाजिभिरुत्थितानि' VI. 33; 'यूथं तदग्रसरगर्वितकृष्णसारम्' 'सवरुणावरुणाग्रसरं रुचा' IX. 55, 61. Amara gives the form अग्रेसर. This question is discussed by Hem. and Châr. for which see ft.-note. किं वा--किं is to be pronounced with a काकु (intonation) and वा expresses विकल्प; किं वा उच्छिनत्ति would your father destroy the foes; नैवोच्छिनत्ति no; certainly he would not. Cf. 'किं वाऽभविष्यदरुणस्तमसां विभेत्ता'। Śák. VII. 4.

The idea here is this—Aruṇa destroys the enemy of the sun (i. e. darkness) only so long as he himself has not taken up the work of destruction. So your father would destroy your enemies only so long as you are not able to take care of yourself. But now you are able (वीर) to take the lead in the battle, so get up and chase your enemies if there be any. Prof. Ray thinks that the enemies here referred to are the morning breeze, the dew drops, the lotuses, &c., which are poetically spoken of as the stealers of Aja's Lakshmí.

Śl. 72. उभयपक्ष &c.—According to Kaiyaṭa, quoted by Malli., the word उभ appearing first in a Comp. always takes the Tad. affix अयच् (अय), i. e. becomes उभय, as indicated by the word 'नित्यम् in the Sûtra 'उभादुदात्तो नित्यम्'। स्तम्बेरमाः—स्तम्ब a clump of grass. See com. मुखर &c.--निन्दितं मुखमस्य। मुखशब्दो लक्षणयात्र वचनपरः। one who has to say something on every topic; garrulous; or मुखं मुखव्यापारं रातीति noisy. Here of course it means 'resounding. शृङ्खल—शृङ्गैः शिञ्जानो वा स्खलतीति। In either case it is of the पृषोदरादि class. तरुणारुण—the newly risen sun (giving reddish light). Cf. वासो वसाना तरुणार्करागं Kum. III. 54. भिन्नाद्रि०—गिरौ भवं गैरिकं (fr. गिरि+ठञ् i. e. इक) a reddish brown mineral; गैरिकप्रचुरा तटाः गैरिकतटाः a comp. of the शाकपार्थिव class. अद्रेः गैरिकतटा अद्रि०; भिन्ना अद्रिगैरिकतटा यैस्ते. दन्तकोशाः—bud-like, i. e. beautiful tusks (Malli.).

Śl. 73. दीर्घेषु &c.—shows that Aja had a large number of horses with him. वनजाक्ष—वने जायते इति वनजं; वनजे इव अक्षिणी यस्य स वनजाक्षः. वनायुदेश्याः—वनायुः देशः तत्र भवाः। ०देश+यत्. A grammatical inaccuracy, for the Tad. affix, though added to देश in this sense, is not available in the case of compounds ending in देश. Vanâyu is a country in the North-West of India, celebrated for its breed of horses. लेह्यानि—The reason of making the horses lick pieces of Rock-salt is given in the Sanj. सैन्धव—सिन्धुषु भवः (produced in

Sindhu) सैन्धवः Páṇ. IV. 2. 133; तस्य शिलास्तासां शकलानि. वाहाः—वाहन्ते प्रयत्नातिशयं कुर्वन्तीति वाहाः fr. वाहृ + अच्; horses.

Śl. 74. विरलभक्ति—विरलं भक्तिर्यस्य । नपुंसकपूर्वपदो बहुव्रीहिः । If we dissolve as विरला भक्तिर्यस्य we shall not get विरल, पुंवद्भाव being prohibited with words of the प्रियादि class to which भक्ति belongs. According to भोजराज, however, विरला भक्तिर्यस्य will also do, if भक्ति be derived from भज् by adding ति भावे (meaning 'arrangement'). See Malli. on दृढभक्ति XII. 19. पुष्पोपहारः—the garlands or boquets of flowers presented to Aja. See IV. 84. As the flowers faded in the morning and shrank up, the garlands got loosened. स्वकिरण &c.—The lamps lost their halo of rays, it being broad day-light now. The three s'lokas show that the sun is above the horizon (and not below it as S. P. Pandit supposes) and it is already late. See notes, s'l. 66. "प्रयुक्ता—mark the sense of युज् with प्र which means 'to utter or pronounce' (when used with words).

Śl. 75. विरचित०—This also shows that the verses were composed for the occasion. *Cf.* विरचितपदं गेयमुद्गातुकामा Meg. II. 26. विगतनिद्रः—Here विगत is equal to विगमित (त्याजित) the sense of the causal being expressed without the affix; or गम् may be taken in its primitive sense; विगता नष्टा निद्रा यस्य, the instr. बन्दिपुत्रैः being हेतौ. राजहंसैः—हंसानां राजानो राजहंसाः । a comp. of the राजदन्तादि class. गाङ्गं सैकतम्—सिकताः सन्त्यस्मिन्निति सैकतं a sandy place; अण् is added to सिकता and शर्करा in the sense of मत् (the affix showing possession), so शार्कर also. सुप्रतीकः—शोभनाः प्रतीकाः limit अस्य. The simile is probably intended to indicate the purity of Aja's bed, who, unlike many of the other princes assembled there was a bachelor.

Śl. 76. अवसाय्य—Indec. p. p. of सो cau. with अव. दिवसमुखो०—दिवसस्य मुखं दिवस० तस्य उचितम्. अश्लिताक्षिपक्ष्मा—अक्ष्णोः पक्ष्माणि अक्षिपक्ष्माणि the eyelashes. See Sanj and ft.-note. अनुकूल—अनुगतः कूलमनुकूलः. क्षितिपसमाजम्—क्षितिं पान्तीति क्षितिपाः तेषाम् । समजान्ति संघीभवन्त्यस्मिन्निति संवीयतेऽनेति वा समाजः (सम् + अज् + घञ्) a multitude; Páṇ. III. 3. 19. But समजः (सम् + अज् + अप्) a group of lower animals, birds &c. *Cf.* Páṇ. III. 3. 69. 'पशूनां समजोऽन्येषां समाजः' Amara. *Cf.* कूजन्बकानां समजो विरेजे । Ras. *Cf.* Eng. 'flock' or 'herd'. स्वयंवर थः—स्वयं व्रियते अस्मिन् इति स्वयंवरः the place of selection, fr. वृ with अ (अप्)added अधिकरणे. स्वयंवरे तिष्ठतीति. क्षितिपगात्—This shows that the other kings were already there when Aja went.
